LIVING LANGUAGE®

PORTUGUESE
DICTIONARY

PORTUGUESE–ENGLISH
ENGLISH–PORTUGUESE

REVISED & UPDATED

PORTUGUESE DICTIONARY

PORTUGUESE–ENGLISH
ENGLISH–PORTUGUESE

REVISED & UPDATED

REVISED BY JURA D. OLIVEIRA, PH.D.

Senior Lecturer in Portuguese
Cornell University

◆

Based on the original by

Oscar Fernández

LIVING LANGUAGE®
A Random House Company

This work was previously published under the title *Living Language™ Common Usage Dictionary—Portuguese* by Oscar Fernández, based on the dictionary developed by Ralph Weiman.

Published by Living Language®, A Random House Company, New York, New York.

Living Language is a member of the Random House Information Group

Random House, Inc., New York, Toronto, London, Sydney, Auckland

www.livinglanguage.com

Living Language and colophon are registered trademarks of Random House, Inc.

If you are traveling, we recommend **Fodor's guides**

Living Language® publications are available at special discounts for bulk purchases for sales promotions or premiums, as well as for fund-raising or educational use. Special editions can be created in large quantities for special needs. For more information, write to Special Sales Manager, Living Language, 1745 Broadway, New York, NY 10019.

Printed in the United States of America

ISBN 1-4000-2025-5

10 9 8 7 6 5

CONTENTS

INTRODUCTION

The *Living Language® Portuguese Dictionary* lists more than 18,000 of the most frequently used Portuguese words, gives their most important meanings, and illustrates their uses. This revised edition contains updated phrases and expressions as well as many new entries related to business, technology, and the media.

1. More than 1,000 of the most essential words are capitalized to make them easy to find.

2. Numerous meanings are illustrated with everyday phrases, sentences, and idiomatic expressions. If there is no close English equivalent for a Portuguese word, or if the English equivalent has several meanings, the context of the illustrative sentences helps to clarify the meanings.

3. Because of these useful phrases, the *Living Language® Portuguese Dictionary* also serves as a phrase book and conversation guide. The dictionary is helpful both to beginners who are building their vocabulary and to advanced students who want to perfect their command of colloquial Portuguese.

4. The Portuguese expressions (particularly the idiomatic and colloquial ones) have been translated into their English equivalents. However, literal translations have

been added to help the beginner. For example, under the entry **"ABRAÇO** embrace, hug," you will find: *Rebeca um abraço do seu amigo.* Cordially yours, ("Receive a hug from your friend"). This dual feature also makes the dictionary useful for translation work.

EXPLANATORY NOTES

1. Although the Portuguese spoken in Portugal and Brazil is the same language, there are certain differences, just as there are between British and American English. In this dictionary, the Brazilian Portuguese version of a word is given first. The Continental Portuguese variation follows in parentheses:

DIRETOR (DIRECTOR) *m. director.*

The spelling and accents in this dictionary have been revised in order to conform to the new orthography determined by the Brazilian Law of December 18, 1971 (Law number 5765), which reflects the Orthographic Agreement established between Brazil and Portugal on December 29, 1943.

2. If more than one form is commonly used, both are given:

toicinho

toucinho *m. bacon.*

3. ⒷB will be used to indicate a term or meaning particular to Brazilian Portuguese, and Ⓟ for words particular to Continental Portuguese:

Suéter *m. sweater* Ⓑ.

garage Ⓑ, **garagem** *f. garage.*

ix

ALMOÇO *m. lunch.*

Primeiro almoço. *Breakfast* Ⓟ.

Pequeno almoço. *Breakfast* Ⓟ.

4. The pronunciation of x between vowels is indicated: **abacaxi** *(x = sh);* **exame** *(x = z);* **próximo** *(x = s);* **táxi** *(x = ks).*

5. A few literal translations are given in quotation marks: **o Rio de Janeiro** ("the river of January").

6. Usually only the masculine singular form of an adjective is given.

7. The dictionary uses the following abbreviations:

adj.	adjective
adv.	adverb
conj.	conjunction
f.	feminine
fam.	familiar
fig.	figurative
ind.	indefinite
m.	masculine
n.	noun
pro.	pronoun
prep.	preposition

Portuguese-English

A

A *to, in, at, by, for, the, her, it, on, with.*
   Vou à cidade. *I'm going to the city.*
   A tempo. *In time.*
   A que horas? *At what time?*
   Um a um. *One by one.*
   A janela está aberta. *The window is open.*
   Não a vimos. *We did not see her.*
   Ele a comprou ontem. *He bought it (fem.)*
     yesterday.
   Vamos a pé. *We're going on foot.*
abacate *m. avocado.*
abacaxi (x = sh) **(ananás)** *m. pineapple;*
   difficult situation, mess ⑧.
abafado *adj. stuffy, close, sultry, hidden,*
   oppressed; annoyed, very busy,
   swamped ⑧.
abaixar (x = sh) *to lower, to bring down, to*
   humiliate.
abaixar-se (x = sh) *to stoop down, to humble*
   oneself.
ABAIXO (x = sh) *below, under.*
   Abaixo e acima. *Up and down.*
abalado *shaken, loose; moved, touched (fig.).*
abanar *to fan, to shake.*
   Ele abanou a cabeça. *He shook his head.*
abandonado *adj. abandoned, forsaken;*
   friendless.
abandonar *to abandon, to give up, to leave.*
   Ele abandonou a família. *He abandoned*
     his family.
abandono *m. abandonment, desertion;*
   neglect, destitution.
abanico *m. a small hand-held fan.*
abarcar *to comprise, to enclose, to contain, to*
   grasp.
   Quem muito abarca, pouco aperta. *Those*
     who try to have it all end up with only
     a little.
abastado *adj. wealthy, rich, well-off.*
abastar *to supply, to provide.*
abastecer *to provide, to supply.*
abastecimento *m. supplies, provisions.*
abatido *adj. depressed, discouraged.*
abatimento *m. decrease, reduction, discount;*
   low spirits, depression.
abdicar *to abdicate, to renounce, to resign.*
abdome, abdômen (abdómen) *m. abdomen.*
abecedário *m. the alphabet; primer.*
abelha *f. bee.*
abençoado *adj. blessed; happy.*
abençoar *to bless; to make happy.*
abertamente *openly, frankly, plainly.*
ABERTO *adj. open, opened; frank.*
   A loja está aberta? *Is the store open?*
   João não tinha aberto as janelas. *John had*
     not opened the windows.

abertura *f. opening.*
abismo *m. abyss, chasm.*
abjurar *to renounce, to repudiate.*
abolição *f. abolition.*
abolir *to abolish, to revoke, to cancel.*
abominável *adj. abominable.*
abonado *adj. trustworthy, creditable; wealthy,*
   well-off ⑧.
abonar *to guarantee, to vouch for; to advance*
   (money) to.
abono *m. loan; warranty, surety.*
abordar *to go aboard, to board; to accost, to*
   broach.
   Ela não quis abordar o assunto. *She did not*
     wish to broach the subject.
aborrecer *to hate, to detest; to annoy, to*
   bother.
   Tudo isto nos aborrece. *All this annoys us.*
aborrecido *adj. annoyed, bored; tiresome.*
aborrecimento *m. annoyance, nuisance, bore.*
aborto *m. abortion.*
abotoar *to button; to bud.*
abraçar *to embrace, to hug; to encompass.*
   Os dois amigos se abraçaram. *The two*
     friends embraced each other.
ABRAÇO *m. embrace, hug.*
   Receba um abraço do seu amigo. *Receive a*
     hug from your friend (in a letter, a
     complimentary close, "Cordially
     yours," or equivalent.)
abreviar *to shorten, to abbreviate, to*
   summarize.
abreviatura *f. abbreviation.*
abricó, abricote, albricote *m. apricot.*
abridor *m. opener.*
abrigar *to shelter, to protect.*
ABRIGO *m. shelter, protection, sanctuary.*
ABRIL *m. April.*
ABRIR *to open; to unlock; to begin; to*
   turn on.
   Faça o favor de abrir a porta. *Please open*
     the door.
   Não abra a torneira. *Don't turn on the*
     faucet.
abrupto *adj. abrupt, sudden.*
abscesso *m. abscess.*
absoluto *adj. absolute, complete,*
   independent.
absolver *to absolve, to acquit, to pardon.*
absolvido *adj. absolved, acquitted,*
   pardoned.
absorto *adj. absorbed, enraptured.*
abster *to abstain, to refrain, to repress.*
abstinência *f. abstinence; fasting.*
absurdo *adj. absurd, foolish; n. m. absurdity,*
   nonsense.
abundância *f. abundance, plenty.*
abundante *adj. abundant, plentiful.*
abundar *to abound.*

abusar *to abuse, to take advantage of.*
   O oficial abusou de sua autoridade. *The officer abused his authority.*
abuso *m. abuse, misuse.*
abutre *m. vulture.*
ACABADO *adj. finished, complete; exhausted.*
ACABAR *to finish, to complete, to end, to have just (with de).*
   Você já acabou o trabalho? *Did you already finish the work?*
   Acabamos de jantar. *We have just had dinner.*
acabrunhar *to oppress, to distress, to afflict.*
academia *f. academy, school; learned society.*
acalmar *to calm, to appease, to soothe.*
   Eu vou acalmá-lo. *I'm going to calm him down.*
acampar *to camp, to pitch camp.*
acanhado *adj. shy, bashful, timid; miserly; close, narrow.*
AÇÃO (ACÇÃO) *f. action, act, deed; share of stock.*
   Houve muito falar e pouca ação. *There was much talk and little action.*
acariciar *to caress, to pet, to cherish.*
ACASO *adj. by chance, perhaps, possibly; n. m. chance, accident.*
   Por acaso. *By chance.*
   Escolhemos ao acaso. *We picked at random.*
   Foram os acasos da fortuna. *They were the hazards of fortune.*
aceder *to accede, to assent, to agree.*
ACEITAÇÃO *f. acceptance.*
ACEITAR *to accept, to take.*
   Aceitam cheque de viagem? *Will you accept a traveler's check?*
ACEITÁVEL *adj. acceptable.*
ACEITE *m. acceptance; adj. accepted.*
ACEITO *adj. accepted.*
acelerador *adj. accelerating; m. accelerator.*
acelerar *to accelerate, to speed up.*
ACENDER *to light (up), to ignite, to turn on (a light); to animate.*
   Deixe-me acender um fósforo. *Let me light a match.*
ACENTO *m. accent, accent mark.*
   Escreva o acento circunflexo, e não o agudo. *Write a circumflex accent, not an acute one.*
acentuar *to accent, to stress.*
acepção *f. meaning, sense.*
acerca de *about, concerning.*
   Escrevemos-lhe acerca de nossa viagem. *We wrote him about our trip.*
acercar *to approach, to enclose.*
acertado *adj. proper, right.*

ACERTAR *to hit the mark, to be right, to accomplish, to set right.*
   Acertámos no alvo. *We hit the mark.*
   Tenho que acertar o relógio. *I have to set my watch.*
acerto *m. hit; discretion.*
   Com acerto. *Properly.*
acessório *adj. accessory, additional; n. m. accessory.*
ACHAR *to find, to discover; to think, to believe.*
   Não achei o livro. *I did not find the book.*
   Acho que ele não vem. *I don't think he's coming.*
   Acho que sim. *I think so.*
acidental *adj. accidental, incidental.*
ACIDENTE *m. accident.*
   Foi um acidente. *It was an accident.*
ácido *adj. acid, sour; n. m. acid.*
ACIMA *above, up.*
   Eles foram pela rua acima. *They went up the street.*
   Acima de tudo. *Above all.*
acionista (accionista) *m. and f. stockholder, shareholder.*
aclamar *to acclaim, to proclaim, to applaud.*
aclarar *to explain, to make clear, to clear up; to illuminate.*
aclimar *to acclimate.*
aço *m. steel.*
acolá *there, to that place.*
   Cá e acolá. *Here and there.*
ACOLHER *to receive, to welcome; to heed.*
ACOLHIDA *f. welcome, reception.*
   Todos tiveram boa acolhida. *They all received a good welcome.*
acomodar *to accommodate.*
ACOMPANHAR *to accompany, to escort, to attend.*
   Queremos que ele nos acompanhe. *We want him to accompany us.*
ACONSELHAR *to advise, to recommend.*
   Eles me aconselham a estudar mais. *They advise me to study more.*
ACONTECER *to happen, to take place.*
   Não aconteceu nada. *Nothing happened.*
ACONTECIMENTO *m. event, happening.*
ACORDAR *to awake; to come to an agreement.*
   Ele ainda não acordou. *He hasn't woken up yet.*
acordeão *m. accordion.*
ACORDO *m. agreement, accord.*
   Chegamos a um acordo com eles. *We came to an agreement with them.*
ACOSTUMADO *adj. accustomed, used to; usual.*
   Estamos acostumados a deitar-nos tarde. *We are used to going to bed late.*

ACOSTUMAR *to accustom, to be in the habit of.*
AÇOUGUE *butcher shop, meat market.*
AÇOUGUEIRO *m. butcher.*
acre *adj. sour, bitter; n. m. acre.*
ACREDITAR *to believe; to believe in.*
    Não acredito nisso. *I don't believe in that.*
    Você acredita? *Do you believe it?*
AÇÚCAR *m. sugar.*
açucena *f. Easter lily.*
açude *m. dam, reservoir.*
acudir *to assist, to help, to run to help.*
acumulador *m. storage battery, accumulator.*
acumular *to accumulate, to collect.*
acusação *f. accusation, charge, indictment.*
acusado *adj. accused, charged.*
acusar *to accuse, to charge; to acknowledge.*
    Acusamos o recebimento de sua carta. *We acknowledge the receipt of your letter.*
adaptação *f. adaptation.*
adaptar *to adapt, to adjust.*
adequado *adj. adequate, proper.*
aderente *adj. adherent, attached.*
aderir *to adhere; to unite, to join.*
adestramento *m. training.*
adestrar *to train, to instruct.*
ADEUS *good-bye, farewell.*
adiantado *adj. advanced, ahead.*
ADIANTAR(-SE) *to advance, to get ahead; to be fast (clock).*
    Meu relógio (se) adianta. *My watch is fast.*
    Não adianta. *It doesn't do any good.*
ADIANTE *ahead, forward.*
    Adiante! *Go on!*
adiar *to postpone, to defer.*
adição *f. addition, sum; bill, check (restaurant).*
adicional *adj. additional.*
adido *m. attaché.*
adivinha *f. puzzle, riddle; female fortune-teller.*
adivinhar *to guess, to find out; to predict.*
    Acho que você nunca adivinha. *I think you'll never guess.*
adivinho *m. male fortune-teller.*
adjetivo (adjectivo) *m. adjective.*
adjunto *adj. joined; n. m. adjunct, assistant, deputy.*
administração *f. administration.*
administrador *m. administrator, manager.*
administrar *to administer, to manage.*
admiração *f. admiration, wonder, surprise.*
admirador *m. admirer.*
admirar *to admire; to be surprised.*
    Não é de admirar. *It's not surprising.*
admirável *adj. admirable, wonderful.*
ADMISSÃO *f. admission, entrance.*
    Exame de admissão. *Entrance examination.*

ADMITIR *to admit, to accept, to grant.*
adoção *f. adoption.*
adoecer *to become ill.*
adolescência *f. adolescence.*
adoração *f. adoration, worship.*
adorar *to adore, to worship, to like very much.*
adorável *adj. adorable.*
ADORMECER *to put to sleep; to fall asleep.*
adornar *to adorn, to dress, to ornament.*
adotar (adoptar) *to adopt.*
adquirir *to acquire, to get.*
aduaneiro *adj. customs, of customs (in an airport, etc.); n. m. customhouse officer.*
adulador *m. flatterer.*
adular *to flatter.*
adultério *m. adultery.*
adulto *adj. adult; n. m. adult.*
advérbio *m. adverb.*
adversário *adj. adverse; n. m. opponent, adversary.*
adversidade *f. adversity.*
advertência *f. warning, notice.*
    Você recebeu a advertência? *Did you receive the warning?*
advertir *to warn, to advise.*
advogado *m. lawyer, attorney.*
aéreo *adj. aerial, air.*
    Por via aérea. *By airmail.*
aeródromo *m. aerodrome, airport.*
aeronáutica *f. aeronautics.*
aeroplano *m. airplane.*
aeroporto *m. airport.*
afã *m. enthusiasm; effort; eagerness.*
afanar *to work hard; to steal* ⑧.
afastado *adj. apart, distant.*
afastar *to separate, to remove.*
afeição *f. affection, fondness.*
afetar (afectar) *to affect, to pretend.*
afeto (afecto) *adj. affectionate, friendly; n. m. affection, friendship.*
afetuoso (afectuoso) *adj. affectionate, kind.*
afiar *to sharpen; to make pointed.*
aficionado *adj. fond, enthusiastic; n. m. fan (sports), follower.*
afilhado *m. godchild, protégé.*
afiliado *adj. affiliated.*
afiliar *to affiliate.*
afinal *finally, at last.*
    Afinal de contas. *After all.*
afirmação *f. affirmation.*
afirmar *to affirm, to state.*
afirmativamente *affirmatively.*
afixar *(x = ks) to fix, to fasten, to post (posters, etc.).*
aflição *f. affliction, distress, grief, agony.*
afligir-se *to grieve, to worry.*
    Não se aflija. *Don't worry.*
aflito *adj. grieved, worried, distressed.*

afogar (-se) *to drown, to suffocate, to stifle.*
Ele se afoga em pouca água. *It doesn't take much to bother him.*

aforismo *m. maxim, aphorism.*

AFORTUNADAMENTE *fortunately, luckily.*

AFORTUNADO *adj. fortunate, lucky, happy.*

afrontar *to affront, to insult; to strike, to meet.*

afundamento *m. sinking.*

afundar *to sink.*

agarrar *to grasp, to hold, to seize.*

agasalhar *to receive, to welcome, to shelter.*

agência *f. agency, bureau, office.*

agenda *f. agenda, memorandum, diary notebook.*

agente *adj. acting; n. m. agent.*

ágil *adj. agile, quick.*

agir *to act, to do.*

agitação *f. agitation, commotion, trouble.*

agitar *to agitate, to disturb, to shake.*

agonia *f. agony, great grief, suffering.*

AGORA *now, at the present time.*
Vamos agora. *We are going now.*
Agora mesmo. *Right now.*
Agora não. *Not now.*

AGOSTO *m. August.*

AGRADAR *to please, to like.*
Isso não me agrada. *I don't like that.*

AGRADÁVEL *adj. pleasant, agreeable, nice.*
Ela é muito agradável. *She is very nice.*

AGRADECER *to be grateful (for), to thank.*
Agradeço muito a sua bondade. *I thank you for your kindness.*

AGRADECIDO *adj. grateful, thankful.*
Fico-lhe muito agradecido. *I am very grateful to you.*

agradecimento *m. gratitude, thanks.*

agrado *m. pleasure, liking, satisfaction.*

agravar *to aggravate, to make worse.*

agregar *to bring together, to accumulate.*

agressão *f. aggression, offense.*

agressivo *adj. aggressive.*

agressor *m. aggressor.*

agrícola *adj. agricultural.*

agricultor *m. farmer.*

agricultura *f. agriculture, farming.*

agrupamento *m. grouping, group.*

agrupar *to group, to gather.*

ÁGUA *f. water.*
Água corrente. *Running water.*
Água doce. *Fresh water.*
Água mineral. *Mineral water.*
Água potável. *Drinking water.*
Água gelada. *Ice water.*

aguaceiro *m. shower (rain).*

água-marinha *f. (pl. águas-marinhas) aquamarine.*

aguardar *to wait for, to expect, to observe (laws).*

Aguardo a sua resposta. *I'm waiting for your answer.*

aguardente *m. brandy; distilled liquor.*

agudo *adj. sharp; acute; witty.*

agüentar (aguentar) *to bear, to stand, to put up with.*
Não agüento mais. *I can't stand any more.*

águia *f. eagle; m. talented person; an untrustworthy person* ⑬.

AGULHA *f. needle.*
Isso é procurar agulha em palheiro. *That's like looking for a needle in a haystack.*

ah! *ah! oh!*

ai! *oh! (exclamation of surprise, pain, etc.)*
Ai de mim! *Poor me!*

AÍ *there, over there (near you).*
Aí mesmo. *Right there.*
Ponha-o aí. *Put it there.*
Por aí. *That way. Over there.*

AIDS *f. AIDS.*

AINDA *still, yet.*
Ele ainda nos escreve. *He still writes us.*
Ele chegou? Ainda não. *Did he arrive? Not yet.*

AINDA QUE *although.*

aipo *m. celery.*

ajoelhar (-se) *to kneel.*

AJUDA *f. help, assistance.*

ajudante *m. and f. assistant, helper.*

AJUDAR *to help, to assist, to aid.*
Você quer que ajude? *Do you want me to help?*

ajustar *to arrange, to fix, to settle.*
Vamos ajustar contas. *Let's settle accounts.*

ala *f. wing, row.*

alarde *m. show, display, parade.*

alargar *to enlarge, to widen.*

alarma *f. alarm.*

alarmar *to alarm.*

alarmar-se *to become frightened.*

alarme *m. alarm.*

alavanca *f. lever.*

albergue *m. inn, shelter.*

albricoque *m. apricot.*

álbum *m. album.*

alcachofra (alcachofa) *f. artichoke.*

alcançar *to reach, to attain, to catch up with, to be ahead.*
Não o alcancei. *I did not catch up with him.*

alcance *m. extent, reach, scope.*
Está ao alcance de todos. *It is within everyone's reach.*

alçar *to raise, to lift.*

alcatrão *m. tar, pitch.*

álcool *m. alcohol.*

Alcorão *m. the Koran.*

alcunha *f. nickname.*

aldeia *f. village.*

aldraba, aldrava *f. latch, knocker (of door).*

alecrim *m. rosemary.*

alegação *f. allegation, claim.*

alegar *to allege, to claim.*

alegrar *to cheer, to make happy.*

alegre *adj. cheerful, happy.*

alegria *f. joy, gladness.*

aleijado *adj. lame, crippled.*

aleijar *to cripple, to maim.*

ALÉM *beyond, besides, farther.*
> Além disso. *Besides, furthermore.*
> Muito além. *Much farther.*

alemão *adj., n. m. German.*

alento *m. breath, courage.*

alerta *adj. alert, vigilant.*

alfabeto *m. alphabet.*

alface *f. lettuce.*
> Salada de alface. *Lettuce salad.*

alfaiataria *f. tailor shop.*

alfaiate *m. tailor.*

alfândega *f. customhouse; customs (in an airport, etc.).*

alfinete *m. pin.*
> Alfinete de gravata. *Tie pin.*

algarismo *m. number, figure.*

algibeira *f. pocket.*

algo *some, something; adv. somewhat.*

ALGODÃO *m. cotton.*
> Tecido de algodão. *Cotton fabric.*

ALGUÉM *somebody, someone*
> Alguém entrou. *Somebody came in.*

ALGUM *adj. some, any; pl. a few.*
> Alguma coisa. *Something.*
> Algum dia. *Some day.*
> Algumas vezes. *Sometimes.*
> Quero alguns. *I want a few.*

alheio *adj. belonging to somebody else; foreign; alienated.*

alho *m. garlic.*

ALI *there, over there (away from person spoken to).*
> Está ali. *It's over there.*
> Ali mesmo. *Right there.*
> Ele desapareceu por ali. *He disappeared that way.*

aliança *f. alliance, association, wedding ring.*

aliás *however, besides; otherwise.*

alicate *m. pliers.*

ALIMENTO *food, nourishment.*

alisar *to smooth (out).*

alistar *to enlist, to enroll.*

aliviar *to alleviate, to mitigate.*

ALMA *f. soul, heart, spirit, essence.*
> Não apareceu nenhuma alma. *Not a soul (person) appeared.*
> Ele tem boa alma. *He has a good heart (is kind).*

almanaque *m. almanac.*

almirante *m. admiral.*

ALMOÇAR *to have lunch.*
> Sempre almoçamos ao meio-dia. *We always have lunch at noon.*

ALMOÇO *m. lunch.*
> Primeiro almoço. *Breakfast* ℗.
> Pequeno almoço. *Breakfast* ℗.

almôndega *f. meatball.*

almotolia *f. oilcan.*

alô! *hello!*

alojamento *m. lodging.*

alojar *to lodge, to billet.*

alparca, alparcata, alpercata *f. sandal.*

alteração *f. alteration, change, disturbance.*

alterar *to alter, to change, to disturb.*

alternar *to alternate.*

alternativa *f. alternative, choice.*

altitude *f. altitude.*

altivo *adj. haughty, proud, lofty.*

ALTO *adj. high, tall; loud; n. m. top, height.*
> Ele é alto e magro. *He is tall and thin.*
> Aconteceu no alto mar. *It happened on the high seas.*
> Fale mais alto, por favor. *Speak louder, please.*
> A vida tem muitos altos e baixos. *Life has many ups and downs.*

alto! *halt! stop!*

alto-falante *m. loudspeaker.*

altura *f. height, point (of time).*
> Não sei a altura. *I don't know its height.*
> Nessa altura. *At that point.*

aludir *to allude to.*

ALUGAR *to rent, to hire.*
> Aluguei a casa para o verão. *I rented the house for the summer.*
> Alugam-se quartos. *Rooms for rent.*

ALUGUEL *m. rent, hiring.*
> Quanto é o aluguel? *How much is the rent?*

alumiado *adj. illuminated, light.*

alumiar *to illuminate, to light (up).*

alumínio *m. aluminum.*

ALUNO *m. pupil, student.*
> Você conhece esse aluno? *Do you know that student?*

alva *f. dawn.*

alvo *m. target, aim, white.*
> Ele deu no alvo. *He hit the target.*

ama *f. housekeeper, nursemaid, governess.*

AMABILIDADE *f. amiability, kindliness.*

amado *adj. loved, beloved.*

amador *adj. loving; n. m. amateur, fan.*

amadurecer *to ripen.*

amaldiçoado *adj. cursed, damned.*

amaldiçoar *to curse, to damn.*

AMANHÃ *m. tomorrow.*
> Eles chegam amanhã. *They are arriving tomorrow.*
> Vou depois de amanhã. *I'm going the day after tomorrow.*

Até amanhã. *See you tomorrow.*

amanhecer *to dawn.*

amante *m. and f. lover.*

AMAR *to love, to like.*

AMARELO *yellow.*

amargo *bitter.*

amarra *f. chain, cable.*

amarrar *to tie (up), to fasten, to moor.*

amassar *to knead, to mix, to beat.*

AMÁVEL *adj. kind, amiable.*

   O senhor é muito amável. *You are very kind.*

ambição *f. ambition.*

ambicioso *adj. ambitious.*

ambiente *m. atmosphere, milieu, environment.*

AMBOS *both.*

   Fico com ambos. *I'll take both.*

ambulância *f. ambulance.*

ameaça *f. threat.*

ameaçar *to threaten.*

ameixa *(x = sh) f. plum.*

ameixa *(x = sh)* **passada** *or* **preta** *f. prune.*

amêndoa *f. almond.*

amendoim *m. peanut.*

ameno *adj. pleasant, gentle, mild.*

AMERICANO *adj., n. m. American.*

amido *m. starch.*

AMIGO *m. friend.*

   Apresento(-lhe) o meu amigo, João. *This is my friend John. ("I am introducing my friend John [to you].")*

   Meu caro amigo: *My dear friend:*

   Você é amigo da onça! *You're a fine friend! (disapprovingly).*

amiúde *often.*

amizade *f. friendship.*

amo *m. master.*

amolação *f. sharpening; bother, annoyance* Ⓑ.

   Desculpe a amolação. *Please excuse the bother.*

amolar *to sharpen; to bother, to annoy* Ⓑ.

   Não me amole com isso! *Don't bother me with that!*

AMOR *m. love, affection, a lovely person or thing.*

   O amor é cego. *Love is blind.*

   Julieta é um amor. *Julie is a lovely person.*

amostra *f. sample.*

   Ele me deu (deu-me) uma amostra. *He gave me a sample.*

amparar *to protect, to shelter.*

ampliação *f. amplification, enlargement.*

ampliar *to amplify, to enlarge.*

amplo *adj. ample.*

ampola *f. blister.*

amputar *to amputate, to cut off.*

analfabeto *m. illiterate.*

analisar *to analyze.*

análise *f. analysis.*

ananás (abacaxi Ⓑ**)** *m. pineapple.*

anão *m. (anã f.) dwarf.*

anatomia *f. anatomy.*

âncora *f. anchor.*

ANDAR *to walk, to go, to be.*

   Andamos à casa de João. *We walked to John's house.*

   Anda! *Get going!*

   Não ando muito bem hoje. *I don't feel very well today.*

andorinha *f. swallow.*

anedota *f. anecdote.*

anel *m. ring, link.*

   Ele esqueceu o anel de casamento. *He forgot the wedding ring.*

ângulo *m. angle, corner.*

angústia *f. anguish, distress.*

animado *adj. lively, animated.*

   Desenho animado. *Animated cartoon.*

animal *m. animal.*

animar *to animate, to encourage.*

ânimo *m. courage, mind.*

aniversário *m. anniversary, birthday.*

   Quando é o seu aniversário? *When is your birthday?*

anjo *m. angel.*

ANO *m. year.*

   Quantos anos você tem? *How old are you?*

   Tenho vinte e dois anos. *I am twenty-two years old.*

   Quando você faz anos? *When is your birthday?*

   Ano bissexto. *Leap year.*

   Ano bom. *New Year.*

   Ano novo. *New Year.*

   Feliz ano novo! *Happy New Year!*

   Em que ano aconteceu? *In what year did it happen?*

   Vamos todos os anos. *We go every year.*

   Eles não vão no ano que vem. *They are not going next year.*

   Elas foram no ano passado. *They went last year.*

anoitecer *to become dark.*

   Ao anoitecer. *At nightfall.*

anônimo (anónimo) *adj. anonymous.*

anormal *adj. abnormal.*

anotar *to note, to record, to comment.*

ânsia *f. anxiety, anguish, sorrow.*

ansiedade *f. anxiety, care, concern, yearning.*

ansioso *adj. anxious, desirous.*

   Estamos muito ansiosos para fazer a viagem. *We are very anxious to take the trip.*

ante *before.*

antecedente *adj., n. m. antecedent.*

antecessor *m. predecessor.*

   Antecessores. *Ancestors.*

antecipação *f. anticipation.*

antecipado *adj.* anticipated, expected.

antecipar *to* anticipate, to expect, to precipitate.

antemão, de antemão *beforehand.*

antena *f.* antenna.

anteontem *the day before yesterday.*

antepassado *adj.* past; *n. pl.* ancestors.

anterior *adj.* anterior; previous, former, preceding.

ANTES *before, rather.*

    Quanto antes. *As soon as possible.*

    Telefone-me antes de partir. *Phone me before you leave.*

    Antes tarde do que nunca. *Better late than never.*

ANTIGO *adj.* old, ancient; former.

    Lisboa antiga. *Old Lisbon.*

antiguidade *f.* antiquity, ancient times.

antipatia *f.* antipathy.

antipático *adj.* unpleasant.

antiquado *adj.* old, obsolete.

anual *adj.* yearly.

anular *to* cancel, to void.

ANUNCIAR *to* announce, to advertise.

    Anunciaram-no ontem. *They announced it yesterday.*

ANÚNCIO *m.* announcement, notice, sign, advertisement.

    Sempre leio os anúncios nos jornais. *I always read the ads in the papers.*

AO (*contr. of* **a** + **o**) *to the, at the; on, when.*

    Vamos ao teatro. *We are going to the theatre.*

    Ao anoitecer. *At nightfall.*

    Ao contrário. *On the contrary.*

    Ao chegarem, disseram-nos tudo. *When they arrived, they told us everything.*

AONDE *where.*

    Aonde foram? *Where did you go?*

apagador *m.* extinguisher, eraser.

apagar *to* extinguish, to erase.

apaixonado (*x* = *sh*) *to* fall in love.

    Apaixonaram-se. *They fell in love.*

apanhar *to* catch, to get, to take, to pick.

    Apanhei um resfriado. *I caught a cold.*

    Eles foram apanhados dois dias mais tarde. *They were caught two days later.*

aparador *m.* sideboard, buffet.

APARECER *to* appear, to show up, to turn up.

    Ele não apareceu ontem. *He didn't show up yesterday.*

aparelho *m.* apparatus, device; phone Ⓑ.

    Não tenho aparelho de rádio. *I don't have a radio set.*

    Quem está no aparelho? Ⓑ *Who's on the phone?*

aparência *f.* appearance.

aparentar *to* seem, to appear, to feign.

aparente *adj.* apparent, evident.

apartado *adj.* apart, remote.

apartamento *m.* apartment; separation.

apartar *to* separate, to set apart.

apelar *to* appeal.

apelido *m.* surname, nickname Ⓑ.

apenas *only, hardly.*

    Ele apenas me falou. *He hardly spoke to me.*

aperitivo *m.* apéritif.

apertado *adj.* tight, close.

APESAR DE *in spite of.*

    Apesar de ser tarde, vamos. *In spite of the fact that it is late, we are going.*

apetecer *to* long for, to have an appetite for.

apetite *m.* appetite, hunger.

    Quando ouvi isso, perdi o apetite. *When I heard that, I lost my appetite.*

apinhar *to* crowd.

apitar *to* whistle.

apito *m.* whistle.

aplaudir *to* applaud.

aplauso *m.* applause.

aplicação *f.* application, use.

aplicado *adj.* applied; industrious, studious.

aplicar *to* apply.

aplicar-se *to* apply oneself, to be diligent.

apoderar-se de *to* take possession of.

apodo *m.* nickname.

apoiar *to* support, to favor, to defend, to aid, to lean.

apoio *m.* support.

apólice *f.* policy, bond, share.

    Apólice de seguro. *Insurance policy.*

apontar *to* sharpen; to point out, to indicate.

aportuguesar *to* render in Portuguese.

após *after, behind.*

aposentar *to* lodge, to pension; to dwell.

aposta *f.* bet.

apostar *to* bet.

    Quanto você apostou? *How much did you bet?*

apóstrofo *m.* apostrophe.

aprazer *to* please.

apreciar *to* appreciate, to value.

apreço *appreciation, esteem.*

APRENDER *to* learn.

    Paulo não aprendeu muito português. *Paul did not learn very much Portuguese.*

    Ela o aprenderá de cor. *She will learn it by heart.*

APRESENTAR *to* present, to introduce.

    Apresento(-lhe) os meus cumprimentos. *I send you my regards.*

    Vou apresentar(-lhe) o meu amigo Carlos Costa. *I'm going to introduce my friend Carlos Costa to you.*

apressar-se *to* hurry.

apropriar *to* appropriate.

aprovação *f. approval, praise; passing grade.*

aprovado *adj. approved; passed (in an examination).*

  João não foi aprovado. *John did not pass (was not passed).*

aprovar *to approve; to pass (a student in an examination).*

aproveitar *to make good use of, to profit.*

  Ele aproveita tudo. *He makes good use of everything.*

aproveitar-se de *to take advantage of, to make good use of.*

  Ele se aproveitou da oportunidade para escapar. *He took advantage of the opportunity to escape.*

aprovisionar *to supply.*

aproximar *(x = s) to approach.*

aptidão *f. aptitude, ability.*

apto *adj. apt, able.*

apunhalar *to stab.*

apurar *to improve, to select, to settle.*

apuro *m. precision, elegance; plight.*

  Ele se veste com apuro. *He dresses very well.*

  Agora estamos em apuros. *We're in a mess now.*

aquarela *f. watercolor.*

aqueceder *m. heater.*

aquecer *to heat, to warm.*

aquecimento *m. heating.*

AQUELA *(f. of* **aquele***) that, that one; the former.*

  Aquela jovem dança muito bem. *That girl dances very well.*

  Esta cadeira é mais nova que aquela. *This chair is newer than that one.*

AQUELE *that, that one; the former.*

  Não quero aquele, prefiro este. *I don't want that one (over there); I prefer this one.*

  José e Eduardo chegaram ontem. Este (Eduardo) me telefonou, mas aquele (José) ainda não comunicou comigo. *Joseph and Edward arrived yesterday. The latter telephoned me, but the former has not communicated with me yet.*

AQUI *here, in this place.*

  Ficamos aqui? *Do we stay here?*

  Aqui mesmo. *Right here.*

  Daqui a nove dias. *In nine days.*

  Venha por aqui. *Come this way.*

aquilo *that (neuter form).*

AR *m. air, wind; aspect, look.*

  Vamos sair ao ar livre. *Let's go out into the open air.*

  Quero quarto com ar condicionado. *I want an air-conditioned room.*

  Ele tem ar de inteligente. *He has an intelligent look.*

arado *m. plow.*

arame *m. wire.*

aranha *f. spider.*

arar *to plow.*

arbitrar *to arbitrate.*

árbitro *m. arbiter, umpire, referee.*

arbusto *m. bush, shrub.*

arca *f. chest, ark.*

arcar *to arch, to bow.*

arcebispo *m. archbishop.*

arco *m. arc, arch.*

arco-íris *rainbow.*

arder *to burn, to glow.*

área *f. area, region.*

areia *f. sand.*

arengar *to harangue.*

argamassa *f. mortar.*

argola *f. ring; door knocker.*

argumento *m. argument, reason, topic, plot.*

  Esse argumento não me convence. *That argument does not convince me.*

árido *adj. arid, dry.*

aritmética *f. arithmetic.*

arma *f. weapon, arm.*

  Não temos armas de fogo. *We have no firearms.*

armada *f. fleet.*

armamento *m. armament.*

armar *to arm.*

armário *m. cupboard, closet.*

armazém *m. grocery store, warehouse.*

armistício *m. armistice.*

arquiteto (arquitecto) *m. architect.*

arquitetura (arquitectura) *f. architecture.*

arquivo *m. record, filing cabinet.*

arrancar *to pull out, to tear out, to start (as a motor).*

  O motor não arrancava. *The motor wouldn't start.*

arranha-céu *m. (pl.* **arranha-céus***) skyscraper.*

  Há muitos arranha-céus em Nova Iorque. *There are many skyscrapers in New York.*

arranhar *to scratch.*

ARRANJAR *to arrange.*

  Não se preocupe, nós arranjamos tudo. *Don't worry, we'll arrange everything.*

arranjo *m. arrangement.*

arrastar *to haul, to drag.*

arrebatar *to grab, to carry off.*

arrebentar *to burst, to explode.*

arredores *m. pl. outskirts, suburbs.*

arregalar *to open the eyes wide, to stare.*

arrendar *to rent, to hire.*

arrepender-se *to repent, to be sorry for.*

arrepiar *to frighten, to terrify.*

arriba *up, above.*

arribar *to put in to port.*

arriscar *to risk, to dare.*
> Quem não arrisca, não petisca. *Nothing ventured, nothing gained.*

arrogante *adj. arrogant.*

arroio *m. brook.*

arrojar *to throw, to hurl.*

arrolhar *to cork.*

arroz *m. rice.*

arruinar *to ruin, to destroy.*

arrumar *to arrange, to put in order.*
> Ainda não arrumaram as malas? *Haven't you packed your bags yet?*
> Ela arruma tudo. *She keeps everything in order.*

arte *f. art, skill; way.*
> É uma verdadeira obra de arte. *It is a true work of art.*
> Belas artes. *Fine arts.*

ártico (árctico) *adj. arctic.*

artigo *m. article.*
> Não gostei do artigo de fundo. *I did not like the main editorial (or main article).*

artista *m. and f. artist.*

árvore *f. tree; shaft.*
> Árvore de Natal. *Christmas tree.*
> O tronco da árvore. *The trunk of a tree.*
> A árvore não tem folhas. *The tree doesn't have any leaves.*

ás *m. ace.*

asa *f. wing.*
> Vamos cortar-lhe as asas. *We're going to clip his wings.*

ascender *to rise.*

ascensão *f. ascension, elevation.*

ascensor *m. elevator.*

asfalto *m. asphalt.*

asilo *m. asylum, shelter.*

asneira *f. foolish thing, nonsense.*
> Mas isso é asneira! *But that's nonsense!*

asno *m. ass, fool.*

aspas *f. pl. quotation marks.*

aspecto, aspeto (aspecto, aspeito) *m. aspect, appearance.*

aspirador de pó *m. vacuum cleaner.*

aspirante *m. and f. aspirant, candidate; m. cadet.*
> Aspirante de marinha. *Midshipman.*

aspirina *f. aspirin.*

assado *adj. roast, roasted, baked.*
> Frango assado. *Roast chicken.*
> Assado de carneiro. *Roast lamb.*

assaltar *to assault, to attack.*

assalto *m. assault, attack.*

assar *to roast, to broil, to burn.*

assassinar *to assassinate, to murder, to kill.*

assassinato *m. assassination, murder.*

assassínio *m. assassination, murder.*

assassino *m. assassin, murderer.*

asseado *adj. clean, neat.*

assear *to clean, to tidy up.*

assear-se *to be neat, to dress well.*

assegurar *to insure, to secure, to fasten; to assure; to affirm, to assert.*

assembléia (assembleia) *f. assembly, meeting.*
> Assembléia legislativa. *Legislative assembly.*

assemelhar-se *to be similar, to resemble.*

assentar *to set, to place, to seat, to adjust.*

assento *m. seat, chair; place; record, entry.*

ASSIM *so, thus, in this manner, therefore, so that.*
> Assim espero. *I hope so.*
> Você deve fazê-lo assim. *You should do it this way.*
> Não é assim, asseguro-lhe. *I assure you that's not so.*
> Assim, assim. *So-so.*
> Assim que ele chegar, falaremos. *We'll talk as soon as he arrives.*

assinado *adj. signed.*

assinar *to sign, to assign, to subscribe.*
> Faça o favor de assinar o cheque. *Please sign the check.*

assinatura *f. subscription, signature.*
> Quero uma assinatura anual. *I would like a year's subscription.*

assistir *to attend, to be present; to help, to assist.*
> Ele não asistiu à aula. *He did not attend (the) class.*

assoar *to blow the nose.*

assobiar *to whistle.*

assobio *m. whistle, whistling.*

associação *f. association, company, society, club.*

assomar *to arise, to appear.*

assomar-se *to become angry.*

assombrado *adj. astonished, frightened.*

assombrar *to astonish, to frighten.*

assombro *m. astonishment, fright.*

ASSUNTO *m. subject, matter, business.*
> Preciso de mais detalhes sobre este assunto. *I need more information on this matter.*
> Conheço a fundo o assunto. *I am thoroughly acquainted with the matter.*
> Qual é o assunto dessa peça? *What is that play about?*

assustar *to startle, to frighten.*

asterisco *m. asterisk.*

astro *m. star (astronomy).*

astucioso *adj. cunning, astute.*

atacado *adj. attacked.*
> Por atacado. *Wholesale.*

atacar *to attack, to assail.*

ataque *m. attack.*

atar *to tie, to tighten.*

atarefado *adj. busy, occupied, "tied up."*

atas *f. pl. proceedings, minutes (of a meeting).*

ataúde *m. coffin, tomb.*

ATÉ *until; as far as; up to; also, even.*

Até logo. *So long. See you later.*

Até a vista. *See you soon. See you later.*

Até amanhã. *See you tomorrow.*

Até breve. *See you soon.*

Até segunda. *See you Monday.*

Fomos até o parque. *We went as far as the park.*

O elevador sobe até o quinto andar. *The elevator goes up to the fifth floor.*

Até onde vai este caminho? *How far does this road go?*

ATENÇÃO *f. attention.*

Quero chamar a sua atenção para isto. *I want to call your attention to this.*

Em atenção a sua carta. *With regard to your letter.*

Atenção! *Watch out!*

atencioso *adj. attentive, thoughtful, polite.*

atender *to attend (to), to take care of; to answer (the telephone).*

Maria, atenda o telefone, por favor. *Mary, please answer the telephone.*

atentar *to attempt.*

atento *adj. attentive, courteous.*

Ele é muito atento. *He is very attentive.*

Atento e obrigado. *Very truly yours.*

aterragem *f. landing (aircraft).*

aterrar *to cover with earth; to frighten.*

aterrissagem *f. landing (aircraft).*

aterrissar *to land (aircraft).*

aterrorizar *to terrify, to frighten.*

atestar *to attest.*

atinar *to hit on (discover), to find out.*

atingir *to attain, to reach.*

atitude *f. attitude, position.*

atividade (actividade) *f. activity.*

Em plena atividade. *In full swing (activity).*

ativo (activo) *adj. active.*

atlântico *adj. Atlantic.*

atleta *m. and f. athlete.*

atlético *adj. athletic.*

atmosfera *f. atmosphere.*

ATO (ACTO) *m. act, action, deed; meeting.*

No primeiro ato não acontece nada. *Nothing happens in the first act.*

átomo *m. atom.*

átono *adj. atonic, unaccented.*

ator (actor) *m. actor.*

atormentar *to torment.*

atração (atracção) *f. attraction.*

atracar *to come alongside, to tie up (a ship), to dock.*

atraente *adj. attractive.*

atrair *to attract*

ATRÁS *behind, backward; past; ago.*

Eu fiquei atrás. *I stayed behind.*

Eles tiveram que voltar para atrás. *They had to turn back.*

Que há atrás da caixa? *(x = sh) What's behind the box?*

atrasado *adj. behind, backward, late.*

Os meninos vão chegar atrasados. *The children are going to be late.*

Parece que meu relógio está atrasado. *It seems my watch is slow.*

atrasar(-se) *to hold back, to delay, to run slow (watch).*

atraso *m. delay.*

atrativo (atractivo) *adj. attractive.*

através *through.*

atravessar *to cross, to pass over; to hinder.*

atrever-se *to dare.*

Alfredo não se atreveu a fazê-lo. *Alfred did not dare to do it.*

atrevido *adj. daring, bold.*

atribuir *to attribute.*

atriz (actriz) *f. actress.*

atroar *to thunder, to roar.*

atrocidade *f. atrocity.*

atropelar *to step on, to trample, to run over.*

Ele foi atropelado por um automóvel. *He was run over by an automobile.*

atropelo *m. trampling, running over.*

atroz *adj. atrocious, cruel.*

atuação (actuação) *f. performance, acting.*

ATUAL (ACTUAL) *adj. actual, present.*

atualidade (actualidade) *f. the present, today.*

ATUALMENTE (ACTUALMENTE) *today, nowadays, at the present time.*

Atualmente eles estão em São Paulo. *At the present time they are in São Paulo.*

atuar (actuar) *to act, to put into action.*

atum *m. tuna.*

aturdido *adj. bewildered.*

audácia *f. audacity, boldness, presumption.*

audacioso *adj. bold, audacious.*

audição *f. audition.*

auditório *m. auditorium, audience.*

auge *m. height, summit.*

augusto *adj. august, venerable.*

aula *f. class, recitation.*

Hoje não tenho aulas. *I don't have any classes today.*

aumentar *to increase, to augment, to enlarge.*

aumento *m. increase.*

Aumento de preços sem aumento de ordenado, não adianta. *An increase in prices without an increase in salary doesn't help.*

áureo *adj. golden, brilliant.*

aurora *f. dawn, daybreak.*

ausência *f. absence.*

ausentar-se *to be absent, to be away.*

AUSENTE *adj. absent.*

autêntico *adj. authentic, true.*

auto *m. automobile, auto; document; public act; short dramatic work.*

autocarro *m. bus* Ⓟ.

automático *adj. automatic.*

automóvel *m. automobile.*

autor *m. author.*

autoridade *f. authority.*

autorização *f. authorization.*

autorizar *to authorize.*

auxiliar *(x = s) to aid, to help; adj. auxiliary.*

auxílio *(x = s) m. help, aid, assistance.*

avaliar *to evaluate, to judge.*

avançado *adj. advanced.*

avançar *to advance, to go ahead, to progress.*

avante *forward.*
    Avante! *Forward!*

avaria *f. damage, loss.*

avariado *adj. damaged.*

avariar *to damage.*

avaro *adj. miserly, greedy.*

ave *f. bird, fowl; hail!*
    Ave, Maria, cheia de graça. *Hail, Mary, full of grace.*

aveia *f. oat, oats.*

avenida *f. avenue.*

avental *m. apron.*

aventura *f. adventure.*

averiguar *to inquire, to find out, to investigate.*
    Averigue a que horas sai o trem. *Find out (at) what time the train leaves.*

avesso *adj. opposite, contrary.*

avestruz *m. and f. ostrich.*

aviação *f. aviation.*

aviador *m. aviator.*

avião *m. airplane.*

aviar *to get ready, to prescribe (medicine), to supply.*
    Numa farmácia aviam receitas. *In a pharmacy they fill prescriptions.*

avisado *adj. notified, advised.*

avisar *to inform, to notify, to let know; to warn.*
    Eu o avisarei assim que souber. *I'll notify you as soon as I know.*

aviso *m. notice, warning.*

avistar *to sight, to see.*

avô *m. grandfather.*

avó *f. grandmother.*

azar *m. misfortune, bad luck, mishap.*

azeite *m. oil.*
    Ele sempre deita azeite no fogo. *He's always adding fuel to the fire.*

azeiteira (almotolia) *f. oilcan.*

azeitona *f. olive.*

AZUL *blue.*
    Gosto mais do vestido azul. *I like the blue dress better.*

    Tudo azul! *Everything's fine!*

azulejo *m. glazed tile.*

B

babá *f. nursemaid* Ⓑ.

bacalhau *m. codfish.*

bacharel *m. bachelor (graduate).*

bacia *f. basin.*

báculo *m. staff, rod.*

badalada *f. sound, stroke (of a bell).*

badalar *to ring, to toll; to hype up* Ⓑ.

bagagem *f. baggage, luggage.*
    Onde posso deixar *(x = sh)* a bagagem? *Where can I leave my luggage?*

bagatela *f. bagatelle, trifle.*

bagunça *f. confusion, mess* Ⓑ.

baía *f. bay.*

bailar *to dance.*

baile *m. dance.*

bairro *m. district, neighborhood, suburb.*
    Moro no bairro residencial. *I live in the residential district (suburb).*

baixa *(x = sh) f. fall, depreciation (price); casualty.*

BAIXAR *(x = sh) to go (come down); to get (bring) down; to get off; to lower, let down; to drop (fever, temperature, etc.).*
    Quando voces vão baixar os preços? *When are you going to lower prices?*

BAIXO *(x = sh) adj. low; under, below; short.*
    Ele é baixo e gordo. *He is short and fat.*
    Fale mais baixo. *Speak more softly.*

bala *f. bullet.*

balança *f. balance, scale; justice.*
    Balança de plataforma. *Platform scale.*

balanço *m. swinging, balancing, balance.*
    Diga-me o balanço para este mês. *Give me the balance for this month.*

balar *to bleat.*

balbuciar *to stutter, to stammer, to blubber, to babble.*

balbúrdia *f. disorder, confusion.*

balcão *m. balcony; counter (in store, etc.).*

balde *m. pail, bucket.*

baldear *to bail (water); to tranship; to transfer; to change trains.*
    Temos que baldear antes de chegar ao Rio? *Do we have to change trains before we arrive in Rio?*

baleia *f. whale.*

balneário *m. boathouse, health resort.*

baluarte *m. bulwark, stronghold; shelter.*

bambu *m. bamboo.*

banal *adj. banal, trite, commonplace.*

banana *f. banana.*

banca *f. table, desk, stand; board (examining).*
   Comprei na banca (no quiosque) de
   jornais. *I bought it at the newsstand.*
banco *m. bank (commercial); bank, bar, reef;*
   bench; seat (car).
   Hoje o banco está fechado. *Today the bank*
   is closed.
   Elas se sentaram no banco. *They sat down*
   on the bench.
banda *f. band; strip, stripe.*
   Aqui vem uma banda de música. *Here*
   comes a brass band.
bandeira *f. flag, pennant, banner; colonial*
   exploratory expedition Ⓑ.
bandeirante *m. member of a bandeira* Ⓑ.
bandeja *f. tray, platter.*
bandido *m. bandit, robber.*
bando *m. band, gang; flock.*
banhar(-se) *to bathe, to wash.*
banheira *f. bathtub.*
BANHEIRO *m. bathroom* Ⓑ.
BANHO *m. bath, bathing.*
   Gostaria de tomar banho de chuveiro. *I'd*
   like to take a shower.
   Casa de banho Ⓟ. *Bathroom.*
banir *to banish, to forbid.*
banqueiro *m. banker.*
bar *m. bar, tavern.*
baralhar *to shuffle (cards); to mix up.*
barata *f. cockroach.*
BARATO *adj. cheap, inexpensive.*
barba *f. chin; beard.*
   Eu ainda não fiz a barba. *I haven't shaved*
   yet.
   Pincel de barba. *Shaving brush.*
bárbaro *adj. barbaric, coarse, brutal.*
barbear *to shave* (**barbeio,** *etc.*).
barbearia *f. barbershop.*
barbear-se *to shave (oneself)* (**barbeio-me,**
   etc.).
   Primeiro vou barbear-me. *First I'm going*
   to shave.
   Sempre me barbeio antes de sair de casa. *I*
   always shave before leaving home.
barbeiro *m. barber.*
barbudo *adj. heavily bearded.*
barca *f. boat, barge.*
barco *m. boat, ship, vessel.*
   Barco a motor. *Motorboat.*
   Barco a vapor. *Steamship.*
   Barco a vela. *Sailboat.*
barômetro (barómetro) *m. barometer.*
barquinha *f. small boat; ship's log.*
barra *f. bar, ingot; strip, band; sandbar.*
barraca *f. hut, tent, shelter.*
barragem *f. dam, barrier.*
barranco *m. ravine, gully; ecipice.*
barrar *to make metal bars; to bar, to obstruct.*
barreira *f. barrier, bar, obstruction.*

barriga *f. belly, stomach.*
barril *m. barrel, cask.*
barro *m. mud, clay.*
barulho *m. noise.*
   Meninos, isso é muito barulho. *Children,*
   that's too much noise.
base *f. base, basis.*
basear *to base.*
básico *adj. basic.*
basquetbol *m. basketball.*
BASTANTE *enough, sufficient; quite.*
   Ele não tem bastante dinheiro. *He does not*
   have enough money.
   Acho bastante caro. *I think it's pretty*
   expensive.
bastão *m. cane, walking stick.*
BASTAR *to suffice, to be enough.*
   Isso basta. *That's enough.*
   Basta! *Enough! Stop!*
bata *f. dressing gown; smock.*
batalha *f. battle, combat, fight.*
batalhão *m. battalion.*
batalhar *to battle, to fight, to struggle.*
batata *f. potato.*
   Batatas fritas. *Fried potatoes.*
   Purê de batatas. *Mashed potatoes.*
   Batata-doce. *Sweet potato.*
BATER *to beat, to strike; to knock.*
   Quem bate à porta? *Who's knocking at the*
   door?
bateria *f. battery, drums (music).*
   Bateria de cozinha. *Kitchen utensils.*
batida *f. blow, knock; collision; a mixed drink*
   with a brandy base Ⓑ.
batismo (baptismo) *m. baptism, christening.*
batizar (baptizar) *to baptize, to christen.*
batuque *m. Afro-Brazilian dance* Ⓑ.
baú *m. trunk, chest.*
baunilha *f. vanilla.*
bazar *m. bazaar, store.*
bêbado *adj. drunk, intoxicated; m. drunkard.*
bebê (bebé) *m. baby.*
BEBER *to drink.*
bebida *f. drink, beverage.*
   Ele se deu à bebida. *He took to drink.*
beco *m. alley, lane, side street.*
   Beco sem saída. *Blind alley.*
beijar *to kiss.*
beijo *m. kiss.*
beira *f. brink, edge, bank.*
beira-mar *f. seashore, coast.*
beleza *f. beauty.*
bélico *adj. bellicose, warlike.*
belicoso *adj. bellicose, warlike; hostile.*
BELO *adj. beautiful.*
   Ela é bela! *She is beautiful!*
   O belo sexo (x = ks). *The fair sex.*
   As belas artes. *The fine arts.*
BEM *well, right; m. loved one, darling.*

Você está bem? *Are you all right?*
Muito bem, obrigado. *Very well, thank you.*
Não muito bem. *Not very well.*
Passe bem. *Good luck. Good-bye.*
Está bem. *All right. O.K.*
Bem educado. *Well brought up.*
É bem longe. *It's quite far.*
É bem pouco. *It's not very much.*
Por que chora, meu bem? *Why are you crying, my darling?*
bem-estar *m. well-being, welfare.*
bênção *f. blessing, benediction.*
bendito *adj. blessed.*
bendizer *to praise; to bless.*
beneficiar *to benefit, to profit.*
beneficiário *adj. beneficiary.*
benefício *m. benefit, profit, advantage.*
benfeitor *m. benefactor.*
bengala *f. cane, walking stick.*
benigno *adj. kind.*
bens *m. pl. property, possessions.*
bento *adj. blessed, holy.*
benzer *to bless.*
benzer-se *to make the sign of the cross.*
    Ela se benzeu ao entrar na igreja. *She made the sign of the cross on entering the church.*
berço *m. cradle, crib; birthplace, birth.*
    Desde o berço até a morte, o estado entra na nossa vida. *The state enters our life from birth to death.*
berinjela *f. eggplant.*
berrar *to roar, to shout.*
berro *m. roar, shout.*
besta *f. beast; fool.*
besteira *f. foolish thing, nonsense.*
    Eles só dizem besteiras. *They speak nothing but nonsense.*
beterraba *f. beet.*
bexiga *(x = sh) f. bladder; smallpox.*
bezerro *m. calf.*
Bíblia *f. Bible.*
bibliografia *f. bibliography.*
biblioteca *f. library.*
bicarbonato *m. bicarbonate.*
bicho *m. animal, insect, worm; unpleasant person; crafty person.*
    Ele é um bicho. *He's a nasty guy.*
    Jogo do bicho. *A type of lottery in Brazil.*
bicicleta *f. bicycle.*
bico *m. beak, bill, point.*
bife *m. steak, beefsteak.*
bigode *m. moustache.*
bilhar *m. billiards.*
BILHETE *m. ticket, note.*
    Quero bilhete de ida e volta. *I want a round-trip ticket.*
    Ontem Carlos recebeu o bilhete azul. *Charles was fired yesterday.*

Bilhete postal. *Postcard* Ⓑ.
bilheteria (bilheteira) *f. ticket office.*
binóculo *m. binoculars, opera glasses.*
biombo *m. screen.*
bip *m. beeper, pager.*
    Mandar chamar por bip. *To page someone.*
bis *again; encore!*
bisavô *m. great-grandfather.*
bisavó *f. great-grandmother.*
biscoito *m. biscuit, cookie, cracker.*
bisneto *m. great-grandson.*
bispo *m. bishop.*
bissexto *adj. bissextile.*
    Ano bissexto. *Leap year.*
bitola *f. gauge (railroad); measure.*
blindado *adj. armored.*
blindar *to armor, to cover.*
bloco *m. block; writing pad.*
    Compre-me um bloco de papel. *Buy me a writing pad.*
BOA *adj. f. of* **bom.**
boas-vindas *f. pl. welcome.*
bobagem *f. nonsense, foolishness.*
bobo *adj. foolish, silly; m. fool, clown.*
BOCA *f. mouth.*
bocadinho *m. bit.*
    Espere um bocadinho. *Wait a bit.*
bocado *m. bite, piece; short while.*
bocejar *to yawn.*
bochecha *f. cheek.*
boda *f. wedding.*
bofetada *f. slap in the face, blow.*
boi *m. ox, bull.*
BOLA *f. ball, globe; wits.*
    Bola de tênis (ténis). *Tennis ball.*
    Ora bolas! *Baloney! Nuts!*
boletim *m. bulletin, report.*
bolo *m. cake; stake, kitty.*
BOLSA *f. purse, bag, scholarship.*
    Bolsa de estudos. *Scholarship.*
    Bolsa de valores. *Stock exchange.*
BOLSO *m. pocket.*
    Esta é uma edição de bolso. *This is a pocket edition.*
BOM *adj. good; kind; satisfactory; suited, fit; well.*
    Bom dia. *Good morning.*
    Boa tarde. *Good afternoon. Good evening.*
    Boa noite. *Good night.*
    É uma boa idéia (ideia). *That's a good idea.*
    Eu acho muito bom. *I think it's great.*
    Ele está bom. *He's well.*
    Nós lhe fizemos uma boa! *We played a fine trick on him!*
bomba *f. pump; fire engine; bomb.*
bombeiro *m. fireman; plumber.*
bombom *m. bonbon, candy.*
BONDADE *f. goodness, kindness.*

Tenha a bondade de sentar-se. *Please sit down.*

bonde *m. streetcar* Ⓑ.

bondoso *adj. kind.*

boné *m. cap.*

bonitão *m.* **(bonitona** *f.) adj. good-looking.*

bonito *adj. pretty, good.*

borboleta *f. butterfly; wing nut.*

bordar *to embroider; to edge.*

bordo *m. board (ship); border; course, tack (boat).*

Peço licença para ir a bordo. *I ask permission to go aboard.*

borracha *f. rubber; eraser.*

borrasca *f. storm.*

bosque *m. forest, woods.*

bosquejo *m. sketch, draft.*

bossa nova *f. type of Brazilian popular music.*

bota *f. boot.*

botão *m. button; bud.*

BOTAR *to cast, to throw; to put, to place* Ⓑ.

Bote fora! *Throw it out!*

Botou cinco dólares no balcão. *He put five dollars on the counter.*

bote *m. boat.*

botica *f. pharmacy.*

boticário *m. pharmacist, druggist.*

boxe (*x* = *ks*) *m. boxing.*

boxeador (*x* = *ks*) *m. boxer.*

boxear (*x* = *ks*) *to box.*

BRAÇO *m. arm.*

Eles ficaram com os braços cruzados. *They stayed there with their arms folded.*

bradar *to roar, to shout.*

BRANCO *white, pale, blank.*

Quero seis camisas brancas. *I want six white shirts.*

Você pode deixá-lo (*x* = *sh*) em branco. *You can leave it blank.*

Verso branco. *Blank verse.*

brando *adj. soft, smooth.*

brasa *f. live coal, ember.*

Eles estão sobre brasas. *They're very worried about it.*

BRASIL *m. Brazil.*

BRASILEIRO *adj. Brazilian; n. m. Brazilian.*

bravo *adj. brave, wild; bravo!*

BREVE *brief, short, soon, shortly.*

Até breve. *See you soon.*

Em breve. *Soon.*

Faça-o o mais breve possível! *Do it as soon as possible!*

brevidade *f. briefness, brevity.*

briga *f. quarrel, fight.*

brigada *f. brigade.*

brigar *to quarrel, to fight.*

brilhante *adj. brilliant, sparkling; n. m. diamond.*

brilhar *to shine, to sparkle.*

brincadeira *f. joke; jest, prank.*

Chega de brincadeiras! *That's enough joking!*

brincar *to joke; to play.*

Os meninos estão brincando. *The children are playing.*

Mas ele só estava brincando! *But he was only joking!*

brindar *to toast.*

brinde *m. toast; offering.*

brinquedo *m. toy.*

brisa *f. breeze.*

broche *m. clasp; brooch.*

brochura *f. brochure, pamphlet; paperback.*

bronze *m. bronze, brass.*

brotar *to bud; to produce; to burst out.*

brusco *adj. brusque, rude, rough.*

brutal *adj. brutal, rough.*

bruto *adj. brutal; rude.*

Foi um ato (acto) muito bruto. *It was a very brutal act.*

bruxaria (*x* = *sh*) *f. witchcraft.*

bruxo (*x* = *sh*) *m.* **(bruxa** *f.) sorcerer, medicine man; witch.*

budista *n. m. and f. Buddhist.*

bufão *m. braggart, joker.*

bufete *m. buffet, sideboard, dresser.*

bugia *f. wax candle.*

bugigangas *f. pl. trinkets, knickknacks.*

buraco *m. hole, opening.*

Buraco de fechadura. *Keyhole.*

burla *f. joke; trick; deceit.*

burlar *to joke, to jest; to trick; to deceive.*

burro *m. donkey, ass.*

busca *f. search, pursuit.*

Ele vai em busca de fama. *He's in pursuit of fame.*

buscar *to look for, to go for.*

busto *m. bust.*

buzina *f. horn (music, car, etc.).*

buzinar *to blow a horn; to honk a car horn.*

C

CÁ *here, this way.*

Venha cá! *Come here!*

cabana *f. hut, cabin.*

CABEÇA *f. head.*

Tenho dor de cabeça. *I have a headache.*

Dos pés à cabeça. *From head to foot.*

Isso não tem pés nem cabeça. *That doesn't make sense.*

cabeceira *f. head of a bed, table, or list.*

Mesa de cabeceira. *Bedside table.*

CABELO *m. hair.*

caber *to fit into; to have enough room; to contain.*

Não cabe mais nada no baú. *There's no more room in the trunk.*

cabide *m. coat hanger, hat rack, peg.*

cabina, cabine *f. cabin, booth.*

Cabina telefônica (cabine telefónica). *Telephone booth.*

cabo *m tip, extremity, end; cape; handle; cable; rope; corporal.*

Ao cabo do dia. *At the end of the day.*

Ele nunca leva nada ao cabo. *He never finishes anything.*

Cabo da Boa Esperança. *Cape of Good Hope.*

caboclo *m.* Ⓑ. *backwoodsman; Brazilian Indian, half-breed; adj. copper-colored.*

cabra *f. female goat; m.* Ⓑ *half-breed; bandit; ruffian.*

caça *f. hunting; game.*

caçador *m. hunter.*

caçar *to hunt, to chase.*

cacarejar *to cackle; to chatter.*

caçarola *f. saucepan, casserole.*

cacau *m. cocoa, cacao.*

cacete *m. club, stick; adj. unpleasant, boring* Ⓑ.

cachaça *f. Brazilian sugar cane liquor or rum.*

cachimbo *m. pipe (for smoking).*

cachoeira *f. waterfall.*

cachorro *m. dog.*

Cachorro quente. *Hot dog.*

caçoar *to tease, to make fun of.*

CADA *adj. m. and f. each, every.*

Cada hora. *Each hour.*

Cada qual. *Each one. Every one.*

Cada vez que ele vem. *Each time he comes.*

Dar a cada um. *To give each one.*

Cada dia ele fala português melhor. *Every day he speaks Portuguese better.*

cadáver *m. corpse, cadaver.*

cadeia *f. chain.*

CADEIRA *f. chair.*

caderno *m. notebook.*

cadete *m. cadet.*

CAFÉ *m. coffee; coffeehouse.*

Uma xícara (*x* = *sh*) de café. *A cup of coffee.*

Café com leite. *Coffee with milk.*

Café preto. *Black coffee.*

CAFÉ DA MANHÃ *m. breakfast* Ⓑ.

Tomo o café da manhã às nove. *I have breakfast at nine o'clock.*

cafeteira *f. coffeepot.*

CAFEZINHO *m. small cup of black coffee* Ⓑ.

caída *f. fall, downfall.*

caído *adj. fallen.*

CAIR *to fall; to tumble down; to drop; to become, to fit.*

Caía chuva no telhado. *Rain was falling on the roof.*

Esse vestido lhe cai bem. *That dress looks good on you.*

O aniversário de João cai no mesmo dia que o meu. *John's birthday falls on the same day as mine.*

cais *m. dock, pier.*

CAIXA (*x* = *sh*) *f. box, case; chest; cabinet.*

Essa caixa é muito pequena. *That box is very small.*

Faça o favor de pagar na caixa. *Please pay the cashier.*

caixão (*x* = *sh*) *m. large box, chest; coffin.*

caixeiro (*x* = *sh*) *m. salesman, clerk.*

cajadada *f. blow with a stick.*

caju *m. cashew.*

cal *m. lime; whitewash.*

calabouço *m. jail, prison.*

calado *adj. quiet, silent, reserved.*

calamidade *f. calamity.*

calar *to keep quiet, to be silent; to conceal.*

Cale-se! *Be quiet!*

calçada *f. sidewalk; pavement.*

calçado *m. footwear, shoes.*

calção *m. shorts, trunks.*

Calção de banho. *Bathing trunks.*

calçar *to put on (shoes, socks, etc.); to tread on.*

calças *f. pl. trousers; panties.*

calcular *to calculate, to estimate, to presume.*

cálculo *m. computation, estimate; calculus.*

caldo *m. soup, broth; juice.*

calefação (calefacção) *f. heat, heating system.*

calendário *m. calendar, almanac.*

calibre *m. caliber, bore; gauge.*

caligrafia *f. penmanship, handwriting.*

calmo *adj. calm, quiet.*

calo *m. corn, callus.*

CALOR *m. heat, warmth.*

Sempre faz calor no verão. *It's always warm in the summer.*

calouro *m. beginner, freshman, greenhorn.*

calúnia *f. calumny, slander.*

caluniar *to slander.*

calvície *f. baldness.*

calvo *adj. bald; bare, barren.*

CAMA *bed; couch; layer.*

Fazer a cama. *To make the bed.*

Ele foi para a cama às dez. *He went to bed at ten.*

câmara *f. chamber; room, camera.*

Câmara municipal. *City council.*

Câmara cinematográfica. *Movie camera.*

camarada *m. and f. friend, companion.*

camarão *m. shrimp, prawn.*

camareira *f. chambermaid.*

camareiro *m. steward; room servant (hotel).*

camarote *m. box (theatre); cabin (ship).*

cambiar to change, to exchange.
câmbio m. change, exchange.
   Câmbio exterior. Foreign exchange.
   Eu perdi no câmbio. I lost in the exchange.
caminhão m. truck.
CAMINHAR to walk; to march; to move along.
CAMINHO m. road, way, highway.
   Qual é o caminho mais curto para a cidade? Which is the shortest way to the city?
   Todos os caminhos levam a Roma. All roads lead to Rome.
CAMISA f. shirt, chemise.
   Ela me comprou três camisas. She bought me three shirts.
   Eu prefiro trabalhar em mangas de camisa. I prefer to work in shirtsleeves.
camisaria f. haberdashery; shirt factory.
camisola f. nightgown; undershirt Ⓟ.
campainha f. bell, buzzer.
campeão m. champion.
campestre adj. rural, rustic, country.
campo m. field, country; space.
cana f. cane, reed.
   Cana-de-açúcar. Sugar cane.
canal m. canal; channel (maritime; TV).
   Passamos pelo canal do Panamá. We went through the Panama Canal.
canalha m. rascal, scoundrel; f. rabble, mob.
canário m. canary.
CANÇÃO f. song.
cancelar to cancel.
câncer m. cancer (sign of the zodiac).
cancioneiro m. songbook.
cancro m. cancer (med.); chancre, canker.
candeeiro m. lamp; chandelier.
candeia f. oil lamp, lamp.
candelabro m. candelabrum.
candidato m. candidate.
candidatura f. candidacy.
candidez f. candor; simplicity.
cândido adj. candid, frank.
caneca f. mug.
canela f. cinnamon; shin.
   Gabriela, Cravo e Canela. Gabriela, Clove and Cinnamon. (Title of a novel by Jorge Amado.)
caneta f. penholder, pen.
   Caneta esferográfica. Ballpoint pen.
   Caneta-tinteiro. Fountain pen.
cânfora f. camphor.
cangaceiro m. outlaw, bandit Ⓑ.
canhão m. cannon, gun; canyon.
caniço m. reed, rod.
canino adj. canine.
   Estou com uma fome canina. I'm ravenous.
canivete m. penknife, pocketknife.

canja f. chicken soup with rice; a cinch, easy Ⓑ.
   É canja! That's a cinch! That's easy!
cano m. pipe, tube.
   Os seus planos foram pelo cano a baixo. His plans went down the drain.
canoa f. canoe.
cansaço m. weariness, fatigue.
CANSADO adj. tired, weary; tedious; annoying.
   Ficamos muito cansados. We are very tired.
cansar to tire, to annoy, to bore.
cansar-se to get tired, to get annoyed, to become bored.
cantador m. singer (of popular songs).
CANTAR to sing.
cântaro m. pot, jar, pitcher.
cantarolar to hum.
cântico m. song, hymn.
cantiga f. popular song, ballad.
cantina f. canteen.
canto m. song; corner, nook.
cantor m. singer.
CÃO m. dog.
   Quem não tem cão, caça com gato. One does the best one can. You have to make the best of things.
capa f. cape, cloak, coat; cover.
   Capa de chuva. Raincoat.
   Capa de livro. Book cover, binding.
capacidade f. capacity.
capataz m. foreman, boss.
capaz adj. capable, able.
   Ele é capaz de fazê-lo. He's capable of doing it.
capela f. chapel.
capelão m. chaplain.
capital adj. principal, main; n. m. principal (money); capital (stock); n. f. capital (city).
   Quanto capital precisa para essa empresa? How much capital do you need for that undertaking?
   Qual é a capital do estado? What is the state capital?
capitão m. captain.
capitólio m. capitol.
capítulo m. chapter.
capote m. cape, cloak, overcoat.
captar to capture, to catch.
capturar to capture, arrest.
CARA f. face, look, appearance.
   Encontraram-se cara a cara. They met face to face.
   Ele tem boa cara. He looks like a decent guy.
   Você tem cara de fome. You look like you're starving.
   Cara ou coroa? Heads or tails?

caranguejo *m. crab.*

caráter (carácter) *m. character.*

carbono *m. carbon; carbon paper.*

cárcere *m. jail, prison.*

cardápio *m. menu.*

cardeal *adj., n. m. cardinal.*
> Pontos cardeais. *Cardinal points.*

cardinal *adj. cardinal, principal.*
> Números cardinais. *Cardinal numbers.*

careca *adj. bald; n. m. bald person.*

CARECER *to lack, to need.*

carga *f. load, burden, freight, cargo.*
> O asno é animal de carga. *The donkey is a beast of burden.*
> Toda a carga chegou? *Did all of the cargo arrive?*

cargo *m. obligation, charge, responsibility; employment.*
> Alberto assumiu o cargo. *Albert took on the responsibility.*

carícia *f. caress.*

caridade *f. charity, pity.*

carimbar *to stamp, to seal.*

carinho *m. love, affection.*

carinhoso *adj. affectionate, kind.*

CARIOCA *adj. of the city of Rio de Janeiro; n. m. and f. inhabitant of Rio de Janeiro.*
> Ele é carioca da gema. *He's a real carioca.*

caritativo *adj. charitable.*

CARNAVAL *m. carnival.*
> É um samba de carnaval. *It's a carnival samba.*

CARNE *f. meat; flesh; pulp (of fruit).*
> Gosto mais de carne de vaca. *I like beef better.*
> Carne de carneiro. *Mutton.*
> Carne de vitela. *Veal.*
> Carne de porco. *Pork.*
> Nem carne nem peixe. *Neither fish nor fowl.*

carneiro *m. sheep.*

CARO *adj. expensive; dear (cherished).*
> Tudo é muito caro. *Everything is really expensive.*
> Meu caro amigo. *My dear friend.*
> Minha cara metade não concorda. *My better half does not agree.*

carpinteiro *m. carpenter; woodpecker.*

carregado *adj. loaded, heavy.*

carregar *to load, to burden.*

carreira *f. career, race (running).*

carreta *f. cart, wagon.*

carro *m. car, automobile; cart.*
> Carro-restaurante. *Dining car.*
> Carro eléctrico. *Streetcar Ⓟ.*

carroça *f. cart.*

CARTA *f. letter; map, chart; charter; playing card.*

> Nem uma carta recebi dele. *I didn't receive even one letter from him.*
> Carta registrada (registada). *Registered letter.*
> Carta expressa. *Special delivery letter.*
> Carta de crédito. *Letter of credit.*
> Carta de naturalização. *Naturalization papers.*

cartão *m. cardboard; card; calling card.*
> Ele me mandou (mandou-me) vários cartões (bilhetes) postais. *He sent me several postcards.*
> Deixei (x = sh) meu cartão. *I left my calling card.*

cartaz *m. poster, placard.*

carteira *f. wallet, pocketbook; portfolio; license.*
> Roubaram-me a carteira. *They stole my wallet.*
> Carteira de motorista. *Driver's license.*

carteiro *m. mailman, postman.*

cartilha *f. primer.*

carvalho *m. oak tree.*

carvão *m. coal, charcoal.*

CASA *f. house, home; firm, concern; room Ⓟ.*
> Ela mora na casa da tia. *She lives in her aunt's home.*
> Vamos para casa. *Let's go home.*
> Estarei em casa o dia todo. *I'll be home all day.*
> Eles estão em casa de João. *They're at John's house.*
> A casa editora ainda não me escreveu. *The publishing house did not write me yet.*
> O Presidente mora na Casa Branca. *The President lives in the White House.*
> Casa de banho Ⓟ. *Bathroom.*

casado *adj. married.*

casal *m. couple; married couple.*

casamento *m. marriage, wedding.*

casar *to marry.*

CASAR-SE *to get married.*
> Ela se casou com o filho do prefeito Ⓑ. *She married the mayor's son.*

casca *f. peel, husk, shell, bark.*

caseiro *adj. pertaining to the home, domestic; homemade.*
> É um remédio caseiro. *It's a home remedy.*

casimira *f. cashmere, woolen cloth.*

CASO *case, event.*
> É um caso raro! *It's a strange case!*
> Bem, vamos ao caso. *Well, let's get to the point.*
> Ele não faz caso de nada. *He doesn't pay attention to anything.*
> Caso que quer . . . *In case you want to . . .*

caspa *f. dandruff.*

castanha *f. chestnut.*
> Castanha-do-Pará. *Brazil nut.*

castiço *adj. pure; of good birth.*

castigar *to punish.*

castigo *m. punishment, penalty.*

casual *adj. accidental, casual.*

casualidade *f. chance, coincidence, accident.*
> Eu o encontrei por casualidade. *I met him by chance.*

catálogo *m. catalog.*

catarata *f. cataract; waterfall.*

catedral *f. cathedral.*

catedrático *m. professor (especially of a university).*

categoria *f. category, class.*

catolicismo *m. Catholicism.*

católico *adj. Catholic.*

CATORZE *fourteen.*

caução *f. bond, bail, security.*

cauda *f. tail; end; extermity.*
> Piano de cauda. *Grand piano.*

caudilho *m. chief, leader.*

CAUSA *f. cause, motive.*
> Por causa disso, ninguém veio. *For that reason, nobody came.*

causar *to cause.*
> Causou muito dano. *It caused great damage.*

cautela *f. caution, prudence.*

cauteloso *adj. cautious.*

cavala *f. mackerel.*

cavalaria *f. cavalry.*

cavaleiro *m. horseman, rider.*

cavalheiro *m. gentleman.*

cavalo *m. horse; knight (chess); jack (cards).*

cavar *to dig.*

caverna *f. cavern, cave.*

cavidade *f. cavity.*

cear *to eat supper (**ceio**, etc.).*

cebola *f. onion.*

ceder *to grant; to give in, to yield.*

CEDO *early, soon.*
> Ainda é muito cedo. *It's still too early.*
> Mais cedo ou mais tarde. *Sooner or later.*

cedro *m. cedar.*

cédula *f. certificate, bill, promissory note.*

cego *adj. blind; n. m. blind person.*

cegonha *f. stork.*

cegueira *f. blindness.*

ceia *f. supper.*

CELEBRAR *to celebrate; to praise; to commemorate.*
> Vamos celebrar a ocasião com uma festa no sábado. *We are going to celebrate the occasion with a party on Saturday.*

célebre *adj. famous; celebrated.*

célula *f. cell.*

CEM *hundred.*
> Custa mais de cem dólares. *It costs more than a hundred dollars.*

cemento *m. cement.*

cemitério *m. cemetery.*

cena *f. scene; stage.*
> Não gostei nada da primeira cena da peça. *I didn't like the first scene of the play at all.*

cenário *m. stage, setting, scenery.*

cenoura *f. carrot.*

censura *f. censorship; censure.*

censurar *to censor; to censure.*

CENTAVO *m. centavo; cent.*

centeio *m. rye.*

centelha *f. spark.*

centena *f. hundred, about a hundred.*

centenário *m. centenary.*

centésimo *adj. hundredth.*

centígrado *adj. centigrade.*

cêntimo *m. cent ($^1/_{100}$ euro).*

CENTO *hundred.*
> Vasco da Gama chegou à Índia em mil quatrocentos e noventa e oito. *Vasco da Gama reached India in 1498.*

CENTRAL *adj. central; f. main office.*
> América Central. *Central America.*
> Onde é a central do correio? *Where is the main post office?*

CENTRO *m. center, middle; core; club, social circle.*

cera *f. wax.*

cerca *f. fence, hedge; enclosed land.*

cerca de *about, approximately.*
> Creio que vi cerca de quarenta quadros modernos. *I believe I saw about forty modern paintings.*

cercar *to fence in, to enclose, to surround; to besiege.*

cereal *m. cereal.*

cérebro *m. brain, mind.*

cereja *f. cherry.*

cerejeira *f. cherry tree.*

cerimônia (cerimónia) *f. ceremony; formality.*

ceroulas *f. pl. long underwear, drawers.*

cerração *f. fog, mist.*

cerrado *adj. thick; dense; closed.*

cerrar *to close, to lock; to enclose.*

cerro *m. small hill.*

certeza *f. certainty.*
> Temos certeza de que ele não vem hoje. *We are sure he is not coming today.*
> Com certeza. *Of course.*

certidão *f. certificate.*
> É preciso apresentar a certidão de nascimento. *You must show your birth certificate.*

certificado *m. certificate.*

certificar *to certify; to attest.*

CERTO *adj. sure, certain; right; true.*
> Eu estou certo disso. *I'm sure of that.*
> Está certo. *That's right.*

Certo amigo me disse isso. *A certain friend told me that.*

Nunca vai dar certo! *It'll never work!*

cerveja *f. beer, ale.*

cervejaria *f. brewery; beer hall.*

cervo *m. deer.*

cessar *to stop, to cease.*

cesto *m. basket.*

cetim *m. satin.*

céu *m. sky; heaven.*

cevada *f. barley.*

CHÁ *m. tea.*

Quer café ou prefere chá? *Do you want some coffee or do you prefer tea?*

Colher de chá. *Teaspoon.*

chácara *f. country house* Ⓑ.

chaleira *f. teakettle; m. and f. flatterer* Ⓑ.

chama *f. flame.*

chamada *f. call.*

Chamada interurbana. *Long-distance call.*

O professor sempre faz a chamada. *The teacher always calls the roll.*

CHAMAR *to call; to appeal; to name; to send for.*

O senhor chamou? *Did you call?*

Chamar pelo telefone. *To phone.*

Chame um táxi (x = ks), por favor. *Please call a taxi.*

CHAMAR-SE *to be called, to be named.*

Como se chama ele? *What is his name?*

Ele se chama (chama-se) João Costa. *His name is John Costa.*

chaminé *f. chimney; smokestack.*

chão *m. floor, ground.*

chapa *f. plate, license plate.*

CHAPÉU *m. hat.*

Não sei onde deixei (x = sh) o chapéu. *I don't know where I left my hat.*

Chapéu de feltro. *Felt hat.*

Quando ela entrou, ele tirou o chapéu. *When she entered, he took off his hat.*

charlatão *m. quack, impostor.*

charque *m. beef jerky* Ⓑ.

charuto *m. cigar.*

chatear *to bore, to annoy.*

chato *adj. flat; boring.*

Ele é muito chato. *He's a big bore.*

CHAVE *f. key; wrench.*

Não posso abrir a porta sem a chave. *I can't open the door without the key.*

Chave de parafusos. *Screwdriver.*

Chave inglesa. *Monkey wrench.*

chávena *f. cup, teacup.*

chefe *m. and f. chief, director.*

CHEGADA *f. arrival.*

CHEGAR *to arrive, to come; to be enough.*

Quando chegaram? *When did you arrive?*

Chega para hoje. *That's enough for today.*

Chega aqui! *Get over here!*

Ele chegou a ser presidente da firma. *He got to be president of the firm.*

CHEIO *adj. full.*

Foi um dia bem cheio. *It was quite a full day.*

cheirar *to smell.*

cheiro *m. odor, smell.*

cheque *m. check.*

Quando viajo sempre levo comigo cheques de viagem. *When I travel I always take travelers' checks with me.*

chiado *m. squeaking, squealing, chirping.*

chiar *to squeak, to screech, to chirp.*

chifre *m. horn.*

chinela *f. house slipper.*

chinelo *m. slipper.*

chique *adj. chic, stylish.*

chiqueiro *m. pigpen.*

chispa *f. spark.*

chiste *m. joke, wisecrack.*

chita *f. calico, cotton cloth.*

choça *f. hut, shack.*

chocolate *m. chocolate.*

chofer *m. driver, chauffeur.*

Chofer de praça. *Cab driver, cabby.*

chope *m. draft beer* Ⓑ.

Chope-duplo. *A double-sized glass of draft beer; double-decker bus* Ⓑ.

choque *m. jolt, shock, collision.*

choramingar *to whimper, to whine.*

CHORAR *to cry, to weep, to mourn, to lament.*

Quando ouviram a notícia, choraram. *When they heard the news, they cried.*

Quem não chora não mama. *The squeaky wheel gets the most grease.*

choro *m. crying, weeping; type of Brazilian popular music.*

CHOVER *to rain.*

Se chover não vamos. *If it rains, we won't go.*

chumbo *m. lead.*

CHUVA *f. rain, rainfall.*

Há muita chuva em março (Março). *There is a lot of rainfall in March.*

chuveiro *m. shower.*

chuviscar *to drizzle.*

chuvisco *m. drizzle.*

cicatriz *f. scar.*

cicerone *m. and f. guide.*

ciclista *m. and f. cyclist.*

ciclone *m. cyclone.*

cidadania *f. citizenship.*

cidadão *m. citizen.*

CIDADE *f. city.*

Rio de Janeiro, cidade maravilhosa. *Rio de Janeiro, marvelous city.*

Em que cidade o senhor nasceu? *In what city were you born?*

cidra *f. cider; citron.*

ciência *f. science.*

ciente *adj. aware, cognizant.*

científico *adj. scientific.*

cifra *f. figure, cipher, number; code.*

cigano *m. gypsy.*

cigarra *f. cicada.*

cigarreira *f. cigarette case.*

CIGARRO *m. cigarette.*

cilindro *m. cylinder, roller.*

cima *f. top, highest part.*

> O livro está em cima da mesa. *The book is on top of the table.*

cimento *m. cement.*

CINCO *five.*

CINEMA *m. movies; movie theater.*

> Vamos ao cinema todos os domingos. *We go to the movies every Sunday.*

CINQUENTA (CINQUENTA) *fifty.*

cinta *f. belt, girdle, band.*

cinto *m. belt, sash.*

cintura *f. waist.*

cinza *f. ash, powder; adj. gray, ashen.*

cinzeiro *m. ashtray.*

cinzento *adj. gray, ashen.*

cipreste *m. cypress.*

circo *m. circus, ring.*

circulação *f. circulation.*

circular *to circulate.*

círculo *m. circle.*

circunflexo *(x = ks) adj. circumflex.*

circunstância *f. circumstance.*

cirurgião *m. surgeon.*

cismar *to think about, to ponder, to meditate.*

> Em cismar sozinho à noite. *In meditation alone by night.*

cisne *m. swan.*

cita *f. quotation, citation.*

citação *f. quotation, citation.*

citar *to quote, to cite.*

ciúme *m. jealousy.*

> Acho que ele tem ciúmes dela. *I think he's jealous of her.*

ciumento *adj. jealous.*

> Ele é muito ciumento. *He is very jealous.*

civil *adj. civil, civilian; courteous.*

civilização *f. civilization.*

clamar *to shout, to cry out.*

claridade *f. clearness; light; distinctness.*

clarim *m. bugle, trumpet.*

clarinete *m. clarinet.*

CLARO *adj. clear, bright; evident; intelligible, obvious; plain, frank; transparent, pure; light (color); n. m. blank, space.*

> Escreva claro. *Write clearly.*
> Claro! *Of course!*
> Claro que sim! *Of course!*
> Claro que não! *Of course not!*

CLASSE *f. class; kind; sort; order.*

> É obra de primeira classe. *It's a top-notch work.*

clérigo *m. clergyman, priest.*

clero *m. clergymen, clergy.*

cliente *m. and f. client; customer; patient.*

clima *m. climate.*

clínica *f. clinic.*

cloaca *f. sewer, cesspool, latrine.*

clorofórmio *m. chloroform.*

clube *m. club (social organization; nightspot).*

cobertor *m. blanket.*

cobra *f. snake.*

cobrador *m. collector.*

COBRAR *to charge, to collect, to receive (money).*

> Quanto cobraram? *How much did they charge?*
> Ele está cobrando ânimo. *He is feeling much encouraged.*

cobre *m. copper.*

COBRIR *to cover.*

coçar *to scratch; to thrash.*

coceira *f. itch; itchiness.*

coche *m. coach, carriage.*

cochichar *to whisper.*

cochicho *m. whispering, whisper.*

cochilo *m. nap, dozing; oversight ℝ.*

coco *m. coconut.*

cócoras, *f. pl. de cócoras squatting.*

codorniz *f. quail.*

coelho *m. rabbit.*

> Matar dois coelhos com uma só cajadada. *To kill two birds with one stone.*

cofre *m. safe, chest.*

coincidência *f. coincidence.*

> Encontramo-nos por coincidência. *We met by chance.*

coincidir *to coincide.*

COISA (COUSA) *f. thing, matter.*

> Não há tal coisa. *There is no such thing.*
> Alguma coisa. *Something.*
> O senhor deseja outra coisa? *Do you want something else?*
> É a mesma coisa. *It's the same thing.*
> Será coisa de três dias. *It will take about three days.*
> Como vão as coisas? *How are things?*

coitado *adj. poor, unfortunate; n. m. poor fellow, poor thing.*

> Coitado de mim! *Poor me!*

cola *f. glue.*

colaboração *f. collaboration.*

colaborar *to collaborate.*

colar *m. necklace, collar.*

colcha *f. bedspread.*

colchão *m. mattress.*

coleção (colecção) *f. collection.*

colecionar (coleccionar) *to collect.*

colega *co-worker*

colégio *m. school (below college level—elementary or secondary).*

cólera *f. anger; cholera.*

colete *m. vest.*

colheita *f. crop, harvest.*

COLHER *f. spoon.*
> Você esqueceu as colheres. *You forgot the spoons.*
> Colher de café. *Coffee spoon.*
> Colher de chá. *Teaspoon.*
> Colher de sopa. *Soupspoon. Tablespoon.*

COLHER *to gather, to take, to obtain; to harvest; to pick.*
> Quer colher-me algumas flores? *Would you pick some flowers for me?*

colibri *m. hummingbird.*

colina *f. hill.*

colmeia *f. beehive.*

colo *m. lap, neck.*

colocar *to place; to give employment to.*
> Coloque tudo em seu lugar. *Put everything in its place.*
> Meu pai o colocou numa casa de comércio. *My father got him a position in a business firm.*

colônia (colónia) *f. colony.*

colonial *adj. colonial.*

coluna *f. column, pillar.*

COM *with.*
> Nós vamos com ele. *We are going with him.*
> Com muito prazer. *Gladly. With great pleasure.*
> Estamos com pressa. *We are in a hurry.*
> Eles o prepararam com cuidado. *They prepared it carefully.*
> Estou com frio. *I am cold.*

comandante *m. commander; captain of a ship.*

comando *m. command.*

comarca *f. district.*

combate *m. combat, military action.*
> Pôr fora de combate. *To put out of action.*

combatente *adj. fighting; m. fighter, combatant.*
> Não-combatente. *Noncombatant.*

combater *to combat, to fight.*

combinação *f. combination; slip (lady's garment).*

combinar *to combine.*

comboio *m. convoy; train* Ⓟ.

combustível *m. fuel.*

COMEÇAR *to begin, to commence.*
> A que horas começa o programa? *At what time does the program begin?*

começo *m. beginning, start.*

comédia *f. comedy.*

comemoração *f. commemoration, celebration.*

comemorar *to commemorate, to celebrate.*

comentar *to comment on, to discuss.*
> Ele gosta de comentar as notícias. *He likes to comment on the news.*

comentário *m. comment.*

COMER *to eat.*
> Os meninos comem demais. *The children eat too much.*

comerciante *m. businessman.*

comerciar *to trade, to do business.*

comércio *m. business, trade, commerce.*

comestíveis *m. pl. food.*

cometer *to commit.*
> Todos cometemos erros. *We all make mistakes.*

cometida *f. attack.*

cômico (cómico) *adj. comical, funny.*

comida *f. food.*
> Comida e bebida. *Food and drink.*
> Quarto e comida. *Room and board.*

comigo *with me.*
> Quer ir comigo? *Do you want to go with me?*

comissão *f. commission, committee.*

comissário *m. commissioner.*

comitê (comité) *m. committee.*

comitiva *f. train, retinue.*

COMO *how, how much; as, like.*
> Como vai o senhor? *How are you?*
> Como se chama ela? *What is her name?*
> Como o senhor quiser. *As you wish.*
> Ele entrou como se estivesse em casa. *He came in as if he were in his own home.*

cômoda (cómoda) *f. dresser, chest of drawers.*

comodidade *f. comfort, ease; convenience.*
> Este apartamento tem todas as comodidades. *This apartment has all the conveniences.*

cômodo (cómodo) *adj. comfortable, convenient.*

compadecer *to pity, to sympathize with.*

compaixão *(x = sh) f. compassion, pity, sympathy.*

companheiro *m. companion, comrade, colleague.*
> Ele é meu companheiro de quarto. *He's my roommate.*
> Eles sempre têm sido bons companheiros. *They have always been good companions.*

companhia *f. company; business firm.*
> Gomes & Cia. *Gomes and Co.*

comparação *f. comparison.*

COMPARAR *to compare.*

comparecer *to appear; to attend a meeting.*

compartilhar *to share.*

compartimento *m. compartment; room.*

compatível *adj. compatible.*

compatriota *m. and f. compatriot.*

compensação *f. compensation.*

compensar *to compensate, to pay.*
competência *f. competence, ability; competition.*
competente *adj. competent, fit.*
competição *f. competition, rivalry; contest.*
competir *to compete, to contend; to behoove.*
   Compete a eles começar. *It is up to them to begin.*
complacente *adj. accommodating, agreeable, pleasing.*
complemento *m. complement.*
COMPLETAMENTE *completely.*
COMPLETAR *to complete, to finish.*
   Completar um trabalho. *To finish a task (job).*
COMPLETO *adj. complete, finished, full.*
   Por completo. *Completely.*
complicado *adj. complicated.*
complicar *to complicate.*
compor *to compose, to constitute.*
   Ele compôs dois poemas épicos. *He composed two epic poems.*
comportamento *m. behavior.*
comportar *to allow, to stand, to include.*
comportar-se *to behave, to act.*
composição *f. composition.*
compositor *m. composer; typesetter.*
composto *adj. composed, compound; n. m. compound, combination.*
compostura *f. composure; composition; falsity.*
compota *f. compote, preserves, stewed fruit.*
COMPRA *f. purchase.*
   Hoje vamos de compras. *We are going shopping today.*
comprador *m. buyer.*
COMPRAR *to buy.*
   Comprar a crédito. *To buy on credit.*
   Comprar a dinheiro. *To buy with cash.*
   Comprar a prestações. *To buy on installments.*
   Comprar por atacado. *To buy wholesale.*
   Eu comprei tudo muito barato. *I bought everything very cheap.*
COMPREENDER *to understand; to comprise, to include.*
   Compreende o que estou dizendo (a dizer)? *Do you understand what I am saying?*
   Não compreendi nada. *I didn't understand a thing.*
compreendido *adj. understood; including.*
compreensão *f. comprehension, understanding.*
compreensível *adj. comprehensible.*
compreensivo *adj. comprehensive.*
comprido *adj. long.*
comprimento *m. length.*

comprimir *to compress, to restrain, to repress.*
comprometer-se *to commit oneself.*
compromisso *m. compromise; engagement, commitment.*
comprovante *adj. confirming.*
comprovar *to prove, to confirm.*
compulsório *adj. compulsory.*
computador *m. computer.*
   Computador portátil. *Laptop computer.*
computadorizar *to computerize.*
computar *to compute.*
COMUM *adj. common.*
   Em comum. *In common.*
   De acordo comum. *By mutual consent.*
   Senso comum. *Common sense.*
comunicação *f. communication.*
   Telefonista, ponha-me em comunicação com o número . . . *Operator, connect me with number . . .*
comunicar *to communicate, to announce, to inform.*
comunidade *f. community.*
comunismo *m. communism.*
comunista *m. communist.*
conceber *to conceive.*
conceder *to grant.*
conceito *m. concept, idea.*
concelho *m. council of a municipality.*
concentrar *to concentrate.*
concepção *f. conception, idea.*
concernir *to concern.*
concerto *m. concert.*
concessão *f. concession.*
concha *f. shell.*
conciliação *f. conciliation.*
conciliar *to conciliate, to reconcile.*
conciso *adj. concise.*
concluir *to conclude, to finish; to settle.*
conclusão *f. conclusion.*
   Todos chegaram à mesma conclusão. *They all arrived at the same conclusion.*
concordância *f. agreement, harmony.*
concordar *to agree.*
concorrência *f. competition.*
concorrer *to compete; to concur.*
concreto *adj. concrete.*
concurso *m. contest, competition.*
conde *m. count.*
condecoração *f. decoration, medal.*
condenado *adj. condemned.*
condenar *to condemn, to convict; to disapprove.*
   Ele foi condenado ontem. *He was convicted yesterday.*
condição *f. condition.*
   Eles aceitaram sob a condição de que ele não voltasse. *They accepted on condition that he not return.*

Tudo está em boas condições. *Everything is in good order.*

condicionado *adj. conditioned.*
　Com ar condicionado. *Air conditioned.*

condicional *adj. conditional.*

condimentar *to season.*

condiscípulo *m. classmate.*

condolência *f. condolence; sympathy.*
　Aceite as minhas condolências. *Please accept my condolences.*

condor *m. condor.*

conduta *f. conduct, behavior.*

conduto *m. conduit, pipe; canal.*

condutor *m. conductor.*

CONDUZIR *to drive; to conduct; to carry; to lead.*
　Este caminho conduz ao lago. *This road goes to the lake.*

confeitaria *f. confectionary, candy store.*

conferência *f. conference, lecture.*

conferencista *m. and f. lecturer.*

conferir *to confer, to bestow.*

confessar *to admit, to confess.*
　Confesso que não pensei nisso. *I admit I didn't think of that.*

confiança *f. confidence, faith; familiarity.*
　Ele é digno de confiança. *He is reliable.*
　Eu lhe digo isto em confiança. *I'm telling you this in confidence.*
　Todos têm confiança nele. *Everybody has confidence in him.*

confiar *to confide; to trust.*

confidência *f. confidence.*

confidencial *adj. confidential.*

confirmação *f. confirmation.*

confirmar *to confirm, to ratify.*

confissão *f. confession; acknowledgment.*

conflito *m. conflict, strife.*

conformar *to conform; to fit; to agree; to comply with.*

conformar-se com *to be satisfied with.*

CONFORME *according to; agreed.*
　Estar conforme. *To be in agreement.*

conformidade *f. conformity; resemblance.*
　De conformidade com. *In accordance with.*

confortante *adj. comforting.*

confortar *to comfort.*

confortável *adj. comfortable.*

conforto *m. comfort, ease.*

confundir *to confuse; to mistake.*

confundir-se *to become confused; to be perplexed.*

confusão *f. confusion, perplexity.*

confuso *adj. confused.*

congelar *to freeze.*

congestão *f. congestion.*

congratulação *f. congratulation.*

congratular *to congratulate.*

congregação *f. congregation.*

congresso *m. congress; assembly; conference.*

conhaque *m. cognac, brandy.*

CONHECER *to know, to understand, to be acquainted with.*
　Você conhece Maria? *Do you know Maria?*
　Não a conheço. *I don't know her.*
　Vocês se conhecem? *Do you know each other?*
　Muito prazer em conhecê-lo. *Very glad to know you.*

conhecido *adj. known; n. m. acquaintance.*
　A obra dele é bem conhecida. *His work is well known.*

conhecimento *m. knowledge, understanding, acquaintance.*
　Tudo chegou ao conhecimento de nossos amigos. *Everything came to the knowledge of our friends.*
　Tomar conhecimento de. *To take notice of.*

conjetura (conjectura) *f. conjecture, guess.*

conjeturar (conjecturar) *to conjecture, to guess.*

conjugação *f. conjugation.*

conjugar *to conjugate.*

conjunção *f. conjunction.*

conjunto *adj. joint, united; n. m. whole.*

conjuração *f. conspiracy.*

conquista *f. conquest.*

conquistar *to conquer, to win over.*

consciência *f. conscience.*

consciente *adj. conscious, aware.*

conseguinte *adj. consequent; consecutive.*
　Por conseguinte, perdemos. *Consequently, we lost.*

CONSEGUIR *to obtain, to attain, to get, to succeed in.*
　Será difícil conseguir um aumento. *It will be difficult to get a raise.*
　Não consegui convencê-lo. *I did not succeed in convincing him.*

conselheiro *m. member of a board (council); adviser; counselor.*

conselho *m. advice; council, advisory board.*
　Seguirei seu conselho. *I will follow your advice.*
　Conselho de ministros. *Cabinet.*
　Conselho de guerra. *War council. Court-martial.*

consentimento *m. consent.*

consentir *to consent; to agree, to be willing; to tolerate.*
　Você consente nisso? *Do you agree to that?*
　Não consentirei nunca. *I'll never consent.*

conseqüência (consequência) *f. consequence.*
　Em consequência. *Therefore. As a result.*

25

Você terá que aceitar as conseqüências. *You will have to accept the consequences.*

consertar *to fix, to repair.*

  O senhor pode consertar meu relógio? *Can you fix my watch?*

conserto *m. repair, mending.*

conservação *f. conservation.*

conservador *adj., n. m. conservative.*

conservar *to conserve, to keep, to preserve.*

  Ela não conserva nada. *She doesn't keep anything.*

  Conserve à sua direita. *Keep to the right.*

conservas *f. preserves; canned food.*

consideração *f. consideration, regard.*

considerar *to consider, to take into account.*

considerável *adj. considerable, large.*

consignar *to consign, to assign.*

consigo *with him, with her, with you, with them.*

  Eles o levaram consigo. *They took it with them.*

consistência *f. consistency; stability; firmness.*

consistente *adj. consistent, solid, firm.*

consistir *to consist, to be composed of.*

consoante *f. consonant.*

consolação *f. consolation.*

consolar *to console, to comfort.*

conspícuo *adj. conspicuous.*

constante *adj. constant.*

constar *to be evident; to consist of.*

  Consta que eles nunca o fizeram. *The fact is that they never did it.*

constipação *f. a cold.*

constituição *f. constitution.*

constituir *to constitute.*

construção *f. construction, building.*

CONSTRUIR *to construct, to build.*

cônsul *m. consul.*

consulado *m. consulate.*

consulta *f. consultation.*

consultar *to consult, to seek advice.*

  Você deve consultar um médico. *You should consult a doctor.*

consultório *m. doctor's office.*

consumidor *m. consumer.*

consumir *to consume, to use.*

consumo *m. consumption; expenditure.*

  Artigos de consumo. *Consumer goods.*

CONTA *f. count; account; statement; bill; bead.*

  Traga-me a conta, por favor. *Please bring me the bill.*

  Ponha tudo na minha conta. *Charge it all to my account.*

  Conta corrente. *Current account.*

  Dar conta de. *To give an account of, to report.*

  Tenha em conta que ele não sabe nada disto. *Keep in mind that he knows nothing about this.*

  Afinal de contas, que mais poderia eu ter feito? *After all, what more could I have done?*

contabilidade *f. bookkeeping, accounting.*

contador *m. accountant; purser; meter (gas, etc.).*

contagiar *to infect, to contaminate.*

contagioso *adj. contagious.*

conta-gotas *m. dropper.*

contaminar *to contaminate.*

CONTAR *to count; to tell.*

  Você tem alguma coisa que me contar? *Do you have something to tell me?*

  Vocês podem contar comigo. *You can count on me.*

contemplação *f. contemplation.*

contemplar *to comtemplate, to consider, to have in view.*

contemporâneo *adj., n. m. contemporary.*

contenda *f. quarrel, dispute, fight.*

contentamento *m. contentment.*

contentar *to please, to satisfy.*

CONTENTE *adj. content, happy, pleased.*

  Ela está muito contente. *She is very happy.*

conter *to contain, to include, to hold.*

conter-se *to refrain, to restrain oneself.*

contestação *f. answer, reply.*

contestar *to contest; to reply.*

conteúdo *m. contents.*

contigo *with you (fam. sing.).*

contíguo *adj. contiguous; close, near.*

continente *m. continent.*

continuação *f. continuation.*

CONTINUAR *to continue.*

CONTO *m. story, tale; a thousand cruzeiros or escudos.*

  Conto de fadas. *Fairy tale.*

  Conto policial. *Detective story.*

CONTRA *against, contrary to, counter to.*

  Ele o fez contra a sua vontade. *He did it against his will.*

  Eu sou contra isso. *I am against that.*

contrabando *m. contraband; smuggling.*

contradição *f. contradiction.*

  Ele diz o contrário do que sente. *He says the opposite of what he thinks.*

  Ao contrário. *On the contrary.*

contradizer *to contradict.*

contrafazer *to counterfeit.*

contrafeito *adj. counterfeit.*

contrariar *to contradict; to annoy, to vex.*

contrariedade *f. mishap; disappointment; vexation.*

contrário *adj. contrary, opposite; n. m. opponent.*

  Aconteceu-me o contrário. *The opposite happened to me.*

contra-senha f. countersign; password.

contrastar to contrast.

contraste m. contrast.

contratar to engage, to hire; to bargain, to trade; to contract.

contratempo m. mishap, setback; disappointment.

contrato m. contract.

contribuição f. contribution; tax.

contribuir to contribute.

controlar to control Ⓑ.

controle m. control Ⓑ.

    Fora do controle. Out of control.

contudo nevertheless, however.

conturbar to trouble, to disturb.

contusão f. bruise, contusion.

convalescença f. convalescence.

convenção f. convention, agreement; pact.

convencer to convince.

convencido adj. convinced.

conveniência f. convenience, fitness.

conveniente adj. convenient, suitable.

convento m. convent.

CONVERSA f. conversation, talk, chatter.

    Acho que é conversa demais. In my opinion, that's enough chatter.

    Conversa mole. Idle chatter.

CONVERSAÇÃO f. conversation, talk.

CONVERSAR to chatter, to converse.

    Tenho que conversar com você. I have to talk to you.

converter to convert, to change.

convés m. deck (ship).

convicção f. conviction, belief, certainty.

convidado adj. invited; m. guest.

convidar to invite.

convir to suit; to agree.

convite m. invitation.

cooperação f. cooperation.

cooperar to cooperate.

coordenar to coordinate.

copa f. pantry; crown (hat); pl. hearts (cards).

cópia f. copy.

    Tirar copias. To make copies.

copiadora f. copier.

    Copiadora de cor. Color copier.

copiar to copy.

COPO m. glass (drinking); goblet, cup.

    Por favor, um copo dágua. A glass of water, please.

coqueiro m. coconut palm; palm tree.

coquete adj. coquettish; n. f. coquette.

coquetel m. cocktail, cocktail party Ⓑ.

COR f. color.

    Esta cor está na moda. This color is very stylish.

    Esta cor vai bem com essa. This color goes well with that one.

    Cor fixa (x = ks). Fast color.

    Cor viva. Bright color

    Cor de laranja. Orange.

    Um homem de cor. A colored man.

    Ela vê tudo cor de rosa. She sees everything through rose-colored glasses.

CORAÇÃO m. heart; core.

    Com todo o meu coração. With all my heart.

    Mãos frias, coração quente. Cold hands, warm heart.

coragem f. courage.

    Coragem! Have courage! Cheer up!

corcovado adj. humped; hunchbacked.

corda f. cord, rope; string; spring (watch).

    Esqueci dar corda ao relógio. I forgot to wind my watch.

    Cordas vocais. Vocal cords.

cordão m. cord, string, lace.

    Cordões de sapato. Shoelaces.

cordeiro m. lamb.

cordel m. twine, string, cord.

cordial adj. cordial, affectionate.

cordilheira f. mountain range.

cordura f. good sense.

corneta f. bugle, horn.

corno m. horn, antler.

coro m. choir, chorus.

coroa f. crown; wreath, garland.

coroar to crown; to complete.

coronel m. colonel.

CORPO m. body; corps.

    Corpo e alma. Body and soul.

    Corpo diplomático. Diplomatic corps.

    Corpo de Paz. Peace Corps.

corredor m. corridor, runner.

correia f. leather strap, leash, thong.

CORREIO m. mail; post office.

    A que horas sai o correio? At what time does the mail leave?

    Correio aéreo. Airmail.

    Correio electronic. E-mail.

    Correio de voz. Voice mail.

corrente adj. current, present (month); f. current; stream; draft (air).

    Conta corrente. Current account.

    Recebi (a) sua estimada carta de 15 do corrente. I have received your letter of the 15th of this month.

    Sinto uma corrente de ar. I feel a draft.

    Estar ao corrente. To be acquainted with. To be up-to-date on.

    Corrente alternada. Alternating current.

    Corrente contínua. Direct current.

    Água corrente. Running water.

CORRER to run; to flow; to elapse; to blow (wind); to draw (curtains).

    Eles vêm correndo. They come running.

    Corra as cortinas. Draw the curtains.

correspondência f. correspondence, mail.

Eu estou em correspondência com eles. *I am in correspondence with them.*
correspondente *adj. corresponding.*
corresponder *to correspond.*
correto (correcto) *adj. correct.*
corrida *f. run, race, course.*
Corrida de cavalos. *Horse race.*
corrigir *to correct.*
corroborar *to corroborate.*
corromper *to corrupt.*
corrupção *f. corruption.*
corrupto *adj. corrupt.*
CORTAR *to cut; to cut off, to shorten.*
Esta faca não corta. *This knife doesn't cut.*
Vou cortar o cabelo. *I'm going to get a haircut.*
corte *m. cut; edge (knife); f. court, house of parliament, assembly; courting.*
cortejar *to court; to flatter.*
cortês *adj. courteous, gentle, polite.*
Ele é muito cortês. *He's very polite.*
cortesia *f. courtesy, politeness.*
cortiça *f. cork; bark.*
cortiço *m. beehive; tenement.*
cortina *f. curtain, screen.*
Cortina de ferro. *Iron curtain.*
Faça o favor de correr as cortinas. *Please draw the curtains.*
coruja *f. owl.*
corvo *m. crow, raven.*
coser *to sew.*
cosmético *adj. cosmetic.*
COSTA *f. coast, shore; pl. back.*
A costa atlântica. *The Atlantic coast.*
As costas da mão. *The back of the hand.*
Ele me deu as costas. *He turned his back on me.*
costela *f. rib; wife (fam.).*
costeleta *f. chop.*
Costeleta de porco. *Pork chop.*
costumado *adj. customary.*
costumar *to be accustomed, to be in the habit of; to accustom.*
costume *m. custom, habit, practice.*
costura *f. sewing.*
Máquina de costura. *Sewing machine.*
cotidiano *adj. daily.*
cotovelo *m. elbow.*
couraçado *adj. armored; n. m. battleship.*
couro *m. leather; hide; skin.*
cousa *f. see* **COISA.**
couve-flor *f. cauliflower.*
cova *f. cave, cavern.*
covarde *m. coward.*
cozer *to cook, to bake, to boil.*
cozinha *f. kitchen; cuisine.*
cozinhar *to cook.*
cozinheiro *m. cook, chef.*
crânio *m. skull, cranium.*

cravo *m. nail, tack; clove.*
Você deu no cravo. *You hit the nail on the head.*
crédito *m. credit; credence; reputation, standing.*
Comprar a crédito. *To buy on credit.*
Vender a crédito. *To sell on credit.*
Dar crédito. *To give credit.*
Carta de crédito. *Letter of credit.*
creme *m. cream.*
CRER *to believe, to think.*
Creio que sim. *I think so.*
Creio que não. *I think not.*
Ver é crer. *Seeing is believing.*
crescer *to grow, to increase.*
crescimento *m. growth, increase.*
criada *f. servant.*
criado *m. servant.*
CRIANÇA *f. child.*
criar *to create, to produce; to nurse; to rear; to bring up.*
criatura *f. creature, person.*
crime *m. crime.*
criminal *adj. criminal.*
criminoso *adj. criminal; n. m. outlaw, criminal.*
crioulo *adj. native; creole; n. m. creole, Portuguese dialect spoken in Cabo Verde.*
crise *f. crisis; depression.*
cristal *m. crystal.*
cristão *m. Christian.*
cristianismo *m. Christianity.*
critério *m. criterion.*
crítica *f. criticism, judgment, comment; review.*
A crítica não gostou da peça. *The critics did not like the play.*
criticar *to criticize, to judge.*
crítico *m. critic, reviewer.*
crônica (crónica) *f. chronicle; newspaper article or column.*
cronista *m. and f. chronicler; columnist.*
croquete *m. croquette.*
cruz *f. cross.*
cruzar *to cross; to cruise.*
CRUZEIRO *m. Brazilian monetary unit; large cross; cruise; cruiser (ship).*
Custa duzentos cruzeiros. *It costs 200 cruzeiros.*
Cruzeiro do Sul. *Southern Cross.*
cubano *adj. Cuban; m. Cuban.*
cubo *m. cube.*
cuecas *f. pl. men's undershorts.*
CUIDADO *m. care, attention; anxiety, worry.*
Cuidado! *Be careful!*
Ter cuidado. *To be careful.*
Cuidado com o cachorro! *Look out for the dog!*

Ao cuidado de . . . *Care of . . .*

cuidadoso *adj. careful.*

cuidar *to care, to take care, to mind, to look after.*

Quem cuida do jardim? *Who takes care of the garden?*

Cuide-se. *Take care of yourself.*

cujo *whose, of which, of whom.*

O professor Cândido, cujo livro sobre a literatura brasileira acaba de sair . . . *Professor Cândido, whose book on Brazilian literature has just come out . . .*

culpa *f. fault, guilt; sin.*

culpável *adj. guilty.*

cultivar *to cultivate; to till; to improve.*

No Brasil se cultiva (cultiva-se) muito o café. *Much coffee is grown in Brazil.*

Cultivar um talento. *To develop a talent.*

cultivo *m. farming, cultivation, tillage.*

culto *adj. well-educated; polished; n. m. worship, cult, religion.*

Ele é um homem culto. *He is a well-read man.*

cultura *f. culture; refinement.*

cultural *adj. cultural.*

cumprimentar *to greet; to congratulate.*

cumprimento *m. greeting, compliment.*

Meus cumprimentos. *My regards.*

cumprir *to carry out, to fulfill; to behoove.*

Ele sempre cumpre a palavra. *He always keeps his word.*

Eles cumpriram o curso em três anos. *They completed the course in three years.*

Cumpre-me avisá-lo . . . *I am pleased (it behooves me) to inform you . . . (business letter).*

cunha *f. wedge.*

cunhada *f. sister-in-law.*

cunhado *m. brother-in-law.*

cura *f. cure; m. priest.*

curar *to cure, to heal.*

curável *adj. curable.*

curiosidade *f. curiosity; oddity.*

curioso *adj. curious, inquisitive; strange, odd.*

Estou curioso por sabê-lo. *I'm anxious to know (it).*

cursar *to cross, to travel; to study at a university.*

curso *m. course, direction; current; course of studies.*

João fará o curso de filosofia. *John will study philosophy.*

curva *f. curve.*

custa *f. cost.*

À custa de. *At the cost of.*

CUSTAR *to cost.*

Quanto custam estes sapatos? *How much do these shoes cost?*

Custa-me crê-lo. *It's hard for me to believe it.*

Custe o que custar. *Cost what it may. Whatever the cost.*

custear *to defray expenses.*

custo *m. cost, price; difficulty.*

A todo custo. *At all costs.*

custódia *f. custody, guard, detention (legal).*

custodiar *to guard, to take into custody.*

custoso *adj. costly, expensive.*

cútis *f. skin, complexion.*

D

DA *(contr. of* **de** + **a**) *of the, from the.*

O irmão da menina. *The girl's brother.*

Feche a porta da sala. *Close the door of the room.*

datilógrafa (dactilógrafa) *f. typist.*

datilógrafo (dactilógrafo) *m. typist.*

dádiva *f. gift, present.*

dadivoso *adj. liberal, generous.*

DAÍ *from there, of there; therefore.*

Daí a pouco. *A little later.*

dalém *from beyond* Ⓟ.

DALI *from there, of there; therefore.*

Saiu dali. *It came from over there.*

Dali a pouco. *A little later.*

dália *f. dahlia.*

dama *f. lady, dame.*

Jogo de damas. *Checkers.*

damasco *m. apricot; damask.*

danado *adj. spoiled, damaged.*

danar *to damage, to hurt.*

dança *f. dance.*

dançar *to dance.*

daninho *adj. harmful.*

dano *m. damage, loss; hurt, harm.*

DAQUELA *(contr. of* **de** + **aquela**) *f. of that, from that.*

Não conheço nenhum professor daquela escola. *I don't know any teacher of that school.*

DAQUELE *(contr. of* **de** + **aquele**) *m. of that, from that.*

O chapéu é daquele senhor. *The hat belongs to that man.*

DAQUI *(contr. of* **de** + **aqui**) *from here, of here.*

Ele não é daqui. *He's not from this area.*

Daqui a oito dias. *In a week.*

DAQUILO *(contr. of* **de** + **aquilo**) *of that, from that.*

DAR *to give; to show; to strike (hour); to hit; to take (a walk).*

Faça o favor de me dar (dar-me) o seu endereço. *Please give me your address.*

Eu lhe dou quatro dólares por esse livro. *I'll give you four dollars for that book.*

Vamos dar um passeio. *Let's take a walk.*

Vamos dar uma volta. *Let's go for a walk.*

Eu lhe dou (dou-lhe) as boas-vindas. *I welcome you.*

O relógio acaba de dar seis horas. *The clock has just struck six.*

Ele me deu as costas. *He turned his back on me.*

Vamos dar fim a todo isso. *We're going to put an end to all that.*

Isso me dá cuidado. *That worries me.* ℗

Eles se dão muito bem. *They get along very well.*

Eu lhe dou (dou-lhe) a minha palavra. *I give you my word.*

É preciso dar corda ao relógio. *You must wind the watch.*

Você dá as cartas. *You deal.*

Eles vão dar uma festa no sábado. *They are going to have a party on Saturday.*

Eu dei com eles ontem. *I ran into (came upon) them yesterday.*

A mãe deu pancadas ao filho. *The mother struck her son.*

Dê-se pressa! *Hurry up!* ℗

Dar um jeito. *To find a way, to finagle a solution.*

Dar-se conta de. *To realize.*

Dar à luz. *To give birth.*

Dar gritos. *To cry out.*

Dar os parabéns. *To congratulate.*

Dar a conhecer. *To make known.*

Tudo deu em nada. *It all came to naught.*

Dar de comer. *To feed.*

Dar de beber. *To give water to.*

Dar aula. *To conduct a class.*

Dá licença? *May I?*

dardo *m. dart.*

data *f. date.*

datar *to date.*

DE *of; from; for; by; on; to; with.*

Essa é a casa de meu amigo. *That's my friend's house.*

De quem é este livro? *Whose book is this?*

O que é feito dele? *What has become of him?*

O livro é dela. *The book is hers.*

Ele é do Brasil. *He's from Brazil.*

Eu sou de Lisboa. *I'm from Lisbon.*

Um copo d'água. *A glass of water.*

Uma casa de pedra. *A stone house.*

Uma xícara (x = sh) de café. *A cup of coffee.*

Máquina de costura. *Sewing machine.*

Está na hora do jantar. *It's time for dinner.*

De dia. *During the day.*

De noite. *At night.*

De nada. *Don't mention it.*

Ela está vestida de azul. *She is dressed in blue.*

De vez em quando. *From time to time.*

Aquela jovem de olhos azuis. *That girl with the blue eyes.*

Eles estão de pé. *They are standing.*

Carlos está de cama. *Charles is sick in bed.*

deão *m. dean.*

DEBAIXO *(x = sh) under, underneath.*

A carta estava debaixo dos papéis. *The letter was under the papers.*

debate *m. debate.*

debater *to debate, to discuss.*

débil *adj. feeble, weak.*

debilidade *f. feebleness, weakness.*

debilitar *to weaken, to debilitate.*

débito *m. debt.*

debruçar *to lean.*

debuxo *(x = sh) sketch.*

década *f. decade.*

decadência *f. decay, decadence; decline.*

decair *to decay, to decline, to die down.*

decano *m. dean.*

decente *adj. decent, honest; neat.*

decepção *f. disappointment.*

decidido *adj. decided; firm; determined.*

DECIDIR *to decide, to resolve, to determine.*

DECIDIR-SE *to decide, to make up one's mind.*

decifrar *to decipher, to decode.*

decímetro *m. decimeter.*

décimo *adj., n. m. tenth.*

Décimo primeiro. *Eleventh.*

Décimo segundo. *Twelfth.*

Décimo terceiro. *Thirteenth.*

Décimo quarto. *Fourteenth.*

Décimo quinto. *Fifteenth.*

Décimo sexto. *Sixteenth.*

Décimo sétimo. *Seventeenth.*

Décimo oitavo. *Eighteenth.*

Décimo nono. *Nineteenth.*

decisão *f. decision, determination.*

decisivo *adj. decisive.*

declaração *f. declaration.*

declarar *to declare, to state; to testify.*

Tem alguma coisa a declarar? *Do you have anything to declare (customs)?*

declinar *to decline.*

decoração *f. decoration; stage scenery.*

decorar *to decorate; to learn by heart, to memorize.*

decoro *m. decency, decorum, honor.*

decotado *adj. low-necked.*

decrescente *adj. decreasing.*

decrescer *to decrease.*

decrescimento *m. decrease.*

decretar *to decree.*

decreto *m. decree.*

dedal *m. thimble.*

dedicação *f. dedication.*

dedicado *adj. dedicated, devoted.*

dedicar *to dedicate; to devote.*
Ele se dedicou à pintura. *He devoted himself to painting.*

dedicatória *f. dedication.*

DEDO *m. finger; toe.*
Dedo mínimo. *Little finger.*
Dedo indicador. *Index finger.*
Dedo polegar. *Thumb.*
Dedo médio. *Middle finger.*
Dedo anular. *Ring finger.*

dedução *f. deduction.*

deduzir *to deduce, to understand.*

defeito *m. fault, defect.*

defeituoso *adj. defective.*

defender *to defend.*

defensiva *f. defensive.*

defensor *m. supporter, defender.*

defesa *f. defense.*

deficiência *f. deficiency.*

déficit *m. shortage, deficit.*

definição *f. definition, explanation.*

definido *adj. definite.*

definir *to define, to determine.*

definitivo *adj. definitive.*

deformação *f. deformation.*

deformar *to deform.*

deformidade *f. deformity.*

defraudar *to defraud, to swindle.*

defronte *facing.*

defunto *adj. deceased; n. m. deceased; dead person.*

degelo *m. thawing; thaw.*

degeneração *f. degeneration.*

degenerar *to deteriorate, to degenerate.*

degradante *adj. degrading.*

degradar *to degrade.*

degrau *m. step; rung (ladder); degree.*

degredar *to banish, to exile.*

DEITAR *to throw, to cast, to lay.*
Isso é deitar lenha no fogo. *That's adding fuel to the fire.*

DEITAR-SE *to lie down, to go to bed.*
Nós nos deitamos às dez. *We go to bed at ten.*

DEIXAR *(x = sh) to leave, to let; to quit, to give up.*
Deixe-me vê-lo. *Let me see it.*
Não nos deixaram entrar. *They did not let us enter.*
Posso deixar meus livros aqui? *May I leave my books here?*
Deixe para amanhã. *Leave it for tomorrow.*
Deixe-me em paz! *Leave me alone!*
Ele deixou de escrever-me. *He stopped writing me.*

Ele deixou seu emprego. *He gave up his job.*
Isso deixa muito a desejar. *That leaves much to be desired.*
Não deixe de telefonar-me. *Don't fail (be sure) to telephone me.*
Deixar um recado. *To leave a message.*

delegação *f. delegation.*

delegacia *f. delegacy.*
Delegacia de polícia. *Police headquarters.*

delegado *m. delegate, deputy, commissioner.*

deleitar *to please, to delight.*

deleite *m. delight, pleasure.*

delgado *adj. thin, slender.*

deliberação *f. deliberation.*

deliberar *to deliberate.*

delicado *adj. delicate; dainty, nice; exquisite; fragile.*

delícia *f. delight, pleasure.*

delicioso *adj. delicious, delightful.*
A sobremesa está deliciosa. *The dessert is delicious.*

delinquente (delinquente) *m. delinquent, offender.*

delirar *to rave, to be delirious.*

delírio *m. delirium, raving; enthusiasm; frenzy.*

delito *m. misdemeanor, offense, crime.*

DEMAIS *other; rest; too much, too many.*
Custa demais. *It costs too much.*
Você bebe demais. *You drink too much.*
Dois é bom; três é demais. *Two's company, three's a crowd.*
Os demais. *The others; the rest.*

demanda *f. claim, demand, request; lawsuit.*

demandar *to demand, to claim; to take legal action; to enter a claim; to sue.*

demarcação *f. demarcation.*

demasiado *too much; too; excessive.*

demência *f. insanity, madness.*

demente *adj. insane, crazy.*

demissão *f. dismissal; firing; resignation.*

demitido *adj. dismissed; fired.*

demitir *to dismiss, to fire.*

demitir-se *to resign.*

democracia *f. democracy.*

democrata *m. and f. democrat.*

democrático *adj. democratic.*

demolição *f. demolition.*

demolir *to demolish.*

demônio (demónio) *m. devil, demon.*
Como um demônio. *Like the devil.*

demonstração *f. demonstration.*

demonstrar *to demonstrate, to prove, to show.*

demora *f. delay.*
Sem mais demora. *Without further delay.*

demorar(-se) *to delay, to tarry; to stay.*
Você se demorou muito. *You are very late.*

denegar *to refuse, to deny.*

denominação f. denomination.
denominar to name.
denotar to denote, to indicate, to express.
densidade f. density.
denso adj. dense, thick.
dentadura f. denture, set of teeth.
dental adj. dental.
DENTE m. tooth.
  Escova de dentes. Toothbrush.
  Dente molar. Molar.
  Dor de dentes. Toothache.
  Dentes postiços. False teeth.
dentifrício m. toothpaste, dentifrice.
dentista m. and f. dentist.
DENTRO within, inside.
  Dentro de alguns dias. Within a few days.
  Dentro em pouco. In a short while.
  Que está acontecendo (a acontecer) lá dentro? What's going on inside there?
denúncia f. denunciation; accusation.
denunciar to denounce, to accuse; to give notice; to inform.
departamento m. department.
dependência f. dependence, dependency; annex.
DEPENDER to depend, be dependent on.
  Muito depende do que você faça. A great deal depends on what you do.
deplorar to deplore, to be sorry, to regret.
  Deploro muito o acontecido. I'm sorry about what happened.
deplorável adj. deplorable.
DEPOIS after, afterward, later.
  Dois dias depois. Two days later.
  Depois de pagar a conta ele saiu. After he payed the bill he left.
  Depois de amanhã. The day after tomorrow.
deportar to deport.
depositar to deposit, to place; to put in a safe place; to entrust.
  Eles depositaram o dinheiro. They deposited the money.
depósito m. deposit; depot; warehouse; reservoir; tank.
  Depósito de bagagem. Baggage room.
  Depósito de água. Water reservoir.
DEPRESSA fast; rapidly; in haste.
  Mais depressa! Faster!
  Depressa! Hurry!
depressão f. depression.
deprimir to depress.
deputado m. deputy, congressman.
derivar to derive.
derradeiro adj. last, final.
derramamento m. spilling, shedding.
derramar to spill; to shed; to scatter; to spread.
derredor around, about.

derreter to melt, to dissolve.
derribamento m. knocking down, felling.
derribar to demolish, to knock down, to bring down.
derrocar to overthrow; to demolish; to destroy.
derrota f. defeat, rout; ship's course.
derrotar to rout, to defeat.
derrubar to knock down, to bring down, to overthrow.
desabafar to free, to uncover; to unburden oneself.
desabitado adj. uninhabited, unoccupied.
desabitar to vacate.
desabotoar to unbutton.
desabrido adj. rude, insolent.
desabrigado adj. uncovered; without shelter, exposed.
desabrigar to uncover; to leave without shelter.
desabrigo m. lack of shelter.
desabrochar to unbutton, to unclasp, to unfasten; to open (flowers).
  Desabrochar-se. To free oneself.
desacerto m. mistake, error.
desacordo m. disagreement.
desacreditar to discredit.
desafiar to challenge, to defy.
desafinar to get out of tune, to play out of tune.
desafio m. challenge; competition.
desafogar-se to unburden oneself.
desafogo m. ease, relief.
desafortunado adj. unlucky, unfortunate.
desagradar to displease.
desagradável adj. unpleasant, disagreeable.
  Tudo isso foi muito desagradável. It was all very unpleasant.
desagradecer to be ungrateful.
desagradecido adj. ungrateful.
desagrado m. displeasure, discontent.
desagravar to vindicate, to avenge.
desagravo m. amends, vindication.
desaguamento m. drainage, draining.
desaguar to drain.
desairoso adj. clumsy, awkward.
desalentar to discourage.
desalento m. discouragement, dismay.
desalojar to dispossess, to evict; to dislodge; to drive out.
desalugado adj. vacant, unrented.
  Atualmente o apartamento está desalugado. At present, the apartment is vacant.
desalugar to vacate.
desamparado adj. abandoned.
desanimado adj. discouraged.
desanimar to discourage.
desânimo m. discouragement.

desaparecer *to disappear.*
  Meu cachorro desapareceu. *My dog disappeared.*
desapercebido *adj. unprepared, not ready.*
desaprovar *to disapprove of.*
desaproveitar *to misuse, not to make good use of.*
desarmado *adj. unarmed.*
desarmar *to disarm; to dismount, to take apart.*
desarrolhar *to uncork.*
desassossegar *to disturb.*
desassossego *uneasiness, restlessness.*
desastre *m. disaster, calamity.*
desatar *to untie, to loosen.*
desatento *adj. inattentive, thoughtless, negligent.*
desatino *m. lack of tact; folly, madness.*
desbaratar *to thwart, to upset (a plan); to destroy; to disperse, to rout, to spoil, to run.*
descabelado *adj. disheveled; hairless; impetuous.*
descalabro *m. calamity, great loss.*
descalçar *to take off shoes, gloves.*
  Ela se sentou e se descalçou (Ela sentou-se e descalçou-se). *She sat down and took her shoes off.*
descalço *adj. barefoot.*
descamisado *adj. shirtless.*
DESCANSAR *to rest.*
  O senhor não quer descansar um pouco? *Don't you want to rest a little?*
descanso *m. rest, calm, support.*
descarado *adj. brazen, impudent.*
descarga *f. discharge, unloading.*
descargo *m. discharge of an obligation.*
DESCARREGAR *to unload, to discharge; to fire (a gun).*
  Vão descarregar o navio amanhã. *They will unload the ship tomorrow.*
descarrilamento *m. derailment.*
descarrilar *to become derailed.*
descartar *to discard, to dismiss.*
descendência *f. descent, origin.*
descendente *adj. descendent; n. m. and f. descendant.*
descender *to descend from.*
descenso *m. descent.*
DESCER *to descend, to go down; to drop.*
  Desçam já! *Come down right away!*
descoberta *f. discovery.*
descoberto *adj. discovered, uncovered; bareheaded.*
descobrimento *m. discovery.*
DESCOBRIR *to discover, to uncover; to find out; to disclose.*
  Descobrimos que não era verdade. *We found out that it was not true.*

O Brasil foi descoberto em mil e quinhentos. *Brazil was discovered in 1500.*
descolorido *adj. discolored, faded.*
descomedido *adj. immoderate; excessive; impolite; rude.*
descompor *to discompose, to disarrange.*
descompor-se *to become upset.*
descomposto *adj. out of order; upset.*
desconcertante *adj. disconcerting; confusing.*
desconcertar *to disturb, to confuse, to baffle.*
desconfiança *f. distrust.*
desconfiar *to distrust, to suspect.*
  Nós desconfiamos deles. *We distrust them.*
desconhecer *not to recognize, not to know; to ignore.*
desconhecido *adj. unknown; n. m. stranger.*
  Quem é aquele desconhecido? *Who is that stranger?*
desconhecimento *m. ignorance; ingratitude.*
desconsiderado *adj. thoughtless, inconsiderate.*
desconsolação *f. disconsolation.*
desconsolador *adj. disheartening, sad.*
descontar *to discount, to deduct.*
descontentamento *m. discontent, dissatisfaction.*
descontente *adj. discontented.*
descortês *adj. discourteous, impolite.*
descoser *to unstitch, to rip.*
descrédito *m. discredit.*
DESCREVER *to describe.*
descrição *f. description.*
descuidado *adj. careless; negligent; slovenly.*
descuidar *to neglect, to overlook.*
  Não descuide de preparar a lista. *Don't neglect to prepare the list.*
descuido *m. negligence, carelessness, omission, oversight.*
desculpa *f. excuse, apology.*
desculpar *to excuse, to pardon.*
DESCULPE! *Excuse me! Pardon me! I'm sorry!*
DESDE *since, after, from.*
  Ela está de cama desde ontem. *She's been (sick) in bed since yesterday.*
  Desde então. *Since then.*
  Desde criança. *From childhood.*
  Desde agora. *From now on.*
  Desde já. *Immediately, from now on.*
desdém *m. disdain, scorn, contempt.*
desdenhar *to disdain, to scorn.*
desdita *f. misfortune, calamity, unhappiness.*
desditado *adj. wretched; unfortunate; unhappy.*
desdizer *to retract, to deny, to contradict.*
DESEJAR *to desire, to wish.*
  Não desejo nada. *I don't want anything.*

João deseja falar com você. *John wants to talk to you.*

Eu lhe desejo felicidade. *I wish you happiness.*

desejável *adj. desirable.*

DESEJO *m. desire, wish.*

Esses são (os) meus desejos. *Those are my wishes.*

desejoso *adj. desirous.*

desembaraçar *to free, to disentangle.*

desembaraçar-se *to get rid of.*

desembarcadouro *m. landing place, dock.*

desembarcar *to disembark, to go ashore.*

desembarque *m. landing.*

desembolsar *to pay out, to disburse.*

desembolso *m. disbursement.*

desempacotar *to unpack.*

desempenhar *to perform; to accomplish; to carry out; to redeem, to take out of pawn; to free from debt.*

O ator principal desempenhou bem seu papel. *The main actor (the male lead) played his part well.*

desemprego *m. unemployment.*

desencantar *to disappoint, to disillusion.*

desenfreado *adj. unbridled, unrestrained.*

desenganado *disappointed, disillusioned.*

desenganar *to disappoint, to disillusion.*

desengano *m. disappointment, disillusionment.*

desenhar *to design, to sketch.*

desenho *m. design, sketch.*

desenlace *m. outcome, result, dénouement.*

O desenlace da peça é muito fraco. *The play's dénouement is very weak.*

desenredar *to disentangle.*

desenredo *m. outcome, result, dénouement.*

desenrolar *to unwind, to unroll.*

desentender *to misunderstand.*

desentendido *adj. not understanding; misunderstood.*

desentoar *to be out of tune.*

desenvoltura *f. ease, boldness; impudence.*

DESENVOLVER *to develop, to grow; to unfold.*

desenvolvido *adj. developed.*

desenvolvimento *m. development.*

desequilibrar *to unbalance.*

desertar *to desert.*

deserto *adj. deserted; n. m. desert.*

A cidade ficou deserta. *The city remained deserted.*

desertor *m. deserter.*

desesperação *f. desperation, despair; fury.*

desesperado *adj. hopeless; desperate; furious.*

desesperar *to despair; to exasperate.*

Isso me desespera. *That exasperates me.*

desespero *m. desperation, despair; fury.*

desfalecer *to faint; to weaken.*

desfalecimento *m. faint; weakness.*

desfazer *to undo; to take apart; to dissolve.*

Foi preciso desfazer a maior parte do que elas tinham feito. *It was necessary to undo most of what they had done.*

desfeito *adj. destroyed; in pieces; undone.*

desfiar *to ravel, to fray.*

desfigurar *to disfigure; to misshape; to distort.*

desfilar *to parade, to march in review.*

desfile *m. parade, review.*

desfolhar *to strip (as of leaves).*

desfrutar *to enjoy; to make fun of.*

desgastar *to wear out.*

desgaste *m. wear and tear.*

desgostar *to displease.*

desgosto *m. displeasure; sorrow.*

Ela sofreu muitos desgostos. *She suffered many sorrows.*

desgraça *f. misfortune, sorrow.*

Que desgraça! *What a misfortune!*

Por desgraça. *Unfortunately.*

Nunca uma desgraça vem só. *It never rains but it pours.*

desgraçado *adj. unfortunate, unlucky; unhappy; m. poor soul, wretch.*

Ele é um desgraçado. *He's a poor (unfortunate) soul.*

designar *to designate, to appoint.*

designio *m. design; plan.*

desigual *adj. uneven.*

desigualar *to make uneven.*

desigualdade *f. inequality; unevenness.*

desilusão *f. disillusion.*

desinfestar *to disinfest.*

desinfetante *adj., n. m. disinfectant.*

desinfetar *to disinfect.*

desinteresse *m. disinterest.*

desistir *to desist; to give up.*

desleal *adj. unfaithful; disloyal; bad-faith.*

deslealdade *f. unfaithfulness; disloyalty.*

desligado *adj. disconnected; off (light, radio, etc.).*

desligar *to disconnect; to turn off.*

Faça o favor de desligar o televisor. *Please turn off the TV.*

Espere um momento; não desligue. *Wait a minute; don't hang up (telephone).*

deslizar *to slip, to slide.*

deslize *m. slip, slipping.*

deslocação *f. dislocation; displacement.*

deslocar *to dislocate; to displace.*

deslumbramento *m. dazzling (great) light.*

deslumbrar *to dazzle, to daze.*

desmaiar *to faint, to turn pale.*

desmaio *m. faint, fainting spell; paleness.*

desmedido *adj. immoderate, excessive.*

desmemoriado *adj. forgetful.*

desmentir *to deny, to contradict.*

34

desmobiliar (desmobilar) *to remove the furniture.*

desmontar *to dismount; to take apart (a machine, etc.).*

desmoralizado *adj. demoralized.*

desmoralizar *to demoralize.*

desnatar *to skim (milk).*

desnudar *to undress, to bare.*

desnudo *adj. naked.*

desobedecer *to disobey.*

desobediência *f. disobedience.*

desobediente *adj. disobedient.*

desocupado *adj. not busy; unemployed.*

Eu lhe falarei quando você estiver desocupado. *I'll speak to you when you are not busy.*

desocupar *to vacate, to empty.*

desonesto *adj. dishonest, indecent.*

desonra *f. dishonor; disgrace.*

Ser pobre não é desonra. *Poverty is no disgrace.*

desonrar *to dishonor; to disgrace.*

desonroso *adj. dishonorable; disgraceful.*

desordem *f. disorder.*

desordenado *adj. disorderly, unruly.*

A vida do Eduardo é bastante desordenada. *Edward's life is pretty wild.*

desorganizar *to disorganize.*

desorientar *to lead astray; to confuse.*

despachar *to dispatch, to forward, to expedite, to send.*

despedaçar *to tear or break into bits.*

despedida *f. farewell; dismissal.*

A despedida foi uma ocasião muito triste. *The farewell was a very sad occasion.*
Jantar de despedida. *Farewell dinner.*

despedir *to send away, to dismiss.*

despedir-se *to say farewell, to say good-bye to; to take leave.*

Despedimo-nos deles na estação. *We said good-bye to them at the station.*

despeito *m. spite.*

A despeito de. *In spite of.*

despejar *to empty; to throw out.*

despensa *f. pantry.*

desperdiçar *to waste.*

desperdício *m. waste.*

despertador *m. alarm clock.*

despertar *to awaken; to wake up.*

desperto *adj. awake.*

DESPESA *f. expense, cost.*

Cada ano tenho ainda mais despesas. *Each year I have even more expenses.*
Sempre há despesas imprevistas. *There are always some unforeseen expenses.*

DESPIR *to undress; to strip.*

Ela se despiu e deitou-se. *She undressed and went to bed.*

despistar *to throw off the track, to mislead.*

despojar *to despoil; to strip.*

desposar *to marry.*

déspota *m. and f. despot.*

desprazer *to displease; displeasure.*

desprender *to unpin; to unfasten; to separate.*

desprendido *adj. unfastened; generous.*

despreocupado *adj. unconcerned.*

despreocupar *not to worry.*

desprezar *to despise, to scorn; to slight; to look down on.*

desprezo *m. contempt, scorn.*

Todos o trataram com desprezo. *Everyone treated him with contempt.*

desproporcionado *adj. disproportionate, unequal.*

despropósito *m. nonsense, absurdity; excessive amount.*

desprovido *adj. lacking.*

desqualificar *to disqualify.*

desquitar *to free; to separate.*

desquitar-se *to separate legally.*

desquite *m. (kind of) legal separation.*

O casamento terminou por desquite. *The marriage ended in separation.*

destacamento *m. detachment.*

destacar *to detach, to stand out.*

destapar *to uncover, to open.*

desterrado *adj. exiled, banished; n. m. exile.*

desterrar *to exile, to banish, to deport.*

Alguns dos chefes foram desterrados. *Some of the leaders were exiled.*

destinar *to appoint; to destine.*

destinatário *m. addressee.*

Escreva no envelope o nome do destinatário. *Write the name of the addressee on the envelope.*

destino *m. fate, destiny; destination.*

Com destino a Lisboa. *Bound for Lisbon.*

destreza *f. skill.*

destro *adj. skillful, adroit.*

destróier (destruidor) *m. destroyer (ship).*

destruição *f. destruction.*

destruidor *adj. destructive; n. m. destroyer.*

destruir *to destroy.*

É mais fácil destruir (do) que construir. *It is easier to destroy than to build.*

desumanidade *f. inhumanity.*

desumano *adj. inhumane, inhuman.*

desvanecer *to vanish; to dispel.*

desvantagem *f. disadvantage.*

desvantajoso *adj. disadvantageous.*

desvão *m. attic; hiding place.*

desvelar *to keep awake; to watch over; to unveil.*

desvelo *m. watching over; solicitude.*

desventurado *adj. unfortunate.*

desviar *to divert, to deviate, to dissuade.*

Ele se desviou do assunto. *He digressed from the subject.*

desvio m. deviation; detour.

detalhe m. detail.

Conte-me em detalhe o que aconteceu. *Tell me in detail what happened.*

Detalhes biográficos. *Biographical data.*

detenção f. detention.

DETER to detain, to hold back, to stop.

Meu amigo me deteve. *My friend detained me.*

detergente adj., n. m. detergent.

deteriorar to deteriorate.

determinação f. determination, decision, courage.

Ele sempre fala com determinação. *He always speaks with conviction.*

determinado adj. determined, resolute.

determinar to determine, to decide.

determinar-se to resolve, to make up one's mind.

DETER-SE to hold oneself back; to delay; to stop.

detestar to detest, to abhor.

detestável adj. detestable.

detetive (detective) m. detective.

detido adj. detained; arrested.

O ladrão foi detido pela polícia. *The thief was arrested by the police.*

DETRÁS behind.

Detrás da porta. *Behind the door.*

Falam dele por detrás. *They talk about him behind his back.*

DEUS God.

Meu Deus! *Good Lord! Heavens!*

Se Deus quiser. *God willing.*

Pelo amor de Deus! *For heaven's sake!*

Deus me livre! *Heaven forbid!*

Graças a Deus! *Thank God!*

O homem propõe e Deus dispõe. *Man proposes, and God disposes.*

Deus lhe pague! *God bless you!*

DEVAGAR slow, slowly.

Devagar se vai ao longe. *Easy does it.*

Faça o favor de falar mais devagar. *Please speak more slowly.*

devastação f. devastation.

devastar to devastate, to ruin.

DEVER to owe; should, must, ought; m. duty, task.

Quanto lhe devo? *How much do I owe you?*

Devemos ir já. *We should go now.*

Você devia comer mais. *You should eat more.*

Que devemos fazer? *What should we do?*

Ele sempre cumpre o seu dever. *He always does his duty.*

deveras really, truly.

devido adj. due; owing to, on account of; proper.

Devido à hora, não esperemos mais. *Owing to the time, let's not wait any longer.*

devoção f. restitution, return.

devolver to return, to give back.

João nunca me devolveu o dinheiro. *John never returned the money to me.*

devorar to devour, to consume.

devoto adj. devout, pious; devoted.

DEZ ten.

DEZANOVE nineteen ℗.

DEZASSEIS sixteen ℗.

DEZASSETE seventeen ℗.

DEZEMBRO December.

DEZENOVE nineteen Ⓑ.

DEZESSEIS sixteen Ⓑ.

DEZESSETE seventeen Ⓑ.

DEZOITO eighteen.

DIA m. day.

Bom dia! *Good morning!*

Que dia é hoje? *What day is it?*

Daqui a cinco dias. *Five days from now.*

Estarei em casa o dia todo. *I'll be home all day.*

Eu o vejo todos os dias. *I see him every day.*

De dia. *During the day.*

Um dia sim um dia não. *Every other day.*

No dia seguinte. *On the following day.*

De dia em dia. *From day to day.*

Dia feriado. *Holiday.*

Dia de trabalho. *Workday.*

Dia útil. *Workday. Weekday.*

Dia de Ano Bom. *New Year's Day.*

De quatro em quatro dias. *Every four days.*

O dia todo. *All day long.*

Dia de folga. *Day off.*

diabete, diabetes m. and f. diabetes.

diabo m. devil.

Pobre diabo! *Poor devil! Poor fellow!*

Pintar o diabo. *To raise the devil.*

diagnóstico adj. diagnostic; n. m. diagnosis.

diagrama m. diagram, chart.

dialeto (dialecto) m. dialect.

diálogo m. dialog.

diamante m. diamond.

diâmetro m. diameter.

DIANTE before, in front, in the presence of.

Ele está esperando diante do clube. *He is waiting in front of the club.*

Daqui em diante. *From now on.*

dianteira f. front, lead.

dianteiro adj. leading, front; m. forward (sports).

DIÁRIO adj. daily; n. m. daily, daily newspaper; diary.

O diário ainda não chegou. *The paper isn't here yet.*

Eu gostaria de ver o diário dela. *I'd like to see her diary.*

diarréia (diarreia) *f. diarrhea.*

dicionário *m. dictionary.*

dieta *f. diet.*

difamação *f. defamation.*

difamar *to defame.*

DIFERENÇA *f. difference.*

Partir a diferença. *To split the difference.*

DIFERENTE *adj. different.*

diferir *to defer, to put off; to differ.*

DIFÍCIL *adj. difficult.*

A lição é muito difícil. *The lesson is very difficult.*

dificuldade *f. difficulty.*

dificultar *to make difficult, to obstruct.*

dificultoso *adj. difficult.*

difteria *f. diphtheria.*

difundir *to diffuse; to divulge; to broadcast.*

difusão *f. diffusion; broadcasting.*

digerir *to digest.*

digestão *f. digestion.*

dignar-se *to deign, to condescend.*

dignidade *f. dignity.*

digno *adj. deserving, worthy; honorable.*

Digno de confiança. *Trustworthy.*

digressão *f. digression.*

dilação *f. delay.*

dilatar *to put off, to delay; to expand.*

dilema *m. dilemma.*

dileto *adj. loved, beloved.*

diligência *f. diligence; legal arrangement; stagecoach.*

diligente *adj. diligent; active.*

diluir *to dilute.*

dilúvio *m. flood.*

dimensão *f. dimension.*

diminuir *to diminish, to decrease.*

diminutivo *adj. diminutive.*

diminuto *adj. diminutive, minute.*

dinamite *f. dynamite.*

dínamo *m. dynamo.*

dinheirão *m. large amount of money.*

DINHEIRO *m. money, currency.*

Dinheiro em caixa (x = sh). *Cash on hand.*

Estou sem dinheiro. *I'm broke.*

Dinheiro é um bom companheiro mas mal conselheiro. *Money is a good friend but a bad master.*

diploma *m. diploma.*

diplomacia *f. diplomacy.*

diplomático *adj. diplomatic.*

DIREÇÃO (DIRECÇÃO) *f. direction; address; guidance; management; administration.*

O volante de direção. *Steering wheel.*

Em direção a. *Toward.*

DIREITO *adj. straight, direct; proper; n. m.*

law, justice; claim, title; right; royalty; duty (import), tax.

À direita. *To the right. On the right.*

A mão direita. *The right hand.*

Faculdade de direito. *Law school.*

É preciso proteger os direitos do indivíduo. *It is necessary to protect the rights of the individual.*

Siga sempre direito. *Continue straight ahead.*

O senhor não tem direito a queixar-se (x = sh). *You have no right to complain.*

Direitos. *Rights. Fees. Duties.*

DIRETO (DIRECTO) *adj. direct, straight; nonstop; frank.*

Este trem (este comboio) é direto? *Is this a through train?*

DIRETOR (DIRECTOR) *adj. directing, managing; n. m. director, manager, administrator.*

Diretor de escola. *Principal (school).*

Diretor geral. *General manager.*

diretório (directório) *m. directory, directorate.*

DIRIGIR *to direct; to address; to conduct, to control, to guide; to drive.*

Vou dirigir-lhe uma carta. *I am going to write a letter to him.*

Ela sabe dirigir (um) automóvel? *Does she know how to drive a car?*

dirigir-se *to address oneself to, to speak to; to apply.*

A quem devo dirigir-me? *To whom should I apply?*

O senhor se dirige a nós? *Are you speaking to us?*

dirigível *m. dirigible.*

discar *to dial (telephone)* Ⓑ.

discernante *adj. discerning, discriminating.*

discernimento *m. discernment.*

discernir *to discern; to distinguish.*

disciplina *f. discipline.*

discípulo *m. disciple, follower; student.*

disco *m. disk; record (phonograph); dial (telephone).*

disco compacto *m. compact disk.*

Disco compacto em ROM. *CD-ROM.*

disco rígido *m. hard disk.*

discordante *adj. discordant.*

discórdia *f. discord, disagreement; dissension.*

discrepância *f. discrepancy.*

discrepar *to disagree, to differ.*

discreto *adj. discreet.*

discurso *m. speech.*

Fazer um discurso. *To make a speech.*

discussão *f. discussion; dispute.*

DISCUTIR *to discuss; to argue.*

disenteria *f. dysentery.*

disfarçar-se *to disguise.*

disfarce *m. disguise; mask.*

díspar *adj. unequal.*

disparar *to shoot, to fire, to discharge.*

disparatado *adj. nonsensical, absurd.*

disparatar *to blunder; to talk nonsense.*

disparate *m. nonsense.*

disparo *m. discharge, shot.*

dispendioso *adj. expensive, costly.*

dispensar *to dispense, to exempt; to bestow, to extend.*

dispensário *m. dispensary.*

disperso *adj. dispersed, scattered.*

disponível *adj. available.*

dispor *to dispose, to arrange, to provide for; to determine; to prepare; m. disposal.*
> Eu estou ao seu dispor. *I'm at your disposal.*
> Disponho de pouco tempo. *I have very little time now.*
> O homem põe, Deus dispõe. *Man proposes, God disposes.*

disposição *f. disposition; service; state of mind, condition.*
> Estou à sua disposição. *I'm at your disposal.*
> Ela está com disposição de aceitar. *She is inclined to accept.*

disposto *adj. disposed, ready, inclined; arranged.*
> Eles estão dispostos a fazê-lo. *They are inclined to do it.*
> Eu estou bem disposto. *I feel fine.*

disputa *f. dispute, quarrel; contest.*

disputar *to dispute, to quarrel.*

disquete *m. diskette, floppy disk.*

disseminar *to disseminate, to scatter.*

dissenção *f. dissension, strife.*

dissidente *adj. dissident; n. m. dissenter; nonconformist.*

dissimulação *f. dissimulation; pretense.*

dissimular *to pretend; to disguise.*

dissolver *to dissolve, to melt; to break up.*

dissuadir *to dissuade; to deter.*

DISTÂNCIA *f. distance.*
> É a pouca distância. *It's not far.*

DISTANTE *adj. far, distant.*

distinção *f. distinction; discrimination; difference.*
> Ele é um homem de grande distinção. *He is a very distinguished man.*
> Aqui é preciso fazer distinção. *It is necessary to make a distinction here.*

distinguir *to distinguish; to discriminate; to tell apart.*
> Não posso distinguir um do outro. *I can't tell one from the other.*

distinguir-se *to distinguish oneself.*

DISTINTO *adj. distinct; different; distinguished.*
> Um homem distinto. *A man of distinction.*

distração (distracção) *f. distraction; absentmindedness.*

distraído *adj. inattentive, absentminded.*

distrair *to distract; to entertain.*

distrair-se *to enjoy oneself.*
> Ela se distraiu na festa. *She had a good time at the party.*

distribuição *f. distribution.*

distribuidor *adj. distributing; n. m. distributor.*

distribuir *to distribute; to divide; to allot, to allocate.*

distrito *m. district; region.*

disturbar *to disturb.*

distúrbio *m. disturbance.*

ditado *m. dictation; saying, proverb.*

ditador *m. dictator.*

ditar *to dictate.*
> Escreva o que vou ditar. *Write what I am going to dictate.*

dito *adj. said; n. m. saying.*
> Dito e feito. *No sooner said than done.*

ditongo *m. diphthong.*

divã *m. divan, couch.*

divagação *f. wandering, digression.*

divergência *f. divergence.*

diversão *f. diversion, amusement, recreation.*

diversidade *f. diversity, variety.*

DIVERSO *adj. different, diverse; pl. several, various.*
> Eu o vi em diversas ocasiões. *I saw him on several occasions.*

DIVERTIDO *adj. entertaining, amusing; funny.*
> Tudo isto é muito divertido. *This is all very amusing.*

divertimento *m. diversion, amusement; sport.*

DIVERTIR *to amuse, to divert, to entertain.*

DIVERTIR-SE *to amuse oneself, to have a good time.*
> Nós nos divertimos na festa. *We had a good time at the party.*
> Divirta-se! *Have a good time!*

dívida *f. debt.*
> Ela pagou todas as dívidas. *She paid all her debts.*
> Dívida ativa (activa). *Outstanding debt.*
> Contrair dívidas. *To incur debts.*

dividendo *m. dividend.*

DIVIDIR *to divide.*

divindade *f. divinity.*

divino *adj. divine; heavenly.*

divisa *f. motto, slogan; emblem.*

divisão *f. division; partition, compartment; section.*

divisar *to perceive, to catch sight of.*

divorciar *to divorce.*

divorciar-se *to get a divorce, to be divorced.*

divórcio m. divorce.

divulgar to divulge, to disclose.

DIZER to say; to speak; to tell; m. saying.

  Diga-me, por favor. Please tell me.

  Pode dizer-me onde é a estação? Can you tell me where the station is?

  Eu lhe direi. I'll tell him.

  Não me diga! You don't say!

  Que quer dizer esta palavra? What does this word mean?

  Dizer adeus. To say good-bye.

  Dizer bem (mal) de alguém. To speak well (ill) of someone.

  Para dizer a verdade . . . To tell the truth . . .

  Ouvi dizer que . . . I heard that . . .

DO (contr. of de + o) of the, with the, from the.

  Qual é a capital do estado? What is the capital of the state?

  Ele é do norte. He's from the North.

dó m. do (music); pity; mourning.

doação f. donation, gift.

doar to give, to donate.

DOBRAR to turn; to double; to fold; to bend; to dub.

  Dobrar (Virar) a esquina. To turn the corner.

  Dobre bem a carta. Fold the letter well.

doca f. dock.

DOCE adj. sweet; agreeable, pleasant; n. m. candy; sweet.

dócil adj. docile, obedient; gentle.

documentação f. documentation.

documento m. document.

doçura f. sweetness; gentleness.

DOENÇA f. illness; malady.

  Apanhar uma doença. To catch a disease.

  Doença contagiosa. Contagious disease.

DOENTE adj. ill, sick; n. m. and f. sick person.

  Ela está doente. She is ill.

doer to ache, to pain.

doido adj. crazy, mad; n. m. madman; fool.

doirado adj. golden, gilded.

DOIS two.

  Dois a dois. Two by two.

  De dois em dois meses. Every two months.

  Dois é bom, três é demais. Two's company, three's a crowd.

DÓLAR m. dollar.

dolência f. sorrow, grief.

dolorosa f. bill (for a meal) (slang).

doloroso adj. painful.

dom m. gift; talent; dom (title).

  Dom Pedro I foi o primeiro imperador do Brasil. Dom Pedro I was the first emperor of Brazil.

domar to tame; to break in.

doméstico adj. domestic; n. m. servant.

domicílio m. residence, domicile.

dominação f. domination.

dominante adj. dominant.

dominar to dominate.

DOMINGO m. Sunday.

  Domingo de Ramos. Palm Sunday.

  Domingo de Páscoa. Easter Sunday.

domínio m. dominion; command; control.

DONA f. lady; title (used with the first name) meaning Mrs. or Miss.

  Dona da casa. Lady of the house.

  Dona Ana. Miss (or Mrs.) Anne.

donaire m. grace; elegance; witty saying.

donativo m. gift, donation.

DONDE (contr. of de + onde) from where, from which.

  Donde é o senhor? Where are you from?

dono m. owner.

DOR f. ache, pain, sorrow.

  Dor de cabeça. Headache.

  Dor de dente(s). Toothache.

  Dor de garganta. Sore throat.

dormente adj. dormant, sleeping; n. m. beam (house); cross tie (railroad).

DORMIR to sleep.

  Dormiu bem? Did you sleep well?

  Eu não pude dormir. I couldn't sleep.

  Dormir como uma pedra. To sleep like a log.

  Dormir a sesta. To take a nap.

dormitar to doze.

dormitório m. dormitory; bedroom Ⓑ.

dose f. dose.

dotação f. endowment; allocation.

dotar to allocate; to endow.

dote m. dowry, talent.

dourado adj. golden, gilded.

doutor m. doctor.

doutrina f. doctrine.

DOZE twelve.

drama m. drama.

dramalhão m. melodrama.

dramático adj. dramatic.

dramatizar to dramatize.

dramaturgo m. dramatist, playwright.

drástico adj. drastic.

droga f. drug.

drogaria f. drugstore, pharmacy.

DUAS (f. of dois) two.

  Duas semanas. Two weeks.

  Às duas horas. At two o'clock.

duelo m. duel.

duende m. ghost; goblin.

duo m. duo, duet.

duodécimo adj., n. m. twelfth.

duplicado adj. duplicate; n. m. duplicate, copy.

duplicar to duplicate; to repeat; to double.

duplo adj. double; duplicate, n. m. double.

duque *m. duke; deuce (cards).*
duquesa *f. duchess.*
duração *f. duration.*
duradouro *adj. durable; lasting.*
DURANTE *during.*
> Durante o dia. *During the day.*
> Durante a noite. *During the night.*
> Durante algum tempo. *For some time.*
DURAR *to last; to continue; to wear well.*
> A viagem durou quatro dias. *The trip lasted four days.*
durável *adj. durable, lasting.*
dureza *f. hardness; harshness.*
DURO *adj. hard, difficult; firm; n. m. Spanish five pesos.*
> A vida dele foi muito dura. *His life was a very difficult one.*
> Não seja duro com ele. *Don't be hard on him.*
> Pão duro. *Tightwad.*
DÚVIDA *f. doubt.*
> Sem dúvida. *Without a doubt.*
> Pôr em dúvida. *To doubt.*
DUVIDAR *to doubt; to hesitate.*
> Duvidamos que ela venha. *We doubt she will come.*
duvidoso *adj. doubtful; uncertain.*
DUZENTAS *f. two hundred.*
DUZENTOS *m. two hundred.*
DÚZIA *f. dozen.*
> Por dúzia. *By the dozen.*

E

e *(pron. as Eng. e in be) and.*
> Maria e João chegaram tarde. *Mary and John arrived late.*
ébrio *adj. intoxicated, drunk.*
economia *f. economy, thrift.*
> Economia política. *Political economy.*
econômico (económico) *adj. economic; economical.*
economizar *to economize; to save.*
edição *f. edition, issue; publication.*
edificar *to construct, to build.*
> Vão edificar uma nova escola. *They are going to build a new school.*
edifício *m. building.*
> Este edifício é um edifício público. *This building is a public building.*
editar *to edit; to publish.*
editor *adj. publishing; n. m. publisher.*
> Casa editora. *Publishing house.*
> O editor não aceitou o livro. *The publisher did not accept the book.*
editorial *adj. editorial; n. m. newspaper editorial; n. f. publishing house.*

educação *f. education; upbringing; training.*
> Ele é um senhor de boa educação. *He is a man of good manners.*
educar *to educate; to bring up; to train.*
> Ele é muito mal educado. *He is very ill-bred.*
educativo *adj. educational, instructive.*
EFEITO *m. effect, result, consequence; impression; pl. effects, assets, goods, belongings.*
> As palavras causaram mau efeito. *The words had a bad effect.*
> Com efeito, ela não sabe nada. *In fact, she doesn't know anything.*
> Levar a efeito. *To carry out. To put into practice.*
> Sem efeito. *Without effect.*
efetivo (efectivo) *adj. effective; real; actual.*
eficaz *adj. effective; efficient.*
eficiente *adj. efficient; effective.*
égua *f. mare.*
eis *behold; here is; there is.*
> Eis a razão. *That's the reason.*
> Eis porque não fomos. *That's why we didn't go.*
eixo *(x = sh) m. axle; axis.*
ELA *she; her; it.*
> Ela não sabe nada. *She doesn't know anything.*
> O vestido é para ela. *The dress is for her.*
elaboração *f. elaboration.*
elaborado *adj. elaborate.*
elaborar *to elaborate; to work out.*
ELAS *f. they; them.*
> Elas são irmãs. *They are sisters.*
elasticidade *f. elasticity.*
elástico *adj. elastic; n. m. elastic; rubber band.*
ELE *he; him; it.*
> Ele vem amanhã. *He's coming tomorrow.*
> A carta é para ele. *The letter is for him.*
electricidade ℗ **(eletricidade** Ⓑ**)** *f. electricity.*
eléctrico ℗ **(elétrico** Ⓑ**)** *adj. electric.*
elefante *m. elephant.*
eleger *to elect; to choose.*
eleição *f. election; choice.*
eleito *adj. elected; selected.*
> Carlos foi eleito presidente do clube. *Charles was elected president of the club.*
elementar *adj. elementary; elemental.*
elemento *m. element; pl. rudiments, first principles.*
elenco *m. cast (theater); catalog; list; index.*
> A peça é boa mas o elenco é muito ruim. *The play is good, but the cast is very bad.*
ELES *m. they; them.*
> Eles gostaram muito do filme. *They liked the film very much.*

Eduardo partiu com eles. *Edward left with them.*

eletricidade (electricidade) *f. electricity.*

elétrico (eléctrico) *adj. electric.*

elevação *f. elevation.*

elevador *m. elevator; lift.*

O prédio tem elevador? *Does the building have an elevator?*

elevar *to elevate; to lift up.*

eliminação *f. elimination.*

eliminar *to eliminate.*

elo *m. link; tie.*

elogiar *to praise.*

elogio *m. praise, eulogy.*

eloqüência (eloquência) *f. eloquence.*

elucidação *f. elucidation, explanation.*

eludir *to elude, to evade.*

EM *in, into, on, at, by.*

Eu o tenho na mão. *I have it in my hand.*

O senhor chegou em boa hora. *You arrived at the right time.*

Entremos nesta loja. *Let's go into this store.*

Em que dia? *On what day?*

Ela está em casa. *She is home.*

Tudo foi em vão. *It was all in vain.*

Em geral. *In general. Generally.*

Em vez de. *Instead of.*

Em toda a parte. *Everywhere.*

Em meio de. *In the middle (midst) of.*

Em breve. *Soon.*

Em fim. *Finally.*

Em verdade. *In truth. Truly.*

Eu estava pensando nisso. *I was thinking about that.*

emagrecer *to become thin.*

embaixada *(x = sh) f. embassy.*

embaixador *(x = sh) m. ambassador.*

embaixo *(x = sh) below, under.*

Lá embaixo. *Down there.*

embandeirar *to deck out or decorate with flags.*

embaraçar *to embarrass; to hinder.*

embaraço *m. embarrassment; difficulty.*

embaralhar *to shuffle (cards); to mix.*

embarcação *f. vessel, ship, boat; embarkation.*

embarcar *to embark, to go aboard.*

Vamos embarcar em vinte minutos. *We are going aboard in twenty minutes.*

embargar *to embargo; to hinder.*

Sem embargo. *Nevertheless.*

embarque *m. embarkation; shipment*

emblema *m. emblem, symbol.*

EMBORA *although, away.*

Vamos embora! *Let's go!*

Embora não tivéssemos dinheiro saímos de casa. *Although we did not have any money, we went out of the house.*

emborrachar-se *to become drunk.*

emboscada *f. ambush, trap.*

emboscar *to ambush.*

embriagar *to intoxicate; to enchant.*

embriagar-se *to become intoxicated; to become enchanted.*

embrulhar *to wrap up; to confuse; to disturb.*

embrulho *m. package; parcel; trick; swindle* ⑬.

Deixei *(x = sh)* os embrulhos na mesa. *I left the packages on the table.*

embrutecer *to brutalize; to make coarse.*

embrutecer-se *to be or to become stupid or coarse.*

embuste *m. lie; trick.*

embusteiro *m. liar; deceiver; cheater.*

embutido *adj. inlaid; n. m. inlaid work; mosaic.*

emendar *to amend, to correct.*

ementa *f. menu* ⑫.

emergência *f. emergency.*

emigração *f. emigration.*

emigrante *adj., n. m. and f. emigrant.*

eminente *adj. eminent.*

emissor *adj. issuing; n. m. transmitter.*

emissora *f. broadcasting station.*

emitir *to emit, to send forth; to issue (bonds); to utter; to broadcast.*

emoção *f. emotion.*

emocionante *adj. moving, touching.*

emocionar *to move, to excite.*

empachar *to stuff; to overload.*

empacotar *to package; to pack.*

empalmar *to palm; to pilfer.*

empanada *f. meat turnover.*

empapar *to soak.*

Ficamos empapados. *We were soaked.*

emparelhar *to pair; to join.*

empatar *to tie (score); to tie up (money).*

Os quadros empataram. *The teams tied.*

empate *m. tie, draw.*

empeçar *to entangle.*

empecilho *m. hindrance; difficulty.*

empenhar *to pawn; to pledge; to engage.*

Eu empenhei minha palavra. *I pledged (gave) my word.*

empenho *m. pledge, obligation; pawning; determination; persistence.*

Elas estudam com empenho. *They study diligently.*

empertigado *adj. haughty.*

empolgante *adj. thrilling, gripping.*

empório *m. trading center; grocery store* ⑬.

empreender *to undertake.*

empregado *adj. used, occupied; n. m. employee; servant.*

Isso foi bem empregado. *That was put to good use.*

Ela tem um empregado e duas empregadas.

She has one male servant and two
maids.

EMPREGAR *to employ, to hire; to spend.*

Em que o senhor empregou a tarde? *How
did you spend the afternoon?*

Empregamos dois dias em fazê-lo. *It took
us two days to do it.*

EMPREGO *m. employment, job, occupation;
use.*

Mário tem um bom emprego. *Mario has a
good job.*

empresa *f. undertaking; enterprise; company.*

empresário *m. impresario; contractor;
manager.*

emprestar *to lend.*

Emprestar de. *To borrow* ⑬.

Pedir emprestado. Tomar emprestado. *To
borrow.*

empréstimo *m. loan.*

empurrar *to push, to shove.*

enamorar-se *to fall in love.*

encabeçar *to head, to direct; to start.*

Quem encabeçou a revolução? *Who
headed the revolution?*

encadear *to chain; to link.*

encadernado *adj. bound (book).*

Eu prefiro o livro encadernado. *I prefer the
book bound.*

encaixar *(x = sh) to fit; to inlay; to box, to put
in a box; to come in handy.*

Isto encaixa sem dificuldade. *This fits
easily.*

encalhar *to run aground; to stick.*

encaminhar *to guide, to direct.*

encaminhar-se *to take the road to; to set
out for.*

encanamento *m. plumbing; pipelines.*

encanecer *to turn gray; to grow old; to
mature.*

encantado *adj. charmed; delighted,
enchanted.*

encantador *adj. charming, delightful,
enchanting.*

encantamento *m. charm; delight; fascination;
enchantment; marvel.*

encanto *m. charm; enchantment; delight;
spell.*

Como por encanto. *As if by magic.*

Ela é um encanto de menina. *She is a
charming little girl.*

encarar *to face; to look straight at.*

Temos que encarar o problema. *We have to
face the problem.*

encarcerar *to imprison.*

encarecer *to raise the price; to entreat.*

encargo *m. charge; duty; tax.*

Os meus encargos vão crescendo. *My
duties are growing.*

encarnado *adj. red; scarlet.*

encarregado *adj. in charge; n. m. person in
charge.*

encarregar *to put in charge, to charge (with).*

encarregar-se *to take charge, to take care.*

Eu me encarrego de tudo. *I'll take care of
everything.*

encenação *f. staging.*

encenador *m. director (theatre); producer
(theatre).*

encenar *to stage (play); to display.*

enceradeira *f. floor waxer.*

encerar *to wax; to polish.*

encerrar *to close in; to enclose; to confine; to
contain.*

encetar *to start; to begin.*

Encetar um assunto. *To broach a subject.*

encharcar *to drench; to soak.*

enchente *f. flood.*

As enchentes causam muito dano. *Floods
cause great damage.*

ENCHER *to fill, to fill up.*

Encha o tanque. *Fill 'er up (fill up the
tank).*

enchova *f. anchovy.*

enciclopédia *f. encyclopedia.*

encoberto *adj. covered; hidden.*

O céu está encoberto. *The sky is overcast.*

encobrir *to cover; to conceal.*

encolher *to shrink; to contract.*

Encolher os ombros. *To shrug the
shoulders.*

encomenda *f. an order (purchase);
commission.*

encomendar *to order; to commission.*

Ela encomendou os cinco volumes. *She
ordered the five volumes.*

ENCONTRAR *to find; to meet; to meet by
chance.*

O senhor encontrou o que procurava? *Did
you find what you were looking for?*

Eles devem nos encontrar aqui. *They are to
meet us here.*

ENCONTRAR-SE *to find oneself; to be; to
meet.*

Eu me encontrei sozinho. *I found myself
all alone.*

Vamos encontrar-nos amanhã. *We are
going to meet tomorrow.*

ENCONTRO *m. meeting; encounter.*

encrenca *f. difficulty; obstacle.*

Deixe-me de encrencas. *I don't want any
trouble.*

encrespar *to curl; to frizzle.*

encruzilhada *f. crossroads.*

endereçar *to address; to direct.*

Um momento. Vou endereçar esta carta.
*Just a moment. I'm going to address
this letter.*

endereço *m. address.*

endossar *to endorse.*

endurecer *to harden.*

energia *f. energy, power.*

enérgico *adj. energetic, active.*

enfadar *to irk, to annoy.*

enfado *m. displeasure; annoyance.*

enfartar *to glut; to stuff.*

ênfase *f. emphasis.*

enfático *adj. emphatic.*

enfeitar *to adorn, to decorate.*

enfermar *to become ill.*

    Se ela continua assim vai enfermar. *If she continues that way, she is going to become ill.*

enfermeira *f. nurse.*

enfermeiro *m. male nurse; hospital orderly.*

enfermo *adj. sick; n. m. patient, sick person.*

ENFIM *finally, at last; in short.*

enforcar *to hang (a person).*

enfrear *to curb; to brake.*

    É preciso enfrear nas colinas. *You have to use your brakes on the hills.*

enfrentar *to face; to confront.*

    Temos que enfrentar o problema hoje. *We have to face the problem today.*

enfurecer *to become angry; to become furious.*

engaiolar *to cage; to lock up.*

engalanar *to decorate, to adorn.*

enganar *to deceive, to fool.*

enganar-se *to deceive oneself; to be mistaken.*

    Sinto muito! Enganei-me. *I'm very sorry! I was mistaken.*

enganchar *to hook.*

engano *error, mistake; deceit.*

enganoso *adj. misleading; deceiving.*

engarrafar *to bottle.*

engendrar *to engender.*

engenharia *f. engineering.*

engenheiro *m. engineer; owner of a mill ℗.*

engenho *m. ingenuity; skill; wit; mill.*

    Engenho de açúcar. *Sugar mill.*

engolir *to swallow; to gulp down.*

    Engula a pílula! *Swallow the pill!*

    Faça o favor de falar mais alto e de não engolir as palavras. *Please speak louder, and do not swallow your words.*

engomar *to starch.*

engordar *to fatten; to grow fat.*

ENGRAÇADO *adj. amusing; funny.*

    Não acho muito engraçado. *I don't think it's very funny.*

engraxar *(x = sh) to wax; to shine shoes, to grease.*

engraxate (engraxador) *(x = sh) bootblack.*

engrenagem *f. gear.*

enguia *f. eel.*

enjoado *adj. nauseated; carsick; seasick.*

enjoar *to nauseate; to feel nausea.*

enjôo *m. nausea; seasickness; car sickness.*

enlaçar *to join, to connect; to bind; to tie.*

enlace *m. union; marriage.*

    Enlace matrimonial. *Marriage.*

enlatado *adj. canned.*

enlatar *to can (food).*

enlouquecer *to go mad; to drive mad.*

enojar *to nauseate; to feel nausea; to disgust.*

enojo *m. nausea; disgust.*

ENQUANTO *while.*

    Enquanto nós estudávamos eles escreviam cartas. *While we studied, they wrote letters.*

    Por enquanto. *For the time being.*

enredar *to entangle; to catch with a net.*

enredo *m. plot (of book); story; complication.*

    O enredo do romance é muito fraco. *The novel's plot is quite weak.*

enriquecer *to enrich; to become rich.*

enrolar *to wind; to roll up; to wrap up.*

ensaboar *to soap; to lather.*

ensaiar *to try; to rehearse; to test.*

ensaio *m. trial; rehearsal; essay.*

    Balão de ensaio. *Trial balloon.*

ensejo *m. opportunity; occasion.*

    Aproveitamos o ensejo para . . . *We take this opportunity to . . .*

ensinamento *m. teaching, instruction.*

ENSINAR *to teach; to show; to train.*

    Quer que lhe ensine? *Would you like me to teach you?*

ensino *m. teaching, instruction; training.*

ensurdecer *to deafen; to stun.*

ENTANTO *meanwhile.*

    No entanto. *Nevertheless. However.*

ENTÃO *then; in that case; at that time.*

    Então o senhor não quer ir comigo. *Then you don't want to go with me.*

    Desde então. *Since that time.*

ENTENDER *to understand.*

    Não entendi nada. *I didn't understand a thing.*

    João entende disso. *John is familiar with that.*

    Entendi mal. *I misunderstood.*

    Ela me deu a entender que já era tarde. *She led me to believe that it was already too late.*

    Não posso me entender com elas. *I can't come to an understanding with them.*

    Agora nos entendemos. *Now we understand each other.*

entendimento *m. understanding.*

enternecer *to soften; to move to pity.*

enterrar *to bury.*

enterro *m. burial; interment; funeral.*

entidade *f. entity.*

entoação *f. intonation; tone.*

entoar *to tune; to intone; to be in tune.*

ENTRADA f. entrance; entry; admission; ticket; entree.

Quanto é a entrada? *How much is the admission?*

A entrada é gratuita. *(The) admission is free.*

Devemos comprar as entradas agora. *We should buy the tickets now.*

É proibida a entrada. *No admittance.*

Meia entrada. *Half-price ticket.*

ENTRAR to enter; to go in; to fit.

Entre! *Come in!*

Que não entre ninguém. *Don't let anybody in.*

Entramos no cinema às três. *We went into the movie theatre at three.*

Entrar com o pé direito. *To have a good start. To get off on the right foot.*

Ela entrou na universidade no ano passado. *She entered the university last year.*

Entrar por um ouvido e sair pelo outro. *To go in one ear and out the other.*

ENTRE between; among.

Fizeram-no entre os dois. *They did it between the two of them.*

Procure entre os papéis. *Look among the papers.*

Entre nós. *Between ourselves.*

Entre a espada e a parede. *Between a rock and a hard place.*

entreato (entreacto) m. intermission.

entrega f. delivery; delivering.

Entrega urgente. *Special delivery (mail).*

ENTREGAR to deliver; to hand over.

A quem entregou a carta? *To whom did you deliver the letter?*

entregar-se to surrender; to give oneself up; to devote oneself (to).

O criminoso se entregou à polícia. *The criminal gave himself up to the police.*

Entregar os pontos. *To give up.*

entregue adj. delivered.

entrementes meanwhile.

entremeter to insert; to place between.

ENTRETANTO meanwhile; however.

entretenimento m. entertainment, amusement.

entrevista f. interview; conference.

entrevistar to interview.

entristecer to become sad.

entusiasmar to fill with enthusiasm.

entusiasmar-se to become enthusiastic.

entusiasmo m. enthusiasm.

entusiasta adj. enthusiastic; n. m. and f. enthusiast, fan.

entusiástico adj. enthusiastic.

envasar to bottle; to put in pots (flowers).

envelhecer to make old; to grow old.

envelope m. envelope.

Não esqueça de escrever o endereço no envelope. *Don't forget to write the address on the envelope.*

envenenar to poison.

ENVIAR to send; to dispatch.

Envie-me uma dúzia. *Send me a dozen.*

Enviar por correio electrónico. *To e-mail.*

Enviar um fax. *To fax, to send a fax.*

envio m. shipment; shipping.

enviuvar to become a widow or widower.

envolver to wrap up; to make into a package; to envelop; to surround.

enxaguar (x = sh) to rinse.

época f. epoch, age, era.

equipa f. team Ⓟ.

equipamento m. equipment.

equipar to equip; to furnish.

equipe f. team (business, etc.) Ⓑ.

equivocação f. mistake.

equivocado adj. mistaken.

equivocar to make a mistake; to mistake.

equívoco adj. equivocal; n. m. mistake; pun; misunderstanding.

Acho que tudo foi um equívoco. *I believe it was all a misunderstanding.*

era f. era; age; period.

ereto (erecto) adj. erect; upright.

erguer to erect, to raise.

erigir to erect, to build.

errado adj. wrong, in error.

ERRAR to err, to make a mistake.

Errámos o caminho. *We lost our way.*

errata f. erratum, error in writing or printing.

ERRO m. error, mistake.

erudição f. erudition, learning.

erudito adj. erudite, learned; n. m. scholar, erudite person.

erva f. herb, plant.

Erva-mate. *Paraguay tea; maté.*

ervilha f. pea.

esbelto adj. slim, slender; elegant.

esboço m. sketch; outline.

escabroso adj. rough; uneven; difficult.

escada f. stairs; staircase; ladder.

Escada de incêndio. *Fire escape.*

Escada de mão. *Stepladder.*

Escada de serviço. *Service stairway.*

Escada rolante. *Escalator.*

escala f. scale; ladder; stop.

Em grande escala. *On a large scale.*

Porto de escala. *Port of call.*

escandir to scan.

escáner m. scanner.

escapar to escape, to flee.

escape m. escape.

escapo adj. escaped; free.

escarmentar to punish; to reprimand.

escárnio m. scorn.

escasso adj. scarce, scanty.

esclarecer *to clarify; to enlighten.*
escoamento *m. drainage.*
escoar *to drain; to flow.*
ESCOLA *f. school.*
    Escola elementar. *Elementary school.*
    Escola secundária. *Secondary school.*
ESCOLHER *to choose, to pick.*
escolhido *adj. chosen, select.*
escolta *f. escort.*
escoltar *to escort.*
escombros *m. pl. ruins.*
esconder *to hide, to conceal.*
escondido *adj. hidden.*
escorrer *to trickle; to drip.*
escoteira *f. girl scout.*
escoteiro *m. boy scout.*
ESCOVA *f. brush.*
    Escova de cabelo. *Hairbrush.*
    Escova de dentes. *Toothbrush.*
    Escova de roupa. *Clothes brush.*
escovar *to brush, to scrub.*
escravatura *f. slavery.*
escravidão *f. slavery.*
escravo *m. slave.*
ESCREVER *to write.*
    Escreva claramente. *Write clearly.*
    Como se escreve esta palavra? *How do you write (spell) that word?*
    Prefiro que escreva a carta à máquina. *I prefer that you type the letter.*
    Máquina de escrever. *Typewriter.*
    Escrever à maquina. *To type.*
escrito *adj. written; n. m. something written, writing.*
    Escrito à mão. *Handwritten.*
    Escrito à máquina. *Typewritten.*
    Pôr por escrito. *To put in writing.*
escritor *m. writer, author.*
escritório *m. office; study.*
escritura *f. writing; writ; document; deed.*
escrivão *m. notary, scribe.*
escrutínio *m. scrutiny; balloting; voting.*
escudo *m. shield.*
escurecer *to grow dark.*
escuridão *f. darkness.*
escusa *f. excuse.*
ESCUTAR *to listen; to heed.*
    Escute! *Listen!*
esfera *f. sphere.*
esforçar *to strengthen; to encourage.*
esforçar-se *to try hard, to endeavor, to strive.*
esforço *m. effort; endeavor.*
esfregar *to rub; to scrub; to scratch.*
esfriar *to cool off; to grow cold.*
esgotado *adj. exhausted; sold out; out of print.*

    Essa edição já está esgotada. *That edition is already sold out.*
esgotar *to drain; to exhaust.*
esgrima *f. fencing (sport).*
eslavo *adj. Slavic; Slav; n. m. Slav.*
esmagar *to overcome; to smash; to crush.*
esmaltar *to enamel.*
esmalte *m. enamel.*
    Esmalte de unhas. *Nail polish.*
esmerado *adj. carefully done; accomplished.*
esmerar *to do with great care; to perfect.*
esmero *m. care; perfection; neatness.*
esmolas *f. pl. alms.*
espaço *m. space, room.*
    Aqui não há espaço. *There's no room here.*
espada *f. sword.*
espaldar *m. back of a chair.*
espalhar *to spread; to scatter; to disseminate.*
espanhol *Spanish.*
espantar *to frighten, to drive away.*
espanto *m. fright.*
espantoso *adj. frightful.*
esparadrapo *m. adhesive tape.*
espargo *m. asparagus.*
espátula *f. spatula; letter opener.*
especial *adj. special.*
especialidade *f. specialty.*
especiarias *f. pl. spices.*
espécie *f. species; kind; sort.*
espectáculo Ⓟ (**espetáculo** Ⓑ) *m. spectacle, show.*
especulação *f. speculation.*
ESPELHO *m. mirror; looking glass.*
    Espelho retrovisor. *Rearview mirror.*
espera *f. wait, waiting.*
    Onde é a sala de espera? *Where is the waiting room?*
esperança *f. hope.*
ESPERAR *to wait for; to expect; to hope.*
    Assim o espero. *I hope so.*
    Espero que não. *I hope not.*
    Espero que sim. *I hope so.*
    Espere-me. *Wait for me.*
    Diga-lhe que espere. *Tell him to wait.*
    Espere um momento. *Wait a moment.*
esperto *adj. smart; alert; clever.*
    Ela é muito esperta. *She's very smart.*
espesso *adj. thick, dense.*
espetáculo (espectáculo) *m. spectacle, show.*
espiar *to spy on.*
espiga *f. spike; ear (corn).*
espinafre *m. spinach.*
espingarda *f. shotgun, rifle.*
espinha *f. spine; fishbone.*
espinho *m. thorn.*
espírito *m. spirit; mind; wit; soul.*
    Espírito prático. *Practical mind.*
    Ele é uma pessoa de espírito. *He is a man of wit.*

Espírito Santo. *Holy Spirit. Holy Ghost.*
espiritual *adj. spiritual.*
espirrar *to sneeze; to burst out.*
espirro *m. sneeze, sneezing.*
esplêndido *adj. splendid; excellent.*
esplendor *m. splendor, magnificence.*
esponja *f. sponge; parasite.*
esporte *m. sport.*
ESPOSA *f. wife, spouse.*
ESPOSO *m. husband, spouse.*
espreguiçadeira *f. chaise lounge, easy chair.*
espreguiçar-se *to stretch oneself out.*
espuma *f. foam, froth.*
   Espuma de sabão. *Lather. Soapsuds.*
esquadra *f. squadron; squad; police station* Ⓟ.
ESQUECER *to forget; to neglect.*
   Não esqueça o que lhe disse. *Don't forget
     what I told you.*
ESQUECER-SE *to forget.*
   Ela se esqueceu de chamar. *She forgot to
     call.*
esquema *m. scheme, drawing.*
ESQUERDA *f. left, left side.*
   À esquerda. *To the left.*
   Esquerda, volver! *Left, face! (Military
     command).*
ESQUERDO *adj. left.*
esqui *m. ski.*
esquilo *m. squirrel.*
ESQUINA *f. corner (of a street).*
   Dobrar (Virar) a esquina. *To turn the
     corner.*
   A loja está na esquina. *The shop is on the
     corner.*
esquisito *adj. peculiar; odd; strange; unusual.*
esquivança *f. disdain, contempt.*
ESSA *f. that; that one; pl. those.*
   Essa senhora. *That lady.*
   Vamos por essa rua. *Let's go down that
     street.*
   Essas coisas não me interessam. *Those
     things don't interest me.*
   Prefiro estas a essas. *I prefer these to
     those.*
   Ora essa! *Come on now!*
ESSE *m. that; that one; pl. those.*
   Esse senhor. *That man.*
   Esses meninos. *Those boys.*
   Não quero esses; prefiro estes. *I don't want
     those; I prefer these.*
essência *f. essence.*
essencial *adj. essential.*
essoutro *that (other) one.*
ESTA *f. this; this one; pl. these.*
   Esta senhora e aquele homem são irmãos.
     *This lady and that man are brother and
     sister.*
   De quem é esta casa? *Whose house is this?*
   Não gosto destas. *I don't like these.*

estabelecer *to establish.*
estabelecimento *m. establishment.*
estábulo *m. stable.*
ESTAÇÃO *f. station, season.*
   Onde é a estação? *Where is the station?*
   O inverno é a estação mais fria do ano.
     Winter is the coldest season of the year.
estacionamento *m. parking.*
   Estacionamento proibido. *No parking.*
estacionar *to park; to stop.*
estada *f. stay; stop.*
estádio *m. stadium; stage, phase.*
ESTADO *m. state; condition.*
   Em bom estado. *In good condition.*
   Homem de estado. *Statesman.*
   Estado-maior. *General staff.*
   Estado de guerra. *State of war.*
   Estados Unidos da América. *United States
     of America.*
estágio *m. period, phase; apprenticeship.*
estalagem *f. inn.*
estalar *to burst, to explode, to crack; to snap.*
estampa *f. picture, print.*
estampar *to stamp; to print.*
estampilha *f. small stamp; revenue stamp* Ⓑ.
estampilhar *to stamp; to put stamps on.*
estancar *to check; to stop.*
estância *f. dwelling, residence; station; stay.*
estanho *m. tin.*
estante *f. bookcase; lectern.*
ESTAR *to be.*
   Estamos prontos. *We are ready.*
   Elas estão cansadas. *They are tired.*
   Que está fazendo? *What are you doing?*
   Eles estão estudando. *They are studying.*
   Eles estão a estudar Ⓟ. *They are studying.*
   Onde está o seu irmão? *Where is your
     brother?*
   Ele está no teatro. *He is at the theater.*
   Deveríamos estar lá antes das nove. *We
     should be there before nine.*
   A janela está aberta. *The window is open.*
   Ela está de pé. *She is standing.*
   Estou certo. *I am sure.*
   Nós estamos de acordo. *We agree.*
   Ela está doente. *She is sick.*
   Estou para sair de viagem. *I am about to
     leave on a trip.*
   Está bem. *Very well. Fine.*
   Está na hora de partir. *It's time to leave.*
   Estou com pressa. *I'm in a hurry.*
estátua *f. statue.*
estatura *f. stature.*
estatuto *m. statute, law.*
este *m. east.*
ESTE *m. this; this one; pl. these.*
   Este senhor. *This man.*
   Estes livros. *These books.*
   Este é o meu. *This one is mine.*

Não quero estes. *I don't want these.*

estender *to extend; to stretch out.*

estenógrafa *f. stenographer.*

estenógrafo *m. stenographer.*

estiagem *f. dry weather, drought.*

esticar *to stretch.*

estilo *m. style.*

estima *f. esteem; appreciation.*

estimar *to esteem; to value.*

estimular *to stimulate.*

estímulo *m. stimulus.*

estio (Estio) *m. summer.*

estirar *to stretch, to extend.*

estirpe *f. stock; ancestry.*

estivador *m. stevedore, longshoreman.*

estojo *m. kit; case, box; set.*

Estojo de barba. *Shaving set.*

estômago *m. stomach.*

estoque *m. stock, supply* ®.

estorvar *to disturb; to hinder.*

estourar *to burst; to explode.*

ESTRADA *f. road, highway.*

Estrada de rodagem. *Highway.*

Estrada de ferro. *Railway.*

ESTRANGEIRO *adj. foreign; n. m. foreigner, alien; stranger.*

Ela está no estrangeiro. *She is abroad.*

estranhar *to be surprised; to find strange.*

estranheza *f. strangeness; surprise.*

estranho *adj. strange; unusual; odd.*

Ele é um pouco estranho. *He's somewhat strange.*

estratégia *f. strategy.*

estratégico *adj. strategic.*

estrear *to try or use for the first time; to make one's debut; to open (play).*

estréia (estreia) *f. opening, première; first showing; debut.*

A estréia de peça vai ser na sexta. *The play will open on Friday.*

estreito *adj. narrow; n. m. strait.*

estrela *f. star.*

estremecer *to shake, to tremble.*

estremecimento *m. shaking, quiver.*

estribo *m. stirrup; running board.*

estropiar *to cripple; to deform.*

estrutura *f. structure.*

estudante *m. and f. student.*

ESTUDAR *to study.*

Os meus filhos não estudam bastante. *My children don't study enough.*

estudioso *adj. studious.*

ESTUDO *m. study.*

Bolsa de estudos. *Scholarship.*

estufa *f. heating stove; hothouse.*

estupendo *adj. stupendous; wonderful.*

estupidez *f. stupidity.*

estúpido *adj. stupid; n. m. stupid person.*

eternidade *f. eternity.*

eterno *adj. eternal.*

ética *f. ethics.*

ético *adj. ethic, ethical.*

etiqueta *etiquette; ceremony; tag (on clothing, etc.).*

euro *m. euro (currency in Portugal).*

europeu *adj. European.*

evacuação *f. evacuation.*

evacuar *to evacuate.*

evadir *to evade.*

evangelho *m. the Gospel.*

evaporar *to evaporate.*

evasão *f. evasion; escape.*

evasivo *adj. evasive.*

evento *m. event, happening.*

evidência *f. evidence; indication.*

evidente *adj. evident, obvious.*

EVITAR *to avoid.*

Quero evitar essa situação, se puder. *I should like to avoid that situation if I can.*

evitável *adj. avoidable.*

evocar *to evoke.*

evolução *f. evolution.*

exageração $(x = z)$ *f. exaggeration.*

exagerar $(x = z)$ *to exaggerate.*

exagero $(x = z)$ *m. exaggeration.*

exaltação $(x = z)$ *f. exaltation.*

exaltar $(x = z)$ *to exalt, to praise.*

exame $(x = z)$ *m. examination.*

Exame de admissão. *Admission examination.*

Exame médico. *Medical examination.*

examinar $(x = z)$ *to examine; to inquire into; to investigate.*

exasperação $(x = z)$ *f. exasperation.*

exasperar $(x = z)$ *to exasperate.*

exatidão (exactidão) $(x = z)$ *f. exactitude, exactness.*

EXATO (EXACTO) $(x = z)$ *adj. exact; correct.*

Exatamente. *Exactly.*

exceção *f. exception.*

exceder *to exceed.*

excelência *f. excellence.*

Vossa Excelência. *Your Excellency.*

excelente *adj. excellent; fine.*

excelentíssimo *adj. most excellent.*

excelso *adj. eminent; exalted.*

excepcional *adj. exceptional; unusual.*

excessivo *adj. excessive; too much.*

excesso *m. excess.*

Em excesso. *In excess. Excessively.*

exceto (excepto) *except.*

excetuar (exceptuar) *to except; to exempt; to exclude.*

excitação *f. excitation; excitement.*

excitante *adj. exciting.*

excitar *to excite; to stimulate.*

excitável *adj. excitable.*
exclamação *f. exclamation.*
exclamar *to exclaim.*
excluir *to exclude; to keep out; to rule out.*
exclusão *f. exclusion.*
exclusivo *adj. exclusive.*
excursão *f. excursion, trip.*
execução *(x = z) f. execution; performance.*
executar *(x = z) to execute; to carry out.*
executivo *(x = z) adj. executive.*
exemplar *(x = z) adj. exemplary; n. m. copy; model.*
    Eu lhe mandarei um exemplar. *I'll send you a copy.*
EXEMPLO *(x = z) m. example, pattern.*
    Por exemplo. *For example.*
exercer *(x = z) to exercise; to carry out; to practice.*
    Exercer a medicina. *To practice medicine.*
exercício *(x = z) m. exercise; drill.*
    Fazer exercício. *To exercise.*
exército *(x = z) m. army.*
exibição *f. exhibition.*
exibir *(x = z) to exhibit.*
exigência *(x = z) f. exigency, urgent need.*
exigente *(x = z) adj. exigent, demanding.*
    Não seja tão exigente. *Don't be so demanding.*
exigir *(x = z) to demand; to require; to exact.*
    As circunstâncias o exigem. *The situation requires it.*
exilar *(x = z) to exile.*
exílio *(x = z) m. exile.*
existência *(x = z) f. existence, stock of goods* Ⓟ.
existente *(x = z) adj. living, existent.*
EXISTIR *(x = z) to exist, to be.*
    Não existe tal coisa. *No such thing exists.*
ÊXITO *(x = z) m. success; hit (song, etc.); result; outcome.*
    Eles tiveram bom êxito. *They were a big success.*
exortar *(x = z) to exhort; to urge.*
expandir *to expand; to spread out.*
expansão *f. expansion.*
expectativa *f. expectation; hope.*
expedição *f. expedition; shipment.*
expediente *adj. expeditious; n. m. expedient; office hours.*
expedir *to expedite; to dispatch, to send.*
expelir *to expel.*
experiência *f. experience; trial.*
experimentar *to experience; to experiment.*
experimento *m. experience; experiment.*
experto *adj. expert; n. m. expert.*
expirar *to expire; to die; to exhale.*
explicação *f. explication.*
EXPLICAR *to explain.*
    Deixe-me explicá-lo. *Let me explain it.*

explicativo *adj. explanatory.*
explicável *adj. explainable.*
explícito *adj. explicit.*
exploração *f. exploration.*
explorador *m. explorer.*
explorar *to explore.*
explosão *f. explosion; outburst.*
expoente *m. and f. exponent.*
expôr *to expound; to explain; to make clear; to expose.*
exportação *f. export.*
exportador *adj. exporting; n. m. exporter.*
    Casa exportadora. *Exporting firm.*
exportar *to export.*
exposição *f. exposition, show, exhibition; exposure.*
expositor *m. exhibitor; expositor.*
exposto *adj. exposed; liable to.*
    Está exposto das dez às quatro horas. *It is being shown from ten to four o'clock.*
expressão *f. expression.*
expresso *adj. express; clear; n. m. express (train); special delivery.*
exprimir *to express.*
expulsão *f. expulsion.*
expulsar *to expel, to eject, to throw out.*
expulso *adj. expelled, expulsed.*
extensão *f. extension; extent.*
    Em toda extensão. *In every sense.*
extensivo *adj. extensive; far-reaching.*
extenso *adj. extensive; vast.*
extenuação *f. extenuation.*
extenuar *to extenuate.*
exterior *adj. exterior; foreign.*
extinguir *to extinguish, to put out.*
extra *extra.*
extrair *to extract, to pull out.*
extra-oficial *adj. unofficial; off the record.*
extraordinário *adj. extraordinary.*
    É um caso extraordinário. *It's an unusual case.*
extratar *to extract.*
extrato (extracto) *m. extract.*
extravagância *f. folly, extravagance.*
extravagante *adj. extravagant; odd.*
extraviado *adj. lost, missing; astray.*
extraviar *to mislead; to mislay.*
extravio *m. loss; deviation; straying.*
extremidade *f. extremity; very end.*
extremo *adj. extreme; last; n. m. extreme; end.*

F

fá *n. musical note.*
fã *m. and f. fan (follower).*
fábrica *f. factory; mill; plant.*
    Preço de fábrica. *Factory price.*

Marca de fábrica. *Trademark.*
fabricação *f. manufacturing; manufacture.*
fabricante *m. and f. manufacturer; maker.*
fabricar *to manufacture, to make; to build.*
fábula *f. fable; story, tale.*
fabuloso *adj. fabulous; incredible.*
FACA *f. knife.*
façanha *f. deed; accomplishment.*
fação Ⓑ **facção** Ⓑ *and* Ⓟ. *f. faction.*
face *f- face; side.*
O negócio tem duas faces. *There are two sides to the matter.*
fachada *f. façade.*
FÁCIL *easy.*
Parece fácil mas é difícil. *It looks easy, but it's difficult.*
Facilmente. *Easily.*
É fácil de aprender. *It's easy to learn.*
facilidade *f. ease, facility.*
facilitar *to facilitate, to make easy.*
facsimile *m. facsimile, fax.*
FACTO Ⓟ **(FATO** Ⓑ**)** *m. fact; occurrence.*
faculdade *f. faculty; school (in a university, etc.).*
Faculdade de direito. *Law school.*
fada *f. fairy.*
Conto de fadas. *Fairy tale.*
fadista *m. and f. singer and player of fados; ruffian.*
FADO *m. fate, destiny; Portuguese popular folk song.*
faina *f. task, chore.*
faixa (x = sh) *f. sash; strip.*
faixar (x = sh) *to bind; to tie up.*
fala *f. speech; language.*
falador *adj. talkative; n. m. talker; gabber.*
FALAR *to speak, to talk.*
O senhor fala português? *Do you speak Portuguese?*
Eu falo português. *I speak Portuguese.*
Aqui se fala inglês. *English is spoken here.*
Fale! *Speak!*
Fale mais devagar. *Speak slower.*
Desejo falar com o gerente. *I wish to speak to the manager.*
Gostaria de falar-lhe sobre um assunto importante. *I would like to speak to you about an important matter.*
Fale mais alto. *Speak louder.*
De que estão falando? *What are they talking about?*
Falemos nisso agora mesmo. *Let's talk about that right now.*
falecer *to die.*
Ele faleceu no ano passado. *He died last year.*
falha *f. fault, flaw.*
falhar *to fail; to miss.*
falho *adj. faulty; defective.*

falsear *to falsify; to distort.*
falsidade *f. falsehood; untruth.*
falsificação *f. falsification; forgery.*
falsificar *to falsify.*
falso *adj. false; incorrect.*
Alarme falso. *False alarm.*
Chave falsa. *Skeleton key.*
FALTA *f. need, lack; absence; fault, defect; mistake.*
Temos que desculpar as faltas dele. *We must excuse his faults.*
Eu corrigirei as faltas. *I'll correct the mistakes.*
Sem falta. *Without fail.*
Estamos com falta de água. *We are short of water.*
Perdemos tudo por falta de dinheiro. *We lost everything for lack of money.*
FALTAR *to need, to lack; to be absent; to fail.*
Aqui faltam três livros. *Three books are missing here.*
Ela faltou à aula hoje. *She missed class today.*
Era o que faltava! *That's the last straw!*
Faltam vinte minutos para as duas. *It's twenty minutes to two.*
Ele nunca falta à palavra. *He never goes back on his word.*
falto *adj. lacking, wanting.*
fama *f. fame, reputation, rumor, report.*
FAMÍLIA *f. family.*
familiar *adj. familiar, pertaining to the family; m. and f. close friend; relative.*
faminto *adj. hungry, famished.*
famoso *adj. famous.*
fanático *adj. fanatic.*
fanfarrão *adj. boasting, bragging; n. m. braggart.*
fantasia *f. fantasy, fancy; fancy dress, carnival costume* Ⓑ.
fantasma *m ghost, phantasm.*
fantástico *adj. fantastic.*
fantoche *m. puppet.*
farda *f. uniform.*
fardo *m. bale; parcel, bundle.*
faringe *f. pharynx.*
farinha *f. flour, meal.*
Farinha de trigo. *Wheat flour.*
farmacêutico *m. pharmacist, druggist.*
farmácia *f. pharmacy, drugstore.*
faro *m. lighthouse; sense of smell (animal).*
farofa *f. a dish made of manioc meal, meat, eggs, vegetables, etc.*
farol *m. lighthouse; beacon; headlight.*
Farol verde. *Green light.*
Farol vermelho. *Red light. Stoplight.*
farrapo *m. rag; ragamuffin.*
farroupilha *m. ragamuffin.*

farsa *f. farce.*

farsante *m. and f. actor, actress in farces; joker.*

farsista *adj. joking; n. m. and f. joker, clown.*

fartar *to fill with, to satiate.*

farto *adj. satiated, full; abundant.*
   Estou farto disto. *I'm sick of this.*

fascinar *to fascinate, to charm.*

fase *f. phase; aspect.*

fastidioso *adj. boring, annoying.*

fastígio *m. apex, summit.*

fastio *m. boredom; lack of appetite.*

fatal *adj. fatal.*

fatalidade *f. fate, destiny; fatality.*

fatia *f. slice.*
   Uma fatia de pão. *A slice of bread.*

fatigador *adj. tiring; boring.*

fatigante *adj. tiring.*

fatigar *to tire; to annoy.*

FATO (FACTO) *m. fact, occurrence; man's suit* ℗.
   De fato. *As a matter of fact.*
   O fato é que já é tarde. *The fact is that it is already too late.*

fator (factor) *m. factor; agent.*

fátuo *adj. fatuous; foolish.*

fatura (factura) *f. invoice, bill.*
   Aqui está a fatura. *Here is the invoice.*

faturar (facturar) *to bill, to invoice.*

fauna *f. fauna.*

fausto *adj. happy; fortunate; n. m. pageantry.*

FAVA *f. a kind of bean.*
   Mandar às favas. *To send someone packing.*

favela *f. slum* ℬ.

favelado *m. slum dweller* ℬ.

FAVOR *m. favor; service; good graces; letter.*
   É um grande favor que me faz. *It's a great favor you are doing me.*
   Por favor. *Please.*
   Faça o favor de chamar-me às sete. *Please call me at seven.*
   Recebemos seu favor de 5 do corrente. *We are in receipt of your favor (letter) of the 5th of this month.*

favorável *adj. favorable.*

favorecer *to favor; to help.*

favorito *adj. favorite.*

fax *m. fax, facsimile.*
   Enviar um fax. *To send a fax.*
   Receber um fax. *To receive a fax.*

fazenda *f. farm; plantation; estate; cloth, material.*
   Fazenda de café. *Coffee plantation.*
   Fazenda de lã. *Woolen cloth.*

fazendeiro *m. farmer, planter; owner of fazenda.*

FAZER *to make; to do; to cause; to be (cold, etc.)*

Faça o favor de dar-me o mapa. *Please give me the map.*

Permite-me fazer-lhe algumas perguntas? *May I ask you some questions?*

Fazem bom pão aqui. *They make good bread here.*

Que faço? *What shall I do?*

Faça como quiser. *Do as you wish.*

Que está fazendo (a fazer)? *What are you doing?*

Que havemos de fazer? *What are we to do?*

Já está feito. *It's already done.*

O navio faz água. *The ship leaks.*

Hoje faço vinte anos. *I am twenty years old today.*

Faço a barba com gilete. *I shave with a safety razor.*

Ela faz a cama todas as manhãs. *She makes her bed every morning.*

Faça chamar o médico. *Have the doctor called* ℗.

Vamos fazer uma viagem no verão (Verão). *We're going on a trip in the summer.*

O deputado fez um discurso. *The congressman made a speech.*

Fazer gazeta. *To play hookey (from school).*

Fazer greve. *To go on strike.*

Fazer a chamada. *To call the roll.*

Fazer caso de. *To pay attention to.*

Fazer o papel. *To play the part.*

Fazer mal. *To do evil, harm.*

Fazer compras. *To go shopping.*

Fazer economias. *To save.*

Fazer exercício. *To exercise.*

Fazer frio. *To be cold (weather).*

Fazer calor. *To be warm (weather).*

Faz bom tempo. *The weather is good.*

Faz mau tempo. *The weather is bad.*

Fazer falta. *To need; To be lacking.*

Fazer alto. *To stop.*

Fazer parte de. *To belong to; to take part in.*

Fazer fila. *To stand in line.*

Não faz mal. *Never mind.*

Fazer um passeio. *To go for a walk.*

FÉ *f. faith; certificate.*

Ela o fez de boa fé. *She did it in good faith.*

Ele o disse de má fé. *He said it in bad faith (deceitfully).*

A fé católica. *The Catholic religion.*

febre *f. fever.*

Febre amarela. *Yellow fever.*

FECHADO *adj. closed; shut; finished.*

A porta não está fechada. *The door is not closed.*

FECHAR *to close; to shut; to finish.*

Amanhã vou fechar a conta. *Tomorrow I am going to close my account.*

Feche a porta à chave. *Lock the door.*

fecundo *adj. fruitful, productive, fecund.*

feder *to smell bad, to stink.*

federação *f. federation.*

FEIJÃO *m. bean, beans.*

feijoada *f. a popular dish made of black beans, meat, vegetables, etc.*

feio *adj. ugly; unpleasant.*

feira *f. fair; market.*

feiticeira *f. witch.*

feiticeiro *m. wizard.*

feitio *m. pattern; style; workmanship.*

FEITO *adj. made; done; finished; n. m. act; fact; deed.*
     Mal feito. *That was wrong. Poorly done (made).*
     Bem feito. *Well done.*
     Dito e feito. *No sooner said than done.*
     Feito! *Agreed!*
     Já feito. *Already made; Ready-made.*
     Feito sob medida. *Tailor-made.*
     Feito à mão. *Handmade.*
     Feito à máquina. *Machine-made.*

feitor *m. administrator; manager; foreman.*

feitura *f. workmanship; work.*

felicidade *f. happiness.*

felicitação *f. congratulation.*
     Felicitações! *Congratulations!*

felicitar *to congratulate, to felicitate.*

FELIZ *adj. happy; fortunate.*
     Feliz Ano Novo! *Happy New Year!*
     Feliz Natal! *Merry Christmas!*
     Foi o dia mais feliz da minha vida. *It was the happiest day of my life.*
     Somos muito felizes. *We are very happy.*
     Felizmente. *Happily. Fortunately.*

fêmea *f. female.*

feminino *adj. feminine.*

fenômeno *m. phenomenon.*

fera *f. wild beast.*

féria *f. wages; pl. holiday, vacation.*
     Vamos passar as férias nas montanhas. *We are going to spend our vacation in the mountains.*

feriado *m. holiday.*

ferido *adj. wounded, injured; n. m. wounded person.*
     Ele foi ferido no braço. *He was wounded in the arm.*
     O ferido está muito melhor. *The wounded man is much better.*

ferir *to wound, to injure, to hurt.*

fermentação *f. fermentation; ferment.*

fermentar *to ferment; to leaven.*

fermento *leaven, yeast.*

feroz *adj. ferocious, fierce; cruel.*

ferradura *f. horseshoe.*

ferragens *f. pl. hardware.*

ferramenta *f. tool.*

ferreiro *m. blacksmith.*

férreo *adj. iron, ferrous.*

FERRO *m. iron; electric iron.*
     Passar a ferro. *To iron (clothes).*
     Estrada de ferro. *Railroad.*

ferrovia *f. railroad.*

ferroviário *adj. railroad.*

ferrugem *f. rust.*

fértil *adj. fertile, fruitful.*

ferver *to boil; to seethe.*

fervor *m. fervor, zeal.*

FESTA *f. feast; party; celebration; holiday.*
     Dona Maria vai dar uma festa no sábado. *Dona Maria is going to give a party on Saturday.*
     Boas Festas! *Merry Christmas! Happy New Year!*

festejar *to celebrate, to party; to praise.*

festividade *f. festival.*

festivo *adj. festive, merry.*

FEVEREIRO *m. February.*
     O segundo mês do ano é fevereiro (Fevereiro). *February is the second month of the year.*

fiado *adj. on credit.*
     Ela não gosta de comprar fiado. *She doesn't like to buy on credit.*

fiador *m. guarantor; bondsman.*

fiambre *m. cold meats.*

fiança *f. bail, bond; security; deposit.*

fiar *to trust, to confide; to sell on credit; to spin, to weave.*
     Todos nós fiamos nele. *All of us trust him.*

fibra *f. fiber; filament.*
     Fibro de vitro. *Fiberglass.*

FICAR *to remain, to stay; to be; to become.*
     Não quero ficar mais aqui. *I don't want to stay here any longer.*
     João ficou com os tios. *John stayed with his aunt and uncle.*
     Quando lhe expliquei a situação ele ficou convencido. *When I explained the situation to him he was convinced.*
     Ela ficou pálida. *She turned pale.*
     Eu fico com este. *I'll take this one.*
     Ficamos sem dinheiro. *We ran out of money.*
     Hoje ela ficou em casa. *Today she stayed home.*
     Fique com o troco. *Keep the change.*
     Ela ficou doente. *She became ill.*

ficção *f. fiction.*

ficha *f. index card, file card; chip (poker).*

fichar *to record, to file.*

fichário *m. file cabinet; card index.*

fidelidade *f. fidelity; loyalty.*
     De alta fidelidade. *High fidelity.*

fiel *adj. faithful, loyal; accurate.*

fígado *m. liver; courage.*

figo *m. fig.*

figueira *f. fig tree.*
figura *f. figure, form, appearance, image.*
figurar *to figure; to appear.*
fila *f. line; row; rank.*
    Em fila. *In line. In a row.*
    Fazer fila. *To line up; To stand in line.*
    Primeira fila. *First row. Front rank.*
filar *to seize, to grasp, to sponge, to mooch.*
filé *m. fillet (meat, fish).*
fileira *f. line, row; tier; rank.*
filete *m. fillet; thread (screw).*
FILHA *f. daughter, child.*
    Eles têm três filhas e um filho. *They have three daughters and one son.*
FILHO *m. son, child; pl. children*
    Não temos filhos. *We don't have any children.*
    Tal pai, tal filho. *Like father, like son.*
filiação *f. filiation; relationship.*
filial *adj. filial; n. f. branch office or store.*
filipino *Philippine.*
filmar *to film.*
FILME *m. film; movie.*
    Não gostei do filme. *I didn't like the film.*
filosofia *f. philosophy.*
filósofo *m. philosopher.*
filtrar *to filter, to strain.*
filtro *m. filter, strainer.*
FIM *m. end; object, purpose, aim.*
    No fim do mês. *At the end of the month.*
    Em fins de junho (Junho). *Toward the end of June.*
    Dar fim a. *To finish.*
    Por fim. *Finally. At last.*
    Sem fim. *Endless. Endlessly.*
    A fim de. *In order that.*
    No fim das contas. *After all.*
finado *adj., n. m. deceased.*
    Dia de Finados. *All Souls' Day.*
FINAL *adj. final; n. m. end.*
    Parte final. *Last part.*
    No final das contas. *After all. In the end*
    Finalmente. *Finally.*
finalizar *to finish, to conclude.*
finanças *f. pl. finances; public funds.*
financeiro *adj. financial; n. m. financier.*
findar *to finish, to end.*
fineza *f. fineness; delicacy; courtesy.*
    Agradeço muito a sua fineza. *I appreciate your courtesy very much.*
fingir *to pretend.*
finlandês *adj. Finnish; n. m. Finn.*
fino *adj. fine, delicate; cunning; keen; polite.*
fio *m. thread, string; filament; edge (knife).*
    Fio de pérolas. *String of pearls.*
    Dias a fio. *Days on end.*
    Ela perdeu o fio da conversa. *She lost the thread of the conversation.*
FIRMA *f. firm; business concern; signature.*

    Ela trabalha com uma firma norte-americana. *She works for an American (North American) firm.*
firmar *to sign, to endorse; to make firm; to secure.*
firme *adj. firm, fast, stable, secure, resolute.*
    Ele se mantem firme. *He holds his ground.*
fiscal *adj. fiscal; n. m. inspector; controller.*
física *f. physics.*
físico *adj. physical; n. m. physicist; physique.*
    Ele tem um defeito físico. *He has a physical defect.*
fisiologia *f. physiology.*
fisionomia *f. appearance; look.*
FITA *f. ribbon; movie film; tape.*
    Fita de máquina de escrever. *Typewriter ribbon.*
fitar *to stare at.*
fixar *(x = ks) to fix, to fasten; to determine; to stare.*
fixo *(x = ks) adj. fixed, set; fast (of color).*
flagrante *adj. flagrant, red-handed; n. m. snapshot.*
    Em flagrante. *In the act. Red-handed.*
flamejar *to flame.*
flamengo *adj. Flemish; n. m. Fleming; flamingo.*
flâmula *f. small flame; pennant; streamer.*
flanela *f. flannel.*
flauta *f. flute.*
flecha *f. arrow, dart.*
flertar *to flirt.*
flexível *adj. flexible, pliable.*
FLOR *f. flower, blossom.*
    Estar em flor. *To be in bloom.*
    Na flor da idade. *In the prime of life.*
florescer *to blossom, to bloom.*
floresta *f. forest.*
florista *m. and f. florist.*
fluente *adj. fluent, flowing.*
fluido *adj. fluid; fluent; n. m. fluid.*
fluminense *adj. of the State of Rio de Janeiro; m. and f. native of the State of Rio de Janeiro.*
flutuar *to float; to fluctuate.*
foca *f. seal, sea lion.*
focalizar *to focus, to focalize.*
focinho *m. snout; nose.*
foco *m. focus.*
    Em foco. *In focus.*
fogão *m. cooking stove.*
FOGO *m. fire.*
    Abrir fogo. *To open fire.*
    Pegar fogo. *To catch fire.*
    Armas de fogo. *Firearms.*
    Fogos de artifício. *Display of fireworks.*
    Não há fumaça sem fogo. *Where there's smoke there's fire.*
fogoso *adj. fiery, impetuous.*

fogueira *f. bonfire; blaze.*

foguete *m. rocket, missile; firecracker; lively person* Ⓑ.

fôlego *m. breath, wind.*
Sem fôlego. *Out of breath.*

folga *f. rest, leisure.*
Dia de folga. *Day off.*

folgar *to rest; to take it easy; to amuse oneself.*

FOLHA *f. leaf; sheet; blade.*
A árvore não tem mais folhas. *The tree has no more leaves.*
Virar a folha. *To change the subject.*
Folha de estanho. *Tinfoil.*
Uma folha de papel. *A sheet of paper.*
Folha de faca. *Knife blade.*

folhagem *f. foliage.*

folhear *to thumb through, to glance at.*

folhetim *m. serial publication.*

folheto *m. pamphlet.*

folia *f. gaiety, merrymaking.*

fólio *m. folio.*

FOME *f. hunger.*
Estou com fome (Tenho fome). *I am hungry.*
Estar com (Ter) uma fome canina. *To be ravenous.*
Estou morrendo (a morrer) de fome. *I'm starving.*

fomentar *to foment, to encourage.*

fonética *f phonetics.*

fonógrafo *m. phonograph, record player.*

FONTE *f. spring, fountain; source.*
Eu sei de boa fonte. *I have it on good authority.*

FORA *outside, out.*
Há mais gente fora de que dentro. *There are more people outside than inside.*
Fora! *Get out!*
Estar fora. *To be absent. To be out.*
Fora disso. *Besides that.*
Fora de si. *Beside oneself. Frantic.*
Deite fora. *Throw it away.*

forasteiro *adj. foreign; strange; n. m. foreigner; stranger.*

FORÇA *f. force, strength, power.*
À força. *By force.*
À força de. *By dint of.*
Força motriz. *Motive power.*
Forças armadas. *Armed forces.*

forçar *to force, to compel, to oblige.*

forçoso *adj. forceful; compelling; compulsory.*

FORMA *f. form, shape; manner, way; mold; pattern.*
A forma desta caixa (x = sh) é interessante. *The shape of this box is interesting.*
Em forma de "U." *U-shaped.*
De nenhuma forma! *By no means!*
Desta forma. *In this way.*

Fora de forma! *Dismissed! (Military.)*
Última forma! *As you were! (Military.)*

formação *f. formation.*

formal *adj. formal.*

formalidade *f. formality.*

formar *to form, to shape.*
Os alunos formaram um círculo. *The students formed a circle.*

formar-se *to graduate.*
O filho dela se formou em direito. *Her son graduated in law.*

formatura *f. graduation, commencement.*

formidável *adj. formidable; excellent; wonderful; terrific.*
Ela é formidável. *She's wonderful.*

formiga *f. ant.*

formoso *adj. beautiful; handsome; lovely; fine.*

formosura *f. beauty.*

fórmula *f. formula; blank form; recipe.*
Faça o favor de preencher esta fórmula ⒫. *Please fill out this form.*

formular *to formulate.*

formulário *m. blank form, application form.*
Primeiro é preciso preencher este formulário. *First you must fill out this form.*

fornalha *f. oven; furnace.*

fornecer *to furnish, to provide.*

forno *m. oven; furnace.*

forrar *to line (a garment, etc.); to cover.*
O sobretudo está forrado. *The overcoat is lined.*

forro *adj. free, freed; m. lining; pudding.*

fortalecer *to fortify.*

fortaleza *f. fortress, stronghold; fortitude, strength.*

FORTE *adj. strong, powerful; n. m. fort; strong point.*
Caixa-forte (x = sh). *Strongbox. Safe.*
Ele sempre joga forte. *He always plays hard.*
O irmão dela é muito forte. *Her brother is very strong.*

fortificação *f. fortification.*

fortificar *to fortify, to strengthen.*

fortuito *adj. fortuitous, accidental.*

fortuna *f. fortune.*
Boa fortuna. *Good luck.*
Por fortuna. *Fortunately.*

fósforo *m. phosphorous; match (to light with).*

fossa *f. pit; hole.*

fotografar *to photograph.*

fotografia *f. photography; photograph, photo, picture.*

foz *f. mouth (of a river).*

fracalhão *m. weakling, coward.*

fração (fracção) *f. fraction.*

fracassar *to fail.*

fracasso m. failure.

fraco adj. lean, thin; weak; n. m. weakling; weakness.

frade m. friar, monk.

fragate f. frigate.

frágil adj. fragile, brittle; weak, frail.

fragmento m. fragment.

fragrância f. fragrance, pleasing odor.

fragrante adj. fragrant.

frágua f. forge.

framboesa f. raspberry.

francês adj. French; n. m. Frenchman; French language.

FRANCO adj. frank, free, open, plain; n. m. franc.

Ele não foi franco conosco. He was not frank with us.

Porto franco. Free port.

Franco de porte. Postpaid.

Entrada franca. Admission free.

frango m. chicken.

Frango assado. Roast chicken.

franqueado adj. franked; free.

franquear to frank, to free from charges; to prepay; to facilitate.

Franqueou as cartas? Did you put stamps on the letters?

Franquear a passagem. To clear the way.

franqueza f. frankness, sincerity.

Fale com franqueza. Speak frankly.

franquia f. franchise; exemption from duties (taxes).

fraqueza f. weakness.

frasco m. flask, bottle.

frase f. phrase, sentence.

Frase feita. Idiom. Common expression.

fraternidade f. fraternity, brotherhood.

fraude f. fraud.

FREAR Ⓑ to put on the brakes; to slow down; to curb.

Freie! Put on the brakes!

freguês m. customer, client.

frei m. friar.

FREIO m. brake; check, curb; bit.

Freio de mão. Hand brake.

Freio de emergência. Emergency brake.

freira f. nun, sister.

frenético adj. mad, frantic.

FRENTE f. front; façade; appearance.

Na frente de. In front of.

Frente a frente. Face to face.

Bem em frente. Straight ahead.

Porta da frente. Front door.

freqüência (frequência) f. frequency.

Eles se viam com freqüência. They saw one another frequently.

freqüente (frequente) adj. frequent.

FRESCO adj. cool; fresh; wet (paint); n. m. fresh air; fresco (painting).

A água está fresca. The water is cool.

Tomar o fresco. To go out for some fresh air.

Tinta fresca. Wet paint.

Ar fresco. Fresh air.

frescura f. freshness; coolness.

fretar to freight; to charter.

frete m. freight; cargo.

fricassé m. fricassee.

fricção f. friction, rubbing.

friccionar to rub, to massage.

frigir to fry; to bother.

frigorífico m. refrigerator Ⓟ; freezer.

FRIO adj. cold, cool; n. m. cold.

Estou com frio (Tenho frio). I am cold.

Está frio hoje. It's cold today.

Sangue frio. Cold blood.

Tempo frio. Cold weather.

friorento adj. sensitive to cold.

fritada f. fried dish.

fritar to fry.

frito adj. fried.

Batatas fritas. Fried potatoes.

Estou frito. I'm in trouble. I'm in a mess Ⓑ.

fronha f. pillowcase; pillow.

fronte f. forehead; front.

fronteira f. frontier, border.

frota f. fleet.

Frota mercante. Merchant fleet.

frouxo (x = sh) adj. loose; slack; flabby.

frugal adj. frugal, thrifty.

frustrar to frustrate.

FRUTA f. fruit.

frutífero adj. fruitful.

frutificar to bear fruit.

FRUTO m. fruit; result; profit.

Em dois anos vai dar fruto. In two years it will show results.

fubá m. Brazilian cornmeal.

fuga f. escape, flight.

Em fuga. In flight.

Pôr em fuga. To put to flight. To rout.

fugaz adj. fleeting, transitory.

fugir to flee, to escape, to run away.

fugitivo adj., n. m. fugitive.

fulano m. person; So-and-So; John Doe.

Fulano de Tal. So-and-So. John Doe.

Fulano, Beltrano e Sicrano. Tom, Dick, and Harry.

fulgir to glow, to shine.

fulgor m. brilliance, glow.

fumaça f. smoke.

Não há fumaça sem fogo. Where there's smoke there's fire.

fumador adj. smoking; n. m. smoker.

FUMAR to smoke.

Ela fuma demais. She smokes too much.

fumo m. smoke; tobacco Ⓑ; fumes.

Quero fumo para cachimbo. *I want some pipe tobacco.*

função *f. function, performance.*

funcionar *to function; to work; to run (machine).*
Esta máquina não funciona. *This machine doesn't work.*
Funcionar bem. *To be in good working condition.*

funcionário *m. functionary; employee.*
Funcionário público. *Government employee.*

fundação *f. foundation.*

fundador *m. founder.*

fundamental *adj. fundamental.*

fundamento *m. foundation, base, ground; reason.*
Sem fundamento. *Groundless.*
Faltar de fundamento. *To be without foundation or reason.*

fundar *to found, to base.*
Foi fundada em 1965. *It was founded in 1965.*

fundear *to anchor.*

fundição *f. foundry; casting, melting.*

fundir *to melt; to fuse.*

FUNDO *adj. deep; bottom; base; background; n. m. pl. funds.*
Fundo duplo. *Double bottom.*
Artigo de fundo. *Main article in a newspaper.*
Conhecer a fundo. *To know well.*
Fundos públicos. *Public funds.*

fúnebre *adj. funereal; sad.*

funeral *adj. funeral, funereal; n. m. funeral.*

funesto *adj. fatal; fateful.*

funil *m. funnel.*

furacão *m. hurricane.*

furar *to penetrate, to break through.*
Furar uma festa. *To crash a party.*

furgão *m. baggage car; van.*

fúria *f. fury, rage, fit of madness.*

furioso *adj. furious, mad, frantic.*

furor *m. fury.*

furtar *to steal; to cheat.*
Furtar-se ao dever. *To shirk one's responsibility.*
Não furtarás. *Thou shalt not steal.*

furto *m. theft.*

fusão *fusion; union.*

fusível *m. fuse.*

fuso *m. spindle, spool; screw; zone (time).*

futebol *m. soccer.*

futebolista *m. and f. soccer fan; soccer player.*

fútil *adj. futile.*

FUTURO *adj. future; n. m. future; fiancé.*
Em futuro próximo. *In the near future.*

Ela nos apresentou seu futuro. *She introduced her fiancé to us.*

fuzil *m. rifle.*

gabardina *f. gabardine.*

gabinete *m. cabinet; study; laboratory; ministry.*
Gabinete de leitura. *Reading room.*

gado *m. cattle, livestock.*

gaiola *f. cage.*

gaita *f. fife; harmonica; "dough," money ⑧; useless things ⑧.*
Não tenho gaita. *I don't have any money.*
Gaita galega. *Bagpipe.*

gaiteiro *m. player of fife, harmonica, or bagpipe.*

gaivão *m. swift (bird).*

gaivota *f. seagull, gull; fool ⑧.*

gala *f. gala occasion; fine or formal dress.*
De gala. *Full or formal dress.*
Fazer gala de. *To boast of; to show off.*

galã *m. main romantic lead (theatre); lover.*

galantaria *f. gallantry; politeness.*

galante *adj. gallant; polite.*

galantear *to court; to compliment.*

galão *m. gallon; stripe (uniform).*

galego *adj. Galician; n. m. Galician; a Portuguese person in Brazil (not complimentary) ⑧.*

galeria *f. gallery; arcade.*

galgo *m. greyhound.*
Correr como um galgo. *To rush, to hurry along.*

galhardete *m. pennant, streamer, banner.*

galho *m. branch (tree).*

galhofa *f. something funny; joke; fun.*

galicismo *m. Gallicism.*

galinha *f. chicken, hen; coward ⑧.*
Deitar-se com as galinhas. *To go to bed with the chickens· To retire early.*
Muita galinha e poucos ovos. *Much talk and little action.*

galinheiro *m. chicken coop; gallery (theatre).*

galo *m. rooster, cock.*
Ao cantar do galo. *At dawn.*
Missa do galo. *Midnight mass.*

galocha *f. galochas, rubber overshoes.*

galopar *to gallop.*

galope *m. gallop.*

gamão *m. backgammon.*

gamo *m. deer, stag.*

gana *f. desire, craving; hate.*

gancho *m. hook; hairpin.*

ganhador *adj. winning; n. m. winner.*

GANHAR *to gain; to earn; to win; to reach.*

Como ganhar amigos. *How to win friends.*

Quanto dinheiro ganhou? *How much money did you earn?*

Não ganhamos. *We did not win.*

Ele não pode ganhar a vida. *He can't make a living.*

ganho *adj.* gained, earned; *n. m.* profit, gain.

ganso *m.* goose, gander.

garage Ⓑ, **garagem** *f.* garage.

garantia *f.* guarantee; guaranty; security.

Garantia por escrito. *Written guarantee.*

garantir *to guarantee; to vouch for.*

garção *m.* waiter Ⓑ.

gardênia (gardénia) *f.* gardenia.

GARFO *m.* fork.

gargalhada *f.* burst of laughter.

GARGANTA *f.* throat; gorge.

Dor de garganta. *Sore throat.*

Estou com ele pela garganta. *I've had enough of him.*

garota *f.* young girl Ⓑ.

garoto *m.* boy; urchin.

garra *f.* claw; finger; hand.

GARRAFA *f.* bottle.

Uma garrafa de cerveja. *A bottle of beer.*

gás *m.* gas.

Gás lacrimogêneo (lacrimogénio). *Tear gas.*

gasolina *f.* gasoline.

gasosa *f.* soda pop.

gasoso *adj.* gaseous.

GASTAR *to spread; to wear out; to use.*

Gastei todo o dinheiro que me deu. *I spent all the money you gave me.*

Não gaste o tempo com ela. *Don't waste your time with her.*

Os meninos gastam tudo em pouco tempo. *The children wear everything out in a short time.*

GASTO *adj.* spent; worn out; *n. m.* cost, expense.

Todo o dinheiro foi gasto em dois meses. *All the money was spent in two months.*

Houve muitos gastos. *There were many expenses.*

gata *f.* cat.

gatilho *m.* trigger.

gatinha *f.* kitten.

Andar de gatinhas. *To crawl on all fours.*

GATO *m.* cat; clever person; slip, error.

Não dê carne ao gato. *Don't give the cat meat.*

Não compre gato por lebre. *Don't buy a pig in a poke.*

Eles vivem como cão e gato. *They fight like cats and dogs.*

Quem não tem cão, caça com gato. *You have to make the best of things.*

Ela cometeu um gato. *She pulled a boner.*

gauchesco *adj.* Gaucho Ⓑ.

gaúcho *adj.* of Rio Grande do Sul in Brazil; *n. m.* native of Rio Grande do Sul; also type of cowboy of Uruguay and of Argentina.

gaveta *f.* drawer (desk).

A carta está na gaveta da mesa. *The letter is in the drawer of the table.*

gavião *m.* hawk; sly person Ⓑ; ladies' man Ⓑ; children's game Ⓟ.

gazeta *f.* gazette, newspaper.

geladeira *f.* icebox, refrigerator.

gelado *adj.* frozen; icy; cold; *n. m.* sherbet; ice cream; cold drink.

gelar *to freeze; to frighten.*

gelatina *f.* gelatin; jelly.

geléia (geleia) *jelly, jam.*

gelo *m.* ice; indifference.

Gelo seco. *Dry ice.*

gema *f.* yolk (egg); core.

Carioca da gema. *A true carioca (native of the city of Rio de Janeiro).*

gêmeo (gémeo) *m.* twin.

gemer *to moan; to creak.*

gemido *m.* groan; sigh.

general *m.* general (military rank).

GÊNERO (GÉNERO) *m.* class, kind, sort; gender, pl. goods.

O gênero humano. *Mankind.*

Gêneros alimentícios. *Foodstuffs.*

generosidade *f.* generosity.

generoso *adj.* generous, liberal.

gengibre *m.* ginger.

gengiva *f.* gum (mouth).

gênio (génio) *m.* genius; talent; nature, disposition; temperament.

Ele tem mau gênio. *He has a bad temper.*

genro *m.* son-in-law.

GENTE *f.* people; personnel; one, they, we.

Há muita gente hoje. *There are many people (here) today.*

A gente não faz isso. *One doesn't do that.*

gentil *adj.* kind; polite; courteous.

gentileza *f.* kindness; courtesy.

Agradeço muito a sua gentileza. *I am very grateful for your kindness.*

gentio *adj. and n. m.* gentile, pagan, heathen.

genuíno *adj.* genuine, real.

geografia *f.* geography.

geometria *f.* geometry.

geração *f.* generation.

gerador *adj.* generating; *n. m.* generator.

GERAL *adj.* general.

Em geral. *In general. Generally.*

Minas Gerais. *Minas Gerais ("General Mines"), name of a state in Brazil.*

gerânio *m.* geranium.

gerar *to generate.*

gerência *f.* management, administration.

gerente *m. manager, administrator.*

gerigonça *f. jargon; slang.*

germânico *adj. Germanic.*

germe *m. germ.*

germinar *to germinate.*

gerúndio *m. gerund.*

gesticular *to gesticulate.*

gesto *m. gesture.*

gigante *adj. giant; n. m. giant.*

gilete *f. safety razor.*
> Não uso navalha, só gilete. *I don't use a straight razor, just a safety razor.*

ginásio *m. high school; gymnasium.*

girar *to rotate, to turn; to circulate.*

girassol *m. sunflower.*

gíria *f. slang; jargon.*

giro *m. turn; stroll; terrific* Ⓟ *(slang).*

giz *m. chalk.*
> Sem giz não so pode escrever no quadro negro. *We can't write on the blackboard without chalk.*

glacial *adj. glacial; cold.*

globo *m. globe, ball.*

glória *f. glory; fame.*

gloriar *to glorify.*

glorioso *adj. glorious.*

glosa *f. comment; criticism.*

goiaba *f. guava.*

goiabada *f. guava paste.*

goiano *adj., n. m. of the state of Goiás in Brazil.*

gol *m. goal (sports).*

gola *f. collar; throat.*

golfe *m. golf.*
> Tacos de golfe. *Golf clubs.*

golfo *m. gulf.*
> Gôlfo do México. *Gulf of Mexico.*

GOLPE *m. blow; coup.*
> De golpe. *Suddenly; All at once.*
> De um só golpe. *At one stroke; With one blow.*
> Um golpe de sorte. *A lucky blow or stroke.*
> Golpe de estado. *Coup d'état.*
> Golpe de mestre. *Master stroke.*
> Golpe de mar. *Surf, heavy sea.*

goma *f. gum; starch.*
> Goma de mascar. *Chewing gum.*

GORDO *adj. fat; n. m. fat person.*
> O pai dele é muito gordo. *His father is very fat.*

gordura *f. fat; grease; stoutness.*

gorila *m. gorilla.*

gorjear *to warble.*

gorjeta *f. tip (money).*

gorro *m. cap.*

GOSTAR *to like; to taste.*
> Gosto muito dele. *I like him very much.*
> Gosto mais deste. *I prefer this one.*

Eu gostaria de ver a peça. *I should like to see the play.*

GOSTO *m. liking; taste; pleasure.*
> Ela tem bom gosto. *She has good taste.*
> Isto é muito a meu gosto. *This is very much to my taste.*

gostoso *adj. tasty, delicious.*

gota *f. drop (liquid); gout.*
> Gota a gota. *Drop by drop.*
> Elas se parecem como duas gotas d'água. *They are as alike as two peas in a pod.*
> Essa foi a gota d'água que fez transbordar o copo. *That was the straw that broke the camel's back.*

gotejar *to trickle, to drip.*

governador *m. governor.*

governante *adj. governing, ruling; n. m. ruler; governor.*

governar *to govern, to rule; to control.*
> E ela quem governa em casa. *She rules the house.*

governo *m. government; control.*
> O novo governo é forte. *The new government is strong.*

gozar *to enjoy.*
> Elas gozam de boa saúde. *They enjoy good health.*

gozo *m. joy; enjoyment.*

gozoso *adj. joyful, merry.*

GRAÇA *f. grace; favor, pardon; wit; charm; name; pl. thanks.*
> Graças a Deus. *Thank God.*
> Eu terminei tudo, graças à sua ajuda. *I finished everything, thanks to your help.*
> Não acho graça nisso. *I don't think that's funny.*
> Tem graça. *That's funny.*
> Lançar graças. *To crack jokes.*
> Qual é sua graça? *What is your name?*

gracejar *to joke.*
> Ele sempre está gracejando (está a gracejar). *He's always joking.*

gracioso *adj. gracious; witty.*

grade *f. grating; grille; latticework.*

gradual *adj. gradual.*

graduar *to grade, to classify; to graduate.*

graduar-se *to graduate (school).*

gráfica *f. writing; spelling.*

gráfico *adj. graphic; n. m. graph; chart.*

gralha *f. crow; jay; magpie; chatterbox, gossip, misprint.*

grama *f. grass; gram.*

gramática *f. grammar.*

grampear *to staple; to clip.*
> Máquina de grampear. *Stapler.*

grampo *m. staple; clip; pin; cramp.*

granada *f. grenade.*

GRANDE adj. great, large, tall.

A casa dele é muito grande. His house is very large.

Ele é um grande artista. He is a great artist.

grandeza f. greatness.

grandioso adj. grandiose, magnificent.

granizar to hail.

granizo m. hail.

granja f. farm.

grão m. grain; kernel.

gratidão f. gratitude.

gratificação f. gratuity, tip.

gratificar to reward; to tip.

grátis free (at no cost).

grato adj. grateful; pleasant.

Fico-lhe muito grato. I remain gratefully yours. I am very grateful to you.

gratuito adj. free (at no cost).

grau m. degree.

Dez graus abaixo (x = sh) de zero. Ten degrees below zero.

Por graus. By degrees.

gravado adj. engraved; recorded.

gravador adj. engraving; recording; n. m. engraver; recorder; tape recorder.

gravar to engrave, to record.

O professor gravou duas fitas. The professor recorded two tapes.

GRAVATA f. necktie.

Vou levar seis gravatas na mala. I'm going to take six neckties in my bag.

Eu prefiro gravata-borboleta. I prefer a bow tie.

grave adj. grave, serious.

Foi muito grave. It was very serious.

Acento grave. Grave accent mark.

gravidade f. seriousness, gravity.

gravura f. etching; engraving; picture.

graxa (x = sh) f. grease; shoe polish.

graxento (x = sh) adj. greasy.

grego adj. Greek.

grelha f. grill.

grelhar to grill, to broil.

grêmio (grémio) m. guild, society.

greve f. strike.

Os operários entraram em greve. The workers went on strike.

grevista m. and f. striker.

grifo m. italics.

Leia a parte em grifo. Read the part in italics.

grilo m. cricket.

gripe f. grippe, influenza.

grisalho adj. grayish; grizzled.

gritar to shout, to scream.

Quem gritou? Who cried out?

gritaria f. shouting; hubbub.

grito m. shout, scream.

Grito de guerra. Battle cry.

groselha f. currant; gooseberry.

grosseiro adj. coarse, rude, impolite.

grosso adj. thick; coarse.

grou m. crane (bird).

grua f. crane (bird); crane, derrick.

grudar to glue, to paste, to stick together.

grude m. glue, paste.

grunhido m. grunt.

grunhir to grunt.

GRUPO m. group.

Vamos dividi-los em quatro grupos diferentes. We are going to divide them into four different groups.

gruta f. grotto, cave.

guarda m. and f. guard; watch; guardian; watchman.

Guarda de honra. Guard of honor.

Quem está de guarda? Who is on duty?

guarda-chuva m. umbrella.

Hoje não precisamos de guarda-chuva. We don't need an umbrella today.

guarda-livros m. and f. bookkeeper.

guarda-marinha m. midshipman.

guardanapo m. napkin.

GUARDAR to keep; to guard; to take care of.

Guarde o dinheiro no banco. Keep your money in the bank.

Ela não sabe guardar segredo. She doesn't know how to keep a secret.

guarda-roupa m. wardrobe; cloakroom.

guarnecer to trim; to garnish; to garrison.

guarnição f. trim; garrison; crew.

Todos os membros da guarnição estão a bordo. All the members of the crew are aboard.

guatemalteco adj., n. m. Guatemalan.

GUERRA f. war.

Fazer guerra. To wage war.

Guerra civil. Civil war.

Guerra atômica (atómica). Nuclear war.

Guerra fria. Cold war.

guerreiro adj. warlike; m. warrior.

GUIA m. guide, leader; guidebook; directory; f. guidance; permit, bill.

Gostaria dos serviços dum guia. I'd like to have the services of a guide.

Não tem guia da cidade? Don't you have a guidebook of the city?

guianês adj., n. m. Guianan.

guiar to guide, to direct; to drive.

O senhor sabe guiar? Do you know how to drive?

guichê (guichet, guiché) m. window (ticket, information).

Guichê de informações. Information window.

guisa f. guise.

À guisa de. Like.

guisado m. stew.

guisar to stew.

guitarra f. guitar.

guitarrista m. and f. guitarist.

H

hã ha!

hábil adj. able; clever; capable.

  Ele é muito hábil. He is very clever.

habilidade f. ability, skill.

habilitado adj. able; qualified.

habilitar to qualify; to enable.

habitação f. dwelling, residence.

habitante m. and f. inhabitant, resident.

  É uma cidade de vinte mil habitantes. It is
  a city of twenty thousand inhabitants.

habitar to inhabit.

hábito m. habit, custom; dress, garb.

  Ele tinha o hábito de levantar-se cedo. He
  was in the habit of getting up early.

  Ela tinha esse mau hábito. She had that
  bad habit.

  O hábito não faz o monge. Clothes don't
  make the man.

habituar to accustom.

habituar-se to become accustomed.

haitiano adj. and n. m. Haitian.

hálito m. breath.

  Mau hálito. Bad breath.

hangar m. hangar.

harmonia f. harmony.

harpa f. harp.

haste f. pole, rod.

hastear to hoist (flag).

havaiano adj. Hawaiian; n. m. Hawaiian.

havana m. and f. Havana cigar.

HAVER to have (auxiliary verb; however,
  today "ter" is replacing it in this use); to
  be, to exist; there to be.

  Há. There is. There are.

  Havia. There was. There were.

  Houve. There was. There were.

  Haverá. There will be.

  Haveria. There would be.

  Haja. There may be.

  Que haja. Let there be.

  Houvesse. There might be.

  Se houvesse. If there were.

  Há havido. There has (have) been.

  Havia havido. There had been. There
  would have been.

  Haveria havido. There would have been.

  Há que. It is necessary.

  Haverá que. It will be necessary.

  Houve que. It was necessary.

  Há de ser. It must be.

  Hei de partir amanhã. I'm to leave
  tomorrow.

  Há pouco tempo. A short while ago.

  Ela havia escrito a carta? Had she written
  the letter?

  Ontem não houve aulas. There were no
  classes yesterday.

  Deve haver cartas para mim. There must be
  some letters for me.

  Há uma semana que a vi. I saw her a
  week ago.

  Que há de novo. What's new?

  O que é que há? What's the matter?

  Haja o que houver. Come what may.

  Não há remédio. It can't be helped.

  Vai haver muita gente lá. There will be
  many people there.

  Não há de quê. Don't mention it.

hebreu adj., n. m. Hebrew.

hectare m. hectare.

hediondo adj. hideous, repugnant.

hélice m. and f. propeller.

hemisfério m. hemisphere.

hera f. ivy.

herança f. inheritance, legacy, heritage.

herdar to inherit.

herdeiro m. heir.

hereditário adj. hereditary.

herói m. hero.

heróico adj. heroic.

hesitar to hesitate.

  Ela hesitou em fazê-lo. She hesitated in
  doing it.

hidráulico adj. hydraulic.

hidroavião m. seaplane.

hidrofobia f. hydrophobia, rabies.

hiena f. hyena.

hífen m. hyphen.

higiene f. hygiene.

higiênico (higiénico) adj. hygienic, sanitary.

hino m. hymn; anthem.

  Hino nacional. National anthem.

hipérbole f. hyperbole.

hipermercado m. large supermarket.

hipertensão f. hypertension.

hipnotismo m. hypnotism.

hipnotizar to hypnotize.

hipocrisia f. hyprocrisy.

hipócrita adj. hypocritical; n. m. and f.
  hypocrite.

hipódromo m. racetrack, hippodrome.

hipopótamo m. hippopotamus.

hipoteca f. mortgage.

hipotecar to mortgage.

hispânico adj. Hispanic.

hispano-americano adj. Spanish-American; n.
  m. Spanish-American.

  Literatura hispano-americana. Spanish-
  American literature.

HISTÓRIA *f. history; story.*
   História antiga. *Ancient history.*
   História moderna. *Modern history.*
   Não me conte mais histórias! *Don't tell me any more stories!*
historiador *m. historian.*
histórico *adj. historic.*
HOJE *m. today.*
   Hoje é segunda-feira. *Today is Monday.*
   Qual é o programa de hoje? *What's today's program?*
   De hoje em diante. *From now on.*
   Hoje em dia. *Nowadays.*
   De hoje a oito dias. *In a week.*
   Hoje à noite. *Tonight. This evening.*
   Hoje à tarde. *This afternoon.*
holandês *adj., n. m. Dutch.*
holofote *m. searchlight.*
HOMEM *m. man.*
   Homem de bem. *Honest man.*
   Homem do mundo. *Man of the world.*
   Homem de letras. *Man of letters.*
   Homem de negócios. *Businessman.*
   Homem de Estado. *Statesman.*
   O homem põe e Deus dispõe. *Man proposes, God disposes.*
homenagem *f. homage, honor, respects.*
   Prestar homenagem. *To render homage to.*
homenzarrão *m. very large man.*
homossexual *m., f. homosexual.*
hondurenho *adj., n. m. Honduran.*
honesto *adj. honest; sincere.*
honra *f. honor, respect.*
   Em honra de. *In honor of.*
honradez *f. honesty, integrity.*
honrar *to honor.*
HORA *f. hour; time.*
   Que horas são? *What time is it?*
   São duas horas e meia. *It's two thirty.*
   À que horas começa a festa? *What time does the party begin?*
   Está na hora de jantar. *It's time for dinner.*
   Hora de verão. *Daylight saving time.*
   Ele chegou na hora. *He arrived on time.*
horário *m. schedule; timetable.*
horizontal *adj. horizontal.*
horizonte *m. horizon.*
horrível *adj. horrible.*
horror *m. horror.*
horroroso *adj. horrible, frightful, dreadful.*
horta *f. vegetable garden.*
hospedagem *f. lodging; board.*
hospedar *to lodge.*
hóspede *m. and f. guest.*
hospício *m. asylum (hospital).*
hospital *m. hospital.*
hospitalizar *to hospitalize.*
hóstia *f. Host (communion bread).*
hostil *adj. hostile.*

hostilidade *f. hostility.*
hostilizar *to antagonize.*
hotel *m. hotel.*
hoteleiro *m. hotelman, innkeeper.*
humanidade *f. humanity, mankind.*
humanitário *adj. humanitarian, philanthropic.*
HUMANO *adj. human, humane; n. m. man, human being.*
   Um ser humano. *A human being.*
humildade *f. humility.*
humilde *adj. humble.*
humilhado *adj. humiliated.*
humilhante *adj. humiliating.*
humilhar *to humiliate, to humble.*
HUMOR *m. humor; disposition.*
   Estar de bom humor. *To be in a good mood.*
   Estar de mau humor. *To be in a bad mood.*
humorado *adj. humored.*
   Mal humorado. *Bad-tempered.*
humorista *m. and f. humorist.*
húngaro *adj. Hungarian; n. m. Hungarian.*
hurra! *hurrah!*

I

iaiá *f. missy, miss Ⓑ.*
iate *m. yacht.*
ibérico *adj., n. m. Iberian.*
ibero *adj., n. m. Iberian.*
içar *to hoist.*
   Içar a bandeira. *To hoist the flag.*
ida *f. departure; one-way (ticket).*
   Bilhete de ida e volta. *Round-trip ticket.*
IDADE *f. age; time, period.*
   Idade de ouro. *Golden Age.*
   Idade Média. *Middle Ages.*
   Certidão de idade. *Birth certificate.*
   Que idade o senhor tem? *How old are you?*
ideal *adj., n. m. ideal.*
idealizar *to idealize.*
idear *to think of, to conceive; to devise; to plan.*
IDÉIA (IDEIA) *f. idea.*
   Não tenho a mínima idéia. *I haven't the slightest idea.*
   É uma boa idéia. *It's a good idea.*
   Mais tarde ela mudou de idéia. *Later she changed her mind.*
idem *the same, ditto.*
idêntico *adj. identical, the same.*
identidade *f. identity.*
   O senhor tem os seus documentos de identidade? *Do you have your identification papers?*
identificação *f. identification.*

identificar *to identify.*
idioma *m. language.*
idiota *adj. idiotic; n. m. and f. idiot, fool.*
idiotice *f. foolishness, foolish thing.*
idiotismo *m. idiocy.*
ídolo *m. idol.*
idoso *adj. aged, old.*
ignomínia *f. infamy; disgrace.*
ignorância *f. ignorance.*
ignorante *adj. ignorant; unaware; n. m. ignoramus, ignorant person.*
　　Ela estava ignorante do que acontecia. *She was unaware of what was happening.*
　　Ele é um ignorante. *He's an ignoramus.*
ignorar *to be ignorant of, not to know, to be unaware.*
　　Ignoro seu nome. *I don't know his name.*
IGREJA *f. church.*
IGUAL *adj. equal; similar, like; even.*
　　Vamos dividi-lo em partes iguais. *We'll divide it in equal parts.*
　　Não ter igual. *To be matchless. To have no equal.*
　　Nunca vi coisa igual. *I never saw anything like it.*
　　Cada qual com seu igual. *Birds of a feather flock together.*
igualar *to equalize, to make even; to compare.*
igualdade *f. equality.*
　　Igualdade de condições. *Equal terms.*
ilegal *adj. illegal.*
ilegítimo *adj. illegitimate.*
ilegível *adj. illegible.*
ileso *adj. unharmed, safe.*
iletrado *adj., n. m. illiterate.*
ilha *f. island, isle.*
ilimitado *adj. unlimited.*
iludir *to deceive.*
iluminação *f. illumination.*
iluminar *to illuminate.*
ilusão *f. illusion.*
ilusivo *adj. illusive.*
ilustração *f. illustration.*
ilustrar *to illustrate; to explain.*
ilustrar-se *to acquire knowledge; to become distinguished.*
ilustre *adj. illustrious, celebrated.*
imagem *f. image, figure.*
imaginação *f. imagination.*
IMAGINAR *to imagine, to think, to suspect.*
　　Imagine! *Just imagine!*
　　Não posso imaginar tal coisa! *I can't imagine such a thing!*
imbecil *adj. imbecileic; n. m. imbecile.*
imediação *f. immediacy; pl. environs.*
imediatamente *immediately.*
imediato *adj. immediate; near; m. second in command.*
imenso *adj. immense.*

imigração *f. immigration.*
imigrante *adj., n. m. immigrant.*
imigrar *to immigrate.*
imitação *f. imitation.*
imitar *to imitate; to mimic.*
imoderado *adj. immoderate.*
imoral *adj. immoral.*
imortal *adj. immortal.*
imóvel *adj. immobile; n. m. real estate* Ⓑ.
impaciência *f. impatience.*
impacientar *to make impatient, to exasperate.*
impaciente *adj. impatient, restless.*
ímpar *adj. odd, uneven (number).*
　　Número ímpar. *Odd number.*
imparcial *adj. impartial, unbiased.*
impávido *adj. fearless.*
impedimento *m. impediment, hindrance, obstacle.*
impedir *to hinder, to prevent.*
　　A linha está impedida Ⓟ. *The line (telephone) is busy.*
impenetrável *adj. impenetrable.*
imperador *m. emperor.*
imperativo *adj., n. m. imperative.*
imperfeito *adj. imperfect, faulty; n. m. imperfect (tense).*
império *m. empire, domain.*
　　Império Romano. *Roman Empire.*
impermeabilizar *to waterproof.*
impermeável *adj. waterproof; n. m. raincoat.*
　　Hoje vou levar o impermeável. *I'm going to take my raincoat today.*
impertinente *adj. impertinent.*
impessoal *adj. impersonal.*
ímpeto *m. impetus.*
impetuoso *adj. impetuous.*
ímpio *adj. wicked, impious; n. m. impious person.*
implicar *to implicate; to imply.*
implícito *adj. implicit.*
implorar *to implore.*
imponente *adj. imposing.*
IMPOR *to impose.*
　　Impor respeito. *To command respect.*
　　Impor condições. *To impose conditions.*
　　Impor um imposto. *To levy a tax.*
importação *f. importation, import.*
IMPORTÂNCIA *f. importance.*
　　Não tem importância. *It doesn't matter.*
　　Sem importância. *Unimportant.*
IMPORTANTE *adj. important.*
　　Isto é importante. *This is important.*
IMPORTAR *to import; to matter, to be important; to amount to.*
　　Esta casa importa café do Brasil. *This firm imports coffee from Brazil.*
　　Que importa? *What does it matter?*
　　Não importa. *It doesn't matter. Never mind.*

Importa muito. *It matters a lot. It's very important.*

Não me importa. *It makes no difference to me.*

Em quanto importa a conta? *How much is the bill? How much does the bill come to?*

importunar *to annoy, to bother.*

imposição *f. imposition.*

impossibilidade *f. impossibility.*

impossibilitar *to make impossible, to preclude.*

IMPOSSÍVEL *adj. impossible.*

É impossível. *It's impossible. It can't be done.*

imposto *adj. imposed, set; n. m. tax, duty.*

Imposto de renda. *Income tax.*

Isento de imposto. *Tax-free.*

impreciso *adj. vague, not clear.*

imprensa *f. press.*

impressão *f. impression; printing, edition.*

impressionar *to impress; to move; to affect.*

impresso *adj. printed; n. m. printed document.*

impressora *f. printer (machine).*

Impressora a laser. *Laser printer.*

Impressora de cor. *Color printer.*

imprevisto *adj. unforeseen, unexpected; sudden.*

Ele chegou de imprevisto. *He arrived unexpectedly.*

imprimir *to print, to imprint.*

impróprio *adj. improper, unfit, unbecoming.*

improvável *adj. unlikely, improbable.*

improvisar *to improvise.*

improviso *adj. unexpected; impromptu.*

De improviso. *Unexpectedly.*

imprudência *f. imprudence, lack of prudence.*

impulsionar *to impel; to drive; to urge.*

impulso *m. impulse.*

impunidade *f. impunity.*

impureza *f. impurity, contamination.*

impuro *adj. impure, contaminated.*

imputar *to impute, to attribute.*

imunizar *to immunize.*

imutável *adj. fixed, unchangeable.*

inaceitável *adj. inadmissible; unacceptable.*

inadaptável *adj. not adaptable.*

inadequado *adj. inadequate.*

inadmissível *adj. inadmissible.*

inadvertido *adj. inadvertent.*

inalterável *adj. unalterable, unchangeable.*

inativo (inactivo) *adj. inactive.*

inauguração *f. inauguration.*

inaugurar *to inaugurate, to begin.*

incansável *adj. untiring.*

incapacidade *f. incapacity, inability, incompetence.*

incapaz *adj. incapable, incompetent.*

Ela é incapaz de fazê-lo. *She is incapable of doing it.*

incendiar *to set on fire.*

incêndio *m. fire.*

incerteza *f. uncertainty.*

incerto *adj. uncertain.*

incessante *adj. incessant, continual, ceaseless.*

inchar *to swell, to puff up.*

incidente *adj., n. m. incident.*

incisão *f. incision.*

inciso *adj. incised, cut.*

incitar *to incite, to stimulate.*

inclemência *f. inclemency.*

A inclemência do tempo não nos permitiu sair. *The bad weather kept us at home.*

inclinação *f. inclination, tendency.*

inclinar *to incline, to bend.*

inclinar-se *to incline; to bow.*

INCLUIR *to include, to enclose.*

Está incluído o vinho? *Is the wine included?*

inclusive *inclusively.*

inclusivo *adj. inclusive.*

incluso *adj. included; enclosed.*

incoerente *adj. incoherent.*

incógnito *adj. incognito; unknown.*

incombustível *adj. incombustible.*

incomodar *to disturb, to inconvenience, to bother.*

Não se incomode. *Don't bother.*

incômodo (incómodo) *adj. uncomfortable, inconvenient.*

incomparável *adj. matchless, without equal.*

incompatível *adj. incompatible.*

incompetência *f. incompetency.*

incompleto *adj. incomplete, unfinished.*

incompreensível *adj. incomprehensible.*

inconcebível *adj. inconceivable, unthinkable.*

incondicional *adj. unconditional.*

inconfidência *f. disloyalty.*

incongruência *f. incongruity.*

inconsciência *f. unconsciousness; lack of conscience.*

inconsciente *adj. unconscious; unaware.*

inconstância *f. inconstancy, fickleness.*

inconstitucional *adj. unconstitutional.*

inconveniente *adj. unseemly, inopportune; n. m. inconvenience, difficulty.*

incorporar *to incorporate.*

incorreto (incorrecto) *adj. incorrect, inaccurate, wrong, improper.*

incorrigível *adj. incorrigible.*

incredulidade *f. incredulity, disbelief.*

incrédulo *adj. incredulous; n. m. unbeliever.*

incremento *m. increment, increase.*

increpar *to reproach, to rebuke.*

incrível *adj. incredible, unbelievable.*

Mas isso é incrível! *But that's incredible!*

incubadora *f. incubator.*

incubar *to incubate, to hatch.*

inculcar *to inculcate.*

inculpar *to blame.*

inculto *adj. uncultivated; uncultured.*

incumbência *f. duty, charge, mission.*

incumbir *to commit, to entrust.*

incurável *adj. incurable.*

indagar *to inquire, to investigate.*

indecente *adj. indecent, shameful.*

indecisão *f. indecision, vacillation.*

indeciso *adj. undecided, vacillating, hesitant.*

indefeso *adj. defenseless.*

indefinido *adj. indefinite.*

indelével *adj. indelible.*

indenização *f. indemnity, reparation.*

indenizar *to indemnify, to reimburse.*

independência *f. independence.*

    Dia de Independência. *Independence Day.*

independente *adj. independent.*

indesejável *adj., n. m. and f. undesirable.*

indeterminado *adj. indeterminate; undecided.*

indevido *adj. improper.*

índex *m. index; index finger, pl. indices.*

indiano *adj., n. m. and f. Indian (from India).*

INDICAR *to indicate, to point out.*

    Faça o favor de me indicar o caminho.
        Please show me the way.

índice *m. index, table of contents.*

    Índice de preços. *Price index.*

    Índice de mortalidade. *Death rate.*

indício *m. indication, sign, mark, clue.*

indiferença *f. indifference.*

indiferente *adj. indifferent.*

indígena *adj., n. m. and f. native.*

indignar *to irritate, to annoy, to anger.*

indigno *adj. unworthy, undeserving, shameful.*

índio *adj., n. m. Indian (native peoples of
    North and South America).*

indireto (indirecto) *adj. indirect.*

indiscreto *adj. indiscreet.*

indiscrição *f. indiscretion.*

indiscutível *adj. unquestionable.*

indispensável *adj. indispensable, essential.*

indispor *to indispose, to upset.*

indisposição *f. indisposition.*

individual *adj. individual.*

indivíduo *m. individual, person.*

índole *f. disposition, nature.*

indulgência *f. indulgence.*

indulgente *adj. indulgent.*

indústria *f. industry.*

industrial *adj. industrial; n. m. and f.
    industrialist.*

induzir *to induce, to influence.*

ineficácia *f. inefficacy.*

ineficaz *adj. inefficacious, ineffectual.*

inegável *adj. undeniable.*

inépcia *f. ineptitude.*

inepto *adj. inept.*

inequívoco *adj. unmistakable, clear.*

inércia *f. inertia.*

inerte *adj. inert; inactive.*

inesgotável *adj. inexhaustible.*

inesperado *adj. unexpected.*

    Inesperadamente. *Suddenly. Unexpectedly.*

inesquecível *adj. unforgettable.*

inevitável *adj. inevitable, unavoidable.*

inexatidão (inexactidão) $(x = z)$ *f. inaccuracy.*

inexato (inexacto) $(x = z)$ *adj. inexact,
    inaccurate.*

inexperto *adj. inexpert, inexperienced.*

inexplicável *adj. inexplicable.*

infalível *adj. infallible.*

infamar *to defame, to malign.*

infame *adj. infamous.*

infâmia *f. infamy.*

infância *f. childhood.*

infantaria *f. infantry.*

infante *adj., n. m. and f. infant.*

infantil *adj. infantile, childish.*

infatigável *adj. tireless.*

infecção (infeção) *f infection.*

infeccionar (infecionar) *to infect, to
    contaminate.*

infeliz *adj. unhappy; unfortunate; n. m.
    unhappy, unfortunate person.*

    Ele é infeliz. *He is unhappy.*

    Infelizmente. *Unfortunately.*

inferior *adj. inferior, lower; subordinate; n.
    m. inferior person; subordinate.*

    É uma fazenda de qualidade inferior. *The
        material is of inferior quality.*

inferioridade *f. inferiority.*

inferir *to infer, to conclude.*

inferno *m. hell, inferno.*

infestar *to infest; to overrun.*

infiel *adj. unfaithful.*

ínfimo *adj. lowest.*

infinidade *f. infinity.*

infinito *adj. infinite.*

inflação *f. inflation.*

inflamação *f. inflammation.*

inflamar *to inflame.*

inflamável *adj. inflammable.*

inflar *to inflate.*

influência *f. influence.*

    Ele tem muita influência no governo. *He is
        quite influential in the government.*

influenciar *to influence.*

INFLUIR *to influence, to inspire.*

INFORMAÇÃO *f. information; inquiry,
    investigation.*

    Eu não recebi essa informação. *I did not
        receive that information.*

informalidade *f. informality.*

INFORMAR *to inform; to report.*

    Ela não me informou disso. *She did not
        inform me about that.*

informática f. computer science.
informe adj. formless; n. m. information.
infortunado adj. unfortunate.
infração (infracção) f. infraction, infringement.
infreqüência (infrequência) f. infrequence.
infreqüente (infrequente) adj. infrequent.
infringir to infringe, to violate.
infrutuoso adj. unsuccessful, fruitless.
infundado adj. unfounded, groundless.
infundir to infuse, to instill.
ingênuo (ingénuo) adj. ingenuous.
INGLÊS adj. English; n. m. Englishman; English language.
    Fala-se inglês. English is spoken here.
    Ela não fala inglês. She does not speak English.
    Ele é inglês. He is English.
ingratidão f. ingratitude.
ingrato adj. ungrateful.
ingressar to enter.
ingresso m. entry, entrance; admission ticket Ⓑ.
inicial adj., n. f. initial.
iniciar to initiate, to begin.
iniciativa f. initiative.
    Tomar a iniciativa. To take the initiative.
início m. beginning.
    De início. At first.
inimigo adj., n. m. enemy.
iniqüidade (iniquidade) f. iniquity, wickedness.
injúria f. insult; injury; offense.
injustiça f. injustice.
injusto adj. unjust, unfair.
inocência f. innocence.
inocente adj. innocent.
inodoro adj. odorless.
inofensivo adj. inoffensive, harmless.
inolvidável adj. unforgettable.
inoportuno adj. inopportune, untimely.
inovar to innovate.
inquebrantável adj. unbreakable; tenacious, unyielding.
inquérito m. inquiry; inquest.
inquietar to disturb, to cause anxiety.
inquieto adj. restless, uneasy.
    Ela passou toda a noite inquieta. She was restless all night.
inquirir to inquire.
insalubre adj. unsanitary, unhealthful.
insano adj. insane, mad.
inscrever to inscribe; to register; to sign up.
inscrever-se to register (at a school, etc.); to sign up.
inscrição f. inscription, registration.
inseguro adj. uncertain; insecure.
insensatez f. foolishness.
insensato adj. foolish; insane.

insensível adj. insensitive, impassive.
inseparável adj. inseparable.
inserir to insert; to introduce.
inseticida (insecticida) f. insecticide.
inseto (insecto) m. insect.
insidioso adj. insidious, treacherous.
insigne adj. famous, noted.
insígnia f. badge, pl. insignia.
insignificante adj. insignificant.
insinuar to insinuate, to hint.
insipidez f. insipidity; lack of flavor (taste); flatness.
insípido adj. insipid; tasteless.
insistência f. insistence, persistence.
insistir to insist.
    Insistimos em que ela venha. We insist that she come.
insolação f. sunstroke.
insolência f. insolence, rudeness.
insolente adj. insolent, rude.
insolvente adj. insolvent.
insônia (insónia) f. insomnia.
inspeção (inspecção) f. inspection.
inspecionar (inspeccionar) to inspect, to examine.
inspetor (inspector) m. inspector, supervisor.
inspiração f. inspiration.
inspirar to inspire; to inhale.
    Ele inspira confiança. He inspires confidence.
instalação f. installation; pl. fixtures.
instalar to install, to set up.
instância f. instance; request.
    Em última instância. As a last resort.
instantâneo adj. instantaneous, immediate; n. m. snapshot.
INSTANTE adj. instant; urgent; n. m. instant, moment.
    Espere um instante. Wait a minute.
    A cada instante. Every minute, All the time.
instar to urge, to press.
instaurar to establish, to initiate.
instinto m. instinct.
instituição f. institution.
instituir to institute, to establish.
instituto m. institute.
instrução f. instruction; education.
    Instrução pública. Public education.
    Instrução primária. Elementary education.
    Instrução secundária. Secondary education.
    Instruções de manejo. Operating instructions.
instruir to instruct, to teach.
instrumento m. instrument.
    Que instrumento você toca? What instrument do you play?
    Instrumento de sopro. Wind instrument.
instrutivo adj. instructive.

instrutor *m. instructor, teacher.*
insubordinado *adj. insubordinate.*
insubordinar-se *to rebel, to revolt.*
insuficiência *f. insufficiency.*
insuficiente *adj. insufficient.*
insultar *to insult.*
insulto *m. insult, offense.*
insuperável *adj. insuperable, insurmountable.*
intato (intacto) *adj. intact, untouched.*
integral *adj. integral, whole.*
    Pão integral. *Whole wheat bread.*
integrar *to integrate.*
integridade *f. integrity.*
íntegro *adj. entire, whole, upright, honest.*
inteirar *to complete.*
inteirar-se *to become informed.*
inteiro *adj. entire, complete.*
inteletual (intelectual) *adj., n. m. and f. intellectual.*
inteligência *f. intelligence; understanding.*
INTELIGENTE *adj. intelligent, bright.*
    Ela é muito inteligente. *She is very intelligent.*
inteligível *adj. intelligible.*
intemperado *adj. intemperate.*
intempérie *f. rough or bad weather.*
INTENÇÃO *f. intention, intent.*
    Ele tinha segundas intenções. *He had ulterior motives.*
    Ter boas intenções. *To have good intentions; To mean well.*
    Ter más intenções. *To have bad intentions; Not to mean well.*
    Ter a intenção de. *To intend to.*
intendência *f. quartermaster (corps); administration.*
intendente *m. quartermaster; superintendent.*
intensidade *f. intensity.*
intenso *adj. intense.*
intentar *to try, to attempt; to intend.*
intento *adj. intent, purpose.*
intercalar *to intercalate, to insert.*
intercâmbio *m. interchange, exchange.*
interceder *to intercede, to plead (in another's behalf).*
interceptar *to intercept; to block.*
INTERESSANTE *adj. interesting.*
    Este romance é muito interessante. *This novel is very interesting.*
INTERESSAR *to interest, to concern.*
    Isso não me interessa. *That doesn't interest me.*
INTERESSAR-SE *to be concerned; to become interested.*
    Não me interesso por isso. *I'm not interested in that.*
INTERESSE *m. interest.*
    Ele não mostra o menor interesse. *He doesn't show the slightest interest.*

interino *adj. provisional, temporary, acting.*
INTERIOR *adj. interior, internal; n. m. interval, inside; country (rural)* ⑬.
    Ministério do Interior. *Department of the Interior.*
interligar *to network (computers).*
intermediar *to intermediate.*
intermediário *adj., n. m. intermediary.*
intermédio *adj. intermediate, n. m. intermediary; intervention; interlude.*
internacional *adj. international.*
internar *to intern.*
interno *adj. internal, interior; n. m. intern; boarding student.*
    Para uso interno. *For internal use.*
interpor *to interpose.*
interpretação *f. interpretation.*
interpretar *to interpret.*
    Acho que o senhor interpretou mal. *I believe you misunderstood.*
intérprete *m. and f. interpreter.*
interrogação *f. interrogation, questioning; question; inquiry; question mark.*
interrogar *to interrogate, to question.*
    Não me interrogue mais. *Don't question me any longer.*
interrogatório *m. interrogation, examination.*
INTERROMPER *to interrupt.*
    Foi preciso interromper o trabalho. *It was necessary to interrupt the work.*
interrupção *f. interruption.*
    Sem interrupção. *Without stopping.*
interruptor *m. switch (electric).*
interurbano *adj. interurban; n. m. long-distance telephone call.*
intervalo *m. interval; intermission.*
    Podemos falar no intervalo. *We can talk during the intermission.*
intervir *to intervene, to mediate.*
intestino *adj. intestinal, internal; n. m. intestine.*
intimar *to summon; to order; to inform.*
intimidade *f. intimacy, closeness, friendship.*
intimidar *to intimidate, to frighten.*
íntimo *adj. intimate, close.*
    Eles eram amigos íntimos. *They were very close friends.*
intitular *to entitle, to give a name to.*
intolerância *f. intolerance.*
intolerante *adj. intolerant.*
intolerável *adj. intolerable, unbearable.*
intoxicação ($x = ks$) *f. intoxication, poisoning.*
intranqüilo (intranquilo) *adj. restless.*
intransigência *f. intransigence.*
intransigente *adj. intransigent, uncompromising, unyielding.*
intransitável *adj. impassable.*
intratável *adj. hard to deal with, stubborn, unsociable.*

intrepidez f. intrepidity, courage.
intrépido adj. intrepid, fearless.
intricado adj. intricate, complicated.
intriga f. intrigue, plot.
    Fazer intriga. To plot.
intrigante adj. intriguing, scheming; n. m. and f. intriguer, schemer.
introdução f. introduction.
introduzir to introduce (not people; see **apresentar**), to initiate.
    O professor introduziu uma nova teoria. The professor introduced (brought out) a new theory.
intromissão f. interference.
intruso adj. intrusive; n. m. intruder.
intuição f. intuition.
inumano adj. inhuman, cruel.
inundar to flood, to overflow.
INÚTIL adj. useless; fruitless; futile.
    É inútil fazer a viagem. There's no use (in) taking the trip.
    Ele é um homem inútil. He's good for nothing. He can't do anything.
inutilidade f. uselessness, inutility.
inutilizar to spoil, to ruin, to disable.
INUTILMENTE uselessly, in vain.
    Fizemos a viagem inutilmente. We took the trip in vain.
invadir to invade.
    Portugal foi invadido nos primeiros anos do século dezenove (dezanove). Portugal was invaded in the early years of the nineteenth century.
invalidar to invalidate, to nullify; to render void.
inválido adj. invalid, disabled; n. m. invalid.
invariável adj. invariable, constant.
invasão f. invasion.
inveja f. envy.
invejar to envy.
invenção f. invention.
inventar to invent.
inventário m. inventory.
invento m. invention.
invernar to spend the winter, to hibernate.
INVERNO m. winter.
    Não gosto nada do inverno (Inverno). I don't like winter at all.
inverossímil adj. unlikely, improbable.
inverter to invert, to reverse; to invest.
investigação f. investigation.
investigar to investigate.
invisível adj. invisible; n. m. the invisible; lady's fine hair net; fine hairpin.
iodo m. iodine.
IR to go; to move; to be.
    Vamos! Let's go!
    Já vou! I'm coming!
    Vou para casa. I'm going home.

    Vá embora! Go away!
    Não posso ir. I can't go.
    Como vai? How are you?
    Vou bem, obrigado. I'm fine, thank you.
    Como vão as coisas? How are things? How is everything?
    Ela vai muito melhor. She is much better.
    Vamos ver. Let's see.
    Vamos, chega. Come on now, that's enough.
    A situação vai de mal a pior. The situation is going from bad to worse.
    Ir a pé. To walk. To go on foot.
    Ir a cavalo. To ride. To go on horseback.
    Ir de carro. To drive. To go by car.
    Ir de avião. To fly. To go by plane.
    Ir a bordo. To go aboard.
    João foi à cidade. John went downtown.
    O chapéu lhe vai bem. The hat looks good on you.
    Acho que vai chover. I think it's going to rain.
    Devagar se vai ao longe. Easy does it.
    Água vem, água vai. Easy come, easy go.
ira f. anger, rage.
    Acesso de ira. Fit of rage.
iracundo adj. irascible.
irlandês adj. Irish; n. m. Irishman.
IRMÃ f. sister.
    Ele tem duas irmãs. He has two sisters.
IRMÃO m. brother.
ironia f. irony.
irônico (irónico) adj. ironic.
irradiar to irradiate; to broadcast; to be on the air.
irreal adj. unreal.
irreflexão (x = ks) f. thoughtlessness.
irregular adj. irregular.
irresponsabilidade f. irresponsibility.
irresponsável adj. irresponsible.
irrigar to irrigate.
irritar to irritate, to exasperate.
irrompível adj. unbreakable.
isentar to exempt, to free.
isolado adj. isolated.
isolar to isolate, to separate.
isqueiro m. cigarette lighter.
ISSO that.
    Isso mesmo. That's it.
    Por isso. Therefore.
    Que é isso? What's that?
    Isso não me importa. That makes no difference to me.
    Nem por isso. Don't mention it. Not at all.
    Só faltava isso. That's the last straw.
ISTO this.
    Que é isto? What's this?
    Para que serve isto? What's this for?
    Tudo isto é muito interessante. All this is very interesting.

Por isto. *Therefore.*
Com isto. *Herewith.*
Isto é. *That is. Namely.*
Além disso. *Besides. Furthermore.*
italiano *adj., n. m. Italian.*
itinerário *m. itinerary.*
iugoslavo *adj., n. m. Yugoslav.*

J

JÁ *already; now; immediately; ever.*
Já me falaram nisso. *They already spoke to me about that.*
Venha já. *Come right now.*
Já esteve na capital? *Were you ever in the capital?*
Já não. *No longer.*
Já vou! *I'm coming!*
Já que. *Since. Inasmuch as.*
Desde já. *Immediately.*
jaça *f. fault, imperfection.*
jacaré *m. alligator.*
jacente *adj. lying down, recumbent.*
jacinto *m. hyacinth.*
jactância *f. boasting.*
jactar-se *to boast, to brag.*
jamais *never.*
JANEIRO *m. January; year.*
Ela tem sessenta janeiros. *She is sixty years old.*
JANELA *f. window.*
A janela de meu quarto é grande. *The window in my room is large.*
jangada *f. raft; sailing raft used in northeastern Brazil.*
JANTAR *m. dinner; to have dinner, to dine.*
Jantamos às sete. *We dine at seven.*
Sala de jantar. *Dining room.*
Jantar fora. *To dine out.*
O jantar está na mesa. *Dinner is served.*
japonês *Japanese.*
jaqueta *f. jacket.*
jaquetão *m. double-breasted jacket.*
jarda *f. yard (36 inches).*
JARDIM *m. garden.*
Jardim botânico. *Botanical garden.*
Jardim da infância. *Kindergarten.*
Jardim público. *Public park.*
Jardim zoológico. *Zoo.*
jardineira *f. female gardener; small table, small bus* Ⓑ.
jardineiro *m. male gardener.*
jarra *f. jar, vase.*
jarro *m. pitcher, jug.*
jato (jacto) *jet, stream.*
Jato de luz. *Flash of light.*
Avião a jato. *Jet plane.*

javali *m. wild boar.*
jazer *to lie, to repose.*
Aqui jaz. *Here lies.*
jazida *f. mineral deposit, bed; resting place.*
jazz *m. jazz.*
JEITO *m. manner, way; aptitude; special knack or ability.*
Ela tem jeito para professora. *She is especially talented at teaching.*
Com jeito. *Skillfully. Adroitly.*
Dar um jeito. *To find a way. To finagle a solution.*
jejuar *to fast.*
jejum *m. fast, fasting.*
Dia de jejum. *Fast day.*
Em jejum. *Fasting.*
jérsei *m. jersey (sweater)* Ⓑ.
jesuíta *m. Jesuit.*
Jesus, Jesus Cristo *m. Jesus, Jesus Christ.*
jibóia *f. boa constrictor.*
joalharia (joalheria) *f. jewelry store.*
jocoso *adj. jocose, funny.*
JOELHO *m. knee.*
De joelhos. *On one's knees. Kneeling.*
Pôr-se de joelhos. *To kneel.*
jogada *f. play, move (in a game); throwing, casting.*
Foi uma boa jogada. *It was a good play (in a game).*
jogador *m. player; gambler.*
JOGAR *to play (game); to gamble; to cast, to throw.*
No Brasil e em Portugal jogam futebol. *In Brazil and in Portugal they play soccer.*
Ele perdeu todo o dinheiro jogando. *He lost all his money gambling.*
Jogue isso fora! *Throw that out!*
JOGO *m. game; play; gambling; set.*
Jogo de cartas. *Card game.*
Jogo de azar. *Game of chance.*
Jogo de damas. *Checkers.*
Jogo do bicho. *Brazilian lottery, numbers game* Ⓑ.
Jogo de palavras. *Play on words.*
Casa de jogo. *Gambling house.*
joguete *m. toy, plaything.*
jóia *f. jewel, gem; pl. jewelry.*
jornada *f. journey; short trip.*
JORNAL *m. newspaper; diary; journal.*
Banca de jornais. *Newsstand* Ⓑ.
jornaleiro *m. day laborer; newsboy.*
jornalismo *m. journalism.*
jornalista *m. and f. journalist; newspaper man or woman.*
jorro *m. torrent, outpouring.*
A jorros. *In torrents.*
JOVEM *adj. young; n. m. young man; n. f. young lady.*

Quem é essa jovem? *Who's that young lady?*

Não conheço esse jovem. *I don't know that young man.*

jubilação *f. jubilation, rejoicing; retirement of a teacher.*

jubilar *to rejoice; to retire.*

judeu *adj. Jewish; n. m. Jew.*

judicial *adj. judicial.*

juiz *m. judge; arbiter; referee; umpire.*

Juiz de paz. *Justice of the peace.*

Juiz de direito. *District judge.*

juízo *m. judgment; opinion; decision; good judgment; mind.*

Você perdeu o juízo? *Have you lost your mind?*

Ele é um homem de juízo. *He's a man of good judgment.*

Chamar a juízo. *To summon to court.*

Dia de juízo. *Judgment day.*

julgado *adj. tried; sentenced; n. m. judicial district.*

julgamento *m. judgment, sentence; trial.*

julgar *to judge; to suppose, believe.*

Julgo que será assim. *I believe that's the way it will be.*

JULHO *m. July.*

jumento *m. donkey.*

JUNHO *m. June.*

júnior *adj. junior.*

junta *f. board, council, junta, committee; junction, union, coupling; joint.*

A que horas foi a junta? *What time did the meeting take place?*

Junta administrativa. *Administrative council.*

Junta de comércio. *Board of trade.*

Junta universal. *Universal joint.*

JUNTAR *to join, to unite; to assemble, to gather; to amass.*

Os dois exércitos juntaram forças. *The two armies joined forces.*

junto *adj. joined; close.*

Deixe *(x = sh)* tudo junto à porta. *Leave it all by the door.*

Fizemos o trabalho juntos. *We did the work together.*

Junto de. *Next to; Near.*

juramento *m. oath, vow.*

jurar *to swear, to take an oath.*

Juro que sim. *I swear it is so.*

júri *m. jury.*

juros *m. pl. interest.*

Juros compostos. *Compound interest.*

justiça *f. justice; fairness; law.*

Fazer justiça. *To do justice. To be just.*

Levar à justiça. *To bring to justice.*

justificar *to justify.*

JUSTO *adj. just; fair; exact; tight; close-fitting.*

Isso não é justo. *That's not fair.*

Este chapéu é muito justo. *This hat is too tight.*

Uma parte justa. *A fair share.*

juventude *f. youth.*

L

la *it, her, you (after verb forms ending in r, s, or z).*

LÁ *over there, there.*

LÃ *f. wool.*

LÁBIO *m. lip.*

Lamber os lábios. *To smack one's lips.*

laborar *to work, to cultivate.*

laboratório *m. laboratory.*

laborioso *adj. laborious; hardworking.*

lacerar *to lacerate, to mangle.*

laço *m. lasso; loop; trap; tie.*

Cair no laço. *To fall into a trap.*

lacônico (lacónico) *adj. laconic, brief.*

ladear *to be or go alongside; to dodge.*

Ele ladeou a questão. *He dodged the issue.*

ladeira *f. slope; hillside.*

Ladeira abaixo *(x = sh)*. *Downhill.*

Ladeira acima. *Uphill.*

ladino *adj. shrewd, crafty, cunning.*

LADO *m. side; party, faction.*

Sente-se a meu lado. *Sit next to me.*

Ao outro lado da rua. *Across the street. On the other side of the street.*

Ela mora na casa do lado. *She lives next door.*

Por outro lado. *On the other hand.*

Não cabe de lado. *It won't fit sideways.*

Trabalharam lado a lado. *They worked side by side.*

Olhar de lado. *To look askance at. To look down at.*

De todos os lados. *From all sides. From all directions.*

Conheço muito bem seu lado fraco. *I know his weakness very well.*

Eu estou do lado de você. *I am on your side.*

ladrão *m. thief, robber.*

ladrar *to bark.*

ladrido *m. barking, bark.*

lagarta *f. caterpillar.*

lagarto *m. lizard.*

lago *m. lake, pond.*

lagoa *f. lagoon, pond.*

lagosta *f. lobster.*

LÁGRIMA *f. tear; teardrop.*

Lágrimas de alegria. *Tears of joy.*

Lágrimas de crocodilo. *Crocodile tears.*

laguna *f. lagoon.*

lama *f. mud.*

lamentar *to lament, to regret, to deplore.*

lamentável *adj. lamentable, regrettable, deplorable.*

É lamentável. *It's regrettable.*

lâmina *f. lamina, blade.*

LÂMPADA *f. lamp; lightbulb.*

Lâmpada de mesa. *Table lamp. Desk lamp.*

Lâmpada néon. *Neon bulb.*

Lâmpada elétrica (eléctrica). *Electric lightbulb.*

Lâmpada de rádio. *Radio tube.*

Mudar uma lâmpada. *To change a lightbulb.*

lançamento *m. launching; throwing, casting.*

LANÇAR *to launch; to throw; to cast; to eject.*

Lançar à água. *To launch (a ship).*

Lançar fora. *To throw out.*

Ele se lançou aos pés dela. *He threw himself at her feet.*

Lançar um livro. *To publish a book.*

Lançar mão de. *To take hold of. To resort to.*

lance *m. throwing, casting; incident; predicament.*

lancha *f. launch, motorboat.*

lânguido *adj. languid, listless.*

lanterna *f. lantern.*

Lanterna elétrica (eléctrica) de mão. *Flashlight.*

lápide *f. a flat stone with an inscription; tombstone.*

LÁPIS *m. pencil.*

lapso *m. lapse; slip.*

lar *m. hearth; home.*

LARANJA *f. orange.*

laranjada *f. orangeade.*

laranjeira *f. orange tree.*

lareira *f. hearth, fireplace.*

largar *to release; to cast off.*

LARGO *adj. wide; ample.*

Um metro de largo. *A meter wide. One meter in width.*

largura *f. width; extent.*

laringe *m. and f. larynx.*

laringite *f. laryngitis.*

lástima *f. pity, compassion.*

É uma lástima! *That's too bad!*

Que lástima! *What a pity!*

lastimar *to feel sorry for; to regret.*

lastimável *adj. lamentable, deplorable.*

lastro *m. ballast.*

LATA *f. tin; tin can.*

Lata de lixo (x = sh). *Garbage can.*

Latas de conservas. *Canned goods.*

Abridor de latas. *Can opener.*

lateral *adj. lateral.*

latido *m. barking, bark.*

latifúndio *m. large landed estate.*

latim *m. Latin.*

latino *adj. Latin.*

latino-americano *adj., n. m. Latin-American.*

latir *to bark, to yelp.*

latitude *f. latitude.*

lavadeira *f. washerwoman; washing machine.*

lavagem *f. washing; wash.*

lavanderia *f. laundry (place where clothes are washed).*

LAVAR *to wash; to bathe; to clean.*

Lave as mãos antes de jantar. *Wash your hands before dinner.*

Lavar a seco. *To dry-clean.*

lavatório *m. lavatory; washbasin.*

lavável *adj. washable.*

lavrador *m. farmer.*

lavrar *to cultivate, to till; to cut; to work.*

laxante *(x = sh) adj. laxative; n. m. laxative.*

lazer *m. leisure.*

leal *adj. loyal.*

lealdade *f. loyalty.*

leão *m. lion.*

lebre *f. hare.*

Comprar gato por lebre. *To buy a pig in a poke.*

lecionar (leccionar) *to teach, to give lessons; to lecture.*

legal *adj. legal; all right, permissible; "cool."*

Tudo legal. *Everything's cool.*

legalizar *to legalize; to validate.*

legar *to bequeath; to delegate.*

legenda *f. legend; inscription.*

legendário *adj. legendary.*

legião *f. legion.*

legislação *f. legislation.*

legislar *to legislate.*

legislatura *f. legislature.*

legitimar *to legitimate, to legalize.*

legítimo *adj. legitimate, authentic.*

legível *adj. legible.*

légua *f. league (measure of distance).*

legume *m. vegetable.*

LEI *f. law, act; rule.*

Lei das médias. *Law of averages.*

Lei de oferta e procura. *Law of supply and demand.*

leitão *m. suckling pig.*

LEITE *m. milk.*

Leite condensado. *Condensed milk.*

Leite magro. *Skim milk.*

Tirar leite de vaca morta. *To draw blood from a stone. ("To extract milk from a dead cow.")*

leiteiro *m. milkman.*

leiteria *f. dairy.*

leito *m. bed.*

leitor *m. reader.*

leitura *f. reading; reading matter.*

lema *m. motto; slogan.*

LEMBRANÇA f. remembrance; reminder; souvenir; pl. regards, greetings.
Lembranças à sua irmã! Give my regards to your sister!
LEMBRAR to remember, to recall; to remind.
LEMBRAR-SE to remember, to recall.
Não me lembro. I don't remember.
Ela não se lembra disso. She doesn't remember that.
leme m. rudder, helm.
LENÇO m. handkerchief.
lençol m. sheet (bed).
lenda f. legend, tale.
lenha f. firewood.
Deitar lenha ao fogo. To add fuel to the fire.
lenhador m. woodcutter.
lenho m. tree trunk.
lentamente adv. slowly.
lente m. teacher, professor; lens.
lentidão f. slowness.
LENTO adj. slow.
leoa f. lioness.
leopardo m. leopard.
LER to read.
Leia em voz alta. Read aloud.
Você leu este romance? Did you read this novel?
lesão f. lesion, injury; wrong.
lesar to hurt; to wound; to injure; to wrong.
leste m. east.
LETRA f. letter; lyrics; handwriting.
Letra maiúscula. Capital letter.
Letra minúscula. Small letter.
Não me lembro da letra dessa canção. I don't remember the lyrics of that song.
Ela tem boa letra. She has good handwriting.
Ao pé da letra. Literally.
Letra de câmbio. Bill of exchange.
letrado adj. learned, erudite; n. m. scholar; lawyer.
letreiro m. inscription; sign; label; poster.
levantamento m. raising; uprising, revolt.
LEVANTAR to raise, to lift, to pick up; to suspend.
Levantar a voz. To raise the voice.
Levantar o pano. To raise the curtain (theatre).
Levantar a mão. To raise one's hand.
Levantar a mesa. To clear the table.
Levantar os ombros. To shrug the shoulders.
Levantar a sessão. To adjourn the meeting.
LEVANTAR-SE to get up.
A que horas se levanta? At what time do you get up?
Levanto-me às sete. I get up at seven.

LEVAR to carry, to take; to wear; to bear; to need.
Leve-me ao seu chefe. Take me to your leader.
Leve este livro a seu pai. Take this book to your father.
Quanto tempo vai levar? How long will it take?
Levar a cabo. To carry out. To bring about.
Eles levam boa vida. They lead a good (easy) life.
Levar em conta. To take into account.
Levar pau. To fail (an examination).
Levar à força. To take by force.
leve adj. light (weight); slight.
leviano adj. frivolous; imprudent.
léxico (x = ks) m. lexicon.
lha (contr. of lhe + a) it to him, to her, to you, etc.
LHE to him, to her, to you, to it.
lho (contr. of lhe + o) it to him, to her, to you, etc.
liar to tie, to bind.
liberação f. liquidation, discharge.
liberal adj., n. m. and f. liberal.
liberar to release.
LIBERDADE f. liberty, freedom.
Tomar a liberdade. To take the liberty.
libertador adj. liberating; n. m. liberator.
libertar to liberate, to free.
libra f. pound.
LIÇÃO f. lesson.
Dar lições. To give lessons.
LICENÇA f. permission; leave; license; permit.
Com licença. Excuse me. May I?
Dá licença? Excuse me. May I?
Pedir licença. To ask for leave; To ask for permission.
Licença de motorista. Driver's license.
licenciado m. person holding a master's degree.
licenciar to license; to allow; to grant leave of absence.
lícito adj. lawful; licit.
licor m. liqueur, liquor.
lidar to combat, to fight.
líder m. leader ®.
lido adj. read; well-read.
liga f. league.
Liga das Nações. League of Nations.
ligado adj. connected; on (TV, radio, etc.).
LIGAR to join, to connect; to tie, to bind; to turn on (radio, etc.).
A ferrovia liga as duas cidades. The railroad joins the two cities.
Ligue-me com . . . Connect me with . . .
Faça o favor de ligar o rádio. Please turn on the radio.

ligeireza f. lightness; quickness.
LIGEIRO adj. light (weight); quick, swift.
lilás adj., n. m. lilac.
lima f. file (tool); lime.
    Lima de unhas. Nail file.
limão m. lemon.
limar to file, to make smooth; to polish.
limitação f. limitation, limit.
limitado adj. limited.
limitar to limit; to restrain; to border on.
limite m. limit; boundary, border.
    Tudo tem os seus limites. There's a limit to everything.
limoeiro m. lemon tree.
limonada f. lemonade.
LIMPAR to clean, to cleanse; to clear.
    Limpar a garganta. To clear the throat.
limpeza f. cleaning; cleanliness.
LIMPO adj. clean; neat; clear.
    Quero uma toalha limpa. I want a clean towel.
    Estou limpo. I'm broke.
linácea f. flax.
lince m. and f. lynx.
linchar to lynch.
lindar to delimit; to border.
linde m. limit, boundary.
LINDO adj. pretty, beautiful.
    Como ela é linda! How pretty she is!
líneo adj. linen.
LÍNGUA f. tongue; language.
    Língua portuguesa. Portuguese language.
    Língua materna. Mother tongue.
    Língua românica. Romance language.
    Tenho na ponta da língua. I have it on the tip of my tongue.
linguagem f. language.
lingüista (linguista) m. and f. linguist.
LINHA f. line; row; string, thread.
    Linha, por favor. Line, please (telephone).
    Linha interurbana. Long-distance line.
    Linha ferroviária. Railway.
    Linha aérea. Airline.
    Manter em linha. To keep in line.
    Linha reta. Straight line.
linimento m. liniment.
linóleo m. linoleum.
linotipista m. and f. linotypist.
linotipo m. linotype.
liqüidação (liquidação) f. liquidation.
liqüidar (liquidar) to liquidate.
líquido (líqüido) adj. liquid; net (profit, etc.); n. m. liquid.
lírico adj. lyric.
lírio m. lily.
LISBOETA adj. of Lisbon; n. m. and f. person from Lisbon.
liso adj. smooth, even.
    Cabelo liso. Straight hair.

lisonja f. praise, flattery.
lisonjear to praise, to flatter; to please.
lisonjeiro adj. flattering; pleasing; n. m. flatterer.
LISTA f. list; stripe; directory; menu.
    Lista telefônica (telefónica). Telephone book.
    Lista negra. Blacklist.
literário adj. literary.
literato m. man of letters.
literatura f. literature.
litigar to litigate.
litígio m. litigation, lawsuit.
litoral adj. coastal; n. m. coastline.
litro m. liter.
lituano adj., n. m. Lithuanian.
livrar to free.
    Deus me livre! God forbid!
livraria f. bookstore.
LIVRE adj. free (unimpeded).
    Quando você estiver livre falaremos. When you are free, we'll talk.
    Livre a bordo. Free on board.
    Ao ar livre. In the open air.
    Tradução livre. Free translation.
    Verso livre. Free verse.
livreiro m. bookseller.
LIVRO m. book.
    Livro brochado. Paperback.
    Livro caixa (x = sh) Cash book.
    Livro de bolso. Pocket book.
    Livro de consulta. Reference book.
lixo (x = sh) m. garbage.
lo (form taking the place of pronoun o after a verb form ending in r, s or z) him, you, it.
lobo m. wolf.
lôbrego adj. murky, dark; sad.
lóbulo m. lobule, lobe.
local adj. local; m. place.
localidade f. locality, place.
localizar to localize, to locate.
loção f. lotion, wash.
locomoção f. locomotion.
locutor m. speaker, announcer.
lodo m. mud, mire.
lógico adj. logical, reasonable.
LOGO right away, immediately; soon; shortly.
    Até logo. So long. See you soon.
    Desde logo. At once.
    Logo depois. Soon after.
    Logo que. As soon as.
lograr to obtain, to get; to attain; to manage; to succeed.
    Elas lograram fazê-lo. They managed to do it.
LOJA f. shop, store; lodge.
    Loja de miudezas. Notions shop.
lona f. canvas.

londrino adj. of London; n. m. Londoner.
LONGE far, distant.
   É muito longe! It's too far!
   É longe daqui? Is it far from here?
   Devagar se vai ao longe. Slow and steady
     wins the race.
   Bem longe. Really far.
   Longe disso. Far from it.
longitude f. longitude.
longo adj. long.
lotação f. capacity; small bus Ⓑ.
lotado adj. filled full (capacity); crowded.
lotar to fill to capacity.
lote m. lot, piece of land; share.
loteria f. lottery.
louça f. dishes, chinaware.
louco adj. crazy, mad, insane; n. m.
   madman.
   Ele está louco. He's crazy.
   Ele está louco por ela. He's crazy about
     her. He's madly in love with her.
loucura f. madness, insanity; folly.
   Isso é uma loucura. That's absurd. That's
     crazy.
louro adj. blond.
louvar to praise.
LUA f. moon.
   Lua nova. New moon.
   Lua-de-mel. Honeymoon.
luar m. moonlight.
lubrificante adj. lubricating; n. m. lubricant.
lubrificar to lubricate.
lucrativo adj. lucrative, profitable.
lucro m. profit, gain.
   Lucros e perdas. Profits and losses.
LUGAR m. place, site; seat; occasion.
   Ponha as coisas em seu lugar. Put things in
     their place.
   Eu em seu lugar não iria. If I were you (in
     your place), I would not go.
   A que horas terá lugar? At what time will it
     take place?
   Em lugar de. Instead of.
   Dar lugar a. To give cause for. To give
     occasion for.
   Em primeiro lugar. In the first place.
lume m. fire; light.
luminoso adj. shining, luminous.
lunático adj., n. m. lunatic.
lusiada adj., n. m. and f. Lusitanian,
   Portuguese.
LUSITANO adj., n. m. Lusitanian,
   Portuguese.
LUSO adj., n. m. Lusitanian, Portuguese.
   Luso-brasileiro. Luso-Brazilian,
     Portuguese-Brazilian.
lustrar to polish, to shine.
lustre m. luster, gloss; splendor.
luta f. fight, struggle, battle.

   A luta pela vida. The struggle for
     existence.
lutador m. fighter, wrestler.
lutar to fight, to wrestle, to struggle.
luto m. mourning; grief, sorrow.
   De luto. In mourning.
LUVA f. glove; coupling.
   Assentar como uma luva. To fit like a
     glove.
luxo (x = sh) m. luxury.
   Edição de luxo. Deluxe edition.
luxuoso (x = sh) adj. luxurious, deluxe.
LUZ f. light.
   Acenda a luz. Turn the light on.
   Apague a luz. Put the light out. Turn the
     light off.
   Luz elétrica (eléctrica). Electric light.
   Dar à luz. To give birth to.
luzir to shine, to brighten.

M

ma (contr. of **me** + **a**) it to me, her to me, you
   to me.
MÁ adj. f. bad, evil.
   Não é má idéia (ideia). That's not a bad
     idea.
   Má fama. Ill repute.
   De má vontade. Unwillingly.
MAÇÃ f. apple.
   Maçã-de-Adão. Adam's apple Ⓟ.
macaco m. monkey; jack (for lifting).
macarrão m. macaroni.
machacaz adj. cunning, sly.
machado m. ax.
machete m. machete; small guitar.
macho adj. male, masculine; vigorous; n. m.
   male, male animal.
machucar to pound; to bruise.
maciço adj. massive; compact; solid; firm.
macio adj. soft, smooth; gentle.
maconha f. marijuana.
mácula f. stain, spot; dishonor.
macumba f. voodoo ceremony of Brazil Ⓑ.
MADEIRA f. wood, lumber, timber.
   A caixa (x = sh) é de madeira. The box is
     made of wood.
madeireiro m. lumber dealer.
madeirense adj. of the island of Madeira; n.
   m. and f. person from the island of
   Madeira.
madeixa (x = sh) f. lock of hair; skein.
madrasta f. stepmother.
madre f. nun.
madressilva f. honeysuckle.
madrileno adj. of Madrid; n. m. person from
   Madrid.

madrinha f. godmother; sponsor; maid of honor.

madrugada f. dawn, early morning.
De madrugada. At dawn.

madrugador m. early riser.

madrugar to get up early; to get ahead of.
A quem madruga, Deus ajuda. The early-bird catches the worm.

madurar to ripen, to mature.

madureza f. maturity, ripeness.

maduro adj. ripe, mature.
A fruta ainda não está madura. The fruit isn't ripe yet.

MÃE f. mother.

magia f. magic.

mágico adj. magic, magical; marvelous.

magistério m. teaching profession; teaching position.

magistrado m. magistrate.

magnânimo adj. magnanimous.

magnésia f. magnesia.

magnético adj. magnetic.

magnífico adj. magnificent, excellent, wonderful.

magnitude f. magnitude.

magno adj. great.

magnólia f. magnolia.

mago adj. magic; m. magician; wizard.

mágoa f. sorrow; anguish.

MAGRO adj. thin.

MAIO m. May.

maionese f. mayonnaise.

MAIOR adj. greater, greatest; bigger, larger; adult, of age.
A major parte. Most. The majority.
Este é maior do que aquele. This one is larger than that one.
Maior de idade. Of age.
Estado maior. General staff (military).

maioria f. majority, plurality.

MAIS more; any more; besides; n. m. rest; most.
Mais ou menos. More or less.
Deseja mais alguma coisa? Would you like something else?
Quer mais café? Would you like more coffee?
Nada mais? Is that all? Nothing else?
Não há mais. There is (there are) no more.
Não tenho mais. I don't have any more.
Ela é mais inteligente (do) que ele. She is more intelligent than him.
É a coisa mais fácil do mundo. It's the easiest thing in the world.
Mais adiante. Further on.
A casa é mais longe. The house is farther.
São mais de dez horas. It's after ten o'clock.
Mais depressa! Faster!

Mais devagar! Slower!
Fale mais alto, por favor. Speak louder, please.
Os mais dos alunos não estudam bastante. Most students don't study enough.
O mais cedo possível. As soon as possible.
Tenho mais de quinze. I have more than fifteen.
Vou trabalhar mais dez anos. I'm going to work ten more years.
Mais tarde. Later. Later on.
Não querem estudar mais. They don't want to study any longer.
Nunca mais. Never again.

maiúscula adj. capital (letter); n. f. capital letter.

majestade f. majesty.

majestoso adj. majestic, imposing.

MAL badly, poorly; hardly; as soon as; n. m. evil; harm; disease, illness.
O livro está mal escrito. The book is poorly written.
De mal a pior. From bad to worse.
Fazer mal. To do harm. To do wrong.
Estar mal de saúde. To be ill.
Não faz mal. It doesn't matter. Don't bother.
O paletó me fica mal. The jacket doesn't fit right.
Eu me sinto mal hoje. I don't feel well today.
Ela mal me falou. She hardly spoke to me.
Mal-agradecido. Ungrateful.
Menos mal. Not so bad.

mala f. suitcase, bag; trunk (of a car).
Fazer as malas. To pack.

malária f. malaria.

malbaratar to squander; to sell at a loss.

malcriado ill-mannered, impolite.

maldade f. wickedness.

maldição f. curse.

maldizer to damn; to curse.

malefício m. evil act; witchcraft.

maleita f. malaria.

mal-estar m. indisposition; discomfort.

maleta f. handbag, suitcase.

malfalante adj. slandering; n. m. and f. slanderer.

malfeitor m. malefactor, criminal.

malgastar to squander, to waste.

malhar to hammer, to beat.
Malhar o ferro enquanto está quente. To strike while the iron is hot.

mal-humorado adj. ill-humored, peevish.

malícia f. malice; cunning.

malicioso adj. malicious; cunning.

malignar to corrupt.

maligno adj. malignant.

mal-intencionado adj. malicious, evil-minded.

malsão *adj. unhealthy, unhealthful.*

maltratar *to treat roughly, to mistreat, to abuse; to harm.*

maltrato *m. ill-treatment.*

maluco *adj. crazy, insane; m. madman.*

malvado *adj. wicked.*

mamã *f. mamma, mother; wet nurse* Ⓑ.

MAMÃE *f. mommy, mother* Ⓑ.

mamar *to suck; to take the breast.*

mamífero *adj. mammalian, m. mammal.*

mana *f. sis, sister.*

manancial *m. fountain, spring; source.*

manar *to flow, to ooze.*

mancha *f. stain, spot, blemish.*

   Mancha solar. *Sunspot.*

manchar *to stain, to spot, to soil.*

manchete *f. headline* Ⓑ.

manco *adj. crippled, lame; n. m. cripple.*

mandado *m. order, command; writ.*

   A mandado de. *By order of.*

MANDAR *to send; to order, to command; to govern.*

   Mande-o à minha casa. *Send it to my home*

   Mandei que chamassem o médico. *I had them call the doctor.*

   Quem manda aqui? *Who's in charge here?*

   Mandar às favas. *To send someone packing.*

   Mandar aviar uma receita. *To have a prescription filled.*

mandatário *adj. mandatory; n. m. attorney; agent; proxy.*

mandato *m. mandate, order.*

mandíbula *f. jaw.*

mandioca *f. manioc, cassava.*

mando *m. command, authority, control.*

mandolina *f. mandolin* *m. mandolin.*

MANEIRA *f. manner, way, method.*

   Faça desta maneira. *Do it this way.*

   Faça de qualquer maneira. *Do it any way you can.*

   Não há maneira de fazê-lo. *There's no way to do it.*

   De maneira que o senhor não vem? *So you're not coming?*

   De maneira nenhuma. *By no means.*

   Escreva-o de maneira que se possa ler. *Write it so that it can be read.*

   Da mesma maneira. *In the same way.*

   Boas maneiras. *Good manners.*

manejar *to handle; to manage; to govern.*

manejo *m. management; handling.*

MANGA *f. sleeve; glass funnel; waterspout.*

   Em mangas de camisa. *In shirtsleeves.*

MANHÃ *f. morning, forenoon.*

   Ontem de manhã. *Yesterday morning.*

   Amanhã de manhã. *Tomorrow morning.*

   Hoje de manhã. *This morning.*

   Todas as manhãs. *Every morning.*

manhoso *adj. skillful, cunning.*

mania *f. mania; whim; obsession.*

maníaco *adj. maniacal; n. m. maniac; crackpot.*

manicômio (manicómio) *m. insane asylum.*

manifestação *f. manifestation, demonstration.*

manifestar *to manifest; to state; to reveal.*

manifesto *adj. manifest, clear; obvious.*

manipulação *f. manipulation, handling.*

manipular *to handle, to manipulate; to manage.*

manivela *f. crank; lever; handle.*

manjar *m. food, coconut pudding* Ⓑ.

mano *m. brother.*

mansão *m. mansion.*

manso *adj. tame, gentle, meek.*

manta *f. blanket; cloak; neckerchief.*

MANTEIGA *f. butter; flattery.*

   Pão e manteiga. *Bread and butter.*

mantel *m. tablecloth.*

manter *to maintain, to support; to keep up; to uphold.*

   Manter ordem. *To maintain order.*

   Manter correspondência. *To keep up a correspondence.*

   Manter a palavra. *To keep one's word.*

manter-se *to carry on, to remain, to keep.*

   Manter-se firme. *To remain firm.*

mantimento *m. maintenance, support.*

manto *m. mantle, cloak.*

manual *adj. manual; n. m. manual, handbook.*

manuelino *adj. of D Manuel I of Portugal, esp. referring to the architecture of the period (early 16th century).*

manufaturar (manufacturar) *to manufacture.*

manuscrito *adj. handwritten; n. m. manuscript.*

manutenção *f. support, maintenance.*

MÃO *f. hand.*

   Ter à mão. *To have at hand.*

   Ter na mão. *To have in the hand.*

   Apertar a mão de alguém. *To shake hands with someone.*

   Aperto de mão. *Handshake.*

   Mão esquerda. *Left hand.*

   Mão direita. *Right hand.*

   Pedir a mão de. *To ask for the hand of (in marriage).*

   Estar em boas mãos. *To be in good hands.*

   Vir às mãos. *To come to blows.*

   Lavar as mãos. *To wash one's hands.*

   De boa mão. *On good authority.*

   As mãos cheias. *Liberally. Abundantly.*

   Feito à mão. *Made by hand.*

   De primeira mão. *Firsthand.*

   Mãos à obra! *Let's get to work!*

   Dar a mão a. *To shake hands with.*

mapa *m. map, chart.*
mapa-múndi *m. world map.*
MÁQUINA *f. machine, engine.*
    Máquina de escrever. *Typewriter.*
    Máquina de lavar. *Washing machine.*
    Máquina de lavar louça. *Dishwasher.*
    Máquina fotográfica. *Camera.*
    Máquina de fax. *Fax machine.*
    Máquina de contestação. *Answering machine.*
maquinaria *f. machinery.*
maquinista *m. machinist; engineer.*
MAR *m. sea.*
    Fazer-se ao mar. *To sail. To put to sea.*
    Por mar. *By sea.*
maracá *m. maraca (musical instrument).*
maranha *f. entanglement.*
maranhense *adj. and n. m. and f. of the state of Maranhão, in Brazil.*
maravilha *f. marvel, wonder.*
maravilhoso *adj. marvelous, wonderful.*
    Cidade maravilhosa. *Marvelous city (literary description of Rio).*
marca *f. mark; brand; make; sign.*
    Marca registrada (registada). *Registered trademark.*
MARCAR *to mark; to brand.*
    Vamos marcar a data. *Let's set the date.*
    Marquemos a hora. *Let's decide on a time.*
marceneiro *m. cabinetmaker.*
marcha *f. march.*
    Praticar marcha. *To go hiking.*
marchar *to march.*
marco *m. window frame; door frame; boundary mark; mark (German monetary unit).*
MARÇO *m. March.*
maré *f. tide.*
mareado *adj. seasick.*
marear *to get seasick.*
marfim *m. ivory.*
margarida *f. daisy.*
margarina *f. margarine.*
margem *f. margin, border, edge; shore, bank (river).*
marido *m. husband.*
marinha *f. navy.*
    Marinha mercante. *Merchant marine.*
    Marinha de guerra. *Navy.*
marinheiro *m. sailor, seaman.*
mariposa *f. moth.*
marítimo *adj. maritime.*
marmelada *f. marmalade.*
marmita *f. dinner pail; mess kit.*
mármore *m. marble.*
marquês *m. marquis.*
marrom *adj. brown Ⓑ; n. m. brown color Ⓑ.*
martelar *to hammer.*
martelo *m. hammer.*

mártir *m. and f. martyr.*
MAS *but, yet, however.*
    Eu esperei duas horas mas ela não chegou. *I waited for two hours, but she did not arrive.*
    Ela é não só bela mas também inteligente. *She is not only pretty but also intelligent.*
    Nem mas nem meio mas. *No ifs, ands, or buts.*
mascar *to chew.*
máscara *f. mask, disguise.*
mascote *f. mascot.*
masculino *adj. masculine.*
    Gênero (género) masculino. *Masculine gender.*
massa *f. dough; mass.*
mastigar *to chew.*
mata *f. forest, woods.*
mata-borrão *m. blotting paper.*
matadouro *m. slaughterhouse.*
matança *f. slaughter.*
MATAR *to kill, to murder.*
    Matar o tempo. *To kill time.*
    Matar a fome. *To satisfy one's hunger.*
mate *m. maté (a kind of tea).*
matemática *f. mathematics.*
matemático *m. mathematician.*
matéria *f. matter, material; subject.*
    Matéria-prima. *Raw material.*
material *adj. material; n. m. material, equipment.*
materializar *to materialize.*
maternal *adj. maternal.*
maternidade *f. maternity.*
materno *adj. maternal, motherly.*
matiz *m. shade (of color).*
mato *m. woods, forest, thicket; country (rural).*
matrícula *f. matriculation, registration.*
matricular *to matriculate, to register.*
    Em que universidade se matriculou? *At what university did you register?*
matrimonial *adj. matrimonial.*
matrimônio (matrimónio) *m. marriage, matrimony.*
matuto *m. backwoodsman, hillbilly.*
MAU (f. MÁ) *adj. bad, wicked; ill; poor.*
    Mau tempo. *Bad weather.*
    Ele é mau. *He's bad.*
    Mau humor. *Bad humor.*
mausoléu *m. mausoleum.*
máximo *(x = ss) adj. maximum, highest, greatest; n. m. maximum.*
    Máxima altura. *Highest point; Peak.*
    Qual é o preço máximo? *What is the top price?*
    Até o máximo. *To the utmost.*
maxixe *(x = sh) m. gherkin; Brazilian dance.*

ME *me; to me; myself.*

João me deu o livro. *John gave me the book.*

Dê-me o endereço, por favor. *Give me the address, please.*

Eu me levanto às seis. *I get up at six.*

Primeiro vou lavar-me. *First I'm going to wash (myself).*

meão (f. meã) *adj. average, mean.*

mecânico *adj. mechanical; n. m. mechanic.*

mecanismo *m. mechanism, machinery.*

mecha *f. wick, fuse.*

medalha *f. medal.*

mediação *f. mediation, intervention.*

mediador *m. mediator, go-between.*

mediano *adj. median, medium.*

mediante *by means of, by virtue of.*

mediar *to mediate, to intercede.*

medicina *f. medicine, remedy.*

médico *adj. medical; n. m. physician, doctor.*

MEDIDA *f measure, measurement; rule.*

Medida padrão. *Standard measure.*

Tomaram-se as medidas necessárias. *The necessary measures were taken.*

Feito sob medida. *Tailor-made. Made to order.*

A medida que ele falava, ela escrevia o que ele dizia. *As he spoke, she wrote what he said.*

médio *adj. mean, medium, average; n. m. half-back (soccer).*

Classe média. *Middle class.*

Médio direito. *Right halfback.*

medíocre *adj. mediocre.*

mediocridade *f. mediocrity.*

medir *to measure.*

Medir as palavras. *To measure one's words.*

meditação *f. meditation.*

meditar *to meditate.*

medo *m. fear, dread.*

Ele está com medo Ⓑ. *He is afraid.*

Elas têm medo dele. *They are afraid of him.*

medula *f. medulla, marrow; pith, essence.*

MEIA *f. stocking; sock.*

Quer meias de lã ou de algodão? *Do you want wool or cotton stockings?*

MEIO *adj. and adv. half, halfway, mean; n. m. sing. and pl. means.*

Quero meio quilo de café. *I want half a kilo of coffee.*

Às duas e meia. *At two thirty.*

Meio irmão. *Half brother.*

Está meio cheio. *It's half full.*

Meio dólar. *Half dollar.*

Meios legais. *Legal means.*

Por meio de. *By means of.*

Meio de transporte. *Means of transportation.*

Por qualquer meio. *By any means.*

MEIO-DIA *m. noon.*

Ao meio-dia. *At noon.*

mel *m. honey.*

Lua-de-mel. *Honeymoon.*

melaço *m. molasses.*

melancia *f. watermelon.*

melancólico *adj. sad, melancholy.*

melão *m. melon.*

MELHOR *adj. and adv. better, best.*

Sinto-me melhor. *I feel better.*

Ele é o melhor aluno de todos. *He's the best student of all.*

Ela fala português melhor de que ele. *She speaks Portuguese better than he does.*

Talvez isso seja melhor. *Perhaps that would be better.*

Eu fiz o melhor que pude. *I did the best I could.*

Eu farei o melhor possível. *I'll do the best I can.*

Tanto melhor! *So much the better!*

Tanto melhor se ela não vem. *So much the better if she doesn't come.*

É melhor que você dirigir. *You better drive.*

Ele está um tanto melhor. *He's somewhat better.*

Cada vez melhor. *Better and better.*

Ele é o meu melhor amigo. *He's my best friend.*

melhora *f. improvement.*

melhorar *to improve.*

O tempo está melhorando (está a melhorar). *The weather is getting better.*

Melhorar de saúde. *To get better (health).*

melodia *f. melody.*

membrana *f. membrane, tissue.*

membro *m. member; part.*

memorável *adj. memorable.*

MEMÓRIA *f. memory; memoir; memorandum.*

Ela tem uma memória extraordinária. *She has an extraordinary memory.*

Eu não tenho boa memória. *I don't have a good memory.*

Aprenda-o de memória. *Learn it by heart.*

Em memória de . . . *In memory of . . .*

menção *f. mention.*

mencionar *to mention.*

mendigar *to beg.*

mendigo *m. beggar.*

menear *to move; to stir; to shake; to wag.*

MENINA *f. child, girl, young lady.*

MENINO *m. child, boy, young man.*

Ele é um menino muito inteligente. *He's a very intelligent boy.*

MENOR *adj. smaller; younger; least; n. m. and f. minor.*

Ele é menor. *He's a minor. He's underage.*

MENOS *adj. and adv.* less; least; minus; except.

É mais ou menos a mesma coisa. *It's more or less the same thing.*

Todos foram menos eu. *Everyone went but me.*

Estaremos lá às sete menos um quarto. *We'll be there at a quarter to seven.*

Não irei a menos que você me acompanhe. *I won't go unless you go with me (accompany me).*

Pelo menos. *At least.*

Menos mal. *Not so bad. It could be worse.*

Estarei em casa em menos de dez minutos. *I'll be home in less than ten minutes.*

Mais dia, menos dia. *Sooner or later.*

Cada vez menos. *Less and less.*

Menos que nunca. *Less than ever.*

menoscabo *m.* disdain, contempt; belittlement.

menosprezar *to* belittle, to disparage; to disdain.

menosprezo *m.* belittlement; scorn.

mensageiro *m.* messenger.

mensagem *f.* message.

Eu não recebi mensagem alguma. *I didn't receive any message at all.*

mensal *adj.* monthly.

mensalidade *f.* monthly allowance; monthly payment.

menta *f.* mint (flavor).

mental *adj.* mental.

mentalidade *f.* mentality.

MENTE *f.* mind, understanding.

Tenha-o sempre em mente. *Always bear it in mind.*

mentecapto *adj.* crazy.

mentir *to* lie.

mentira *f.* lie, falsehood.

mentiroso *adj.* lying, false, deceitful; *n. m.* liar.

menu *m.* menu.

mercado *m.* market, marketplace.

Mercado de valores. *Stock market.*

mercadologia *f.* marketing.

mercador *m.* merchant, dealer.

mercadoria *f.* commodity, merchandise, goods.

mercante *adj.* merchant, commercial; *n. m.* merchant.

Navio mercante. *Merchant ship.*

Marinha mercante. *Merchant marine.*

mercê *f.* favor; reward; mercy.

Estar à mercê de. *To be at the mercy of.*

mercearia *f.* grocery store.

mercenário *adj.* mercenary.

merecer *to* deserve, to merit.

merecido *adj.* deserved.

merenda *f.* light lunch, snack.

merendar *to* have a snack, to eat a light lunch.

merengue *m.* meringue.

mergulhar *to* dive, to plunge.

meridiano *adj., n. m.* meridian.

mérito *m.* merit, worth, value.

mero *adj.* mere, only, pure, simple.

MÊS *m.* month.

Há dois meses. *Two months ago.*

O mês que vem. *Next month.*

O mês passado. *Last month.*

Todos os meses. *Every month.*

MESA *f.* table; board, committee.

Ponha a mesa. *Set the table.*

Os convidados se sentaram à mesa. *The guests sat down at the table.*

mesclar *to* mix, to blend, to mingle.

MESMA *adj. f.* same, equal, self.

Ela mesma o disse. *She said so herself.*

Ele já não é a mesma pessoa. *He's no longer the same person.*

Somos da mesma idade. *We're of the same age.*

MESMO *adj. and adv.* same.

O mesmo dia. *The same day.*

É o mesmo homem que vi ontem. *He's the same man I saw yesterday.*

Eu mesmo o farei. *I'll do it myself.*

Agora mesmo. *Right now.*

Ali mesmo. *Right there. In that very place.*

Eu espero aqui mesmo. *I'll wait right here.*

Mesmo assim, não vou. *Even so, I won't go.*

Hoje mesmo o faço. *This very day I'll do it.*

Não é o mesmo. *It's not the same (thing).*

Ao mesmo tempo. *At the same time.*

É mesmo? *Is that so?*

É isso mesmo! *That's it (exactly)!*

Para mim é o mesmo. *It's all the same to me.*

Por isso mesmo não vamos. *For that very reason we're not going.*

mesquinho *adj.* niggardly, stingy.

mestiço *adj. and n. m.* of mixed blood, mestizo.

mestre *m. and f.* teacher; master; expert.

Cópia mestre. *Master copy.*

meta *f.* goal; end, object, aim.

metade *f.* half; middle, center.

Dê-me a metade. *Give me half.*

Cara metade. *Better half. Wife.*

Eu fui só a metade do caminho a pé. *I went only half of the way on foot.*

metafísica *f.* metaphysics.

metáfora *f.* metaphor.

metal *m.* metal.

metálico *adj.* metallic.

metalurgia *f.* metallurgy.

metamorfose *f.* metamorphosis.

metediço *adj.* meddlesome.

77

meteorito *m. meteorite.*

meteoro *m. meteor.*

meteorologia *f. meteorology.*

METER *to put; to put in, to insert.*

Meter a mão no bolso. *To put one's hand in one's pocket.*

Não consigo meter a chave na fechadura. *I can't get the key in the lock.*

Meter-se com. *To get mixed up with. To interfere.*

Meter-se em camisa de onze varas. *To get into a difficult situation.*

metódico *adj. methodical.*

método *m. method.*

metralhadora *f. machine gun.*

METRO *m. meter (39.37 inches).*

metrópole *f. metropolis.*

MEU *adj., pro. m. my, mine; pl.* **meus.**

Meu livro. (O meu livro.) *My book.*

Meus livros. (Os meus livros.) *My books.*

Este lenço não é meu. *This handkerchief is not mine.*

Eles são amigos meus. *They're friends of mine.*

Isto é meu. *This is mine. This belongs to me.*

O prazer é todo meu. *The pleasure is all mine.*

Meus senhores: *Gentlemen:*

A meu ver. *In my opinion.*

mexer *(x = sh) to stir; to disturb.*

mexer-se *(x = sh) to stir oneself, to move.*

mexicano *(x = sh) adj., n. m. Mexican.*

micróbio *m. microbe, germ.*

microcomputador *m. microcomputer.*

microcosmo *m. microcosm.*

microfilmar *to microfilm.*

microfilme *m. microfilm.*

microfone *m. microphone.*

microonda *f. microwave.*

Forno de microondas. *m. microwave oven.*

microprocessador *m. microprocessor.*

microscópio *m. microscope.*

migalha *f. crumb; bit.*

migrar *to migrate.*

MIL *thousand.*

Mil novecentos e sessenta e seis. *1966.*

Dois mil dólares. *Two thousand dollars.*

Duas mil casas. *Two thousand houses.*

milagre *m. miracle, marvel.*

milagroso *adj. miraculous.*

milésimo *adj., n. m. thousandth.*

milha *f. mile.*

Quantas milhas são daqui a Chicago? *How many miles is it from here to Chicago?*

milhão *m. million.*

MILHO *m. corn.*

miligrama *m. milligram.*

milímetro *m. millimeter.*

milionário *adj., n. m. millionaire.*

militante *adj. militant.*

militar *adj. military; n. m. military man, soldier.*

Serviço militar. *Military service.*

Escola militar. *Military academy.*

mil-réis *m. former monetary unit of Brazil, replaced by the cruzeiro* Ⓡ.

MIM *me, myself (after a prep.).*

Para mim. *For me.*

Para mim tanto faz. *It's all the same to me.*

Ai de mim! *Poor me!*

mimar *to pamper, to spoil (person).*

mina *f. mine.*

mineral *adj., n. m. mineral.*

mingau *m. a soft, mushy food; porridge.*

MINHA *(f. of* **meu**) *adj. and pro. my, mine; pl.* **minhas.**

Esta gravata é minha. *This tie is mine. This is my tie.*

Ela é uma amiga minha. *She is a friend of mine.*

Minhas senhoras: *Ladies:*

Minha casa é sua. *Make yourself at home. You're always welcome here.*

miniatura *f. miniature.*

mínimo *adj. minimum, least, smallest; n. m. minimum.*

Não tenho a mínima idéia (ideia). *I haven't the slightest idea.*

Este é o preço mínimo. *This is the lowest price.*

MINISTÉRIO *m. cabinet; ministry; a department of the government.*

Ministério de Educação e Saúde. *Department of Education and Welfare.*

Ministério da Guerra. *War Department.*

Ministério da Marinha. *Navy Department.*

Ministério da Aeronáutica. *Air Force Department.*

Ministério da Fazenda. *Treasury Department.*

MINISTRO *m. minister; secretary (of government department).*

Ministro da Agricultura. *Secretary of Agriculture.*

minoria *f. minority.*

minuta *f. note, memorandum.*

MINUTO *m. minute.*

Espere um minuto! *Wait a minute!*

miolo *m. core, interior; pl. brains.*

míope *adj. myopic, nearsighted.*

mirar *to look, to behold, to gaze at.*

miserável *adj. miserable, wretched; miserly.*

miséria *f. misery; destitution.*

Eles vivem na miséria. *They live in abject poverty.*

misericórdia *f. mercy.*

MISSA *f. mass.*

Missa cantada. *High mass.*

Missa do galo. *Midnight mass (Christmas).*

Ouvir missa. *To attend mass.*

missão *f. mission.*

missionário *m. missionary.*

mistério *m. mystery.*

misterioso *adj. mysterious.*

misto *adj. mixed.*

Colégio misto. *Coeducational school.*

mistura *f. mixture.*

misturar *to mix.*

mitigar *to mitigate, to ease.*

mito *m. myth.*

mitologia *f. mythology.*

miudeza *f. pl. details; odds and ends; notions.*

Loja de miudezas. *Notions shop.*

miúdo *adj. small; n. m. small child, kid ℗.*

Dinheiro miúdo. *Small change.*

mo *(contr. of* **m + o***) it to me, you to me, him to me.*

Ela escreveu-mo. *She wrote it to me.*

Eles mos mandaram. *They sent them to me.*

mobilar, (mobiliar) *to furnish (apartment, etc.).*

mobília *f. furniture.*

mobiliário *adj. of furniture; n. m. furniture.*

MOÇA *f. girl, young lady.*

moção *f. motion, movement; parliamentary motion.*

mochila *f. knapsack, backpack.*

mocidade *f. youth.*

MOÇO *m. boy, young man.*

Moço de recados. *Messenger.*

moda *f. fashion, style; manner.*

Os chapéus de palha estão fora de moda? *Are straw hats out of style?*

Estar na moda. *To be in style.*

A última moda. *The latest style.*

modalidade *f. modality; form.*

modelo *m. model; pattern.*

modem *m. modem.*

moderação *f. moderation.*

moderado *adj. moderate.*

moderar *to moderate; to restrain.*

MODERNO *adj. modern.*

Métodos modernos. *Modern methods.*

Arte moderna. *Modern art.*

modéstia *f. modesty.*

modesto *adj. modest.*

módico *adj. moderate, reasonable.*

É um preço módico. *It's a reasonable price.*

modificar *to modify, to alter.*

modismo *m. idiom.*

modista *f. dressmaker.*

MODO *m. mode, method, manner; mood.*

É o melhor modo de fazê-lo. *It's the best way to do it.*

Deste modo. *This way.*

De modo que. *So that.*

Fale de modo que todos possam ouvir. *Speak so that all can hear.*

De nenhum modo. *By no means. In no way. Not at all.*

Do mesmo modo. *In the same way.*

Modo condicional. *Conditional mood.*

moeda *f. money; coin.*

Papel moeda. *Paper currency. Bills.*

Pagar na mesma moeda. *To give as good as you get.*

mofa *f. mockery, derision.*

mofar *to mock, to deride.*

mofino *adj. unfortunate, unhappy.*

mogno (mógono) *m. mahogany.*

moído *adj. ground, crushed; worn out, exhausted.*

moinho *m. mill.*

mola *f. spring coiled metal; motivating force.*

Mola de relógio. *Watch spring.*

molde *m. mold, pattern, model.*

moldura *f. molding; picture frame.*

molecada *f. gang of boys, street urchins.*

moleque *m. urchin; black boy ℗.*

molestar *to disturb, to trouble, to bother, to annoy; to tease.*

moléstia *f. illness; discomfort.*

molesto *adj. bothersome; uncomfortable; annoying.*

molhar *to wet, to moisten, to dampen.*

Molhar a garganta. *To wet one's whistle.*

molho *m. gravy, sauce.*

Molho de salada. *Salad dressing.*

molusco *m. mollusk, shellfish.*

momentâneo *adj. momentary.*

MOMENTO *m. moment, instant.*

Não tenho nem um momento livre. *I don't have even a free moment.*

Espere um momento. *Wait a moment.*

A qualquer momento. *At any moment.*

De um momento para outro. *From one moment to the next.*

monarca *m. and f. monarch.*

monarquia *f. monarchy.*

mondar *to weed; to prune.*

monge *m. monk.*

monólogo *m. monologue.*

monopólio *m. monopoly.*

monopolizar *to monopolize.*

monotonia *f. monotony.*

monótono *adj. monotonous.*

monstro *m. monster.*

monstruosidade *f. monstrosity.*

monstruoso *adj. monstrous.*

monta *f. amount, total.*

De pouca monta. *Of little importance.*

montanha *f. mountain.*

montar *to mount; to ride (horseback); to*

amount to; to assemble; to set (a precious stone).

Montar a cavalo. *To get on a horse. To ride a horse.*

A quanto monta a conta? *How much does the bill come to?*

Monte esta máquina. *Assemble this machine.*

monte *m. mountain, hill; pile.*

montra *f. shopwindow, showcase.*

monumental *adj. monumental.*

monumento *m. monument.*

morada *f. dwelling, residence.*

morador *m. resident, inhabitant.*

moral *adj. moral; n. m. morality; morale; n. f. morals, ethics.*

morango *m. strawberry.*

MORAR *to dwell, to reside, to live.*

Onde o senhor mora? *Where do you live?*

mordedura *f. bite.*

morder *to bite.*

morena *adj. dark-complexioned; n. f. brunette.*

moreno *adj. dark-complexioned; n. m. brunet.*

moribundo *adj. dying.*

MORRER *to die.*

Ele morreu de fome. *He died of hunger.*

morro *m. hill, mound.*

Morro abaixo *(x = sh). Downhill.*

Morro acima. *Uphill.*

mortal *adj. mortal, fatal.*

mortalidade *f. mortality, death rate.*

MORTE *f. death.*

Morte súbita. *Sudden death.*

morteiro *m. mortar.*

mortificação *f. mortification.*

mortificar *to humiliate, to mortify; to vex.*

MORTO *adj. dead; m. dead person.*

Estou morto de fome. *I'm famished. I'm starved.*

Ele está morto. *He is dead.*

mosca *f. fly; a bore.*

moscatel *m. muscatel (grape or wine).*

moscovita *adj. and n. m. and f. Muscovite, Russian.*

mosquito *m. mosquito.*

mostarda *f. mustard.*

mostra *f. exhibition, show; pl. gestures.*

À mostra. *On view.*

mostrador *m. face, dial (clock, watch, etc.); showcase.*

MOSTRAR *to show; to exhibit; to prove.*

Ela me mostrou as costas. *She turned her back on me.*

mostruário *m. showcase.*

motivar *to motivate.*

motivo *m. motive, reason; motif.*

Sem motivo. *Groundless. Unfounded.*

motocicleta *f. motorcycle.*

MOTOR *m. motor, engine.*

Não chegamos a tempo porque o motor falhou. *We didn't arrive on time because the motor stalled.*

motorista *m. and f. motorist, driver.*

MÓVEL *adj. movable; n. m. a piece of furniture; motive.*

MOVER *to move.*

movimentar *to move, to get moving.*

movimento *m. movement, motion; traffic.*

Há muito movimento nesta rua. *There is a lot of traffic on this street.*

Pôr em movimento. *To set in motion.*

mucama, mucamba *both* Ⓑ *f. Mammy.*

muçulmano *adj., n. m. Muslim.*

muda *f. change, move.*

mudança *f. change, moving out.*

MUDAR *to change, to alter, to remove; to move out or away.*

Eu mudei de parecer. *I've changed my mind.*

Vamos mudar de casa. *We're going to move.*

Mudar de roupa. *To change clothes.*

Mudar de idéia. *To change one's mind.*

Quando ela chegou eles mudaram de conversa. *When she arrived, they changed the subject.*

mudo *adj. mute, silent.*

mugir *to moo; to roar.*

MUITO *adj. and adv. much, very much, very; pl. many, too many.*

Muito dinheiro *A lot of money.*

Ela escreve muito. *She writes a great deal.*

Muito mais barato. *Much cheaper.*

Muitos livros. *Many books.*

Isto é muito melhor. *This is much better.*

Com muito prazer. *Gladly. With much pleasure.*

Agradeço muito. *I appreciate it very much.*

Há muito tempo. *A long time ago.*

Está muito frio hoje. *It's very cold today.*

Não muito. *Not much.*

Ainda falta muito. *There's still a lot missing. There's still a lot to be done.*

Muito bem! *Fine! Excellent!*

Muitas vezes. *Often. Frequently.*

Muito obrigado. *Thank you very much.*

mula *f. female mule.*

muleta *f. crutch.*

MULHER *f. woman, wife.*

Mulher de casa. *Housewife.*

mulo *m. male mule.*

multa *f. fine, penalty.*

multar *to fine.*

multidão *f. multitude, crowd.*

multiplicar *to multiply.*

multiplicidade *f. multiplicity.*

múltiplo *adj. multiple.*

MUNDO m. world; multitude; great quantity.
  Ela quer ver o mundo. She wants to see the world.
  Tenho que comprar um mundo de coisas. I have to buy a whole lot of things.
  Todo o mundo quer ir. Everybody wants to go.
  O mundo todo. The whole world.
munheca f. wrist.
munição f. ammunition.
municipal adj. municipal.
municipalidade f. municipality; city council.
município m. municipality.
muralha wall (around a city, etc.); rampart.
murmurar to murmur; to whisper; to gossip.
murmúrio m. murmur, whisper.
muro m. wall.
murro m. blow, punch.
músculo m. muscle.
museu m. museum.
  Que dias o museu está aberto? What days is the museum open?
  O museu de Arte Moderna. The Museum of Modern Art.
MÚSICA f. music.
  Música clássica. Classical music.
  Música popular. Popular music.
  Música de dança. Dance music.
musical adj. musical.
músico adj. musical (said of people); n. m. musician.
mutável adj. changeable.
mutilar to mutilate.
mútuo adj. mutual.

N

NA (contr. of **em** + **a**) in the, on the, at the.
  Na cidade. In the city.
na (form of object pronoun **a** when used after a verb ending in a nasal sound) it, her, you
  Compraram-na. They bought it.
nabo m. turnip.
NAÇÃO f. nation.
  Nações Unidas. United Nations.
nacional adj. national.
nacionalidade f. nationality.
NADA nothing; not at all.
  Não desejo nada. I don't want anything.
  Nada de novo. Nothing new.
  Nada mais. Nothing more. Nothing else.
  De nada. Don't mention it.
  Não vale nada. It's worthless.
  Nada disso. None of that. Not at all.
  Não sei nada disso. I don't know anything about it.

Antes de mais nada. First of all.
  Nada de queixas (x = sh). No complaining! Let's have no complaints.
  Eu não tenho nada com isso. I have nothing to do with that.
  Ou tudo ou nada. All or nothing.
nadador m. swimmer.
nadar to swim, to float.
  Ela sabe nadar? Does she know how to swim?
nado m. swimming.
  Nado de peito. Breast stroke.
naipe m. suit (cards).
namorado adj. in love; m. lover, suitor, boyfriend.
namorar to court, to go out with.
namoro m. love affair, courtship.
NÃO no, not.
  Não falo espanhol. I don't speak Spanish.
  Eu tive que dizer que não. I had to say no.
  Ainda não. Not yet.
  Não sei. I don't know.
  Não a conheço. I don't know her.
  Não quer sentar-se? Won't you have a seat? Won't you sit down?
  Não há ninguém na sala. There's no one in the room.
  Não tenho mais. I don't have any more.
  Já não. No longer. Not any more.
  Não tenho muito tempo. I don't have much time.
  Não há de quê. Don't mention it. You're welcome.
  Não importa. It doesn't matter.
  Não me diga! You don't say! Don't tell me!
  A não ser que. Unless.
  Não obstante. Nevertheless. Notwithstanding.
  Acho que não. I don't think so.
  Ela não disse palavra. She didn't say anything.
  Não? or Não é? or Não é verdade? Isn't that so?
  Não faz mal. Don't bother. It's all right.
  Pois não! Certainly! Of course!
napolitano adj. Neapolitan; n. m. Neapolitan.
NAQUELA (contr. of **em** + **aquela**) f. in that, on that, in that one, on that one.
  Não há ninguém naquela sala. There is no one in that room.
NAQUELE (contr. of **em** + **aquele**) m. in that, on that, in that one, on that one.
  Naquele ano. In that year.
NAQUILO (contr. of **em** + **aquilo**) in that, on that.
narcótico adj., n. m. narcotic.
NARIZ m. nose.
  Nariz aquilino. Aquiline nose.

Ele mete o nariz em tudo. *He pokes his nose into everything.*

Torcer o nariz. *To turn up one's nose.*

Assoar o nariz. *To blow one's nose.*

narração *f. account, narration, story.*

narrar *to narrate, to relate.*

NASCER *to be born; to bud; to rise (sun); to originate.*

Ele nasceu em São Paulo mas os pais dele nasceram em Lisboa. *He was born in São Paulo, but his parents were born in Lisbon.*

nascimento *m. birth; origin, source.*

nata *f. cream; the best part.*

natação *f. swimming.*

natal *adj. natal, native; n. m. Christmas.*

natalício *adj.; n. m. birthday.*

nativo *adj. native.*

natural *adj. natural, native; n. m. native.*

Os alimentos naturais são saudáveis. *Natural foods are healthful.*

NATURALMENTE *of course, naturally.*

natureza *f. nature.*

naturismo *m. naturalism; back-to-nature movement.*

naturista *m. naturalist; believer in the back-to-nature movement.*

naufragar *to be shipwrecked; to fail.*

naufrágio *m. shipwreck; failure.*

náusea *f. nausea.*

náutica *f. navigation.*

náutico *adj. nautical.*

naval *adj. naval.*

navalha *f. razor; knife.*

navegação *f. navigation; shipping.*

navegador *m. navigator.*

navegante *m. navigator, seafarer.*

navegar *to navigate; to sail.*

navegável *adj. navigable.*

navio *m. ship.*

Navio mercante. *Merchant ship.*

Navio de guerra. *Warship.*

neblina *f. fog, mist.*

NECESSÁRIO *adj. necessary.*

É necessário fazê-lo hoje. *It must be done today.*

NECESSIDADE *f. necessity; need.*

Não há necessidade de registrar a carta. *It's not necessary to register the letter.*

A necessidade faz lei. *Necessity is its own law.*

necessitado *adj. poor, needy; n. m. person in need.*

NECESSITAR *to need; to be in need.*

Necessita mais alguma coisa? *Do you need anything else?*

necrologia *f. necrology, obituary.*

nefasto *adj. ill-fated; ominous.*

NEGAR *to deny; to refuse; to disown.*

Não o negue. *Don't deny it.*

Não o nego. *I don't deny it.*

Ele se negou a fazê-lo. *He refused to do it.*

negativa *f. refusal.*

negativo *adj. negative.*

Uma resposta negativa. *A negative answer. An answer in the negative.*

negligência *f. negligence, neglect.*

negligente *adj. negligent, careless.*

negociante *m. merchant, trader, businessman.*

negociar *to negotiate.*

NEGÓCIO *m. business; affair; transaction.*

Fazer bons negócios. *To do good business.*

Fazer mau negócio. *To get a bad deal.*

Abandonar os negócios. *To retire from business.*

Homem de negócios. *Businessman.*

Mulher de negócios. *Businesswoman.*

NEGRO *adj. black; gloomy; n. m. Negro.*

Vestir-se de negro. *To dress in black.*

Ele vê tudo negro. *He always looks on the dark side. He takes a gloomy view of everything.*

NELA *(contr. of em + ela) f. in it, on it, in her, on her.*

NELE *(contr. of em + ele) m. in it, on it, in him, on him.*

NEM *neither, either, nor, not.*

Não vou nem com você nem com ele. *I won't go either with you or with him.*

Nem meu irmão nem eu fomos. *Neither my brother nor I went.*

Nem sempre. *Not always.*

Nem sequer. *Not even.*

Nem mais nem menos. *Exactly. Neither more nor less.*

Nem peixe (x = sh) nem carne. *Neither fish nor fowl.*

NENHUM *not any, no, none, any.*

Nenhum homem. *No man.*

De modo nenhum. *By no means. No way.*

A nenhum preço. *Not at any price.*

Nenhuma das meninas. *None of the girls.*

Nenhum de nós. *None of us.*

Estar a nenhum. *To be broke Ⓑ.*

nervo *m. nerve.*

Nervo ótico (óptico). *Optic nerve.*

Ela é uma pilha de nervos. *She's a bundle of nerves.*

nervoso *adj. nervous.*

NESSA *(contr. of em + essa) f. in that, on that, in that one, on that one.*

Ponha o livro nessa mesa. *Put the book on that table.*

NESSE *(contr. of em + esse) m. in that, on that, in that one, on that one.*

Nesse caso eu não vou. *In that case, I won't go.*

NESTA (contr. of **em** + **esta**) f. in this, on this, in this one, on this one.

Não foram a outra cidade; ficaram nesta. They did not go to another city; they stayed in this one.

NESTE (contr. of **em** + **este**) m. in this, on this, in this one, on this one.

Não está nesse, está neste. It's not in that one, it's in this one.

neto m. grandchild.

neurótico adj. neurotic.

neutral adj. neutral.

neutro adj. neutral, neuter; n. m. neuter.

nevar to snow.

Está nevando (a nevar). It's snowing.

neve m. snow.

nevoeiro m. fog.

nicaraguano adj., n. m. Nicaraguan.

nicotina f. nicotine.

NINGUÉM nobody, anybody, no one, anyone, none.

Ninguém veio. Nobody came.

Ele nunca fala mal de ninguém. He never says anything bad about anyone.

Um joão-ninguém. A nobody.

ninho m. nest.

NISSO (contr. of **em** + **isso**) in that, of that.

NISTO (contr. of **em** + **isto**) in this, of this.

nítido adj. clear, bright, sharp.

nível m. level.

NO (contr. of **em** + **o**) in the, on the, at the.

No livro. In the book.

no (form of object pronoun **o** when used after a verb ending in a nasal sound) it, him, you.

Viram-no ontem. They saw him yesterday.

nó m. knot; tie; joint; knuckle.

nobre adj. noble; n. m. nobleman.

nobreza f. nobility.

noção f. notion, idea.

nocivo adj. harmful.

nogueira f. walnut tree; walnut (wood).

NOITE f. night, evening.

Boa noite. Good evening. Good night.

Hoje à noite. Tonight.

Ontem à noite. Last night.

Todas as noites. Every night.

De noite. At night. In the evening.

À meia-noite. At midnight.

noivado m. engagement; wedding.

noivar to get engaged; to be engaged.

Carlos noivou-se com uma Americana. Charles got engaged to an American girl.

noivo m. sweetheart, boyfriend, fiancé, bridegroom.

Os noivos. The newlyweds.

nojo m. nausea; disgust.

NOME m. name; noun.

Ponha aqui o nome e o endereço (a direcção). Put your name and address here.

Eu a conheço de nome. I know her by name.

Nome de batismo (baptismo). Baptismal name.

Nome de família. Family name. Last name.

Qual é o seu nome? What is your name?

Nome coletivo (colectivo). Collective noun.

nomeação f. nomination, appointment.

nomear to appoint, to nominate; to name.

Ele foi nomeado diretor (director). He was appointed director.

nonagésimo adj., n. m. ninetieth.

nono adj., n. m. ninth.

nora f. daughter-in-law.

nordeste adj., n. m. northeast.

norma f. norm, rule, standard, model.

normal adj. normal.

normalidade f. normality, normalcy.

noroeste adj., n. m. northwest.

NORTE adj., n. m. north.

Norte América. North America.

norte-americano adj., n. m. North American.

norueguês adj., n. m. Norwegian.

NOS us, to us, ourselves.

Levantamo-nos imediatamente. We got up immediately.

Elas não nos disseram nada. They didn't say anything to us.

Eles não nos deixaram entrar. They did not let us enter.

NÓS we, us.

Nós vamos hoje; elas vão amanhã. We are going today; they are going tomorrow.

Estes livros são para nós? Are these books for us?

NOSSO our.

Nossa cidade. Our town.

Nossa irmã. Our sister.

Nosso irmão. Our brother.

De quem é? É nossa. Whose is it? It's ours.

NOTA f. note; grade, mark.

Tomar nota. To take note.

Nota promissória. Promissory note.

O aluno recebeu boas notas. The student received good grades.

Digno de nota. Noteworthy.

notar to note, to notice.

Não notei nada. I didn't notice anything.

notário m. notary.

notável adj. notable; worthy of notice.

Ele é um homem notável. He's an outstanding man.

NOTÍCIA f. a piece of news, information, notice; pl. news.

Boa notícia. *A piece of good news.*
As notícias do dia. *The news of the day.*
Más notícias. *Bad news.*
notificação *f. notification.*
notificar *to notify, to inform.*
notório *adj. well-known, evident.*
noturno (nocturno) *adj. nocturnal, night, in the night.*
novato *m. novice, beginner.*
NOVE *nine.*
novecentos *nine hundred.*
novela *f. novelette, novel.*
novelista *m. and f. novelist.*
NOVEMBRO *m. November.*
NOVENTA *ninety.*
noviço *m. novice, apprentice.*
NOVIDADE *f. novelty; news.*
Há alguma novidade? *Anything new?*
Não há novidade. *Nothing new.*
A última novidade. *The latest thing.*
Cheio de novidades. *Full of airs.*
NOVO *adj. new.*
Esse chapéu é novo? *Is that hat new? Is that a new hat?*
Que há de novo? *What's new?*
É preciso fazê-lo de novo. *It's necessary to do it again. It has to be done again.*
Feliz Ano Novo! *Happy New Year!*
O irmão mais novo. *The younger brother.*
noz *f. nut; walnut.*
nu *adj. naked, nude, bare.*
nublado *adj. cloudy.*
nublar *to become cloudy, to cloud.*
nuca *f. nape (neck).*
nuclear *adj. nuclear.*
núcleo *m. nucleus.*
nulidade *f. nullity; nonentity; incompetent person.*
nulo *adj. null, void; n. m. worthless person.*
NUM *(contra. of em + um) in a, on a, to a.*
Num livro. *In a book.*
NUMA *(contr. of em + uma) in a, on a, to a.*
Numa mesa. *On a table.*
numerar *to number.*
NÚMERO *m. number, figure.*
O número de meu telefone é . . . *My telephone number is . . .*
Escreva o número. *Write the number.*
Números arábicos. *Arabic numerals.*
Números pares. *Even numbers.*
Números ímpares. *Odd numbers.*
Número cardinal. *Cardinal number.*
Número ordinal. *Ordinal number.*
Sem número. *Countless. Endless.*
NUNCA *never; ever.*
Nunca! *Never!*
Nunca vou ao cinema. *I never go to the movies.*
Quase nunca. *Hardly ever.*

Nunca mais. *Never again.*
Mais vale tarde do que nunca. *Better late than never.*
nupcial *adj. nuptial.*
núpcias *f. pl. nuptials, wedding.*
nutrição *f. nutrition, nourishment.*
nutrir *to nourish, to feed.*
nutritivo *adj. nutritious, nourishing.*
nuvem *f. cloud.*

O

O *m. the, it, him.*
O livro. *The book.*
Comprei-o. *I bought it.*
Eu não o vi. *I didn't see him.*
Nós não os vimos. *We did not see them.*
Os alunos estão na escola. *The students are in school.*
obcecado *adj. obsessed.*
obedecer *to obey.*
Ele sempre obedece. *He always obeys.*
obediência *f. obedience.*
obediente *adj. obedient.*
obeso *adj. obese, fat.*
objetar (objectar) *to object, to oppose.*
OBJETO (OBJECTO) *m. object, thing; purpose, aim.*
Por fim ele logrou seu objeto. *At last he reached his goal.*
Objeto direto (directo): *Direct object.*
oblíquo *adj. oblique.*
OBRA *f. work (of art, etc.); book; deed; action.*
É uma obra em quatro volumes. *The work is in four volumes.*
Obra-prima. *Masterpiece.*
Obras públicas. *Public works.*
Obra de arte. *Work of art.*
Obra de consulta. *Reference book. Reference work.*
Obra dramática. *Dramatic work. Play.*
Mãos à obra! *Let's get to work! To work!*
obrar *to work; to act; to operate.*
obreiro *m. worker, workman.*
obrigação *f. obligation, duty.*
OBRIGADO *adj. obliged, thankful; thanks, thank you.*
Muito obrigado. *Thank you very much.*
obrigar *to oblige.*
obrigatório *adj. obligatory.*
obscurecer *to darken, to grow dark.*
obscuridade *f. obscurity.*
obscuro *adj. obscure, dark.*
Uma noite obscura. *A dark night.*
obsequiar *to oblige, to favor.*
obséquio *m. favor, kindness.*

Agradeço muito o seu obséquio. *Thank you for your kindness.*

observar *to observe, to notice; to obey.*
   É preciso observar as regras. *One must follow the rules.*

observatório *m. observatory.*

obsessão *f. obsession.*

obstáculo *m. obstacle.*

obstinado *adj. obstinate.*

obstruir *to obstruct, to block.*
   Obstruir o tráfico. *To block traffic.*

obtenção *f. attainment.*

OBTER *to obtain, to get; to attain.*
   Ele obteve um bom emprego. *He got a good job.*

obturador *m. shutter (camera); plug, stopper.*

obtuso *adj. obtuse, blunt.*

obus *m. howitzer.*

óbvio *adj. obvious, evident.*

OCASIÃO *f. occasion, opportunity.*
   Eu perdi uma boa ocasião. *I missed a good opportunity.*
   Eu irei na primeira ocasião que tiver. *I'll go the first chance I have.*
   Em outra ocasião. *Some other time.*
   Por ocasião de. *On the occasion of.*

ocasionar *to cause, to bring about.*

ocaso *m. setting (sun); decline.*

oceano *m. ocean.*
   Oceano Atlântico. *Atlantic Ocean.*
   Oceano Pacífico. *Pacific Ocean.*

ocidental *adj. western, occidental.*

ócio *m. idleness, leisure.*

ociosidade *f. idleness, leisure.*

ocioso *adj. idle; lazy.*

octagésimo *eightieth.*

ocorrência *f. event.*

ocorrer *to happen, to occur.*
   Não me ocorreu. *It didn't occur to me.*

oculista *m. and f. optician.*

óculos *m. pl. eyeglasses.*
   Usar óculos. *To wear glasses.*

ocultar *to conceal, to hide.*

oculto *adj. concealed, hidden.*

ocupação *f. occupation, business; occupancy.*

OCUPADO *adj. busy; occupied; engaged.*
   Estou muito ocupado. *I am very busy.*

OCUPAR *to occupy; to take possession of.*
   Os móveis ocupam muito lugar. *The furniture takes up a lot of space.*

odiar *to hate.*

ódio *m. hatred.*

odioso *adj. hateful.*

OESTE *m. west.*

ofender *to offend.*

ofensa *f. offense.*

ofensiva *f. offensive.*
   Tomar a ofensiva. *To take the offensive.*

OFERECER *to offer; to present.*

Ele me ofereceu dois dólares pelo livro. *He offered me two dollars for the book.*

oferecimento *m. offer.*

oferta *f. offer, offering; gift.*
   É a última oferta. *It's the last (final) offer.*
   Oferta e procura. *Supply and demand.*

oficial *adj. official; n. m. official, officer.*

oficina *f. workshop.*

ofício *m. job, occupation.*

oh *oh.*

oi *popular Brazilian greeting; corresponds to* "hi," "hiya."

oitavo *adj., n. m. eighth.*

OITENTA *eighty.*

OITO *eight.*
   De hoje a oito dias. *A week from today.*

oitocentos *eight hundred.*

olá *hello!*

óleo *m. oil.*
   Óleo de amendoim. *Peanut oil.*
   Óleo combustível. *Fuel oil.*

olfato *m. sense of smell, smell.*

olhada *f. glance, look.*
   Dar uma olhada. *To take a look.*

olhadela *f. glimpse, glance, look.*

OLHAR *to look at, to glance at, to watch; n. m. glance, look.*
   Ele olhou para ela. *He looked at her.*
   Olhar com bons olhos. *To look upon with favor.*

OLHO *m. eye; attention, care.*
   Eu tenho os olhos cansados de tanto ler. *My eyes are tired from reading so much.*
   Olho de agulha. *Eye of a needle.*
   Num abrir e fechar de olhos. *In the blink of an eye.*
   Quatro olhos vêem mais que dois. *Two heads are better than one.*

oliva *f. olive.*

olor *m. fragrance, odor.*

oloroso *adj. fragrant.*

olvidar *to forget.*

olvido *m. forgetfulness.*

ombro *m. shoulder.*
   Encolher os ombros. *To shrug the shoulders.*

omelete, omeleta *f. omelet.*

omissão *f. omission.*

omitir *to omit, to leave out.*
   Você omitiu a primeira parte. *You left out the first part.*

onça *f. ounce; wildcat.*
   Tempo da onça. *Long ago.*
   Amigo da onça. *False friend.*

onda *f. wave.*
   Onda curta. *Shortwave (radio).*
   Onda sonora. *Sound wave.*

ONDE *where.*

Onde está a tinta? *Where is the ink?*
Onde vendem romances brasileiros? *Where do they sell Brazilian novels?*
De onde (or donde) é o seu professor? *Where is your teacher from?*
ondular *to wave.*
ônibus (autocarro) *m. bus.*
ONTEM *yesterday.*
Eles chegaram ontem. *They arrived yesterday.*
ONZE *eleven.*
opa! *wow!*
opaco *adj. opaque; dull.*
opção *f. option, choice.*
ópera *f. opera.*
operação *f. operation.*
operar *to operate (medical); to produce, to work.*
operário *m. worker, workman.*
opinar *to give an opinion.*
opinião *f. opinion.*
Esta é a opinião de todos. *Everyone is of this opinion.*
Eu mudei de opinião. *I changed my opinion.*
opôr *to oppose.*
opôr-se *to oppose.*
Eu me oponho a essa resolução. *I am against that resolution.*
oportunidade *f. opportunity.*
Esta é uma boa oportunidade. *This is a good opportunity.*
oportuno *adj. opportune.*
oposição *f. opposition.*
opositor *adj. opposing; n. m. opponent, competitor.*
oposto *adj. opposed, opposite, contrary.*
opressão *f. oppression.*
opressivo *adj. oppressive.*
opressor *m. oppressor.*
oprimir *to oppress.*
optar *to choose.*
óptico, ótico (óptico) *adj. optic, optical; m. optician.*
ora *now, well.*
Ora! *Well!*
Por ora. *For the time being.*
oração *f. prayer; speech; clause, sentence.*
orador *m. speaker, orator.*
oral *adj. oral.*
orar *to pray; to ask for.*
orçamento *m. budget.*
ORDEM *f. order; method; rule.*
Às suas ordens. *At your service.*
Por ordem de . . . *By order of . . .*
Chamar à ordem. *To call to order.*
Em ordem. *In order.*
A ordem do dia. *The order of the day.*
Fora de ordem. *Out of order.*

ordenado *m. salary.*
ordenança *f. ordinance; m. and f. orderly (military).*
ordenar *to order, to command; to ordain; to arrange.*
ordenhar *to milk.*
ordinal *adj. ordinal.*
ordinário *adj. ordinary, common.*
orelha *f. ear.*
Orelha dum livro. *Flap of a book.*
órfão *m. orphan.*
orgânico *adj. organic.*
organismo *m. organism.*
organização *f. organization.*
organizar *to organize, to form, to arrange.*
órgão *m. organ.*
orgulho *m. pride.*
orgulhoso *adj. proud, haughty.*
oriental *adj. oriental, eastern; n. m. Oriental.*
orientar *to orient.*
orientar-se *to orient oneself, to get one's bearings.*
É difícil orientar-se nesta cidade. *It is difficult to get one's bearings in this city.*
ORIENTE *m. orient, east.*
origem *f. origin, source.*
original *adj. original.*
originalidade *f. originality.*
originar *to cause, to originate.*
ornamento *m. ornament, decoration.*
ornar *to adorn.*
orquestra *f. orchestra.*
ortografia *f. spelling.*
orvalho *m. dew.*
osso *m. bone.*
Em carne e osso. *In the flesh. In person.*
ostentar *to display, to show off, to boast.*
ostra *f. oyster.*
ótico *adj. optical; otic.*
otimismo (optimismo) *m. optimism.*
otimista (optimista) *m. optimist.*
ótimo (óptimo) *adj. excellent, wonderful.*
Ótimo! *Excellent! Great!*
OU *or, either.*
Compre-me dois ou três. *Buy me two or three.*
OURO *m. gold, money; pl. diamonds (cards).*
Sim, tenho um relógio de ouro. *Yes, I have a gold watch.*
ousar *to dare.*
OUTONO *m. autumn, fall.*
outorgar *to grant; to agree to.*
OUTRO *adj. other, another.*
Não quero este, quero outro. *I don't want this one; I want the other one.*
Prefiro os outros. *I prefer the other ones.*
Outro dia. *Another day.*
No outro dia. *The other day.*

Outra garrafa de cerveja! *Another bottle of beer!*
Outra vez. *Again.*
Outras vezes. *Other times.*
OUTUBRO *m. October.*
OUVIDO *m. hearing; ear.*
Dor de ouvido. *Earache.*
Ela tem ouvido para música. *She has an ear for music.*
Entrar por um ouvido e sair pelo outro. *To go in one ear and out the other.*
ouvinte *m. and f. listener; auditor.*
OUVIR *to hear, to listen.*
Não ouço nada. *I can't hear a thing.*
Não ouvi o despertador. *I didn't hear the alarm clock.*
Ouvir missa. *To hear mass.*
Ouvimos dizer que ela é atriz. *We heard that she's an actress.*
ovação *f. ovation.*
oval *adj. oval.*
ovelha *f. sheep.*
OVO *egg.*
Ovos duros. *Hard-boiled eggs.*
Ovos estrelados. *Fried eggs.*
Ovos mexidos (x = sh). *Scrambled eggs.*
A clara do ovo. *The white of the egg.*
A gema do ovo. *The yolk of the egg.*
oxalá (x = sh) *let's hope; God willing.*
Oxalá não esteja chovendo. *Let's hope it's not raining*

P

pá *f. shovel, spade; blade (propeller).*
Pá de hélice. *Propeller blade.*
pacato *adj. quiet, peaceful.*
paciência *f. patience.*
Tenha paciência. *Be patient. Have patience.*
Estou perdendo (a perder) a paciência. *I'm losing my patience.*
paciente *adj., n. m. and f. patient.*
pacífico *adj. peaceful; mild.*
PACOTE *m. package, bundle.*
pacto *m. pact, agreement.*
pactuar *to reach an agreement, to sign a pact.*
padaria *f. bakery.*
padecer *to suffer, to bear.*
padecimento *m. suffering.*
padeiro *m. baker.*
padrão *m. standard; pattern (sewing, etc.).*
Padrão de vida. *Standard of living.*
padrasto *m. stepfather.*
padre *m. priest, Father.*
Padre-nosso. *Our Father. The Lord's Prayer.*

Padre Tomás. *Father Thomas.*
padrinho *m. godfather; best man; sponsor.*
paga *f. payment; pay, wages, fee.*
pagador *m. payer, paymaster, teller.*
pagamento *m. payment; pay.*
Pagamento adiantado. *Payment in advance.*
Dia de pagamento. *Payday.*
Pagamento a (em) prestações. *Payment in installments.*
pagão *adj. pagan; n. m. pagan.*
PAGAR *to pay, to pay for.*
Quanto lhe pagaram? *How much did they pay you?*
Pagar na mesma moeda. *To pay back in the same coin. To give as good as you get.*
Pagar uma visita. *To pay a visit.*
Pagar a prestações. *To pay in installments.*
Pagar caro. *To pay dearly.*
PÁGINA *f. page (book).*
Em que página está? *On what page is it?*
pago *adj. paid; m. pay, wages.*
PAI *m. father; pl. parents.*
Tal pai, tal filho. *Like father, like son.*
pai-de-santo *m. priest of Afro-Brazilian ritual, medicine man* ⑧.
painel *m. panel.*
pairar *to hover.*
país *m. country (nation).*
paisagem *f. landscape, view.*
paisano *adj. civilian; m. civilian; fellow countryman.*
À paisano. *In civilian clothes. In plainclothes.*
paixão (x = sh) *f. passion.*
palácio *m. palace.*
paladar *m. palate; taste.*
PALAVRA *f. word; promise.*
Que quer dizer esta palavra? *What does this word mean?*
Ele me tirou a palavra da boca. *He took the words right out of my mouth.*
Não falte à sua palavra. *Don't go back on your word.*
Peço a palavra? *May I have the floor?*
Ele me deu a sua palavra. *He gave me his word.*
Em poucas palavras. *In short. In a few words.*
Cumprir a palavra. *To keep one's word.*
Em toda a extensão da palavra. *In the full sense of the word.*
Não dizer sequer uma palavra. *Not to say a word.*
palavrão *m. a curse word, an ugly word.*
palco *m. stage.*
palestino *adj., n. m. Palestinian.*
palestra *f. talk, conversation, lecture.*
PALETÓ *n. man's jacket, coat.*
palha *f. straw.*

Chapéu de palha. *Straw hat.*
palhaço *m. clown.*
pálido *adj. pale.*
palito *m. toothpick.*
palma *f. palm; pl. applause.*
    Bater palmas. *To applaud. To clap.*
palmada *f. slap.*
palmeira *f. palm tree.*
palmo *m. span (of the hand).*
palpável *adj. palpable, evident.*
pálpebra *f. eyelid.*
palpitar *to beat, to throb, to palpitate.*
palrar *to chatter.*
paludismo *m. malaria.*
pampa *f. pampa, treeless plain.*
panamenho *adj., n. m. Panamanian.*
pança *f. paunch, belly.*
pancada *f. blow; hit.*
pandeireta *f. small tambourine.*
pandeiro *m. tambourine.*
pane *f. breakdown (due to motor).*
panela *f. pot, pan.*
panfleto *m. pamphlet.*
pânico *adj., n. m. panic.*
PANO *m. cloth, material; curtain (theatre).*
    Pano de mesa. *Tablecloth.*
panorama *m. panorama, landscape, view.*
panqueca Ⓑ *f. pancake.*
pantalha *f. lampshade; screen.*
pântano *m. swamp, marsh.*
panteísmo *m. pantheism.*
pantomima *f. pantomime.*
PÃO *m. bread.*
    Pão com manteiga. *Bread and butter.*
    O pão nosso de cada dia. *Our daily bread.*
pãozinho *m. roll (bread).*
PAPA *m. Pope.*
PAPÁ *m. papa, daddy.*
papagaio *m. parrot; kite.*
PAPAI *m. papa, daddy.*
    Papai Noel. *Santa Claus.*
PAPEL *m. paper; role.*
    Preciso duma folha de papel. *I need a
    sheet of paper.*
    Escreva-o neste papel. *Write it on this
    paper.*
    Há papel de escrever na gaveta. *There's
    some writing paper in the drawer.*
    Papel moeda. *Paper currency. Bills.*
    Papel de seda. *Tissue paper.*
    Papel carbono. *Carbon paper.*
    Papel de embrulho. *Wrapping paper.*
    Papel em branco. *Blank paper.*
    Saco de papel. *Paper bag.*
    Desempenhar um papel. *To play a role. To
    play a part.*
papelão *m. cardboard.*
papelaria *f. stationery shop.*
paquete *m. steamship.*

PAR *adj. equal; par; even (number); n. m.
    pair, couple; peer.*
    O cruzeiro e o escudo estavam ao par. *The
    cruzeiro and the escudo were at par.*
    Um par de luvas. *A pair of gloves.*
    Números pares e ímpares. *Even and odd
    numbers.*
    Ela é uma senhora sem par. *There's
    nobody like her. She's the greatest.*
PARA *for, to, until, about, in order to, toward.*
    Para quê? *What for? For what purpose?*
    Para quem é isto? *Who is this for?*
    Esta carta é para o senhor. *This letter is
    for you.*
    Para que serve isto? *What's this for?
    What's this good for?*
    Deixemos *(x = sh)* para amanhã. *Let's
    leave (it) for tomorrow.*
    Ela tem talento para a música. *She has a
    gift for music.*
    Vou agora para não chegar tarde. *I'm
    leaving now in order not to arrive late.*
    Quando sai o trem (comboio) para a
    capital? *When does the train for the
    capital leave?*
    Para sempre. *Forever.*
    Para onde foram? *Where did they go?*
    Para cá e para lá. *To and fro.*
parabéns *m. pl. congratulations.*
parábola *f. parable, parabola.*
pára-brisa *m. windshield.*
pára-choque *m. bumper (car).*
PARADA *f. stopping place; stop, halt; pause;
    parade; wager.*
    Ponto de parada (paragem). *Stopping
    place.*
    Parada de ônibus Ⓑ (Paragem de autocarro
    Ⓟ). *Bus stop.*
    Cinco minutos de parada. *Five minutes'
    stop.*
paradeiro *m. whereabouts.*
parado *adj. stopped, still.*
paradoxo *(x = ks) m. paradox.*
paraense *adj., n. m. and f. of the state of Pará
    in Brazil.*
parafuso *m. screw.*
    Chave de parafuso. *Screwdriver.*
PARAGEM *f. stopping place; stop.*
    Paragem de autocarro Ⓟ (Parada de ônibus
    Ⓑ). *Bus stop.*
parágrafo *m. paragraph.*
paraguaio *adj., n. m. Paraguayan.*
paraibano *adj., n. m. of the state of Paraíba in
    Brazil.*
paraíso *m. paradise.*
paralelo *adj. and m. parallel.*
paralisar *to paralyze.*
paralisia *f. paralysis.*
paralítico *adj. and m. paralytic.*

paranaense *adj., n. m. and f. of the state of Paraná in Brazil.*

parapeito *m. parapet, rampart; windowsill.*

pára-quedas *m. parachute.*

pára-quedista *m. parachutist.*

PARAR *to stop, to halt, to stay; to bet.*

Por que paramos aqui? *Why are we stopping here?*

Pare em frente da estação. *Stop in front of the station.*

(O) meu relógio parou. *My watch stopped.*

Quando vai parar de chover? *When is it going to stop raining?*

Em que hotel pararam? *At what hotel did you stay?*

Sem parar. *Continuously.*

pára-raios *m. lightning rod.*

parasita *m. and f. parasite.*

pára-sol *m. parasol.*

parceiro *m. partner.*

parcela *f. parcel, portion.*

parcelado *adj. divided.*

parcelar *to parcel out.*

parceria *f. partnership.*

parcial *adj. partial.*

parcialidade *f. partiality, bias.*

parco *adj. economical, thrifty.*

pardo *adj. brown, dark; n. m. mulatto.*

PARECER *to appear, to seem, to look; n. m. opinion; appearance.*

Que lhe parece? *What do you think (of it)?*

Parece-me muito caro. *It seems awfully expensive to me.*

Ao que parece. *Apparently.*

Parece que vai chover. *It looks as if it's going to rain*

Dê-me o seu parecer. *Give me your opinion.*

Eu também sou do mesmo parecer. *I'm also of the same opinion.*

Ela se parece muito com a tia. *She looks very much like her aunt.*

parecido *adj. similar, like.*

PAREDE *f. wall.*

As paredes têm ouvidos. *The walls have ears.*

Estar entre a espada e a parede. *To be between a rock and a hard place.*

parelha *f. matching item, pair.*

PARENTE *m. relative, relation.*

Não tenho parentes nesta cidade. *I don't have family in this city.*

parêntese *m. parenthesis.*

Parênteses quadrados. *Brackets.*

parir *to give birth.*

parisiense *adj., n. m. and f. Parisian.*

parlamento *m. parliament.*

paróquia *f. parish.*

paroquiano *m. parishioner.*

parque *m. park.*

Parque de diversões. *Amusement park.*

parreira *f. trellised grapevine.*

parreiral *m. grape arbor; arbor.*

PARTE *f. part, portion, share; side; role; party (dispute).*

Em que parte da cidade mora? *In what part of the city do you live?*

Cada um pagou a sua parte. *Each one paid his share.*

Trago isto da parte do senhor Nunes. *This is from Mr. Nunes.*

Cumprimente João da minha parte. *Say hi to John for me.*

Li a maior parte do livro. *I read most of the book.*

O senhor o viu (viu-o) em alguma parte? *Did you see him anywhere?*

Em nenhuma parte. *Nowhere.*

Em parte. *In part. Partly.*

Em grande parte. *Largely. In large part.*

Em toda parte. *Everywhere.*

Dar parte. *To inform. To notify.*

Por toda parte. *Everywhere.*

Por minha parte. *For my part. As far as I'm concerned.*

participação *f. participation; share; announcement.*

Participação de casamento. *Marriage announcement.*

participar *to participate, to take part; to share; to announce, to inform, to notify.*

Vocês participaram no jogo? *Did you take part in the game?*

Não poderemos participar da festa. *We won't be able to attend the reception.*

particípio *m. participle.*

Particípio passado. *Past participle.*

Particípio presente. *Present participle.*

particular *adj. particular, private; m. pl. particulars, details.*

Em particular. *In private. In particular.*

Escola particular. *Private school.*

particularidade *f. particularity, peculiarity.*

PARTIDA *f. departure; item, entry; game, match.*

Ponto de partida. *Starting point. Point of departure.*

Uma partida de xadrez (x = sh). *A game of chess.*

Partida dobrada. *Double entry (account).*

partidário *adj., n. m. partisan, follower, supporter.*

Ser partidário de. *To be in favor of.*

Máquina partidária. *Party machinery.*

PARTIDO *adj. divided, split, broken; n. m. party; advantage; side.*

Está partido! *It's broken!*

Que partido vamos tomar? *Which side are we going to take?*

O Partido Democrático. *The Democratic party.*

O Partido Republicano. *The Republican party.*

O Partido Trabalhista. *The Labor party.*

PARTIR *to divide, to split; to leave; to cut; to break.*

O avião está para partir. *The plane is about to leave.*

Vamos partir na sexta. *We are going to leave on Friday.*

Preciso duma faca para partir o pão. *I need a knife to cut the bread.*

A partir de hoje. *From today on.*

Parti-me a perna em criança. *I broke my leg as a child.*

parto *m. childbirth.*

parvo *n. m. blockhead; adj. foolish.*

Páscoa *f. Easter; Passover.*

pasmar *to bewilder; to amaze.*

passa *f. raisin.*

passadiço *m. walkway; passageway.*

PASSADO *adj. past, done; n. m. past; past tense.*

O ano passado. *Last year.*

A semana passada. *Last week.*

Esqueçamos o passado. *Let's forget the past.*

Um bife bem passado. *A well-done steak.*

Mal passado. *Rare (meat)*

passageiro *adj. passing, transitory; m. passenger; traveler.*

passagem *f. passage; fare.*

Passagem de ida e volta. *A round-trip ticket.*

Quanto custa a passagem? *What is the fare?*

passaporte *m. passport.*

PASSAR *to pass, to go by, to go across; to come over, to come in; to spend (time); to approve; to happen.*

Passe-me o sal, por favor. *Please pass the salt.*

Passe por aqui. *Come this way.*

Pode passar por meu escritório amanhã? *Can you drop by my office tomorrow?*

Ele passa por brasileiro mas é americano. *He passes for a Brazilian, but he's an American.*

Os anos passam rapidamente. *The years go by quickly.*

Passe bem. *Good-bye. Take it easy.*

Passar por alto. *To overlook. To omit.*

Passar a ferro. *To iron. To press (clothes).*

Muitos dias ele passava fome. *Many days he would go hungry.*

Passar um telegrama. *To send a telegram.*

Como tem passado? *How have you been?*

pássaro *m. bird.*

Mais vale um pássaro na mão que dois voando (a voar). *A bird in the hand is worth two in the bush.*

passatempo *m. pastime, amusement.*

passe *m. pass, permit; free ticket.*

PASSEAR *to walk, to take a walk; to ride.*

PASSEIO *m. walk, stroll; ride; trip.*

Dar um passeio. *To go for a walk.*

passivo *adj. passive; n. m. liability.*

PASSO *m. step; pass; passageway; gait.*

Está a dois passos daqui. *It's only a few steps from here.*

Passo a passo. *Step by step.*

A cada passo. *At every step. Frequently.*

Ao passo que. *While. As.*

Quem vai dar o primeiro passo? *Who will take the first step?*

pasta *f. paste; dough; briefcase.*

Pasta de dente(s). *Toothpaste.*

pastagem *f. pasture.*

pastel *m. pastry; pastel.*

pastelaria *f. pastry shop.*

pasteleiro *m. pastry cook.*

pastilha *f. lozenge, drop.*

pasto *m. pasture, food.*

pastor *m. shepherd; pastor.*

pata *f. paw; foot; female duck.*

Pata anterior. *Foreleg.*

Pata posterior. *Hind leg.*

Meter a pata. *To put your foot in your mouth. To make a blunder.*

patente *adj. patent, obvious; f. patent; privilege.*

patife *n. m. lowlife, scoundrel, "piece of work."*

patim *m. skate.*

Patins de rodas. *Roller skates.*

Patins de gelo. *Ice skates.*

patinar *to skate.*

pátio *m. patio, courtyard, yard.*

pato *m. drake, male duck.*

patranha *f. lie, fib.*

patrão *m. master; skipper; employer; boss; landlord.*

pátria *f. fatherland, native country.*

patriota *m. and f. patriot.*

patriotismo *m. patriotism.*

patrocinar *to patronize (a business, etc.); to sponsor.*

patrono *m. patron, sponsor.*

patrulha *f. patrol.*

PAU *adj. boring; n. m. pole, stick, club; wood.*

Pau de bandeira. *Flagpole.*

A meio pau. *At half-mast.*

Ele levou pau. *He failed (an examination)* ⑧.

paulista *adj., n. m. and f. of the state of São Paulo in Brazil.*

paulistano *adj., n. m. of the city of São Paulo in Brazil.*

pausa *f. pause.*

pauta *guidelines; ruled lines.*

pavão *m. peacock.*

pavilhão *m. pavilion; tent; pennant.*

pavimento *m. pavement.*

pavio *m. wick.*

> Pavio de vela. *Candlewick.*
> De fio a pavio. *From beginning to end.*

pavor *m. fear, terror.*

PAZ *f. peace.*

> Por que não fazem as pazes? *Why don't you make up? Why don't you bury the hatchet?*
> Em paz. *In peace.*
> Deixe-me *(x = sh)* em paz! *Leave me alone!*

PÉ *m. foot; footing; base; basis.*

> A pé. *On foot.*
> Ao pé da colina. *At the foot of the hill.*
> De *(or em)* pé. *Standing. On foot.*
> Ao pé da letra. *Literally.*
> Pôr-se em pé. *To stand up.*
> Ficar de pé. *To remain standing. To stand (including agreements, etc.).*
> Isso não tem pés nem cabeça. *I can't make heads or tails of that.*
> Ele se levantou (levantou-se) com o pé esquerdo. *He got up on the wrong side of the bed.*

peão *m. pedestrian; peon; pawn (chess).*

PEÇA *f. piece, part; room; article; joke, trick; play (drama).*

> Peça por peça. *Piece by piece.*
> Quantas peças (divisões) tem o apartamento? *How many rooms does the apartment have?*
> A peça é em três atos (actos). *The play has three acts.*
> Pregar uma peça. *To play a trick or practical joke.*

pecado *m. sin.*

pecar *to sin, to do wrong.*

pecuário *adj. of cattle; n. m. cattleman.*

peculiar *adj. peculiar, individual.*

peculiaridade *f. peculiarity.*

PEDAÇO *m. bit, piece*

> Fazer em pedaços. *To break into pieces.*

pedagogo *m. pedagogue, teacher.*

pedal *m. pedal.*

pedestal *m. pedestal, support.*

pedestre *adj., n. m. and f. pedestrian.*

pedido *adj. ordered; asked for; n. m. order, demand, request.*

> O pedido chegou ontem. *The order arrived yesterday.*

> Fazer um pedido. *To order (goods). To place an order.*
> A pedido de. *At the request of.*

PEDIR *to ask for; to demand; to order (goods); to beg.*

> Ela me pediu que lhe fizesse um favor. *She asked me to do her a favor.*
> Pedir licença. *To ask permission.*
> Peço a palavra. *May I have the floor?*
> Pedir informações. *To inquire. To ask for information.*
> Pedir desculpas. *To apologize.*
> Pedir emprestado. *To borrow.*

PEDRA *f. stone, rock; blackboard; gem.*

> Pedras preciosas. *Precious stones.*
> Duro como uma pedra. *Hard as (a) stone.*
> Não deixar pedra sobre pedra. *Not to leave one stone on top of another.*

pedreiro *m. bricklayer; stonemason.*

PEGAR *to glue; to stick; to grasp, to take hold of; to catch.*

> Ele pegou na pasta e saiu. *He took his briefcase and left.*
> Ela já pegou no sono. *She's already fallen asleep.*
> Pegar fogo. *To catch fire.*
> Pegue e pague. *Cash and carry.*

PEITO *m. chest; breast, bosom; heart, courage.*

> Não o tome a peito. *Don't take it to heart.*
> Ele é um homem de peito. *He is a courageous man.*

PEIXE *(x = sh) m. fish (in water).*

pelado *adj. plucked, bare, bald; penniless.*

pelar *to peel; to skin; to rob; to grow bald.*

pele *f. skin; hide; fur.*

> Salvar a pele. *To save one's skin.*

peleja *f. fight, struggle.*

pelejar *to fight, to struggle.*

peleteria *f. furrier's, fur shop.*

película *f. film.*

PELO *(contr. of por + o) for the, through the.*

> Pelo amor de Deus. *For the love of God.*
> Pelo contrário. *On the contrary.*

pêlo *m. fur, fuzz.*

> Montar em pelo. *To ride bareback.*
> Em pelo. *Naked.*

pelota *f. pellet; soccer ball.*

pelotão *m. platoon; group.*

PENA *f. feather; writing pen; penalty, punishment; grief, sorrow.*

> Desenho a bico de pena. *Pen-and-ink drawing.*
> Pena de morte. *Death sentence.*
> É (uma) pena! *That's too bad!*
> Ter pena de. *To feel sorry for.*
> Que pena! *What a pity!*
> Não vale a pena. *It's not worth it. It's not worth the trouble.*

penal *adj. penal.*
penalidade *f. penalty.*
penalizar *to distress, to pain; to penalize.*
pendão *m. pennant, flag.*
pendente *adj. hanging; pending; n. m. pendant, earring.*
pender *to hang; to be pending.*
pendurar *to hang, to suspend; to pawn* Ⓑ*; to put on your credit card/account* Ⓑ*.*
penetrante *adj. penetrating, piercing.*
penetrar *to penetrate; to comprehend.*
penha *f. rock, cliff, bluff.*
penhor *m. pawn, pledge.*
> Dar em penhor. *To pawn. To pledge.*
> Casa de penhores. *Pawnshop.*

península *f. peninsula.*
penitência *f. penitence; penance.*
penitente *adj., n. m. and f. penitent.*
penoso *adj. painful, distressing; arduous.*
pensador *adj. thinking; n. m. thinker.*
pensamento *m. thought, idea.*
pensão *f. pension; board; boardinghouse.*
PENSAR *to think; to consider; to intend.*
> Pense antes de falar. *Think before you speak.*
> Sem pensar. *Without thinking.*
> Ela está pensando (a pensar) nas férias. *She's thinking about her vacation.*
> Pensamos estar no cinema às oito. *We expect to be at the movie theater at eight.*

pensativo *adj. pensive, thoughtful.*
pensionista *m. and f. pensioner, boarder.*
PENTE *m. comb.*
penteado *m. coiffure, hairdo, hairstyle.*
> Que penteado prefere? *Which hairstyle do you prefer?*

pentear *to comb.*
penúltimo *adj. penultimate, next to last.*
penúria *f. penury, poverty.*
pepino *m. cucumber.*
PEQUENO *adj. little, small; n. m. child.*
> Ele é muito pequeno. *He's quite small.*
> Como estão os pequenos? *How are the little ones?*

PÊRA *f. pear.*
peral *m. pear orchard.*
perante *before, in the presence of.*
percal *m. percale.*
perceber *to perceive, to understand, to "get."*
> Dar a perceber. *To imply.*
> Percebemos o que queriam fazer. *We understood what they wanted to do.*
> Não o percebo. *I don't get it.*

percentagem *f. percentage.*
percepção *f. perception.*
percha *f. perch, pole.*
percorrer *to traverse, to cover (distance); to search through.*

perda *f. loss; damage; waste.*
> A perda foi grande. *The loss was heavy. It was a great loss.*
> Perda total. *Total loss.*

perdão *f. pardon.*
> Perdão! *I'm sorry! Excuse me!*

PERDER *to lose; to spoil; to miss.*
> Perdi a caneta. *I lost my pen.*
> Estamos perdendo (a perder) tempo. *We're losing time. We're wasting time.*
> Perder de vista. *To lose sight of.*
> Você perdeu uma boa oportunidade. *You missed a good opportunity.*
> Perdemos a paciência. *We lost patience. We lost our patience.*
> Ele perdeu o avião. *He missed the plane.*
> Depressa! Não há tempo a perder. *Hurry! There's no time to lose.*
> Perder a vez. *To lose one's turn.*

perdição *f. perdition; ruin.*
perdido *adj. lost; ruined.*
perdiz *f. partridge.*
PERDOAR *to excuse, to pardon, to forgive.*
> Perdoe-me. *Pardon me. Excuse me.*
> Perdoe a demora. *Pardon the delay.*

perdurar *to last a long time; to endure.*
perecer *to perish, to die.*
> O menino pereceu de fome. *The child died of hunger.*

peregrino *m. pilgrim.*
perfeição *f. perfection, excellence.*
PERFEITO *adj. perfect; excellent.*
> É um trabalho perfeito. *It's a perfect piece of work.*

perfídia *f. perfidy, treachery.*
perfil *m. profile; outline.*
perfumaria *f. perfume shop.*
perfume *m. perfume; scent, fragrance.*
perfurar *to perforate, to penetrate.*
PERGUNTA *f. question.*
> Fazer perguntas. *To ask questions.*

PERGUNTAR *to ask, to inquire.*
> Por que me pergunta isso? *Why do you ask me that?*
> Ela lhe perguntou (perguntou-lhe) alguma coisa? *Did she ask you something?*
> Quem perguntou por mim? *Who asked for me?*

perícia *f. skill.*
perigo *m. danger, peril.*
> Não há perigo. *There's no danger.*

perigoso *adj. dangerous.*
periódico *adj. periodic, periodical; n. m. periodical.*
periodista *m. and f. journalist, newspaper writer.*
período *m. period, span of time.*
perito *adj. expert, experienced, skillful; n. m. expert; appraiser.*

permanecer *to remain, to stay; to continue.*
> Quanto tempo vai permanecer fora da cidade? *How long will you be out of town?*

permanência *f. permanence; stay.*

PERMANENTE *adj. permanent.*

permeável *adj. permeable.*

PERMISSÃO *f. permission; permit; authorization; consent.*
> Ter permissão. *To have permission.*

PERMITIR *to permit, to let, to allow.*
> Permita-me. *Allow me.*
> Permite que lhe faça uma pergunta? *May I ask you a question?*

permuta *f. permutation; exchange; barter.*

PERNA *f. leg.*
> Estirar as pernas. *To stretch one's legs.*

pernambucano *adj., n. m. of the state of Pernambuco in Brazil.*

pernicioso *adj. pernicious, injurious, harmful.*

pérola *f. pearl.*

perpendicular *adj., n. f. perpendicular.*

perpetrar *to perpetrate.*

perpetuar *to perpetuate.*

perpetuidade *f. perpetuity.*

perpétuo *adj. perpetual, everlasting.*

perplexidade *(x = ks) f. perplexity, bewilderment.*

perplexo *(x = ks) adj. perplexed, bewildered, puzzled.*
> Fico perplexo. *I'm puzzled.*

persa *adj., n. m. and f. Persian.*

perscrutar *to scrutinize, to scan.*

perseguição *f. persecution; pursuit.*

perseguir *to persecute; to pursue; to harass.*

perseverança *f. perseverance.*

perseverar *to persevere, to persist.*

persignar-se *to cross oneself, to make the sign of the cross.*

persistência *f. persistence.*

persistente *adj. persistent, firm.*

persistir *to persist.*

personagem *m. and f. personage; character (in book, play).*

personalidade *personality.*

perspetiva (perspectiva) *f. perspective.*

perspicácia *f. perspicacity.*

perspicaz *adj. perspicacious, acute.*

perspirar *to perspire.*

persuadir *to persuade, to convince.*

persuasão *f. persuasion.*

pertencer *to belong.*
> Não me pertence. *It doesn't belong to me.*

pertinente *adj. pertinent.*

PERTO *near.*
> Fica perto. *It's close. It's nearby.*
> Fica perto da escola. *It's near the school.*

perturbar *to perturb, to disturb.*

peru *m. turkey.*

peruano *adj., n. m. Peruvian.*

perversão *f. perversion.*

perversidade *f. perversity.*

perverso *adj. perverse, wicked.*

perverter *to pervert.*

pesadelo *m. nightmare.*

pesado *adj. heavy; tedious, tiresome.*
> O ferro é pesado. *Iron is heavy.*
> É um trabalho pesado. *It's hard work.*

pêsames *m. pl. condolences.*

PESAR *to weigh; to cause regret or sorrow; n. m. grief, sorrow; regret.*
> Quanto pesa a caixa (x = sh)? *How much does the box weigh?*
> Pesar as palavras. *To weigh one's words.*
> É com grande pesar que lhe escrevo. *It is with great sorrow that I write you.*

pesca *f. fishing; catch.*

pescado *m. catch of fish; fish (after it has been caught; see peixe).*

pescar *to fish; to catch.*
> Pescar em águas turvas. *To fish in troubled waters.*

pescaria *f. fishing.*

pescoço *m. neck.*

peso *m. weight; burden; importance; peso (money).*
> Peso líquido. *Net weight.*
> Peso bruto. *Gross weight.*
> Peso pesado. *Heavyweight (boxing).*

pesquisa *f. research, investigation.*

pêssego *m. peach.*

pessimismo *m. pessimism.*

pessimista *adj. pessimistic; n. m. and f. pessimist.*

péssimo *adj. very bad, terrible.*

PESSOA *f. person.*
> Ela é muito boa pessoa. *She's a very nice person. She's a wonderful person.*
> Pessoa de bem. *Fine person.*
> Ela apareceu em pessoa. *She was there in person.*

pessoal *adj. personal, private; n. m. personnel.*
> Viva, pessoal, apressamo-nos! *OK, people, let's get moving!*

pestana *f. eyelash; fringe, edging.*
> Queimar as pestanas. *To burn the midnight oil.*

peste *f. plague, pestilence; pest.*

petição *f. petition; claim.*

petróleo *m. petroleum.*

pia *f. washbasin; sink; font.*
> Pia da cozinha. *Kitchen sink.*

piada *f. joke, wisecrack.*

pianista *m. and f. pianist.*

piano *m. piano.*

piar *to peep (as a baby chick).*

picada *f. sting; prick; dive (airplane).*

picante *adj. hot, highly seasoned; sharp; caustic; n. m. appetizer.*

pica-pau *m. woodpecker.*

picar *to bite, to sting; to prick; to itch; to chop; to nibble; to spur; to be hot (pepper, etc.); to dive (airplane).*
   Picou-me uma abelha. *A bee stung me.*
   Picar carne. *To chop (up) meat.*

pícaro *adj. crafty, sly.*

pico *m. peak, summit; spine; thorn; sting; a bit.*
   Subiram ao pico mais alto. *They climbed to the highest peak.*
   Ficaram lá um mês e pico. *They stayed there a little more than a month.*

piedade *f. piety; pity; mercy.*

pigarrear *to clear the throat.*

pigarro *m. frog in the throat.*

pijama *m. pajamas.*

pilar *m. pillar, column, post.*

pilha *f. pile, heap; battery (in a car, etc.).*
   Pilha sêca (seca). *Dry battery.*

pilhéria *f. joke, gag.*

piloto *m. pilot.*
   Piloto de provas. *Test pilot.*

pílula *f. pill.*

pimenta *f. pepper.*

pincel *m. brush.*

pindorama *m. country of palms Ⓑ.*

pingar *to drip, to leak.*

pingue-pongue *m. Ping-Pong.*

pinha *f. pinecone; sweetsop, sugar apple (a tropical fruit) Ⓑ.*

pinheiro *m. pine tree.*

pinho *m. pine (wood).*

pino *m. peg; pin; apex.*
   Pino mestre. *Kingpin.*
   No pino de. *At the peak of.*

pinta *f. spot; mole, beauty mark.*

pintado *adj. painted; spotted, speckled, freckled.*

pintar *to paint; to describe.*
   Que está pintando (a pintar)? *What are you painting?*
   Pintar a óleo. *To paint in oil.*
   Pintar o sete. *To raise hell.*

pintor *m. painter.*

pintura *f. painting.*
   Pintura a óleo. *Oil painting.*

pio *adj. pious; n. m. peep, chirp.*

piolho *m. louse.*

pioneiro *m. pioneer.*

PIOR *adj. and adv. worse, worst.*
   O doente está pior. *The patient is worse.*
   Isso é o pior. *That's the worst of it.*
   Ainda pior. *Worse yet.*
   A situação vai de mal a pior. *The situation is going from bad to worse.*
   Cada vez pior. *Worse and worse.*

piorar *to worsen.*

piquenique *m. picnic.*

pirâmide *f. pyramid.*

pirata *m. pirate.*

pires *m. sing. and pl. saucer, saucers.*

pisada *f. footstep; footprint.*

pisar *to tread, to step on; to press; to walk.*

piscar *to wink, to blink.*
   Ele piscou para ela. *He winked at her.*

piscina *f. swimming pool.*

piso *m. floor, ground; tread; gait.*

pista *f. track; landing strip; trail, clue.*
   Seguir a pista. *To follow the trail.*
   Pista de corridas. *Race track.*

pistão *m. piston; cornet.*

pistola *f. pistol, gun.*

pitoresco *adj. picturesque.*

placa *f. plate (metal); plaque; badge.*
   Placa de licença. *License plate.*

placar *to placate, to appease; n. m. placard, poster; badge.*

plaina *f. carpenter's plane.*

plana *f. category, class.*

planalto *m. plateau.*

planejar *to plan.*

planeta *m. planet.*

planície *f. plain.*

plano *adj. smooth, even; n. m. plane; plan.*
   Primeiro plano. *Foreground.*
   Último plano. *Background.*
   Geometria plana. *Plane geometry.*

planta *f. plant; plan.*
   Planta anual. *Annual plant.*

plantação *f. plantation; planting.*

plantar *to plant; to drive into the ground.*
   Vamos plantar algumas árvores perto da casa. *We're going to plant some trees near the house.*

plástica *f. plastic art; plastic surgery.*

plástico *adj., n. m. plastic.*

plataforma *f. platform.*

plátano *m. plane tree; sycamore.*

platéia (plateia) *f. orchestra section (theatre); audience.*

platina *f. platinum.*

platino *adj. of the River Plate region.*

pleito *m. lawsuit; dispute.*

PLENO *adj. full, complete.*
   Plenos poderes. *Full powers.*
   Em pleno dia. *In broad daylight.*

pluma *f. feather, plume; feather pen.*

plural *adj., n. m. plural.*

pneu *m. tire (on a car, etc.).*

pneumático *adj. pneumatic.*

pó *m. dust; powder.*
   Pó de arroz. *Face powder.*

POBRE *adj. poor; n. m. and f. poor person; beggar.*
   Ele é muito pobre. *He is very poor.*
   Pobre homem! *Poor man! Poor fellow!*

pobreza *f. poverty, need.*

poço *m. well; shaft (elevator, mine, etc.); pit.*
    Poço de petróleo. *Oil well.*

podar *to prune.*

PODER *to be able; can; may; n. m. power; authority; command.*
    Em que posso servi-lo? *What can I do for you? (How) may I help you?*
    Não posso ir. *I can't go.*
    Não pode ser! *That can't be! That's impossible!*
    Eu fiz o melhor que pude. *I did the best I could.*
    Quem tem o poder nesse país? *Who has the power in that country?*
    Poder executivo. *Executive power.*
    Plenos poderes. *Full powers.*
    Não posso com eles. *I can't deal with them.*
    Posso entrar?—Pode. *May I come in?— You may.*

poderoso *adj. mighty, powerful.*

podre *adj. rotten; corrupt.*

podridão *f. rottenness; corruption.*

poeira *f. dust.*

poema *m. poem.*

poesia *f. poetry.*

poeta *m. poet.*

POIS *as, since; so; well; then; why; now; indeed.*
    Pois faça-o. *Then do it.*
    Pois vamos. *Then let's go.*
    Pois bem. *Well then.*
    Pois é. *That's it. Of course.*
    Pois não! *Of course! Certainly!*

polaco *adj. Polish; n. m. Pole.*

polar *adj. polar.*
    Estrela polar. *North Star.*

polca *f. polka.*

polcar *to dance the polka.*

polegada *f. inch.*

polegar *m. thumb; big toe.*

poleiro *m. perch; top gallery of theater, peanut gallery* Ⓑ.

polêmica (polémica) *f. polemics; controversy.*

polêmico (polémico) *adj. polemic, polemical.*

polícia *f. police force; m. policeman.*
    Polícia militar. *Military police.*

policial *adj. police; n. m. policeman, officer.*
    Romance policial. *Detective story.*

polido *adj. polished, bright.*

polígamo *adj. polygamous; n. m. polygamist.*

polimento *m. polishing; polish.*

poliomielite *f. poliomyelitis.*

polir *to polish.*

política *f. politics; political science; policy.*
    Política econômica. *Economic policies.*
    Política social. *Social policies.*

político *adj. political; n. m. politician.*

    Ter influência política. *To have good political connections.*
    Economia política. *Political economy.*

pólo *pole; polo.*

polonês *adj. Polish; n. m. Polish person.*

poltrona *f. easy chair; orchestra seat.*

pólvora *f powder, gunpowder.*

pomada *f. pomade.*

pomar *m. orchard.*

pombo *m. pigeon, dove.*
    Pombo de barro. *Clay pigeon.*

pômulo (pómulo) *m. cheek.*

ponche *m. punch (drink).*

ponderação *f. consideration, reflection.*

ponderar *to ponder, to weigh.*

PONTA *f. point; tip.*
    Ter na ponta da língua. *To have on the tip of the tongue.*
    Nas pontas dos pés. *On tiptoe.*

pontapé *m. kick.*

pontaria *f. aim, aiming.*

ponte *f. bridge.*
    Ponte suspensa. *Suspension bridge.*
    Ponte levadiça. *Drawbridge.*

ponteiro *m. pointer; hand (clock).*

pontiagudo *adj. pointed, sharp.*

PONTO *m. point; dot; period; place; stitch; prompter.*
    Ponto de partida. *Starting point. Point of departure.*
    Ponto final. *Period.*
    Ponto e vírgula. *Semicolon.*
    Dois pontos. *Colon.*
    Seis ponto cinco. *6.5.*
    Ponto por ponto. *Point by point.*
    Estarei lá às sete horas em ponto. *I'll be there at seven o'clock sharp.*
    Ponto cardeal. *Cardinal point (N, S, E, W on compass).*
    Ponto culminante. *Climax.*
    Ponto fraco. *Weakness. Weak point.*
    Estávamos a ponto de sair quando chegaram. *We were about to leave when they arrived.*
    Até certo ponto é verdade. *To a certain extent it is true.*

pontual *adj. punctual.*

popa *f. stern.*
    A popa. *Aft.*
    De proa à popa. *From stem to stern.*

popular *adj. popular.*
    E uma canção popular. *It's a popular song.*

popularidade *f. popularity.*

pôquer Ⓑ *m. poker.*

POR *for; by; through; about.*
    Por correio aéreo. *By airmail.*
    Ganharam por dois pontos. *They won by two points.*

Dom Casmurro foi escrito por Machado de Assis. *Dom Casmurro was written by Machado de Assis.*

Entrem pela porta principal. *Enter through the main door.*

Pode pasar pela casa? *Can you pass by the house?*

Por mês. *By the month.*

Por muito tempo. *For a long time.*

Pela manhã. *In the morning.*

Pela tarde. *In the afternoon.*

Pela noite. *In the evening.*

Por agora. *For the present.*

Por dentro. *On the inside.*

Por fora. *On the outside.*

Por conseguinte. *Consequently.*

Por fim. *Finally.*

Por quê? *Why?*

Por toda parte. *Everywhere.*

Por Deus! *Heavens! For heaven's sake!*

Por outro lado. *On the other hand.*

Por exemplo *(x = z). For example.*

Por volta (de). *Around. About.*

Por pouco. *Almost. Nearly.*

Por meio de. *By means of.*

Por atacado. *Wholesale.*

Por aqui. *This way.*

Por acaso. *By chance.*

Por favor. *Please.*

Eu não votei por ele. *I didn't vote for him.*

PÔR *to put; to set (table); to put on; to lay (eggs).*

Ponha o livro na mesa. *Put the book on the table.*

Pôr a mesa. *To set the table.*

Pôr ovos. *To lay eggs.*

Pôr à prova. *To put to the test.*

Pôr em execução *(x = z). To carry out. To execute.*

Pôr em dúvida. *To doubt. To question.*

Pôr mãos à obra. *To get to work.*

Pôr em liberdade. *To free.*

Pôr uma gravata. *To put on a tie.*

Pôr por escrito. *To put in writing.*

Pôr os pontos nos ii. *To dot the i's and cross the t's.*

Pôr mel em boca de asno. *To cast pearls before swine.*

O homem põe e Deus dispõe. *Man proposes, God disposes.*

porão *m. hold (ship), basement* ⑧.

porca *f. sow; nut (for bolt).*

porção *f. portion, part, share; many, much* ⑧.

Dividir em porções. *To divide. To share.*

porcelana *f. porcelain; chinaware.*

porco *adj. dirty, filthy; n. m. pig. pork.*

porém *however, but, nevertheless.*

porfia *f. insistence, obstinacy.*

porfiado *adj. stubborn, obstinate.*

porfiar *to persist.*

pormenor *m. detail.*

PORQUE *because, on account of, for, as, since.*

Ela não veio porque estava ocupada. *She didn't come because she was busy.*

Porque era tarde ficamos em casa. *Since it was late, we stayed home.*

porquê *m. reason, the why, why.*

Não sei porquê. *I don't know why.*

porqueiro *m. swineherd.*

pôr-se *to start, to begin, to get.*

Pôr-se a falar. *To begin to speak.*

Pôr-se de joelhos. *To get on one's knees.*

PORTA *f. door, doorway; gate.*

Abra a porta. *Open the door.*

Feche a porta. *Close the door.*

Feche a porta à chave quando sair. *Lock the door when you leave.*

Porta-malas. *Car trunk.*

Porta principal. *Main entrance. Main door.*

Porta giratória. *Revolving door.*

porta-aviões *m. aircraft carrier.*

portador *m. bearer, carrier; porter, messenger.*

portal *m. portal, doorway.*

portão *m. large door, gate.*

portar *to carry; to reach a port; to arrive.*

portar-se *to behave.*

Portar-se mal. *To behave badly.*

portaria *f. reception desk.*

portátil *adj. portable.*

Máquina de escrever portátil. *Portable typewriter.*

Computador portátil. *Laptop computer.*

porte *m. transportation; freight cost; department; postage.*

Quanto é o porte? *How much is the postage?*

Porte pago. *Postpaid.*

porteiro *m. doorman; janitor.*

portenho *adj., n. m. of the city of Buenos Aires.*

portento *m. wonder, portent, prodigy.*

portentoso *adj. prodigious, marvelous.*

porto *m. port, harbor; port (wine).*

Porto de escala. *Port of call.*

portuense *adj., n. m. of the city of Porto in Portugal.*

PORTUGUÊS *adj., n. m. Portuguese.*

Eu falo português. *I speak Portuguese.*

Uma gramática de português. *A Portuguese grammar.*

Ele é português mas ela não é portuguesa. *He is Portuguese, but she is not Portuguese.*

porvir *m. future.*

pós-guerra *adj. postwar; n. m. postwar period.*

POSIÇÃO f. position, place, situation.

Posição firme. *A firm stand. A firm position.*

positivo adj. positive, sure, certain.

posse f. possession, ownership; pl. possessions; wealth.

Homem de posses. *A man of means.*

possessão f. possession.

possibilidade f. possibility.

POSSÍVEL adj. possible.

Não será possível fazê-lo. *It won't be possible to do it.*

Farei quanto me for possível. *I'll do as much as I can.*

O mais cedo possível. *As soon as possible.*

possuir to possess, to have.

posta f. slice; post, mail.

Posta-restante. *General delivery.*

postal adj. postal; n. m. postcard.

Cartão postal (bilhete postal). *Postcard.*

posteridade f. posterity.

posterior adj. posterior, rear, back.

POSTO adj. put, placed; set (table, sun); n. m. place, post, station.

Posto de gasolina. *Gas station.*

Posto militar. *Military post.*

Posto naval. *Naval station.*

póstumo adj. posthumous

postura f. posture, position.

potável f. potable.

potência f. power, strength, force.

As grandes potências. *The Great Powers.*

potentado m. potentate, ruler.

potente adj. potent, powerful, mighty.

potro m. colt.

POUCO adj. and adv. little; small; scanty; n. m. a little, a small part; pl. a few.

Quer um pouco de café? *Would you like some coffee?*

Ela sabe um pouco de tudo. *She knows a little about everything.*

Fica-me muito pouco dinheiro. *I have very little money left.*

Ele chegará dentro de pouco (tempo). *He'll be here shortly.*

Poucas vezes. *A few times.*

Gosto um pouco. *I like it a bit.*

Aos poucos. *Little by little.*

Acho um pouco caro. *I think it's rather (a little) expensive.*

Há pouco. *A short while ago.*

Tenho uns poucos. *I have a few.*

poupar to save, to economize.

Vou poupar o meu dinheiro. *I'm going to save my money.*

pousar to set down; to put; to stay, to lodge.

POVO m. people; public.

O povo português. *The Portuguese people.*

povoação f. population; town, settlement.

povoar to populate; to stock.

PRAÇA f. plaza, square; market; enlisted man.

Vamos dar uma volta pela praça. *Let's take a stroll around the square.*

Carro de praça. *Taxi.*

prado m. meadow, pasture, field.

praga f. plague; curse.

praia f. beach, shore.

pranto m. weeping, crying.

prata f. silver; silverware.

prateleira f. shelf.

prática f. practice; exercise; talk.

A prática faz o mestre. *Practice makes perfect.*

praticante adj. practicing; n. m. practitioner; apprentice.

praticar to practice; to do (a hobby, etc.).

Ela pratica bordado. *She does embroidery.*

prático adj. practical; skilled; experienced (worker); n. m. harbor pilot.

PRATO m. dish, plate; course (meal).

Este prato é gostoso. *This dish is delicious.*

Qual é o prato do dia? *What's today's special?*

Prato fundo. *Soup plate.*

Prato raso. *Dinner plate.*

Do prato à boca se perde a sopa. *The best laid plans often go awry.*

praxe (x = sh) f. custom, habit.

De praxe. *Usual. Customary.*

PRAZER to please; m. pleasure, enjoyment.

Tenho muito prazer em conhecê-lo. *I am very glad to know you.*

O prazer é todo meu. *The pleasure is all mine.*

Foi um prazer vê-lo de novo. *It was a pleasure to see you again.*

prazo m. term; period of time.

Comprar a prazo. *To buy on time. To buy on the installment plan.*

Prazo de entrega. *Time of delivery.*

preâmbulo m. preamble, introduction.

É um preâmbulo interessante. *It's an interesting preface.*

Deixe (x = sh) de preâmbulos e diga o que quer. *Stop beating around the bush and tell me what you want.*

precário adj. precarious.

precaução f. precaution.

precaver to forewarn, to caution.

precedência f. precedence.

precedente adj. preceding; n. m. precedent.

preceder to precede.

preceito m. precept, rule.

preciosidade f. preciousness; precious or beautiful thing.

precioso adj. precious, dear.

Pedras preciosas. *Precious stones.*

precipício m. precipice.

precipitação f. precipitation.

precipitado adj. precipitate, hasty.

precipitar to precipitate; to hurry; to rush on.

precisão f. precision, accuracy; necessity.
Instrumento de precisão. Precision instrument.

PRECISAR to need; to specify.
Preciso duma dúzia. I need a dozen.
Precisamos (de) estudar mais. We must study more.

PRECISO adj. necessary; exact.
É preciso pagar hoje. It is necessary to pay today.
É preciso que cheguemos antes da seis. It is necessary that we arrive before six.
Não é preciso. It's not necessary.

PREÇO m. price; value.
Por que preço? At what price?
Preço fixo. Fixed price.
Preço de fábrica. At cost.
A qualquer preço. At any price.
Preço de ocasião. Bargain price.
Preço de varejo. Retail price.
Abaixar (x = sh) o preço. To lower the price.

preconceito m. prejudice.
Preconceito de raça. Racial prejudice.

predição f. prediction.

predicar to preach.

predileção f. predilection, preference.
Ter predileção por. To have a fondness for. To have a preference for.

prédio m. building, house; land.
É um prédio de dois andares. It's a building with two floors.

predisposto adj. predisposed, inclined.

predizer to predict, to foretell.

predominar to predominate, to prevail.

preencher to fill (out).
Faça o favor de preencher este formulário. Please fill out this form.
Preencher uma vaga. To fill a vacancy.

prefácio m. preface, introduction.

prefeito (administrador do concelho) m. mayor, administrator.

prefeitura (câmara municipal) f. city hall.

preferência f. preference, choice.
De preferência. Preferably.
Ter preferência. To take preference. To have priority.

preferido adj. preferred, favorite.

PREFERIR to prefer.
Qual prefere? Which do you prefer?
Prefiro este. I prefer this one.

preferível adj. preferable.
É preferível ir pessoalmente. It's better to go in person.

prefixo (x = ks) m. prefix.

prega f. crease, fold.

pregar to nail; to fasten; to stick; to preach.
Pregar um prego. To drive a nail.
Pregar uma peça emalguém. To play a trick on someone.
Não preguei os olhos. I didn't sleep a wink.

prego m. nail.

preguiça f. laziness.

preguiçoso adj. lazy.
O João é muito preguiçoso. John is very lazy.

pré-histórico adj. prehistoric.

prejuízo m. harm, damage; loss.

preliminar adj. preliminary.

prelo m. printing press.

prelúdio m. prelude.

prematuro adj. premature.

premeditação f. premeditation.

premeditar to premeditate.

premiar to reward.

PRÊMIO m. prize, reward; premium.
Ela ganhou o prêmio. She won the prize.

prenda f. gift, present; talent.

prendar to present with.

prendedor m. clasp; fastener.
Prendedor de gravata. Tie clip.

PRENDER to fasten; to catch; to arrest.
Quem prendeu o ladrão? Who arrested (caught) the thief?

prenhe adj. pregnant.

prensa f. printing press; press.
Prensa hidráulica. Hydraulic press.

preocupação f. preoccupation, concern, worry.

preocupar to preoccupy, to concern.
Eles estão muito preocupados. They are quite concerned.

preparação f. preparation.

preparado adj. prepared; preparation (medicinal).

PREPARAR to prepare, to get ready.
Primeiro temos que preparar a lição. First we have to prepare the lesson.

preparativo adj. preparative; n. m. pl. preparations.
Estamos fazendo (a fazer) os preparativos para a viagem. We're making preparations for the trip.

preparatório adj. preparatory.

preponderância f. preponderance.

preponderar to prevail.

preposição f. preposition.

presa f. prey, capture; female prisoner; fang; claw.

prescindir to do without, to dispense with.

prescrever to prescribe.

presença f. presence.
Presença de espírito. Presence of mind.

presenciar *to be present; to witness, to see.*
  Acabamos de presenciar . . . *We've just witnessed . . .*
PRESENTE *adj. present; n. m. gift, present; present time; present tense.*
  Presente! *Present! Here!*
  Presente de aniversário. *Birthday gift.*
  A presente serve para dizer-lhe . . . *(in a letter) This is to inform you . . .*
presépio *m. stable; crèche, Nativity scene.*
preservação *f. preservation.*
preservar *to preserve; to maintain; to keep.*
presidência *f. presidency.*
presidente *m. president; chairman.*
presidiário *m. convict.*
presídio *m. penitentiary, prison.*
presidir *to preside, to direct.*
preso *adj. imprisoned, arrested; n. m. prisoner, convict.*
  Preso em flagrante. *Caught in the act.*
  Ele foi preso como cúmplice. *He was arrested as an accomplice.*
  Está preso! *You're under arrest!*
PRESSA *f. haste, speed, hurry.*
  Estou com pressa (tenho pressa). *I'm in a hurry.*
  Sem pressa. *Leisurely.*
  Por que tanta pressa? *Why the rush?*
pressagiar *to predict, to foretell.*
presságio *m. prediction; omen.*
pressentimento *m. presentiment, premonition.*
prestar *to lend; to aid; to pay (attention).*
  Prestar atenção. *To pay attention.*
  Você me prestou um bom serviço. *You rendered me a great service.*
  Não presta para nada. *It's not good for anything.*
prestes *adj. ready.*
presteza *f. quickness, speed, promptness.*
prestígio *m. prestige.*
prestigioso *adj. famous; influential.*
presumido *adj. vain, conceited; n. m. conceited person.*
presumir *to presume, to assume; to be conceited.*
presunção *f. presumption; conceit.*
presunto *m. ham.*
pretendente *n. m. and f. candidate, claimant; n. m. suitor.*
pretender *to claim, to intend.*
  Pretendemos visitar o Brasil. *We intend to visit Brazil.*
pretensão *f. pretension.*
pretensioso *adj. pretentious; n. m. pretentious person.*
pretexto *(x = sh) m. pretext.*
PRETO *adj. black; dark; difficult.*
  Vestir de preto. *To wear black.*
prevalecer *to prevail.*

prevenção *f. prevention; prejudice.*
prevenir *to prevent; to warn.*
  Estamos prevenidos. *We're prepared. We've been forewarned.*
prever *to foresee; to anticipate.*
  Ele previu essa dificuldade. *He expected (foresaw) that difficulty.*
prévio *adj. previous, prior.*
  Aviso prévio. *Previous notice.*
  Questão prévia. *Previous question (parliamentary procedure).*
previsão *f. foresight, prevision.*
previsto *adj. foreseen, expected.*
prezado *adj. dear, esteemed.*
  Prezado Senhor: *Dear Sir:*
primário *adj. primary.*
  Escola primária. *Elementary school. Primary school.*
PRIMAVERA *f. spring (season).*
PRIMEIRO *adj., n. m. first; foremost.*
  Traga-nos primeiro a sopa. *Bring us the soup first.*
  Bilhete de primeira. *First-class ticket.*
  Eles moram na primeira casa. *They live in the first house.*
  De primeira ordem. *First-rate.*
  A primeira vez. *The first time.*
  O primeiro do mês. *The first of the month.*
  Primeiro andar. *First floor.*
  Em primeiro lugar. *In the first place.*
  Primeiro ministro. *Prime minister.*
  Primeiro prêmio (prémio). *First prize.*
  Primeiros socorros. *First aid.*
  O romance está escrito na primeira pessoa. *The novel is written in the first person.*
  Primeiro plano. *Foreground.*
primitivo *adj. primitive.*
primo *adj. prime; n. m. cousin.*
  Número primo. *Prime number.*
  Obra prima. *Masterpiece.*
  Ela é prima de João. *She is John's cousin.*
primor *m. beauty, excellence.*
princesa *f. princess.*
PRINCIPAL *adj. principal, main, chief; n. m. principal.*
  Quem tem o papel principal? *Who has the main role?*
  O principal é acabar este trabalho antes da sexta. *The main (most important) thing is to finish this work before Friday.*
príncipe *m. prince.*
principiante *adj. beginning; n. m. and f. beginner.*
PRINCÍPIO *m. beginning, origin; principle.*
  No princípio parecia-me fácil. *It seemed easy to me at first.*
  Pagam no princípio de mês. *They pay the first part of the month.*

Em princípio não me parece má idéia
(ideia). *In principle it doesn't seem like
a bad idea.*

prioridade *f. priority.*

prisão *f. imprisonment; prison.*

prisioneiro *m. prisoner.*

privação *f. privation, want.*

privada *f. toilet.*

privado *adj. private, confidential.*
Vida privada. *Private life.*

privar *to deprive.*

privilegiado *adj. privileged.*

privilégio *m. privilege.*

pró *m. pro; argument for.*
Os prós e os contras. *The pros and cons.*
Em pró de. *In favor of.*

proa *f. bow (ship).*

probabilidade *f. probability.*

PROBLEMA *m. problem.*

procaz *adj. insolent, impudent, bold.*

procedência *f. origin, source; validity.*

procedente *adj. coming or proceeding from;
logical.*

proceder *to proceed; to act, to behave; m.
behavior, conduct.*
Ele procedeu corretamente
(correctamente). *He acted properly.*
Proceda com muito cuidado. *Proceed very
carefully.*

procedimento *m. procedure; method.*

processar *to sue; to indict.*

processo *m. process, procedure; lawsuit.*

proclamação *f. proclamation.*

proclamar *to proclaim; to promulgate.*
Nesse mesmo dia proclamaram a paz. *They
declared peace on that very day.*

procriar *to procreate.*

procura *f. search; demand.*
Oferta e procura. *Supply and demand.*
Ela está à procura duma boa gramática de
português. *She is looking for a good
Portuguese grammar.*

PROCURAR *to look for, to seek; to try.*
Estou procurando (a procurar) o chapéu.
I'm looking for my hat.
Procure estar na esquina às nove. *Try to be
on the corner at nine.*

prodígio *m. wonder, marvel.*

prodigioso *adj. prodigious, marvelous.*

produção *f. production, output.*

produtivo *adj. productive.*

produto *m. product, yield.*
Produtos alimentícios. *Food products.
Food.*

PRODUZIR *to produce, to turn out, to yield.*
Essa fábrica produz automóveis. *That
factory produces (turns out)
automobiles.*

proeza *f. prowess; accomplishment.*

profanação *f. profanation.*

profanar *to profane.*

profano *adj. profane, irreverent; worldly.*

profecia *f. prophecy.*

proferir *to utter, to say.*
Ele proferiu um discurso. *He delivered an
address.*

professar *to profess, to declare openly; to
teach.*

professor *m. professor, teacher.*
Professor particular. *Private tutor.*

profeta *m. prophet.*

profético *adj. prophetic.*

profissão *f. profession; declaration.*
Seu nome e profissão, por favor. *Your
name and profession, please.*

profissional *adj. professional.*

profundidade *f. profundity, depth.*
200 metros de profundidade. *200 meters
deep.*

PROFUNDO *adj. profound, deep; intense.*
Silêncio profundo. *Deep silence.*
O poço é muito profundo. *The well is very
deep.*

prognosticar *to prognosticate, to forecast.*

prognóstico *adj. prognostic; n. m. forecast;
prognosis.*

PROGRAMA *m. program; plan.*
O program não foi muito bom. *The
program was not very good.*

progredir *to progress, to advance.*

progresso *m. progress.*
Ordem e progresso. *Order and progress.*

proibição *f. prohibition.*

proibido *adj. prohibited, forbidden.*
É proibido fumar. *No smoking.*
É proibida a entrada. *No admittance.*

PROIBIR *to prohibit, to forbid.*
Proíbo-lhe de fazer isso. *I forbid you to do
that.*

projetado (projectado) *adj projected,
planned.*

projetar (projectar) *to project, to plan.*

projetil, projétil (projéctil) *m. projectile,
missile.*

projeto (projecto) *m. project, plan.*

proletariado *m. proletariat.*

proletário *adj. proletarian.*

prólogo *m. prologue.*

prolongação *f. prolongation, extension.*

prolongar *to prolong, to extend.*

promessa *f. promise.*

PROMETER *to promise.*
Mas você prometeu fazê-lo. *But you
promised to do it.*
Ele nunca cumpre o que promete. *He never
does what he promises.*

prometido *adj. promised; m. promise; fiancé.*
Cumprir o prometido. *To keep a promise.*

promoção f. *promotion.*
promover *to promote, to advance.*
promulgar *to promulgate, to publish.*
pronome m. *pronoun.*
prontidão f. *promptness; swiftness.*
PRONTO adj. *ready, prepared.*
> Estamos prontos. *We are ready.*

prontuário m. *handbook.*
pronúncia f. *pronunciation.*
> Ela tem uma boa pronúncia. *She has good pronunciation. Her pronunciation is good.*

pronunciar *to pronounce; to utter; to give (a speech).*
> A senhora pronuncia muito bem o português. *You pronounce Portuguese very well.*
> Pronunciar (uma) sentença. *To pronounce sentence.*

propagação f. *propagation, dissemination.*
propaganda f. *propaganda, advertisement.*
propagandista m. and f. *propagandist.*
propagar *to propagate; to spread (news, etc.).*
propender *to tend, to incline to.*
propensão f. *propensity, tendency.*
propenso adj. *inclined, disposed.*
propício adj. *propitious, favorable.*
> Um momento propício. *A favorable moment.*

proponente adj., n. m. and f. *proponent.*
propor *to propose; to suggest.*
> Proponho ir vê-lo. *I intend to go to see him.*
> O homem propõe, Deus dispõe. *Man proposes, God disposes.*

proporção f. *proportion.*
proporcionar *to provide, to supply; to proportion, to adjust.*
proposição f. *proposition, proposal.*
propósito m. *purpose, intention.*
> Fizemos isso de propósito. *We did it on purpose.*
> A propósito. *By the way.*
> A propósito de. *Regarding. With regard to.*

proposta f. *proposal, proposition.*
proposto adj. *proposed.*
propriedade f. *property; ownership; propriety.*
> Acabo de comprar essa propriedade. *I've just bought that property.*
> Propriedade literária. *Copyright.*

proprietário m. *proprietor, owner, landlord.*
PRÓPRIO adj. *own; proper, fit, suitable.*
> Essas foram suas próprias palavras. *Those were his/her own words.*
> Esse é um jogo próprio de meninos. *That's a game (suitable) for children.*

prorrogação f. *prorogation, extension.*
prorrogar *to extend (time), to prolong.*
prorromper *to break out, to burst out.*

prosa f. *prose; chatter, gab* Ⓑ.
prosaico adj. *prosaic.*
prosista m. and f. *prose writer; chatterer* Ⓑ.
prosperar *to prosper, to thrive; to be successful.*
prosperidade f. *prosperity.*
próspero adj. *prosperous; successful.*
> Próspero ano novo! *Happy New Year!*

prospecto (prospecto) m. *prospectus; prospect.*
prosseguir *to pursue, to carry on, to go on, to continue, to proceed.*
> Prossiga! *Continue!*

prostrar *to prostrate.*
protagonista m. and f. *protagonist.*
proteção (protecção) f. *protection; support.*
proteger *to protect; to support.*
protestante adj. *protesting, Protestant; n. m. and f. protestor; Protestant.*
protestar *to protest.*
protesto m. *protest, objection; expression.*
> Sob protesto. *Under protest.*
> Com os protestos de minha alta consideração. *Sincerely yours.*

protetor (protector) m. *protector.*
PROVA f. *proof; test, examination; proof sheet; fitting (of garments).*
> Recebi duas provas. *I received two proofs.*
> À prova de fogo. *Fireproof.*
> Prova oral. *Oral test.*
> Prova escrita. *Written test.*

provado adj. *proven, tried.*
PROVAR *to try; to taste; to prove; to try on.*
> Prove este vinho. *Try this wine.*

PROVÁVEL adj. *probable, likely.*
> É pouco provável. *It's not likely.*
> É provável que venha amanhã. *It's likely that he will come tomorrow.*

PROVEITO m. *profit; benefit, advantage.*
> Tirar proveito. *To derive profit from. To turn to advantage.*
> Bom proveito! (said at meals). *Enjoy your meal! Bon appétit!*

proveitoso adj. *profitable, beneficial.*
prover *to provide, to furnish, to supply.*
provérbio m. *proverb.*
providência f. *providence, precaution; pl. steps, measures.*
> Tomar providências. *To take steps. To take measures.*

província f. *province.*
provir *to derive from, to come from.*
provisão f. *provision, supply; pl. provisions.*
> Provisões de guerra. *Munitions.*

provisional adj. *provisional, temporary.*
provisório adj. *provisional, temporary.*
provocação f. *provocation.*
provocador adj. *provocative; n. m. instigator, troublemaker.*
provocar *to provoke, to vex.*

PRÓXIMO (x = s) adj. near, next, neighboring; m. neighbor, fellowman.
Na próxima semana. Next week.
Amar o próximo. To love one's neighbor.

prudência f. prudence, moderation.

prudente adj. prudent, cautious.

pseudónimo (pseudónimo) m. pseudonym.

psicanálise f. psychoanalysis.

psicologia f. psychology.

psicólogo m. psychologist.

psicótico psychotic.

psique m. psyche.

psiquiatra m. and f. psychiatrist.

psiquiatria f. psychiatry.

psíquico adj. psychic.

psiu! pst! shh!

pua f. sharp point, prong; bit (drill).

publicação f. publication.

publicar to publish, to announce.
Ele publicou uma série de artigos sobre a literatura brasileira. He published a series of articles about Brazilian literature.

publicidade f. publicity.

PÚBLICO adj. public; n. m. public; audience.
Biblioteca pública. Public library.
Em público. In public.
O público não gostou da peça. The audience did not like the play.

pudim m. pudding.

pudor m. modesty, shyness; propriety.

pugilista m. pugilist, boxer.

pugna f. struggle, fight.

pular to jump.

pulga f. flea.
Andar com a pulga atrás da orelha. To be suspicious. To smell a rat.

pulmão m. lung.

pulmonia f. pneumonia.

pulo m. jump, skip.
Quando ela ouviu a notícia deu pulos de alegria. When she heard the news, she jumped with joy.
Em dois pulos. Right away. In two shakes of a lamb's tail.
Dar um pulo na casa de alguém. To drop in on someone.

pulôver ⑧ m. pullover, sweater.

pulsar to pulsate, to beat.

pulseira f. bracelet.
Relógio-pulseira. Wristwatch.

pulso m. pulse; wrist; force, strength.
Deixe-me tomar-lhe o pulso. Let me take your pulse.

pum! Bang! Boom!

pundonor m. dignity, self-respect.

pungente adj. pungent, acute.

pungir to prick, to pierce; to torment; to afflict.

punhado m. handful, a few.
Um punhado de soldados defenderam a posição. A handful of soldiers defended the position.

punhal m. dagger.

punhalada f. a stab; stab wound.

punho m. fist, wrist; cuff; handle.
De próprio punho. In one's own handwriting.

punição f. punishment.

punir to punish.

pupilo m. ward; protegé.

purê (puré) m. purée.
Purê de batatas. Mashed potatoes.

pureza f. purity.

purga f. purge; laxative.

purgação f. purge; purification.

purgante adj., n. m. purgative.

purgar to purge; to cleanse.

purgatório m. purgatory.

purificar to purify.

puro adj. pure, clean; plain.
É a pura verdade. That's the plain truth.

púrpura f. crimson, purple.

pusilânime adj. fainthearted, cowardly; n. m. and f. coward, wimp.

pútrido adj. rotten, putrid.

putrificar to putrefy, to rot.

puxa! (x = sh) Gosh! Golly!

puxar (x = sh) to pull; to haul; to take after, to resemble.
Puxar conversa. To strike up a conversation.
Puxa-saco. Apple-polisher ⑧.

quadra f. square area; quatrain; series of four; quarter; block (of street) ⑧; court (sports).

quadragésimo adj., n. m. fortieth.

quadrado adj. square.
Um metro quadrado. One square meter.

quadrilha f. a squadron; a gang; a square dance.
Uma quadrilha de ladrões. A gang of thieves.

quadro m. picture; painting; team; board.
Quadro negro. Blackboard.
Quadro a óleo. Oil painting.
Quadro de avisos. Bulletin board.

QUAL which; what; which one; like; as.
Qual prefere o senhor? Which (one) do you prefer?
Quais são os do senhor? Which (ones) are yours?
Cada qual. Each one.

qualidade *f. quality; kind; grade.*

qualquer *adj. any.*
> A qualquer hora. *At any time.*
> Ele é capaz de qualquer coisa. *He is capable of anything.*
> De qualquer maneira. *By any means. Anyhow.*

QUANDO *when.*
> Quando vai partir? *When are you going to leave?*
> Quando o senhor quiser. *Whenever you wish.*
> Até quando? *Until when?*
> De quando em quando. *From time to time.*
> De vez em quando. *From time to time.*
> Quando ela chegou, ele já tinha partido. *When she arrived, he had already left.*

quantia *f. sum, amount.*

quantidade *f. quantity, amount.*

QUANTO *how much; how; as much as; all that.*
> Quanto? *How much?*
> Quantos? *How many?*
> A quantos do mês estamos? *What day of the month is it?*
> Quanto é? *How much is it?*
> Compre quantos livros você quiser. *Buy as many books as you like.*
> Quanto mais lhe dou, mais me pede. *The more I give him, the more he asks for.*
> Quanto antes. *As soon as possible.*
> Quanto a mim, não irei nunca. *As for me, I'll never go.*

quão *adv. how, as.*

QUARENTA *forty.*

quaresma *f. Lent.*

QUARTA, *f. Wednesday.*

QUARTA-FEIRA *f. Wednesday.*

quarteirão *m. city block.*

quartel *m. barracks; quarter.*
> Quartel-general. *General headquarters.*

QUARTO *adj. fourth, m. quarter, fourth; room, bedroom.*
> Estarei lá às dez menos um quarto. *I'll be there at a quarter to ten.*
> Às quatro e um quarto. *At a quarter past four.*
> Quarto de solteiro. *Single bedroom.*
> Quarto de casal. *Double bedroom.*

QUASE *almost, nearly.*
> Quase nunca leio o jornal. *I hardly ever read the newspaper.*
> Quase sempre. *Almost always.*
> Quase nunca. *Hardly ever.*

QUATRO *four.*
> São quatro horas. *It's four o'clock.*

QUATROCENTOS *four hundred.*

QUE *what, how; that, which; who, whom; than.*

> Que deseja? *What do you want?*
> Que é isto? *What's this?*
> Que horas são? *What time is it?*
> Por que me chamou? *Why did you call me?*
> De que está falando (a falar)? *What are you talking about?*
> Que pena! *What a pity! Too bad!*
> Não sei o que disseram. *I don't know what they said.*
> Isso é o que eu digo. *That's what I say.*
> Maria disse que o faria. *Mary said she would do it.*
> Vale mais do que o senhor pensa. *It's worth more than you think.*
> Espero que sim. *I hope so.*
> Ela é mais inteligente (do) que ele. *She is more intelligent than he is.*
> Temos que partir. *We have to leave.*

quê *(used as an interjection or as an interrogative when it stands alone or in final position) what! why! why? something.*
> Por quê? *Why? (For what reason?)*
> Para quê? *Why? (For what purpose?)*
> Não há de quê. *Don't mention it. You're welcome.*

quebra *f. break; crash; bankruptcy.*

quebradiço *adj. fragile, brittle.*

quebrado *adj. broken; ruptured; m. fraction.*

quebra-luz *m. lampshade.*

quebrantar *to break; to wear out.*

QUEBRAR *to break; to burst; to weaken.*
> Quebrar a palavra. *To break one's word.*

queda *f. fall; inclination.*
> Queda de água. *Waterfall*
> Ela tem queda para as letras. *She has a bent for literature.*

quedar *to stay.*

QUEIJO *m. cheese.*

queimado *adj. burned.*
> Cheira a queimado. *It smells like something's burning.*

queimar *to burn; to parch; to sell at reduced prices; to get angry.*
> Queimar as pestanas. *To burn the midnight oil.*

queixa *(x = sh) f. complaint.*
> Apresentar queixa. *To lodge a complaint.*
> Ter motivo de queixa. *To have grounds for complaint.*

queixar-se *(x = sh) to complain.*
> Eles se queixaram das condições nas escolas. *They complained about conditions in the schools.*

queixo *(x = sh) m. chin; jaw.*

queixoso *(x = sh) adj. constantly complaining.*

QUEM *who, whom; whoever; those who.*
> Quem é ele? *Who is he?*
> Quem são os outros convidados? *Who are the other guests?*

Quem fala? *Who's speaking?*

Para quem é esta caixa (x = sh)? *Who is this box for?*

De quem é? *Whose is it?*

Quem fala assim não conhece o problema. *Whoever says that doesn't know the problem.*

QUENTE *warm, hot.*

Está muito quente hoje. *It's very hot today.*

quer *whether, or.*

Quer ele aceite quer não aceite, eu vou continuar. *Whether he accepts or not, I'm going to continue.*

Quer sim, quer não. *Whether yes or no.*

querença *f. affection, fondness; wish, desire.*

QUERER *to wish, to want, to desire; to like.*

Que quer o senhor? *What do you want? What would you like?*

O senhor quer ver o apartamento? *Do you want (would you like) to see the apartment?*

Eu não o quero. *I don't want it.*

Se o senhor quiser. *If you wish.*

Faça como quiser. *Do as you wish.*

Como quiser. *As you wish.*

Quero comprar um relógio. *I want to buy a watch.*

Não quero mais. *I don't want any more.*

Que quer dizer esta palavra? *What does this word mean?*

Sem querer. *Unintentionally.*

Queira Deus. *God willing.*

Querer é poder. *Where there's a will, there's a way.*

querido *adj. dear, beloved.*

Querida filha. *Beloved daughter.*

QUESTÃO *f. question; dispute; matter.*

Eles resolveram a questão. *They settled the matter.*

Eis a questão. *That's the point.*

questionar *to question.*

questionável *adj. questionable, debatable.*

quiçá *perhaps.*

QUIETO *adj. quiet, still.*

Fique quieto! *Be quiet!*

quilate *m. carat; caliber.*

quilha *f. keel.*

quilo *m. kilo, kilogram.*

quilograma *m. kilogram.*

quilômetro (quilómetro) *m. kilometer.*

química *f. chemistry.*

químico *adj. chemical; m. chemist.*

quimono *m. kimono.*

QUINHENTOS *five hundred.*

quinina *f. quinine.*

qüinquagésimo *adj., n. m. fiftieth.*

QUINTA *f. Thursday; farm; country house.*

QUINTA-FEIRA *f. Thursday.*

quintal *m. backyard.*

QUINTO *adj. fifth.*

O quinto andar. *The fifth floor.*

quintuplicar *to quintuple.*

quíntuplo *adj. quintuple, fivefold.*

QUINZE *fifteen.*

Dentro de quinze dias. *Within fifteen days. In two weeks.*

quinzena *f. period of fifteen days, two weeks.*

quiosque *m. kiosk, stand (for newspapers, etc.).*

quitanda *f. vegetable market or shop.*

quitandeiro *m. greengrocer, operator of a quitanda.*

quitar *to free, to release.*

quite *adj. even, clear.*

Estamos quites. *We're even.*

quota *f. quota; share, portion.*

R

rã *f. frog.*

rábano *m. radish.*

rabi *m. rabbi.*

rabo *m. tail.*

De cabo a rabo. *From head to tail. From end to end.*

raça *f. race; breed.*

Raça humana. *Human race.*

Cavalo de raça. *Thoroughbred horse.*

ração *f. ration.*

racemo *m. bunch (grapes).*

raciocinar *to reason.*

raciocínio *m. reasoning.*

racional *adj. rational; reasonable.*

racionar *to ration.*

racista *m. and f. racist.*

radar *m. radar.*

radiação *f. radiation.*

radiador *m. radiator.*

radiar *to radiate; to shine.*

radical *adj. radical; n. m. and f. radical.*

RÁDIO *m. radio; radius; radium.*

Aparelho de rádio. *Radio set.*

Rádio portátil. *Portable radio.*

radioatividade (radioactividade) *f. radioactivity.*

radiodifusão *f. radio broadcasting; radio broadcast.*

radioemissora *f. radio station.*

radiografia *f. radiography; X-ray photography.*

radiouvinte *m. and f. radio listener.*

raia *f. line; ray.*

Passar as raias. *To go too far.*

raiar *to line; to radiate, to shine; to dawn.*

Estaremos iá no raiar do dia. *We'll be there at daybreak.*

rainha f. queen.

RAIO m. ray, beam; spoke (wheel); lightning; thunderbolt; misfortune; radius.
  Raio de sol. A ray of sunlight.
  Raios X. X rays.
  Como um raio. Like a flash.
  Raio de ação (acção). Sphere of action.

raiva f. anger, rage; rabies.
  Ela estava pálida de raiva. She was livid with rage.

raivar to be furious, to be angry, to rage.
  Raivar por. To be "dying to." To be extremely eager or anxious for something.

raivoso adj. furious, angry; mad

raiz f. root.
  Lançar raízes. To take root.
  Raiz quadrada. Square root.

raja f. stripe, streak.

rajado adj. striped, streaked.

ralar to grate; to annoy.

ralhar to scold; to nag; to get angry.

rama f. branches; foliage.
  Algodão em rama. Raw cotton.

ramal m. branch, line, extension.

ramificação f. ramification.

ramo m. branch; limb; bunch (flowers).
  Não sei nada desse ramo da família. I don't know anything about that branch of the family.
  Domingo de Ramos. Palm Sunday.

rampa f. ramp, slope.

rancho m. mess (military); hut; a group of strollers.

ranço adj. rancid.

ranger to gnash; to creak.
  Quando ouviu isso, ele rangeu os dentes. When he heard that, he gnashed his teeth.

rapado adj. scraped; close-cropped.

rapariga f. prostitute Ⓑ; young lady Ⓟ.

RAPAZ m. young man; fellow.

rapidez f. rapidity, swiftness.

RÁPIDO adj. rapid, fast, swift; n. m. express train; messenger service; rapids.
  Vou tomar o rápido. I'm going to take the express.

raposa f. fox.
  Cova de raposa. Foxhole.

raposo m. fox.

raptar to abduct, to kidnap; to rob.

rapto m. kidnapping, abduction; robbery.

raqueta f. racket (tennis).

rareza f. rarity.

raridade f. rarity.

raro adj. rare, unusual.
  Ele é um homem muito raro. He's a very unusual man.
  Raras vezes. Rarely. Seldom.

rascante adj. bitter, sour.

rascar to scratch.

rascunho m. draft, preliminary copy.

rasgadura f. tear, rip.

rasgão m. tear, rip.

rasgar to tear, to rip.
  Rasgar em pedaços. To tear to pieces.

rasgo m. tear, rip; flash of wit; noble deed.
  Rasgo de eloquiencia (eloquência). Burst of eloquence.

raso flat, even, level; n. m. flat land.
  Soldado raso. Private (military).

raspar to scrape; to rasp; to ease.

rasteiro adj. low; creeping.
  Planta rasteira. Creeping plant.

rasto m. track, trail; trace, sign, clue; footprint.
  Andar de rasto. To crawl.

rata f. rat; blunder.

ratificação f. ratification.

ratificar to ratify, to sanction.

rato m. rat, mouse; thief.
  Calado como um rato. Quiet as a mouse.

ratoeira f. mousetrap; trick.

ratoneiro m. petty thief.

RAZÃO f. reason; cause; rate; right.
  Ter razão. To be right.
  Não ter razão. To be wrong.
  O senhor tem razão. You are right.
  Ela não tem razão. She's wrong.
  À razão de. At the rate of.
  Dar ouvidos à razão. To listen to reason.
  Idade da razão. Age of discretion.
  Perder a razão. To lose one's reason.

razoamento m. reasoning.

razoar to reason, to argue.

razoável adj. reasonable, fair.

ré f. female defendant or criminal; stern.
  Marcha à ré. Reverse speed.
  À ré. Astern.

reabastecer to replenish, to restock.

reabilitar to rehabilitate.

reação (reacção) f. reaction.

reacionário (reaccionário) adj. and m. reactionary.

real adj. real; actual; royal; n. m. monetary unit.

realçar to enhance, to intensify.

realidade f. reality; fact.
  Na realidade. Actually. In fact.

realismo m. realism.

realista adj. realistic; royalist; n. m. and f. realist; royalist.

realizar to realize, to accomplish, to fulfill.
  Ele realizou e que tinha projetado (projectado). He accomplished what he had planned.

reaparecer to reappear.

reator (reactor) m. reactor.

rebaixamento *(x = sh) m. reduction, lowering.*

rebaixar *(x = sh) to reduce, to lower, to diminish.*

Esta semana rebaixaram os preços. *This week they lowered prices.*

rebanho *m. flock, herd.*

rebater *to repel; to refute; to discount (note); to return (sports).*

rebelar *to rebel, to revolt.*

rebelde *adj. rebellious; defiant; n. m. and f. rebel.*

rebelião *f. rebellion.*

rebentar *to burst.*

rebocador *m. plasterer; tugboat.*

reboque *m. tow, towing; trailer.*

Levar a reboque. *To take in tow.*

rebuçar *to hide; to muffle up.*

rebuscar *to search; to glean.*

recado *m. message; errand; pl. greetings.*

Tem algum recado para mim? *Do you have a message for me?*

Dê-lhe meus recados. *Give him my regards.*

recaída *f. relapse.*

recair *to fall back; to relapse.*

recalcar *to trample, to read; to repress.*

recalcitrar *to oppose, to resist.*

recanto *m. nook; retreat.*

recatado *adj. prudent, modest, sober.*

recatar-se *to be cautious.*

recato *m. caution.*

RECEAR *to fear.*

Receio que ele não venha. *I'm afraid he won't come.*

RECEBER *to receive, to accept.*

Hoje recebi duas cartas. *I received two letters today.*

receio *m. fear; doubt.*

receita *f. prescription; recipe; receipts, income.*

Aviar uma receita. *To fill a prescription.*

Receita bruta. *Gross income.*

Receita líquida. *Net income.*

receitar *to prescribe.*

recém-chegado *adj. newly arrived; n. m. newcomer.*

RECENTE *adj. recent, new, fresh; modern.*

Um acontecimento recente. *A recent event.*

Recentemente. *Recently.*

recepção *f. reception.*

receptor *m. receiver.*

rechonchudo *adj. fat, chubby.*

recibo *m. receipt.*

Pode me dar (dar-me) um recibo? *Can you give me a receipt?*

recife *m. reef.*

Recife de coral. *Coral reef.*

recinto *m. enclosed area; enclosure.*

recipiente *adj. recipient, receiving; m. receiver, container.*

reciprocar *to reciprocate.*

reciprocidade *f. reciprocity.*

recíproco *adj. reciprocal, mutual.*

Reciprocamente. *Reciprocally.*

recital *f. recital.*

recitar *to recite, to relate.*

reclamação *f. reclamation, complaint.*

reclamante *m. and f. claimant.*

reclamar *to complain, to protest.*

reclamo *m. claim, complaint.*

recluso *adj. confined; n. m. recluse; convict.*

recobrar *to recover, to regain.*

Recobrar a saúde. *To regain one's health.*

RECOLHER *to pick up; to gather; to collect.*

Ela recolheu todos os documentos. *She gathered all the documents.*

recomendação *f. recommendation.*

Carta de recomendação. *Letter of recommendation.*

RECOMENDAR *to recommend, to advise, to command; to entrust.*

Aquele amigo que você recomendou recebeu o emprego. *That friend you recommended received the job.*

recomendável *adj. recommendable.*

recompensa *f. reward, compensation.*

recompensar *to recompense, to reward.*

reconciliação *f. reconciliation.*

reconciliar *to reconcile.*

RECONHECER *to recognize; to admit; to examine; to appreciate.*

O senhor reconhece esta letra? *Do you recognize this handwriting?*

Reconheço que tudo é como ele indicou. *I admit that everything is as he indicated.*

reconhecimento *m. recognition; acknowledgment; appreciation, gratitude; reconnaissance.*

reconstituinte *n. m. tonic.*

reconstrução *f. reconstruction.*

reconstruir *to reconstruct, to rebuild.*

recopilar *to compile, to collect.*

recordação *f. remembrance.*

recordar *to remember, to recall.*

Não posso recordar o nome dele. *I don't recall his name.*

recorde *m. record (sports, etc.)* ⑧.

Ele bateu o recorde. *He broke the record.*

reco-reco *m. Brazilian musical instrument of bamboo.*

recorrer *to go over, to look over; to appear to.*

Recorremos a todos os meios. *We tried everything. (We resorted to all means.")*

recortar *to cut, to trim, to clip, to shorten.*

recorte *m. clipping; outline.*

Eu lhe mandei um recorte do jornal. *I sent him a newspaper clipping.*

recostar *to lean against.*

recostar-se *to lean back, to recline, to lie down.*

recreação *f. recreation, diversion, amusement.*

recrear *to entertain, to amuse, to delight.*

recrear-se *to have a good time.*

recreio *recreation, diversion, amusement.*

recruta *m. recruit, new member.*

recrutar *to recruit.*

recuar *to recede, to back away.*

recuperar *to recuperate, to recover.*

Recuperar as forças. *To recover one's strength.*

Temos que recuperar o tempo perdido. *We have to make up for lost time.*

recurso *m. recourse; appeal; resource; pl. resources, means.*

Sem recursos. *Without means.*

recusar *to refuse, to deny; to reject; to prohibit.*

Recusamos o projeto (projecto). *We turned down the plan.*

redação *f. editing; editorial office.*

redator (redactor) *m. editor.*

rede *f. net; network; trap.*

Rede ferroviária. *Railroad system.*

O animal caiu na rede. *The animal was trapped. The animal fell into the trap.*

rédea *f. reins; control.*

À rédea solta. *At full tilt, at full speed, unrestrained.*

redenção *f. redemption.*

redigir *to write, to compose.*

REDONDO *adj. round; chubby.*

A mesa é redonda. *The table is round.*

Em números redondos. *In round numbers.*

redor *m. circle, circuit; environs.*

Em redor. *Around. All around.*

Ao redor. *Around. All around.*

redução *f. reduction.*

redundância *f. redundance.*

redundante *adj. redundant.*

redundar *to redound, to result.*

reduzir *to reduce, to cut down.*

De hoje em diante vou reduzir as minhas despesas. *From now on I'll cut down on my expenses.*

Reduzir a cinzas. *To reduce to ashes.*

reeleger *to reelect.*

reeleição *f. reelection.*

reembolsar *to reimburse.*

reembolso *m. reimbursement, refund.*

refazer *to make over, to redo.*

refeição *f. meal.*

Fazer uma refeição. *To have a meal.*

referência *f. reference.*

Com referência a. *With regard to.*

referente *adj. referring, relating.*

referir *to refer.*

refinado *adj. refined, polished.*

refinar *to refine, to improve.*

refinaria *f. refinery.*

refletir (reflectir) *to reflect.*

refletor (reflector) *adj. reflective; n. m. reflector.*

reflexão *(x = ks) f. reflection, thought.*

reflexionar *(x = ks) to think over, to reflect.*

reflexivo *(x = ks) adj. reflexive.*

reflexo *(x = ks) adj. reflected; n. m. reflex.*

Ação (Acção) reflexa. *Reflex action.*

reforçar *to reinforce, to strengthen.*

reforma *f. reform, reformation; alteration; remodeling.*

reformar *to reform; to correct; to alter; to remodel; to retire.*

reformar-se *to retire.*

Depois de quarenta anos de serviço militar, o general se reformou (reformou-se). *After forty years of military service, the general retired.*

reformatório *m. reformatory.*

refrão *m. refrain; chorus; saying, proverb.*

refrear *to curb, to restrain, to refrain.*

refrega *f. fight, skirmish, fray.*

refrescante *adj. cooling; refreshing.*

refrescar *to refresh; to cool.*

Refrescar a memória. *To refresh one's memory.*

refresco *m. refreshment; cold drink.*

refrigerador *adj. refrigerating, cooling; n. m. refrigerator, icebox.*

refrigerar *to refrigerate, to cool.*

refugiado *m. refugee.*

refugiar-se *to take refuge; to take shelter.*

refúgio *m. refuge, shelter, haven.*

regadeira *f. shower; gutter; irrigation ditch.*

regador *adj. irrigating; n. m. sprinkler, watering can.*

regalado *adj. regaled; pleased.*

Ele leva uma vida regalada. *He leads an easy life.*

regalar *to regale; to enjoy.*

regalo *m. regalement; pleasure, gift.*

regar *to water, to irrigate.*

regata *f. boat race, regatta.*

regatear *to bargain, to haggle; to stint.*

regateio *m. haggling.*

regeneração *f. regeneration.*

regenerar *to regenerate.*

regente *m. regent; leader; conductor.*

reger *to rule, to govern.*

região *f. region; district.*

Região campestre. *Country. Countryside.*

regime, regímen *m. regime; diet.*

Eu estou fazendo (a fazer) regime. *I'm on a diet.*

O país mudou de regime. *The country had a change of government.*

regimento *m. regiment.*

régio *adj. royal, regal.*

regional *adj. regional, local.*

registrar, registar *to register, to put on record.*

As compras se registram (registram-se) neste livro. *Purchases are entered in this book.*

Registrar uma carta. *To register a letter.*

registro, registo *m. registration; register; record.*

Registro de nomes. *Directory of names.*

REGRA *f. rule; ruler (for measuring).*

O passaporte está em regra? *Is the passport in order?*

Tudo está em regra. *Everything is in order.*

Estas são as regras do jogo. *These are the rules of the game.*

Não há regra sem exceção (excepção). *There is an exception to every rule.*

regressar *to return, to go back, to come back.*

Regressarei na sexta. *I'll be back Friday.*

regresso *m. return.*

regulamento *m. rule, regulation, law.*

REGULAR *to regulate, to adjust; adj. regular, ordinary; fair, moderate; fairly good.*

Regular o tráfico. *To regulate traffic.*

João recebe um salário regular. *John receives a moderate salary.*

rei *m. king.*

reimprimir *to reprint.*

reinado *m. reign.*

reinar *to reign; to predominate, to prevail.*

O rei reinou durante vinte anos. *The king reigned for twenty years.*

reino *m. kingdom, reign.*

reintegrar *to restore.*

réis *m. pl. former monetary unit of Brazil.*

reiterar *to reiterate.*

reitor *m. rector, dean.*

rejeitar *to reject.*

RELAÇÃO *f. relation, connection; report; pl. connections.*

Não há relação entre estas duas coisas. *There is no relation (connection) between these two things.*

Nós estamos em boas relações com eles. *We are on good terms with them.*

relacionado *adj. acquainted; related.*

relacionar *to relate; to connect.*

relâmpago *m. lightning.*

relampejar *to lighten (lightning).*

relatar *to relate, to tell.*

relativo *adj. relative.*

Relativo a. *With reference to.*

relato *m. account, statement, story.*

Ele fez um relato do que tinha acontecido. *He gave an account of what had happened.*

relatório *m. report; statement.*

reler *to reread.*

relevo *m. relief, projection.*

religião *f. religion.*

religioso *adj. religious.*

RELÓGIO *m. clock, watch.*

Relógio de bolso. *Pocket watch.*

Relógio-pulseira. *Wristwatch.*

Dar corda ao relógio. *To wind a watch.*

O relógio está adiantado. *The watch is fast.*

O relógio está astrasado. *The watch is slow.*

relojoaria *f. watchmaking; watchmaker's shop.*

relojoeiro *m. watchmaker.*

reluzir *to shine, to sparkle.*

Nem tudo que reluz é ouro. *All that glitters is not gold.*

remar *to row, to paddle.*

rematar *to complete; to put the finishing touches on.*

remate *m. end, conclusion, finish.*

remediar *to remedy; to make good; to help.*

Isso não se pode remediar. *That can't be helped.*

REMÉDIO *m. remedy; medicine.*

Isto não tem remédio. *There's no remedy for this. This can't be helped.*

Não há remédio. *It can't be helped.*

Sem remédio. *Irremediable.*

Remédio caseiro. *Household remedy.*

remendar *to mend, to patch.*

remessa *f. remittance; shipment.*

remetente *adj. sending; n. m. and f. sender.*

remeter *to remit, to send.*

Faça o favor de remeter (as) minhas cartas a este endereço. *Please forward my mail to this address.*

remir *to redeem.*

remitente *adj. remittent.*

remitir *to remit, to forgive; to abate.*

remo *m. oar, paddle.*

Remo de duas pás. *Double-bladed paddle*

remodelar *to remodel.*

remoinhar *to spin, to whirl.*

remontar *to remount, to repair; to go up; to go back.*

remorso *m. remorse.*

remover *to remove; to take away.*

remuneração *f. remuneration; reward.*

remunerar *to remunerate, to reward.*

renascença *f. renaissance, rebirth; Renaissance.*

renascer *to be reborn; to grow again.*

renascimento *m. rebirth.*

RENDA *f. income, revenue; rent; lace.*

Imposto de renda. *Income tax.*

Renda bruta. *Gross income.*

render *to subdue; to surrender; to produce, to yield; to tire out.*

Este negócio rende pouco. *This business is not very profitable.*

Render homenagem. *To pay homage.*

rendição *f. surrender.*

rendido *adj. split; submissive; overcome.*

rendimento *m. income, return; surrender.*

Rendimento bruto. *Gross income.*

renegado *m. renegade.*

renegar *to deny; to reject.*

renhido *adj. hard-fought; furious.*

renome *m. renown, fame.*

renomeado *adj. renowned, famous.*

renovação *f. renovation, renewal.*

renovar *to renovate, to renew; to reform.*

rente *adj. close, even with.*

Cortar bem rente. *To cut quite close*

renúncia *f. renunciation; resignation.*

renunciar *to renounce; to reject, to resign.*

Eu renunciei o emprego. *I resigned the position.*

Renunciar um direito. *To give up a right.*

reorganização *f. reorganization.*

reorganizador *adj. reorganizing, reforming; n. m. reorganizer.*

reorganizar *to reorganize.*

reparação *f. reparation, repair; amends; satisfaction.*

reparador *adj. reparative; compensating; n. m. repairer.*

reparar *to repair; to notice.*

Reparei em que todos olhavam para ela. *I noticed that they were all looking at her.*

reparo *m. repair; notice; remark.*

repartição *f. partition; department.*

repartidor *adj. sharing; n. m. sharer.*

repartir *to distribute, to divide.*

Repartiram os lucros. *They divided the profits.*

repassar *to go over, to review; to soak.*

Vamos repassar a lição. *Let's review the lesson.*

repelir *to repel; to reject.*

repente *m. sudden act; outburst.*

De repente. *Suddenly. All of a sudden.*

repentino *adj. sudden.*

repercussão *f. repercussion; reaction.*

repercutir *to echo; to reverberate; to have a repercussion.*

repertório *m. repertory; repertoire; list, index.*

repetente *adj. repeating; n. m. and f. repeater (student).*

repetição *f. repetition.*

O relatório está cheio de repetições *The report is full of repetitions.*

REPETIR *to repeat.*

Faça o favor de repetir o que disse. *Please repeat what you said.*

Repito que eu não vou. *I repeat that I'm not going.*

repicar *to pierce; to ring, to peal, to toll; to mince, to chop.*

repleto *adj. full, replete.*

O ônibus (autocarro) está repleto. *The bus is full.*

réplica *f. reply, answer.*

Não gostamos (gostámos) de (da) sua réplica. *We didn't like your answer.*

replicar *to reply, to retort.*

Não me repliques! *Don't answer back! Don't talk back to me!*

repor *to replace; to restore.*

reportagem *f. reporting, report.*

reportor *to go back in time; to moderate.*

repórter *m. and f. reporter.*

repositório *m. repository.*

repreender *to reprimand, to reprehend.*

represa *f. dam.*

representação *f. representation; performance.*

representante *adj. representative; n. m. and f. representative, agent.*

representar *to represent; to act, perform.*

Que casa representa? *Which firm do you represent?*

Eu vi a peça; ela representou muito mal. *I saw the play; she performed very badly. I saw the play; her acting was very bad.*

repressão *f. repression.*

reprimir *to repress, to check, to hold in check.*

Não me pude reprimir por mais tempo. *I couldn't contain myself any longer.*

reprodução *f. reproduction.*

reproduzir *to reproduce.*

reprovar *to reprove; to fail.*

O aluno foi reprovado. *The student failed.*

reptil (réptil) *m. reptile.*

república *f. republic.*

republicano *adj. republican; n. m. republican.*

repudiar *to repudiate; to disavow.*

repugnância *f. repugnance; dislike.*

repugnante *adj. repugnant, distasteful.*

repugnar *to be distasteful, to be repugnant; to dislike, to detest; to reject; to oppose.*

Isso me repugna. *I detest it.*

repulsa *f. repulsion, aversion.*

repulsar *to repulse, to repeal.*

reputação *f. reputation, name.*

Ele tem uma boa reputação. *He has a good reputation.*

requerer *to require, to request.*

Isso requer muita atenção. *That requires a lot of attention.*

requisito *m. requisite, requirement.*

rés *adj. level; close.*

Rés-do-chão. *Ground floor.*
resenha *f. report; list; summary.*
resenhar *to report; to list.*
reserva *f. reserve; reservation; privacy.*
Reserva mental. *Mental reservation.*
Sem reserva. *Without reservation.*
Unreservedly.
De reserva. *Extra. Spare. In reserve.*
Fundo de reserva. *Reserve fund.*
reservado *adj. reserved; cautious; confidential.*
reservar *to reserve; to keep.*
Queremos que nos reserve um lugar. *We want you to reserve a place (to make a reservation) for us.*
resfriado *m. a cold.*
Apanhei um resfriado. *I caught a cold.*
resfriar *to cool.*
resgatar *to redeem; to release.*
resgate *m. redemption; release.*
resguardar *to protect, to guard.*
resguardo *m. protection; guard.*
residência *f. residence.*
residencial *adj. residential.*
residente *adj. residing, resident; n. m. and f. resident, inhabitant.*
residir *to reside, to live.*
Resido na Rua da Alfândega. *I live on Alfândega Street.*
resíduo *adj. residual; n. m. residue, remainder.*
resignação *f. resignation; patience.*
resignar *to resign.*
resignar-se *to resign oneself, to be resigned.*
resistência *f. resistance.*
resistente *adj. resistant; hardy.*
resistir *to resist, to endure.*
Resistir a tentação. *To resist temptation.*
Resistir à prova. *To stand the test.*
resmungar *to grumble, to mumble.*
resolução *f. resolution; determination; decision; solution.*
É preciso tomarmos uma resolução. *We must come to some decision.*
resoluto *adj. resolute.*
resolver *to resolve, to determine, to decide; to solve; to dissolve; to settle.*
Resolvi fazê-lo eu mesmo. *I was determined to do it myself.*
Este problema é difícil de resolver. *This problem is difficult to solve.*
respeitar *to respect, to honor.*
respeitável *adj. respectable.*
RESPEITO *m. relation; respect; reference; regard.*
Com respeito a. *With regard to. Concerning.*
A respeito de. *With regard to. Concerning.*
Falta de respeito. *Disrespect.*

respeitoso *adj. respectful, polite.*
respiração *f. respiration, breathing.*
Falta de respiração. *Shortness of breath.*
respirar *to breathe.*
Deixe-me *(x = sh)* respirar. *Give me a chance to catch my breath.*
respiro *m. breath, breathing; respite.*
resplandecer *to shine.*
RESPONDER *to answer, to respond; to be responsible for.*
Ele nem sequer me respondeu. *He didn't even answer me.*
Quem responde por ele? *Who answers for (is responsible for) him?*
responsabilidade *f. responsibility.*
responsável *adj. responsible, liable.*
RESPOSTA *f answer, reply, retort, response.*
Resposta favorável. *Favorable reply.*
Resposta negativa. *Negative reply. Refusal.*
ressaltar *to rebound; to stand out; to stress.*
ressentir-se *to resent; to feel.*
Ela se ressentiu por nada. *She became offended over nothing.*
ressoar *to resound.*
ressonância *f. resonance.*
ressonar *to resound.*
ressurgimento *m. resurgence.*
ressurgir *to resurge; to reappear.*
ressuscitar *to resuscitate.*
restabelecer *to reestablish; to restore.*
restante *adj. remaining; n. m. remainder.*
Posta-restante. *General delivery.*
restar *to remain, to be left.*
Restam-me cinco dólares. *I have five dollars left.*
restauração *f. restoration.*
restaurante *m. restaurant.*
restaurar *to restore.*
restituição *f. restitution.*
restituir *to restore*
RESTO *m. rest, remainder; pl. remains; leftovers.*
A cozinheira sabe aproveitar os restos. *The cook knows how to make good use of leftovers.*
De resto. *Besides.*
restrição *f. restriction.*
restringir *to restrain; to curtail; to restrict, to limit.*
RESULTADO *m. result.*
Qual foi o resultado? *What was the result?*
resultar *to result.*
Resultou-nos muito caro. *It was very costly for us.*
resumido *adj. condensed; abridged.*
resumir *to abridge, to cut short; to summarize.*
Resumir um discurso. *To cut a speech short.*

resumo *m. summary.*
retaguarda *f. rear guard.*
retalho *m. piece, scrap.*
  A retalho. *At retail.*
  Colcha de retalhos. *Patchwork quilt.*
retângulo (rectângulo) *m. rectangle.*
retardamento *m. delay.*
retardar *to retard, to delay.*
reter *to retain; to withhold; to keep; to*
  remember.
  A polícia o reteve (reteve-o). *The police*
  detained him.
  Não posso reter tanta informação. *I can't*
  retain so much information.
reticência *f. reticence.*
retificar (rectificar) *to rectify, to correct.*
retina *f. retina.*
retirada *f. retreat, withdrawal.*
retirado *adj. withdrawn; retired.*
retirar *to withdraw; to retire; to take back.*
  O general retirou as tropas. *The general*
  withdrew his troops.
retirar-se *to leave; to retire.*
  Ela se retirou (retirou-se) ao seu quarto.
  She retired to her room.
retiro *m. retreat.*
reto (recto) *adj. straight; just, upright; erect.*
  Ele é um homem reto. *He is an*
  upright man.
  Ângulo reto. *Right angle.*
  Linha reta. *Straight line.*
retocar *to retouch.*
retoque *m. retouch; finishing touch.*
retorcer *to twist.*
retornar *to return; to restore.*
retorno *m. return; exchange.*
retorsão *f. twisting.*
retraído *adj. withdrawn, reserved.*
  Ele é muito retraído. *He is quite*
  withdrawn.
retraimento *m. reserve; retreat; seclusion.*
retrair *to retract, to hold back.*
retratar *to portray; to show.*
retrato *m. portrait; photograph; picture.*
  Tirar o retrato. *To take a picture.*
  Ele é o retrato fiel de seu pai. *He's the*
  living image of his father.
retrete *f. toilet; lavatory.*
retribuição *f. reward.*
retribuir *to pay back; to reward.*
retrocedente *adj. retrocedent, retroceding.*
retroceder *to back up; to draw back; to fall*
  back; to grow worse.
  Ele não pôde retroceder na sua decisão. *He*
  could not reverse his decision.
retrospecção (retrospeção) *f. retrospection.*
retumbar *to resound.*
réu *m. male defendant; convict.*
reumatismo *m. rheumatism.*

reunião *f. reunion; meeting.*
  Haverá uma reunião às cinco. *There will be*
  a meeting at five o'clock.
reunir *to gather; to collect; to bring together.*
  O professor reuniu os alunos numa festa.
  The teacher brought his students
  together at a party.
reunir-se *to get together; to meet; to join.*
  A que horas podíamos reunir-nos? *What*
  time could we get together?
  Reunem-se de dois em dois anos. *They get*
  together every two years.
revelação *f. revelation.*
revelar *to reveal, to show; to disclose; to*
  develop (photography).
  Revelar um segredo. *To reveal a secret.*
  O autor revelou grande talento nesse livro.
  The author showed great talent in that
  book.
revendedor *m. dealer; retailer.*
revender *to resell; to retail.*
reverência *f. reverence; bow.*
  Fazer uma reverência. *To bow.*
reverso *adj. reverse, opposite; n. m. reverse.*
  O reverso da medalha. *The other side of*
  the coin. The other side of the question.
revés *m. reverse; backhand; misfortune.*
  Ao revés. *Upside down. Inside out.*
revisão *f. revision; review.*
revisar *to look over; to revise; to review.*
  Revisar os livros. *To audit the books.*
revisor *m. conductor; reviewer; proofreader.*
REVISTA *f. review; magazine; musical*
  comedy.
  Ainda não recebi esse número da revista. *I*
  haven't yet received that issue of the
  magazine.
reviver *to revive.*
revocação *f. revocation, repeal.*
revocar *to revoke, to repeal, to evoke.*
revolta *f. revolt.*
revoltoso *adj. rebellious.*
revolução *f. revolution.*
revolucionário *adj. n. m. revolutionary.*
revolver *to revolve; to turn; to stir.*
  Revolver céu e terra. *To move heaven and*
  earth.
revólver *m. revolver.*
rezar *to pray; to read, to say.*
  Ela reza todos os dias. *She prays (says her*
  prayers) every day.
  Reza aqui que . . . *It says here that . . .*
riacho *m. brook.*
ribeira *f. bank (river); shore.*
ribeiro *m. stream, brook.*
RICO *adj. rich, wealthy.*
  Se eu fosse rico não trabalharia tanto. *If I*
  were rich, I wouldn't work so much.
ridicularizar *to ridicule.*

ridículo *adj. ridiculous, foolish; n. m. ridiculous thing; ridiculous person.*
    Fazer-se ridículo. *To make a fool of oneself.*

rifa *f. raffle.*

rifar *to raffle.*

rifle *m. rifle.*

rigidez *f. rigidity; sternness.*

rígido *adj. rigid; severe; hard; stern.*

rigor *m. rigor.*

rigoroso *adj. rigorous, severe, strict.*

rijo *adj. rigid.*

rim *m. kidney.*

rima *f. rhyme.*

rinha Ⓑ *f. cockfight; fight.*

rinoceronte *m. rhinoceros.*

RIO *m. river.*
    Rio abaixo *(x = sh). Down the river. Downstream.*
    O Rio de Janeiro. *Rio de Janeiro ("the river of January").*

rio-grandense-do-norte *adj. and n. m. of the state of Rio Grande do Norte of Brazil.*

rio-grandense-do sul *adj. and n. m. of the state of Rio Grande do Sul of Brazil.*

riqueza *f. riches, wealth.*

RIR *to laugh.*
    Rir às gargalhadas. *To laugh out loud. To laugh heartily.*

RIR-SE *to laugh.*
    Por que se ri dele? *Why do you laugh at him?*

risada *f. laughter.*

risco *m. risk.*
    Correr um risco. *To run a risk. To take a chance.*

RISO *m. laughter, laugh.*
    Um frouxo *(x = sh)* Ⓑ de riso. *A fit of laughter.*
    Isso não é motivo de riso. *That's no laughing matter.*

risonho *adj. smiling, pleasing.*

ritmo *m. rhythm.*

rito *m. rite, ceremony.*

rival *adj., n. m. and f. rival.*

rivalidade *f. rivalry.*

rivalizar *to vie, to compete, to rival.*

robusto *adj. robust, strong.*
    Ele é muito robusto. *He is very strong.*

roça *f. rock.*

roça *f. country, backwoods; plot of cleared land.*

rocha *f. stone, boulder.*
    Rocha calcária. *Limestone.*

rochoso *adj. rocky.*

rocio *m. dew.*
    Rocio da manhã. *Morning dew.*

RODA *f. wheel, circle.*
    Roda da sorte. *Wheel of fortune.*

    Roda sobressalente. *Spare wheel.*

rodagem *f. set of wheels.*
    Estrada de rodagem. *Highway.*

rodante *adj. rolling.*
    Material rodante. *Rolling stock.*

rodapé *m. valance; baseboard; newspaper article at bottom of the page.*

rodar *to roll; to revolve; to rake.*

rodeio *m. rodeo; evasion.*
    Deixe *(x = sh)* de rodeios e responda claramente. *Stop beating around the bush and give a straight answer.*

rodovia *f. highway* Ⓑ.

rodoviário *adj. of or for a highway* Ⓑ.

roer *to gnaw; to nibble; to erode.*

rogar *to pray, to beg, to entreat, to request.*
    Rogo-lhe que . . . *I beg you to . . . Please . . .*

rogo *m. request, petition; plea.*

rol *m. roll, list.*

rolante *adj. rolling.*
    Escada rolante. *Escalator.*

rolar *to roll, to revolve.*

roiha *f. cork, stopper.*
    Saca-rolhas. *Corkscrew.*

rolo *m. roll; roller.*

romance *m. novel; romance.*

romanceiro *m. collection of songs, poems, etc.*

romano *adj., n. m. Roman.*

romanticismo *m. romanticism.*

romântico *adj., n. m. romantic.*

romantismo *m. romanticism.*

romaria *f. pilgrimage, excursion, tour.*

romeiro *m. pilgrim.*

ROMPER *to break; to smash; to tear; to rip; to fracture; to start, to begin.*
    De repente ela rompeu o silêncio. *Suddenly, she broke the silence.*
    Nós rompemos com eles. *We broke with them.*
    Romper em pranto. *To burst into tears.*
    Ao romper do dia. *At daybreak.*

roncar *to snore; to roar.*

ronco *m. snore; roar.*

ronda *f. watch, patrol; rounds.*

rondar *to watch, to patrol.*

ronha *f. scabies; malice, ill will.*

roque *m. rock, rock music/song.*

roqueiro (-ra) *rock musician/fan.*

rosa *f. rose.*
    Não há rosa sem espinhos. *No rose without a thorn.*

rosal *m. rose garden.*

rosário *m. rosary.*

rosca *f. ring (bread or cake), thread (of a screw).*

roseira *f. rosebush.*

ROSTO *m. face.*

rota *f. rout; route; course.*

roteiro *m. itinerary, schedule.*

rotina *f. routine; habit; rut.*

roubar *to rob, to steal.*
Roubaram-me a carteira. *They stole my wallet.*

roubo *m. robbery, theft.*

ROUPA *f. wearing apparel, clothing, clothes.*
Tenho que mudar de roupa. *I have to change my clothes.*
Roupa feita. *Ready-made clothes.*
Roupa de cama. *Bed linen.*

roupão *m. bathrobe; dressing gown.*

rouxinol *(x = sh) m. nightingale.*

roxo *(x = sh) adj. purple.*

RUA *f. street.*
Rua de uma mão. *One-way street.*
Rua principal. *Main street.*

rubi *m. ruby.*

rubo *m. brier, bramble.*

ruborizar *to redden, to blush.*

rude *adj. rude; rough; harsh.*

rudez, rudeza *f. rudeness; roughness, harshness.*

rugido *adj. roaring; n. m. roar.*

rugir *to roar; to bellow.*

ruído *m. noise.*

ruim *adj. bad; terrible; inferior.*
Eu achei o filme muito ruim. *I thought the film was terrible.*

ruína *f. ruin; downfall; pl. ruins.*

ruinoso *adj. ruinous.*

rumar *to steer; to head (for).*

rumo *m. course; route, direction.*
Vamos tomar outro rumo. *We'll take another course (road).*
Sem rumo. *Adrift. Without direction.*

rumor *m. rumor; noise.*

ruptura *f. rupture; break.*

rural *adj. rural, rustic.*

russo *adj., n. m. Russian.*

rústico *adj. rustic, rural.*

SÁBADO *m. Saturday.*

SABÃO *m. soap.*

sabedoria *f. learning, knowledge, wisdom.*

SABER *to know; to know how; to be able to; to taste; to find out.*
O senhor sabe a que horas abrem as lojas? *Do you know at what time the stores open?*
O senhor sabe nadar? *Can you (do you know how to) swim?*
Sei lá! *I don't know! How should I know?*
Quem sabe! *Who knows!*

Ela não sabe nada. *She doesn't know anything.*
Como se sabe. *As is known.*
Que eu saiba. *As far as I know.*
Pelo que sei. *As far as I know.*
Saber de cor. *To know by heart.*

sabiá *m. thrush, bird of Brazil.*

sábio *adj. wise, learned; n. m. scholar, sage.*

SABONETE *m. bath soap.*

sabor *m. taste, flavor.*

saborear *to flavor; to savor; to relish.*

saboroso *adj. delicious, tasty; pleasant.*
O jantar foi muito saboroso. *The dinner was delicious.*

sabotagem *f. sabotage.*

sabotar *to sabotage.*

sabre *m. saber.*

saca *f. bag, sack.*

sacar *to draw out.*

saca-rolhas *m. corkscrew.*

saciar *to satiate.*

SACO *m. sack; bag; purse.*
O que há neste saco de papel? *What's in this paper bag?*

sacramento *m. sacrament.*

sacrificar *to sacrifice.*

sacrifício *m. sacrifice.*

sacrilégio *m. sacrilege.*

sacristão *m. sexton.*

sacristia *f. sacristy, vestry.*

sacro *adj. sacred, holy.*

sacrossanto *adj. sacrosanct.*

sacudida *f. shock; shake, shaking, jolt.*

sacudidela *f. shock; shake, shaking, jolt.*

sacudidura *f. shaking.*

sacudir *to shake.*
Sacudir a cabeça. *To shake the head.*

sadio *adj. sound, healthy.*

sagacidade *f. sagacity, shrewdness.*

sagaz *adj. sagacious; shrewd; clever.*

sagrado *adj. sacred.*

saia *f. skirt.*

SAÍDA *f. departure; exit; outlet; loophole.*
Saída de emergência. *Emergency exit.*
Um beco sem saída. *A blind alley.*
Rua sem saída. *Dead-end street.*

sainete *m. short comedy or farce.*

SAIR *to go out; to leave; to depart; to appear; to come out.*
Ela já saiu. *She's already left.*
Ela sai à sua mãe. *She takes after her mother.*
A família saiu de viagem. *The family left on a trip.*
Vou sair ao ar livre. *I'm going out into the open air.*
Tudo saiu bem. *It all came out fine.*
Sair da linha. *To get out of line.*
Sair caro. *To end up costing a lot.*

SAL m. salt; wit.

Sal e pimenta. Salt and pepper.

SALA f. room.

Quantos alunos há na sala de aula? How many students are there in the classroom?

Sala de espera. Waiting room.

Sala de jantar. Dining room.

salada f. salad.

salão m. large room; hall; salon; parlor.

Salão de beleza. Beauty parlor.

Salão de baile. Dance hall. Ballroom.

salário m. salary, wages.

saldar to settle.

saldo m. balance, remainder.

Saldo negativo. Debit balance.

Saldo positivo. Credit balance.

saleiro m. salt shaker.

salgado adj. salty, salted; witty.

salientar to make clear, to point out.

saliente adj. salient, prominent.

saliva f. saliva.

salmão m. salmon.

salmo m. psalm.

salpicar to sprinkle (with).

salpico m. sprinkle; speck, a drop or dash of something.

salsa f. parsley; sauce.

salsicha f. sausage.

SALTAR to jump, to leap; to hop; to skip; to omit.

Você pode saltar a parede? Can you jump over the wall?

Ela saltou várias palavras. She skipped several words.

Saltar do ônibus (autocarro). To get off the bus.

Saltar da cama. To jump out of bed.

saltear to assault, to attack.

SALTO m. jump, leap; heel.

Dar saltos. To jump. To leap.

Salto de borracha. Rubber heel.

salubre adj. salutary, healthy.

salva f. salvo; volley; tray.

Uma salva de aplausos. Thunderous applause.

salvação f. salvation.

salvamento m. salvage; rescue.

salvar to save (also on computer); to salvage; to jump over.

O médico perdeu a esperança de salvá-lo. The doctor lost hope of saving him.

salva-vidas m. life preserver; lifeguard; lifeboat.

salvo adj. safe, saved; prep. besides, except.

São e salvo. Safe and sound.

Em salvo. Safe.

Todos vieram salvo ele. Everyone came except him.

salvo-conduto m. safe-conduct, pass.

samba m. samba (Brazilian music and dance).

sanar to cure, to heal; to recover.

sanatório m. sanatorium, sanitarium.

sanção f. sanction.

sancionar to sanction; to confirm.

sandália f. sandal.

sanduíche m. sandwich.

saneamento m. sanitation.

sanear to make sanitary; to repair.

sangrar to bleed.

sangrento adj. bloody.

SANGUE m. blood.

A sangue e fogo. Without mercy.

A sangue frio. In cold blood.

Ter o sangue quente. To be hot-blooded.

sanha f. anger, fury.

sanitário adj. sanitary, hygienic.

SANTO adj. saintly, holy; n. m. saint.

Semana Santa. Holy Week (the week leading up to Easter).

Santo Antônio (António). Saint Anthony.

Santa Bárbara. Saint Barbara.

Despir um santo para vestir outro. To rob Peter to pay Paul.

SÃO adj. sound, healthy; sane; safe; n. m. saint.

Regressou são e salvo. He returned safe and sound.

São Pedro. Saint Peter.

sapataria f. shoe store; shoe repair shop.

sapateiro m. shoemaker.

SAPATO m. shoe.

Um par de sapatos. A pair of shoes.

Onde aperta o sapato? Where does the shoe pinch?

Sapatos de tênis (ténis). Tennis shoes. Sneakers.

Sapatos de salto alto. High-heeled shoes.

Calçar os sapatos. To put your shoes on.

Descalçar os sapatos. To take your shoes off.

sapo m. toad.

saque m. bank draft; serve (tennis); sack, sacking, plunder.

saquear to sack, to loot, to pillage.

sarampo m. measles.

sarar to cure, to heal; to correct.

sarcasmo m. sarcasm.

sardinha f. sardine.

sargento m. sergeant.

sarna f. scabies, itch.

satanás m. Satan, devil.

satélite m. satellite.

sátira f. satire.

satírico adj. satiric.

SATISFAÇÃO f. satisfaction; pleasure; apology.

Eu tive a satisfação de conhecê-lo. I had the pleasure of meeting him.

Isso foi uma grande satisfação para mim. *That gave me great satisfaction.*

Dar satisfações. *To apologize.*

satisfatório *adj. satisfactory.*

SATISFAZER *to satisfy; to please; to pay (a debt).*

O trabalho dele não me satisfaz. *His work doesn't satisfy me.*

Satisfazer uma dívida. *To pay a debt.*

SATISFEITO *adj. satisfied, content; fulfilled.*

Queremos que todos estejam satisfeitos. *We want everyone to be satisfied.*

Estou satisfeito. *I'm satisfied.*

SAUDADE *f. longing, yearning, nostalgia, wistfulness; pl. regards, greetings; longing.*

Ter saudades de. *To miss. To long for.*

Tenho saudades de minha terra. *I'm homesick (for my country, district).*

saudar *to greet, to salute.*

Ele a saudou (saudou-a) muito afetuosamente (afectuosamente). *He greeted her affectionately.*

saudável *adj. healthful, good for the health; salutary; beneficial.*

SAÚDE *f. health.*

Ela está de boa saúde. *She is in good health.*

Ela está bem de saúde. *She is in good health.*

Ele está mal de saúde. *He is in bad health.*

Estamos gozando de boa saúde. *We are enjoying good health.*

À sua saúde! *To your health! (a toast).*

saudoso *adj. longing, yearning, homesick.*

sazão *f. season; time.*

Em sazão. *At the proper time. In season.*

sazonar *to season; to mature, to ripen.*

SE *(third person reflexive pronoun; also used as reciprocal pronoun and for the passive voice) himself, herself, themselves, etc.*

O menino não se lavou antes de sentar-se à mesa. *The boy did not wash before sitting at the table.*

Cale-se! *Be quiet! Be still!*

Diz-se que . . . *It's said that . . .*

Sabe-se que . . . *It's known that . . .*

Eles se conhecem (conhecem-se). *They know each other.*

Escrevem-se todos os dias. *They write to each other every day.*

Como se chama o senhor? *What is your name?*

Fala-se português. *Portuguese is spoken (here).*

SE *conj. if, whether.*

Se o senhor quiser. *If you wish.*

Se tivesse o dinheiro eu o compraria. *If I had the money, I would buy it.*

Se ela chegar antes das oito iremos ao cinema. *If she arrives before eight, we'll go to the movies.*

Se bem que . . . *Although . . .*

Se não. *If not.*

sé *f. see.*

A Santa Sé. *The Holy See.*

seca *f. drought, dry spell.*

secante *adj. drying, boring; n. m. drying agent; bore.*

secão (secção) *f. section; division; department; cutting, portion.*

Em que seção trabalha? *In what section do you work?*

SECAR *to dry.*

Ela pôs a roupa a secar ao sol. *She put the clothes out to dry in the sun.*

SECO *adj. dry, withered; lean; curt; rude.*

Tenho a garganta seca. *My throat is dry.*

Ele é um homem seco. *He is a very curt ("dry") person.*

Clima seco. *Dry climate.*

Vinho seco. *Dry wine.*

secretaria *f. secretariat; office.*

secretária *f. female secretary; desk.*

secretária electrônica *f. answering machine.*

secretário *m. male secretary.*

secreto *adj. secret; private.*

Serviço secreto. *Secret service.*

século *m. century; age; a long time.*

Estamos no século vinte. *We are in the twentieth century.*

Há um século que não o vejo. *I haven't seen you for ages.*

secundar *to second; to support; to aid.*

Ela o secunda em tudo. *She supports him in everything.*

secundário *adj. secondary.*

seda *f. silk.*

Bicho da seda. *Silkworm.*

Papel de seda. *Tissue paper.*

Gravata de seda. *Silk tie.*

sede *f. seat, headquarters.*

SEDE *f. thirst; desire, craving.*

Estou com sede. (Tenho sede). *I'm thirsty.*

sedento *adj. thirsty.*

sedição *f. sedition; rebellion.*

sedimento *m. sediment.*

sedução *f. seduction, enticement.*

sedutor *adj. seductive, enticing; n. m. seducer.*

seduzir *to seduce; to tempt; to fascinate.*

segredo *m. secret; secrecy; mystery.*

Você pode guardar o segredo? *Can you keep the secret?*

segregacionismo *m. segregation.*

segregacionista *m. and f. segregationist.*

segregar *to segregate, to separate.*

seguido *adj. continued; following.*

Em seguida. *Right away. Immediately. Next.*

SEGUINTE adj. following, next.
  No dia seguinte ele partiu. *The following day he left.*
  Não gosto de todos; mande-me só os seguintes: *I don't like all of them; send me only the following:*
SEGUIR to follow; to pursue; to continue, to go on, to keep on.
  Siga-me. *Follow me.*
  Seguirei os seus conselhos. *I'll follow your advice.*
  Siga bem em frente. *Continue straight ahead.*
  Que segue depois? *What comes afterward?*
  Como segue: *As follows:*
  É preciso seguir as instruções. *You must follow the directions.*
  Quem segue? *Who's next?*
SEGUNDA f. Monday.
SEGUNDA-FEIRA f. Monday.
SEGUNDO adj. second; n. m. second; prep. according to.
  Ela mora no segundo andar. *She lives on the second floor.*
  Desejo o segundo volume. *I want the second volume.*
  Em segundo lugar. *In second place.*
  Um bilhete de segunda. *A coach ticket. ("A second-class ticket.")*
  De segunda mão. *Secondhand.*
  Segundo o relatório. *According to the report.*
segurança f. security; safety; certainty; protection.
  Com segurança. *Assuredly.*
  Freio de segurança. *Emergency brake.*
  Alfinete de segurança. *Safety pin.*
segurar to secure; to assure; to insure.
SEGURO adj. secure, sure, safe, certain; insured; n. m. insurance; security.
  Você não está seguro? *Aren't you sure?*
  Companhia de seguros. *Insurance company.*
  Apólice de seguro. *Insurance policy.*
  Seguro de vida. *Life insurance.*
  Seguro contra acidentes. *Accident insurance.*
seio m, breast, bosom.
SEIS six.
seiscentos six hundred.
selar to seal; to stamp; to saddle.
  Faça o favor de selar estas cartas. *Please put stamps on these letters.*
seleção (selecção) f. selection, choice.
selecionar (seleccionar) to select, to choose.
SELO m. seal; stamp; postage stamp.
  Selo postal. *Postage stamp.*
selvagem adj. savage, wild; n. m. and f. savage.

SEM without, besides.
  Iremos sem ele. *We'll go without him.*
  Não posso ler sem os meus óculos. *I can't read without my glasses.*
  Eu fiz sem pensar. *I did it without thinking.*
  Sem falta. *Without fail.*
  Sem dúvida. *Without a doubt. Undoubtedly.*
  Sem fim. *Endless.*
  Sem mais cerimônias. *Without further ado.*
SEMANA f. week.
  Irei a semana que vem. *I'll go next week.*
  Ela virá a próxima semana. *She'll come next week.*
  A semana passada. *Last week.*
  Numa semana mais ou menos. *In a week or so.*
  Semana Santa. *Holy Week.*
  Fim de semana. *Weekend.*
semanal adj. weekly.
  Uma revista semanal. *A weekly magazine.*
semanário adj. weekly; n. m. weekly (publication).
semblante m. countenance, face; look, aspect.
  Você tem bom semblante hoje. *You look well today.*
semear to sow, to seed; to scatter, to spread.
semelhança f. similarity, resemblance, likeness.
semelhar to resemble, to be like.
semente f. seed.
semestre m. semester.
seminarista m. seminarian.
semítico adj. Semitic.
sem-par adj. unequaled, peerless.
SEMPRE always, ever.
  Ele sempre chega tarde. *He's always late.*
  Como sempre. *As always. As usual.*
  Para sempre. *Forever.*
senado m. senate.
senador m. senator.
senão conj. if not, otherwise.
senda f. path.
senha f. signal; sign; password; readmission theatre ticket, pass.
SENHOR m. mister, sir; gentleman; **o senhor** you (masc.).
  Bom dia, senhor Silva. *Good morning, Mr. Silva.*
  O senhor Silva não estará aqui hoje. *Mr. Silva won't be here today.*
  Muito obrigado, senhor. *Thank you, sir.*
  O senhor é americano? *Are you an American?*
  Não conheço esse senhor. *I don't know that gentleman.*
  Caro Senhor: *Dear Sir:*

Sim, senhor. *Yes, sir.*

SENHORA *f. Mrs., madam, lady; wife;* **a senhora** *you (fem.).*

　A senhora Silva está em casa? *Is Mrs. Silva in?*

　A senhora não está em casa. *The lady of the house is not at home.*

　A senhora é americana? *Are you an American?*

　Não conheço essa senhora. *I don't know that lady.*

　Prezada Senhora: *Dear Madam:*

　Sim, senhora. *Yes, ma'am.*

　Minhas senhoras e meus senhores: *Ladies and gentlemen:*

senhoria *f. lordship, ladyship.*

　Vossa Senhoria. *Your lordship. Your ladyship.*

SENHORINHA *f. miss, young lady* Ⓑ.

SENHORITA *f. miss; young lady.*

senil *adj. senile.*

sensação *f. sensation.*

sensacional *adj. sensational.*

sensatez *f. good sense, discretion.*

sensato *adj. sensible, discreet.*

sensibilidade *f. sensibility; sensitivity.*

sensível *adj. sensitive; appreciable.*

　Os olhos são sensíveis à luz. *The eyes are sensitive to light.*

senso *m. sense.*

　Senso comum. *Common sense.*

sensual *adj. sensual.*

sensualidade *f. sensuality.*

sentado *adj. seated.*

　Ela estava sentada à minha esquerda. *She was seated on my left.*

sentar *to sit, to seat.*

SENTAR-SE *to sit (down).*

　Os convidados se sentaram (sentaram-se) à mesa. *The guests sat at the table.*

　Sentemo-nos. *Let's sit down.*

sentença *f. sentence; verdict; maxim.*

sentenciar *to sentence.*

SENTIDO *adj. felt; experienced; offended; sad; n. m. sense; meaning; direction.*

　Ela ficou muito sentida. *She was very offended.*

sentimental *adj. sentimental, romantic.*

sentimentalismo *m. sentimentalism.*

sentimento *m. sentiment, feeling.*

　Sentimentos nobres. *Noble sentiments.*

　Sentimento de culpa. *Guilty feeling.*

SENTIR *to feel; to be sorry; to hear; to sense; to be (happy, cold, etc.); to appreciate; n. m. feeling; opinion.*

　Sinto muito. *I'm very sorry.*

　Sinto não poder ir. *I'm sorry I can't go.*

　Agora sinto frio. *Now I'm cold.*

　Sentimos falta dela. *We miss her.*

Sentimos que você não pudesse vir. *We are sorry you could not come.*

sentir-se *to feel.*

　Ela se sente (sente-se) muito bem. *She feels very well.*

separação *f. separation.*

separar *to separate.*

　Uma cortina separa as duas salas. *A curtain separates the two rooms.*

separar-se *to separate, to part company.*

　Decidiram separar-se. *They decided to separate.*

septuagésimo *seventieth.*

sepulcro *m. sepulchre, grave, tomb.*

sepultar *to bury, to inter; to hide.*

sepultura *f. burial; grave, tomb.*

seqüência (sequência) *f. sequence; series; order.*

sequer *adv. at least, so much as, even.*

　Nem sequer. *Not even.*

seqüestrar (sequestrar) *to kidnap; to confiscate.*

SER *to be.*

　Quem é? *Who is it?*

　É o João. *It's John.*

　Quem será? *Who can it be?*

　O senhor é o senhor Smith? *Are you Mr. Smith?*

　Donde é o senhor? *Where are you from?*

　Sou de Boston. *I'm from Boston.*

　Somos brasileiros. *We are Brazilians.*

　De quem é este lápis? *Whose pencil is this?*

　É meu. *It's mine.*

　É de João. *It's John's.*

　Esta caixa *(x = sh)* é de madeira. *This box is made of wood.*

　Ela é bonita. *She is pretty.*

　Sou escritor. *I'm a writer.*

　Que é isso? *What is that?*

　Quanto é? *How much is it?*

　Que horas são? *What time is it?*

　É uma hora. *It's one o'clock.*

　São duas (horas). *It's two o'clock.*

　Ainda é cedo. *It's still early.*

　É tarde. *It's late.*

　Quando será a boda? *When will the wedding take place?*

　Que dia é hoje? *What day is today?*

　Hoje é segunda-feira. *Today is Monday.*

　É fácil. *It's easy.*

　É difícil. *It's difficult.*

　É verdade? *Is it true?*

　Não é verdade. *It's not true.*

　Pode ser. *That may be.*

　Farei quanto puder. *I'll do what I can.*

　Fosse quem fosse. *Whoever it might be.*

　Que é feito dele? *What has become of him?*

　A carteira foi achada na rua. *The wallet was found in the street.*

Era uma vez. *Once upon a time.*

É isso mesmo! *That's it exactly!*

serenar *to calm down, to pacify.*

serenata *f. serenade.*

serenidade *f. serenity, coolness.*

sereno *adj. serene, calm; clear; n. m. dew; open air.*

Foi uma noite serena. *It was a calm evening.*

série *f. series.*

seriedade *f. seriousness, gravity.*

seringa *f. syringe.*

seringueira *f. rubber tree.*

seringueiro *m. rubber tapper.*

SÉRIO *adj. serious, earnest.*

Tomar a sério. *To take seriously.*

Você está sério? *Are you serious?*

sermão *m. sermon; lecture.*

serpente *f. serpent, snake.*

serpentina *f. paper streamer.*

serpentino *adj. serpentine.*

serra *f. saw; range of mountains, sierra.*

A serra não corta bem. *The saw doesn't cut well.*

Serra de cadeia. *Chain saw.*

serrar *to saw.*

sertanejo *adj. of the* **sertão**, *of the backwoods; m. backwoodsman.*

sertão *m. backwoods, interior.*

SERVIÇO *m. service, favor; set.*

Serviço de mesa. *Table service.*

Você me prestou (prestou-me) um grande serviço. *You rendered me a great service.*

O serviço neste hotel é muito ruim. *The service in this hotel is terrible.*

Ele está de serviço. *He's on duty.*

Serviço militar. *Military service.*

Serviço de contestação. *Answering service.*

servidão *f. servitude.*

servidor *m. servant, server.*

Servidor público. *Public servant.*

SERVIR *to serve; to do a favor; to do, to be useful; to serve at the table; to wait on a table.*

Em que posso servi-lo? *What can I do for you?*

Pode me servir (servir-me) um pouco de vinho? *Can you serve me a little wine?*

Servir à mesa. *To wait on a table.*

Para que serve esta máquina? *What's this machine for?*

Não serve. *It's no good.*

Não serve para nada. *It's no good. It's good for nothing.*

Ela pode servir de intérprete. *She can act as interpreter.*

servitude *f. servitude.*

sessão *f. session, meeting.*

Estar em sessão. *To be in session.*

SESSENTA *sixty.*

sesta *f. siesta, nap.*

seta *f. arrow.*

SETE *seven.*

Pintar o sete. *To have a wild time.*

Sete de setembro (Setembro). *September 7 (Brazilian Independence Day).*

setecentos *seven hundred.*

SETEMBRO *m. September.*

SETENTA *seventy.*

sententrional *adj. northern.*

sétimo *seventh.*

setuagenário *adj., n. m. septuagenarian.*

SEU *m. adj. and pron. your, his, her, its, their; Mr. (a shortened form of* **senhor** *corresponding to* **dona** *for females).*

João, onde deixou (x = sh) o seu livro? *John, where did you leave your book?*

Os meus filhos estão com os seus avós. *My children are with their grandparents.*

Este procedimento tem as suas vantagens e desvantagens. *This procedure has its advantages and its disadvantages.*

severidade *f. severity, strictness.*

severo *adj. severe, strict.*

sexagenário (x = ks) *adj., n. m. sexagenarian.*

sexagésimo *sixtieth.*

sexo (x = ks) *m. sex.*

SEXTA (x = s) *f. Friday.*

SEXTA-FEIRA *f. Friday.*

sexto *sixth.*

si *yourself, himself, herself, themselves, itself.*

Ela o quer para si mesma. *She wants it for herself.*

sibilo *m. whistle; hiss.*

sicrano *m. Mr. so-and-so.*

Fulano, Beltrano e Sicrano. *Tom, Dick and Harry.*

SIDA *f. AIDS.*

sidra *f. cider.*

significação *f. meaning, significance.*

significado *m. meaning, significance.*

significante *adj. significant.*

significar *to mean, to signify.*

Que significa isso? *What's the meaning of that?*

significativo *adj. significant.*

signo *m. sign (zodiac).*

sílaba *f. syllable.*

silêncio *m. silence.*

Silêncio! *Silence!*

Guardar silêncio. *To remain silent.*

Sofrer em silêncio. *To suffer in silence.*

O silêncio vale ouro. *Silence is golden.*

silencioso *adj. silent, noiseless; n. m. muffler (auto).*

silvar *to whistle, to hiss (wind, etc.).*

silvestre *adj. wild, rustic.*

Plantas silvestres. *Wild plants.*

SIM *adv. yes; indeed; n. m. consent, assent.*

Sim senhor. *Yes, sir.*

Eu lhe disse que sim. *I told him yes.*

Acho que sim. *I think so.*

Um dia sim, um dia não. *Every other day.*

Pois sim! *Fine! All right! or Oh, yeah!*

   Come on now! (depends on inflection).

Dar o sim. *To say yes. To give consent.*

simbolizar *to symbolize.*

símbolo *m. symbol.*

simetria *f. symmetry.*

simétrico *adj. symmetrical.*

similar *adj. similar.*

similitude *f. similitude, similarity, resemblance.*

simpatia *f. sympathy.*

   Ter simpatia por. *To sympathize with. To have sympathy for.*

simpático *adj. nice, pleasant, sympathetic.*

   Ela é muito simpática. *She's very nice.*

simpatizar *to sympathize.*

SIMPLES *adj. simple; plain; n. m. and f. simpleton.*

   É muito simples. *It's quite simple.*

   Simplesmente. *Simply.*

   Juros simples. *Simple interest.*

simplicidade *f. simplicity.*

simplificação *f. simplification.*

simplificar *to simplify.*

simulação *f. simulation; sham.*

simulacro *m. sham; imitation.*

simular *to simulate, to feign.*

simultâneo *adj. simultaneous.*

SINAL *m. sign; mark; signal; token; beauty mark; deposit.*

   Ponha um sinal nessa página. *Put a mark on that page.*

   Ela deu sinal de alarma. *She sounded the alarm.*

   Sinal de perigo. *Danger signal.*

   Sinal aberto. *Green light.*

   Sinal fechado. *Red light.*

   Ela fez o sinal da cruz. *She made the sign of the cross.*

sinalizar *to signal.*

sinceridade *f. sincerity.*

sincero *adj. sincere.*

   Ele é um amigo sincero. *He's a true friend.*

síncope *f. fainting spell.*

sincronizar *to synchronize.*

sindical *adj. pertaining to a trade union; syndical; union.*

sindicato *m. labor union; trade union.*

sinfonia *f. symphony.*

sinfônico (sinfónico) *adj. symphonic.*

singelo *adj. simple; sincere; single.*

singular *adj. singular; unusual; individual; odd.*

"Lápis" é singular e plural: o lápis, os lápis. *"Lápis" is singular and plural: the pencil, the pencils.*

   É um caso singular. *It's a strange case.*

singularidade *f. singularity; peculiarity.*

sinistra *f. left hand.*

sinistro *adj. left; sinister; unfortunate; n. m. accident, loss.*

   Lado sinistro. *Left side.*

   Tem um aspecto sinistro. *It looks sinister.*

   Onde aconteceu o sinistro? *Where did the accident occur?*

sino *m. bell.*

sinônimo (sinónimo) *adj. synonymous; n. m. synonym.*

sinopse *f. synopsis, summary.*

sintaxe (x = ks) *f. syntax.*

síntese *f. synthesis.*

sintético *adj. synthetic.*

sintoma *m. symptom.*

sintonizar *to tune in (radio).*

   O aparelho de rádio está mal sintonizado. *The radio is not properly tuned.*

sirena *f. siren, nymph.*

siri *m. crab.*

sisal *m. sisal.*

sistema *m. system.*

   Sistema métrico. *Metric system.*

   Sistema decimal. *Decimal system.*

sistemático *adj. systematic.*

sisudo *adj. pensive; prudent; calm.*

sitiar *to besiege.*

sítio *m. place, site, location; siege.*

SITUAÇÃO *f. situation; position; circumstances; site, location.*

   Ele está em má situação. *He's in a bad situation.*

situar *to place, to locate, to situate.*

smoking *m. tuxedo, dinner jacket* Ⓑ.

SÓ *adj. alone; single; adv. only.*

   O senhor está só? *Are you alone?*

   Só para adultos. *Adults only.*

soalho *m. floor.*

SOAR *to sound; to ring.*

   O sino soou. *The bell rang.*

sob *prep. under, below.*

   Sob juramento. *Under oath.*

   Sob medida. *Made to order.*

soberania *f. sovereignty.*

soberano *adj., n. m. sovereign.*

soberbo *adj. proud, haughty; magnificent.*

sobra *f. excess, surplus; pl. leftovers.*

   Tenho tempo de sobra. *I have plenty of time.*

sobrado *adj. left over; plenty; n. m. wooden floor; house of two or more stories* Ⓑ; *plantation owner's large home* Ⓑ.

sobrancelha *f. eyebrow.*

Franzir as sobrancelhas. *To frown. To knit one's brows.*

sobrar *to be more than enough; to be left over.*

Sobrou muito alimento. *A great deal of food was left over.*

Parece-me que aqui sobro. *It seems to me that I'm not needed here.*

Sobram seis. *There are six too many.*

SOBRE *on; over; above; about.*

Ponha o copo sobre a mesa. *Put the glass on the table.*

Ele escreveu um livro sobre Portugal. *He wrote a book about Portugal.*

Sobre que falaram? *What did they talk about?*

sobrecarga *f. overload.*

sobrecarregar *to overload.*

sobremaneira *adv. excessively, greatly.*

SOBREMESA *f. dessert.*

sobrenatural *adj., n. m. supernatural.*

sobrenome *m. surname.*

sobrepor *to superimpose, to place over; to overlay; to overlap.*

sobressair *to stand out; to excel.*

sobressalente *adj. spare.*

Pneu sobressalente. *Spare tire.*

sobressaltar *to frighten; to startle; to surprise.*

sobressalto *m. fright; surprise; shock.*

sobretudo *adv. above all, especially; n. m. overcoat.*

sobreviver *to survive.*

sobriedade *f. sobriety, temperance, moderation.*

sobrinha *f. niece.*

sobrinho *m. nephew.*

sóbrio *adj. sober, temperate.*

socar *to strike, to hit, to beat, to punch, to pound.*

social *adj. social.*

Assistência social. *Social work.*

Ordem social. *Social order.*

socialismo *m. socialism.*

socialista *adj., n. m. and f. socialist.*

socializar *to socialize.*

sociável *adj. sociable.*

sociedade *f. society; community; company, corporation; partnership.*

A alta sociedade. *High society.*

Formaram uma sociedade. *They formed a partnership.*

Sociedade anônima (anónima). *Corporation.*

sócio *m. partner, associate; member.*

O senhor é sócio desse clube? *Are you a member of that club?*

Sócio principal. *Senior partner.*

sociologia *f. sociology.*

sociólogo *m. sociologist.*

soco *m. punch, sock.*

Dar um soco a alguém. *To punch someone.*

socorrer *to aid, to help, to assist; to rescue.*

Ninguém quer socorrê-lo. *Nobody wants to help him.*

socorro *m. aid, help, succor.*

soda *f. soda.*

sofá *m. sofa, couch.*

sofrer *to suffer, to stand.*

sofrido *adj. patient, long-suffering.*

sofrimento *m. suffering.*

software *m. software.*

soga *f. rope, lariat.*

sogra *f. mother-in-law.*

sogro *m. father-in-law.*

SOL *m. sun, sunshine.*

Tomar banho de sol. *To have a sunbath.*

Nascer do sol. *Sunrise.*

Pôr do sol. *Sunset.*

De sol a sol. *From sunrise to sunset.*

Queimadura de sol. *Sunburn.*

sola *f. sole (of the foot, of shoe).*

solar *to sole (shoe); to play a solo; adj. solar, manorial; n. m. mansion, manor house.*

Ano solar. *Solar year.*

Mancha solar. *Sunspot.*

soldado *m. soldier.*

Soldado raso. *Buck private.*

Soldado Desconhecido. *Unknown Soldier.*

soldar *to solder; to weld.*

solene *adj. solemn, serious, grave; religious.*

solenidade *f. solemnity.*

soletrar *to spell; to read slowly; to read badly.*

solicitação *f. solicitation, request.*

solicitador *adj. soliciting; n. m. solicitor.*

solicitar *to solicit; to ask; to apply for.*

Ele solicita um emprego. *He's applying for a position.*

solícito *adj. solicitous, concerned.*

solicitude *f. solicitude, concern.*

solidão *f. solitude.*

solidariedade *f. solidarity.*

solidário *adj. joint; mutual.*

solidez *f. solidity, firmness, soundness.*

sólido *adj. solid, sound, strong; firm; n. m. solid.*

Tem uma base muito sólida. *It has a very solid base.*

solitário *adj. solitary, lonely; n. m. hermit.*

solo *m. soil; ground; solo.*

soltar *to untie, to loosen; to set free; to let out; to let go.*

Soltaram o preso. *They set the prisoner free.*

Soltaram as amarras. *They loosened the cables.*

De repente ele soltou uma gargalhada. *Suddenly he burst into laughter.*

Soltar o cabelo. *To let one's hair down.*

soltar-se *to get loose.*

solteirão *m. confirmed bachelor.*

solteiro *adj. single, unmarried, bachelor; n. m. bachelor.*

O senhor é casado ou solteiro? *Are you married or single?*

Ainda sou solteiro. *I'm still a bachelor.*

solteirona *f. old maid, spinster.*

solto *adj. loose; free; licentious.*

Verso solto. *Blank verse.*

Ela tem a língua muito solta. *She has a very loose tongue.*

SOLUÇÃO *f. solution; answer; dénouement, outcome; payment.*

Isto não tem solução. *There's no solution to this.*

Essa é a melhor solução. *That's the best solution.*

soluço *m. sob.*

solúvel *adj. soluble; solvable.*

solvência *f. solvency.*

solvente *adj. solvent.*

solver *to solve; to resolve.*

SOM *m. sound; tone; noise; manner, way.*

Sem tom nem som. *Without rhyme or reason.*

À prova de som. *Soundproof.*

Em alto e bom som. *Loud and clear.*

soma *f. sum, amount, addition.*

Quanto é a soma total? *What's the total amount?*

somar *to add up, to sum up.*

SOMBRA *f. shadow; shade; darkness.*

Ela se sentou (sentou-se) à sombra duma árvore. *She sat down in the shade of a tree.*

Não há nem sombra de verdade no que ele diz. *There isn't a shadow of truth in what he says.*

sombrinha *f. parasol.*

sombrio *adj. shady; gloomy; somber.*

SOMENTE *solely, only.*

Aprendi somente um pouco de português. *I learned only a little Portuguese.*

sonâmbulo *m. sleepwalker.*

sonata *f. sonata.*

sondagem *f. sounding; survey, poll.*

sondar *to sound, to sound out.*

Estavam sondando (a sondar) a baía. *They were sounding the bay.*

soneca *f. nap (short sleep).*

Ele está tirando (a tirar) uma soneca. *He is taking a nap.*

soneto *m. sonnet.*

sonhador *m. dreamer.*

sonhar *to dream.*

Ela sonha com dias passados. *She dreams of days gone by.*

sonho *m. dream.*

Tudo parece um sonho. *It all seems like a dream.*

SONO *m. sleep.*

Você está com sono? (Você tem sono?) *Are you sleepy?*

Ele pegou no sono. *He fell asleep.*

sonoridade *f. sonority.*

sonoro *adj. sonorous.*

Um filme sonoro. *A talkie, a film with sound.*

SOPA *f. soup; easy, simple* Ⓑ.

Quer mais sopa? *Do you want more soup?*

Isto é sopa. *This is easy. There's nothing to this.*

sopapo *m. blow, slap.*

soprano *m. and f. soprano.*

soprar *to blow; to whisper.*

sopro *m. blowing; breath; puff.*

Instrumento de sopro. *Wind instrument.*

soro *m. serum; whey (milk).*

sorrir *to smile.*

Todos sorriram. *They all smiled.*

sorriso *m. smile.*

SORTE *f. chance, lot, fortune, luck; fate; manner; kind.*

Boa sorte! *Good luck!*

Ela tem muita sorte. *She is very lucky.*

Deitemos sorte. *Let's cast lots.*

Má sorte. *Bad luck.*

Quem tirou a sorte grande? *Who won the grand prize?*

sortear *to cast lots; to raffle.*

sorteio *m. raffle; drawing of lots.*

sortir *to supply; to mix.*

sorver *to sip; to absorb; to swallow.*

sorvete *m. ice cream; sherbet.*

soslaio *m. slant.*

De soslaio. *Askance.*

sossegado *adj. calm, quiet.*

sossegar *to calm, to quiet.*

Quando você sossegar, falaremos. *When you calm down we'll talk.*

sossego *m. peace, calm, quiet.*

Não tivemos um minuto de sossego. *We didn't have a moment's peace.*

sótão *m. attic.*

sotaque *m. accent, foreign accent.*

Ela fala português com um sotaque espanhol. *She speaks Portuguese with a Spanish accent.*

soviético *adj. Soviet.*

sozinho *adj. alone, all alone.*

SUA *f. adj. and pron. your, his, her, its, their, yours, hers, theirs.*

José, onde está (a) sua irmã? *Joseph, where is your sister?*

Ela está com (a) sua amiga Maria. *She is with her friend Mary.*

suar *to sweat, to perspire.*
suave *adj. soft; mild; gentle; mellow; sweet.*
Ele tem maneiras suaves. *He has gentle manners.*
suavidade *f. softness, gentleness.*
suavizar *to soften, to soothe.*
subalterno *adj., n. m. subaltern, subordinate.*
subarrendar *to sublet, to sublease.*
subconsciente *adj., n. m. subconscious.*
subdiretor (subdirector) *m. subdirector, assistant director.*
subdivisão *f. subdivision.*
SUBIR *to go up, to ascend, to rise; to climb; to mount; to raise.*
Subamos. *Let's go up.*
Suba ao quarto andar. *Go up to the fourth floor.*
Ela já subiu para o trem. *She has already boarded the train.*
Os preços vão subindo. *Prices keep going up.*
súbito *adj. sudden.*
De súbito. *Suddenly. All of a sudden.*
subjetividade (subjectividade) *f. subjectivity.*
subjetivo (subjectivo) *adj. subjective.*
subjugar *to subjugate, to overpower.*
subjuntivo *adj., n. m. subjunctive.*
sublevação *f. insurrection, uprising.*
sublevar *to stir up, to rebel.*
sublime *adj. sublime.*
sublinhar *to underline; to emphasize.*
submarino *adj., n. m. submarine.*
submeter *to submit; to subdue.*
Submeter à votação. *To put to a vote.*
subordinado *adj. subordinate.*
subordinar *to subordinate.*
subornar *to bribe.*
suborno *m. bribe, bribery.*
subscrever *to subscribe.*
O senhor quer subscrever a esta revista? *Would you like to subscribe to this magazine?*
subscrição *f. subscription.*
subscritor *m. subscriber.*
subsecretário *m. undersecretary.*
subseqüente (subsequente) *adj. subsequent.*
subsidiar *to subsidize, to aid.*
subsídio *m. subsidy, aid.*
subsistência *f. subsistence.*
subsistir *to subsist; to exist; to survive.*
substância *f. substance; essence.*
Em substância. *In substance. In short.*
substancial *adj. substantial.*
substanciar *to substantiate.*
substancioso *adj. substantial; nourishing.*
substantivo *adj. substantive; n. m. substantive, noun.*

substituição *f. substitution.*
substituir *to substitute.*
Ele substituiu o seu amigo. *He substituted for his friend.*
substituto *m. substitute.*
subterrâneo *adj. subterranean, underground.*
subtítulo *m. subtitle.*
subtração *f. subtraction.*
subúrbio *m. suburb.*
subvenção *f. subsidy, grant.*
subvencionar *to subsidize.*
subversão *f. subversion.*
suceder *to happen; to succeed.*
Que sucedeu depois? *What happened then (next)?*
Suceda o que suceda, eu estarei aqui. *No matter what happens, I'll be here.*
Crê-se que o filho dele lhe sucederá. *It is believed that his son will succeed him.*
sucessão *f. succession.*
sucessivo *adj. successive.*
sucesso *m. event, incident; result; success.*
A peça teve grande sucesso. *The play was a hit.*
sucessor *m. successor.*
suco *m. juice.*
Suco de laranja. *Orange juice.*
sucumbir *to succumb; to die; to yield.*
sucursal *adj., n. m. branch (post office, etc.).*
sudeste *adj., n. m. southeast.*
sudoeste *adj., n. m. southwest.*
sueco *adj. Swedish; n. m. Swede.*
suéter *m. sweater ®.*
suficiência *f. sufficiency, adequacy.*
suficiente *adj. sufficient, enough.*
Isso não é suficiente. *That's not enough.*
sufixo *(x) ks) m. suffix.*
sufocar *to suffocate; to strangle.*
sufrágio *m. suffrage, voting.*
sugerir *to suggest, to hint.*
Que me sugere o senhor? *What do you suggest (to me)?*
sugestão *f. suggestion; hint.*
Essa foi uma boa sugestão. *That was a good suggestion.*
sugestivo *adj. suggestive.*
suicida *m. f. suicide (person).*
suicidar-se *to commit suicide.*
suicídio *m. suicide (act).*
suíço *adj. Swiss; n. m. Swiss person.*
sujeitar *to subject; to subdue.*
SUJEITO *adj. subject; liable; n. m. subject; theme; fellow, guy.*
Estar sujeito a. *To be subject to.*
Quem é esse sujeito? *Who is that fellow?*
sujo *adj. dirty, soiled; foul.*
SUL *adj. south, southern; n. m. south.*

Cruzeiro do Sul. *Southern Cross.*
sulcar *to plow.*
súlfur *m. sulfur.*
sulista *adj. southern; n. m. southerner.*
sumário *m. summary.*
sumir, sumir-se *to disappear, to fade away.*
sumo *adj. great, high, supreme; n. m. juice; top.*
Ao sumo. *At most.*
suntuosidade *f. sumptuousness.*
suntuoso *adj. sumptuous, magnificent.*
suor *m. sweat, perspiration; hard work.*
superabundância *f. superabundance, oversupply.*
superabundante *adj. superabundant, very abundant.*
superar *to exceed, to excel, to surpass; to overcome.*
Esse trabalho supera todas as expectativas. *That work exceeds all expectations.*
superficial *adj. superficial.*
superficialidade *f. superficiality.*
superfície *f. surface, area.*
Superfície da terra. *Surface of the earth.*
supérfluo *adj. superfluous.*
superintendente *m. superintendent, supervisor.*
superior *adj. superior; higher; better; n. m. superior.*
Ele é um homem superior. *He's a great man.*
Este é um vinho superior. *This is an excellent wine.*
superioridade *f. superiority.*
superlativo *adj. superlative.*
supermercado *m. supermarket.*
supernumerário *adj. supernumerary.*
superprodução *f. overproduction.*
superstição *f. superstition.*
supersticioso *adj. superstitious.*
suplantar *to supplant, to displace.*
suplemento *m. supplement.*
suplente *adj., n. m. substitute, alternate.*
súplica *f. request, entreaty, petition.*
Ele não cedeu às súplicas dela. *He did not give in to her pleas.*
suplicar *to beg, to implore, to beseech, to entreat.*
Suplico-lhe que o perdoe. *I entreat (beg) you to forgive him.*
suplício *m. ordeal; torment; torture; execution.*
Ele passou pelo suplício de . . . *He went through the ordeal of . . .*
supor *to suppose, to imagine, to presume.*
Você bem pode supor o que aconteceu. *You can well imagine what happened.*
suportar *to support; to bear.*
suportável *adj. supportable, bearable.*

suposição *f. supposition, conjecture, assumption.*
suposto *adj. supposed, presumed.*
supremacia *f. supremacy.*
supremo *adj. supreme, highest.*
A Corte Suprema. *The Supreme Court.*
supressão *f. suppression.*
suprimir *to suppress; to eliminate; to omit.*
surdez *f. deafness.*
surdo *adj. deaf; muffled; n. m. deaf person.*
surgir *to arise, to emerge.*
surpreendente *adj. surprising.*
surpreender *to surprise.*
A chegada dele surpreendeu a todos. *His arrival surprised everybody.*
surpreendido *adj. surprised.*
surpresa *f. surprise.*
surpreso *adj. surprised.*
surrar *to beat, to thrash.*
surtir *to cause, to bring about.*
suscetibilidade (susceptibilidade) *f. susceptibility.*
suscetível (susceptível) *adj. susceptible, sensitive.*
suscitar *to stir up, to excite.*
suspeita *f. suspicion, doubt.*
suspeitar *to suspect, to distrust.*
Suspeito dele. *I'm suspicious of him. I suspect him.*
suspeito *adj. suspected; suspect; n. m. suspect.*
suspeitoso *adj. suspicious, doubtful.*
suspender *to suspend; to postpone; to put off; to discontinue; to stop; to adjourn.*
Suspendeu-se a publicação da revista. *The publication of the magazine was suspended.*
Suspender os pagamentos. *To stop payment.*
Suspender a sessão. *To adjourn the meeting.*
suspensão *f. suspension, cessation.*
suspenso *adj. suspended, hanging.*
Em suspenso. *In suspense. Pending.*
Deixar (x = sh) em suspenso. *To hold over. To hold in abeyance.*
suspirar *to sigh.*
Suspirar por. *To long for.*
suspiro *m. sigh.*
sussurrar *to whisper, to murmur.*
sussurro *m. whisper, murmur.*
sustância, substância *f. substance.*
sustentar *to support; to sustain; to assert.*
Devemos sustentar as artes. *We should support the arts.*
sustento *m. maintenance, support.*
suster *to support, to sustain.*
susto *m. fright.*
sutil (subtil) *adj. subtle.*
sutileza, subtileza *f. subtleness, subtlety.*

T

ta (*contr. of* **te + a**) *it to you (fam.); her to you.*

tabacaria *f. tobacco shop.*

tabaco *m. tobacco.*

Tabaco em folha. *Leaf tobacco.*

taberna *f. tavern, inn, bar.*

taberneiro *m. tavern keeper, innkeeper.*

tabique *m. partition wall, partition.*

tablado *m. stage, platform; scaffold.*

tábua *f. table (of information); board, plank.*

Tábua de multiplicação. *Multiplication table.*

Tábua de mesa. *Leaf of a table.*

taça *f. cup (including measurement); trophy.*

tacanho *adj. stingy, miserly, narrow-minded; short.*

tacão *m. shoe heel.*

tacha *f. tack, nail; blemish, fault.*

tachar *to criticize; to stain.*

tácito *adj. tacit.*

taciturno *adj. taciturn.*

taco *m. golf club; billiard cue; hockey stick.*

tagarelar *to chatter, to gossip.*

TAL *adj. such, so, as.*

Que tal? *What do you think about it?*

Que tal uma cerveja? *How about a beer?*

Não permitirei tal coisa. *I won't allow such a thing.*

Um tal Smith o disse (disse-o). *A certain Smith said it.*

Fulano de tal. *John Doe.*

Tal pai, tal filho. *Like father, like son.*

talão *m. heel; check; stub; receipt.*

Talão de bagagem. *Baggage check.*

talco *m. talcum, talc.*

talento *m. talent, ability.*

Ele é um escritor de grande talento. *He's a very talented writer.*

talhar *to carve; to engrave; to cut.*

talhe *m. shape, figure.*

talher *m. table cutlery (set of knife, fork, and spoon).*

TALHO *m. butcher's shop, meat market* Ⓟ.

TALVEZ *perhaps, maybe.*

Talvez aconteça como você disse. *Perhaps it will turn out as you said.*

tamanho *adj. such, so great, so big; n. m. size, dimensions.*

Nunca vi tamanho medo. *I never saw such fear.*

Qual é o tamanho? *What size is it?*

De grande tamanho. *Very large.*

tâmara *f. date (fruit).*

TAMBÉM *also, too; as well; likewise.*

Eu também. *Me too.*

Ela também comprou dois romances. *She also bought two novels.*

tambor *m. drum; drummer; barrel.*

tampa *f. cover, lid; cap.*

tampão *m. cover; stopper, plug.*

tampar *to cover, to cap.*

tampouco *neither.*

Ele não quer vê-la. Nem eu tampouco. *He doesn't want to see her. Neither do I.*

tanger *to play (musical instrument), to pluck (strings), to ring (a bell).*

tangerina *f. tangerine.*

tangível *adj. tangible.*

tango *m. tango.*

tanque *m. tank, vat.*

Tanque de gasolina. *Gasoline tank.*

Encher o tanque. *To fill the tank.*

TANTO *adj. so much, as much; pl. so many; adv. so, in such a manner, so much; n. m. some.*

Não beba tanto. *Don't drink so much.*

Por que tanta pressa? *Why the hurry?*

Tanta gente. *So many people.*

Ter tantos anos de idade. *To be so many years old.*

Custou tanto? *Did it cost that much?*

A tanto o metro. *So much a meter.*

Algum tanto. *A little. Somewhat.*

Outro tanto. *Just as much. As much more.*

Outros tantos. *Just as many.*

Tanto um como outro. *One as well as the other. Both of them.*

Quanto mais lhe dou, tanto mais pede. *The more I give him, the more he asks for (wants).*

Tanto melhor. *So much the better.*

Tanto pior. *So much the worse.*

Tantas vezes. *So often.*

Estou um tanto cansado. *I'm somewhat tired.*

TÃO *adv. so, as, such.*

Por que voltou tão cedo? *Why did you return so soon?*

Ele é tão alto quanto o pai. *He's as tall as his father.*

Tão bem. *So well. As well.*

Tão mal. *So bad. As bad.*

tapar *to cover; to conceal, to hide.*

tapeçaria *f. tapestry; upholstery.*

tapete *m. carpet, rug, mat.*

tapioca *f. tapioca.*

taquígrafa *f. female stenographer.*

taquigrafia *f. shorthand.*

taquígrafo *m. male stenographer.*

tardança *f. delay, slowness.*

Perdoe a minha tardança. *Pardon my delay.*

tardar *to delay; to be late.*

Não tarde. *Don't be long. Don't take too long.*

Não tardarei em voltar. *I'll be back before long.*

TARDE *adv. late; n. m. afternoon.*
  Boa tarde! *Good afternoon!*
  Hoje à tarde. *This afternoon.*
  Mais tarde. *Later.*
  Amanhã à tarde. *Tomorrow afternoon.*
  Ontem à tarde. *Yesterday afternoon.*
  É tarde. *It's late.*
  Fazer-se tarde. *To grow late.*
  Antes tarde do que nunca. *Better late than never.*
tardio *adj. tardy; slow; late.*
tarefa *f. job; task, chore.*
  A tarefa está concluída. *The job is finished.*
tarifa *f. tariff; table of rates.*
tartamudear *to stammer, to stutter.*
tartamudo *adj. stammering, stuttering; n. m. stammerer, stutterer.*
tartaruga *f. tortoise.*
tatear *to feel; to feel one's way; to probe.*
tática *f. tactics.*
tático (táctico) *adj. tactical; n. m. touch.*
tato (tacto) *m. sense of touch; tact.*
  Ele é um homem de muito tato. *He's a very tactful man.*
  É suave ao tato. *It feels soft. ("It's soft to the touch.")*
tatuagem *f. tattoo; tattooing.*
tatuar *to tattoo*
taxa $(x = sh)$ *f. tax, duty, toll; rate.*
  Taxa de exportação. *Export duty.*
  Taxa de juro. *Rate of interest.*
taxar $(x = sh)$ *to tax; to price.*
TÁXI $(x = ks)$ *m. taxi, taxicab.*
taxímetro $(x = ks)$ *m. meter in a taxi.*
te *to, for you (fam.)*
teatral *adj. theatrical.*
TEATRO *m. theater.*
  Peça de teatro. *Play.*
teatrólogo *m. playwright.*
tecer *to spin, to weave; to intrigue.*
tecido *adj. woven; n. m. textile, fabric.*
  Tecido de algodão. *Cotton fabric.*
tecla *f. key (piano, computer, etc.).*
teclado *m. keyboard (piano, computer, etc.).*
técnica *f. technique.*
técnico *adj. technical; n. m. technician.*
tédio *m. boredom, tediousness.*
tedioso *adj. tiresome, tedious.*
teia *f. cloth, material; web.*
  Teia de aranha. *Cobweb. Spiderweb.*
teimar *to persist, to insist.*
teimoso *adj. stubborn; willful.*
tela *f. network, web; canvas (painting); screen (movie, computer, etc.).*
  Tela de cinema. *Movie screen.*
telão *drop curtain (theater).*
telecomando *m. remote control.*
telecomunicação *f. telecommunication.*
teleférico *m. cable lift.*

TELEFONAR *to telephone.*
  Telefone-me às cinco. *Call me at five.*
TELEFONE *m. telephone.*
  Telefone celular. *Cellular phone.*
  Telefone sem fio. *Cordless phone.*
telefonema *m. telephone call.*
telefônico (telefónico) *adj. telephonic, telephone.*
  Lista telefônica. *Telephone directory.*
  Cabine (or cabina) telefônica. *Telephone booth.*
telefonista *f. telephone operator.*
telegrafar *to telegraph, to wire.*
  Teremos que telegrafar-lhe. *We'll have to wire him.*
telegrafista *m. and f. telegraph operator.*
telégrafo *m. telegraph; telegraph office.*
  Onde é o telégrafo? *Where is the telegraph office?*
telegrama *m. telegram.*
  Quero passar um telegrama. *I want to send a telegram.*
teleguiado *adj. guided (missile).*
telenovela *f. TV soap opera.*
telepatia *f. telepathy.*
telescópio *m. telescope.*
telespectador(-a) *TV viewer.*
televisão *f. television.*
  Aparelho de televisão. *Television set.*
televisionar *to televise.*
televisor *m. television set.*
televisora *f. television station.*
telha *f. tile (roofing).*
telhado *m. roof.*
tema *m. theme, subject; written composition.*
TEMER *to fear, to dread, to be afraid.*
  Temo que seja muito tarde. *I'm afraid it's too late.*
temerário *adj. reckless, rash.*
temeroso *adj. afraid, fearful.*
temido *adj. fearsome, frightening.*
temível *adj. fearsome.*
temor *m. fear, dread.*
temperamento *m. temperament, nature.*
temperatura *f. temperature.*
  Ver a temperatura. *To take one's temperature.*
tempero *m. seasoning.*
tempestade *f. tempest, storm.*
TEMPO *m. time, tense; weather; tempo.*
  Por muito tempo. *For a long time.*
  Há muito tempo. *It's been a long time. A long time ago.*
  Há pouco tempo. *Lately. Not long ago.*
  Há quanto tempo você mora aqui? *How long have you been living here?*
  Quanto tempo? *How long?*
  Há tempo de sobra. *There's plenty of time.*
  Não tenho tempo. *I have no time.*

A tempo. *In time.*
Perder tempo. *To lose time. To waste time.*
Bom tempo. *Good weather.*
Mau tempo. *Bad weather.*
O tempo está péssimo. *The weather is terrible.*
Fora de tempo. *Out of season.*
O tempo é dinheiro. *Time is money.*
temporada *f. season, period.*
Esta peça é a melhor da temporada. *This play is the best of the season.*
tenacidade *f. tenacity.*
tenaz *adj. tenacious, stubborn; n. f. tongs.*
tencionar *to intend.*
Tencionamos visitá-lo mais tarde. *We intend to visit him later.*
tenda *f. tent; stall, booth.*
tendência *f. tendency, leaning, trend.*
tender *to spread out; to tend.*
tenebroso *adj. dark, gloomy.*
tenente *m. lieutenant.*
tênis (ténis) *m. tennis.*
Jogar tênis. *To play tennis.*
tenor *m. tenor.*
tenro *adj. soft, tender.*
tensão *f. tension, pressure.*
tenso *adj. tense, tight.*
tentação *f. temptation.*
Não nos deixeis cair em tentação. *Lead us not into temptation.*
tentar *to try, to attempt; to tempt.*
Vou tentá-lo hoje. *I'm going to try it today.*
tentativa *f. attempt.*
tentativo *adj. tentative.*
teor *m. meaning; content.*
Teor alcoólico. *Alcohol content.*
teoria *f. theory.*
teórico *adj. theoretical.*
TER *to have, to possess; to keep; to hold, to contain; to take; to be (hungry, tired, etc.).*
Que tem na mão? *What do you have in your hand?*
Você terá que partir hoje. *You will have to leave today.*
Não tenho muito tempo. *I haven't much time.*
Tenho muito que fazer antes de partir. *I have a lot to do before I leave.*
Não tenho troco. *I don't have any change.*
Não tenho mais. *I don't have any more.*
Que idade tem Maria? *How old is Mary?*
Quantos anos tem Maria? *How old is Mary?*
Maria tem dezoito anos. *Mary is eighteen years old.*
Aqui tem um livro interessante. *Here's an interesting book.*
Que é que você tem? *What's the matter with you?*

Não tenho nada. *There's nothing the matter with me.*
Tenho fome. *I'm hungry.*
Tenho sede. *I'm thirsty.*
Tenho vontade de almoçar agora. *I feel like having lunch now.*
Tenho muito frio. *I'm very cold.*
Tenho dor de cabeça. *I have a headache.*
Ela tem sono. *She is sleepy.*
Elas têm razão. *They are right.*
Elas não têm razão. *They are wrong.*
Tenha cuidado! *Be careful!*
Ter sorte. *To be lucky.*
Ter pressa. *To be in a hurry.*
Ter lugar. *To take place. To happen.*
Ter em conta. *To bear in mind.*
Ter em muito (em pouco). *To think much (little) of.*
Ter jeito. *To have a special skill or talent.*
Ter saudades de. *To miss. To long for.*
Ter notícias de. *To hear from.*
Tenha a bondade de repetir. *Please repeat.*
Não tem importância. *It doesn't matter.*
Quando eu cheguei, eles já tinham partido. *When I arrived, they had already left.*
TERÇA *f. Tuesday.*
TERÇA-FEIRA *f. Tuesday.*
TERCEIRO *adj. third; n. m. third person, mediator, intermediary.*
O terceiro capítulo. *The third chapter.*
A terceira lição. *The third lesson.*
Ele serviu de terceiro nas negociações. *He was an intermediary in the negotiations.*
TERÇO *m. third.*
terminação *f. termination, ending.*
terminal *adj. terminal.*
terminante *adj. terminating; decisive.*
TERMINAR *to end, to terminate, to finish.*
Quase terminei. *I'm almost finished.*
A reunião terminou às três. *The meeting ended at three o'clock.*
término *m. terminus; end; boundary, limit.*
terminologia *f. terminology.*
termo *m. Thermos; term; limit; span; end.*
Pôr termo a. *To put an end to.*
Termos técnicos. *Technical terms.*
termômetro (termómetro) *m. thermometer.*
termostato *m. thermostat.*
terno *adj. tender, affectionate; n. m. trio, group of three; man's suit* Ⓑ.
ternura *f. tenderness, fondness.*
TERRA *f. earth; soil; ground; land, country.*
Viajar por terra. *To travel by land.*
Terra natal. *Fatherland. Native land.*
Terra Santa. *Holy Land.*
Descer à terra. *To land. To go ashore.*
Minha terra. *My land. My country.*
terraço *m. terrace.*

terremoto *m. earthquake.*

terreno *m. land, soil, piece of ground; field.*
Partiram o terreno em vários lotes. *They divided the land into several lots.*
Sondar o terreno. *To sound out the situation.*
Perder terreno. *To lose ground.*

terrestre *adj. ground, terrestrial.*

território *m. territory.*

TERRÍVEL *adj. terrible, dreadful.*

terror *m. terror.*

tertúlia *f. social gathering.*

tese *f. thesis.*

teso *adj. taut, stiff.*

tesoura *f. scissors, shears.*

tesouraria *f. treasury, bursar's office.*

tesoureiro *m. treasurer, bursar.*

tesouro *m. treasury.*

testa *f. forehead, brow; front.*
Pôr-se à testa de. *To put oneself at the head of.*
Testa de ferro. *Figurehead. Straw man.*

testar *to will; to bequeath; to testify.*

teste *m. test, examination; trial.*

testemunha *f. witness.*

testemunhar *to testify; to witness.*

testemunho *m. testimony; proof.*

testificar *to testify, to declare.*

teto (tecto) *m. ceiling; roof.*
Preço teto. *Ceiling price.*

teu *m. adj. and pron. your, yours (fam.).*

têxtil *(x = sh) adj. textile.*

texto *(x = sh) m. text.*

tez *f. complexion; skin.*
Ela tem uma tez muito suave. *Her skin is very smooth.*

ti *you (fam.) (used after a preposition).*

tíbia *f. tibia, shinbone.*

tíbio *adj. lukewarm, indifferent.*

tico *m. a bit.*

tifo *m. typhoid fever.*

tifóide *adj. typhoid.*
Febre tifóide. *Typhoid fever.*

tigela *f. bowl, dish; cup.*

tigre *m. tiger.*

tijolo *m. brick.*

til *m. tilde (wavy line over a nasal vowel; ~).*

timbre *m. stamp; seal; timbre, tone.*

time *m. team ⑬.*

timidez *f. timidity, shyness.*

tímido *adj. timid, shy.*
Maria é muito tímida. *Mary is very shy.*

timoneiro *m. helmsman.*

tina *f. vat, tub.*

tingir *to dye, to tinge.*

tino *m. judgment, prudence, discretion.*

tinta *f. ink; paint.*
Não há tinta no tinteiro. *There's no ink in the inkwell.*

Tinta fresca! *Wet paint!*

tinteiro *m. inkwell.*

tinto *adj. dyed, colored.*
Vinho tinto. *Red wine.*

tintura *f. dye, dyeing.*

tinturaria *f. cleaner's, dry cleaning shop.*

tintureiro *m. (dry) cleaner, dyer.*

TIO *m. uncle.*
Os meus tios. *My uncle and aunt.*
O tio Sam. *Uncle Sam.*
Ela foi ao cinema com a tia. *She went to the movies with her aunt.*

típico *adj. typical, characteristic.*

tipo *m. type, class; fellow, guy.*
Tipo negrito. *Boldface type.*
Tipo grifo. *Italic type.*
Ele é um tipo esquisito. *He's a weird guy.*

tipografia *f. printing; printing shop.*

tipógrafo *m. printer, typographer, typesetter.*

tique-taque *m. tick-tock.*

tira *f. band, strip.*

tirada *f. drawing; tirade.*

tiragem *f. printing, circulation; drawing, draft.*

tirania *f. tyranny.*

tirano *m. tyrant.*

tirante *adj. pulling, drawing.*

TIRAR *to take, to take out, to withdraw; to deduct; to remove; to drag; to win; to draw out; to pull; to throw.*
Ela tirou um lápis da gaveta. *She took a pencil out of the drawer.*
O professor tirou a sorte grande. *The teacher won the grand prize.*
A mãe retirou o filho da escola. *The mother withdrew her son from school.*
Ao entrar na igreja ele tirou o chapéu. *On entering the church, he took off his hat.*
Tirámos proveito do negócio. *We benefited from the business.*
Tirar a prova. *To check (a computation).*
Tirar uma fotografia. *To take a photograph.*

tiritar *to shiver.*

tiro *m. shot; shooting; drawing, hauling.*
O tiro errou. *The shot missed.*
Ao sairmos de casa depois de jantar, ouvimos um tiro. *On leaving home after dinner, we heard a shot.*
Tiro ao alvo. *Target practice.*

tirotear *to fire, to volley.*

tiroteio *m. firing, volley.*

tísica *f. tuberculosis.*

tísico *adj. tubercular; n. m. consumptive, person with tuberculosis.*

tisnar *to blacken.*

titã *m. titan.*

títere *m. puppet, marionette.*

titubear *to hesitate; to stagger.*

A testemunha respondia sem titubear. *The witness answered without hesitation.*

titular *to title, to entitle; adj. titular; n. m. and f. person holding a title; head.*

título *m. title; degree; inscription; bond.*

Qual é o título do livro? *What is the title of the book?*

Título honorífico. *Honorary title.*

to *(contr. of* **te** + **o***) it (m) to you, him to you (fam.).*

toada *f. tune, melody.*

TOALHA *f. towel; cloth.*

Toalha de rosto. *Face towel.*

Toalha de banho. *Bath towel.*

Toalha de mesa. *Tablecloth.*

toar *to sound; to be in tune with.*

toca-discos *m. record player.*

tocador *m. player (music).*

tocante *adj. touching, affecting, regarding.*

No tocante a. *Concerning. Regarding.*

TOCAR *to touch, to play (music); to concern, to interest; to ring (bells); to be one's turn; to be one's share; to call (at a port).*

Não toque! *Don't touch! Hands off!*

Tocar o violão. *To play the guitar.*

Tocar bem. *To play well.*

Tocar mal. *To play badly.*

A orquestra está tocando (a tocar) um samba. *The orchestra is playing a samba.*

A quem lhe toca agora? *Whose turn is it now?*

Agora toca a ele. *It's his turn now.*

O navio tocou em Lisboa. *The ship called (stopped) at Lisbon.*

Pelo que me toca. *As far as I'm concerned.*

Tocar de ouvido. *To play by ear.*

Tocar o piano. *To play the piano.*

tocha *f. torch, large candle.*

todavia *adv. however, yet.*

TODO *adj. each, every; all; n. m. all, whole; pl. all, everyone.*

Ele perdeu todo o seu dinheiro. *He lost all his money.*

Ela estudou toda a manhã. *She studied all morning.*

Todos dizem o mesmo. *They all say the same thing.*

Todo o dia. *All day.*

O dia todo. *All day long.*

Todos os dias. *Every day.*

Toda a família. *The whole family.*

Todo o mundo. *Everybody.*

Todos de uma vez. *All at once. All at the same time.*

Todos nós. *All of us.*

Em todo caso. *In any case.*

Todo homem. *Every man.*

A cidade toda. *The entire city.*

toldo *m. awning.*

tolerância *f. tolerance.*

tolerante *adj. tolerant.*

tolerar *to tolerate.*

Não podemos tolerar tal barulho. *We can't tolerate such noise.*

Não posso tolerá-lo. *I can't stand him.*

tolerável *adj. tolerable.*

tolice *f. foolishness, nonsense.*

Que tolice! *What nonsense!*

Não diga tolices. *Don't speak foolishness.*

tolo *adj. foolish; crazy; n. m. fool.*

Não seja tolo. *Don't be a fool.*

tom *m. tone; sound; color.*

Sem tom nem som. *Without rhyme or reason.*

TOMAR *to take; to get; to seize; to have (drink, food).*

Que quer tomar? *What will you have (to eat/drink)?*

Nunca tomo vinho. *I never drink wine.*

Tome o remédio às horas indicadas. *Take the medicine at the times indicated.*

Tomemos um táxi *(x = ks). Let's take a taxi.*

Aconselho-lhe a tomar o trem (comboio) das oito. *I advise you to take the eight o'clock train.*

Tomar nota de. *To take note of.*

Tomaram as medidas necessárias. *They took the necessary measures.*

Tomar emprestado. *To borrow.*

Não quer tomar uma bebida? *Don't you want a drink?*

É preciso tomar uma decisão. *You have to make a decision.*

Tomar a palavra. *To take the floor.*

Tomar em conta. *To take into account.*

Tomar banho. *To take a bath.*

Não o tome a mal. *Don't take it wrong. Don't take it the wrong way.*

Tomar a peito. *To take to heart.*

Tomar o pulso. *To take the pulse.*

Tomar posse de. *To take possession of.*

Eu o tomei (tomei-o) por outro. *I took (mistook) you for somebody else.*

tomara *I hope. Would that* ⓇⒷ.

Tomara! *I hope so!*

Tomara que não! *I hope not!*

tomate *m. tomato.*

tombar *to fell, to bring down; to fall.*

tomo *m. volume (book)*

É uma obra em três tomos. *It's a three-volume work.*

tonelada *f. ton.*

tônico (tónico) *adj. stressed (syllable); tonic; n. m. tonic.*

tonsilite *f. tonsillitis.*

tontear *to act foolishly, to talk nonsense; to feel dizzy.*

tonto *adj. silly, foolish; dizzy; n. m. fool.*

topar *to meet by chance, to "run into."*
> Topei com ele no cinema. *I ran into him (came across him) at the movies.*

topázio *m. topaz.*

tope *m. top, summit; clash, collision.*

topete *m. forelock; audacity, "nerve."*

tópico *adj. topical.*

topografia *f. topography.*

topógrafo *m. topographer.*

toque *m. touch; bugle call.*
> Toque de alvorada. *Reveille.*
> Toque de silêncio. *Taps.*

tora *f. portion; nap* Ⓑ.
> Tirar uma tora. *To take a nap (slang)* Ⓑ.

tórax (x = ks) *m. thorax.*

torcedura *f. twisting; sprain.*

torcer *to twist; to sprain; to distort.*
> Torcer o nariz. *To turn up one's nose.*
> João torceu o tornozelo. *John sprained his ankle.*

torcida *f. group of rooters, cheering section.*

torcido *adj. twisted, crooked.*

tormenta *f. storm, tempest.*

tormento *m. torment, distress.*

tormentoso *adj. stormy.*

tornar *to come back; to change;* **tornar a** *to do again.*
> Ela tornou a cantar. *She sang again.*

tornar-se *to become.*
> José se tornou (tornou-se) chefe do grupo. *Joseph became leader of the group.*

torneio *m. tournament.*

torneira *f. faucet, spigot.*
> Abrir a torneira. *To turn the faucet on.*
> Fechar a torneira. *To turn the faucet off.*

torno *m. lathe; vise; faucet.*

tornozelo *m. ankle.*

toronja *f. grapefruit.*

torpe *adj. base, lowly.*

torpedeiro *m. torpedo boat.*

torpedo *m. torpedo.*

torrada *f. toast (bread).*

torrado *adj. toasted, roasted.*

torre *f. tower; turret; belfry; rook (chess).*
> Torre de igreja. *Steeple.*

torrente *f. torrent.*

tórrido *adj. torrid.*

torta *f. pie, tart, cake.*
> Torta de maçã. *Apple pie.*

torto *adj. twisted, crooked.*
> A torto e a direito. *By hook or by crook.*

tortura *f. torture.*

torturar *to torture.*

torvar *to disturb, to upset.*

torvelinho, torvelino *m. whirlwind, eddy.*

tosar *to shear.*

tosco *adj. rough, clumsy, coarse.*

tosquiar *to shear.*
> Ir buscar lã e vir tosquiado. *To go for wool and return shorn.*

tosse *f. cough.*

tossir *to cough.*

tostão *m. former Portuguese coin; Brazilian coin.*
> Não vale um tostão. *It isn't worth peanuts. It's worthless.*

tostar *to toast, to brown, to tan.*

total *adj., n. m. total, whole.*
> Quantos há no total? *How many are there in all?*

totalidade *f. totality, all.*

touca *f. bonnet, cap, coif.*

toucador *m. vanity, dressing table; dressing room.*

toucinho, toicinho *m. bacon, fatback, salt pork.*

tourada *f. bullfight.*
> As touradas em Madrid. *The bullfights in Madrid.*

tourear *to fight bulls.*

toureiro *m. bullfighter.*

touro *m. bull.*

tóxico (x = ks) *adj. toxic, poisonous; n. m. poison.*

trabalhador *adj. hard-working, industrious; n. m. worker, laborer.*
> O filho dele é muito trabalhador. *His son is very industrious.*

TRABALHAR *to work, to labor.*
> Alberto trabalha como um mouro. *Albert works like a horse.*
> Acho que ele não trabalha muito. *I don't think he works too hard.*

TRABALHO *m. work, labor; job; product, result.*
> Garantimos o trabalho. *We guarantee the work.*
> Tudo isto é trabalho perdido. *All this is wasted effort.*
> Sem trabalho. *Unemployed. Out of work.*
> Trabalho de noite. *Night work.*
> Trabalhos forçados. *Hard labor.*

trabalhoso *adj. laborious, arduous.*

traçar *to draw, to sketch; to outline; to plan.*
> Traçar uma linha. *To draw a line.*
> Os engenheiros traçaram os planos para uma nova ponte. *The engineers drew up the plans for a new bridge.*

tracejar *to trace, to outline.*

tradição *f. tradition.*

tradicional *adj. traditional.*

tradução *f. translation.*
> Tradução literal. *Literal translation.*
> Tradução livre. *Free translation.*

tradutor *m. translator.*

traduzir *to translate.*
   Traduza esta carta para o inglês. *Translate this letter into English.*
   Não há maneira de traduzi-lo. *There's no way to translate it.*
tráfego *m. traffic; trading, trade.*
   Sinal de tráfego. *Traffic light.*
traficante *adj. dishonest; n. m. swindler.*
traficar *to traffic, to trade; to swindle.*
tráfico *m. traffic, trafficking, trade.*
tragar *to swallow; to devour.*
tragédia *f. tragedy.*
trágico *adj. tragic.*
trago *m. swallow, swig, drink.*
   Vamos tomar um trago. *Let's have a drink.*
traição *f. treason, treachery.*
traidor *adj. treacherous; n. m. traitor.*
trair *to betray; to divulge.*
traje, trajo *m. clothing, suit, dress.*
   Traje de banho (fato de banho). *Bathing suit.*
trama *f. weft (weaving); n. m. and f. web; plot, conspiracy.*
tramar *to weave; to plot, to scheme.*
tranca *f. crossbar, bar; obstacle.*
tranqüilidade (tranquilidade) *f. tranquility, peace.*
tranqüilo (tranquilo) *adj. tranquil, quiet, calm.*
   Este lugar é muito tranqüilo. *This place is very quiet.*
transação (transacção) *f. transaction.*
transatlântico *adj. transatlantic; n. m. ocean liner.*
transbordar *to overflow.*
transcendental *adj. transcendental.*
transcendente *adj. transcendent.*
transcender *to transcend.*
transcorrer *to pass, to elapse (time).*
transcrever *to transcribe.*
transcurso *m. course, lapse (time).*
transeunte *m. and f. pedestrian, passerby.*
transferência *f. transference, transfer.*
transferir *to transfer; to defer.*
transformação *f. transformation.*
transformador *adj. transforming; n. m. transformer.*
transformar *to transform.*
   A cidra se transformou (transformou-se) em vinagre. *The cider turned into vinegar.*
transfusão *f. transfusion.*
transgredir *to transgress.*
transição *f. transition, passage.*
transigir *to compromise, to agree.*
transistor *m. transistor.*
trânsito *m. passage, transit, transition; traffic.*
   Trânsito impedido. *No thoroughfare.*
transitório *adj. transitory.*

transmissão *f. transmission, broadcast.*
transmissor *adj. transmitting; n. m. transmitter.*
transmissora *f. transmitter.*
transmitir *to transmit, to send, to convey.*
transparente *adj. transparent; clear.*
transpiração *f. transpiration; perspiration.*
transpirar *to transpire; to perspire; to become known.*
transpor *to transpose, to cross over.*
transportar *to transport, to convey; to transpose.*
   Não sei se podem transportar tanta bagagem. *I don't know whether they can carry so much baggage.*
transporte *m. transport, transportation.*
   Transporte pago. *Carriage paid.*
transtornar *to overturn; to upset, to disturb.*
trapalhada *f. predicament, mess.*
   Que trapalhada! *What a mess!*
trapo *m. rag; pl. old clothes.*
   Boneca de trapos. *Rag doll.*
TRÁS *after, behind.*
   Ir para trás. *To go back, backward.*
   Um trás outro. *One after the other.*
traseiro *adj. back, rear.*
   A porta traseira dá para o jardim. *The back door opens out into the garden.*
trasladar *to transport, to move, to transfer; to postpone; to transcribe, to translate.*
traslado *m. transfer; transcript; translation; copy.*
traspassar *to cross; to transfer; to trespass.*
   Traspassar de um lado a outro. *To cross from one side to the other.*
   Traspassar um negócio. *To transfer a business.*
traste *m. household item of little value.*
tratado *m. treaty.*
tratamento *m. treatment; form of address.*
TRATAR *to treat, to deal with; to discuss.*
   De que se trata? *What's it about?*
   Trata-se dum assunto importante. *The matter in question is important.*
   De que trata este artigo? *What's this article about?*
   Este livro trata da vida de Camões. *This book is about the life of Camões.*
   Prefiro tratar com pessoas sérias. *I prefer to deal with serious people.*
   Você tem de tratar com esses problemas. *You must deal with those problems.*
   Tratam mal (os) seus empregados. *They don't treat their employees well.*
trato *m. treatment; form of address; contract, agreement.*
   Tenho tido pouco trato com eles. *I haven't had much to do with them.*
   Façamos um trato. *Let's make a deal.*

trator (tractor) *m. tractor.*

travar *to join, to unite, to bind, to link.*

Travar conversa. *To strike up a
conversation.*

Travar amizade. *To make friends.*

Travar conhecimento. *To make someone's
acquaintance. To strike up an
acquaintance.*

través *m. bias, slant.*

Olhar de través. *To look sideways. To look
out the corner of one's eyes.*

travessa *f. crosspiece, crossbeam; alley.*

travessão *crossbar, crossbeam; dash
(punctuation).*

travesseiro *m. pillow.*

travessia *ocean crossing, sea voyage,
crossing, passage.*

travessura *f. mischief, prank, trick.*

TRAZER *to bring, to carry; to wear.*

Traga-me uma cerveja. *Bring me a beer.*

Trouxeram (x = s) tudo o que lhes pedi.
They brought everything I asked for.

Você trouxe (x = s) consigo (or com você)?
Did you bring it with you?

Ela traz um chapéu novo. *She is wearing a
new hat.*

trecho *m. distance, interval.*

A trechos. *At intervals.*

trégua *f. truce, respite.*

treinador *m. trainer, coach.*

treinamento *m. training, coaching.*

treinar *to train, to coach.*

TREM *m. train Ⓑ; pl. gear, belongings,
"stuff."*

A que horas sai o trem (comboio) para São
Paulo? *At what time does the train for
São Paulo leave?*

Este trem pára em todas as estações? *Does
this train stop at all stations?*

Vamos tomar o trem das oito. *Let's take
the eight o' clock train.*

Os meus trens estão na mala. *My stuff is in
the trunk.*

tremendo *adj. tremendous, dreadful, awful.*

tremer *to tremble, to shake.*

trenó *m. sled, sleigh.*

trepar *to climb.*

TRÊS *three.*

Às duas por três. *Two out of three times.*

Dois é bom, três é demais. *Two's
company; three's a crowd.*

trevas *f. pl. darkness.*

trevo *m. clover.*

Trevo de quatro folhas. *Four-leaf clover.*

treze *thirteen.*

trezentos *three hundred.*

triângulo *m. triangle.*

tribo *f. tribe.*

tribuna *f. tribune, platform.*

tribunal *m. tribunal (of justice).*

tributar *to pay taxes; to pay tribute; to tax, to
assess.*

tributo *m. tribute, tax.*

tricotar *to knit.*

trigésimo *adj., n. m. thirtieth.*

trigo *m. wheat.*

Farinha de trigo. *Wheat flour.*

trigonometria *f. trigonometry.*

trilhar *to thresh; to tread.*

trilho *m. trail, way; track, rail Ⓑ.*

trimestre *m. trimester; quarter (of a year).*

trinar *to warble.*

trincar *to bite, to crunch; to grit (teeth).*

trinchar *to carve (meat).*

trincheira *f. trench, ditch.*

trindade *f. trinity, Trinity.*

TRINTA *thirty.*

trio *m. trio.*

tripa *f. tripe, intestines.*

triplicar *to triple.*

triplo *adj., n. m. triple.*

tripulação *f. crew.*

tripulante *m. and f. member of a crew.*

TRISTE *adj. sad, gloomy.*

Ele faz um papel triste. *He cuts a sorry
figure.*

Isto é muito triste. *That's (this is) very sad.*

Ao ouvir a notícia ela ficou muito triste.
*She became very sad when she heard
the news.*

tristeza *f. sadness, grief, gloom.*

Tristeza não tem fim. *There's no end to
sadness.*

triunfante *adj. triumphant.*

triunfar *to triumph, to succeed.*

triunfo *m. triumph.*

trivial *adj. trivial.*

troar *to thunder; to rumble.*

troça *f. mockery, derision; joke.*

Fazer troça de. *To make fun of.*

trocadilho *m. pun, play on words.*

trocar *to change, to exchange, to barter.*

Trocar dinheiro. *To change money.*

Trocar uma coisa por outra. *To exchange
one thing for another.*

Trocar roupa. *To change clothes.*

troçar *to joke; to ridicule.*

trocista *m. and f. joker; mocker.*

troco *m. change (money); exchange.*

Fique com o troco. *Keep the change.*

trombada *f. crash, collision.*

trombeta *f. trumpet, horn.*

trombone *m. trombone.*

trompa *f. horn; tube.*

tronar *to thunder; to roar.*

tronco *m. trunk (wood, body); stem.*

trono *m. throne.*

tropa *f. troop.*

tropeçar *to stumble, to trip; to make a mistake.*

tropeço *m. stumbling, tripping; obstacle.*

tropical *adj. tropical.*

trópico *m. tropic.*
> Trópico de Câncer. *Tropic of Cancer.*

trotar *to trot.*

trote *m. trot.*

trovão *m. thunder.*

trovoada *f. thunderstorm.*

trovoar *to thunder.*

truta *f. trout.*

tu *you (fam.).*

tua *f. adj. and pron. your (fam.).*

tuberculose *f. tuberculosis.*

tuberculoso *adj. tubercular; n. m. person with tuberculosis.*

tubo *m. tube, pipe.*

TUDO *all, everything.*
> Ou tudo ou nada. *All or nothing.*
> Ele sabe um pouco de tudo. *He knows a little about everything.*
> Tudo está pronto. *Everything is ready.*
> Antes de tudo. *First of all.*
> Tudo quanto lhe digo é verdade. *Everything I'm telling you is the truth.*
> Apesar de tudo. *Nevertheless.*

tule *m. tulle, silk net.*

tulipa (túlipa) *f. tulip.*

tumba *f. tomb, grave.*

tumor *m. tumor.*

túmulo *m. tomb, grave, vault.*

túnel *m. tunnel.*

tupi *adj., n. m. Tupi, Indian tribes of Brazil.*

tupi-guarani *adj., n. m. the Tupi-Guarani tribes.*

turba *f. mob, rabble, crowd.*

turbação *f. disturbance.*

turbante *m. turban.*

turbar *to disturb, to upset; to darken, to muddy.*

turbina *f. turbine.*

turbulência *f. turbulence, disturbance.*

turbulento *turbulent.*

turco *adj. Turkish; n. m. Turk.*

turismo *m. touring, tourism.*
> Agência de turismo. *Travel agency.*

turista *m. and f. tourist.*
> No ano passado houve muitos turistas em Portugal. *Last year there were many tourists in Portugal.*

turma *f. group, gang; class (school).*

turno *m. turn; shift; school period.*
> Por turnos. *By turns.*
> Turno de noite. *Night shift.*

turquesa *f. turquoise.*

turrão *adj. stubborn.*

turvar *to confuse, to upset; to darken, to muddy.*

tutear *to address someone in the familiar form, to use the "tu" form.*

tutela *f. guardianship, tutelage.*

tutor *m. tutor, guardian.*

U

ufa! *whew!*

ufanar-se *to be proud, to boast.*

ufano *adj. proud, haughty.*

ui! *oh! ouch! ow! ugh!*

uísque *m. whiskey* ⑧.

uivar *to howl.*

uivo *m. howl.*

úlcera *f. ulcer.*

ulterior *adj. ulterior.*

ultimato *m. ultimatum.*

ÚLTIMO *adj. last, latest; final, ultimate.*
> José foi último a chegar. *Joseph was the last one to arrive.*
> Por último. *Finally. At last.*
> No último momento. *At the last moment.*
> Ultimamente. *Recently.*

ultramar *m. overseas lands or areas.*

ultramarino *adj. overseas.*

ulular *to wail.*

UM, UMA *one; (ind. article) a, an.*
> Um homem. *A man.*
> Uma mulher. *A woman.*
> Um pouco. *A little.*
> Uma vez. *Once.*
> Vou comprar somente um livro. *I'm going to buy only one book.*
> Um dia sim, um dia não. *Every other day.*

umbral *m. threshold, doorway.*

umedecer *to moisten, to dampen.*

umidade *f. humidity, dampness, moisture.*

úmido *adj. humid, moist, damp.*

unânime *adj. unanimous.*

unanimidade *f. unanimity.*

undécimo *adj., n. m. eleventh.*

ungüento (unguento) *m. unguent, ointment.*

UNHA *f. fingernail, toenail; claw; hoof.*
> Fazer as unhas. *To trim the nails.*

união *f. union, unity; coupling.*
> A união faz a força. *there is strength in unity.*
> Traço de união. *Hyphen.*

único *adj. only, only one, unique, singular.*
> Essa foi a única vez que ele me falou. *That was the only time he spoke to me.*

unidade *f. unity; unit.*
> Unidade de disco. *Disk drive.*

unido *adj. united, joined.*

unificar *to unify.*

uniforme *adj., n. m. uniform.*

uniformidade *f. uniformity.*

unir *to unite, to join together, to put together.*
   Vamos fazer tudo possível para uni-los.
     We're going to do everything possible to unite them.

unir-se *to come together, to unite, to join.*
   As duas firmas se uniram (uniram-se). *The two firms merged.*

universal *adj. universal.*

universidade *f. university.*

universitário *adj. of a university, academic; n. m. university faculty member or student.*

universo *m. universe.*

uno *adj. one, only one.*

untar *to grease, to anoint.*

urânio *m. uranium.*

urbanidade *f. urbanity, good manners, politeness.*

urbano *adj. urban; urbane, refined, polite.*

urdir *to warp; to scheme, to hatch a plot.*

urgência *f. urgency, pressure.*
   Com urgência. *Urgently.*
   A urgência dos negócios. *The pressure of business.*

urgente *adj. urgent.*
   Entrega urgente. *Special delivery (mail).*
   É urgente que você venha amanhã às oito horas. *It's urgent that you come tomorrow at eight o'clock.*

urgir *to urge, to press, to be urgent, to be pressing.*

urna *f. urn; ballot box.*

urrar *to roar, to yell.*

urro *m. roar, yell.*

urso *m. bear; rude individual.*
   Urso-branco. *Polar bear.*
   Amigo urso. *False friend.*
   Ursa Maior. *Great Bear (constellation).*

urubu *m. black vulture.*

uruguaio *adj., n. m. Uruguayan.*

usança *f. usage, custom.*

USAR *to use; to be accustomed to; to wear.*
   Usar o telefone. *To use the telephone.*
   Sempre uso óculos para ler. *I always wear (use) glasses to read.*
   No verão uso camisa de manga curta. *In the summer, I wear short-sleeved shirts.*

usina *f. factory, mill.*
   Usina de aço. *Steel mill.*
   Usina de açúcar. *Sugar mill.*
   Usina hidrelétrica (hidroeléctrica). *Hydroelectric power station.*

USO *m. use; usage; custom; wear.*
   Para uso externo. *For external use.*
   Em uso. *In use.*
   Fora de uso. *Out of use.*

USUAL *adj. usual, customary.*
   Isso é muito usual. *That's very common.*
   O usual. *The usual.*

usura *f. usury.*

usurário *m. usurer.*

usurpação *f. usurpation.*

usurpador *m. usurper.*

usurpar *to usurp.*

utensílio *m. utensil.*
   Utensílios de cozinha. *Kitchen utensils.*

ÚTIL *adj. useful, profitable.*
   Você o encontrará útil. *You'll find it very useful.*
   Dias úteis. *Workdays. Weekdays.*

utilidade *f. utility, usefulness.*

utilizar *to utilize.*

Utopia *f. Utopia.*

uva *f. grape.*

V

VACA *f. cow.*
   Carne de vaca. *Beef.*

vacante *adj. vacant; in abeyance.*

vacar *to vacate; to be vacant; to be free.*

vacilação *f. vacillation, hesitation.*

vacilante *adj. vacillating, wavering, uncertain, hesitating.*

vacilar *to vacillate, to waver, to hesitate.*
   Eles não vacilaram em fazê-lo. *They did not hesitate to do it.*

vacina *f. vaccination; vaccine.*

vacinar *to vaccinate.*

vadear *to ford; to wade.*

vadiar *to waste time, to loaf.*

vadio *adj. lazy, idle; n. m. idler, loafer.*

vaga *f. vacancy.*

vagabundo *adj. vagabond, vagrant; cheap, shoddy; n. m. idler, vagabond, tramp.*

vagão *m. coach, car; wagon; freight car.*
   Vagão restaurante. *Dining car.*

vagar *to rove, to roam; to vacate, to be vacant; to idle.*

vagem *f. string bean, green bean.*

vago *adj. vague, indefinite; vacant; vagrant.*
   Horas vagas. *Spare time.*

vaia *f. boo, jeer.*

vaiar *to boo, to jeer at.*

vaidade *f. vanity.*
   Ela o faz (fá-lo) por vaidade. *She does it out of vanity.*

vaidoso *adj. vain, conceited.*

vaivém *m. coming and going; vicissitude.*
   Os vaivéns da sorte. *The ups and downs of life (of fortune).*

vale *m. IOU, voucher; valley.*
   Vale postal. *Postal money order.*
   O jogador assinou o vale. *The gambler signed the IOU.*

valente *adj. brave, valiant.*

valentia *f. valor, courage, bravery.*

VALER *to be worth, to amount to; to cost; to merit; to assist; to be of use.*
  Quanto vale? *How much is it worth?*
  Não vale nada. *It's worthless. It isn't worth anything.*
  Acho que este vale mais (do) que esse. *I believe this one is better than that one.*
  Mais vale tarde do que nunca. *Better late than never.*
  Valer a pena. *To be worthwhile.*
  Valha-me Deus! *God help me!*

validar *to validate.*

validez *f. validity.*

válido *adj. valid; sound.*
  O passaporte é válido por um ano. *The passport is valid (good) for a year.*

valioso *adj. valuable, worthy.*

valise *f. valise, grip, traveling bag.*

VALOR *m. value; price; worth; valor, courage; pl. securities.*
  De pouco valor. *Of little value.*
  Sem valor. *Of no value. Worthless.*
  Dar valor a. *To value.*
  Valor nominal. *Face value. Par value.*
  Bolsa de valores. *Stock exchange.*

valorizar *to value, to appraise; to increase in value.*

valsa *f. waltz.*

válvula *f. valve.*
  Válvula de segurança. *Safety valve.*

VAMOS! *Come! Come on! Let's go! Hurry up!*

vanguarda *f. vanguard.*

vantagem *f. advantage; profit; odds (games), handicap (sports).*
  Este procedimento tem as suas vantagens e desvantagens. *This procedure has its advantages and disadvantages.*
  Levar vantagem. *To have the advantage. To gain the upper hand.*

vão *adj. (vã fem.) vain; futile; n. m. space, opening.*
  Toda tentativa foi em vão. *Every attempt was in vain.*

vapor *m. vapor, steam; steamship.*
  A todo vapor. *At full steam.*
  Cavalo-vapor. *Horsepower.*

vaqueiro *m. cowboy.*

vara *f. rod, pole, stick, wand; judgeship; jurisdiction; measurement of 43.3 inches.*

varanda *f. veranda, balcony.*

varão *adj. male; n. m. man, male.*

varar *to pierce, to stick; to beat with a stick; to ford (a stream); to beach (a boat).*

varejo *m. retail Ⓑ; search, raid.*
  Vender a varejo. *To sell at retail.*

variação *f. variation, change.*
  Sem variação. *Unchanged.*

variado *adj. varied.*

variante *adj. varying, variant; f. variant, variation.*

variar *to vary, to change.*
  Não varia nada. *It doesn't change (vary) a bit.*

variável *adj. variable, changeable.*

varicela *f. chicken pox.*

variedade *f. variety.*

VÁRIO *adj. different, changeable; pl. several, some.*
  Hoje comprei vários livros sobre Portugal e o Brasil. *Today I bought several (some) books about Portugal and Brazil.*

varíola *f. smallpox.*

varonil *adj. manly, virile.*

varredor *adj. sweeping; n. m. sweeper.*

varrer *to sweep.*

várzea *f. meadow, field.*

vaselina *f. Vaseline.*

vasilha *f. vessel (for liquids).*

vaso *m. vase, bowl, vessel.*
  Vaso de flores. *Flowerpot. Vase for flowers.*

vassoura *f. broom.*

vastidão *f. vastness.*

vasto *adj. vast.*

vatapá *m. a seasoned Brazilian meat dish Ⓑ.*

vaticano *adj., n. m. Vatican.*

vau *m. river crossing, ford; opportunity.*

vazar *to empty; to flow out; to drain.*

vazio *adj. empty, vacant; n. m. void, vacuum.*

veado *m. deer.*

vedar *to prohibit, to stop.*

vedeta *f. advanced guard, sentry; star (movies, theater).*

vegetação *f. vegetation.*

vegetal *adj., n. m. vegetable.*

veia *f. vein.*
  Veia artéria. *Pulmonary artery.*
  Continuamos na mesma veia. *Let's keep going in the same vein.*

veículo *m. vehicle.*

veio *m. grain (wood), streak, vein.*

vela *f. candle; sail.*
  Apagar as velas. *To blow out the candles.*
  Vela de cera. *Wax candle.*
  Vela de ignição. *Spark plug.*
  Barco à vela. *Sailboat.*

velar *to watch; to keep vigil; to veil.*

veleiro *m. sailboat.*

velhaco *adj., crooked; n. m. crook, lowlife.*

velhice *f. old age; old people.*

VELHO *adj. old; ancient; worn-out; old man.*
  Somos velhos amigos. *We're old friends.*

A mãe dela é muito velha. *Her mother is very old.*

Esse velho é rico. *That old man is rich.*

Mais velho. *Older. Senior.*

Meu velho. *Old fellow. My friend* ®.

velocidade *f. velocity, speed; gear.*

Primeira, segunda, e terceira velocidade. *First, second, and third gear.*

Passaram a toda velocidade. *They went by at full speed.*

veloz *adj. swift, fast.*

veludo *adj. velvety; n. m. velvet; velour.*

vencer *to conquer, to vanquish, to win.*

vencido *adj. defeated; due, outstanding.*

Dar-se por vencido. *To give up.*

venda *f. sale; store; blindfold.*

vendar *to blindfold.*

vendedor *m. seller, trader, dealer.*

VENDER *to sell; to trade; to betray.*

Não vendemos a varejo; só por atacado. *We don't sell retail; only wholesale.*

Também não vendemos a crédito (or fiado); só a dinheiro. *We also don't sell on credit; only cash.*

veneno *m. venom, poison.*

venenoso *adj. poisonous.*

veneração *f. veneration.*

venerar *to venerate.*

venezuelano *adj., n. m. Venezuelan.*

venta *f. nostril.*

ventilação *f. ventilation.*

ventilador *m. ventilator, electric fan.*

ventilar *to ventilate, to air.*

VENTO *m. wind; breeze; air.*

Ir de vento em popa. *To get along very well. To be progressing. ("To go with the wind at your stern.")*

ventre *m. stomach, belly, paunch.*

ventura *f. happiness; fortune, chance; venture; risk.*

Por ventura. *By chance. Perchance.*

venturoso *adj. lucky, fortunate, happy.*

VER *to see; to look at; to visit; to meet; n. m. sense of sight; opinion.*

Deixe-me (*x = sh*) ver. *Let me see.*

Vamos ver. *Let's see.*

Que quadros deseja ver? *What paintings do you wish to see?*

Veja esta carta. *Look at this letter.*

Não ter nada que ver com. *To have nothing to do with.*

A meu ver. *In my view. As I see it.*

Tenha a bondade de ver quem é. *Please see who it is.*

Já se vê. *It is clear. It is evident.*

Agora estou vendo. *I see now. I understand.*

Vamos vê-los no sábado. *We're going to see them on Saturday.*

Veja só! *Just imagine!*

Quatro olhos vêem melhor que dois. *Two heads are better than one.*

Ver para crer. *Seeing is believing.*

VERÁO *m. summer.*

veras *f. pl. truth, reality.*

Com todas as veras. *Truthfully. In all truth.*

verba *f. item; entry; appropriation.*

verbal *adj. verbal, oral.*

verbete *m. entry; note.*

verbo *m. verb.*

VERDADE *f. truth.*

Diga a verdade. *Tell the truth.*

Quero saber se é verdade. *I want to know if it is true.*

Você chegou tarde, não é verdade? *You arrived late, didn't you?*

É verdade. *That's right. That's true.*

De verdade? *Really?*

Para dizer a verdade. *To tell the truth.*

verdadeiro *adj. true; real; sincere.*

VERDE *adj. green; not ripe; immature; n. m. green.*

verdugo *m. executioner, hangman, jerk (nasty person).*

verdura *f. greeness; pl. vegetables, greens.*

vereador *m. alderman, councilman.*

vereda *f. path, footpath, trail.*

veredicto *m. verdict.*

verga *f. stick, switch.*

vergar *to bend, to curve; to stoop.*

vergonha *f. shame, disgrace; timidity, embarrassment.*

Não tem vergonha? *Aren't you ashamed?*

Que vergonha! *What a shame!*

Sem vergonha. *Shameless.*

É uma vergonha. *It's a shame.*

vergonhoso *adj. shameful, disgraceful.*

verídico *adj. truthful, veracious.*

verificação *f. verification.*

verificar *to check, to verify.*

Verifique tudo. *Check everything.*

verificar-se *to take place.*

verme *m. worm, vermin, larva.*

VERMELHO *adj., n. m. red.*

A Cruz Vermelha. *The Red Cross.*

verminose *f. verminosis, disease caused by worms.*

verniz *m. varnish.*

verossímil (verosímil) *adj. verisimilar.*

verossimilhança (verosimilhança) *f. verisimilitude.*

versão *f. version, rendition.*

Cada um deles deu a sua versão. *Each one of them gave his own version.*

versar *to deal with; to be about; to examine; to put into verse.*

versátil *adj. versatile, fickle.*

ver-se *to see oneself, to find oneself, to be.*

verso *m. verse; back side.*
Verso branco. *Blank verse.*

vértebra *f. vertebra.*

vertedor *m. water pitcher, jug.*

verter *to pour; to spill; to translate.*
Verter lágrimas. *To weep. To shed tears.*

vertical *adj. vertical.*

vértice *m. vertex, apex, top.*

vertigem *f. dizziness; fainting.*

vesgo *adj. cross-eyed; n. m. cross-eyed person.*

vesguear *to squint.*

vespa *f. wasp, hornet.*

véspera *f. eve.*
Véspera de Natal. *Christmas Eve.*

vespertino *m. evening newspaper.*

vestiário *m. checkroom, cloakroom.*

vestíbulo *m. vestibule, lobby, hall, foyer.*
Encontrámo-nos no vestíbulo do teatro às oito. *We met in the lobby of the theater at eight.*

VESTIDO *adj. dressed; n. m. dress; garment; clothing.*
Ela estava bem vestida. *She was well dressed.*
Vestido de baile. *Evening dress.*

vestígio *m. vestige, trace.*

VESTIR *to dress, to put on.*
Ele veste bem. *He dresses well.*
A mãe está vestindo (a vestir) os filhos. *The mother is dressing her children.*

VESTIR-SE *to dress oneself, to get dressed.*
Os meninos ainda não se vestiram. *The children haven't dressed yet.*

vestuário *m. wardrobe; clothing, apparel.*

veterano *adj., n. m. veteran.*

veterinário *m. veterinarian.*

veto *m. veto.*

vetusto *adj. old, ancient.*

vexar *(x = sh) to vex, to annoy.*

VEZ *f. time, turn.*
Uma vez. *Once.*
Duas vezes. *Twice.*
Outra vez. *Again.*
Repetidas vezes. *Again and again.*
De uma vez para sempre. *Once (and) for all.*
Raras vezes. *Seldom.*
Muitas vezes. *Often.*
Cada vez. *Each time. Every time.*
Cada vez mais. *More and more.*
De vez em quando. *Now and then.*
Algumas vezes. *Sometimes.*
Fazer as vezes de. *To take the place of.*
Duas vezes três são seis. *Two times three are six.*
É minha vez. *It's my turn.*

Um de cada vez. *One at a time.*

via *f. road, way; manner; prep. via.*
Por via de regra. *As a general rule.*
Via férrea. *Railroad. Railway.*
Via aérea. *By airmail.*
Via pública. *Public road. Thoroughfare.*
Via expressa. *Express highway.*

viação *f. traffic; transit system.*

viaduto *m. viaduct.*

viageiro *adj. traveling; n. m. traveler, passenger, voyager.*

VIAGEM *f. trip, voyage, journey, travel.*
Boa viagem! *Pleasant journey! Bon voyage!*
Estar de viagem. *To be on a trip.*
Viagem de ida e volta. *Round trip.*

viajante *adj. traveling; n. m. and f. traveler.*
Caixeiro-viajante. *Traveling salesman.*

VIAJAR *to travel.*
Viajar de trem (comboio). *To go by train.*
Eu viajei por Portugal. *I traveled through Portugal.*

viatura *f. vehicle.*

víbora *f. viper.*

vibração *f. vibration.*

vibrar *to vibrate, to throb; to brandish; to touch, to sound (stringed instrument).*

vice-almirante *m. vice admiral.*

vice-cônsul *m. vice-consul.*

vice-presidente *m. vice-president.*

vice-versa *adj. vice versa.*

viciado *adj. addicted; n. m. addict.*
Viciado em. *Addicted to.*

viciar *to addict; to falsify.*

vício *m. vice; bad habit; failing; addiction.*

vicissitude *f. vicissitude, fluctuation.*

VIDA *f. life, living.*
Ganhar a vida. *To earn a living.*
Assim é a vida. *That's life. Such is life.*
Seguro de vida. *Life insurance.*
Custo de vida. *Cost of living.*

vidente *m. and f. seer.*

vídeo *m. video.*

videocassette *m. videocassette; VCR.*

videoclube *m. video rental club.*

videodisco *m. videodisk.*

videojogo *m. videogame.*

videoteipe *m. videotape.*

vidraça *f. windowpane.*

vidro *m. glass; bottle.*
Vidro de aumento. *Magnifying glass.*
Fábrica de vidro. *Glassworks.*

vienense *adj., n. m. and f. Viennese.*

viga *f. beam, girder.*

vigário *m. vicar.*
Conto do vigário. *Swindle, fraud.*

vigésimo *adj. twentieth; n. m. twentieth.*

vigiar *to watch; to stand guard.*

vigilância *f. vigilance.*

vigília f. vigil.

vigor m. vigor, strength.

    Em vigor. In force.

vigoroso adj. vigorous, strong.

vil adj. mean, low, vile, despicable.

vila f. village; villa.

vilão adj. villainous; rustic; n. m. villain, scoundrel; peasant.

vime m. wicker.

    Cadeira de vime. Wicker chair.

vinagre m. vinegar.

vinda f. arrival.

    Eu lhe dou as boas vindas. I welcome you.

vindicar to vindicate.

vingador adj. avenging, vindictive; n. m. avenger.

vingança f. vengeance, revenge.

vingar to avenge, to take vengeance.

vingativo adj. vindictive.

vinha f. vineyard, vine.

vinho m. wine.

    Vinho branco. White wine.

    Vinho tinto. Red wine.

    Vinho do Porto. Port.

VINTE twenty.

vintém m. former coin of Portugal and Brazil.

    Eu estou sem um vintém. I don't have two cents to rub together.

viola f. viola.

violação f. violation, breach.

violão m. guitar.

violar to violate; to offend.

violência f. violence.

violento adj. violent.

violeta adj. violet; n. m. violet (color); n. f. violet (flower).

violinista m. violinist, fiddler.

violino m. violin, fiddle.

violoncelo m. cello.

VIR to come, to approach.

    Venha cá! Come here!

    O mês que vem. Next month.

    Venha o que vier. Come what may.

    Vem a ser a mesma coisa. It's all the same.

    Eles vieram do sul do país. They came from the southern part of the country.

virar to turn; to upset.

    Vire à esquerda. Turn to the left.

    Virar as costas. To turn one's back on.

viravolta f. turnabout, sudden change.

vírgula f. comma.

viril adj. virile, manly.

virilidade f. virility.

virtude f. virtue.

    Em virtude de. By virtue of.

virtuoso adj. virtuous.

virulência f. virulence.

virulento adj. virulent.

visar to endorse; to visa; to aim at.

viscosidade f. viscosity.

viscoso adj. viscous, sticky.

visibilidade f. visibility.

VISITA f. visit, call; visitor.

    Temos visitas. We have company.

    Fazer uma visita. To call on.

    Cartão de visita. Calling card.

VISITAR to visit, to call on.

    Eu os visito (visito-os) de vez em quando. I visit them from time to time.

VISTA f. sight, view; glance, look; scenery.

    Conheço-o de vista. I know him by sight.

    Não o perca de vista. Don't lose sight of him.

    À primeira vista. At first sight.

    Em vista de. In view of. Considering.

    Ponto de vista. Point of view.

    Vista curta. Nearsightedness.

    Até à vista. So long. See you soon.

visto adj. seen; visaed; n. m. visa.

    Está visto. It's obvious. It's evident.

    Visto que. Considering that.

vistoso adj. showy, colorful, attractive.

visual adj. visual.

vital adj. vital.

vitalício adj. lifelong.

vitalidade f. vitality.

vitalizar to vitalize.

vitamina f. vitamin.

vitela f. female calf; veal.

vitelo m. male calf.

vítima f. victim.

vitória f. victory.

    Vitória moral. Moral victory.

vitorioso adj. victorious.

vitrina f. show window.

viuva f. widow.

viuvez f. widowhood.

viúvo m. widower.

    Ele é viúvo e tem três filhos. He's a widower and has three children.

viva! Hooray for! Long live!

    Viva o Brasil! Long live Brazil!

vivacidade f. vivacity.

vivaz adj. lively, spirited; perennial.

viveiro m. plant nursery; hatchery; aquarium.

VIVER to live, to exist; n. m. life, living.

    Ele vive só. He lives alone.

    Eles vivem bem. They live well. They lead a good life.

    Comer para viver e não viver para comer. To eat to live and not live to eat.

víveres m. pl. provisions, victuals.

viveza f. liveliness, vivacity.

vivificar to vivify, to animate.

VIVO *adj. living, alive; lively; smart, bright.*

Ele está vivo. *He's alive.*

De viva voz. *By word of mouth.*

Cor viva. *Bright color.*

Os vivos e os mortos. *The quick and the dead.*

vizinhança *f. vicinity, neighborhood.*

vizinho *adj. neighboring, next; n. m. neighbor.*

Um bom vizinho. *A good neighbor.*

VOAR *to fly; to flee; to blow up.*

As horas voaram. *The hours flew (by).*

vocabulário *m. vocabulary.*

vocábulo *m. word, term.*

vocação *f. vocation.*

vocal *adj. vocal, oral.*

VOCÊ *you; pl. vocês.*

Você tem razão. *You are right.*

vociferar *to vociferate, to shout, to cry out.*

vodu *m. voodoo.*

volante *adj. flying, mobile; n. m. steering wheel; balance wheel (watch); shuttlecock.*

volátil *adj. volatile, changeable.*

vo-lo *(contr. of vos + o, direct object) it to you, her to you.*

VOLTA *f. turn, turning; return; curve; change; walk.*

Estar de volta. *To be back.*

Dar uma volta. *To take a walk. To go for a stroll.*

Passagem de ida e volta. *Round-trip ticket.*

Meia volta, volver! *About, face!*

VOLTAR *to turn; to return; to change.*

Volte amanhã. *Come back tomorrow.*

Ela ainda não voltou. *She hasn't returned yet.*

Voltar as costas. *To turn one's back.*

volume *m. volume; bulk; tome; piece of luggage; package.*

volumoso *adj. voluminous, bulky.*

voluntário *adj. voluntary, willing; volunteer.*

voluptuoso *adj. voluptuous, sensual.*

volver *to turn, to revolve.*

À direita, volver! *Right face!*

Volver a si. *To regain consciousness.*

vomitar *to vomit.*

vômito *m. vomiting.*

VONTADE *f. will; desire; intention.*

Esteja à vontade. *Make yourself at home. Make yourself comfortable.*

Estou com vontade de ir ao cinema. *I feel like going to the movies.*

Ela o fará de boa vontade. *She will do it willingly.*

vôo *m. flight, flying.*

Levantar vôo. *To take off. To take flight.*

voracidade *f. voracity, greediness.*

voragem *f. whirlpool, maelstrom.*

vórtice *m. vortex.*

vos *direct and indirect object, fam. pl. you, to you.*

vós *fam. pl. you.*

vosso *fam. pl. your.*

Vossa Excelência. *Your Excellency.*

Vossa Senhoria. *Informal correspondence or announcements this phrase is often used to translate "you."*

votação *f. ballot, voting.*

Votação secreta. *Secret ballot. Secret vote.*

votante *m. and f. voter, elector.*

votar *to vote; to vow.*

Eu não votarei nele. *I won't vote for him.*

voto *m. vote; ballot; vow; wish.*

Voto de confiança. *Vote of confidence.*

VOZ *f. voice; outcry; word; rumor.*

À meia voz. *In an undertone. In a whisper.*

Em voz alta. *Aloud.*

Em voz baixa *(x = sh). In a low voice.*

Levantar a voz. *To raise one's voice.*

A voz do povo. *Public opinion.*

vulcanizar *to vulcanize.*

vulgar *adj. vulgar, common, ordinary.*

vulgo *m. the masses, the common people.*

vulnerável *adj. vulnerable.*

vulto *m. form, figure; bulk; important person.*

X

xadrez *(x = sh) m. chess.*

xale *(x = sh) m. shawl.*

xampu *(x = sh) m. shampoo.*

xaropada *(x = sh) f. cough syrup; boring talk, blather.*

xarope *(x = sh) m. syrup, remedy.*

xavante *(x = sh) adj., n. m. and f. Chavante (Indian tribe of Brazil).*

XÍCARA *(x = sh) f. cup.*

Uma xícara de chá. *A cup of tea.*

xingar *(x = sh) to call names, to abuse.*

Z

zagal *m. shepherd.*

zangado *adj. angry.*

zangar *to anger, to annoy.*

zangar-se *to get angry.*

Zangaram-se quando ouviram as palavras do rapaz. *They got mad when they heard the young man's words.*

zarpar *to weigh anchor, to set sail.*
zebra *f. zebra.*
zéfiro *m. zephyr.*
zelador *m. caretaker.*
zelar *to watch over, to take care of.*
zelo *m. zeal, devotion.*
zeloso *adj. zealous, dedicated.*
zênite (zénite) *m. zenith.*
ZERO *m. zero, nothing.*
   Acima de zero. *Above zero.*

ziguezague *m. zigzag.*
ziguezaguear *to zigzag.*
zinco *m. zinc.*
zoar *to hum, to buzz.*
zona *f. zone, area, region.*
   Zona temperada. *Temperate zone.*
   Zona de silêncio. *Quiet zone.*
zorro *m. fox.*
zumbido *m. buzzing, hum.*
zumbir *to buzz, to hum.*

GLOSSARY OF PROPER NAMES

Adolfo Adolph
Afonso Alphonse
Alberto Albert
Alexandre Alexander
Alfredo Alfred
Alice Alice
Ana Ann, Anne, Anna
André Andrew
Antônio (António) Anthony
Artur Arthur
Augusto Augustus
Aurélio Aurelius

Bárbara Barbara
Beatriz Beatrice
Bernardo Bernard

Camilo Camillus
Carlos Charles
Carlota Charlotte
Carolina Caroline
Cecília Cecilia
Cláudio Claude, Claudius

Diogo James
Dorotéia (Doroteia) Dorothy

Edmundo Edmund
Eduardo Edward
Emília Emily
Ernesto Ernest
Ester Esther
Eugênio (Eugénio) Eugene
Eva Eve

Fernando Ferdinand
Filipe Philip
Francisco Francis
Frederico Frederick

Gertrudes Gertrude
Gil Giles
Glória Gloria
Guilherme William

Gustavo Gustave

Heitor Hector
Henrique Henry

Inácio Ignatius
Inês Agnes, Inez
Isabel Elizabeth

Jesus Jesus
João John
Joaquim Joachim
Jorge George
José Joseph
Josefa Josephine
Josefina Josephine
Júlio Julius

Leonardo Leonard
Leonor Eleanor
Lúcia Lucy
Luís Louis
Luísa Louise

Manuel Emanuel, Manuel
Margarida Margaret
Maria Mary
Mário Mario, Marius
Marta Martha
Maurício Maurice, Morris
Miguel Michael

Paulo Paul
Pedro Peter

Raimundo Raymond
Raquel Rachel
Ricardo Richard
Roberto Robert
Rodolfo Rudolph, Ralph
Rodrigo Roderic
Rosa Rose

Sebastião Sebastian

Teresa Theresa
Tomás Thomas

Vicente Vincent

GLOSSARY OF GEOGRAPHICAL NAMES

Açores Azores
África Africa
Alemanha Germany
Alpes Alps
América America
América do Norte North America
América do Sul South America
América Espanhola Spanish America
Andes Andes
Angola Angola
Argentina Argentina
Ásia Asia
Atenas Athens
Atlântico Atlantic
Austrália Australia

Barcelona Barcelona
Belém Belem; Bethlehem
Bélgica Belgium
Bolívia Bolivia
Brasil Brazil
Brasília Brasilia
Bruxelas (x = sh) Brussels
Buenos Aires Buenos Aires

Chile Chile
China China
Coimbra Coimbra
Colômbia Colombia
Costa Rica Costa Rica
Cuba Cuba

Dinamarca Denmark

Egito, Egipto Egypt
El Salvador El Salvador
Equador Ecuador
Escandinávia Scandinavia
Escócia Scotland
Eslováquia Slovakia
Espanha Spain.
Estados Unidos da América (E.U.A.) United States of America
Estônia Estonia
Europa Europe

Filipinas Philippines
Finlândia Finland
França France

Galícia Galicia
Genebra Geneva

Grã-Bretanha Great Britain
Grécia Greece
Guatemala Guatemala

Haiti Haiti
Havaí Hawaii
Havana Havana
Hispano-América Spanish America
Holanda Holland
Honduras Honduras
Hungria Hungary

Inglaterra England
Irlanda Ireland
Israel Israel
Itália Italy

Japão Japan

Letônia Latvia
Lisboa Lisbon
Londres London

Macau Macao
Madeira Madeira
Madrid Madrid
Mediterrâneo Mediterranean
México (x = sh) Mexico
Moçambique Mozambique
Moscou, Moscóvia, Moscovo Moscow.

Nicarágua Nicaragua
Noruega Norway
Nova Iorque New York
Nova Zelândia New Zealand

Oceânia Oceania

Pacífico Pacific
Países Baixos (x = sh) Low Countries, Netherlands
Paraguai Paraguay
Paris Paris
Peru Peru
Pireneus, Pirenéus Pyrenees
Polônia, Polónia Poland
Porto Oporto
Porto Rico Puerto Rico
Portugal Portugal

República Checa Czech Republic
República Dominicana Dominican Republic
Rio de Janeiro Rio de Janeiro
Roma Rome

Romênia (Roménia)
Romania
Rússia Russia

São Paulo São Paulo
Sicília Sicily
Suécia Sweden
Suíça Switzerland

Timor Timor
Turquia Turkey

Ucrânia Ukraine
Uruguai Uruguay

Vaticano Vatican
Viena Vienna

English-Portuguese

A

a, an um, uma.
ability capacidade, habilidade; aptidão, talento.
able capaz.
    to be able to poder *(to have the capability of);* saber *(to know how).*
abnormal anormal.
aboard a bordo.
abolish abolir, suprimir.
abortion aborto.
about cerca de, quase, mais ou menos; sobre; em volta de.
    to be about (book, movie, etc.) tratar de.
    How about a beer? Que tal uma cerveja?
above sobre, acima de; acima.
abroad no estrangeiro, para o exterior, fora de casa.
absence ausência.
absent ausente.
absent-minded distraído.
absolute absoluto.
absorb (to) absorver, incorporar.
absurd absurdo, ridículo.
abundant abundante.
abuse abuso.
abuse (to) abusar, maltratar.
academic académico (académico).
academy academia, colégio.
accent acento *(mark on letter),* sotaque *(regional pronunciation).*
accent (to) acentuar.
accept (to) aceitar, receber; reconhecer.
acceptance aceitação.
accident acidente.
accommodate (to) acomodar.
accommodations acomodações, alojamento.
accompany (to) acompanhar.
accomplish (to) efetuar (efectuar), realizar.
according to segundo, conforme.
account conta; relato, narrativa.
accuracy exatidão (exactidão) (x = z), precisão.
accusative acusativo.
accuse (to) acusar, denunciar.
accustomed acostumado.
    to get accustomed to acostumar-se a.
ache dor.
achieve (to) conseguir, realizar, ganhar.
acid ácido *(n. and adj.).*
acknowledge (to) reconhecer, admitir; acusar recebimento de.
acknowledgment reconhecimento; confirmação.
acquaintance conhecimento; conhecido (person).
acre acre.

across através; através de; no outro lado de.
act ato (acto); ação (acção).
act (to) agir, atuar (actuar) *(to do);* portar-se, comportar-se, conduzir-se *(to behave);* representar (theater).
action ação (acção).
active ativo (activo).
activity actividade (actividade).
actor ator (actor).
actual real, verdadeiro.
add (to) adicionar, aumentar.
addict *n.* viciado.
addicted viciado.
    to get addicted viciar-se.
addiction vício.
address endereço *(on letter),* discurso *(speech).*
address (to) endereçar, dirigir-se a.
adequate adequado.
adjective adjetivo (adjectivo).
adjoining contíguo, adjacente, vizinho.
administrative administrativo.
admiral almirante.
admiration admiração.
admire (to) admirar.
admirer admirador.
admission admissão, entrada.
    Free admission. Entrada gratuita.
admit (to) admitir, conceder; reconhecer.
admittance admissão, entrada.
    No admittance. Entrada proibida.
admonish (to) advertir, prevenir; repreender.
adopt (to) adotar (adoptar).
adoption adoção (adopção); aceitação.
adult adulto.
advance adiantamento, antecipação; avanço.
advance (to) avançar, adiantar.
advantage vantagem, benefício, proveito.
advantageous vantajoso, proveitoso.
adventure aventura.
adverb advérbio.
adversity adversidade.
advertise (to) anunciar, publicar, fazer propaganda.
advertisement anúncio, aviso.
advice conselho.
advise (to) aconselhar, recomendar.
affair assunto; negócio.
affected afetado (afectado), comovido.
affection afeição; amor.
affectionate afetuoso (afectuoso), carinhoso.
    Affectionately yours. Afetuosamente.
affirm (to) afirmar, confirmar.
affirmative afirmativo.
after depois de, após; atrás de; depois que.
afternoon tarde.
    Good afternoon! Boa tarde!
afterward depois, mais tarde.
again outra vez, de novo.

against contra.
age idade *(of person)*, época *(time period)*.
age (to) envelhecer.
agency agência.
aggravate (to) agravar, piorar; irritar.
aggressive agressivo.
ago há.
    a long time ago há muito tempo.
    How long ago? Quanto tempo há? Há
        quanto tempo?
agony angústia, agonia.
agree (to) concordar, estar de acordo.
agreeable agradável; satisfatório.
agreed combinado; de acordo.
agreement convênio (convénio), acordo.
agricultural agrícola.
agriculture agricultura, lavoura.
ahead avante, adiante.
    straight ahead bem em frente.
aid auxílio (x = s).
aid (to) auxiliar (x = s).
AIDS SIDA.
aim objetivo, meta.
air ar.
    open air ar livre.
    air conditioning condicionamento de ar.
airmail correio aéreo.
airplane avião.
airport aeroporto.
aisle passagem, corredor.
alarm alarme.
alarm (to) alarmar.
alarm clock despertador.
album álbum.
alcohol álcool.
alike parecido, semelhante.
alive vivo.
all todo; tudo.
    all day o dia todo.
    after all afinal de contas.
    not at all de modo algum.
allied aliado.
allow (to) permitir, deixar (x = sh).
    Allow me. Permita-me.
allowed permitido.
ally aliado.
almond amêndoa.
almost quase.
alone só, sozinho.
along ao longo de, ao lado de.
    along with junto com, com.
    all along sempre, continuamente.
    to get along with entender-se com.
    to go along with acompanhar.
alright bem.
    It's alright. Está bem.
also também, além disso.
alternate (to) alternar.
alternately alternativamente.

although embora, ainda que, posto que.
always sempre.
ambassador embaixador (x = sh).
amber âmbar.
ambition ambição.
ambitious ambicioso.
amen amém.
amend (to) emendar.
America América.
    North America América do Norte.
American americano, norte-americano.
among entre.
amount quantia, quantidade, soma.
ample amplo.
amuse (to) divertir.
amusement divertimento.
amusing divertido; engraçado.
analyze (to) analisar.
anchor âncora.
ancient antigo.
and e.
anecdote anedota.
angel anjo.
anger raiva, ira.
anger (to) irritar.
angry zangado, irado.
    to get angry zangar-se.
animal animal.
animate (to) animar.
ankle tornozelo.
annex anexo (x = ks).
annex (to) anexar (x = ks).
anniversary aniversário.
announce (to) anunciar.
annoy (to) aborrecer, irritar.
annual anual.
anonymous anônimo (anónimo).
another outro.
answer resposta, contestação.
answer (to) responder.
    answering machine máquina de
        contestação.
    answering service serviço de
        contestação.
ant formiga.
anxious ansioso.
any qualquer, algum, alguma.
anybody qualquer pessoa, alguém.
anyhow de qualquer maneira, de qualquer
    forma.
anyone qualquer pessoa, alguém.
anything qualquer coisa, alguma coisa.
anyway de qualquer maneria, em qualquer
    caso.
anywhere em qualquer parte, em qualquer
    lugar.
apart à parte; separado.
apartment apartamento.
apiece cada um.

apologize (to) desculpar-se, apresentar desculpas, pedir desculpas.

apology desculpa.

apparatus aparelho.

appeal apelação (*law*); súplica, apelo (*request*); atração (atracção), simpatia (*attraction*).

appear (to) aparecer, comparecer; parecer (*seem*).

appetite apetite.

applaud (to) aplaudir, aclamar, bater palmas.

applause aplauso.

apple maçã.

applicable aplicável.

applicant pretendente, requerente, candidato.

application aplicação; requerimento, solicitação, petição (*application for something*).

apply (to) aplicar.

    to apply for solicitar, pedir.

appointment hora marcada (*with doctor, etc.*); compromisso (*to meet someone*).

appreciate (to) apreciar, prezar.

appreciation apreciação, gratidão, reconhecimento.

approach acesso (access); enfoque (*manner of doing something*).

approach (to) aproximar-se (x = s) de (*to come near*); abordar (a subject).

approval aprovação, autorização.

approve (to) aprovar, autorizar.

April abril (Abril).

apron avental.

arbitrary arbitrário.

architect arquiteto (arquitecto).

architecture arquitetura (arquitectura).

area área, superfície, região.

Argentinean, Argentine argentino.

argument argumento; discussão.

arid árido, seco.

arm braço (*part of body*).

armed forces forças armadas.

arms armas (*weapons*).

army exército (x = z) força.

around em torno de, em redor de, em volta de

    Is there any coffee around? Há café por aí?

arrange (to) arranjar, preparar.

arrangement arranjo.

arrival chegada.

arrive (to) chegar.

article artigo.

artificial artificial.

artist artista.

artistic artístico.

as como.

    as ... as ... tão ... como ...

    as it were por assim dizer.

    as much tanto.

    as much as tanto quanto, tanto como.

    as many as tantos quanto.

ascertain (to) averiguar, indagar, verificar.

ashamed envergonhado.

aside à parte, de lado.

ask (to) perguntar (*question*); pedir (*request*).

asleep adormecido.

    He's asleep. Ele está dormindo (a dormir).

    to fall asleep adormecer, pegar no sono.

aspire (to) aspirar, ansiar.

aspirin aspirina.

assemble (to) reunir (*to gather*); montar, armar (*a machine*); ajuntar, acumular (*to collect*).

assembly assembléia (assembleia), reunião.

assets ativo (activo); bens.

assign (to) designar, nomear.

assimilate (to) assimilar.

assist (to) auxiliar (x = s).

assistance auxílio (x = s).

associate sócio, associado.

associate (to) associar, associar-se a.

assume (to) assumir, supor.

assumption suposição.

assurance segurança, certeza.

assure (to) assegurar, convencer, garantir.

astonish (to) assombrar, espantar.

astounded pasmado, assombrado.

astounding assombroso, pasmante.

at a, em.

    at first a princípio, no início.

    at last finalmente.

    at least pelo menos.

    at once imediatamente.

    at the same time ao mesmo tempo, à vez.

    at two o'clock às duas (horas).

    at that time naquele tempo.

    We were at John's. Estávamos na casa de João.

athlete atleta.

athletic atlético.

athletics atletismo.

atmosphere atmosfera; ambiente (*fig.*).

atom átomo.

attach (to) afixar (x = ks), unir, juntar.

attack ataque.

attack (to) atacar.

attempt tentativa, ensaio.

attempt (to) tentar, procurar; experimentar.

attend (to) assistir, estar presente (*be present*); tomar conta de (*take care of*); prestar atenção (*pay attention*).

attention atenção.

attentive atento, atencioso.

attic sótão.

attitude atitude.

attorney advogado.

attract (to) atrair.

attraction atração (atracção).

attractive atrativo (atractivo), atraente.
audience audiência; platéia (plateia) *(in theater);* público.
August agosto (Agosto).
aunt tia.
author autor.
authority autoridade.
authorize (to) autorizar.
automobile automóvel.
autumn outono (Outono).
available disponível, acessível.
avenue avenida.
average média.
avoid (to) evitar.
await (to) aguardar.
awake acordado.
awake (to) acordar.
aware ciente.
away ausente, fora, longe.
    to go away ir-se embora.
    ten miles away a dez milhas de distância.
awful terrível; horrível.
awkward desajeitado *(clumsy);* embaraçoso, difícil *(embarassing, difficult).*
ax, axe machado.

B

babble (to) balbuciar, palrar.
baby bebê (bebé) *(infant);* nenê (nené) *(term of endearment).*
bachelor solteiro.
back costas *(of the body);* posterior; atrás, para trás; reverso, verso; espaldar, encosto *(of a chair).*
    behind one's back nas costas.
    back door porta dos fundos.
    to go back voltar.
    to be back estar de volta.
    to call back telefonar de volta.
background fundo *(scenery, painting, etc.);* educação *(education);* experiência.
backward atrasado, retrógrado; acanhado.
    to go backwards ir para trás, ir de costas.
backwoods sertão ; interior .
bacon toicinho, toucinho.
bad *adv.* mal; *adj.* mau.
    Too bad! Que pena!
badge emblema, crachá.
bag saco, saca; bolsa.
baggage bagagem.
bait isca.
baker padeiro.
bakery padaria.
balance balança; equilíbrio; saldo *(account).*
bald calvo, careca.

ball bola.
balloon balão; globo.
banana banana.
band banda.
bandage bandagem, atadura.
banister corrimão.
bank banco; margem *(of river).*
bankruptcy bancarrota.
baptize batizar (baptizar).
bar bar *(where liquor is served);* barra *(of metal, etc.);* tribunal; sabonete *(of soap).*
barber barbeiro.
barbershop barbearia.
bare nu, despido.
barefoot descalço.
bargain contrato, negócio *(business deal);* pechincha *(good buy).*
barge barcaça.
bark cortiça, casca *(of a tree);* latido *(of a dog).*
barley cevada.
barn celeiro; estábulo.
barrel barril.
barren estéril.
base base.
baseball basebol.
basic básico.
basin bacia.
basis base.
basket cesto, cesta.
bath banho.
bathe (to) banhar; banhar-se; tomar banho.
bathing suit roupa de banho.
battery bateria *(car),* pilha.
battle batalha, luta.
be (to) ser; estar; ficar.
    to be hungry estar com fome, ter fome.
    to be right ter razão.
    to be sleepy estar com sono, ter sono.
    to be slow ser lento; estar atrasado (of a watch).
    to be sorry sentir.
    to be thirsty estar com sede, ter sede.
    to be used to estar acostumado a.
    to be wrong estar errado.
beach praia.
beam viga *(of wood, etc.);* raio *(of light).*
beaming radiante, brilhante.
bean feijão.
bear urso.
bear (to) agüentar (aguentar), suportar, sofrer *(to endure, to suffer);* carregar, levar *(to carry);* parir, dar à luz *(children, etc.);* produzir *(fruit, etc.).*
    to bear a grudge ter ressentimento.
    to bear in mind guardar na memória, ter em mente.
beard barba.
bearer portador.

beat (to) palpitar *(heart)*; bater, espancar *(strike)*; tocar *(a drum)*; bater *(eggs, etc.)*; vencer, derrotar *(in a game)*.

beating surra, açoitamento *(whipping)*; palpitação, pulsação *(heart)*.

beautiful belo, formoso.

beauty beleza.

because porque.
    because of devido a, por causa de.

become tornar-se, vir a ser, fazer-se.

bed cama.

bed linens roupa de cama.

bedroom quarto de dormir.

bee abelha.

beech faia.

beef carne de vaca.

beehive colméia.

beeper bip.

beer cerveja.

beet beterraba.

before antes; antes que *(time)*; diante de; na frente de *(position)*.

beforehand de antemão, anteriormente.

beg (to) mendigar *(for money)*; suplicar *(for a favor)*.

beggar mendigo.

begin (to) principiar, começar, iniciar.

beginning princípio, começo, início.
    in the beginning no início.

behind atrás, detrás.

Belgian belga.

belief crença, opinião.

believe (to) crer, acreditar, pensar, achar.

bell campainha, sino.

belong (to) pertencer, ser de.

below abaixo (x = sh), debaixo (x = sh).

belt cinto.

bench banco *(seat)*; tribunal *(court)*.

bend (to) dobrar, curvar, dobrar-se, inclinar-se.

beneath debaixo (x = sh), abaixo (x = sh).

benefit benefício.

benefit (to) beneficiar.

beside ao lado de.

besides além disso, também; além de.

best melhor.

bet aposta.

bet (to) apostar.

better melhor.

between entre, no meio de.

beyond mais longe, além; além de.

Bible Bíblia.

bicycle bicicleta.

big grande.

bill conta, nota *(check, account)*; fatura (factura) *(invoice)*.

billiards bilhar.

billion bilhão.

bind (to) atar, unir; encadernar *(book)*.

binding encadernação *(book)*.

birch vidoeiro.

bird pássaro.

birth nascimento.
    to give birth dar à luz.

birthday aniversário; data de nascimento *(date of birth)*.
    My birthday is on November 21. Faço anos no vinte e um de Novembro.

biscuit biscoito.

bishop bispo.

bit bocado, pouquinho *(small amount)*.

bite mordedura.

bite (to) morder.

bitter amargo.

bitterness amargor, amargura.

black preto, negro.

blackbird melro.

blackboard quadro-negro, lousa.

blacken (to) enegrecer; escurecer.

blade lâmina.

blame culpa.

blame (to) culpar, acusar.

blank *adj.* em branco; *n.* espaço em branco.

blanket cobertor.

bleed (to) sangrar.

bless (to) benzer, abençoar.

blessing bênção.

blind *adj.* cego.

blind (to) cegar.

blindness cegueira.

blister empola, bolha.

block (city) quadra, quarteirão.

block (to) obstruir, tapar.

blood sangue.

blouse blusa.

blow golpe, pancada.

blow (to) soprar.

blue azul.

blush rubor.

blush (to) ruborizar-se.

board tábua *(wood)*; junta, conselho *(of directors, etc.)*; tabuleiro *(for games)*.
    on board a bordo.

boarder pensionista.

boardinghouse pensão.

boast jactância.

boast (to) jactar-se, vangloriar-se.

boat bote *(small)*, barco *(medium)*, navio *(large; ship)*.

body corpo.

boil furúnculo.

boil (to) ferver.

boiler caldeira.

boiling fervendo, fervente.

bold corajoso, valente.

Bolivian boliviano.

bomb bomba.

bond união, laço, ligação; título *(stocks)*.

bone osso.

book livro.
bookseller livreiro.
bookstore livraria.
boom! pum!
boot bota.
border fronteira, limite *(boundary)*; beira, margem.
bore (to) aborrecer, amolar; furar, perfurar *(to make holes)*.
boring aborrecido, tedioso.
born nascido.
    to be born nascer.
borrow (to) pedir emprestado, tomar emprestado.
boss chefe, patrão.
both ambos, os dois.
bother amolação, incômodo (incómodo).
bother (to) aborrecer, amolar.
bottle garrafa.
bottom fundo.
bound for com destino a, rumo a.
bound up atado, amarrado.
boundless ilimitado.
bow saudação, reverência *(greeting)*; arco *(weapon, bow of a violin)*; proa *(ship)*.
bow (to) saudar, fazer uma reverência *(to bow in reverence)*; ceder, submeter-se *(to submit or yield)*.
bowl tijela, bacia.
bow tie gravata borboleta.
box caixa (x = sh).
box office bilheteria (bilheteira).
boy menino, garoto, moço, jovem.
bracelet bracelete, pulseira.
braid trança.
brain cérebro.
brake freio.
bran farelo.
branch ramo, galho *(of tree)*; ramal *(railroad, etc.)*; filial, sucursal *(local office, etc.)*
brand marca *(of goods)*.
brave bravo, corajoso, valente.
Brazilian brasileiro.
bread pão.
break ruptura, quebra.
break (to) romper, quebrar.
breakfast café da manhã (pequeno almoço, primeiro almoço).
    to have breakfast tomar o café da manhã (tomar o pequeno almoço, tomar o primeiro almoço).
breath respiração, fôlego.
breathe respirar.
breeze brisa.
bribe suborno.
bribe (to) subornar.
bride noiva.
bridge ponte.
brief breve, curto.

briefcase pasta.
briefly brevemente.
bright claro *(opposite of dark)*; radiante *(radiant)*; inteligente; vivo *(color)*.
brighten clarear, tornar claro *(to make clearer)*; alegrar, animar *(to make cheerful)*.
brilliant brilhante, luminoso.
brim aba *(hat)*.
bring (to) trazer.
    to bring together juntar, unir, reunir.
    to bring toward aproximar (x = s), trazer.
    to bring up educar, criar *(to rear)*; introduzir *(a matter, etc.)*.
British britânico.
broad largo.
broadcast radiodifusão, emissão.
broil (to) grelhar *(meat)*.
brook riacho.
broom vassoura.
brother irmão.
brother-in-law cunhado.
brotherly fraternal.
brown castanho.
bruise contusão, hematoma.
bruise (to) machucar.
brush escova; mato *(thicket, small shrubs)*.
    clothes brush escova de roupa.
    toothbrush escova de dentes.
brute bruto.
bubble bolha.
bucket balde.
buckle fivela.
bud botão; broto Ⓑ.
budget orçamento.
buffet bufê Ⓑ.
bug inseto (insecto), bicho.
build (to) construir.
building edifício.
bull touro.
bulletin boletim.
bullfighter toureiro.
bundle pacote, embrulho.
burden carga, peso.
bureau cômoda (cómoda) *(in a bedroom)*; escritório, departmento, agência *(office)*.
burglar ladrão.
burial enterro.
burn queimadura.
burn (to) queimar.
    to burn up queimar-se, consumir-se.
burst estouro, explosão.
burst (to) estourar, explodir, rebentar.
    to burst out laughing cair na gargalhada.
    to burst into tears desatar a chorar.
bury (to) enterrar.
bus ônibus (ónibus, autocarro).
bush arbusto.
bushel alqueire.

business trabalho, ocupação; negócio.
businessman negociante, comerciante, homem de negócios.
businesswoman mulher de negócios.
busy ocupado.
but mas.
butcher açougueiro.
butcher shop açougue (talho).
butter manteiga.
button botão.
buy (to) comprar.
buyer comprador.
by por, a, em, de, para; junto a, perto de *(near)*.
　　by and by daqui a pouco, logo.
　　by and large de modo geral.
　　by hand à mão.
　　by reason of por causa de.
　　by the way a propósito.
　　by virtue of em virtude de.
　　Finish it by Sunday. Termine-o antes do domingo.
　　Send it by airmail. Envie-o por correio aéreo.

C

cab táxi (x = ks).
cabbage repolho, couve.
cabin cabana; cabine, camarote *(ship)*.
cabinet gabinete *(political)*; armário *(furniture)*.
cable cabo.
cable car teleférico.
cadet cadete.
café café, restaurante; bar.
cage gaiola.
cake bolo; sabonete *(soap)*.
calendar calendário.
calf bezerro.
call chamada *(summons)*; telefonema *(telephone)*; visita *(visit)*.
call (to) chamar; convocar *(a meeting)*; citar *(to summon to court)*.
　　to call (someone) back telefonar de volta.
　　to call on visitar.
　　to call out gritar, bradar.
calling card cartão telefônico.
calm *adj.* calmo, quieto, tranqüilo (tranquilo); *n.* calma, silêncio.
camera câmara; máquina fotográfica.
camp acampamento.
camp (to) acampar.
campaign campanha.
can lata.
can poder *(to be able)*; saber *(to know how)*; enlatar *(to put in a can)*.

canal canal.
candidate candidato.
candle vela.
candy bala, doce, bombom.
can opener abridor de latas.
cap boné, gorro *(hat)*; tampa *(on bottle)*.
capable capaz.
capital capital.
　　capital letter letra maiúscula.
capitalism capitalismo.
captain capitão; comandante *(skipper of ship)*; capitão de mar-e-guerra *(navy captain)*.
capture (to) capturar.
car carro; automóvel; vagão *(train)*.
card cartão; carta *(playing card)*.
cardboard cartão, papelão.
care cuidado.
　　to take care ter cuidado, tomar cuidado.
　　to take care of cuidar de, tomar conta de.
　　in care of (c/o) ao cuidado de (a/c).
care (to) interessar-se, importar-se.
　　I don't care to go. Não me interessa ir.
　　He doesn't care at all. Não lhe importa nada.
　　I don't care. Não me importa.
career carreira.
careful cuidadoso.
　　Be careful! Cuidado!
careless descuidado.
carnival carnaval.
carpenter carpinteiro.
carpet tapete.
carry (to) levar, conduzir, carregar.
　　to carry out levar a cabo *(finish)*.
　　to carry on continuar *(continue)*.
cart carreta, carroça.
carve (to) trinchar, cortar *(meat)*; esculpir, entalhar *(marble, wood, etc.)*.
case caso *(a particular instance; grammar, etc.)*; estojo *(carrying box)*; caixa (x = sh) *(case of beer, etc.)*.
　　in case of em caso de.
　　in case you want to . . . caso que quer . . .
cash dinheiro disponível, dinheiro em caixa (x = sh).
　　cash on hand dinheiro em caixa.
　　cash payment pagamento à vista.
cash (to) cobrar *(a check)*.
cashier o caixa (x = sh).
castle castelo.
casual casual.
casually casualmente.
cat gato.
catch (to) apanhar, agarrar.
　　to catch cold pegar um resfriado.
　　to catch on compreender, dar-se conta.
　　to catch (on) fire pegar fogo.
　　to catch up alcançar.
Catholic católico.

cattle gado.
cause causa, motivo, razão.
cause (to) causar.
caution cautela.
cavalry cavalaria.
CD disco compacto, disco laser.
ceiling teto.
celebrate (to) celebrar.
celebration celebração, comemoração.
celery aipo.
cellar adega; porão Ⓑ.
cellular phone telefone celular.
cement cimento.
cemetery cemitério.
cent centavo Ⓑ; cêntimo Ⓟ.
center centro.
century século.
ceremony cerimônia (cerimónia).
certain seguro, certo; claro, evidente.
certainly certamente, sem dúvida, seguramente.
certificate certidão, certificado, atestado.
chain cadeia.
chain (to) encadear.
chair cadeira.
chairman presidente *(of a meeting)*.
chalk giz.
chance acaso, casualidade *(random probability, chance)*; oportunidade *(opportunity)*; probabilidade *(probability)*; risco *(risk)*.
    by chance por casualidade, por acaso.
    to take a chance arriscar-se.
chance (to) aventurar, arriscar.
change troco *(money)*; mudança *(alteration)*.
change (to) mudar, trocar; cambiar *(money)*.
    to change your mind mudar de ideia.
    to change clothes trocar de roupa.
channel canal.
chapel capela.
chapter capítulo.
character caráter (carácter).
characteristic *adj.* característico, típico; *n.* característica.
charge carga *(load; quantity of powder, electricity, etc.)*; ordem, comando *(order)*; custo, preço *(price)*; acusação *(accusation)*; carga, ataque *(attack)*.
    in charge of encarregado de.
charge (to) carregar *(a battery, etc.; to load)*; cobrar *(a price)*; acusar *(to accuse)*.
    How much do you charge for this? Quanto cobra por isto?
charges despesas *(expenses)*; instruções *(to a jury, etc.)*.
charitable caridoso, caritativo, generoso.
charity caridade.
charm encanto.
charming encantador.

chart carta *(for the use of navigators)*; mapa *(outline, map)*; quadro, gráfico *(graph)*.
chase (to) perseguir.
chat (to) conversar; bater papo Ⓑ.
cheap barato.
check cheque *(banking)*; talão *(claim check)*; conta, nota *(in a restaurant)*; xeque (x = sh) *(chess)*; controle Ⓑ, supervisão *(control)*; restrição *(restraint)*; obstáculo, empecilho *(hindrance)*; verificação *(verification)*.
check (to) investigar *(to investigate)*; verificar *(to verify)*; frear, reprimir *(to restrain)*; depositar, enviar *(baggage)*; dar xeque, pôr em xeque (x = sh) *(chess)*.
cheek bochecha.
cheer *n.* alegria, bom humor; *pl.* vivas, aplausos *(applause)*.
    Cheers! Saúde!
cheerful alegre, animado.
cheese queijo.
chemical químico.
chemist químico.
cherish (to) apreciar, estimar *(to hold dear)*.
cherished estimado *(dear)*; caro *(dear)*.
cherry cereja.
chest peito *(body)*; arca, caixa (x = sh) *(f.)*; caixão (x = sh) *(m.)*.
chestnut castanha.
chew (to) mastigar, mascar.
chicken galinha, frango.
chief *adj.* principal; *n.* chefe.
child criança; menino *(m.)*; menina *(f.)*.
childhood infância, meninice.
Chilean chileno.
chimney chaminé.
chin queixo (x = sh).
china louça, porcelana.
chocolate chocolate.
choice *adj.* seleto (selecto), escolhido; *n.* escolha, seleção (selecção).
choir coro.
choke (to) sufocar, afogar.
choose (to) escolher, eleger.
chop costeleta *(cut of meat)*.
chop (to) cortar *(wood, etc.)*; picar *(meat)*.
chore tarefa.
Christian cristão.
Christmas Natal.
church igreja.
cider sidra.
cigar charuto.
cigarette cigarro.
cigarette lighter isqueiro.
cinnamon canela.
circle círculo.
circulation circulação.
citizen cidadão.
city cidade.

city hall prefeitura (câmara municipal).
civil civil.
　　civil rights direitos civis.
civilization civilização.
civilize (to) civilizar.
claim pretensão, reclamação, título, direito.
claim (to) reclamar, pretender *(rights, etc.);* affirmar, a legar *(to assert).*
clam marisco.
clamor clamor, gritaria, tumulto.
clap (to) aplaudir, bater palmas.
class classe *(school).*
classify (to) classificar.
clause cláusula.
claw garra *(talon);* unha *(cats, etc.).*
clay argila.
clean limpo.
clean (to) limpar.
cleanliness asseio, limpeza.
clear claro.
clear (to) aclarar *(to clarify);* absolver *(of blame, guilt);* liqüidar (liquidar), pagar *(debts, accounts, etc.).*
　　The weather is clearing up. O tempo está a melhorar.
　　to clear the table tirar (levantar) a mesa.
clearly claramente.
clerk caixeiro (x = sh); escrivão.
clever destro, hábil; inteligente.
climate clima.
climb (to) subir.
cloak capa, manto.
clock relógio.
close (near) perto; próximo.
　　close by muito perto.
close (to) fechar *(to shut, to shut down);* terminar *(to end);* encerrar *(a meeting);* fechar *(a deal).*
closed fechado.
closet armário *(piece of furniture);* guarda-roupa *(walk-in.).*
cloth tecido, fazenda, pano.
clothe (to) vestir.
clothes roupa.
　　clothes brush escova de roupa.
　　clothes dryer secador de roupa.
clothing roupa.
cloud nuvem.
cloudy nublado *(sky);* turvo *(liquids).*
clover trevo.
club clube, *(social group, nightspot);* sociedade, associação; *(association);* cacete, porrete *(stick).*
coach treinador *(sports, etc.).*
coach (to) treinar.
coal carvão.
coast costa.
coat paletó, casaco *(jacket);* sobretudo *(overcoat);* camada *(paint, etc.).*

cocktail coquetel.
coconut coco.
code código.
coffee café.
coffin caixão (x = sh).
coin moeda.
coincidence coincidência.
　　by coincidence por casualidade.
cold frio.
cold cuts frios.
coldness frialdade.
collaborate colaborar.
collar colarinho.
collect (to) colecionar (coleccionar); cobrar *(money due).*
collection coleção (colecção).
collective coletivo (colectivo).
college escola de estudos universitários; colégio *(of cardinals, etc.).*
Colombian colombiano.
colonial colonial.
colony colônia (colónia).
color cor.
color (to) colorir, dar cor a.
colored de cor.
colt potro.
column coluna.
comb pente.
combination combinação.
combine (to) combinar.
come (to) vir.
　　to come back voltar.
　　to come forward adiantar; apresentar-se.
　　to come across dar com, encontrar-se com.
　　to come for vir por.
　　to come in entrar.
　　to come down descer, baixar (x = sh).
　　to come up subir.
　　Come on! Vamos!
　　to come out well sair bem.
comedy comédia.
comet cometa.
comfort conforto, comodidade; consolo *(consolation).*
comfort (to) confortar, consolar.
comfortable comodo, confortável.
comma vírgula.
command ordem *(order);* mandado, comando *(authority to command).*
command (to) mandar, comandar.
commence (to) começar, iniciar.
commercial comercial.
commission comissão.
commit (to) cometer.
committee comissão, comitê Ⓑ.
common comum.
　　common sense senso comum.
communicate (to) comunicar.
communism comunismo.

communist comunista.
community comunidade.
compact disc disco compacto.
companion companheiro.
company companhia *(firm)*; hóspedes *(guests)*; visitas *(visitors)*.
compare (to) comparar.
comparison comparação.
   by comparison em comparação.
compete (to) competir.
competition concurso; concorrência, competição.
complain (to) queixar-se (x = sh), lamentar-se.
complaint queixa (x = sh).
complete completo.
complete (to) completar, acabar.
complex complexo (x = ks).
complexion cútis, tez *(skin)*; aspecto *(appearance)*.
complicate (to) complicar.
complicated complicado.
complication complicação.
compliment cumprimento.
compliment (to) cumprimentar.
compose (to) compor.
composition composição.
comprise (to) compreender, abranger.
compromise compromisso, acordo.
compromise (to) transigir, fazer concessão *(to settle by mutual concessions)*; resolver, ajustar *(a difference between parties)*; comprometer *(to endanger)*.
compute (to) computar, calcular.
computer computador.
   laptop computer computador portátil.
   computer science informática.
computerize (to) computadorizar.
comrade camarada.
conceit presunção, vaidade.
conceive (to) conceber.
concentrate (to) concentrar.
concentration concentração.
concern assunto, negócio *(subject, business, affair)*; interesse; firma, empresa comercial *(a business organization)*; ansiedade, inquietação *(worry)*.
concern (to) concernir; interessar, preocupar.
concert concerto.
conclusion conclusão.
concrete concreto.
condemn (to) condenar.
condense (to) condensar.
condition condição.
conduct conduta, comportamento *(behavior)*.
conduct (to) conduzir, guiar *(to lead)*; comportar-se *(to conduct oneself)*.
conductor condutor.
cone cone.

confer (to) conferir *(to grant)*; conferenciar *(to hold a conference)*; consultar *(to consult, to compare views)*.
confidence confiança.
confident seguro, confiado.
confidential confidencial, de confiança, secreto.
confirm (to) confirmar, verificar.
confirmation confirmação.
conflict conflito.
confusion confusão.
congratulate (to) felicitar, congratular.
congratulations felicitações, parabéns.
   Congratulations! Parabéns!
congress congresso.
congressman congressista; deputado; senador.
conjunction conjunção.
connect (to) ligar, juntar.
connection ligação, união, conexão (x = ks).
conquer (to) conquistar, vencer.
conquest conquista.
conscience consciência.
conscientious consciencioso, escrupuloso.
conscious consciente.
consent consentimento, permissão.
consent (to) consentir.
consequence conseqüência (consequência).
consequently por conseguinte, portanto.
conservative conservador.
consider (to) considerar.
considerable considerável.
consideration consideração.
consist (to) consistir, constar.
consistent constante *(in ideas, etc.)*; congruente *(congruous)*.
consonant consoante.
constable guarda, policial.
constant constante.
constitution constituição.
constitutional constitucional.
construct (to) construir.
consul cônsul.
consume (to) consumir.
consumer consumidor.
consumption consumo *(use of goods)*; consumpção, consunção (consumpão) *(tuberculosis)*.
contagion contágio.
contagious contagioso.
contain (to) conter.
container recipiente.
contemplation contemplação.
contemporary contemporâneo.
contend (to) sustentar, afirmar *(to assert, to maintain)*; contender, disputar, competir *(to strive, to compete)*.
content contente.
contents conteúdo.
continent continente.

continuation continuação.
continue (to) continuar.
contract contrato.
contract (to) contratar.
contractor contratante.
contradict (to) contradizer.
contradiction contradição.
contradictory contraditório.
contrary contrário.
    on the contrary ao contrário, pelo
      contrário.
contrast contraste.
contrast (to) contrastar, comparar.
contribute (to) contribuir.
contribution contribuição.
control controle Ⓑ; domínio, direção
    (direcção).
    out of control fora do controle.
control (to) controlar Ⓑ; dominar, dirigir.
convenience conveniência.
    at your convenience quando lhe convier.
convenient conveniente.
    if it's convenient for you ... se for
      conveniente para você ...
convent convento.
convention convenção, assembléia
    (assembleia).
conversation conversação, conversa.
converse (to) conversar.
convert (to) converter.
conviction convicção.
convince (to) convencer.
cook cozinheiro.
cook (to) cozinhar.
cool fresco *(temperature)*; legal *("neat")*.
cooperation cooperação.
cooperative cooperativo.
copier copidora.
    color copier copiadora de cor.
copy cópia; exemplar (x = z) *(of a
    publication)*.
copy (to) copiar.
cordial cordial.
cordless sem fio.
cork cortiça *(in sheets)*; rolha *(stopper for
    wine bottle)*.
corn milho.
corner esquina *(street)*, canto *(nook, corner of
    a room)*.
corporation corporação, sociedade anônima
    (anónima).
correct correto.
correct (to) corrigir.
correction correção (correcção).
correspond (to) corresponder.
correspondence correspondência.
correspondent correspondente.
corresponding correspondente.
corrupt corrupto.

corrupt (to) corromper.
cost custo, preço.
    cost of living custo de vida.
cost (to) custar.
Costa Rican costarriquense, costarriquenho.
costume traje, costume *(suit of clothes)*;
    fantasia *(for carnaval, Halloween, etc.)*.
cottage casa pequena, casa de campo.
cotton algodão.
couch sofá, divã.
cough tosse.
    cough drop pastilha para a tosse.
cough (to) tossir.
council junta, concelho.
counsel conselho.
count conde *(title)*; conta *(number of)*.
count (to) contar.
counter balcão *(in a store)*.
countess condessa.
countless incontável, sem conta, sem número.
country país *(nation)*; região rural, campo
    (opposed to city); pátria *(fatherland)*.
countryman compatriota; camponês.
couple casal *(romantic)*; par *(two of
    something)*.
courage coragem, valentia.
course curso; pista *(racing)*; prato *(of a meal)*;
    rumo *(route)*.
    of course claro que.
court tribunal *(law)*.
courteous cortês.
courtesy cortesia.
courtyard pátio, quintal.
cousin primo.
cover cobertura *(covering)*; tampa *(lid)*.
cover (to) cobrir; tampar *(to place a lid on)*;
    percorrer *(a distance)*; incluir,
    compreender *(to include)*.
cow vaca.
cowboy vaqueiro.
crab caranguejo.
crack quebra, fenda *(split)*.
crack (to) fender, rachar, quebrar, estalar.
cradle berço.
cramp cãibra (cãimbra).
crash estrépito, estrondo *(noise)*; quebra, ruína
    (business); colisão *(collision)*.
crash (to) estalar; colidir; espatifar-se *(a
    plane, etc.)*.
crazy louco, demente, doido.
cream creme, nata.
create (to) criar; causar.
creation criação.
credit crédito.
creditor credor.
cricket grilo *(insect)*.
crime crime, delito.
crisis crise.
critic crítico.

criticism criticismo, crítica.

criticize (to) criticar, censurar.

crook ladrão *(thief)*, vigarista *(criminal)*.

crooked torcido *(bent)*.

crop colheita *(harvest)*.

cross cruz *(symbol)*.

cross (to) cruzar, atravessar *(a street)*; riscar, cancelar *(to cross out)*.

    to make the sign of the cross fazer o sinal da cruz, persignar-se.

    to cross one's mind ocorrer-lhe.

    to cross over atravessar.

    cross-examination interrogatório.

    cross-eyed vesgo, estrábico.

crouch (to) agachar-se.

crow corvo.

crowd multidão.

crowded apinhado, cheio.

crown coroa.

crown (to) coroar.

cruel cruel.

cruelty crueldade.

cruise cruzeiro, viagem.

crumb migalha.

cry grito; choro *(weeping)*.

cry (to) gritar *(shout)*; chorar *(weep)*.

crystal cristal.

Cuban cubano.

cube cubo.

cucumber pepino.

cuff punho.

culture cultura.

cup xícara (x = sh), chávena.

cure cura.

cure (to) curar.

curiosity curiosidade.

curious curioso.

curl caracol *(hair)*.

curl (to) enrolar, encaracolar.

current corrente.

curtain cortina; pano *(theater)*.

curve curva.

cushion almofada.

custom costume.

customer freguês.

customhouse alfândega.

customs direitos aduaneiros *(duties)*.

customs officer oficial alfandegário.

cut corte.

cut (to) cortar.

    Cut it out! Corte essa!

D

dad papai, papá Ⓟ.

dagger punhal, adaga.

daily diário, cotidiano.

    daily newspaper jornal diário, diário.

dainty delicado.

dairy leitaria.

dam açude, represa (dique).

damage dano, prejuízo.

damp úmido.

dampness umidade.

dance baile.

dance (to) dançar.

dancer dançarino *(professional)*; bailarino.

dandruff caspa.

danger perigo.

dangerous perigoso.

Danish dinamarquês.

dare (to) atrever-se, ousar *(venture)*; desafiar *(challenge)*.

dark escuro.

darkness escuridão.

darling querido, amado; caro.

darn (to) cerzir.

data dados.

date encontro *(romantic)*; data *(of month)*; datil, tâmara (fruit).

date (to) datar *(memo, etc.)*; namorar *(romantic)*.

daughter filha.

daughter-in-law nora.

dawn alvorada, madrugada.

    at dawn ao amanhecer, de madrugada.

day dia.

    the day after tomorrow depois de amanhã.

    the day before véspera.

    the day before yesterday anteontem.

    every day todos os dias.

daze ofuscação, confusão, entorpecimento.

    in a daze aturdido.

dead morto; falecido *(deceased)*.

deadly mortal, fatal.

deaf surdo.

deal negócio, negociação, acordo.

    to deal with tratar com.

dealer negociante, mercador *(merchandise)*; traficante *(drugs)*.

dear querido, amado; caro, prezado.

death morte.

debatable contestável, discutível.

debate debate, discussão.

debate (to) discutir, disputar.

debt dívida.

debtor devedor.

decade década.

decadence decadência.

decay decadência *(decadence)*; declínio *(decrease)*; podridão *(rot)*.

decay (to) decair, declinar *(decline)*; deteriorar *(deteriorate)*; apodrecer *(fruit)*; cariar *(teeth)*.

deceit engano.

deceive (to) enganar.

December dezembro (Dezembro).

decency decência.

decent decente, decoroso.

decide (to) decidir tomor uma decisão; resolver, solucionar *(a dispute)*.

decidedly decididamente.

decision decisão.

decisive decisivo.

deck convés *(of ship)*, baralho *(of cards)*.

declaration declaração.

declare (to) declarar, afirmar.

decrease diminuição, redução.

decrease (to) diminuir, minguar.

decree decreto.

dedicate (to) dedicar.

deduct (to) deduzir, diminuir.

deduction dedução, redução, desconto.

deep fundo, profundo.

deeply profundamente.

defeat derrota.

defeat (to) derrotar, vencer.

defect defeito.

defective defectivo, defeituoso.

defend (to) defender, proteger.

defender defensor.

defense defesa.

defer (to) diferir *(to put off)*.

defiance desafio.

definite definido, definitivo, preciso.

definition definição.

defy (to) desafiar.

degenerate (to) degenerar.

degree grau.

delay demora, atraso, tardança.

delay (to) demorar, atrasar, tardar.

delegate delegado.

delegate (to) delegar.

delegation delegação.

deliberate circunspeto (circunspecto). acautelado *(careful)*; deliberado, considerado *(carefully thought out)* intencional *(intentional)*.

deliberate (to) deliberar.

delicacy delicadeza *(finesse)*; iguaria, guloseima *(food)*.

delicate delicado.

delicious delicioso, saboroso.

delight delícia, encanto, alegria, prazer.

delight (to) encantar, deleitar.

delinquency delinqüência (delinquência).

deliver (to) entregar *(hand over)*; livrar de *(deliver from)*; pronunciar, proferir *(a speech)*.

delivery entrega *(of goods)*; distribuição *(mail)*.

deluxe de luxo (x = sh).

demand demanda.

demand (to) demandar, exigir.

democracy democracia.

democrat democrata.

democratic democrático.

demon demônio.

demonstrate (to) demonstrar.

demonstration demonstração, exibição (x = z).

denial negativa, denegação.

denounce (to) denunciar.

dense denso.

density densidade.

dentist dentista.

deny (to) negar; recusar *(to refuse to grant)*.

depart (to) partir.

department departamento.

depend (to) depender.

dependable de confiança, seguro.

dependence dependência.

dependent *adj.* dependente, pendente, sujeito; *n.* dependente.

deplore (to) deplorar, lamentar.

deposit depósito.

deposit (to) depositar.

depth profundidade.

descend (to) descer, baixar (x = sh).

descendant descendente.

descent descida.

describe (to) descrever.

description descrição.

desegregate (to) dessegregar.

desegregation dessegregação.

desert deserto.

desert (to) desertar, abandonar.

deserve (to) merecer.

desirable desejável.

desire desejo.

desire (to) desejar.

desirous desejoso, ansioso.

desk escrivaninha, secretária.

desolation desolação.

despair desespero.

despair (to) desesperar.

desperate desesperado.

despite apesar de, a despeito de.

dessert sobremesa.

destiny destino, fado.

destroy (to) destruir.

destruction destruição.

detach (to) separar, despegar *(to separate)*; destacar *(soldiers)*.

detail detalhe, pormenor.

detain (to) deter.

determination determinação.

determine (to) determinar.

detour desvio.

develop (to) desenvolver; revelar *(photography)*.

development desenvolvimento; revelação *(photography)*.

devil diabo.

devote (to) dedicar.
devotion devoção.
devour (to) devorar, engolir.
dew orvalho, rocio.
diabolical diabólico.
dial mostrador *(watch)*; disco.
dial (to) discar.
dialogue diálogo.
diameter diâmetro.
diamond diamante; ouros *(cards)*.
dictate (to) ditar.
dictator ditador.
dictionary dicionário.
die (to) morrer, falecer.
diet regime, dieta.
differ (to) diferençar *(to stand apart)*; dissentir, não estar de acordo *(to disagree)*.
difference diferença.
different diferente, distinto.
difficult difícil.
difficulty dificuldade.
diffuse (to) difundir.
dig (to) cavar, escavar.
digest (to) digerir.
digestion digestão.
dignity dignidade.
dim escuro, pouco claro.
dimple covinha.
dine (to) jantar.
dinner jantar.
diplomacy diplomacia.
diplomat diplomata.
diplomatic diplomático.
direct direito, em linha reta (recta).
    direct current corrente contínua.
direct (to) dirigir.
direction direção (direcção).
directly diretamente (directamente).
director diretor (director).
directory lista, catálogo.
    telephone directory lista telefônica (telefónica).
dirt sujeira, imundície (filth); solo *(soil)*.
dirty sujo.
disadvantage desvantagem.
disagree (to) discordar, não concordar.
disagreeable desagradável.
disappear (to) desaparecer.
disappearance desaparição.
disappoint (to) desapontar.
disappointment desapontamento, decepção.
disapprove (to) desaprovar.
disarm (to) desarmar.
disaster desastre.
disastrous desastroso.
discipline disciplina.
discontent descontente.
discord discórdia, desacordo.

discourage (to) desanimar, dissuadir.
discouragement desânimo.
discover (to) descobrir.
discoverer descobridor.
discovery descoberta, descobrimento.
discreet discreto.
discretion discrição, prudência.
discuss (to) discutir, tratar de.
discussion discussão.
disease doença.
disgrace desonra, vergonha, desgraça.
disgust repugnância, asco.
disgust (to) repugnar, desagradar, enojar.
disgusting repugnante, nojento.
dish prato.
dishonest desonesto.
disk disco.
    floppy disk disquete.
    hard disk disco rígido.
    disk drive unidade de disco.
dismal lúgubre, triste, funesto *(morose)*; sombre *(weather)*.
dismiss (to) despedir.
disobey (to) desobedecer.
disorder desordem.
dispatch despacho, mensagem.
dispatch (to) despachar, enviar.
display exibição (x = z) *(show)*; ostentação *(ostentation)*.
display (to) exibir (x = z), mostrar *(to show)*; ostentar *(to flaunt)*.
displease (to) desagradar.
dispute disputa.
dispute (to) disputar, discutir.
dissolve (to) dissolver.
distance distância.
distinct distinto, claro.
distinction distinção.
distinguish (to) distinguir.
distinguished distinguido.
distort (to) falsear, corromper, torcer.
distract (to) distrair.
distraction distração (distracção).
distribute (to) distribuir, repartir.
distribution distribuição.
district distrito, bairro.
disturb (to) perturbar, incomodar.
disturbance perturbação, desordem.
dive mergulho *(into water)*; picada *(a plane)*.
dive (to) mergulhar *(into water)*; dar picada, descer a pique *(aviation)*.
divide (to) dividir.
dividend dividendo.
divine divino.
diving board trampolim.
division divisão.
divorce divórcio, separação.
divorce (to) divorciar, separar-se de.
dizzy tonto, aturdido.

do (to) fazer *(perform action);* praticar *(crafts, hobbies, etc.).*
    How do you do? Como vai? Como está?
    to do one's best fazer o possível.
    to do without passar sem.
    to have to do with ter que ver com.
    That will do. Chega. Basta. Isto serve.
    Do you believe it? Você crê? Você acredita? Você acha?
    to do your hair arrumar o cabelo.
dock doca, cais.
dock (to) atracar *(ship).*
doctor doutor, médico.
doctrine doutrina.
document documento.
dog cão, cachorro.
dogma dogma.
doll boneca.
dollar dólar.
dome cúpula.
domestic doméstico *(pertaining to the household);* do país, nacional *(trade, etc.).*
Dominican dominicano.
don dom.
door porta.
doorman portéiro.
double duplo.
doubt dúvida.
doubt (to) duvidar.
doubtful duvidoso.
doubtless sem dúvida, certo.
dough massa de farinha, pasta.
down abaixo (x = sh), para baixo (x = sh).
    to go down baixar (x = sh), descer.
    to come down baixar (x = sh), descer.
    down there lá em baixo.
downstairs em baixo (x = sh), para baixo (x = sh), no andar-térreo.
downtown na cidade, para a cidade, o centro.
dozen dúzia.
drain cāno de esgoto.
    His business went down the drain. A sua empresa foi pelo cano abaixo.
draft corrente de ar *(air);* saque, letra de câmbio *(bank);* sorteio *(military);* desenho, esboço rascunho *(sketch, outline).*
draft (to) rascunhar, esboçar *(to outline).*
drag (to) arrastar.
drama drama.
dramatist dramaturgo.
draw (to) debuxar (x = sh), desenhar *(to sketch);* tirar *(money, liquids, etc.);* correr *(curtains);* sacar *(bank draft);* ganhar, receber *(a salary);* formular, escrever *(to draw up).*
drawer gaveta.
drawing desenho.
dread (to) temer.
dreaded temido.

dreadful terrível, horrível.
dream sonho.
dreamer sonhador.
dress vestido, traje, roupa.
dress (to) vestir-se *(to get dressed);* limpar, medicar *(a wound).*
dresser cómoda (cômoda) *(furniture).*
drink bebida.
drink (to) beber, tomar.
drip (to) pingar, gotejar.
drive volta, passeio *(a ride in a car, etc.);* passeio, estrada *(a road);* campanha *(to raise money, etc.).*
drive (to) conduzir, dirigir *(a car, etc.);* cravar *(a nail)*
    to drive away expulsar, expelir.
driver motorista, chofer ⑱.
    driver's license carteira de chofer ⑱, carteira de motorista.
drop gota *(liquid);* queda, caída *(fall).*
    cough drops pastilhas para tosse.
drop (to) soltar, deixar (x = sh) cair *(to release, to let fall);* pingar, gotejar *(fall in drops);* abandonar, renunciar, desistir de, deixar *(to let go).*
    to drop in visitar, dar pula na cosa de.
    to drop a subject mudar de assunto.
drown (to) afogar, afogar-se.
drug droga (also **drugs**).
drugstore farmácia, drogaria.
drum tambor.
drunk bêbado, ébrio.
drunkard bêbado, ébrio.
drunkenness embriaguez, ebriedade.
dry seco.
dry (to) secar.
dry cleaning lavagem a seco.
dryness seca, secura, aridez.
duchess duquesa.
duck pato.
due devido; pagável *(payable);* suficiente, bastante *(enough).*
    due to circumstances . . . devido às circunstâncias . . .
duke duque.
dull opaco; apagada *(color);* pesado, aborrecido, grosseiro *(slow, boring).*
dumb estúpido *(stupid).*
durable durável.
during durante.
dusk crepúsculo, escuridāo.
dust pó, poeira.
dust (to) tirar o pó, limpar do pó.
dusty poeirento, empoeirado, coberto de pó.
Dutch holandés.
duty dever.
dwelling morada, habitação, residência.
dye tintura, tinta.
dye (to) tingir, corar.

E

each cada.
   each one cada um.
   each other mutamente, um ao outro, uns aos outros.
eager ansioso.
eagle águia.
ear ouvido *(the organ of hearing, the internal ear)*; orelha *(the external ear)*; espiga *(of corn)*.
early cedo.
earn (to) ganhar.
earnest sério *(serious)*; ansioso *(eager)*.
   in earnest a sério, de boa fé.
earth terra.
earthquake terremoto.
ease tranqüilidade (tranquilidade), alívio *(rest)*; facilidade *(facility)*.
   at ease a vontade.
ease (to) aliviar, mitigar.
easily facilmente.
east leste, este, oriente.
Easter Páscoa.
eastern oriental.
easy fácil.
eat (to) comer.
economic econômico (económico).
economics economia.
economy economia.
Ecuadorian equatoriano.
edge beira, margem *(of a stream, of collapse, etc.)*; canto *(of a table)*; gume, fio *(of a blade)*.
edit (to) red; gir *(writing)*; editar *(tape)*.
edition edição.
editor redator (redactor), director (director).
educate (to) educar, ensinar.
education educação.
eel enguia.
effect efeito.
effect (to) efectuar (efectuar).
efficiency eficiência, eficácia.
effort esforço.
egg ovo.
eggplant berinjela.
eggshell casca de ovo.
egoism egoísmo.
eight oito.
eighteen dezoito.
eighteenth décimo oitavo.
eighth oitavo.
eightieth octagésimo.
eighty oitenta.
either ou; qualquer.
   one or the other um ou o outro.
   either of the two qualquer dos dois.
elastic elástico.

elbow cotovelo.
elderly idoso.
elect (to) eleger.
elected eleito.
election eleição.
elector eleitor.
electric elétrico (eléctrico).
electricity eletricidade (electricidade).
electronics eletrônica (electrónica).
elegance elegância.
elegant elegante.
element elemento.
elementary elementar.
elephant elefante.
elevation elevação, altura.
elevator elevador, ascensor.
eleven onze.
eleventh décimo-primeiro.
eligible elegível.
eliminate (to) eliminar.
eloquence eloqüência (eloquência).
eloquent eloqüente (eloquente).
else outro, mais, além disso.
   nothing else nada mais.
   something else outra coisa.
   or else senão, ou então.
   nobody else ninguém mais.
elsewhere em qualquer outra parte, noutra parte.
elude (to) eludir, evitar.
e-mail correio eletrônico.
e-mail (to) enviar por correio eletrônico.
embark (to) embarcar.
embarrass (to) embaraçar.
embarrassing embaraçante, embaraçoso.
embassy embaixada (x = sh).
embody (to) encarnar, incorporar.
embrace abraço.
embrace (to) abraçar.
embroidery bordado.
emerge (to) emergir, surgir.
emergency emergência, urgência.
emigrant emigrante.
emigrate (to) emigrar.
emigration emigração.
eminent eminente.
eminently eminentemente.
emotion emoção.
emphasis ênfase.
emphasize (to) enfatizar, acentuar.
emphatic enfático.
empire império.
employ (to) empregar.
employee empregado.
employer empregador.
employment emprego.
empty vazio.
empty (to) esvaziar, evacuar.
enclose (to) cercar *(ground, etc.)*; incluir.

enclosed anexo (x = ks), incluso.
encourage (to) animar, estimular.
encouragement encorajamento, estímulo.
end fim; conclusão.
end (to) acabar, terminar.
endeavor esforço.
endeavor (to) esforçar-se.
endorse (to) endossar.
endow (to) dotar.
endure (to) suportar, resistir, agüentar
  (aguentar).
enemy inimigo.
energetic enérgico.
energy energia.
enforce (to) fazer cumprir, executar (x = z) *(a law)*, forçar, compelir *(to compel)*.
engage (to) empregar, contratar *(services)*.
engagement compromisso, encontro
  (appointment, date); noivado *(for marriage)*; contrato *(for employment)*.
engine motor, máquina.
engineer engenheiro.
English inglês.
engrave (to) gravar.
enjoy (to) gozar, gostar de.
  to enjoy oneself divertir-se.
enjoyment gozo.
enlarge (to) aumentar, ampliar.
enlargement ampliação, aumento.
enlist (to) alistar, alistar-se.
enlistment alistamento.
enough bastante, suficiente.
enrich (to) enriquecer.
enroll (to) matricular, registrar *(school)*.
entangle (to) enredar, complicar.
enter (to) entrar *(a house, etc.)*; anotar,
  registrar *(in a register, etc.)*; ingressar,
  matricular-se *(a school)*.
entertain (to) divertir, entreter; considerar
  (ideas).
entertainment entretenimento, diversão.
enthusiasm entusiasmo.
enthusiastic entusiástico.
entire inteiro, todo.
entirely completamente, totalmente.
entrance entrada.
entrust (to) confiar.
entry entrada *(entrance)*; registro, entrada
  (books, records); verbete *(dictionary)*.
enumerate (to) enumerar.
envelope envelope.
enviable invejável.
envious invejoso.
environment ambiente.
envy inveja.
episode episódio.
epoch época, era.
equal igual.
equal (to) igualar.

equality igualdade.
equator equador.
equilibrium equilíbrio.
equip (to) equipar, guarnecer.
equipment equipamento.
equity eqüidade *(equidade)*.
era era, época.
erase (to) apagar, riscar, extinguir.
eraser apagador, borracha.
err (to) errar, enganar-se.
errand recado, mandado, mensagem.
error erro.
escape fuga, escape.
escape (to) escapar, fugir.
escort escolta *(a body of soldiers, etc.)*;
  acompanhante *(an individual)*.
escort (to) escoltar, acompanhar.
especially especialmente, particularmente.
essay ensaio, composição.
essence essência.
essential essencial, indispensável.
establish (to) estabelecer.
establishment estabelecimento.
estate herança *(inheritance)*; bens,
  propriedade *(properties, possessions)*;
  fazenda *(a country estate)*.
esteem estima, apreço.
esteem (to) estimar.
estimable estimável.
estimate cálculo; avaliação.
estimate (to) calcular, avaliar.
eternal eterno.
eternity eternidade.
euro euro.
European europeu.
evacuate (to) evacuar.
eve véspera.
even *adj.* par *(numbers)*; plano, liso *(level)*;
  adv. ainda, até, mesmo.
  to be even with estar quite com.
  even if mesmo que.
  even though embora.
  even so mesmo assim.
  even that até isso.
  not even nem sequer.
evening tarde, noite.
  Good evening! Boa tarde! Boa noite!
  yesterday evening ontem à noite.
event acontecimento.
  in the event that no caso de, caso que.
ever sempre.
  as ever como sempre.
  ever since desde então.
  not . . . ever nunca.
  nor . . . ever nem nunca.
every cada.
  every bit inteiramente.
  every day todos os dias.
  every other day um dia sim, um dia não.

every one cada um, todos eles.

     every once in a while de vez em quando.

everybody todos, todo o mundo.

everyone todos, todo o mundo.

everything tudo.

everywhere em toda parte.

evidence evidência, testemunho *(court)*, prova *(proof)*.

evident evidente, claro.

evil *adj.* mau; *n.* mal.

evoke (to) evocar.

exact exato (exacto) (x = z), preciso.

exaggerate (to) exagerar (x = z).

exaggeration exageração (x = z), exagero (x = z).

exalt (to) exaltar (x = z).

examination exame (x = z).

examine (to) examinar (x = z).

example exemplo (x = z).

exasperate (to) exasperar (x = z), irritar.

excavate (to) escavar, cavar.

exceed (to) exceder (x = s), superar.

excel (to) sobressair, distinguir-se.

excellence excelência (x = s).

excellent excelente (x = s).

except exceto (excepto) (x = s), menos, a menos que, a não ser que.

except (to) excetuar (exceptuar) (x = s), excluir (x = sh).

exception exceção (excepção) (x = s).

exceptional excepcional (x = s).

exceptionally excepcionalmente (x = s).

excess excesso (x = s).

excessive excessivo (x = s).

exchange troca, câmbio.

     in exchange for em troca de.

exchange (to) trocar, cambiar.

excite (to) excitar (x = s).

excitement excitação (x = s), agitação.

exclaim (to) exclamar (x = sh).

exclamation exclamação (x = sh).

exclude (to) excluir (x = sh), eliminar.

exclusive exclusivo (x = sh).

excursion excursão (x = sh).

excuse escusa.

excuse (to) escusar, dispensar, desculpar.

execute (to) executar (x = z).

executive executivo (x = z).

exempt (to) isentar, eximir (x = z).

exercise exercício (x = z).

exercise (to) exercer (x = z) *(power, etc.)*, fazer exercícios (x = z), *(work out)*.

exhaust (to) esgotar.

exhausted esgotado, exausto (x = z).

exhausting exaustivo (x = z).

exhibition exibição (x = z).

exile exílio (x = z), desterro, degredo.

exile (to) exilar (x = z), desterrar.

exist (to) existir (x = z).

existence existência (x = z).

existentialism existencialismo (x = z).

exit saída.

expand (to) expandir (x = sh), espalhar, desenvolver.

expansion expansão (x = sh).

expansive expansivo (x = sh).

expect (to) esperar, aguardar.

expectation expectativa (x = sh) Ⓑ, expectação, esperança.

expel (to) expelir (x = sh), expulsar (x = sh).

expense despesa.

     at one's expense à custa de.

expensive caro.

experience experiência (x = sh).

experience (to) experimentar (x = sh).

experiment experimento (x = sh).

experiment (to) experimentar (x = sh).

experimental experimental (x = sh).

expert perito.

expire (to) expirar (x = sh).

explain (to) explicar (x = sh).

explanation explicação (x = sh).

explanatory explicativo (x = sh).

explode (to) explodir (x = sh), estourar.

exploit façanha.

exploit (to) explorar (x = sh), utilizar.

exploration exploração (x = sh).

explore (to) explorar (x = sh).

explorer explorador (x = sh).

explosion explosão (x = sh), estouro (estoiro).

export exportação (x = sh).

export (to) exportar (x = sh).

expose (to) expor (x = sh).

express *adj.* expresso (x = sh); *n.* rapido.

express (to) expressar (x = sh), exprimir.

expression expressão (x = sh).

expulsion expulsão (x = sh).

extend (to) estender.

extension extensão (x = sh).

extensive extensivo (x = sh).

extent extensão (x = sh).

     to a certain extent até certo ponto.

exterior exterior (x = sh).

exterminate (to) exterminar (x = sh).

external externo (x = sh).

extinguish (to) extinguir (x = sh).

extra extra (x = sh).

extract extrato (extracto) (x = sh).

extract (to) extrair (x = sh).

extraordinary extraordinário (x = sh).

extravagance extravagância (x = sh).

extravagant extravagante (x = sh).

extreme extremo (x = sh).

extremely extremamente (x = sh), sumamente.

extremity extremidade (x = sh).

eye olho.

eyebrow sobrancelha.
eyeglasses óculos.
eyelash pestana.
eyelid pálpebra.

F

fable fábula.
fabulous fabuloso.
face face, rosto, cara.
facsimile fac-símile, fax.
fact fato (facto).
   in fact de fato.
factory fábrica.
faculty faculdade *(ability)*; corpo docente *(teaching staff)*.
fade (to) murchar, enfraquecer.
fail (to) fracassar (in an undertaking); ser reprovado (in an examination); faltar (to fail to do something); malograr *(plans, etc.)*.
   Don't fail to do it. Não deixe de fazê-lo.
failure fracasso; falha, falta (fault, defect); quebra (bankruptcy); avaria (motor).
faint (to) desmaiar, desfalecer.
fair *adj.* louro (loiro) *(hair)*; branco *(complexion)*; claro *(clear)*; justo *(just)*; regular *(moderate)*; bom *(weather)*; *n.* feira.
fairness justiça, eqüidade (equidade).
fairy tale conto de fadas.
faith fé.
faithful fiel, leal
fall queda, caída; outono (Outono) (autumn).
fall (to) cair.
false falso *(statement)*; postiço *(teeth, etc.)*
fame fama.
familiar familiar.
familiarity familiaridade, confiança.
family família.
famine fome.
famous famoso, célebre.
fan leque *(hand)*; ventilador *(electric)*; fã, aficionado *(of sports, etc.)*.
fantastic fantástico.
far longe.
   How far? A que distância?
   far away muito longe.
   so far até agora.
   As far as I'm concerned. Quanto a mim.
fare preço *(trains, buses, etc.)*; torifa *(taxis)*.
farewell despedida.
farmer fazendeiro, agricultor (lavrador).
farming lavoura, agricultura.
farther mais longe, mais distante.
fashion moda, uso.

fashionable à moda, da moda.
fast depressa, rapidamente.
fasten (to) prender, fixar (x = ks), segurar.
fat *adj.* gordo; *n.* gordura.
fate fado, destino.
father pai; padre *(priest)*.
fatherhood paternidade.
father-in-law sogro.
fatherland pátria.
faucet torneira.
fault falta.
favor favor, serviço.
   in favor of a favor de.
favor (to) favorecer.
favorable favorável.
favorite favorito.
fax fax.
   to send a fax enviar un fax.
   to receive a fax receber um fax.
   fax machine máquina de fax.
fear medo, temor, receio.
fear (to) temer, recear.
fearless intrépido.
feast festa.
feather pena, pluma.
feature traço, característica.
February fevereiro (Fevereiro).
federal federal.
fee taxa, remuneração, honorários.
feeble débil, fraco; delicado.
feed (to) alimentar, dar de comer a.
feeding alimentação.
feel (to) sentir; tocar *(touch)*.
feeling tato (tacto) *(tact)*; sentimento *(sentiment)*; sensibilidade *(sensitivity)*.
fellow sujeito; companheiro.
   fellow student colega.
   fellow traveler companheiro de viagem.
female fêmea.
feminine feminino.
fence cerca.
ferment (to) fermentar.
fermentation fermentação.
ferry barco de passagem, barca.
fertile fértil, fecundo.
fertilize (to) fertilizar, fecundar.
fertilizer fertilizante, adubo.
fervent fervente.
fervor fervor.
festival festa, festival.
fever febre.
feverish febril, febricitante.
few poucos.
   a few alguns, algumas.
   quite a few muitos.
fewer menos.
fiber fibra.
fiberglass fibra de vidro.
fiction ficção.

field campo; campanha, campo de batalha *(military)*; especialidade, ramo Ⓑ *(career, etc.)*.

fierce feroz.

fiery veemente, impetuoso.

fifteen quinze.

fifteenth décimo quinto.

fifth quinto.

fiftieth qüinquagésimo.

fifty cinqüenta (cinquenta).

fig figo, figueira.

fight luta, batalha, peleja, briga.

fight (to) lutar, batalhar, pelejar, brigar.
    to put up a fight dar luta.

figure figura.

file lima *(for nails, etc.,)*; arquivo, fichário *(for papers, etc.)*.

file (to) limar *(with an instrument)*; arquivar *(papers, etc.)*; arquivo *(computer)*.
    filing cabinet arquivo, fichário.
    file card ficha.

Filipino filipino.

fill (to) encher.
    to fill out a form preencher um formulário.

film filme *(residue)*; fita *(recording medium)*; película *(movie)*.

filthy imundo sujo.

final final.

finally finalmente.

finance finança, finanças.

financial financeiro, financial.

find (to) achar, encontrar.
    to find out saber.

fine *adj.* fino, bom, magnífico, excelente; *n.* multa, penalidade, pena.

finger dedo.

finish (to) terminar, acabar.

fire fogo; incêndio.

fire (to) disparar *(a gun)*; demitir, despedir *(an employee)*.
    to set a fire incendiar.

firm *adj.* firme; *n.* firma, empresa *(business)*.

firmness firmeza.

first *adj.* primeiro; *adv.* primeiramente.
    first of all antes de tudo, antes de mais nada.
    the first time a primeira vez.
    in the first place em primeiro lugar.
    first floor primeiro andar.

fish peixe (x = sh) *(in water)*; pescado *(when caught)*.

fish (to) pescar.

fisherman pescador.

fishing pesca.

fist punho.

fit *adj.* conveniente, apropriado, justo, digno.
    to see fit achar conveniente.

fit (to) servir *(clothes)*; caber *(object into a space)*.
    to fit something into a space encaixar (x = sh).
    It fits you well. Une serve muito bem.
    It fits badly. Lhe serve mal.

fitness saúde, boa forma.

fitting (be) ser apropriado.

five cinco.

five hundred quinhentos.

fix (to) fixar (x = ks) *(secure)*; consertar *(repair)*.

flag bandeira.

flagrant flagrante.

flame chama.

flannel flanela.

flash jato (jacto) de luz; relâmpago, clarão *(lightning)*.

flashlight lanterna elétrica (eléctrica).

flat plano, liso; chato, insípido *(taste, etc.)*.

flatten (to) nivelar, alisar *(smooth out)*; achatar *(smash)*.

flatter (to) lisonjear, adular.

flattery lisonja, adulação.

flavor sabor, gosto.

flavor (to) condimentar, sazonar.

flax linho.

flea pulga.

fleet frota, armada.

flesh carne; polpa *(fruit)*.

flexibility flexibilidade (x = ks).

flexible flexível (x = ks).

flight vôo *(in the air)*; fuga *(escape)*.

flint pederneira; pedra *(of lighter)*.

float (to) flutuar.

flood enchente, inundação, cheia.

flood (to) inundar.

floor chão, soalho *(of room)*; andar *(of building)*.
    ground floor andar térreo, res-do-chão.

flour farinha.

flow (to) fluir, correr.

flower flor.

flowery florido.

fluid fluido.

fly mosca

fly (to) voar.

foam espuma.

foam (to) espumar.

focus foco.

fog nevoeiro, névoa, cerração.

fold prega, dobra.

fold (to) preguear, dobrar.

foliage folhagem.

folks pais *(parents)*; gente *(people)*.

follow (to) seguir.

following seguinte.

food alimento, comida.

fool tolo.

fool (to) enganar.
foolish tolo, ridículo.
foolishness tolice.
foot pé.
    on foot a pé.
football futebol.
for para, por.
    This is for her. Isto é para ela.
    for example por exemplo (x = z).
    for the first time pela primeira vez.
    for the present por agora.
forbid (to) proibir.
forbidden proibido.
force força.
force (to) forçar, obrigar.
forced forçado, obrigado.
ford vau.
forecast prognóstico, previsão.
forecast (to) prognosticar, prever.
forehead fronte, testa.
foreign estrangeiro, alheio, estranho.
foreigner estrangeiro, forasteiro.
foresee prever.
forest floresta, selva.
forever para sempre.
forget (to) esquecer, esquecer-se.
forgetfulness esquecimento, olvido.
forgive (to) perdoar.
forgiveness perdão.
fork garfo.
form forma *(shape)*; formulário *(paper)*.
form (to) formar.
formal formal, cerimonioso, solene.
formality formalidade, cerimônia (cerimónia).
formation formação.
former anterior.
former (the) aquele, aquela, aqueles *(vs. latter)*; antigo *(previous)*.
formerly antigamente, em tempos passados.
formula fórmula.
forsake (to) deixar (x = sh), abandonar.
fortieth quadragésimo.
fortunate afortunado.
fortunately afortunadamente.
fortune fortuna, sorte.
fortune-teller adivinho; cartomante *(card reader)*, quiromante *(palm reader)*.
fortune-telling adivinhação, cartomancia, quiromancia.
forty quarenta.
forward adiante, avante.
forward (to) expedir, enviar, transmitir.
found (to) fundar.
foundation fundação.
founder fundador.
fountain fonte.
four quatro.
four hundred quatrocentos.
fourteen catorze.

fourteenth décimo quarto.
fourth quarto.
fowl ave, ave doméstica.
fragment fragmento.
fragrance fragrância, aroma.
fragrant fragrante, aromático.
frail débil, delicado, frágil.
frame quadro, moldura *(of a picture, etc.)*; armação, estrutura *(structure)*.
    frame of mind estado de espírito.
frame (to) enquadrar, emoldurar *(a picture, etc.)*
frank franco, sincero.
frankly francamente.
frankness franqueza.
free livre *(at liberty)*; gratuito, grátis *(at no cost)*.
free (to) livrar, libertar.
freedom liberdade.
freeze (to) gelar, congelar.
freight carga, frete.
French francês.
frequent freqüente (frequente).
frequent (to) freqüentar (frequentar).
frequently freqüentemente (frequentemente).
fresh fresco.
Friday sexta-feira, sexta.
friend amigo.
friendly amigável, amistoso, cordial.
friendship amizade.
frighten (to) assustar.
frightening assustador, alarmante.
frivolity frivolidade.
frivolous frívolo.
frog rã.
from de, desde.
    from a distance de longe.
    from memory de memória.
    from page one to page four desde a página um até a página quatro.
front *adj.* anterior, dianteiro, da frente; *n.* frente.
    in front of à frente de.
frown olhar carrancudo.
frown (to) franzir as sobrancelhas.
fruit fruta.
fry (to) fritar.
frying pan frigideira.
fuel combustível.
fugitive fugitivo.
fulfill (to) cumprir.
full cheio; lotado.
fully completamente.
fun divertimento, diversão.
    to have fun divertir-se.
    to make fun of fazer troça de, zombar de.
function função.
function (to) funcionar.
fundamental fundamental.

funds fundos.
funeral funeral, enterro.
funny engraçado, divertido, cômico (cómico).
fur pele.
furious furioso.
furnace fornalha, forno.
furnish (to) mobiliar (mobilar) *(a room, house, etc.)*; fornecer *(supply, provide)*.
furniture mobília, móveis.
furrow sulco.
further mais longe, mais distante; além, ademais.
furthermore além disso.
fury fúria.
future futuro.
    in the future no futuro.

G

gain ganho.
gain (to) ganhar.
    to gain weight engordar.
Galician galego.
gallant galante.
gamble (to) jogar.
game jogo; partida *(match)*; caça *(hunting)*.
    a game of chess uma partida de xadrez (x = sh).
garage garagem, garage Ⓑ.
garbage lixo (x = sh).
garden jardim.
gardener jardineiro.
gargle (to) gargarejar, fazer gargarejo.
garlic alho.
garment peça de roupa.
garter liga.
gas gás *(oxyen, natural gas, etc.)*; gasolina *(gasoline)*.
    gas station posto de gasolina.
    gas tank tanque de gasolina.
    gas pump bomba de gasolina.
gate portão, porta.
gather (to) reunir, juntar, recolher.
gay homossexual, gay.
gear engrenagem *(mechanics)*; marcha *(car)*.
gem gema.
general *adj.* geral; *n.* general.
    in general em geral.
generality generalidade.
generalize (to) generalizar.
generally geralmente.
generation geração.
generosity generosidade.
generous generoso.
genius gênio (génio).
gentle suave; brando, meigo *(of a person)*.

gentleman cavalheiro.
    gentlemen senhores; prezados senhores *(in a letter)*.
gentleness brandura, meiguice; suavidade.
gently suavemente, meigamente.
genuine genuíno, autêntico.
geographic geográfico.
geography geografia.
geometric geométrico.
geometry geometria.
germ germe, micróbio.
German alemão.
gesture *n.* gesto.
get (to) conseguir, obter, adquirir, receber.
    to get ahead adiantar.
    to get away partir, ir-se embora, fugir.
    to get back voltar, regressar.
    to get home chegar em casa.
    to get old envelhecer.
    to get dark escurecer.
    to get better melhorar.
    to get worse piorar.
    to get in entrar.
    to get married casar-se.
    to get off descer, saltar, desmontar.
    to get on subir, montar.
    to get out sair; descer *(car)*.
    to get up levantar-se; subir.
    Get over here! Chega aqui!
    Get out of here! Vá lá!
giant gigante.
gift presente, dá diva.
gifted talentoso, dotado.
gin gim Ⓑ, genebra.
ginger gengibre.
girl menina *(child)*, moça *(preteen, teen)*.
girlfriend noiva *(of man)*; amiga *(of woman)*.
girl scout escoteira.
give (to) dar.
    to give in ceder.
    to give up desistir.
    to give a gift presentear.
    He doesn't give a darn. Não lhe importa nado.
giver doador.
glad contente, alegre.
gladness alegria.
glance relance. olhadela.
glance (to) olhar de relance.
glass vidro; copo *(for drinking)*.
    glasses óculos *(for eyes)*.
glimpse *n.* olhadela.
glitter (to) brilhar, resplandecer.
globe globo.
gloomy sombrio; melancólico, triste *(sad)*.
glorious glorioso.
glory glória.
glove luva.
glue cola, grude.

go (to) ir; percorrer (*to cover a distance*).
   to go away ir-se embora, partir.
   to go back regressar, voltar.
   to go down descer, baixar.
   to go forward ir adiante, avançar.
   to go out sair; apagar-se (*a light, fire, etc.*).
   to go up subir.
   to go with acompanhar.
   to go without passar sem.
goal meta, objetivo (objectivo), firm; gol (*sports*).
   to reach one's goal conseguir o objetivo (objectivo).
God Deus.
godchild afilhado.
godfather padrinho.
godmother madrinha.
godparents padrinhos.
gold ouro.
golf golfe.
golf club taco de golfe.
good bom.
   good morning bom dia.
   good afternoon boa tarde.
   good night boa noite.
good-bye adeus.
goodness bondade.
   Goodness! Goodness gracious! Meu Deus!
   Goodness knows! Quem sabe!
goods mercadorias.
goodwill boa vontade.
goose ganso.
Gosh! Puxa! (x = sh)
gossip fofocas, mexerico (x = sh).
gossip (to) fofocar, mexericar (x = sh).
govern (to) governar.
government governo.
governor governador.
gown vestido, beca.
grab (to) agarrar, pegar em.
grace graça.
graceful gracioso.
gracious cortês, afável.
grade grau.
gradual gradual.
gradually gradualmente.
graduate diplomado, graduado.
graduate (to) formar-se, graduar-se.
grain grão.
grammar gramática.
grammatical gramatical.
grand grande, grandioso, magnífico.
grandchildren netos.
granddaughter neta.
grandfather avô.
grandmother avó.
grandparents avós.
grandson neto.

grant subvenção, subsídio.
grant (to) conceder, outorgar.
   to take for granted tomar por certo, achar natural.
   granting (granted) that admitido que.
grape uva.
grapefruit toronja.
grasp (to) agarrar, segurar; compreender, entender.
grass relva, grama.
grasshopper gafanhoto.
grateful agradecido.
gratefully agradecidamente.
gratitude gratidão, agradecimento.
grave *adj.* grave, sério; *n.* túmulo, sepultura.
gravity gravidade.
gravy molho.
gray cinza Ⓑ, cinzento.
grease graxa (x = sh).
great grande; *informal* ótimo, bacana.
   a great man um grande homem.
   a great many muitos.
   a great deal muito.
   Great! Estupendo! Magnífico! Ótimo!
greatness grandeza.
greedy avarento, ganancioso.
green verde.
greet (to) cumprimentar.
greeting cumprimento.
grief pesar, dor.
grieve (to) afligir-se, sofrer.
grill (to) grelhar.
grin sorriso largo.
grin (to) sorrir abertamente.
grind (to) moer.
groan gemido.
groan (to) gemer.
grocer merceeiro.
groceries comestíveis.
grocery store mercearia, armazém.
groom noivo.
groove ranhura.
grope (to) tatear (tactear).
ground *n.* terra, terreno; chão.
group grupo.
group (to) agrupar.
grow (to) crescer.
growth crescimento.
grudge rancor, ressentimento.
gruff brusco, áspero.
grumble (to) grunhir (*make a grumbling sound*); resmungar (*complain*).
guarantee garantia.
guarantee (to) garantir.
guard guarda.
guard (to) guardar, vigiar.
   to guard against guardar-se de.
Guatemalan guatemalteco.
guess conjetura (conjectura), suposição.

guess (to) adivinhar, conjeturar (conjecturar); supor *(suppose)*.
   to guess right acertar.
guest hóspede *(at an inn, etc.); convidado* (at a party); visita *(visitor)*.
guide guia.
guide (to) guiar, conduzir.
guidebook guia de viagem.
guilt culpa.
guilty culpado.
guitar violão.
gulf golfo.
gum chiclete *(for chewing); pl.* gengivas *(teeth)*.
gun arma de fogo, revólver, pistola, fuzil *(rifle)*.
guy tipo.
gymnasium ginásio.
gypsy cigano.

H

habit costume, hábito.
   to be in the habit of costumar, ter o hábito de.
habitual habitual, costumeiro.
habitually habitualmente.
hail granizo *(during storm);* viva, salve *(cheering, greeting)*.
hail (to) granizar *(in a thunderstorm);* saudar *(to greet)*.
hair cabelo.
   hairbrush escova para cabelo.
   haircut corte de cabelo.
   hair dye tintura para o cabelo.
   hairpin grampo para o cabelo.
   to do your hair arrumar cabelo.
hairdo penteado.
half meio; metade.
   half and half meio a meio; metades iguais.
   half past two duas (horas) e meia.
   half-hour meia hora.
half brother meio-irmão.
half sister meia-irmã.
halfway a meio caminho.
hall vestíbulo *(entrance, foyer);* salão *(assembly room);* corredor.
halt alto, parado (paragem).
halt (to) parar, deter, deter-se.
   Halt! Alto!
ham presunto.
hammer martelo.
hammer (to) martelar.
hand mão; ponteiro *(of a watch)*.
   by hand à mão, manual.
   in hand em mão.

   on hand à mão; em estoque *(in stock)*.
   on the one hand por um lado.
   on the other hand por outro lado.
hand (to) passar *(pass)*.
   to hand over entregar.
handbag bolsa.
handbook manual.
handful punhado.
handkerchief lenço.
handle asa *(of cup, etc.);* cabo *(of knife, etc.);* monivela *(of car door)*.
handmade feito à mão.
handshake aperto de mãos.
hang (to) pendurar.
hanger cabide *(clothes)*.
happen (to) acontecer.
happening acontecimento.
happiness felicidade.
happy feliz, contente.
harbor porto.
hard duro, difícil.
   hard luck má sorte.
   hard work trabalho difícil.
   to rain hard chover a cântaros.
harden (to) endurecer.
hardly apenas, mal, quase.
hardness dureza.
hardware ferragens *(tools);* hardware *(computer)*.
hardware store loja de ferragens.
hardy forte, robusto.
hare lebre.
harm mal, prejuízo, dano.
harmful prejudicial, nocivo, daninho.
harmless inofensivo.
harmonious harmonioso.
harmonize (to) harmonizar.
harmony harmonia.
harness arreios.
harsh severo, áspero.
harshness aspereza.
harvest colheita.
haste pressa.
   in haste à pressa, às pressas.
hasten (to) apressar-se, acelerar.
hastily apressadamente.
hasty apressado.
hat chapéu.
hatch (to) incubar, chocar.
hate ódio.
hate (to) odiar, detestar.
hateful odioso.
hatred ódio.
haughty soberbo, arrogante.
Havana Havana.
have (to) ter, possuir *(to possess);* ter, haver *(auxiliary)*.
   to have in mind ter em mente.
   to have to ter que, ter de.

    to have a mind to estar disposto a.

hay feno.

he ele.

head cabeça; chefe *(chief)*.

head (to) encabeçar.

    to head for dirigir-se a.

    heading for rumo a.

headache dor de cabeça.

headline título, cabeçalho, manchete Ⓑ.

headquarters sede *(business)*; quartel-general *(military)*.

heal (to) curar; recobrar a saúde.

health saúde.

    to be in good health estar bem de saúde.

healthful saudável.

healthy são *(sã f.)*, sadio *(in good health)*; saudável *(healthful)*.

heap montão, pilha.

heap (to) acumular, amontoar.

hear (to) ouvir.

    to hear from ter notícias de.

heart coração.

    by heart de cor.

    at heart no fundo.

    to take to heart tomar a sério.

heart attack ataque cardíaco.

hearth lareira, lar.

hearty cordial *(warm)*, entusiástico.

heat calor.

heat (to) aquecer.

heater aquecedor.

heating aquecimento.

heaven céu.

    Heavens! Céus!

heavy pesado.

hedge cerca viva, sebe.

heel calcanhar *(of foot)*; salto *(of shoe)*.

height altura.

heir herdeiro.

helicopter helicóptero.

hell inferno.

Hello! Alô! Olá!

help ajuda, auxílio (x = s).

help (to) ajudar.

    to help oneself to servir-se.

helper ajudante.

helpful útil, proveitoso *(thing)*; prestativo *(person)*.

hemisphere hemisfério.

hen galinha.

her a ela, seu, sua, lhe.

herb erva.

here aqui; cá.

    Here it is. Aqui está.

    Come here. Venha cá.

    around here por aqui.

    Here I go! Aí vou eu!

    near here perto daqui.

hereafter daqui em diante.

herein incluso, anexo (x = ks).

hero herói.

heroic heróico.

heroine heroína.

heroism heroísmo.

herring arenque.

hers seu, sua, dela; o seu, a sua, os seus, as suas.

herself ela mesma, si mesma; se, si.

    by herself sozinha.

    she herself ela mesma.

hesitant hesitante, indeciso.

hesitate (to) hesitar, vacilar.

hesitation hesitação, indecisão.

Hi! Oi!

    to say hi to cumprimentar.

hidden escondido, oculto.

hide (to) esconder, esconder-se, ocultar.

hideous horrível, horrendo.

high alto, elevado; caro *(price)*.

    It is two meters high. Tem dois metros de altura.

higher mais alto; superior.

highway rodovia, estrada.

hill colina, morro; ladeira *(slope)*.

him o, ele, lhe.

himself ele mesmo; si mesmo; se, si.

hinder (to) impedir, estorvar.

hindrance impedimento, estorvo, obstáculo.

hinge dobradiça, gonzo.

hint insinuação, alusão, sugestão.

    Give me a hint. Me dá uma pista.

    to take the hint compreender.

hip quadril, anca.

hire (to) contratar.

his seu, sua, seus, suas, o seu, a sua, os seus, as suas, dele.

Hispanic hispânico.

hiss (to) silvar *(wind, etc.)*; chiar *(steam)*.

historian historiador.

historic histórico.

history história.

hit golpe, pancada *(blow)*; êxito *(song, etc.)*.

hit (to) bater em.

hive colméia.

hoarse rouco.

hoe enxada (x = sh).

hog porco.

hold (to) ter *(in one's hands, arms, etc.)*; agarrar, segurar *(to grasp, hold on to)*; caber, conter *(to contain)*; ter, ocupar *(a job, etc.)*.

    to hold a meeting realizar uma reunião.

    to hold one's own manter-se.

    to be on hold ficar pendurado.

    to hold hands dar mãos.

hole buraco.

holiday feriado.

holy santo.
    Holy cow! Credo!
homage homenagem.
home casa, lar, residência.
    at home em casa.
homely feio.
homemade caseiro, feito em casa.
homosexual homossexual; bicha *(colloquial)*.
Honduran hondurenho.
honest honesto; sincero, franco.
honesty honestidade.
honey mel.
honeymoon lua-de-mel.
honk (to) buzinar *(car horn)*.
honor honra.
honor (to) honrar.
honorable honroso, honrado.
hoof casco, pata.
hook gancho; anzol *(for fishing)*.
hope esperança.
hope (to) esperar.
hopeful esperançoso.
hopeless desesperado *(depressed)*; incorrigível *(irremediable)*.
horizon horizonte.
horizontal horizontal.
horn chifre *(of animals)*; buzina *(of car)*; corneta, trompa *(music)*.
horrible horrível.
horror horror.
horse cavalo.
    on horseback a cavalo.
hosiery meias.
hospitable hospitaleiro.
hospital hospital.
hospitality hospitalidade.
host hospedeiro *(in hotel, etc.)* anfitrião *(of party)*.
hostess hospedeira; anfitriã.
hot quente.
hot dog cachorro-quente.
hotel hotel.
hour hora.
house casa.
household família, casa.
housekeeper governanta.
housemaid empregada.
housewife dona de casa.
how como; que; quanto.
    How are you? Como vai? Como está?
    How many? Quantos?
    How much? Quanto?
    How far? A que distância?
    How long? Quanto tempo?
    How pretty! Que linda!
    How old is she? Quantos anos ela tem?
    How about a beer? Que tal uma cerveja?
however porém, todavia.
hug abraço.

huge imenso, enorme.
human humano.
    human race raça humana.
humane humano, humano, humanitário.
humanity humanidade.
humble humilde.
humiliate (to) humilhar.
humiliation humilhação.
humility humildade.
humor humor.
humorous cômico (cómico), engraçado.
hundred cem.
    two hundred duzentos.
hundredth centésimo.
hunger fome.
hungry (be) estar com fome, ter fome.
hunt (to) caçar.
hunter caçador.
hunting caça.
hurry pressa.
    to be in a hurry estar com pressa, ter pressa.
hurt (to) machucar, ferir *(physically)*; ofender *(one's feelings)*.
husband marido, esposo.
hydrant hidrante.
hygiene higiene.
hymn hino.
hyperbole hipérbole.
hypertension hipertensão.
hyphen hífen.
hypnotism hipnotismo.
hypnotize (to) hipnotizar.
hypocrisy hipocrisia.
hypocrite hipócrita.
hysteria histeria.
hysterical histérico.

I

I eu.
    I'm the one eu é.
Iberian ibero, ibérico.
ice gelo.
ice cream sorvete.
ice skate (to) patinar (no gelo).
idea idéia (ideia).
ideal ideal.
idealism idealismo.
identical idêntico.
identification identificação.
identify (to) identificar.
identity identidade.
idiocy idiotismo.
idiot idiota, imbecil.
idle ocioso.
idleness ociosidade, ócio.

if se.
   if not senão.
   even if ainda que, mesmo que.
   If I may. Com licença.
ignorance ignorância.
ignorant ignorante.
ignore (to) não saber; não fazer caso de; ignorar.
ill doente *(sick)*; mau *(bad)*; mal *(badly)*.
   ill will má vontade.
illegal ilegal.
illegible ilegível.
illiteracy analfabetismo.
illiterate analfabeto.
illness doença.
illogical ilógico, absurdo.
illuminate (to) iluminar, alumiar.
illumination iluminação.
illusion ilusão.
illustrate (to) ilustrar.
illustration ilustração, gravura.
image imagem.
imagery imaginação, fantasia.
imaginary imaginário.
imagination imaginação.
imaginative imaginativo.
imagine (to) imaginar, supor.
   Just imagine! Imagine!
imitate (to) imitar.
imitation imitação.
immediate imediato.
immediately imediatamente.
immense imenso.
immigrant imigrante.
immigrate (to) imigrar.
immigration imigração.
imminent iminente.
immoderate imoderado, excessivo.
immoral imoral.
immorality imortalidade.
immortal imortal.
immortality imoralidade.
impartial imparcial.
impatience impaciência.
impatient impaciente.
imperative imperativo.
imperceptible imperceptível.
imperfect imperfeito.
impersonal impessoal.
impertinence impertinência.
impertinent impertinente.
impetuous impetuoso, impulsivo.
implement instrumento, utensílio, ferramenta.
implied implícito.
imply (to) implicar, significar.
impolite descortês.
import (to) importar.
importance importância.
important importante.

importation importação.
importer importador.
impose (to) impor *(rules, etc.)*. abusar de *(impose on)*.
imposing imponente.
impossibility impossibilidade.
impossible impossível.
impress (to) impressionar.
impression impressão.
   to have the impression ter a impressão.
impressive impressionante.
imprison (to) encarcerar.
improbable improvável.
improper impróprio.
improve (to) melhorar; progredir *(pupils, etc.)*. melhorar-se, restabelecer-se *(health)*.
improvement melhora, melhoria, progresso.
improvise (to) improvisar.
imprudence imprudência.
imprudent imprudente.
impure impuro.
in em.
   in fact de fato (de facto).
   in the afternoon de tarde, pela tarde.
   in a week daqui a uma semana, daqui a oito dias.
   to be in (the office) estar em casa, estar no escritório.
   in general em geral.
   in part em parte.
   in reality na verdade.
   in spite of apesar de.
   in vain em vão.
   in writing por escrito.
inability inabilidade, inaptidão, incapacidade.
inaccessible inacessível.
inaccuracy inexatidão (inexactidão) (x = z).
inaccurate inexato (inexacto) (x = z), incorreto (incorrecto).
inactive inativo (inactivo).
inadequate inadequado.
inaugurate (to) inaugurar.
incapability incapacidade.
incapable incapaz.
incapacity incapacidade.
inch polegada.
incident incidente.
inclination inclinação.
include (to) incluir, abranger, compreender.
inclusive inclusivo.
incoherent incoerente.
income renda.
   income tax imposto de renda.
incomparable incomparável.
incompatible incompatível.
incomprehensible incompreensível.
inconsistent inconsistente.
inconvenience inconveniência.
inconvenience (to) incomodar.

inconvenient inconveniente.
incorrect incorreto (incorrecto).
increase aumento.
increase (to) aumentar.
incredible incrível.
incurable incurável.
indebted em dívida; reconhecido, obrigado
   (for kindness shown).
indecent indecente, imoral.
indeed realmente, na verdade, de fato (facto),
   certamente, naturalmente.
indefinite indefinido.
independence independência.
independent independente; auto-suficiente.
indescribable indescritível.
index índice, índex.
index finger dedo indicador, índice, índex.
indicate (to) indicar.
indifference indiferença.
indifferent indiferente.
indigestion indigestão.
indignant indignado, furioso.
indignation indignação, raiva.
indirect indireto (indirecto).
indiscreet indiscreto, imprudente.
indispensable indispensável.
indisputable indisputável.
indistinct indistinto.
individual *adj.* individual, particular; *n.*
   indivíduo.
individuality individualidade.
individually individualmente.
indivisible indivisível.
indolence indolência, preguiça.
indolent indolente, preguiçoso.
indoors dentro de casa, em casa.
indulge (to) comprazer *(a person);* entregar-se
   a *(to indulge in).*
indulgence indulgência, tolerância.
indulgent indulgente.
industrial industrial.
industrious industrioso, trabalhador, diligente.
industry indústria.
inequality desigualdade.
inevitable inevitável.
inexcusable indesculpável, imperdoável.
inexhaustible inesgotável.
inexpensive barato.
inexperience inexperiência.
inexperienced inexperiente, sem experiência.
infallible infalível.
infant bebê (bebé).
infantry infantaria.
infection infecção.
infectious infeccioso, contagioso.
infer (to) inferir, deduzir, concluir.
inference inferência, dedução.
inferior inferior.
inferiority inferioridade.

infinite infinito.
infinitive infinitivo.
infinity infinidade, infinito.
influence influência.
influence (to) influenciar, influir.
influential influente.
influenza gripe, influenza.
information informação.
   information desk guichê (guichet) de
      informações.
infrequent infreqüente (infrequente), raro.
infrequently infreqüentemente
   (infrequentemente), raramente.
ingenious engenhoso.
ingenuity engenho.
ingratitude ingratidão.
inhabit (to) habitar, ocupar, morar.
inhabitant habitante.
inherit (to) herdar.
inheritance herança.
initial inicial.
initiative iniciativa.
injure (to) ferir, machucar *(physically);*
   prejudicar *(reputation, etc.).*
injurious prejudicial.
injury ferimento *(physical);* dano *(damage).*
injustice injustiça.
ink tinta.
inkwell tinteiro.
inland interior.
inn hospedaria, estalagem, pousada.
innate inato.
inner interno, interior.
innkeeper hospedeiro, estalajadeiro.
innocence inocência.
innocent inocente.
insane insano, demente.
insanity insanidade; demência.
inscribe (to) inscrever.
inscription inscrição, dedicatória.
insect inseto (insecto).
insecticide inseticida (insecticida).
insecure inseguro.
insecurity insegurança.
insensible insensível.
inseparable inseparável.
insert (to) inserir, introduzir.
insertion inserção.
inside dentro; interior.
   on the inside por dentro.
   toward the inside para dentro.
   inside out às avessas.
insignificance insignificância.
insignificant insignificante, sem importância.
insincere insincero, não sincero.
insincerity insinceridade, falta de sinceridade.
insist (to) insistir.
insistence insistência.
insolence insolência.

insolent insolente.

inspect (to) inspecionar (inspeccionar), examinar (x = z).

inspection inspeção (inspecção).

inspector inspetor (inspector).

inspiration inspiração.

install (to) instalar.

installation instalação.

instance instância; exemplo (x = z); caso.
    for instance por exemplo.
    in this instance neste caso.

instead of em lugar de, em vez de.

instinct instinto.

institute instituto.

institute (to) instituir, estabelecer.

institution instituição.

instruct (to) instruir, ensinar.

instruction instrução, ensino.

instructive instrutivo.

instructor instrutor.

instrument instrumento.

insufficiency insuficiência, deficiência.

insufficient insuficiente, deficiente.

insult insulto.

insult (to) insultar, ofender.

insulting insultante, ofensivo.

insuperable insuperável.

insurance seguro.

intact intato (intacto).

integral integral.

intellectual inteletual (intelectual).

intelligence inteligência.

intelligent inteligente.

intend (to) intentar, tencionar.
    to be intended for ter por finalidade.

intense intenso.

intensity intensidade.

intention intenção, propósito.

intentional intencional.

intentionally intencionalmente, de propósito.

interest interesse; juros (bank).

interest (to) interessar.

interesting interessante.

interior interior, interno.

intermission intervalo.

internal interno.

international internacional.

interpose (to) interpor.

interpret (to) interpretar.

interpretation interpretação.

interpreter intérprete.

interrupt (to) interromper.

interruption interrupção.

intersection cruzamento (roads); intersecção (lines, etc.).

interval intervalo.

intervention intervenção.

interview entrevista.

interview (to) entrevistar.

intestine intestino.

intimacy intimidade.

intimate íntimo.

intimidate (to) intimidar.

into em, dentro, para dentro.

intonation entonação.

intoxicate (to) embriagar.

intoxicating inebriante.

intoxication embriaguez.

intricate intricado, complicado, complexo (x = ks).

intrigue intriga, trama.

intrinsic intrínseco.

introduce (to) introduzir (a subject, etc.); apresentar (a person).

introduction introdução; apresentação (people).

intruder intruso.

intuition intuição.

invade (to) invadir.

invalid adj. inválido (person); inválido, nulo (void); n. inválido.

invasion invasão.

invent (to) inventar.

invention invenção.

inventor inventor.

invert (to) inverter (upside down, backwards); virar (inside out).

invest (to) investir.

investigate (to) investigar.

investigation investigação; inquérito (inquest).

investment investimento.

investor investidor.

invisible invisível.

invitation convite.

invite (to) convidar.

invoice fatura (factura).

involuntary involuntário.

involve (to) implicar, comprometer, envolver.

iodine iodo.

iris íris.

iron ferro (metal, and for ironing).

iron (to) passar a ferro (clothes).

ironic irônico (irónico).

ironing roupa a ser passada.

irony ironia.

irregular irregular.

irresolute irresoluto, indeciso.

irresponsible irresponsável.

irrigate (to) irrigar.

irrigation irrigação.

irritable irritável.

irritate (to) irritar.

irritation irritação.

island ilha.

isolation isolamento.

issue questão, assunto, tema (subject); número (magazine).

issue (to) publicar, lançar *(report, etc.);* distribuir *(equipment).*

it ele, ela, o, a, lhe; isto, este, esta. ["It" is not translated in phrases like "it's raining" (chove), "it's late" (é tarde), "it's two o'clock" (são duas horas), etc.].
  I have it. Tenho. Tenho-o *(m.).*
  I have it. Tenho. Tenho-a *(f.).*
  I said it. Eu o disse. Disse-o.
  Isn't it? Não é verdade? Não é?
  That's it. Isso é. E desta *(It's over). (indicating an object).*

Italian italiano.

itinerary itinerário.

its seu, sua, seus, suas, dele, dela, deles, delas.

itself si mesmo, si, si próprio, se.
  by itself por si, por si mesmo.
  in itself em si.

ivory marfim.

ivy hera.

J

jack macaco *(tool);* valete *(cards).*

jacket paletó, jaqueta; sobrecapa, capa (book).

jail cadeia, cárcere; xadrez (x = sh) Ⓑ.

jam geléia (geleia); aperto (a fix); engarrafamento *(traffic)*

janitor zelador, porteiro.

January janeiro (Janeiro).

Japanese japonês.

jar jarro *(large);* pote *(small)*

jaw mandíbula.

jazz jazz.

jealous ciumento.

jealousy ciúme.

jelly geléia (geleia); gelatina.

jerk (to) arrancar, sacudir.

Jesuit jesuíta.

jet jato (jacto).
  jet plane avião a jato.

Jew judeu *(male);* judia *(female).*

jewel jóia.

jewelry jóias.

jewelry store joalheria.

Jewish judeu, judaico.

job emprego *(position);* trabalho *(duties at work);* tarefa *(task).*

John Doe Fulano de Tal.

join (to) unir, juntar *(to put together);* unir-se, associar-se *(to unite);* afiliar-se a, incorporar-se a *(an organization).*

joint encaixe (x = sh) *(woodworking);* articulação *(body).*

joke piada, pilhéria, brincadeira.
  to play a joke on pregar peça em.
  to crack jokes lançar graças.

joke (to) gracejar, brincar.

jolly *adj.* alegre, jovial, convival.

jostle (to) acotovelar, empurrar.

journal diário *(diary),* jornal.

journalist jornalista.

journalistic jornalístico.

journey viagem.

jovial jovial.

joy alegria.

joyful alegre.

judge juiz.

judge (to) julgar.

judgment julgamento.

judicial judicial, judiciário.

juice suco, sumo.

juicy suculento; picante *(gossip, etc.).*

July julho (Julho).

jump salto, pulo.

jump (to) saltar, pular.
  Go jump in a lake! Vai ver se chove!

June junho (Junho).

junior *adj.* júnior, mais jovem, mais novo, mais moço; subordinado.
  junior partner sócio mais novo.
  Paul Fountain Jr. Paulo Fontes Júnior.

juror jurado.

jury júri.

just *adj.* justo; *adv.* justamente, exatamente (exactamente) (x = z), somente.
  just as I came in no momento em que eu entrava.
  just a moment um momento.
  just now agora mesmo.
  I just wanted to eu somente queria.
  to have just acabar de.
  I have just come. Acabo de chegar.
  Just as you please. Como você quiser.
  He's just a loser. Ele é apenas um falhado.

justice justiça.

justifiable justificável.

justification justificação.

justify (to) justificar.

juvenile *adj.* juvenil, menor de idade.

K

keep (to) guardar, manter, reter.
  to keep away manter afastado.
  to keep for oneself reter, deter.
  to keep from impedir *(hinder);* abster-se *(refrain).*
  to keep quiet calar-se, ficar quieto.
  to keep in mind ter em mente.
  to keep one's word cumprir (a) sua promessa.
  to keep a secret guardar um segredo.
  to keep in touch manter-se em contacto.

keep to the right conserve (à) sua direita.
kernel semente, grão.
kerosene querosene.
kettle bule *(for tea)*; caldeirão, chaleira
(cauldron).
key chave *(for doors, etc.)*; tecla *(piano,*
computer, etc.).
keyboard teclado.
kick pontapé, chute.
kick (to) dar pontapé, chutar.
kidney rim.
kill (to) matar.
kilo quilo *(kilogram).*
kilogram quilograma.
kilometer quilômetro (quilómetro).
kin família, parentes.
kind *adj.* bom, amável, bondoso; *n.* classe,
espécie, gênero (género).
kindergarten jardim de infância.
kind-hearted bondoso, de bom coração.
kindly amavelmente, cordialmente.
   Kindly do it. Tenha a bondade de fazê-lo.
kindness bondade, amabilidade.
king rei.
kiss beijo.
kiss (to) beijar.
kitchen cozinha.
kite papagaio, pipa.
kitten gatinho.
knee joelho.
kneel (to) ajoelhar(-se).
knife faca.
knit (to) tricotar.
knock golpe, pancada; batida *(on door).*
knock (to) dar pancadas, bater *(on door).*
knot nó.
know (to) saber; conhecer *(be acquainted*
with).
knowledge conhecimento.
knuckle nó dos dedos.

L

label rótulo, etiqueta.
labor trabalho, labor.
laboratory laboratório.
laborer trabalhador, operário.
lace *n.* renda.
lack falta, carência, deficiência.
lack (to) carecer de, faltar.
ladder escada de mão.
lady senhora.
   Ladies and gentlemen. Senhoras e
   senhores. Meus senhores e minhas
   senhoras.
lake lago.
lamb cordeiro.

lame coxo (x = sh), manco, aleijado.
lame (be) coxear (x = sh), manear.
lameness coxeadura (x = sh).
lament lamento, queixa.
lament (to) lamentar, lamentar, se de.
lamp lâmpada.
land terra *(ground)*; terreno *(terrain)*; país,
terra *(country).*
land (to) desembarcar *(ship)*; aterrar *(plane).*
landing desembarque *(from a ship)*;
aterrissagem *(of an airplane)*; patamar *(a*
staircase).
landlady proprietária.
landlord proprietário.
landscape paisagem.
language língua, idioma.
languid lânguido.
languish (to) languir.
languor langor, languidez.
lantern lanterna.
lap colo *(body)*; volta *(around track).*
laptop computer computador portátil.
lard toucinho, banha.
large grande.
   at large em liberdade.
large-scale em grande escala.
lark cotovia.
larynx laringe.
laser printer impresora a laser.
last *adj.* último, derradeiro, passado; *adv.* por
fim, finalmente, por último.
   at last finalmente.
   last night ontem à noite.
   last week a semana passada.
   last year o ano passado.
   the last time I saw her ... A última vez
   que a vi ...
last (to) durar.
lasting duradouro, durável.
latch trinco.
late *adj.* tarde.
   to be late chegar tarde.
   late in the year no fim do ano.
lately ultimamente, recentemente, há pouco
tempo.
lateness atraso, demora.
later mais tarde.
latest último.
   the latest style a última moda.
   at the latest no mais tardar.
lather espuma.
Latin *adj.* latino; *n.* latim.
Latin American latino-americano.
laudable louvável.
laugh riso, risada; gargalhada *(guffaw).*
laugh (to) rir, rir-se.
   to make someone laugh fazer rir.
   to laugh at rir de.
laughable risível, ridículo.

laughter riso, risada.

launder (to) lavar e passar.

laundry lavanderia *(laundry shop)*; roupa para lavar *(clothes to be washed)*; roupa lavada *(laundered clothes)*.

lavish pródigo, generoso *(spending)*; luxuoso *(party, etc.)*.

law lei; jurisprudência *(legal science)*; direito *(body of laws)*; regra *(rule)*.
  law school faculdade de direito.
  international law direito internacional.

lawful legal, lícito.

lawn gramado.

lawyer avogado.

laxative laxativo (x = ch).

lay (to) pôr.
  to lay aside pôr de lado.
  to lay hold of agarrar.
  to lay off despedir.

laziness preguiça.

lazy preguiçoso.

lead *(metal)* chumbo.

lead (to) conduzir, guiar.
  to lead to levar a.
  to lead the way mostrar o caminho.

leader líder ⑧, condutor, chefe; guia *(guide)*; diretor *(director)*.

leadership liderança, direção (direcção), chefia, comando.

leading principal, primeiro.
  leading article artigo de fundo.
  leading man galã, ator principal.

leaf folha.

lean (to) inclinar-se.
  to lean back encostar-se.
  to lean out or over debruçar-se.

leaning inclinação, propensão, tendência.

leap salto, pulo.

leap (to) saltar, pular.
  by leaps and bounds em flecha.

learn (to) aprender *(to acquire knowledge, skill)*; tomar conhecimento de, saber de *(to find out about)*.

learned erudito, douto.

learning erudição, saber.

lease arrendamento.

lease (to) arrendar, alugar.

least mínimo, o mínimo, menor, menos.
  at least pelo menos, ao menos.
  not in the least de maneira alguma, de modo algum.
  the least possible o menos possível.

leather couro.

leave (to) deixar.
  to leave a message deixar um recado.

lecture *n.* conferência, discurso, palestra *(a speech)*; repreensão *(reprimand)*.

lecturer conferencista.

left *adj.* esquerdo; *n.* esquerda.

left hand mão esquerda.
  to the left à esquerda.
  left-handed canhoto.
  There are two left. Ficam (restam) dois.

leg perna *(person)*; pata *(table)*.

legal legal, lícito.

legend lenda *(story)*; legenda *(caption)*.

legible legível.

legislation legislação.

legislator legislador.

legislature legislatura.

leisure lazer, folga, ócio.

lemon limão.

lemonade limonada.

lend (to) emprestar, dar emprestado.
  to lend an ear prestar atenção.
  to lend a hand ajudar.

length comprimento.
  at length finalmente; detalhadamente *(extensively)*.

less menos.
  more or less mais ou menos.
  less and less cada vez menos.

lessen (to) reduzir, diminuir.

lesson lição.

let (to) deixar (x = sh), permitir.
  Let's go. Vamos.
  Let's see. Vejamos. Vamos ver.
  Let them go. Que se vão.
  to let someone alone deixar alguém em paz.
  to let go soltar.
  to let in deixar entrar.
  to let know avisar.

letter carta; letra *(of the alphabet)*.

lettuce alface.

level *adj.* plano, raso, nivelado; *n.* nível.

level off (to) nivelar.

liable sujeito, exposto *(exposed to)*; responsável por *(accountable)*; capaz de *(likely)*.

liar mentiroso.

liberal liberal.

liberty liberdade.

library biblioteca.

license licença, autorização.

lick (to) lamber.

lid tampa.

lie mentira.

lie (to) mentir *(tell a falsehood)*; deitar-se *(to lie down)*; jazer *(dead, in grave)*.

lieutenant tenente.

life vida.
  life preserver salva-vidas.
  lifeboat barco salva-vidas.
  life insurance seguro de vida.

lifetime tempo de vida.

lift (to) levantar, alçar.

light *n.* luz, lume, claridade, iluminação; *adj.* leve, ligeiro *(in weight)*; claro *(color)*.

light-hearted despreocupado, alegre.

light (to) acender *(a cigarette)*; iluminar *(to illuminate)*.

lightbulb lâmpada, lâmpada elétrica (eléctrica).

lighten (to) aliviar, mitigar.

lighthouse farol.

lighting iluminação.

lightness leveza.

lightning relâmpago, raio.

like parecido, semelhante *(similar)*.

    to be like ser semelhante.

    I've never seen anything like this. Nunca vi coisa destas.

like (to) querer, gostar de.

    I like him very much. Gosto muito dele.

    As you like. Como você quiser.

    Do you like it? Você gosta?

    I like it. Gosto.

    I don't like it. Não gosto.

    She looks like her mother. Ela se parece com a mãe.

likely provável.

likeness semelhança.

likewise igualmente, do mesmo modo.

liking afeição, simpatia, gosto.

limb membro.

lime cal.

limit limite.

limit (to) limitar.

limp (to) coxear (x = sh), mancar.

line linha.

line (to) forrar *(coat, etc.)*; linear *(streets)*.

to line up (to) alinhar, alinhar-se.

linen linho.

lining forro.

link elo.

link (to) unir, ligar.

lip lábio.

lipstick batom.

liquid líquido.

liquor bebida alcoólica, licor.

lisp cicio.

list lista.

listen (to) escutar.

literal literal, ao pé da letra.

literally literalmente, ao pé da letra.

literary literário.

literature literatura.

little pequeno *(size)*; pouco *(amount)*.

    a little um pouco.

    very little muito pouco.

    the little ones os pequenos, as crianças.

    little by little pouco a pouco.

live *adj.* vivo; ao vivo *(broadcast)*.

live (to) viver; morar *(to reside)*.

lively vivo, animado.

liver fígado.

living *adj.* vivo.

to make a living ganhar a vida.

living room sala de estar.

load carga.

load (to) carregar.

loaf pão.

loan empréstimo.

loan (to) emprestar.

lobby vestíbulo.

lobster lagosta.

local local.

locate (to) localizar, situar *(find)*; colocar *(situate)*.

location local, sítio *(place, locality)*; posição *(position)*.

lock fechadura.

lock (to) fechar à chave, trancar.

locomotive locomotiva.

locust gafanhoto.

lodging alojamento.

lodging house hospedaria, pensão.

log tora, tronco, lenho.

    logbook diário de bordo *(ship)*.

logic lógica.

logical lógico.

lonely solitário, só.

long *adj.* comprido, longo; *adv.* muito tempo, muito.

    It's five meters long. Tem cinco metros de comprimento.

    a long time ago há muito tempo.

    long-distance call telefonema interurbano.

    long ago há muito tempo.

    all day long o dia todo.

    not long ago não há muito tempo.

    How long ago? Quanto tempo há?

    How long? Quanto tempo?

longer *adj.* mais comprido; *adv.* mais tempo.

    How much longer? Quanto tempo mais?

    no longer não mais; já não.

    to long for ter saudades de, anelar por.

longing desejo, ânsia, saudade.

look olhar, olhada.

look (to) ver, olhar.

    Look! Olhe!

    to look for procurar, buscar.

    to look after cuidar de.

    to look like parecer-se com.

    to look forward to esperar.

    to look into examinar (x = z).

    to look as though it's going to rain parecer que vai chover.

    to look out ter cuidado (be careful).

    Look out! Cuidado!

    to look over (review) repassar.

    That dress looks good on you. Esse vestido lhe cai bem.

loose solto *(free)*; frouxo (x = sh) *(not tight)*.

loosen (to) desatar, soltar.

Lord Senhor, Deus.

lose (to) perder.
    to lose weight emagrecer.
loss perda.
    at a loss perplexo (x = ks), confuso.
lot (a) muito.
    a lot of money muito dinheiro.
loud alto.
love amor.
    to fall in love apaixonar-se (x = sh).
    to be in love estar apaixonado (x = sh).
love (to) amar, querer.
lovely encantador, lindo.
low baixo (x = sh).
lower mais baixo (x = sh), inferior.
    lower case letters letras minúsculas.
lower (to) baixar (x = sh), abaixar (x = sh),
    reduzir; arriar *(sails)*.
lowlife velhaco.
loyal leal, fiel.
loyalty lealdade.
luck sorte, fortuna.
    good luck boa sorte.
    bad luck azar.
    to have luck estar com sorte, ter sorte.
luckily felizmente, afortunadamente.
lucky afortunado.
luggage bagagem.
lukewarm morno, tépido *(water)*; indiferente
    (reaction).
lumber madeira.
luminous luminoso.
lunch almoço.
    to have lunch almoçar.
lung pulmão.
luxurious luxuoso (x = sh).
luxury luxo (x = sh).
    deluxe de luxo (x = sh).

M

machine máquina.
    answering machine máquina de
    contestação.
machinery maquinaria.
mad zangado *(angry)*.
    to get mad zangar-se.
made feito, fabricado.
madness loucura.
magazine revista.
magic *adj.* mágico; *n.* magia.
magistrate magistrado.
magnanimous magnânimo, generoso.
magnet ímã.
magnetic magnético.
magnificent magnífico.
magnify (to) aumentar, exagerar (x = z).
magnifying glass lente de aumento.

maid empregada, criada.
mail correio.
    e-mail correio eletrónico.
mailbox caixa (x = sh) de correio.
mailman carteiro.
main principal.
    main street rua principal.
    main reason motivo principal, razão
    principal.
mainly principalmente.
maintain (to) manter, conservar, sustentar
    (insist).
maintenance manutenção, conservação.
majestic majestoso.
majesty majestade.
major *adj.* maior, principal; *n.* major *(military)*.
majority maioria.
make (to) fazer, fabricar, produzir.
    to make sad entristecer, tornar triste.
    to make happy alegrar, tornar alegre.
    to make a living ganhar a vida.
    to make possible fazer possível.
    to make room for dar lugar para.
    to make known dar a conhecer.
    to make a mistake errar, enganar-se.
    to make a stop parar, fazer uma parada.
    to make friends fazer amizade com.
    to make fun of fazer troça de, zombar de.
    to make haste apressar-se.
    to make headway progredir, avançar.
    to make into converter.
    to make no difference não importar.
    to make out compreender, decifrar
    (understand).
    That makes me sick! Isso me enche o
    saco!
    to make the best of tirar o maior proveito
    de, tirar o melhor partido de.
    to make up one's mind decidir-se,
    resolver-se.
maker fabricante, criador.
malady doença.
male macho *(animal)*; masculino *(person)*.
malice malícia.
malicious malicioso, maligno.
man homem.
    young man jovem.
    Men *(as on a sign)* Senhores. Homens.
    Cavalheiros.
manage (to) administrar, governar, dirigir
    (organization); conseguir *(to succeed)*.
management administração, direção.
manager administrador, diretor (director);
    gerente *(sports)*.
manifest (to) manifestar.
mankind humanidade, raça humano.
manly másculo, viril, varonil.
manner maneira, modo.
manners maneiras, educação.

mansion mansão.

manual manual.

manufacture (to) manufaturar (manufacturar), fabricar.

manufacturer fabricante.

manuscript manuscrito.

many muitos.
 many times muitas vezes.
 as many as tantos quanto, tantos como.
 How many? Quantos?

map mapa.

maple bordo.

marble mármore; bolinha de gude (for children).

March março (Março).

march marcha.

march (to) marchar.

margin margem.

marijuana maconha.

marine marinho.

mark marca.

mark (to) marcar.

market mercado.

marketing marketing, mercadologia.

marriage matrimônio (matrimónio), casamento.

marry (to) casar-se com, casar.
 to get married casar-se.

marvel n. maravilha, prodígio.

marvel (to) maravilhar-se, admirar-se, estranhar.

marvelous maravilhoso.

marvelously maravilhosamente.

masculine masculino.

mask máscara.

mason pedreiro.

mass massa; missa (religious).

massage massagem.

massage (to) fazer massagem, dar massagem.

massive maciço, sólido.

mast mastro.

master mestre; dono, senhor.
 master copy cópia mestre.

masterpiece obra prima.

mat esteira.

match fósforo (to light with); partida, jogo (sports); aliança, casamento (marriage).

match (to) emparelhar, igualar; combinar (colors).

material material; pano, lecido (cloth).

maternal materno, maternal.

mathematical matemático.

mathematics matemática.

matinee matinê Ⓑ, vesperal.

matter matérial (substance); assunto, questão (question).
 an important matter um assunto importante.
 What's the matter? O que é que há?

no matter how bad it is . . . tão mal que seja . . .
 no matter what happens aconteça o que a conteçer.

matter (to) importar.
 It doesn't matter. Não importa.

mattress colchão.

mature adj. maduro.

mature (to) madurar, amadurecer.

maturity maturidade, madureza.

maximum máximo (x = s).

May maio (Maio).

may poder, ser possível.
 It may be. Pode ser. É possível.
 It may be true. Pode ser verdade.
 May I? Com licença. O senhor permite?

maybe talvez.

mayonnaise maionese.

mayor prefeito (administrador do concelho, presidente da câmara municipal).

maze labirinto.

me eu, me, mim.
 It's me! Sou eu!

meadow prado.

meal refeição.

mean adj. maldoso, cruel (unkind).

mean (to) significar, querer dizer; tencionar (intend).
 What do you mean? O que você quer dizer?

meaning propósito, intenção (intent); sentido, significado.

means meio, meios, recursos.
 by all means sem dúvida, certamente.
 by no means de nenhuma maneira.

meantime interim.

meanwhile entretanto, entrementes.

measure medida.
 in great measure em grande parte.
 to take measures tomar medidas.

measure (to) medir.

measurement medição, medida.

meat carne.

mechanic mecânico.

mechanical mecânico.

mechanically mecanicamente, maquinalmente.

mechanism mecanismo.

medal medalha.

meddle (to) intrometer-se, meter-se.

mediate (to) mediar.

medical médico.
 medical school faculdade de medicina.

medicine medicina (in general), remédio, medicamento (particular remedy).

medieval medieval.

meditate (to) meditar.

meditation meditação, contemplação.

Mediterranean Mediterrâneo.

medium *adj.* médio, mediano.
   medium-sized de tamanho médio.
meet (to) encontrar, encontrar-se, dar com *(to come across)*; conhecer *(for the first time)*; reunir-se *(to get together)*.
   Glad to meet you. (Tenho muito) prazer em conhecê-lo.
   I hope to meet you again. Espero ter o prazer de vê-lo de novo (tornar a vê-lo).
   Till we meet again. Até a vista.
meeting *n.* reunião; sessão *(congress, etc.)*.
melancholy *adj.* melancólico.
melody melodia.
melon melão.
melt (to) derreter; fundir *(metals)*.
member membro, sócio.
memorable memorável.
memorandum memorando.
memory memória.
mend (to) emendar, consertar; corrigir-se *(mend one's ways)*.
mental mental.
mention menção, alusão.
mention (to) mencionar.
menu menu, cardápio (ementa).
merchandise mercadorias.
merchant comerciante, negociante.
merciful misericordioso, compassivo, piedoso.
merciless impiedoso, despiadoso.
mercury mercúrio.
mercy piedade, misericórdia.
merit mérito.
merry alegre.
mess desordem, bagunça.
   to mess up bobeiar *(make a mistake)*.
message mensagem, recado.
messenger mensageiro.
metal *adj.* metálico; *n.* metal.
metamorphosis metamorfose.
metaphor metáfora.
metaphysics metafísica.
meteor meteoro.
meter metro *(measurement)*; medidor *(for gas, etc.)*.
method método.
methodical metódico.
methodically metodicamente.
metric métrico.
   metric system sistema métrico.
metropolis metrópole.
metropolitan metropolitano.
Mexican mexicano (x = sh).
microbe micróbio.
microcosm microcosmo.
microfiche microficha.
microfilm microfilme.
microfilm (to) microfilmar.
microphone microfone.

microscope microscópio.
microscopic microscópico.
microwave microonda.
   microwave oven forno de microondas.
midday meio-dia.
middle *adj.* médio; *n.* meio, centro.
   Middle Ages Idade Média.
   middle-aged de meia idade.
   middle-class da classe média.
   in the middle no meio, no centro.
midnight meia-noite.
might poder, força.
mighty poderoso, forte.
mild suave, brando, meigo; moderado *(moderate)*.
mile milha.
military militar.
milk leite.
milkman leiteiro.
milk shake milk-shake, batido de leite.
mill moinho; fábrica, engenho *(factory)*; usina *(steel mill, etc.)*.
miller moleiro.
million milhão.
millionaire milionário.
mind mente; idéia.
   to have in mind ter em mente, pensar em.
   to change one's mind mudar de idéia.
   to my mind . . . na minha idéia . . .
mine *pron.* meu, minha, meus, minhas, o meu, a minha, os meus, as minhas; *n.* mina.
   a friend of mine um amigo meu.
   your friends and mine (os) seus amigos e os meus.
miner mineiro.
mineral mineral.
miniature miniatura.
minimum mínimo.
minister ministro *(government)*; pastor *(religion)*.
minor *adj.* menor, secundário; *n.* menor de idade.
minority minoria; menoridade *(age)*.
mint menta *(plant)*; casa da moeda *(money)*.
minus menos.
minute minuto *(time)*.
   minute hand ponteiro dos minutos.
   Just a minute, please. Um minuto, por favor. Um momento, por favor.
   any minute de minuto em minuto.
   Wait a minute! Aguarde um momento!
miracle milagre.
miraculous milagroso, miraculoso.
mirror espelho.
misbehave (to) comportar-se mal.
misbehavior mau comportamento, má conduta.
mischief travessura, diabrura.
mischievous travesso.

miser avaro, sovina.
miserable miserável; tristonho *(unhappy)*.
misfortune infortúnio, desventura.
Miss senhorita, senhorinha.
miss (to) ter saudades de *(someone or something)*; perder *(bus, etc.)*; errar, não acertar *(mark, etc.)*.
   to miss the point não compreender o verdadeiro sentido.
mission missão.
missionary missionário.
mistake erro, engano, equívoco.
   by mistake por engano.
mistake (to) confundir com.
   to be mistaken enganar-se.
Mister senhor.
mistrust desconfiança.
mistrust (to) desconfiar de, suspeitar de.
misunderstand (to) entender mal, compreender mal.
misunderstanding malentendido, desentendimento.
mix (to) misturar, mesclar.
mixture mistura, mescla.
moan gemido.
moan (to) gemer.
mobilization mobilização.
mobilize (to) mobilizar.
mode modo.
model modelo.
modem modem.
moderate *adj.* moderado.
moderate (to) moderar.
moderately moderadamente.
moderation moderação.
modern moderno.
modest modesto.
modesty modéstia.
modify (to) modificar.
moist úmido.
moisten (to) umedecer.
moisture umidade.
moment momento.
   Just a moment! Um momento!
momentary momentâneo.
momentous importantíssimo.
monarch monaraca.
monarchy monarquia.
Monday segunda-feira, segunda.
money dinheiro.
monk monge.
monkey macaco.
monologue monólogo.
monopoly monopólio.
monosyllable monossílabo.
monotonous monótono.
monotony monotonia.
monster monstro.
monstrous monstruoso.

month mês.
monthly mensal.
monument monumento.
monumental monumental.
mood humor.
   to be in a good mood estar de bom humor.
moon lua.
moonlight luar.
moral *adj.* moral, ético.
morale moral, estado de espírito.
morbid mórbido.
more mais.
   more or less mais ou menos.
   one more outra vez, mais uma vez.
   no more não mais.
   the more . . . the better quanto mais . . . tanto melhor.
moreover além disso.
morning manhã.
   Good morning! Bom dia!
morsel bocado.
mortal mortal.
mortgage hipoteca.
mosquito mosquito.
moss musgo.
most o mais, os mais, o maior número, a maior parte, a maioria.
   at most quando muito.
   for the most part em geral, na maior parte.
   most of us a maior parte de nós.
moth traça.
mother mãe.
mother-in-law sogra.
motion movimento; moção, proposta *(at meeting)*.
motive motivo.
motor *n.* motor.
mount (to) montar.
mounting base, montagem *(base)*; suporte *(for instruments, etc.)*.
mountain montanha.
mountainous montanhoso.
mourn (to) lamentar.
mournful triste, pesaroso.
mourning luto.
   in mourning de luto.
mouse camundongo; rato.
mouth boca.
mouthful bocado.
movable móvel, móbil.
move (to) mexer-se, mover-se *(change position)*; mexer *(to cause to move)*, mudar-se *(to another house)*, afastar, deslocar *(to change places)*, jogar, fazer uma jogada *(in a game)*.
movement movimento.
movie filme.

movies cinema.
moving *adj.* comovente, tocante *(emotionally)*.
Mr. senhor, Sr.
Mrs. senhora, Sra.
much muito.
    as much tanto.
    as much as tanto . . . quanto,
        tanto . . . como.
    How much? Quanto?
    too much demais, demasiado.
    much the same quase o mesmo, mais ou
        menos o mesmo.
    much money muito dinheiro.
    so much the better tanto melhor.
    so much the worse tanto pior.
mud lama, lodo, barro.
muddy turvo, barrento.
mule mulo *(male)*, mula *(female)*.
multiple múltiplo.
multiplication multiplicação.
multiply (to) multiplicar.
murder assassínio.
murder (to) assassinar.
murderer assassino.
murmur *n.* murmúrio.
muscle músculo.
museum museu.
music música.
musical musical, músico.
musician músico.
must ter que, ter de, dever.
    I must go. Tenho que ir.
    It must be. Deve ser.
mustache bigode.
mustard mostarda.
mute mudo.
mutton carne de carneiro.
mutual mútuo.
my meu, minha, meus, minhas, o meu, a
    minha, os meus, as minhas.
    Oh my God! Meu Deus!
myself eu mesmo, me, para mim.
mysterious misterioso.
mystery mistério.

N

nail unha *(of finger)*; cravo *(for hammering)*.
nail polish esmalte de unhas.
nail (to) cravar, pregar.
naive ingênuo (ingénuo).
naked nu, despido.
name nome.
    first name prenome.
    surname sobrenome; apelido.
    What is your name? Qual é o seu nome?
        Como se chama?

    My name is . . . Chamo-me . . .
namely isto é, a saber.
nap soneca, cochilo.
napkin guardanapo.
narration narração.
narrative narrativa.
narrow estreito.
nation nação.
national nacional.
nationality nacionalidade.
nationalization nacionalização.
nationalize (to) nacionalizar.
native *adj.* nativo, indígena; *n.* natural.
    native land terra natal, pátria.
natural natural.
naturalist naturalista.
naturally naturalmente, claro.
naturalness naturalidade.
nature natureza; caráter (carácter), índole.
    good nature boa índole.
naughty travesso, levado.
naval naval.
navigable navegável.
navigator navegador, navegante.
navy marinha, armada.
near perto, perto de.
nearby perto, à mão; ali perto.
nearly quase, por pouco.
nearsighted míope.
nearsightedness miopia.
neat asseado, esmerado; em ordem,
    arrumado.
neatness asseio, limpeza.
necessarily necessariamente.
necessary necessário.
    to be necessary ser necessário, ser
        preciso.
necessitate (to) exigir, tornar necessário.
necessity necessidade.
    of necessity necessariamente.
neck pescoço.
necklace colar.
necktie gravata.
need necessidade.
need (to) necessitar, precisar de; faltar.
    to be in need of ter necessidade de,
        precisar de.
    to be in need estar necessitado.
    I need to go. Preciso ir.
needle agulha.
negative negativo.
    a negative answer uma resposta negativa.
neglect descuido, negligência.
neglect (to) descuidar.
neighbor vizinho.
neighborhood vizinhança.
neither *conj.* nem; *adj.* nenhum, nenhum dos
    dois; *pron.* nenhum.
    neither . . . nor nem . . . nem.

    neither one nor the other nem um nem outro.

nephew sobrinho.

nerve nervo; topete (*audacity*).

nervous nervoso.

nest ninho.

net rede.

network interligar (*computer*); rede (*broadcasting*).

neuter neutro.

neutral neutro; ponto mortu (*car*).

never nunca, jamais.

    never again nunca mais.

nevertheless não obstante, todavia, contudo.

new novo.

    new moon lua nova.

    New Year ano novo.

news notícias, notícia (*piece of news*).

newspaper jornal, diário.

newsstand banca de jornais, quiosque.

New York Nova Iorque.

next seguinte, próximo (x = s). ~

    the next day no dia seguinte.

    (the) next week a semana que vem.

    (the) next time a próxima vez.

    next to ao lado de, junto a.

    Who's next? Quem segue?

nice agradável, simpático, amável; bonito, lindo; bom.

nickname apelido, alcunha.

niece sobrinha.

night noite.

    by night de noite.

    good night boa noite.

    last night ontem à noite.

nightclub boate, clube.

nightfall anoitecer.

nightmare pesadelo.

nighttime noite.

nine nove.

nine hundred novecentos.

nineteen dezenove (dezanove).

nineteenth décimo nono.

ninetieth nonagésimo.

ninety noventa.

ninth nono, nona parte.

no não; nenhum, nenhuma.

    no other nenhum outro.

    no one ninguém.

    no longer já não.

    no more não mais.

    no matter não importa.

    (in) no way de modo algum.

    No admittance. É proibida a entrada.

    No smoking. É proibido fumar.

    No it's not. Nãoé não.

nobility nobreza.

noble nobre.

nobody ninguém.

    nobody else ninguém mais.

nod (to) inclinar a cabeça, acenar com a cabeça; cabecear (*become sleepy*).

noise barulho, ruído.

noisy barulhento, ruidoso.

nominative nominativo.

none ninguém, nenhum, nada.

    none of us nenhum de nós.

nonsense tolice, asneira.

noon meio-dia.

nor nem.

    neither . . . nor . . . nem . . . nem . . .

normal normal.

normally normalmente.

north norte.

    North America América do Norte.

    North American norte-americano.

northeast nordeste.

northern do norte, setentrional.

nose nariz.

nostril narina.

not não; nem.

    if not se não.

    not any nenhum.

    not one nem um.

    not a word nem uma palavra.

    not at all de modo algum.

    not yet ainda não.

    not even nem sequer.

notable notável.

note nota, bilhete; cédula (bank note).

note (to) anotar, notar; reparar em, observar.

notebook caderno.

nothing nada.

    nothing doing nada disso, não pode ser.

    It's nothing. Não é nada.

    nothing much pouca coisa.

    for nothing grátis; em vão (in vain).

notice aviso, anúncio.

notice (to) notar, observar, perceber; dar conta de.

notwithstanding não obstante, apesar de, embora, ainda que.

noun nome, substantivo.

nourish (to) alimentar, nutrir.

nourishment alimento, nutrição.

novel romance, novela.

novelist romancista, novelista.

novelty novidade, inovação.

November novembro (Novembro).

now agora, pois bem.

    for now para já.

    until now até agora.

    now and then de vez em quando.

    Is it ready now? Já está pronto?

nowadays hoje em dia.

nowhere em nenhuma parte, em lugar algum.

nuclear nuclear.

nucleus núcleo.

number número.
numerous numeroso.
nun freira, monja.
nurse *n.* enfermeira *(f.)*, enfermeiro *(m.)*.
nursery quarto de crianças.
nut noz; amêndoa; porca *(for a bolt)*.

O

oak carvalho.
oar remo.
oat aveia.
oath juramento.
oatmeal farinha de aveia.
obedience obediência.
obedient obediente.
obey (to) obedecer.
object objeto (objecto), objetivo (objectivo); complemento *(grammar)*.
object (to) opor-se, objetar (objectar).
objection objeção (objecção).
objective objetivo (objectivo), propósito.
obligation obrigação.
oblige (to) obrigar, forçar.
oblique oblíquo.
obscure obscuro, pouco conhecido.
observation observação.
observatory observatório.
observe (to) observar, notar, perceber.
observer observador.
observing observador, atento.
obstacle obstáculo.
obstinacy teimosia, obstinação.
obstinate teimoso, obstinado.
obstruct (to) obstruir.
obstruction obstrução, impedimento.
obtain (to) obter, conseguir.
obvious óbvio.
occasion ocasião, oportunidade.
occasional pouco freqüente (frequente).
occasionally de vez em quando.
occidental ocidental.
occupation ocupação; emprego, profissão *(job)*.
occupy (to) ocupar.
occur (to) ocorrer, acontecer.
occurrence ocorrência, acontecimento.
ocean oceano.
  ocean liner vapor, transatlântico.
o'clock horas.
  at nine o'clock às nove (horas).
  It's ten o'clock. São dez (horas).
October outubro (Outubro).
odd ímpar *(number)*; raro, estranho *(strange)*.
  odds and ends miudezas.
of de, do, da.
  to think of pensar em.

of course claro que, naturalmente.
of himself por si mesmo.
It's twenty of two. Faltam vinte para as duas. É uma hora e quarenta minutos.
That's very kind of you. O senhor é muito amável.
off desligado *(TV, etc.)*; apagado *(light)*; fechado *(faucet)*.
  off and on de vez em quando.
  The meeting is off. Cancelaram a reunião.
  off the coast perto da costa.
  day off dia de folga.
  to take off tirar *(coat, etc.)*.
offend (to) ofender.
  to be offended ressentir-se.
offense ofensa, injúria.
offensive *adj.* ofensivo, desagradável; *n.* ofensiva, ataque.
offer oferta, oferecimento, proposta.
offer (to) oferecer, propor.
offering oferecimento; oferenda, oblação *(gift, oblation)*.
office escritório, repartição *(a building, a room, etc.)*; cargo, posição, posto *(position)*.
officer oficial.
official oficial.
often muitas vezes, freqüentemente (frequentemente).
oil óleo, petróleo; azeite *(olive or vegetable)*.
  oil painting pintura a óleo.
ointment ungüento (unguento).
old velho, antigo.
  to be twenty years old ter vinte anos.
  old man velho.
  old age velhice.
  old maid solteirona.
olive azeitona, oliva.
  olive oil azeite (de oliva).
  olive tree oliveira.
omelette omeleta.
omission omissão.
omit (to) omitir.
on sobre, em cima de, em; a, ao; com, por; ligado *(TV, etc.)*; aceso *(light)*; aberto *(faucet)*.
  on the table sobre a mesa.
  on the train no trem (comboio).
  on that occasion naquela ocasião.
  on the left à esquerda.
  on board a bordo.
  on foot a pé.
  on credit a crédito.
  on time na hora.
  on my part de minha parte.
  on the average em média.
  on the contrary pelo contrário.
  on the whole geralmente, em geral.
  on Monday na segunda.

once uma vez.
    once and for all uma vez por todas.
    at once imediatamente.
    all at once de repente, subitamente.
one um, uma.
    one by one um por um.
    this one este.
    the blue one o azul.
one hundred cem.
oneself si, se, si mesmo.
one thousand mil.
one-way de mão única (de um sentido, sentido
    único) (street).
onion cebola.
only adj. só, único; adv. só, somente, apenas.
opaque opaco.
open aberto.
    open air ar livre.
open (to) abrir.
opening abertura.
opera ópera.
operate (to) funcionar, fazer funcionar
    (machine); operar (surgery).
operation operação (surgery); funcionamento
    (machine).
opinion opinião.
    in my opinion a meu ver.
opponent oponente, antagonista.
opportune oportuno.
opportunity oportunidade.
oppose (to) opor-se, resistir.
opposite oposto, contrário.
opposition oposição.
oppress (to) oprimir.
oppression opressão.
optic(al) ótico (óptico).
optician ótico (óptico), oculista.
optimism otimismo (optimismo).
optimistic otimista (optimista).
or ou.
oracle oráculo.
oral oral, verbal.
orange laranja.
oratory oratória.
orchard pomar.
orchestra orquestra.
order ordem, pedido (of goods).
    in order that a fim de que, para que.
order (to) mandar, comandar; pedir,
    encomendar (goods).
ordinal ordinal.
    ordinal number número ordinal.
ordinarily geralmente, ordinariamente.
ordinary usual, ordinário.
organ órgão.
organic orgânico.
organism organismo.
organization organização.
organize (to) organizar.

organizer organizador.
orient oriente.
oriental oriental.
origin origem.
original original.
originality originalidade.
originate (to) originar; originar-se, surgir.
ornament ornamento, adorno.
orphan órfão.
ostentation ostentação.
other outro, outra, outros, outras.
    the other day o outro dia.
    the others os outros.
    Give me the other one. Dê-me o outro.
ouch! ui!
ought dever.
    You ought to do it. Você devia fazê-lo.
ounce onça.
our, ours nosso, nossa, nossos, nossas, o
    nosso, a nossa, os nossos, as nossas.
out fora.
    out of breath sem fôlego, esbaforido.
    out of date antiquado, fora de moda.
    out of doors ao ar livre.
    out of order avariado, enguiçado.
    out of place fora do seu lugar, deslocado.
    out of print esgotado.
    out of respect for por respeito a.
    out of style fora de moda.
    out of work sem trabalho, desempregado.
    out of control fora do controle.
outcome resultado.
outdoor(s) ao ar livre.
outline perfil, esboço, esquema, contorno,
    croqui Ⓑ.
outline (to) esboçar, delinear.
output produção, rendimento.
outrage ultraje.
outrageous ultrajante.
outside externo, exterior; fora, fora de.
outstanding saliente, eminente,
    extraordinário; pendente, a pagar (to be
    paid).
outward externo, exterior; aparente.
    outward bound rumo ao exterior.
oven forno.
over sobre, por cima de; ao outro lado; mais
    de; por; em.
    overnight durante a noite.
    to stay over the weekend passar o fim de
        semana.
    to be over ter passado; acabar-se;
        terminar-se (done).
    all over por toda parte.
    all over the world por todo o mundo.
    over again outra vez, mais uma vez.
    over and over repetidas vezes.
overcoat sobretudo.
overcome (to) vencer, superar, conquistar.

overflow (to) transbordar.
overseas ultramarino, de ultramar.
oversight inadvertência, descuido.
overtake (to) ultrapassar.
overwhelm (to) esmagar, sobrepujar.
overwhelming esmagador, irresistível.
overwork trabalho excessivo, trabalho em
    excesso.
overwork (to) trabalhar demais, fazer
    trabalhar demais.
owe (to) dever.
    owing to devido a.
owl coruja.
own próprio.
    This is your own. Isto é o seu.
    I'll do it on my own. Eu farei por minha
        própria conta.
    our own (o) nosso próprio.
    to be on your own estar por sua conta.
own (to) possuir, ter, ser dono de.
owner dono, proprietário.
ox boi.
oyster ostra.

P

pace passo.
pack (to) empacotar, carregar, fazer a mala.
package pacote, embrulho.
packaging embalagem.
paddle remo curto *(oar)*.
paddle (to) remar *(boat)*.
page página.
page (to) mandar chamar por bip.
pager bip.
pail balde.
pain dor.
    He is such a pain! Ele é um tão bicho!
painful doloroso, penoso.
paint pintura, tinta de pintar.
paint (to) pintar.
painter pintor.
painting pintura, quadro.
pair *n.* par *(shoes, etc.);* casal *(couple);* dupla
    (duo).
pajamas pijama.
palace palácio.
palate palato, paladar.
pale pálido.
    to turn pale empalidecer.
paleness palidez.
palm palma *(of the hand).*
palm tree palmeira.
pamphlet panfleto.
pan panela, caçarola.
pancake panqueca.
pane vidraça.

panel painel.
panic pânico.
pant (to) ofegar, arfar.
pantry despensa, copa.
pants calças.
papa papai, papá ℗.
paper papel.
    writing paper papel de escrever.
    newspaper jornal, diário.
paperback brochura.
paperwork papelada.
parade parada, desfile.
paradise paraíso.
paragraph parágrafo.
parallel paralelo.
paralysis paralisia.
paralyze (to) paralisar.
parcel pacote, embrulho.
    parcel post encomenda postal.
pardon perdão.
    I beg your pardon. Perdoe(-me).
        Desculpe (-me).
pardon (to) perdoar, desculpar.
parentheses parêntese, parêntesis.
parents pais.
parish paróquia, freguesia.
park parque.
park (to) estacionar.
parking estacionamento.
    parking lot parque de estacionamento.
    parking space vaga.
parliament parlamento.
parliamentary parlamentar.
parlor sala, salão.
parrot papagaio.
parsley salsa.
part parte.
    a great part of, most of a maior parte de.
    for my part de minha parte.
    he did his part ele cumpriu com o seu
        dever.
    to play the part of desempenhar o
        papel de.
    to play a part in desempenhar um
        papel em.
partial parcial.
partiality parcialidade.
partially parcialmente.
participant participante.
participle particípio.
particular particular.
particularly particularmente.
partly em parte, parcialmente.
partner sócio, companheiro.
party partido *(political);* festa, recepção
    (social, entertainment).
pass passagem; passe *(permit).*
pass (to) passar; ser aprovado *(in an exam);*
    ultrapassar *(in car).*

passage passagem.
passenger passageiro, viajante.
passerby transeunte.
passion paixão (x = sh).
passive passivo.
passport passaporte.
past *prep.* além de, depois de; *adj.* passado; *n.* passado.
    the past year o ano passado.
    half past two as duas e meia.
paste pasta, massa; cola, grude *(for sticking).*
paste (to) grudar.
pastime passatempo, diversão.
pastry massa, bolos.
past tense pretérito, pretérito perfeito.
patent patente.
paternal paternal, paterno.
path caminho, senda, trilha.
patience paciência.
patient *adj.* paciente; *n.* paciente, doente.
patriot patriota.
patriotic patriótico.
patriotism patriotismo.
pave (to) pavimentar.
    to pave the way abrir caminho.
pavement pavimento.
pavilion pavilhão.
paw pata.
pawn (to) penhorar, empenhar.
pawnshop casa de penhores.
pay pagamento, paga, ordenado, salário.
pay (to) pagar; prestar *(attention);* fazer *(a visit).*
    to pay in installments pagar a prestações.
    to pay on account pagar por conta.
    to prepay pagar adiantado.
    to pay dearly pagar caro.
payment pagamento, paga.
pea ervilha.
peace paz.
peach pêssego, pessegueiro.
peanut amendoim.
pear pêra.
pear tree pereira.
pearl pérola.
peasant camponês.
peculiar peculiar.
peddler camelô, mascate Ⓑ.
pedestal pedestal, base.
pedestrian pedestre.
peel casca.
peel (to) descascar.
peg cavilha.
pen caneta.
penalty pena; multa *(fine).*
pencil lápis.
penetrate (to) penetrar.
penetration penetração.
peninsula península.

pension pensão.
pensive pensativo.
people gente, povo; pessoal.
    many people muita gente.
    people say dizem, diz-se.
    Hey, people, let's go! Eh, pessoal, andamos!
pepper pimenta.
perceive (to) perceber.
percent por cento.
percentage percentagem, porcentagem.
perfect perfeito.
perfection perfeição.
perform (to) executar (x = z), realizar.
performance execução (x = z), cumprimento; representação *(theater).*
perfume perfume.
perfume (to) perfumar.
perhaps talvez.
period período; ponto *(punctuation).*
periodical periódico.
perish (to) perecer.
permanent permanente.
permanently permanentemente.
permission permissão, licença.
permit (to) permitir.
perpendicular perpendicular.
persecute (to) perseguir.
persecution perseguição.
persistent persistente.
person pessoa.
personal pessoal.
personality personalidade.
personally pessoalmente.
personnel pessoal.
persuade (to) persuadir.
persuasion persuasão.
persuasive persuasivo.
pertaining pertencente, relativo.
pessimist pessimista.
pessimistic pessimista.
petal pétala.
petition petição.
petroleum petróleo.
petty insignificante, trivial, pequeno.
    petty cash dinheiro para despesas menores.
pharmacist farmacêutico.
pharmacy farmácia.
phase fase.
phenomenon fenômeno (fenómeno).
philosopher filósofo.
philosophical filosófico.
philosophy filosofia.
phone telefone.
phone (to) telefonar.
phonograph fonógrafo.
photograph fotografia.
photograph (to) fotografar.

to take a photograph tirar uma
  fotografia.
physical físico.
physician médico.
physics física.
piano piano.
pick picareta (tool); escolha (choice).
pick (to) escolher (choose).
  to pick up pegar, apanhar; acelerar
    (speed); arrumar (tidy up).
  to have a bone to pick with ter conta a
    ajustar com.
  to pick on atormentar, perseguir.
pickle pepino em escabeche, picles pl. Ⓑ.
picnic piquenique.
picture quadro, foto, fotografia.
  to take a picture tirar uma fotografia.
picturesque pitoresco.
pie pastelão; torta (tart).
piece pedaço, parte.
pier cais, molhe.
pig porco.
pigeon pombo.
pill pílula.
pillow travesseiro (almofada).
pilot piloto.
pin alfinete.
pinch (to) beliscar.
pineapple abacaxi (ananás).
pink cor de rosa.
pipe cachimbo (smoking); tubo, cano
  (plumbing).
pistol pistola.
pitch arremesso, lance (throw); inclinação
  (slope).
pitcher jarro, cântaro (for water, etc.);
  lançador (baseball).
pitiful lastimável.
pity pena, piedade, compaixão (x = sh).
  It's a pity. É pena. É uma pena.
  What a pity! Que pena!
pity (to) ter pena de, compadecer-se de.
place lugar, posição.
  in the first place em primeiro lugar.
  in place no seu lugar.
  in place of em lugar de, em vez de.
  out of place fora do seu lugar.
  to take place realizar-se.
place (to) colocar, pôr.
plain plano, liso; simples; franco.
  the plain truth a pura verdade.
plan plano, projeto (projecto).
plan (to) planejar, projetar (projectar).
planet planeta.
plant planta.
plant (to) plantar.
plantation plantação.
plaster reboco (for walls); gesso (of Paris).
plastic plástico.

plate prato (food); chapa, lâmina (metal in
  sheets); chapa (photography).
  a bowl of soup um prato de sopa.
plateau planalto.
platform plataforma.
play jogo (game); peça (theater).
play (to) jogar (sports); tocar (music); brincar
  (games, recreation); representar (theater).
  to play a part representar, fazer um papel.
  to play a game jogar uma partida.
  to play a joke on pregar uma peça em.
player jogador.
playful brincalhão.
playground pátio de recreio.
plea rogo, apelo, argumento, pleito (law).
plead (to) rogar, suplicar; pleitear (law).
pleasant agradável, amável.
please (to) agradar, dar prazer a.
  I'm pleased. Estou satisfeito. Estou
    contente.
  It pleases me. Agrada-me.
  It doesn't please me. Não me agrada.
  He was quite pleased. Ele ficou contente.
  please faça o favor (de), tenha a bondade
    (de), queira, por favor.
  Please tell me. Faça o favor de me dizer
    (dizer-me).
  Pleased to meet you. Prazer em
    conhecê-lo.
pleasing agradável, amável.
pleasure prazer, gosto.
plenty abundância.
plot conspiração, intriga (scheme); lote Ⓑ,
  pedaço de terra (land); trama, enredo
  (novel, etc.).
plow arado.
plug tomada (electric); tampão (stopper).
plum ameixa (x = sh).
plumber bombeiro, encanador.
plumbing encanamento.
plump rechonchudo, roliço.
plural plural.
plus mais.
pocket bolso (algibeira).
poem poema.
poet poeta.
poetic poético.
poetry poesia.
point ponto; ponta (of a pin, etc.)
  point of view ponto de vista.
  cardinal points pontos cardeais.
  6.5 seis ponto cinco.
point (to) apontar, indicar.
pointed pontudo, aguçado.
poise porte, equilíbrio.
poison veneno.
poison (to) envenenar.
poisonous venenoso.
polar polar.

pole poste, vara; pólo *(of the earth)*.
police polícia.
policeman polícia, policial.
police station delegacia (esquadra).
policy política *(of a government)*; costume, plano; apólice *(insurance)*.
polish polimento, requinte *(manners)*; graxa (x = sh) *(for shoes)*; esmalte *(for nails)*.
polish (to) polir, lustrar; engraxar (x = sh) *(shoes)*.
polite cortês.
political político.
politician político.
politics política.
pond lagoa.
pool piscina *(for swimming)*.
poor pobre.
Poor me! Coitado de mim!
pope papa.
poppy papoula.
popular popular.
population população.
porch varanda, pórtico.
pork carne de porco.
pork chop costeleta de porco.
port porto; vinho do Porto *(wine)*.
portable portátil.
porter carregador.
portion porção, parte.
portrait retrato.
Portuguese português.
position posição.
positive positivo.
positively certamente, positivamente.
possess (to) possuir.
possession possessão, posse.
to take possession of tomar posse de.
possessor possessor.
possibility possibilidade.
possible possível.
as soon as possible o mais cedo possível.
possibly possivelmente, talvez.
post poste; posto guarnição *(military)*.
postcard cartão postal, bilhete postal.
post office correio.
postage porte.
postage stamp selo postal.
posterity posteridade.
postman carteiro.
postscript pós-escrito.
pot panela, caçarola *(cooking)*; pote *(for plants)*.
potato batata.
fried potatoes batatas fritas.
mashed potatoes purê (puré) de batatas.
pound libra.
pour despejar; chover a cântaros *(rain)*.
poverty pobreza.

powder pó; pó de arroz *(for face)*; pólvora *(gunpowder)*.
power poder, força, potência.
electric power força elétrica (eléctrica).
horsepower cavalo-vapor.
the great powers as grandes potências.
power of attorney procuração.
powerful poderoso.
practicable praticável.
practical prático.
practice prática; uso, costume *(usage)*; desempenho *(of a profession)*; ensaiao *(rehearsal)*.
practice (to) praticar; desempenhar *(a profession)*; ensaiar *(to rehearse)*.
praise elogio, louvor.
praise (to) elogiar, louvar.
prank peça, brincadeira, travessura.
pray (to) rezar, orar; suplicar.
prayer oração; súplica.
precede (to) preceder.
precedent precedente.
preceding precedente.
precept preceito.
precious precioso, de grande valor.
precipice precipício.
precise preciso, exato (exacto) (x = z).
precisely precisamente, exatamente (exactamente) (x = z).
precision precisão.
precocious precoce.
predecessor antecessor.
predicament apuro.
predict (to) predizer, profetizar.
prediction predição, profecia.
predominant predominante.
preface prefácio.
prefer (to) preferir.
preferable preferível.
preferably preferivelmenta, de preferência.
preference preferência.
prejudice preconceito.
preliminary preliminar.
premature prematuro.
premonition pressentimento.
preparation preparação.
prepare (to) preparar.
preposition preposição.
prescribe (to) prescrever; receitar *(medicine)*.
prescription receita *(medicine)*.
presence presença.
present presente, oferta.
at present atualmente (actualmente).
for the present por agora.
present participle particípio presente.
present-day atual (actual).
the present month o corrente.
to give a present fazer presente, dar de presente.

to be present estar presente.
present (to) apresentar *(introduce);* dar de presente, ofertar.
presentation apresentação.
preservation preservação, conservação.
preserve (to) preservar, conservar.
preside (to) presidir.
president presidente.
press prensa; imprensa *(printing, "the press").*
press (to) apertar; passar a ferro *(clothes);* insistir, urgir *(to urge).*
pressing urgente.
pressure pressão.
prestige prestígio.
presumable presumível.
presume (to) presumir, supor.
pretend (to) fingir, pretender.
pretense pretensão, pretexto, simulação.
    under the pretense of sob o pretexto de.
    under false pretenses sob falsos pretextos.
pretension pretensão, pretexto.
preterit, preterite pretérito.
pretext pretexto.
pretty *adj.* belo, bonito, lindo; *adv.* um tanto, bastante, um pouco.
    pretty tired um tanto cansado.
    pretty good bastante bom.
    pretty much quase *(almost).*
    pretty much the same quase o mesmo.
prevail (to) prevalecer, predominar.
    to prevail over vencer, triunfar.
    to prevail upon persuadir, convencer.
prevent (to) prevenir, impedir.
prevention prevenção, impedimento.
previous prévio.
    previous to antes de.
previously previamente, antes.
price preço.
pride orgulho.
priest sacerdote, padre.
primarily principalmente.
primary primário, principal *(first in importance);* elementar *(elementary).*
    primary color cor primária.
    primary school escola primária.
prince príncipe.
principal principal.
principally principalmente.
principle princípio.
    in principle em princípio.
print (to) imprimir, publicar.
printed impresso, publicado.
    printed matter impressos.
printer impressora.
    laser printer impressora a laser.
    color printer impressora de cor.
prior anterior, precedente, prévio.
    prior to antes de.
prison prisão, cadeia, cárcere.

prisoner prisioneiro, preso.
private privado, particular, pessoal, confidencial, reservado, secreto.
    private office escritório particular.
    private secretary secretária particular.
    in private em particular.
privately em segredo, confidencialmente.
privilege privilégio.
prize prêmio (prémio).
pro pro *(advantage);* profissional *(sports).*
probability probabilidade.
probable provável.
probably provavelmente.
problem problema.
procedure procedimento.
proceed (to) seguir, prosseguir, continuar.
process processo, procedimento, método *(method);* curso, marcha *(of time);* citação *(law).*
    in the process of no decurso de.
procession procissão, cortejo.
proclaim (to) proclamar.
proclamation proclamação.
produce (to) produzir, fabricar, render.
product produto.
production produção.
productive produtivo.
profession profissão.
professional profissional.
professor professor.
proficient proficiente, competente.
profile perfil.
profit lucro, ganho.
profit (to) lucrar, tirar proveito.
profitable lucrativo, proveitoso.
program programa.
progress progresso.
progressive progressivo.
prohibit (to) proibir.
prohibition proibição.
project projeto (projecto), plano.
project (to) projetar (projectar); ressaltar *(to jut out).*
prolong (to) prolongar.
prominent proeminente, saliente.
promise promessa.
promise (to) prometer.
promote (to) promover *(advertise);* elevar *(in grade).*
promotion promoção, elevação.
prompt pronto, preparado; pontual.
promptly prontamente.
promptness prontidão, pontualidade.
pronoun pronome.
pronounce (to) pronunciar.
pronunciation pronúncia.
proof prova.
propaganda propaganda.
propeller hélice.

proper próprio, correto (correcto), apropriado.
properly propriamente, corretamente (correctamente).
property propriedade; bens.
prophecy profecia, predição.
prophesy (to) profetizar, predizer.
proportion proporção.
    in proportion em proporção.
    out of proportion fora de proporção, desproporcionado.
proposal proposta, oferta.
propose (to) propor, sugerir.
proprietor proprietário, dono.
prosaic prosaico.
prose prosa.
prosper (to) prosperar.
prosperity prosperidade.
prosperous próspero.
protect (to) proteger.
protection proteção (protecção).
protector protetor (protector).
protest protesto.
protest (to) protestar.
Protestant protestante.
proud orgulhoso *(pleased)*; soberbo *(arrogant)*.
prove (to) provar, demonstrar, comprovar; revelar-se, mostrar-se *(to turn out)*.
proverb provérbio, rifão.
provide (to) prover, fornecer.
    to provide oneself with prover-se de.
    provided that sempre que, contanto que.
providence providência.
province província.
provincial provinciano.
provisions mantimentos, víveres *(supplies)*; provisões *(plans)*.
prudence prudência.
prudent prudente.
psalm salmo.
pseudonym pseudônimo.
pst! psiu!
psyche psique.
psychiatrist psiquiatra.
psychiatry psiquiatria.
psychic *n.* médium; *adj.* psíquico.
psychoanalysis psicanálise.
psychological psicológico.
psychology psicologia.
psychotic psicótico.
public público.
publication publicação.
publicity publicidade.
publish (to) publicar.
publisher editor.
publishing house casa editora.
pudding pudim.
pull (to) puxar (x = sh).

to pull in chegar, entrar *(train)*; encostar *(to a parking space)*.
to pull out sair, partir *(train)*; arrancar *(of a parking space)*.
to pull apart separar, romper.
to pull through sair bem.
pulpit púlpito.
pulse pulso.
pump bomba.
punch soco *(blow)*; ponche *(drink)*.
punch (to) socar.
punctual pontual.
punctuate (to) pontuar.
punctuation pontuação.
puncture puntura (punctura).
punish (to) punir, castigar.
punishment castigo, punição.
pupil aluno *(school)*; pupila *(eye)*.
purchase compra.
purchase (to) comprar.
purchaser comprador.
pure puro.
purely puramente, simplesmente.
purple púrpura.
purpose propósito, fim, finalidade, objetivo (objectivo), intenção.
    on purpose de propósito.
    to no purpose inutilmente, em vão.
    for the purpose of com o fim de.
    With what purpose? Com que finalidade?
purse bolsa.
pursue (to) perseguir *(chase)*; prosseguir *(a matter, etc.)*.
pursuit perseguição, procura.
push (to) empurrar.
put (to) pôr, colocar.
    to put away guardar, pôr de lado.
    to put in order pôr em ordem.
    to put off adiar.
    to put up for sale pôr à venda.
    to put up with suportar, agüentar (aguentar), aturar.
    to put on vestir, pôr.
    to put out publicar *(a book)*; apagar *(a light)*.
    to put to bed pôr na cama, fazer deitar.
    to put to sleep fazer dormir *(anesthetize)*.
    to put together juntar.
    to put to a vote submeter a votação.
puzzle quebra-cabeça; enigma, problema.
    to be puzzled estar perplexo (x = ks).

quaint curioso, raro, singular,
qualify (to) qualificar.
quality qualidade.

quantity quantidade.
quarrel briga, disputa.
quart quarto.
quarter quarto, quarta parte.
   a quarter hour um quarto de hora.
quarters alojamento; quartel *(military)*.
queen rainha.
quell (to) esmagar, sufocar.
quench (to) matar *(thirst)*; apagar.
question pergunta *(query)*; questão *(matter)*.
   to ask a question fazer uma pergunta.
   to be a question of tratar-se de, ser uma questão de.
   question mark ponto de interrogação.
   What's the question? De que se trata?
   without any question sem dúvida.
   to be out of the question ser impossível.
quick rápido.
quickly depressa, rapidamente.
quiet quieto, sossegado, tranqüilo (tranquilo).
quietly quietamente, tranqüilamente (tranquilamente).
quietness quietude.
quilt colcha, acolchoado.
quinine quinina.
quit deixar (x = sh), parar, cessar *(to stop)*; desistir *(give up)*.
   to quit smoking deixar de fumar.
quite completamente, muito, realmente, bem.
   quite good muito bom.
   quite soon bem cedo.
   quite difficult bem difícil.
   quite well done muito bem feito.
   She seems quite different. Ela parece outra.
quotation citação, cotação.
   quotation marks aspas.
quote (to) citar.

R

rabbit coelho.
race raça *(ethnic)*; corrida, carreira.
racial racial.
radiance brilho, esplendor.
radiant radiante, brilhante.
radiator radiador.
radio rádio.
   radio set aparelho de rádio.
   radio station estação de rádio, radioemissora.
radish rabanete.
radium rádio.
rag trapo, farrapo.
rage raiva, ira.
ragged esfarrapado, andrajoso.
rail barreira, barra; trilho *(train)*.

railroad estrada de ferro (caminho de ferro), ferrovia.
rain chuva.
rain (to) chover.
rainbow arco-íris.
raincoat impermeável.
rainfall chuva.
rainy chuvoso.
raise aumento.
   to get a raise conseguir um aumento.
raise (to) levantar, elevar; aumentar, subir *(prices, salary)*; criar *(children)*; cultivar *(a crop)*.
   to raise an objection levantar uma objeção (objecção), objetar (objectar).
   to raise money angariar fundos.
raisin passa.
rake ancinho.
rake (to) usar ancinho.
ranch fazenda, estância.
range alcance *(reach)*; extensão (x = sh) *(voice)*; cadeia *(mountains)*.
rank posto *(military, etc.)*; fileira *(line of soldiers)*; posição.
   rank and file gente comum.
rapid rápido.
rapidly rapidamente.
rare raro *(unusual)*; mal passado *(meat)*.
rarely raramente.
rash *adj.* precipitado, temerário; *n.* erupção *(skin)*; vaga *(of deaths, etc.)*.
rat rato.
rate preço, taxa (x = sh).
   at the rate of à razão de.
   rate of exchange taxa de câmbio.
   at any rate de qualquer maneira.
rather um pouco, antes, meio um tanto.
   rather expensive um tanto caro, meio caro.
   rather than em vez de.
ratio proporção.
ration ração.
rational racional.
raw cru *(food)*; bruto *(materials)*.
ray raio.
rayon raiom.
razor navalha *(straight)*; gilete *(safety)*.
   razor blade lâmina (de borbear).
reach alcance *(range)*.
   out of reach fora do alcance.
   within reach ao alcance.
reach (to) alcançar, chegar a, chegar até.
   to reach the end terminar, chegar ao fim, conseguir o objetivo (objectivo).
   to reach out one's hand estender a mão.
   to reach someone chegar a alguem *(get through to their heart)*.
react (to) reagir.
reaction reação (reacção).

reactionary reacionário (reaccionário).
read (to) ler.
reader leitor.
reading leitura.
reading room gabinete de leitura.
ready pronto, disposto.
   to get ready arrumar-se (bathe and dress).
ready-made feito, já feito.
   ready-made clothes roupa feita.
real real, verdadeiro.
   real estate bens imóveis.
realist realista.
reality realidade.
realization realização; compreensão.
realize (to) dar-se conta de, compreender;
   realizar, conseguir (obtain, achieve), levar
   a cabo (bring to reality).
   to realize a danger dar-se conta do perigo.
   to realize a project levar a cabo um
     projeto (projecto).
   to realize a profit tirar proveito, tirar
     lucro.
really de fato (facto), realmente (in reality);
   muito, bem (very).
reap (to) colher, segar.
rear adj. traseiro, posterior; n. parte traseira,
   fundo.
   to bring up the rear fechar a retaguardo.
reason razão, motivo, causa.
   by reason of por causa de.
   for this reason por isto.
   without reason sem razão.
reason (to) raciocinar, pensar.
reasonable razoável, módico.
reasonably razoavelmente, moderadamente.
reasoning raciocínio.
rebel rebelde.
rebel (to) rebelar-se, revoltar-se.
rebellion rebelião, revolta.
rebellious rebelde, revoltoso.
recall (to) lembrar, recordar.
receipt recibo (document); recebimento
   (action).
   to acknowledge receipt acusar o
     recebimento.
receive (to) receber.
receiver fone (telephone); recebedor,
   destinatário (mail, etc.).
recent recente.
recently recentemente.
reception recepção, recebimento, acolhida.
recipe receita.
recite (to) recitar.
reckless temerário, imprudente.
recklessly temerariamente, imprudentemente.
recline (to) reclinar-se, recostar-se.
recognition reconhecimento.
recognize (to) reconhecer.
recollect (to) recordar, lembrar (to remember).

recollection recordação, lembrança.
recommend (to) recomendar.
recommendation recomendação.
reconcile (to) reconciliar, harmonizar.
reconciliation reconciliação.
record registro; disco (phonograph); recorde
   Ⓑ (sports); evidência; pl. arquivo, anais.
   on record registrado.
recover (to) recuperar (from illness); recobrar
   (to get back).
recovery recuperação.
recreation recreio, divertimento, passatempo.
recuperate (to) recuperar-se, restabelecer-se.
red vermelho.
   Red Cross Cruz Vermelha.
reduce (to) reduzir, diminuir.
reduction redução, abatimento, desconto
   (prices).
refer (to) referir.
reference referência.
   reference book livro de consulta.
refine (to) refinar.
refinement refinamento, requinte.
reflect (to) refletir (reflectir), pensar.
reflection reflexão (x = ks), reflexo (x = ks).
reflexive reflexivo (x = ks).
reform reforma.
reform (to) reformar, corrigir.
refrain (to : . . from) abster-se de.
refresh (to) refrescar.
refreshment refresco.
refrigerator refrigerador, geladeira.
refuge refúgio, asilo, amparo.
refugee refugiado.
refusal recusa.
refuse (to) recusar, negar.
refute (to) refutar.
regard consideração, respeito, estima.
   in regard to com referência a.
   in this regard a esse respeito, neste
     respeito.
   with regard to com referência a.
   without any regard to sem nenhuma
     consideração para.
regard (to) considerar, estimar, julgar.
regarding com respeito a, quanto a.
regardless of não obstante, apesar de.
regards lembranças, cumprimentos.
   regards to lembranças a.
regime regime.
regiment regimento.
region região, área.
register registro.
register (to) inscrever, registrar.
   registered letter carta registrada.
regret pesar, remorso.
regret (to) sentir, deplorar, lamentar.
   I regret it very much. Sinto(-o) muito.
   I regret that . . . Sinto que . . .

regular regular.
regularity regularidade.
regularly regularmente.
regulation regulamento, regra, ordem.
rehearsal ensaio.
rehearse (to) ensaiar.
reign reinado.
reign (to) reinar.
reject (to) rejeitar.
rejection rejeição.
rejoice (to) alegrar, regozijar.
rejoicing alegria, júbilo, regozijo.
relate (to) relatar, narrar, contar *(story);* relacionar *(be connected).*
   everything relating to quanto se relaciona com.
relation relação; parente *(family member).*
relationship relação; parentesco *(family).*
relative *adj.* relativo, respectivo; *n.* parente *(family).*
relax descontrair-se.
release (to) soltar, libertar; permitir *(publication, etc.).*
reliability confiança.
reliable de confiança.
relief alívio *(from pain);* socorro, auxílio *(aid).*
religion religião.
religious religioso.
relish (to) saborear, gostar de.
reluctance relutância, resistência.
reluctant relutante, hesitante.
reluctantly relutantemente, de má vontade.
rely on (to) confiar em, contar com.
remain (to) ficar, permanecer, restar.
   to remain silent ficar quieto, calar.
   to remain to be done ficar por fazer.
remains restos.
remark observação, comentário.
   to make a remark fazer um comentário.
remark (to) observar, comentar, notar *(notice).*
remarkable notável, extraordinário.
remarkably notavelmente.
remedy remédio.
remedy (to) remediar, corrigir.
remember (to) lembrar, lembrar-se, recordar.
   I don't remember. Não me lembro.
   Remember me to him. Dê-lhe (as) minhas lembranças.
remembrance lembrança.
remind (to) lembrar.
reminder lembrete, aviso.
remit (to) remeter.
remorse remorso.
remote control (TV) controle remoto; telecomando ℗.
removal remoção, demissão.
remove (to) tirar, retirar; demitir *(from a job).*
renew (to) renovar, recomeçar.

to renew a subscription renovar uma assinatura.
rent aluguel, renda.
   for rent aluga-se.
rent (to) alugar.
repair conserto.
   in good repair em bom estado.
repair (to) consertar.
repeal (to) revogar, anular.
repeat (to) repetir.
repeatedly repetidamente.
repetition repetição.
reply resposta, réplica.
reply (to) responder, replicar.
report relatório, informação.
report (to) informar, comunicar, fazer relatório; denunciar *(to the police).*
   it is reported diz-se que, dizem que.
reporter repórter, jornalista.
represent (to) representar.
representation representação.
representative representante, agente; deputado *(political).*
reproach censura, repreensão.
reproach (to) censurar, repreender.
reproduce (to) reproduzir.
reproduction reprodução.
reptile réptil.
republic república.
republican republicano.
reputation reputação, renome, fama.
request pedido, petição.
request (to) pedir, rogar.
rescue salvamento.
rescue (to) salvar, socorrer.
resemblance semelhança.
resemble (to) parecer-se com.
   He resembles his father. Ele se parece com o pai.
resent (to) ressentir-se.
reservation reserva.
reserve reserva.
   without reserve sem reserva.
reserve (to) reservar.
reside (to) morar, residir.
residence residência, domicílio.
resident residente.
resign (to) demitir-se; resignar-se *(to resign oneself).*
resignation renúncia, demissão; resignação *(despair).*
resist (to) resistir, opor-se.
resistance resistência, oposição.
resolute resoluto, determinado.
resolution resolução, solução.
resolve (to) resolver, determinar, decidir.
resource recurso.
respect respeito.
   in this respect neste respeito.

with respect to com respeito a.
with all due respect com todo respeito.
in all respects em todo sentido, sob todos os pontos de vista.
in every respect em todo sentido.
respect (to) respeitar, estimar.
respectable respeitável.
respectful respeitoso.
    respectfully yours atenciosamente.
respective respectivo.
response resposta, réplica.
responsibility responsabilidade.
responsible responsável.
rest resto *(remainder)*; descanso, repouso *(when tired).*
rest (to) descansar, repousar.
restaurant restaurante.
restful sossegado, tranqüilo (tranquilo).
restless inquieto, impaciente.
restore (to) restaurar, restabelecer.
restrict (to) restringir, limitar, confinar.
result resultado, conseqüência (consequência).
result (to) resultar.
    to result in acabar em, terminar em, resultar em.
retail venda a varejo, venda a retalho Ⓟ.
retail (to) vender a retalho, vender a varejo.
retire (to) reformar-se.
    She is retired now. Ela já é reformada.
return volta.
    in return for em troca de.
    by return mail à volta do correio.
    return trip viagem de volta.
return (to) voltar, regressar; devolver *(to return something).*
    to return a book devolver um livro.
    to return a favor retribuir um favor.
    to return home voltar para casa.
review revista *(summary)*; revisão, repasso *(recheck);* exame (x = z).
review (to) rever, revisar, repassar; criticar *(movies, etc.).*
revise (to) revisar.
revision revisão.
revive (to) ressuscitar *(person)*; restaurar *(custom).*
revolt revolta, rebelião.
revolt (to) revoltar(-se), rebelar(-se).
revolution revolução.
reward recompensa.
reward (to) recompensar.
rewind rebobinagem.
rhyme rima.
rhythm ritmo.
rib costela.
ribbon fita.
rice arroz.
rich rico; forte *(food).*
riches riquezas.

riddle adivinha, enigma.
ride passeio.
ride (to) montar a cavalo, andar a cavalo *(on horseback)*; viajar.
ridiculous ridículo.
rifle rifle.
right *adj.* direito; justo *(just);* correto (correcto); *n.* direito; *adv.* bem; certo; certamente; justamente; perfeitamente; mesmo.
    the right man o homem certo.
    right hand mão direita.
    right-handed destro.
    the right time a hora certa.
    right or wrong com razão ou sem razão.
    right side lado direito.
    Is this right? Está certo?
    It's right. Está certo.
    to be right ter razão.
    to the right à direita.
    keep to the right conserve a sua direita.
    to have a right ter direito.
    by rights de direito.
    right here aqui mesmo.
    right away imediatemente, já.
    right now agora mesmo.
    all right está bem, bem.
    Everything is all right. Tudo vai bem.
ring anel *(for finger).*
ring (to) tocar, soar *(bells).*
riot motim, desordem.
riot (to) amotinar-se.
ripe maduro.
ripen (to) amadurecer.
rise aumento, subida.
    sunrise nascer do sol, levantar do sol.
rise (to) subir; levantar-se *(to get up)*; sair *(sun);* revoltar-se *(revolt);* aumentar *(taxes).*
risk risco, perigo.
    to run a risk correr um perigo, arriscar.
risk (to) arriscar.
river rio.
road estrada, caminho.
    main road estrada principal, caminho principal.
roar rugido, berro.
roar (to) rugir, berrar.
roast assado.
    roast beef rosbife, carne assada.
roast (to) assar.
rob (to) roubar.
robber ladrão.
robbery roubo, furto.
rock rocha; rock *(music).*
rock (to) balançar, embalar *(to sleep).*
rocket foguete, projétil (projéctil).
rocking chair cadeira de balanço.
roll rolo; pãozinho *(bread);* lista *(list).*

roll (to) enrolar, rolar.
romance romance.
romantic romântico.
roof telhado *(house)*; teto (tecto) *(car)*.
room sala, quarto, peça (divisão).
    to make room dar lugar, fazer lugar.
    There's not enough room. Não há
        bastante espaço.
    There's no room for doubt. Não cabe
        dúvida.
    living room sala de estar.
    dining room sala de jantar.
rooster galo.
root raiz.
rooted enraizado, radicado.
rope corda.
    to be at the end of one's rope estar na
        última.
rose rosa.
rosebush roseira.
rotary giratório, rotativo.
    rotary press rotiva.
rough áspero.
    rough draft rascunho.
round *adj.* redondo; *n.* rodada *(drinks)*.
    a round table uma mesa redonda.
    round number número redondo.
    round trip viagem de ida e volta.
    all year round o ano todo.
route rota, rumo, caminho, curso.
routine rotina.
row fila, fileira.
row (to) remar.
rub (to) esfregar, friccionar.
rubber borracha.
rude rude, grosso, descortês.
rudeness rudeza, grosseria.
rug tapete.
ruin ruína.
rule regra, norma; reinado, dominio *(reign)*.
    as a rule em regra.
    to be the rule ser regra, ser uso.
rule (to) reger *(king)*; governar *(government)*;
    determinar *(court)*.
    to rule out excluir, eliminar.
    to rule over governar.
ruler soberano *(monarch)*; régua *(for drawing*
    lines).
rumor rumor.
run (to) correr; andar, funcionar *(a watch, a*
    machine, etc.).
    to run across someone encontrar, dar com.
    to run into someone encontrar-se com,
        topar com.
    to run away escapar, fugir.
    to run the risk of correr o risco de,
        arriscar.
    to run up and down correr de cá para lá
        (acolá).

    to run a business dirigir um negócio.
rural rural.
rush pressa *(haste)*.
    to be in a rush estar com pressa.
rush (to) ir depressa, apressar-se.
    to rush in entrar correndo, entrar
        precipitadamente.
    to rush through fazer depressa.
Russian russo.
rusty enferrujado, ferrugento.
rye centeio.

S

Sabbath sábado.
saccharine sacarina.
sack saco, saca.
sacred sagrado, sacro.
sacrifice sacrifício.
sacrifice (to) sacrificar.
sad triste.
saddle sela.
sadly tristemente.
sadness tristeza.
safe *n.* cofre, caixa (x = sh) forte; *adj.* seguro;
    salvo, ileso *(unhurt)*; sem perigo *(safe from*
    danger); sem risco *(safe from risk)*.
    safe and sound são e salvo.
    Have a safe trip! Feliz viagem! Boa
        viagem!
safely a salvo.
safety segurança.
sail vela.
    sailboat barco a vela, veleiro.
sail (to) velejar, navegar; fazer à vela *(set sail)*.
sailor marinheiro, marujo.
saint santo, são.
    Saint Paul São Paulo.
    Saint Barbara Santa Bárbara.
    Saint Andrew Santo André.
sake causa, motivo, amor, bem, consideração.
    for your sake para seu próprio bem.
    for the sake of por, por amor a, por
        causa de.
    for the sake of brevity por brevidade.
    for mercy's sake por misericórdia.
    for God's sake, for the love of God por
        Deus, pelo amor de Deus.
salad salada.
salary salário, ordenado.
sale venda.
    for sale à venda.
salesgirl caixeira, vendedora.
salesman caixeiro, vendedor.
    traveling salesman caixeiro viajante.
salmon salmão.
salt sal.

salt (to) salgar, pôr sal.
   salt shaker saleiro.
same mesmo, igual.
   the same o mesmo, os mesmos.
   It's all the same to me. Tanto faz. Para
     mim é o mesmo.
   much the same quase o mesmo.
   the same as o mesmo que, os mesmos que.
sample amostra.
sand areia.
sandpaper lixa (x = sh).
sandwich sanduíche.
sandy arenoso.
sane são.
sanatorium, sanitarium sanatório.
sanitary sanitário.
sanitation saneamento.
sanity sanidade *(medical)*; juízo, razão
   (sensibility).
sap seiva.
sarcasm sarcasmo.
sarcastic sarcástico.
sardine sardinha.
Satan satanás, satã.
satisfaction satisfação.
satisfactorily satisfatoriamente.
satisfactory satisfatório.
satisfy (to) satisfazer.
Saturday sábado.
sauce molho.
saucer pires.
sausage salsicha, lingüiça (linguiça).
savage selvagem.
save *prep.* salvo, exceto (excepto), menos;
   conj. a não ser.
save (to) salvar, resgatar *(a person)*; poupar,
   economizar. *(money)*; salvar *(computer).*
   to save face salvar as aparências.
savings poupanças, economias.
   savings bank caixa (x = sh) econômica
     (económica).
saw serra; serrote *(hand saw).*
say (to) dizer.
   that is to say quer dizer, isto é.
   it is said diz-se, dizem.
saying dito, provérbio, rifão.
   as the saying goes como diz o provérbio,
     como se costuma dizer.
scale *n.* balança *(for weighing)*; escala
   (proportion); escama *(of fish, etc.).*
scalp couro cabeludo.
scan (to) escandir.
scandal escândalo.
Scandinavian escandinavo.
scanner escáner.
scanty escasso, pouco, insuficiente.
scar cicatriz.
scarce escasso, raro.
scarcely apenas, mal, quase não.

scarcity escassez.
scarf cachecol *(long)*; lença *(square).*
scarlet escarlate.
scene cena.
scenery cenário, decoração *(theater)*;
   paisagem, vista *(view).*
scent cheiro, aroma, odor.
schedule horário *(timetable)*; programa lista
   (of events); *(list).*
scheme plano, esquema; projeto (projecto).
scholarship bolsa de estudos.
school escola.
   schoolteacher professor.
   schoolbook livro escolar.
   schoolmate colega, condiscípulo.
   schoolroom sala de aula.
science ciência.
scientific científico.
scientist cientista.
scissors tesoura.
scold (to) ralhar, repreender.
score escore, contagem; partitura *(music).*
score (to) fazer pontos, marcar os pontos;
   riscar *(for cutting, etc.).*
scorn dezprezo, desdém.
scorn (to) desprezar, desdenhar.
scornful desdenhoso.
Scottish escocês.
scrape (to) raspar *(on a surface).*
scratch arranhadura, arranhão *(on the hand,
   etc.)*; raspadura *(on a table, etc.).*
scratch (to) arranhar *(with the nails)*; rasgar *(a
   table, etc.)*; cancelar, apagar *(eliminate).*
scream (to) berrar, gritar.
screen biombo *(partition)*; tela *(windows,
   movie, computer)*; cortina, barreira.
screw parafuso.
screw (to) parafusar, atarraxar (x = sh).
scruple escrúpulo.
sculptor escultor.
sculpture escultura.
sea mar.
seal selo.
seal (to) selar; lacrar.
seam costura.
search busca, procura *(act of looking for)*;
   pesquisa, investigação *(research,
   investigation).*
   in search of em procura de, em busca de.
search (to) procurar, buscar *(to search for)*;
   examinar *(to comb through)*, revistar *(a
   place)*; explorar *(to explore).*
   to search after indagar, perguntar por.
   to search for procurar, buscar.
seasick enjoado.
season estação *(of the year)*; temporada
   (sports).
   in season na época.
   out of season fora da época.

season (to) sazonar, condimentar *(food)*.
seat *n.* assento; banco *(car)*; sede
  (government, etc.).
  to take a seat sentar-se, tomar assento.
  front seat assento dianteiro.
  back seat assento traseiro.
  seat belt cinto de seguiança.
second segundo; em segundo lugar.
  second-class de segunda classe.
  second year o segundo ano.
  Wait a second! Espere um momento!
  on second thought depois de pensá-lo bem.
  second to none sem par.
secondary secundário.
secondary school escola secundária.
secondhand de segunda mão, usado.
secrecy segredo, reserva, silêncio.
secret secreto.
  in secret em segredo, secretamente.
secretary secretário, secretária.
section seção (secção).
secure seguro, certo, firme.
secure (to) assegurar; garantir; conseguir
  (obtain).
securely seguramente, certamente.
security segurança *(assurance; crime
  prevention)*, garantia.
see (to) ver.
  See? Sabe? Compreende?
  I see. Já estou compreendendo. Já estou
    vendo.
  Let's see. Vamos ver.
  to see about averiguar, indagar.
  to see someone off despedir-se.
  See ya! Até logo!
  to see someone home acompanhar à
    casa.
  to see the point perceber, compreender.
  to see a thing through terminar, levar a
    cabo.
  to see fit achar conveniente.
  to see one's way clear ver o modo de
    fazer alguma coisa.
  to see to cuidar de, encarregar-se de.
  seeing that visto que, desde que.
seed semente.
seek (to) procurar, buscar.
seem (to) parecer.
  it seems to me parece-me.
  it seems parece.
seize (to) agarrar *(to grasp)*; pegar, apanhar *(to
  get hold of, to take)*; apoderar-se de *(to
  take possession of)*.
seldom raramente, poucas vezes.
select seleto (selecto), escolhido.
select (to) escolher, selecionar (seleccionar).
selection seleção (selecção).
self mesmo, por si mesmo; si, se.
  myself eu mesmo.

I said to myself. Disse para mim. Eu me
  disse.
yourself você mesmo; o senhor mesmo.
himself ele mesmo.
He said to himself. Ele disse para si. Ele
  se disse.
She said to herself. Ela disse para si. Ela
  se disse.
ourselves nós mesmos.
yourselves vocês mesmos; os senhores
  mesmos.
themselves eles mesmos.
Wash yourself. Lave-se. Lave-te *(fam.)*.
by himself por si mesmo.
self-confidence autoconfiança.
self-defense autodefesa.
self-determination autodeterminação.
self-evident evidente, claro, patente.
selfish egoísta.
selfishness egoísmo.
self-taught autodidata (autodidacta).
sell (to) vender.
semester semestre.
senate senado.
senator senador.
send (to) enviar, mandar, expedir, transmitir.
  to send away despedir, mandar embora.
  to send word mandar recado, mandar
    dizer.
  to send back devolver.
  to send in mandar entrar.
  to send for mandar buscar.
senior mais velho, mais antigo, superior.
  John Williams, Sr. João Guimarães
    Senior.
sense sentido, senso.
  common sense senso comum.
  to be out of one's senses ter perdido o
    juízo.
  sense of humor senso de humor.
sensible sensato, razoável.
sensibly sensatamente.
sentence frase *(grammar)*; sentença,
  julgamento *(court)*.
sentence (to) sentenciar, condenar.
sentiment sentimento.
sentimental sentimental.
separate separado, distinto.
separate (to) separar, afastar.
separately separadamente.
separation separação.
September setembro (Setembro).
serene sereno.
sergeant sargento.
serial em série, serial.
series série.
serious sério.
seriously seriamente.
  to take seriously levar a sério.

seriousness seriedade, gravidade.
sermon sermão.
servant empregado, criado.
serve (to) servir.
    to serve the purpose servir.
    to serve notice notificar, fazer saber, avisar.
    to serve one right ser bem feito, ser merecido.
    to serve as servir de.
service serviço.
    at your service às suas ordens.
    to be of service ser útil, servir.
session sessão.
set *adj.* fixo (x = ks), estabelecido, determinado; *n.* jogo, aparelho.
    set price preço fixo.
    set of dishes jogo de copos.
    aparelho de TV TV set.
set (to) pôr.
    to set aside pôr de lado.
    to set back impedir; atrasar *(watch).*
    to set free liberar.
    to set in order pôr em ordem.
    to set on fire incendiar.
    to set to work começar a trabalhar.
    to set up cadastrar.
settle (to) arranjar, arrumar *(arrange);* pagar, liquidar, saldar *(an account, a debt);* fixar residência, estabelecer-se *(to settle down);* pousar, assentar *(to go down, as liquids).*
    to settle an account saldar uma conta.
settlement acordo, entendimento *(adjustment, agreement);* colônia (colónia), povoção *(village);* colonização *(colonization).*
seven sete.
seven hundred setecentos.
seventeen dezessete (dezassete).
seventeenth décimo sétimo.
seventh sétimo.
seventieth septuagésimo.
seventy setenta.
several vários, alguns.
    several times várias vezes.
severe severo.
severity severidade, gravidade.
sew (to) coser, costurar.
sewing costura.
    sewing machine máquina de costura.
sex sexo (x = ks).
sexual sexual (x = ks).
shade sombra.
shade (to) sombrear.
shadow sombra.
shady sombreado; suspeito *(disreputable).*
shake sacudida, tremor; aperto de mãos *(handshake);* batida *(drink).*
shake (to) sacudir; estremecer *(to tremble);* apertar a mão *(shake hands).*

    to shake your head abanar a cabeça.
shame vergonha.
shame (to) envergonhar.
shameful vergonhoso, escandaloso.
shameless desavergonhado, sem vergonha.
shampoo xampu (x = sh), lavagem de cabeça.
shape forma, figura.
shape (to) formar, dar forma.
share porção, parte; ação (acção) *(stock).*
share (to) partilhar, repartir *(to apportion);* participar, tomar parte em *(to share in).*
shareholder acionista (accionista).
sharp agudo, afiado, pontiagudo *(sharp-pointed).*
    a sharp pain uma dor aguda.
    a sharp curve uma curva fechada.
    sharp-witted esperto, inteligente.
    at two o'clock sharp às duas horas em ponto.
sharpen (to) afiar, aguçar; apontar, fazer a ponta *(a pencil).*
shatter (to) despedaçar, estilhaçar, espatifar.
shave (to) barbear, fazer a barba.
    shaving brush pincel de barba.
    shaving cream creme de barbear.
shawl xale (x = sh).
she ela.
shears tesoura.
shed alpendre, galpão, barracão.
shed (to) perder *(fur, etc.),* derramar *(tears, etc.).*
sheep carneiro, ovelha.
sheet lençol *(bed);* folha *(paper).*
shelf estante, prateleira.
shell concha, carapaça; casca *(egg, nut);* granada, bomba *(military).*
shelter refúgio, abrigo.
    to take shelter abrigar-se.
    to give shelter abrigar, proteger.
shelter (to) abrigar, proteger, dar asilo.
shepherd pastor.
sheriff xerife (x = sh).
sherry xerez (x = sh).
Shh! Psiu!
shield escudo, defesa.
shield (to) proteger, defender, servir de escudo.
shift mudança *(change);* turno *(work).*
shift (to) mudar.
shine (to) brilhar, iluminar; polir, lustrar *(shoes, etc.).*
shining brilhante, reluzente, lustroso.
shiny lustroso, brilhante.
ship navio, vapor.
    merchant ship navio mercante.
ship (to) embarcar, despachar, enviar, mandar.
shipment embarque, despacho, carregamento.
shipwreck naufrágio.
shipyard estaleiro.

shirt camisa.
    sport shirt camisa-esporte.
shiver tremor, arrepio, calafrio.
shiver (to) tremer *(from cold)*, tiritar.
shock choque; descarga *(electrical)*.
shock (to) chocar, abalar.
shoe sapato.
    shoe store sapataria.
    shoelaces cordões de sapato.
    shoe polish graxa (x = sh) para sapato.
shoehorn calçadeira.
shoemaker sapateiro.
shoot (to) atirar, disparar; filmar *(to film)*.
shop loja.
    to go shopping ir às compras.
shore costa, praia *(sea)*; margem *(lake)*.
short curto *(not long)*; baixo (x = sh) *(not tall)*; breve, conciso *(brief)*; com falta de *(of goods)*.
    shortcut atalho.
    short circuit curto-circuito.
    short story conto.
    in short em resumo.
    in a short while dentro de pouco, em breve.
    a short time ago há pouco tempo.
shorten (to) encurtar, abreviar.
shorts calças curtas.
shot tiro, descarga.
should deve, deveria, devia.
    I should go eu devia ir.
    The window should be open. A janela devia estar aberta.
shoulder ombro.
    shoulder to shoulder ombro a ombro.
shout grito, berro.
shout (to) gritar, berrar.
shovel pá.
show exposição (x = sh) *(exhibition)*; espetáculo (espectáculo) *(spectacle)*; entretenimento *(entertainment)*.
    show window vitrina (montra).
show (to) mostrar, ensinar, provar, demonstrar.
    to show someone in mandar entrar.
    to show to the door acompanhar até a porta.
    to show off exibir-se.
    to show up apresentar-se, aparecer.
shower aguaceiro, chuveiro.
    shower bath (banho de) chuveiro.
shrewd astuto, sutil.
shrimp camarão.
shrink (to) encolher, contrair-se.
shrub arbusto.
shrug (to) encolher os ombros.
shut (to) fechar.
    to shut in encerrar, confinar.
    to shut out excluir.
    to shut up calar, fazer calar.

shutter veneziana; obturador *(photography)*.
shy tímido, acanhado.
sick doente.
    to feel sick sentir-se mal, sentir-se doente.
    I'm sick of this! Estou farto disto!
sickness doença.
side lado.
    side by side lado a lado.
    on this side deste lado.
    on that side desse lado.
    on the other side de outro lado.
    wrong side out ao revés.
    I'm on your side. Estou do seu lado.
sidewalk calçada.
sieve peneira.
sigh suspiro.
sigh (to) suspirar.
sight vista *(sense)*; espetáculo *(spectacle)*.
    at first sight à primeira vista.
    to keep in sight não perder de vista.
sightseeing (to go) ver as coisas de interesse, visitar os lugares notáveis.
sign sinal *(mark)*; letreiro, tabuleta *(as over a shop)*.
    sign of the cross sinal da cruz.
sign (to) assinar.
    to sign a check assinar um cheque.
    to sign up alistar-se.
signal sinal, aviso.
signal (to) fazer sinal, fazer sináis, comunicar por meio de sinais.
signature assinatura.
significance significado, importância.
significant significante, importante.
silence silêncio.
silence (to) silenciar, fazer calar.
silent silencioso; calado *(person)*.
silently silenciosamente.
silk seda.
silly tolo, bobo.
silver prata.
silverware prataria.
similar semelhante, similar.
similarity semelhança, similaridade.
simple simples.
simplicity simplicidade.
simplification simplificação.
simplify (to) simplificar.
simply simplesmente.
sin pecado.
sin (to) pecar.
since *adj.* desde então, depois; *conj.* já que, desde que, visto que *(because, seeing that)*; *prep.* desde, depois de.
    since then desde então.
sincere sincero.
sincerely sinceramente.
    sincerely yours atenciosamente.
sincerity sinceridade.

sing (to) cantar.

singer cantor.

single só, único; solteiro *(unmarried).*
>**not a single word** nem uma só palavra.
>**single room** quarto de solteiro.

singly individualmente, separadamente.

singular singular.

sink pia, bacia.

sink (to) afundar, ir a pique.

sinner pecador.

sip sorvo, golinho.

sip (to) sorver, beber em golinhos.

sir senhor.
>**Dear Sir:** Prezado Senhor:

siren sirena *(alarm);* sereia *(mythology).*

sister irmã.

sister-in-law cunhada.

sit (to) sentar-se.

situated situado.

situation situação.

six seis.

six hundred seiscentos.

sixteen dezesseis (dezasseis).

sixteenth décimo sexto.

sixth sexto, sexta parte.

sixtieth sexagésimo.

sixty sessenta.

size tamanho, medida.

skate patim.
>**ice skate** patim para o gelo.
>**roller skate** patim de rodas.

skate (to) patinar.

skeleton esqueleto.

sketch esboço, desenho.

sketch (to) esboçar.

skill destreza, habilidade.

skillful destro, habilidoso.

skin pele.

skinny magro.

skirt saia.

skull crânio, caveira.

sky céu.
>**sky blue** azul-celeste.

slander calúnia.

slang gíria.

slap bofetada, palmada, tapa.

slap (to) dar tapa, dar bofetada, esbofetear.

slate ardósia.

slaughter matança.

slave escravo.

slavery escravidão.

slay (to) matar, assassinar.

sleep sono.
>**to go to sleep** deitar-se, adormecer.

sleepy sonolento.
>**to be sleepy** estar com sono, ter sono.

sleeve manga.

slender delgado, magro, esbelto.

slice fatia.

slice (to) cortar, cortar em fatias.

slide (to) escorregar, deslizar.

slight ligeiro, leve; insignificante.

slight (to) menosprezar.

slightly ligeiramente, levemente; um pouco.

slim delgado, magro, esbelto.

sling tipóia *(medical).*

slip escorregão *(slide);* combinação *(underwear).*

slip (to) escorregar, deslizar.
>**to slip one's mind** escapar à memória.
>**to slip away** fugir, escapulir(-se).

slippers chinelos.

slippery escorregadio, escorregadiço, resvaladiço.

slope inclinação, declive.

slow lento, devagar.
>**to be slow** *(as a watch)* atrasar-se.
>**to slow down** reduzir a velocidade.

slowly lentamente, devagar.
>**Drive slowly.** Dirija devagar.
>**Go slowly.** Vá devagar.

slowness lentidão.

slumber sono leve.

slumber (to) dormitar.

slums bairros pobres; favelas Ⓑ.

sly astuto.

small pequeno.
>**small change** troco.

smallness pequenez.

smart esperto.

smash (to) esmagar, escangalhar.

smell cheiro, odor.

smell (to) cheirar.

smile sorriso.

smile (to) sorrir.

smoke fumaça, fumo; cigarro *(a cigarette).*

smoke (to) fumar *(tobacco);* fumegar.
>**No smoking.** É proibido fumar.

smoker fumante (fumador).

smokestack chaminé.

smooth liso, macio, plano, suave.

snail caracol.

snake cobra, serpente.

snatch (to) agarrar. arrebatar.

sneeze espirro.

sneeze (to) espirrar.

snore (to) roncar (resonar).

snow neve.

snow (to) nevar.

snowflake floco de neve.

snowy nevoso *(weather);* coberto de neve *(streets, etc.).*

so assim, tal; do modo que, de maneira que.
>**That is so.** Assim é.
>**so-and-so** fulano de tal.
>**so much** tanto.
>**at so much a meter** a tanto o metro.
>**so that** para que, de modo que.

so-so regular; mais ou menos; assim, assim.

So long! Até logo!

Is that so? Realmente? É verdade?

I think so. Acredito. Acho que sim.

soak (to) embeber, pôr de molho.

soap sabão, sabonete *(bar of soap)*.

soap opera telenovela.

sob soluço.

sob (to) soluçar.

sober sóbrio *(not drunk);* sério, solene.

so-called chamado.

sociable sociável.

social social.

socialism socialismo.

society sociedade.

socket cavidade; tomada *(electric)*.

eye socket órbita de olho.

socks meias.

soda soda; soda pop.

soda water água gasosa, água com gás.

sofa sofá.

soft macio, suave, mole.

soft-boiled eggs ovos quentes.

soften (to) amolecer, suavizar.

softness moleza, maciez, suavidade.

software software.

soil solo, terra.

soil (to) sujar, manchar.

soiled sujo.

solar solar.

sold vendido.

sold out esgotado.

soldier soldado.

sole *adj.* só, único; *n.* sola *(shoe);* linguado *(fish)*.

solemn solene.

solemnity solenidade.

solid sólido *(object);* contínuo *(line)*.

solidity solidez.

solidly solidamente.

solitary solitário.

solitude solidão.

soluble solúvel.

solution solução.

solve (to) solver, resolver.

some um pouco; algum, alguns, alguma, algumas, uns, umas.

Some people think so. Há quem pensa assim.

at some time or other em qualquer ocasião.

Bring me some cigars. Traga-me alguns charutos.

There are some left. Ainda ficam alguns.

some of his books alguns dos seus livros.

some two hundred uns duzentos.

somebody alguém.

somebody else alguém mais.

somehow de algum modo, de alguma maneira.

something alguma coisa, algo.

Something else? Mais alguma coisa?

sometime algum dia, alguma vez.

sometimes algumas vezes, às vezes.

somewhat um tanto.

somewhat busy um tanto ocupado.

somewhere em alguma parte, algures.

somewhere else em outra parte.

son filho.

song canção, canto.

son-in-law genro.

soon logo, breve, cedo.

as soon as logo que, assim que.

as soon as possible o mais cedo possível.

sooner or later mais cedo ou mais tarde.

the sooner the better quanto antes melhor.

How soon will you finish? Quanto tempo demorará para terminar?

soothe (to) aliviar, acalmar, suavizar.

sore *adj.* dolorido, doído; *n.* chaga *(on the body)*.

sore throat dor de garganta.

sorrow dor, tristeza, pesar, mágoa.

sorry arrependido; lamentável *(pathetic)*.

to be sorry sentir.

Sorry. Desculpe.

I'm very sorry. Sinto muito.

sort espécie, classe, maneira.

all sorts of people toda classe de gente.

a sort of uma espécie de.

nothing of the sort nada disso.

soul alma.

sound *adj.* são, firme; *n.* som, ruido, barulho.

safe and sound são e salvo.

sound sleep sono profundo.

soup sopa.

soup plate prato de sopa, prato fundo.

vegetable soup sopa de legumes.

sour azedo, ácido.

source fonte.

south sul.

South America América do Sul.

South American sul-americano.

southern do sul, meridional, sulista.

souvenir lembrança.

soviet soviético.

sow (to) semear.

space espaço.

spaceship nave espacial.

spacious espaçoso, amplo, vasto.

spade pá.

Spaniard espanhol.

Spanish espanhol.

Spanish America América Espanhola, Hispano-América.

Spanish American hispano-americano.

spare de sobra; sobressalente, de reserva.

spare time horas vagas, tempo livre.
spare money dinheiro de reserva.
spare room quarto de hóspedes.
spare parts peças sobressalentes.
spare tire pneu sobressalente.
spare (to) poupar *(to save)*; perdoar *(to forgive)*.
sparingly frugalmente.
spark faísca.
spark (to) faiscar.
spark plug vela.
sparrow pardal.
speak (to) falar.
  to speak for falar em favor de, falar em nome de.
  to speak for itself ser evidente, ser claro.
  to speak one's mind dizer o que se pensa.
  to speak out falar claramente.
  to speak to falar a.
  to speak up falar, dizer.
speaker orador, locutor.
spear lança.
spearmint hortelã.
special especial.
  special delivery entrega urgente.
specialist especialista.
specialize (to) especializar.
specially especialmente.
specialty especialidade; ramo especializado *(medicine, etc.)*.
specific específico.
specifically especificamente.
specify (to) especificar.
specimen espécime, amostra.
spectacle espetáculo (espectáculo).
spectacles óculos.
spectator espectador.
speculation especulação.
speech fala; discurso; língua.
  to make a speech fazer um discurso.
speechless estupefato.
speed velocidade.
  at full speed a toda velocidade.
  speed limit velocidade máxima (x = s).
  to speed up acelerar, apressar-se.
speed (to) ir em alta velocidade.
spell (to) soletrar.
spelling ortografia.
spend (to) gastar *(money)*; passar *(time)*.
  to spend time passar tempo.
  to spend the night passar a noite.
  I'll spend the winter in the south. Vou passar o inverno (Inverno) no sul.
spice especiaria, condimento.
spicy condimentado, picante.
spider aranha.
spin giro, volta; parafuso *(aviation)*.
spin (to) fiar *(thread, etc.)*; girar, virar, rodar.
spinach espinafre.

spine espinha *(thorn)*; espinha dorsal *(backbone)*.
spiral espiral.
spirit espírito.
spiritual espiritual.
spit espeto *(for roasting)*; cuspe *(saliva)*.
spit (to) cuspir.
spite rancor, despeito, ressentimento.
  in spite of apesar de.
spiteful rancoroso, vingativo.
splash (to) borrifar; salpicar *(splash with)*.
splendid esplêndido, ótimo (óptimo), magnífico.
splendor esplendor.
split fendido, dividido, partido.
split (to) fender, dividir, partir, repartir.
  They split the difference. Repartiram a diferença.
  to split hairs perder-se em minúcias.
spoil (to) danificar, arruinar, estragar *(to ruin)*; apodrecer *(to rot)*.
spoke raio *(of a wheel)*.
sponge esponja.
sponsor patrocinador *(TV, etc.)*, padrinho.
spontaneity espontaneidade.
spontaneous espontâneo.
spool carretel, bobina.
spoon colher.
  teaspoon colher de chá.
  tablespoon colher de sopa.
spoonful colherada.
sport *adj.* esportivo, de esporte; *n.* esporte (desporto).
  sport shirt camisa-esporte.
sports esportes (desportos).
spot mancha *(stain)*; borrão *(of ink, paint)*; lugar, ponto *(place)*.
  on the spot no lugar, no mesmo lugar; imediatamente; em apuros *(in trouble)*.
sprain torcedura, distensão.
sprain (to) torcer.
spray (to) pulverizar, borrifar.
sprayer pulverizador.
spread difusão, extensão.
spread (to) espalhar; propagar, difundir *(news, etc.)*; estender, distribuir.
spring primavera (Primavera) *(season)*; fonte, manancial *(water)*; salto, pulo *(jump)*; mola *(of wire, etc.)*.
  box spring colchão de molas.
spring (to) saltar, pular.
  to spring at lançar-se sobre.
sprinkle (to) regar *(lawn)*; chuviscar *(rain)*; salpicar *(in cooking)*.
sprout (to) brotar, germinar.
spy espião.
spy (to) espiar, espionar.
squad pelotão, esquadra.
squadron esquadra, esquadrão, esquadrilha.

square quadrado; praça *(town)*.
   two square meters dois metros quadrados.
squash abóbora.
squash (to) esmagar.
squeeze (to) espremer, comprimir, apertar.
squirrel esquilo.
stab punhalada.
stab (to) apunhalar.
staff pau *(pole)*; bastão, bengala *(rod, stick)*; pessoal *(personnel)*; estado-maior *(military)*.
   office staff pessoal de escritório.
   editorial staff redação.
   staff officer oficial de estado-maior.
stage palco, tablado *(theater)*; etapa *(life, etc.)*.
   by stages por etapas.
stage (to) representar, encenar *(theater)*.
stain mancha; tinta, tintura *(coloring)*.
stain (to) manchar.
stair degrau; *pl.* escada.
stake estaca, poste *(for driving into the ground)*.
   at stake arriscado, em perigo.
stake (to) estacar, estaquear *(into the ground)*; apostar, arriscar *(money)*.
stammer (to) gaguejar, tartamudear.
stamp selo; timbre; carimbo *(rubber)*.
   postage stamp selo de correio.
stand posto, banca (quiosque) *(stall)*; tribuna, plataforma *(platform)*; posição, opinião *(opinion)*; resistência *(defense)*.
   newsstand banca (quiosque) de jornais.
stand (to) colocar, pôr em pé *(to set upright)*; levantar-se, pôr-se em pé, estar em pé *(to stand, be standing)*; resistir, sustentar, agüentar (aguentar) *(put up with)*; parar *(to stop moving)*.
   Stand up! Levante-se!
   I'm up. I'm standing. Estou em pé.
   I can't stand him. Não o posso agüentar (aguentar).
   to stand a chance ter uma probabilidade.
   to stand by estar a postos, estar de prontidão.
   to stand for estar por, favorecer, aprovar; significar, querer dizer *(to mean)*; agüentar (aguentar), tolerar, permitir *(to tolerate)*.
   to stand in line fazer fila.
   to stand off manter-se à distância.
   to stand on one's own two feet ser independente.
   to stand one's ground resistir, manter-se firme.
   to stand out salientar-se, distinguir-se.
   to stand up levantar-se, pôr-se em pé.
standard norma, padrão, modelo; estandarte, bandeira *(flag)*.
   standard of living padrão de vida.

   standard time hora oficial.
standpoint ponto de vista.
star estrela, astro.
starch amido *(food)*; goma *(for clothes)*.
start princípio, começo *(beginning)*; partida, começo, saída *(starting point, departure)*; arranque *(of car, engine)*.
start (to) começar *(to begin)*; principiar, partir, sair *(to start out)*; arrancar *(an engine)*.
starvation fome, morte de fome.
starve (to) morrer de fome.
state estado, condição, situação.
state (to) afirmar, declarar.
statement declaração, afirmação; relatório *(report)*; extrato (extracto) de contas, conta *(of account, bill)*.
stateroom camarote *(ship)*, cabina.
statesman estadista.
station estação.
   broadcast station emissora.
   railroad station estação ferroviária.
   police station delegacia.
stationary estacionário, parado.
stationery artigos de papelaria, papel de carta.
stationery store papelaria.
statistical estatístico.
statistics estatística.
statue estátua.
stay estadia, permanência; suspensão *(legal)*.
stay (to) ficar, permanecer, morar, residir; parar; suspender *(to put off)*.
   to stay in ficar em casa.
   to stay in bed ficar na cama.
   to stay away estar ausente, não voltar.
steadily constantemente.
steady firme, fixo (x = ks), estável, constante.
steak bife.
steal (to) roubar, furtar.
steam vapor.
steamboat barco a vapor.
steam engine máquina a vapor.
steamer navio a vapor, vapor.
steamship navio a vapor.
   steamship line companhia de navegação.
steel aço.
steep íngreme, escarpado.
steer (to) g. iar, dirigir, pilotar, conduzir.
steering wheel volante.
stem talo, tronco; raiz *(grammar)*.
stenographer taquígrafo, estenógrafo.
stenography taquigrafia, estenografia.
step passo; degrau *(stair)*.
   step by step passo a passo.
   in step em cadência.
   out of step fora de cadência.
   steps escada *(stairs)*.
step (to) dar um passo, pisar, andar, caminhar.
   to step aside dar passagem.
   to step back retroceder.

to step down descer.
to step in entrar; intervir *(intervene)*.
to step on pisar.
to step out sair; descer *(down)*.
stepbrother meio-irmão.
stepchild enteado.
stepdaughter enteada.
stepfather padrasto.
stepmother madrasta.
stepsister meia-irmã.
stepson enteado.
stern *adj.* austero, severo; *n.* popa, ré.
stew cozido, guisado.
steward camareiro, aeromoço.
stewardess camareira, aeromoça.
stick pau, vara; bastão, bengala *(cane)*.
stick (to) apunhalar *(to stab)*; transpassar,
    perfurar *(to penetrate)*; colar, grudar *(to
    glue)*; fixar (x = ks).
    to stick by manter-se fiel a.
    to stick out pôr para fora; salientar.
    to stick it out aguentar *(aguentar)* firme.
    to stick up for defender, tomar a defesa de.
    to stick to perseverar, sustentar, manter,
        aderir a.
stiff rígido, duro, teso; afetado *(not natural in
    manners)*; cerimonioso *(formal)*; forte
    (wind, drink); caro *(of prices)*.
    stiff collar colarinho engomado.
    stiff neck torcicolo.
stiffen (to) endurecer, fortalecer; obstinar-se.
stiffness rigidez, dureza.
still *adj.* quieto, imóvel, tranquilo *(tranquilo)*;
    adv. ainda, não obstante, entretanto.
    to stand still ficar quieto.
    still life natureza morta.
    Stay still! Não se mexa!
    She's still at home. Ela ainda está em
        casa.
stillness calma, quietude, silêncio.
sting picada.
sting (to) picar.
stir (to) mexer, agitar, misturar; mexer-se
    (move).
    to stir the fire atiçar o fogo.
    to stir up comover, excitar.
stirrup estribo.
stock estoque (existência), mercadoria
    (supply of goods); ações (acções) *(stocks,
    shares)*; gado *(animals)*; estirpe *(lineage,
    race)*.
    stock market Bolsa, mercado de valores.
    in stock em estoque (em existência).
    out of stock esgotado.
stockings meias.
stomach estômago.
stone pedra.
stool banquinho, banco, tamborete.
stop parada (paragem).

stop (to) parar, deter, deter-se; parar, ficar *(to
    stay)*.
    to stop raining deixar (x = sh) de chover.
    Stop! Alto!
    Stop that! Basta! *(That's enough!)*
    Stop a minute. Fique um momento.
store loja, armazém.
    department store magazine, grande
        armazém.
stork cegonha.
storm tempestade.
stormy tempestuoso.
story história, conto *(tale)*; andar *(building)*;
    mentira *(lie)*.
    short story conto.
    as the story goes conforme consta,
        segundo consta.
stout sólido, corpulento, gordo.
stove fogão *(for cooking)*; estufa *(for heating)*.
straight direito, reto (recto).
    straight line linha reta.
    Go straight ahead. Siga bem em frente.
straighten (to) endireitar, pôr em ordem.
straightforward direito; reto (recto); franco
    (frank); honesto, honrado *(honest)*.
strain tensão *(tension)*; esforço *(force)*.
strain (to) coar *(through a strainer)*; cansar
    (the eyes, etc.); esforçar-se *(to make an
    effort)*.
    to stand the strain aguentar (aguentar) o
        esforço.
strainer coador, peneira.
strange èstranho, raro *(odd)*; desconhecido
    (not known).
strangeness estranheza, singularidade.
stranger estrangeiro, estranho,
    desconhecido.
strap correia.
strategic estratégico.
strategy estratégia.
straw palha.
    straw hat chapéu de palha.
    to be on the last straw a última gota, o
        cúmulo.
strawberry morango.
stream corrente, riacho.
street rua.
streetcar bonde Ⓑ (carro eléctrico).
strength força.
strengthen (to) fortalecer(-se), reforçar(-se).
stress stress *(mental strain)*; força *(force)*;
    esforço *(effort)*; tensão *(strain)*; pressão
    (pressure); acento *(accent)*; ênfase
    (emphasis); importância *(importance)*.
stress (to) acentuar, dar ênfase a.
stretch (to) estirar, esticar.
stretcher maca, padiola.
strict estrito (estricto), rigoroso, severo.
strike greve *(of workers)*.

strike (to) bater, dar pancada, golpear; entrar em greve *(workers)*.
  to strike at atacar.
  to strike a match acender um fósforo.
  to strike against chocar-se contra, colidir com.
  to strike back revidar.
  to strike home acertar, acertar no alvo.
striking surpreendente, extraordinário.
string barbante, fio, cordel, corda.
strip faixa *(land);* tiro *(paper).*
stroll passeio, volta.
  to go for a stroll dar uma volta.
stroll (to) passear.
strong forte, poderoso.
stronghold fortaleza, baluarte.
structure estrutura, construção.
struggle luta.
struggle (to) lutar.
stubborn teimoso, obstinado, cabeçudo.
student estudante, aluno.
studious estudioso.
study estudo.
study (to) estudar.
stuff fazenda, pano *(cloth, material);* troços, trens *(belongings);* coisas, trastes, bugigangas *(miscellaneous things);* bobagem, tolice *(foolishness).*
stumble (to) tropeçar.
stump toco *(tree);* coto *(limb).*
stupid estúpido.
  to be stupid ser estúpido.
stupidity estupidez.
stupor estupor.
style estilo, maneira, modo; moda *(fashion).*
subdue (to) subjugar.
subject súdito *(of king);* matéria, assunto, tema *(subject matter).*
subject (to) submeter.
submarine submarino.
submission submissão.
submit (to) submeter, submeter-se.
subordinate subordinado.
subscribe (to) subscrever.
subscriber assinante, subscritor.
subscription subscrição; assinatura *(to magazine).*
subsequent subseqüente (subsequente), seguinte, ulterior.
substance substância.
substantial substancial.
substitute substituto.
substitute (to) substituir.
substitution substituição.
subtract (to) subtrair, deduzir.
suburb subúrbio.
subway metrô.
succeed (to) sair bem, suceder, ter sucesso, ter êxito (x = z); lograr.

success sucesso, êxito (x = z).
successful feliz, bem sucedido, próspero.
successive sucessivo, consecutivo.
successor sucessor.
such tal *(pl.* tais); semelhante.
  such as tal como.
  in such a way de tal modo, de tal maneira.
  such that de modo que, de forma que.
sudden repentino, súbito.
  all of a sudden de repente.
suddenly repentinamente, subitamente.
suffer (to) sofrer.
suffering sofrimento, padecimento.
suffice (to) ser suficiente, bastar.
sugar açúcar.
suggest (to) sugerir.
suggestion sugestão.
suicide suicídio.
  to commit suicide suicidar-se.
suit terno *(fato),* traje completo *(clothes);* processo *(court);* naipe *(cards).*
suit (to) acomodar, adaptar *(to make suitable);* satisfazer, agradar *(to please, to satisfy);* vestir *(to clothe).*
suitable adequado, apropriado.
suitably adequadamente, apropriadamente.
suitcase mala.
sulfur enxofre.
sum soma, total.
summary sumário.
summer verão (Verão).
  summer resort lugar de veraneio.
summit topo, cume; cúmulo.
summon (to) convocar, chamar.
summons citação *(to court).*
sun sol.
  sunbath banho de sol.
  to take a sunbath tomar banho de sol.
sunbeam raio de sol.
sunburn queimadura de sol.
sunburnt queimado pelo sol.
Sunday domingo.
sunlight luz do sol.
sunny de sol, ensolarado *(weather);* alegre, jovial *(disposition).*
sunrise nascer do sol, levantar do sol.
sunset pôr do sol.
sunshine luz solar.
superb esplêndido, soberbo, magnífico.
superfluous supérfluo.
superintendent superintendente.
superior superior.
superiority superioridade.
superstition superstição.
superstitious supersticioso.
supper jantar, ceia.
supplement suplemento.
supply abastecimento.
  supply and demand oferta e procura.

supply (to) abastecer, fornecer, prover.
support apoio, sustento; manutenção (*act of providing for*).
support (to) apoiar, sustentar; manter (*to provide for*).
suppose (to) supor.
supposition suposição, conjetura (conjectura).
suppress (to) suprimir.
suppression supressão.
supreme supremo.
   Supreme Court Corte Suprema.
sure certo, seguro.
   to be sure estar certo.
   be sure to não deixe (x = sh) de.
   for sure ao certo.
surely seguramente, certamente.
surface superfície.
surgeon cirurgião.
surgery cirurgia.
surname apelido, sobrenome.
surprise surpresa.
surprise (to) surpreender.
surprising surpreendente.
surprisingly surpreendentemente.
surrender rendição, entrega.
surrender (to) render(-se), entregar(-se).
surround (to) cercar, rodear.
surrounding circundante.
surroundings arredores, vizinhança; meio, ambiente (*atmosphere*).
survey sondagem (*poll*); exame (x = z), estudo; inspeção (inspecção) (*inspection*); levantamento topográfico (*land*).
survey (to) examinar (x = z), estudar; inspecionar (inspeccionar) (*to inspect*); levantar um plano (*land*).
survival sobrevivência.
survivor sobrevivente.
susceptible suscetível (susceptível).
suspect suspeito.
suspect (to) suspeitar.
suspend (to) suspender.
suspenders suspensórios.
suspicion suspeição, suspeita.
suspicious suspeito (*suspect*); suspeitoso (*distrustful*).
swallow andorinha (bird); bocado (*food*); trago (*drink*).
swallow (to) engolir.
swamp pântano.
swan cisne.
swarm enxame (x = sh).
swarm (to) enxamear (x = sh).
swear (to) jurar, prestar juramento.
   to swear by jurar por.
sweat suor.
sweet doce.
   sweet potato batata doce.

   to have a sweet tooth ser guloso.
sweetheart noivo, noiva.
sweetness doçura.
swell (to) inchar (*medical*), engrossar.
swift rápido, veloz.
swiftly rapidamente, velozmente.
swim (to) nadar.
   My head's swimming. Estou com a cabeça zonza.
swimmer nadador.
swimming pool piscina.
swing balanço (*in playground*); balanceio, oscilação.
   in full swing em plena atividade (actividade).
swing (to) balançar, oscilar, fazer girar.
switch chave (*key*); interruptor, comutador (*electric switch*); agulha (*railroad*).
switch (to) ligar, desligar (*to turn electric switch on or off*); desviar (*railroad*); trocar (*to change*).
sword espada.
syllable sílaba.
symbol símbolo.
sympathetic simpático.
sympathize (to) compadecer-se, simpatizar.
sympathy compaixão, simpatia, pêsames (*condolences*).
symphony sinfonia.
   symphony orchestra orquestra sinfônica (sinfónica).
symptom sintoma.
synthetic sintético.
syrup xarope (x = sh).
system sistema.
systematic sistemático, metódico.

T

table mesa; tabela (*of measures, etc.*).
   to set the table pôr a mesa.
tablecloth toalha de mesa.
table lamp lâmpada de mesa.
tablespoon colher de sopa; colherada (*measurement*).
tablet comprimido (*of aspirin, etc.*); bloco de papel (*for writing*); tábua, chapa, placa (*with an inscription*).
tableware utensílios de mesa.
tact tato (tacto).
tactful com tato (tacto), diplomático.
tactical tático (táctico).
tactics tática (táctica).
tactless sem tato (tacto), indelicado.
tag etiqueta (*on clothing*).
tail rabo; cauda (*of comet, etc.*).
tailor alfaiate.

take (to) tomar; pegar em *(to grasp)*; ganhar *(prize)*.
  to take a bath tomar banho, banhar-se.
  to take a picture tirar uma fotografia, tirar uma foto.
  to take a walk dar um passeio, dar uma volta.
  to take a nap tirar uma soneca.
  to take a trip fazer uma viagem.
  to take an oath prestar juramento.
  to take apart desarmar *(a machine)*.
  to take a step dar um passo.
  to take away levar.
  to take back levar de volta, receber de volta.
  to take into account levar em conta.
  to take advantage of aproveitar-se de.
  to take advice tomar conselho.
  to take care of ter cuidado de.
  to take charge of encarregar-se de.
  to take into consideration levar em consideração.
  to take to heart levar a sério.
  to take it easy ir com calma.
  to take leave despedir-se.
  to take notes tomar notas.
  to take notice observar, notar.
  to take out tirar; levar para fora.
  to take after parecer-se com *(resemble)*.
  to take off decolar, levantar vôo *(plane)*; tirar *(a piece of clothing)*.
  to take one's clothes off despir-se, desnudar-se.
  to take one's shoes off descalçar-se.
  to take part tomar parte.
  to take place acontecer.
  to take possession tomar posse.
  to take refuge refugiar-se.
  to take upon oneself encarregar-se de.

talcum talco.
  talcum powder talco em pó.

tale conto, história, narrativa.

talent talento.

talk conversa, conversação *(conversation)*; palestra, conferência, discurso *(speech)*; rumor, boato *(rumor)*.

talk (to) falar, conversar, dizer.
  to talk back retrucar.
  to talk over discutir.
  to talk to falar a.

talkative loquaz, tagarela.

tall alto.

tame domesticado, manso.

tame (to) domar, domesticar.

tan *n.* bronzeado *(from sun)*; *adj.* bronzeado, marrom, moreno.

tan (to) bronzear-se, amorenar; curtir *(hides)*.

tangled emaranhado.

tank tanque; aquário *(for fish)*.

tape fita.
  tape measure fita métrica.
  tape recorder gravador.

tapestry tapeçaria, tapete.

tar breu, alcatrão.

target alvo, objetivo (objectivo).
  to hit the target dar no alvo.

task tarefa.

taste gosto, sabor.
  in bad taste de mau gosto.
  in good taste de bom gosto.
  to have a taste for ter gosto por.

taste (to) sentir o gosto, saborear; provar *(to try)*; ter gosto de.
  The soup tastes of onion. A sopa tem gosto de cebola.

tavern taverna.

tax taxa (x = sh), imposto.
  income tax imposto de renda.

tax (to) tributar, taxar (x = sh); sobrecarregar *(to test)*.

taxi táxi (x = ks).

tea chá.

teach (to) ensinar.

teacher professor.

teacup xícara de chá, chávena de chá.

teakettle chaleira.

team equipe, time ⑧; junta, parelha *(horses, etc.)*.
  teamwork trabalho de equipe.

teapot bule.

tear lágrima *(from weeping)*; vasgão *(rip)*.
  in tears em pranto, chorando.

tear (to) rasgar.
  to tear down derrubar, demolir.
  to tear to pieces despedaçar, estraçalhar.
  to tear one's hair out arrancar-se os cabelos.

tease (to) implicar com, zombar de.

teaspoon colher de chá.

technical técnico.

technique técnica.

tedious tedioso, chato.

teeth dentes.
  false teeth dentes postiços, dentadura postiça.
  set of teeth dentadura.

telecommunications telecomunicções.

telegram telegrama.

telegraph telégrafo.

telegraph (to) telegrafar.

telepathy telepatia.

telephone telefone.
  telephone book lista telefônica.
  telephone booth cabina telefônica (telefónica).
  telephone call telefonema, chamada telefônica.
  telephone exchange estação telefônica.

telephone operator telefonista.
telephone directory lista telefônica.
telephone (to) telefonar.
telescope telescópio.
television televisão *(the technology);* televisor, aparelho de televisão *(set).*
on television em televisão.
tell (to) dizer; contar, narrar.
to tell a story contar uma história.
Who told you so? Quem lhe disse isso?
Tell him to stop. Manda-lhe parar.
temper temperamento, disposição, humor.
bad temper mau humor.
to lose one's temper perder a paciência.
temperament temperamento, disposição.
tempest tempestade, temporal.
temple templo; têmpora, fonte *(of the head).*
temporarily temporariamente.
temporary temporário, provisório.
tempt (to) tentar, provocar.
temptation tentação.
tempting tentado.
ten dez.
tenacious tenaz.
tenant inquilino, locatário.
tendency tendência.
tender tenro, macio; carinhoso,
tender-hearted compassivo.
tennis tênis (ténis).
tennis court quadra de tênis.
tense tenso.
tension tensão.
tent tenda, barraca.
tentative provisório, tentativo.
tenth décimo.
term termo, prazo; *pl.* condições; mandato *(office).*
to be on good terms with ter boas relações com.
to come to terms chegar a um acordo.
terminal *adj.* terminal, final, último; *n.* terminal, estação final.
terrace terraço.
terrible terrível.
terribly terrivelmente.
territory território.
terror terror, pavor.
terse conciso, breve, sucinto.
terseness concisão, brevidade.
test prova, ensaio *(trial);* exame (x = z), análise.
test (to) ensaiar, experimentar, examinar (x = z).
testify (to) testemunhar testificar.
text texto.
textbook livro escolar.
than que, do que.
more than that mais (do) que isso.
fewer than menos que, menos de.

He is richer than I am. Ele é mais rico (do) que eu.
thank (to) agradecer.
Thank you. Obrigado.
Thank God! Graças a Deus!
thankful agradecido, reconhecido.
thanks obrigado.
thanks to graças a.
that *dem. adj. and pron.* esse, essa, isso, aquele, aquela, aquilo; *rel. pron.* que, quem, o qual, a qual; *adv.* tão; *conj.* que, para que.
that man aquele homem, esse homem.
that woman aquela mulher, essa mulher.
That's it. Isso é. Isso mesmo.
That is to say. Isto é.
That may be. É possível. Talvez.
That's all. É tudo.
That way. Por ali.
That's how it's done. Assim é como se faz.
not that far não tão longe.
so that de modo que, para que.
in order that para que, de maneira que.
the o, a, os, as.
the man o homem.
the men os homens.
the woman a mulher.
the women as mulheres.
the sooner the better quanto antes melhor.
theater teatro.
theatrical teatral.
their seu, sua, seus, suas, deles, delas.
them os, as, lhes, eles, elas.
theme tema.
themselves eles mesmos, elas mesmas, si mesmos, se.
then então, nesse tempo.
now and then de vez em quando.
and then e então.
just then nesse mesmo momento.
by then naquela altura.
what then? e então?
theoretical teórico.
theory teoria.
there ali, aí *(near the person addressed),* lá, acolá *(more remote).*
Put it there. Ponha-o aí.
I was there. Eu estive ali.
Go there. Vá lá.
Over there. Por ali. Lá.
there is há.
there are há.
thereabouts por aí, por ali.
thereafter depois disso, daí em diante.
thereby assim, desse modo.
therefore portanto, por isso.
thermometer termômetro (termómetro).
these estes, estas.

thesis tese.
they eles, elas.
thick grosso, denso.
   three inches thick três polegadas de grossura.
   thick-headed estúpido.
thickness espessura, grossura.
thief ladrão.
thigh coxa (x = sh).
thimble dedal.
thin magro, delgado (person); ralo (liquid).
thing coisa, objeto (objecto).
   something alguma coisa.
   anything qualquer coisa.
think (to) pensar, crer, achar.
   to think of pensar em.
   to think well of pensar bem de.
   As you think fit. Como você quiser.
   to think it over pensá-lo.
   to think nothing of não ligar a mínima importância.
   to think twice pensar bem.
   I don't think so. Não acho. Acho que não.
   I think so. Acho que sim.
   Don't even think it! Nem pensar!
thinness magreza.
third terceiro, terceira parte.
   a third person um terceiro.
thirst sede.
   to be thirsty estar com sede, ter sede.
thirteen treze.
thirteenth décimo terceiro.
thirtieth trigésimo.
thirty trinta.
this este, esta.
   this man este homem.
   this woman esta mulher.
   this evening hoje à noite.
   this one and that one este e aquele.
   this and that isto e aquilo.
   like this assim.
thorn espinho.
thorough completo, minucioso, profundo.
thoroughfare via, passagem.
thoroughly completamente, minuciosamente.
those aqueles, aquelas.
though embora, ainda que.
   as though como se.
   even though mesmo que.
thought pensamento.
   to give thought to pensar em.
thoughtful pensativo, atento; atencioso, solícito.
thoughtfully atenciosamente, pensativamente.
thoughtfulness reflexão (x = ks), meditação, atenção.
thoughtless descuidado, imprudente.
thoughtlessly descuidadamente, sem reflexão (x = ks).

thousand mil; pl. milhares.
thousandth milésimo.
thread linha, fio; rosca (of screw).
thread (to) enfiar.
threat ameaça.
threaten (to) ameaçar.
three três.
three hundred trezentos.
threshold limiar, soleira.
thrift economia, frugalidade.
thrifty frugal, econômico (económico).
thrill emoção, sensação.
thrill (to) emocionar(-se), excitar.
throat garganta.
   sore throat dor de garganta.
throne trono.
through adj. direto (directo); adv. de uma parte a outra, de lado a lado, completamente, totalmente; prep. por, através de, por meio de, devido a, por causa de.
   through and through completamente.
   to be through ter terminado.
   to be through with cortar relações com, ter acabado com.
   a through train um trem direto (um comboio directo).
   through the door pela porta.
   through his influence devido a sua influência.
   through the years ao longo dos anos.
   health through honey saúde atraves do mel.
throughout prep. durante todo, por todo, em todo; adv. por toda parte, completamente.
throw (to) atirar, lançar.
   to throw out deitar fora, jogar fora.
   to throw light on esclarecer.
thumb polegar.
thumbnail unha do polegar.
thumbtack percevejo.
thunder trovão.
thunder (to) trovejar.
thunderbolt raio.
thunderstorm trovoada.
Thursday quinta-feira, quinta.
thus assim, deste modo, como segue.
   thus far até aqui, até este ponto.
ticket bilhete.
   round-trip ticket bilhete de ida e volta.
   ticket window guichê (guichet), bilheteria (bilheteira).
tickle (to) fazer cócegas.
tide maré.
   high tide maré alta.
   low tide maré baixa (x = sh).
tie gravata (necktie); vínculo, laço (bond); nó (knot); dormente (of railroad); empate (score); jogo empatado (tie game).

tie (to) atar, amarrar.
tiger tigre.
tight apertado, justo, firme; escasso *(money)*.
tighten (to) apertar.
tile telha *(for roof)*, azulejo.
till até, até que.
    till now até agora.
till (to) cultivar.
timber madeira.
time tempo; hora; vez; época.
    What time is it? Que horas são?
    the first time a primeira vez.
    What time is dinner? A que horas vamos jantar?
    on time a tempo, na hora.
    a long time ago há muito tempo.
    at the same time ao mesmo tempo.
    at no time nunca.
    one at a time um por vez.
    at this time agora *(now)*.
    at that time a estas horas *(time of day)*.
    at times às vezes.
    for the time being por agora.
    from time to time de vez em quando.
    in no time imediatamente, num instante.
    to be on time estar na hora.
    Have a good time! Divirta-se!
    spare time horas vagas.
timely *adj.* oportuno, conveniente.
timetable horário.
time zone fuso horário.
timid tímido.
timidity timidez.
tin estanho.
    tin can lata.
tincture tintura.
    tincture of iodine tintura de iodo.
tinfoil papel de estanho.
tint matiz.
tip ponta, extremidade *(point, end)*; gorjeta *(gratuity)*; palpite *(inside information)*; aviso dica *(suggestion)*.
tip (to) inclinar *(to slant)*; dar uma gorjeta *(to give a gratuity)*; avisar *(to tip off)*.
tire pneu.
    flat tire pneu vazio.
tire (to) cansar, fatigar; aborrecer *(to bore)*.
tireless incansável, infatigável.
tissue tecido *(skin, etc.)*; lenço de papel *(for blowing nose)*.
    tissue paper papel de seda.
title título.
    title page frontispício, página de rosto.
to a, para, de, por, até, que.
    to give to dar a.
    to go to ir a.
    ready to go pronto para ir-se embora.
    It's time to leave. Está na hora de sair.
    the time has come chegou a hora.

    from house to house de casa em casa.
    to be done por fazer.
    letters to be written cartas por escrever.
    to this day até agora.
    in order to para, a fim de.
    to and fro para cá e para lá.
    I have to go. Tenho que ir-me. Tenho de ir-me.
    I have something to do. Tenho alguma coisa para fazer.
    It's twenty (minutes) to three. Faltam vinte para as três. São duas horas e quarenta minutos.
toad sapo.
toast torradas *(bread)*; brinde *(drink)*.
toast (to) torrar; brindar.
toaster torradeira.
tobacco tabaco, fumo.
    tobacco shop tabacaria.
today hoje.
    a week from today daqui a oito dias.
toe dedo do pé.
together juntos; juntamente, ao mesmo tempo.
    Let's go together. Vamos juntos.
    together with junto com.
    to call together reunir.
toil labuta.
toilet banheiro *(bathroom)*.
    toilet soap sabonete.
    toilet paper papel higiênico (higiénico).
    toilet bowl vaso sanitário.
    toilet water água-de-colônia (colónia) *(cologne)*.
tolerance tolerância.
tolerant tolerante.
tolerate (to) tolerar.
tomato tomate.
    tomato juice suco de tomate.
tomb túmulo, sepultura.
tomorrow amanhã.
    the day after tomorrow depois de amanhã.
    tomorrow morning amanhã de manhã.
ton tonelada.
tone tom.
tongs tenaz.
tongue língua.
    to hold one's tongue calar-se.
tonic tônico (tónico).
tonight hoje à noite, esta noite.
tonsil amígdala.
tonsilitis amigdalite.
too demais *(too much)*, também *(also)*.
    too much demais, muito.
    too many demais, muitos.
    Too bad! Que pena!
    It's too early. É cedo demais.
    That's too much. That's the last straw. É o cúmulo.

me (I) too eu também.
one dollar too much um dólar demais.
That's too little. Isso é muito pouco.
tool ferramenta.
tooth dente.
    toothache dor de dente(s).
toothbrush escova de dentes.
toothpaste pasta de dentes.
toothpick palito.
top pico, cume; parte superior; superfície, topo; pião *(toy)*; top *(shirt)*.
    the top of the mountain o cume da montanha.
    at top speed a toda velocidade.
    from top to bottom de cima para baixo (x = sh).
    from top to toe da cabeça aos pés.
topcoat sobretudo.
torch tocha.
torment tormento.
torrent torrente, toró, borbotão.
torrid tórrido.
    torrid zone zona tórrida.
tortoise tartaruga.
torture tortura, tormento.
torture (to) torturar, atormentar.
total total.
touch toque, contato (contacto).
    to be in touch with estar em contato com.
touch (to) tocar.
touching comovedor, comovente, tocante.
tough duro, forte; difícil.
toughen (to) endurecer(-se).
tour viagem, viagem de turismo; turnê, digressão *(by musician)*.
    to go on tour fazer turnê.
tour (to) percorrer, viajar por.
touring turismo.
tourist turista.
    tourist agency agência de turismo.
    tourist guide guia de turismo.
tournament torneio.
toward para, para com, em direção a.
    to go toward a place ir para um lugar.
    his attitude toward me a atitude dele para mim.
towel toalha.
    face towel toalha de rosto.
    bath towel toalha de banho.
tower torre.
town cidade.
    town hall prefeitura (câmara municipal).
tow truck reboque.
toy brinquedo.
trace indício, rasto.
trace (to) seguir a pista de, investigar; traçar, esboçar *(to mark out)*.
track rasto, pista; trilho *(rail)*; pista *(race)*.
trade comércio, ofício *(skill, job)*.

trademark marca registrada, marca de fábrica, marca de comércio.
    trade union sindicato.
trading comércio.
tradition tradição.
traditional tradicional.
traffic tráfego, trânsito; tráfico *(illegal)*.
tragedy tragédia.
tragic trágico.
train trem (comboio).
    train car vagão.
train (to) treinar, instruir; amestrar *(dogs)*.
training treinamento, treino.
traitor traidor.
tramp vagabundo.
tranquil tranqüilo (tranquilo).
transatlantic transatlântico.
transfer transferência; passagem, bilhete *(bus, etc.)*; transporte.
transfer (to) transferir, transportar.
translate (to) traduzir.
translation tradução.
translator tradutor.
transparent transparente.
transport transporte.
transport (to) transportar.
transportation transporte.
trap armadilha.
trap (to) apanhar, capturar.
trash lixo.
travel (to) viajar.
traveler viajante.
tray bandeja.
treacherous traiçoeiro; perigoso *(dangerous)*.
treachery traição.
tread passo, pisada.
tread (to) pisar.
treason traição.
treasure tesouro.
treasure (to) prezar, apreciar.
treasurer tesoureiro.
treasury tesouraria.
treat (to) tratar; convidar *(with food, etc.)*.
    to treat a patient tratar de um paciente.
    to treat well (badly) dar bom (mau) tratamento.
treatment tratamento.
treaty tratado.
tree árvore.
tremble (to) tremer, estremecer.
trembling *adj.* trêmulo (trémulo); *n.* tremor, estremecimento.
tremendous tremendo, enorme; sensacional *(wonderful)*.
trench trincheira.
trend tendência.
    to set the trend dar o tom.
trial prova, ensaio, tentativa; julgamento *(law)*.

triangle triângulo.
tribe tribo.
tribunal tribunal.
trick truque, trapaça, peça.
  to do the trick resolver o problema.
  to play a trick pregar uma peça.
trifle bagatela, insignificância.
trim (to) cortar, aparar *(hair)*; podar *(trees)*; adornar, decorar *(clothes)*.
trimming adorno, decoração.
trinket buginganga, berloque.
trip viagem *(voyage)*; tropeço *(stumble)*.
  one-way trip viagem de ida.
  round trip viagem de ida e volta.
trip (to) tropeçar, fazer tropeçar.
triple triplo.
triumph triunfo.
triumph (to) triunfar.
triumphant triunfante.
trivial insignificante, trivial.
trolley bonde (carro eléctrico).
troops tropas.
trophy troféu.
tropic trópico.
tropical tropical.
trot (to) trotar.
trouble dificuldade *(difficulty)*; incômodo *(bother)*; desordem *(disorder)*; doença *(illness)*.
  to be in trouble estar em apuros.
  not to be worth the trouble não valer a pena.
  It's no trouble at all. Incômodo (incômodo) nenhum.
trouble (to) preocupar, perturbar; importunar *(ask)*.
troubled preocupado, perturbado.
troublesome importuno, difícil, desagradável.
trousers calças.
trout truta.
truck caminhão.
true certo, exato (exacto) (x = z), verdadeiro; fiel, leal *(faithful)*.
  It's true. É verdade.
trunk tronco *(tree)*; baú, mala *(for packing)*; mala *(of car)*.
trust confiança.
  in trust em fideicomisso.
trust (to) confiar em, ter confiança em.
  I trust her. Confio nela.
trustworthy digno de confiança.
truth verdade.
truthful verdadeiro, verídico.
truthfulness veracidade, autenticidade.
try (to) tentar; experimentar; provar *(test)*; procurar *(try and)*.
  to try on clothes provar roupa.
  Try to do it. Tente fazê-lo.

Try the shrimp! Experimento os camarões!
tub tina.
  bathtub banheira.
tube tubo, cano.
Tuesday terça-feira, terça.
tuna atum.
tune toada, melodia.
  to be out of tune estar desafinado.
tune (to) afinar *(musical instrument)*; sintonizar *(radio)*.
tunnel túnel.
turkey peru.
turn turno, período, vez *(time, order)*; volta, giro *(motion)*; favor *(favor)*.
  by turns alternativamente.
  in turn por sua vez.
  to take turns cada uma ter a sua vez.
  It's my turn now. Agora é a minha vez.
turn (to) girar *(key in lock)*, rodar *(wheel)*; dobrar, virar *(to change direction)*; tornar-se *(to become)*.
  to turn around virar.
  to turn down recusar, rejeitar *(to refuse)*; abaixar (x = sh), diminuir *(lights, etc.)*.
  to turn into transformar, converter.
  to turn off fechar *(faucet)*; desligar *(radio, etc.)*; apagar *(light)*.
  to turn on ligar *(radio, etc.)*; abrir *(faucet)*; acender *(light)*.
  to turn back voltar atrás.
  to turn one's back on dar as costas a.
  to turn over transferir *(to transfer)* entregar, dar *(to hand over)*; ponderar, considerar *(to think about)*; fazer girar *(motor)*.
  to turn sour azedar.
  to turn up aparecer.
  in turn por sua vez.
turnip nabo.
turtle cágado.
tweezers pinças.
twelfth décimo segundo.
twelve doze.
twentieth vigésimo.
twenty vinte.
twice duas vezes.
twilight crepúsculo.
twin gêmeo.
  twin brother irmão gêmeo.
twist (to) torcer, retorcer.
two dois, f. duas.
two hundred duzentos.
type tipo.
type (to) escrever à máquina.
typewriter máquina de escrever.
  portable typewriter máquina de escrever portátil.

typewriter ribbon fita de máquina de escrever.
typical típico.
typist datilógrafo.
tyrannical tirânico.
tyranny tirania.
tyrant tirano.

U

ugly feio.
ulcer úlcera.
umbrella guarda-chuva.
umpire árbitro.
unable incapaz.
 I was unable to do it. Não pude fazê-lo. Foi-me impossível.
unanimous unânime.
unaware inconsciente.
unbearable insuportável.
unbutton (to) desabotoar.
uncertain incerto.
uncertainty incerteza.
unchangeable imutável, permanente.
uncle tio.
uncomfortable incômodo (incómodo) *(accommodations)*; desagradável *(situation)*.
unconquered invicto, indomado.
undecided indeciso.
under debaixo (x = sh), em; menos, sob.
 under the table debaixo da mesa.
 under consideration em consideração.
 under penalty of sob pena de.
 underage menor de idade.
 under contract conforme o contrato.
 under the circumstances em tais circunstâncias.
 under obligation dever favores.
 under one's nose nas barbas.
 in under an hour em menos de uma hora.
undergo (to) agüentar (aguentar), passar por, sofrer, submeter-se.
 to undergo an operation submeter-se a uma operação.
underground subterrâneo.
underline (to) sublinhar.
underneath embaixo (x = sh), debaixo (x = sh), sob.
understand (to) compreender, entender.
 Do you understand? Compreende?
understanding entendimento, acordo.
 to come to an understanding chegar a um acordo.
undertake (to) empreender, encarregar-se de.
undertaking empresa, compromisso, promessa *(promise)*.

underwear ropa de baixo.
undo (to) desfazer, desatar; desprender *(belt, etc.)*.
undress (to) despir-se.
uneasiness inquietude, desassossego.
uneasy inquieto, desassossegado.
unequal desigual.
uneven desigual; irregular *(surface)*.
unexpected inesperado.
unfair injusto.
unfaithful infiel, desleal.
unfavorable desfavorável.
unfinished inacabado, incompleto.
unfit inadequado, impróprio.
unfold (to) desdobrar, estender; revelar, esclarecer *(plot, etc.)*.
unforeseen imprevisto.
unforgettable inespecível.
unfortunate desventurado, infeliz.
unfortunately infelizmente.
unfurnished desmobiliado (desmobilado), sem móveis.
 unfurnished apartment apartamento sem móveis.
ungrateful ingrato.
unhappy infeliz, descontente com *(with something)*.
unhealthy doentio *(person)*; malsão.
unheard of inaudito *(extraordinary)*; desconhecido *(unknown)*.
unhurt ileso.
uniform uniforme.
union sindicato.
unit unidade; grupo *(team)*.
unite (to) unir(-se).
united unido.
 United States Estados Unidos.
unity unidade.
universal universal.
universality universalidade.
universe universo.
university universidade.
unjust injusto.
unkind cruel.
unknown desconhecido.
unless a menos que, a não ser que, se não.
unlike ao contrário de.
unlikely improvável *(results, etc.)*; inverossímil *(explanation)*.
unload (to) descarregar.
unlucky desafortunado, infeliz.
unmarried solteiro.
 bachelor, unmarried man solteiro.
 unmarried woman solteira.
unmoved impassível, indiferente, frio.
unnecessary desnecessário.
unpaid a pagar, não pago *(bills)*, não remunerado *(worker)*.
unpleasant desagradável.

unquestionable indiscutível, indisputável.
unreasonable irracional, injusto.
unrest desassossego, inquietação; distúrbios *(political)*.
unruly ingovernável, rebelde.
unsatisfactory insatisfatório, inadequado.
unseen não visto, inobservado.
unselfish desinteressado.
unsettled inquieto; variável, inconstante *(not stable)*; não pago, não saldado *(not paid)*.
unsteady instável; inconstante, inseguro.
unsuccessful sem exito *(artist)*; malogrado, frustrado *(plan)*.
unsuitable impróprio, inadequado, inconveniente.
until até.
untiring incansável, infatigável.
unusual extraordinário, raro, incomum, insólito.
unwelcome mal acolhido *(feeling)*; indesejável *(occurrence, etc.)*.
unwilling relutante, sem vontade.
unwillingly de má vontade.
unwise imprudente.
unworthy indigno.
unwritten não escrito; tácito *(secret)*.
up para cima; em pé, de pé.
   up and down para cima e para baixo (x = sh), de um lado para outro.
   to go up a mountain ir montanha acima.
   to go up subir.
   to go upstairs subir a escada.
   What's up? Que (se) passa? O que é que há?
   She's not up yet. Ela ainda não se levantou.
   up-to-date moderno, contemporaneo; atualizad *(updated)*.
update (to) atualizar.
upon sobre, em cima de.
upper superior, de cima.
   upper floor andar superior.
   upper lip lábio superior.
upright vertical; direito, justo *(character)*.
upset (to) transtornar *(disrupt)*; perturbar *(make someone upset)*.
upside down invertido; de cabeça para baixo (x = sh).
upstairs andar superior; em cima, para cima.
   to go upstairs subir.
upstart arrivista.
upward para cima, acima.
urgency urgência.
urgent urgente.
Uruguyan uruguaio.
use uso.
   to make use of utilizar, servir-se de.
   in use em uso.
   of no use inútil, não servir para nada.

   It's no use. Não adianta. É inútil.
   What's the use? Para quê? É inútil. Não adianta.
use (to) usar, servir-se de, utilizar, empregar.
   to use up gastar, esgotar, consumir.
   to get used to acostumar-se a.
   I'm used to it. Estou acostumado.
   I used to see her every day. Eu acostumava vê-la todos os dias. Eu a via (via-a) todos os dias.
used usado, de segunda mão.
useful útil.
useless inútil, vão.
usher indicador, lanterninha *(theater, etc.)*.
usual usual, habitual, costumeiro.
   as usual como de costume.
usually normalmente, geralmente.
   I usually get up early. Geralmente eu me levanto (levanto-me) cedo.
utensil utensílio.
   kitchen utensils utensílios de cozinha.
utility utilidade.
utilize (to) utilizar, empregar.
utmost maior, máximo (x = s).
utterly inteiramente, totalmente, completamente.

V

vacancy vaga, vacância; quarto livre.
vacant vago *(post)*; vazio *(house)*; livre *(rental, seat)*.
vacation férias.
   to go on vacation ir de férias.
vaccinate (to) vacinar.
vaccine vacina.
vacuum vácuo.
vacuum cleaner aspirador de pó.
vague vago.
vain vão.
   in vain em vão.
vainly inutilmente, futilmente.
valid válido.
valley vale.
valuable valioso, de valor.
value valor, valia; preço *(price)*; apreço, estima *(regard)*.
value (to) avaliar *(to estimate the value)*; apreciar, estimar *(to think highly of)*.
valve válvula.
vanilla baunilha.
vanish (to) desaparecer.
vanity vaidade.
variable variável.
variety variedade.
various vários, diversos.
varnish verniz.

vary (to) variar.
vaseline vaselina.
vast vasto, imenso, enorme.
VCR videocassete.
veal carne de vitela.
    veal cutlet costeleta de vitela.
vegetable legume, *pl.* verduras.
vegetation vegetação.
vehement veemente.
vehicle veículo.
veil véu.
vein veia *(body)*, veio, filão *(mineral)*.
    Let's continue in the same vein.
        Continuamos no mesmo veio.
velvet veludo.
vendor vendedor; camelô *(street)*.
Venezuelan venezuelano.
vengeance vingança.
    with a vengeance para valer.
ventilate (to) ventilar.
ventilation ventilação.
veranda varanda.
verb verbo.
verdict veredicto, decisão.
verse verso *(poetry)*; estrote *(stanza)*;
    versículo *(in scripture)*.
vertical vertical.
very muito.
    very much muito, muitíssimo.
    very many muitíssimos, muitíssimas.
    very much money muito dinheiro.
    (Very) much obliged. Muito
        agradecido.
    Very well, thank you. Muito bem,
        obrigado.
    the very same man o mesmo homem.
    on the very same day precisamente no
        mesmo dia.
vessel vaso, vasilha *(for liquids)*; navio *(ship)*;
    vaso *(blood)*.
vest colete.
veteran veterano.
veterinary veterinário.
vex (to) irritar, amolar.
vexation amolação, irritação.
vibration vibração.
vice vício.
vice-president vice-presidente.
vice versa vice versa.
vicinity vizinhança.
vicious vicioso, malvado, malévolo.
    vicious circle círculo vicioso.
victim vítima.
victor vencedor.
victorious vitorioso.
victory vitória.
video vídeo.
videocassette videocassete.
videodisk videodisco.

video game videogame, videojogo.
video recorder videocassete.
videotape videoteipe.
view vista, panorama, paisagem.
    in view of em vista de.
    point of view ponto de vista.
    What a view! Que vista! Que paisagem!
view (to) olhar, ver.
vigil vigília.
vigilant vigilante.
vigor vigor, força, vitalidade.
vigorous vigoroso.
vile vil, baixo (x = sh).
villa casa de campo.
village aldeia, povoado.
villager aldeão.
villain vilão.
vine vinha, videira.
vinegar vinagre.
vineyard vinha.
violate (to) violar.
violation violação.
violence violência.
violent violento.
violet violeta.
violin violino.
violinist violinista.
virgin virgem.
virtue virtude.
virtuous virtuoso.
visa visto.
visible visível.
vision visão.
visit visita.
    to pay a visit visitar, fazer uma visita.
visitor visitante, visita.
visual visual.
vital vital, essencial.
vitamin vitamina.
vivid vívido, vivo.
vocal vocal.
    vocal cords cordas vocais.
voice voz.
    voice mail correio de voz.
void *adj.* inválido, nulo; *n.* vazio.
volcano vulcão.
volt volt.
volume volume; tomo *(book)*.
voluntary voluntário.
volunteer voluntário.
vomit vômito (vómito).
vomit (to) vomitar.
vote voto; votação *(voting)*; sufrágio *(right to vote)*.
vote (to) votar.
voter votante, eleitor.
vow voto.
vow (to) fazer voto.
voyage viagem.

voyager viajante.
vulgar vulgar.
vulture abutre.

W

wade (to) vadear.
wage (to) empreender, fazer.
    to wage war fazer guerra.
wager aposta.
wager (to) fazer aposta.
wages salário, ordenado.
wagon carroça (horse-drawn); carro de mão
    (child's).
waist cintura.
wait (to) esperar; aguardar (to await).
    Wait for me. Espere-me.
    to keep waiting fazer esperar, deixar
        esperando.
    to wait on servir.
waiting room sala de espera.
waiter garçom (empregado).
waitress garçonete (empregada).
wake (to) acordar, despertar.
    to wake up acordar, despertar.
    I woke up at seven. Acordei às sete.
walk passeio.
    to take a walk dar um passeio.
walk (to) andar, caminhar.
    to walk away from afastar-se.
    to walk down descer.
    to walk up subir.
    to walk out sair.
    to walk out on abandonar, desertar.
    to go for a walk dar um passeio.
    walking cane bengala.
wall parede; muro (exterior); muralha
    (city, etc.).
    wallpaper papel de parede.
walnut noz; nogueira (tree).
waltz valsa.
waltz (to) valsar, dançar uma valsa.
wand vara, varinha.
wander (to) vagar; desviar-se (to go astray).
want necessidade, falta.
    to be in want estar necessitado.
    for want of por falta de.
want (to) querer, desejar (to desire); precisar
    de, necessitar (to need).
    What do you want? Que deseja o senhor?
    Don't you want to come? Não quer vir?
    Cook wanted. Precisa-se cozinheiro.
wanting falto, insuficiente.
    to be wanting faltar.
war guerra.
    War Department Ministério da Guerra.
    to wage war fazer guerra.

ward ala, divisão (hospital); bairro, distrito
    (city); pupilo, tutelado (under a guardian).
warden administrador, diretor (prison).
ward off (to) aparar, desviar, repelir.
wardrobe guarda-roupa.
warehouse armazém.
wares mercadorias.
warfare guerra, combate.
warlike bélico, belicoso.
warm quente; cordial (welcome, etc.).
    It's warm. Está quente.
    I am warm. Estou com calor. Tenho calor.
    warm water água quente.
warm (to) aquecer.
    to warm up aquecer (leftovers, etc.);
        esquentar (athletic).
warmly calorosamente, cordialmente.
warn (to) advertir, prevenir, avisar.
warning advertência, aviso.
    to give warning advertir.
warrant autorização; mandado (legal).
warrior guerreiro.
wash lavagem, roupa para lavar, roupa lavada.
    washbasin lavatório, bacia.
    washing machine máquina de lavar roupa.
wash (to) lavar(-se).
    to wash one's hands lavar as mãos.
waste desperdício; perda (time).
waste (to) desgastar, desperdiçar; perder
    (time).
wastebasket cesto para papéis.
watch relógio; guarda (guard).
    wristwatch relógio-pulseira.
    to wind a watch dar corda a.
watch (to) ver, olhar; guardar, vigiar (to watch
    over).
    to watch out ter cuidado.
    to watch TV ver televisão.
watchful alerta, vigilante, atento.
watchmaker relojoeiro.
watchman guarda, vigia.
watchword lema.
water água.
    fresh water água doce.
    hot water água quente.
    mineral water água mineral.
    running water água corrente.
    seltzer water água gasosa.
    water faucet torneira.
    water power força hidráulica.
    to make one's mouth water dar água na
        boca.
water (to) regar (houseplants); irrigar (fields);
    lacrimejar (eyes).
waterfall cachoeira, queda d'água.
watermelon melancia.
waterproof impermeável, à prova d'água.
wave onda, ondulação; vaga (of people, etc.).
    short wave onda curta.

long wave onda longa.
sound wave onda sonora.
wavelength comprimento de onda.
wave (to) ondular; fazer sinais (to signal by waving); agitar (an object).
   to wave one's hand fazer sinais com a mão.
   to wave to someone acenar.
waver (to) vacilar, hesitar.
wavering vacilante, hesitante.
wavy ondulado.
wax cera.
   wax candle vela de cera.
   wax paper papel encerado.
wax (to) encerar.
way caminho, via, rumo (path, direction); modo, maneira (manner).
   way in entrada.
   way out saída.
   by way of via.
   by the way a propósito.
   in such a way de tal maneira.
   in this way deste modo.
   any way de qualquer modo.
   in no way de nenhum modo, de maneira alguma.
   this way assim, desta maneira.
   Go this way. Vá por aqui.
   on the way to a caminho para, rumo de.
   out of the way fora do caminho; longe; raro.
   Which way? Por onde?
   Step this way. Venha por aqui. Venda cá.
   No way! De modo nenhum!
   in some way or other de um modo ou de outro.
   under way a caminho, em marcha.
   the other way around ao contrário.
   I'm on my way. Já vou.
   all the way todo o caminho.
   to give way ceder.
   to make way abrir caminho.
we nós.
   the five of us nós cinco.
weak débil, fraco.
weaken (to) debilitar(-se), enfraquecer(-se).
weakness debilidade, fraqueza.
wealth riqueza, abundância.
wealthy rico, abastado.
weapon arma.
wear (to) usar, vestir.
   to wear down desgastar.
   to wear off passar, diminuir.
   to wear out gastar-se, desgastar.
   to wear well durar (to last).
weariness cansaço, fadiga.
weary cansado, fatigado.
weary (to) cansar(-se), fatigar(-se).
weather tempo.

bad weather mau tempo.
   nice weather bom tempo.
weave (to) tecer.
web teia; rede (network).
   spider web teia de aranha.
wedding boda, casamento.
   wedding dress vestido de noiva.
   wedding ring aliança.
wedge cunha.
Wednesday quarta-feira, quarta.
weed erva daninha.
week semana.
   weekday dia útil.
   last week a semana passada.
   next week a semana que vem.
weekend fim de semana.
weekly adj. semanal; adv. semanalmente.
   weekly publication semanário.
weep (to) chorar.
   to weep for, to weep over chorar por.
weigh (to) pesar; levantar ferro (to weigh anchor).
weight peso.
   gross weight peso bruto.
   net weight peso líquido.
   to gain weight engordecer.
   to lose weight emagrecer.
   weights and measures pesos e medidas.
weighty pesado; importante.
weird esquisito, estranho.
welcome adj. bem-vindo; n. acolhimento, recepção.
   Welcome! Bem-vindo!
   You're welcome. De nada (answer to "Thank you.").
welcome (to) dar as boas-vindas.
welfare assistência social (public dole).
well poço.
well adj. bom; adv. bem.
   to be well sentir-se bem.
   very well muito bem.
   I don't feel well. Não me sinto bem.
   well-being bem-estar.
   well-bred bem educado.
   well-done bem feito; bem passado (meat).
   well-to-do rico, abastado, próspero.
   well-known conhecido.
   well-timed oportuno.
   as well as assim como, tanto como, tanto quanto.
   Well then? E agora?
   Very well! Está bem!
   Well, I'm not sure. Bem, não tenho certo.
west oeste, ocidente.
western ocidental.
wet molhado, úmido.
   to get wet molhar-se.
wet (to) molhar.
wharf cais.

what que, o que.

   What's that? Que é isso?

   What's the matter? O que é que há?

   What else? Que mais?

   What for? Para quê?

whatever qualquer que, tudo quanto.

   whatever you like o que você quiser.

wheat trigo.

wheel roda.

   steering wheel volante.

   wheelchair cadeira de rodas.

wheelbarrow carrinho de mão.

when quando.

   Since when? Desde quando?

whenever quando, sempre que, quando quer que.

   whenever you like quando você quiser.

where onde.

   Where is Onde está; cadê *(colloquial).*

   Where are you from? Donde (de onde) é o senhor?

   Where are you going? Para onde vai?

whereby pelo qual, por meio de que, por meio do qual.

wherever onde quer que.

whether se, quer, ou.

   I doubt whether duvido que.

   whether he likes it or not quer queira quer não.

which qual, que, o qual, a qual.

   Which book? Que livro?

   Which way? Por onde? Por que caminho?

   Which of these? Qual destes?

   all of which todo o qual, todos dos quais.

whichever qualquer.

while *n.* momento, tempo; *conj.* enquanto; embora *(whereas).*

   in a little while daquia pouco.

   a little while ago há pouco tempo.

   for a while por algum tempo.

   once in a while de vez em quando.

   to be worthwhile valer a pena.

whim capricho.

whip açoite, chicote, látego.

whip (to) chicotear, açoitar; bater *(cream, eggs, etc.).*

   whipped cream nata batida.

whirl remoinho, rodopio.

whirl (to) girar, rodopiar, redemoinhar.

whirlpool remoinho.

whirlwind remoinho de vento, furacão.

whisper sussurro, cochicho, murmúrio.

whisper (to) sussurrar, cochichar, murmurar.

   in a whisper em voz baixa (x = sh).

whistle apito, assobio.

whistle (to) assobiar, apitar.

white branco.

   white of egg clara de ovo.

   white lie mentira inofensiva.

White House Casa Branca.

whiten (to) branquear.

who quem, que, qual, o qual, a qual, os quais, as quais, aquele, aquela.

   Who is it? Quem é?

whoever quem quer que, qualquer que.

   whoever it may be quem quer que for, seja quem for.

whole todo, inteiro, completo.

   the whole of Portugal todo Portugal.

   whole wheat bread pão integral.

   on the whole em geral.

   whole number número inteiro.

wholehearted sincero, dedicado.

wholesale por atacado.

wholesome salubre, sádio.

wholly totalmente, inteiramente.

whom quem, que.

whose de quem *(used as first word in questions);* cujo *(of whom, of which).*

why por que.

   Why not? Por que não?

wicked mau, malvado.

wickedness maldade.

wide largo, vasto, amplo, extenso.

   two inches wide duas polegadas de largura.

   wide open aberto de par em par.

   wide awake bem acordado, desperto, vivo.

widely muito, extensamente.

   widely different completamente diferente.

   widely used muito usado.

   widely known muito conhecido.

widen (to) alargar, ampliar.

widespread difundido, muito espalhado, comum.

widow viúva.

widower viúvo.

width largura.

wife mulher, esposa.

wig peruca.

wild selvagem *(savage);* silvestre *(plants);* não domesticado *(not tamed);* bárbaro; desenfreado *(unruly).*

wilderness ermo.

will vontade; testamento *(legal).*

   at will à vontade.

   against one's will contra a vontade.

will (to) querer, desejar; legar.

   Will you tell me the time? Quer ter a bondade de me dizer (dizer-me) que horas são?

   Will you do me a favor? Quer me fazer (fazer-me) um favor?

   I won't go. Não irei. Não quero ir.

   You won't do it, will you? Não o farei, tá?

   auxiliary the future tense of the indicative is formed by adding -ei, (-ás), -á, -emos, (-eis), -ão to the infinitive.

I will go irei.
   you will go *(fam.)* irás.
   he will go irá.
   we will go iremos.
   you will go ireis.
   they will go irão.
willing disposto, pronto, inclinado.
   to be willing estar disposto, querer.
   God willing. Se Deus quiser.
willingly de boa vontade, de bom grado.
willingness boa vontade.
win (to) ganhar, vencer, triunfar.
   to win out sair bem, triunfar.
wind vento.
   wind instrument instrumento de sopro.
wind (to) enrolar *(roll up)*; dar corda a *(a watch)*; serpentear *(river, road)*.
windmill moinho de vento.
window janela.
   windowpane vidro, vidraça.
windshield pára-brisa.
windy com muito vento.
   It's windy. Está ventando.
wine vinho.
   red wine vinho tinto.
   white wine vinho branco.
wing asa; ala *(of building)*.
wink piscadela.
wink (to) piscar.
winner vencedor.
winter inverno (Inverno).
wintry invernal. -
wipe (to) limpar.
   to wipe out eliminar, destruir.
   wiped out arrasado *(tired)*.
wire arame *(metal)*; telegrama *(telegram)*.
   barbed wire arame farpado.
wire (to) telegrafar.
wisdom sabedoria, prudência, bom senso.
   wisdom tooth dente do siso.
wise sábio, prudente.
wish desejo.
wish (to) desejar, querer.
wit engenho *(humor)*; agudeza *(mental sharpness)*.
witch bruxa (x = sh).
with com, de, a, em, por meio de, contra.
   coffee with milk café com leite.
   to touch with the hand tocar com a mão.
   She came with a friend. Ela veio com um amigo.
   to identify oneself with identificar-se com.
   to struggle with lutar contra.
   with respect to com respeito a.
   the young girl with the red dress on a jovem de vestido vermelho.
   That always happens with friends. Isso sempre acontece entre amigos.

   with much study por meio de muito estudo.
withdraw (to) retrair, tirar, remover.
withdrawal retirada.
within dentro de, dentro, a pouco de.
   within a week dentro de uma semana.
   within a short distance a pouca distância.
without sem.
   coffee without sugar café sem açúcar.
   without fail sem falta.
   without a doubt sem dúvida.
   without thinking it over well sem pensar bem. -
witness testemunha.
witness (to) presenciar, ver, testemunhar.
witty engenhoso, gracioso.
wolf lobo.
woman mulher.
   young woman mulher jovem.
wonder maravilha.
   no wonder não é de admirar.
wonder (to) admirar-se *(be amazed)*; perguntar-se *(to be unsure)*.
   I wonder whether it's true. Eu me pergunto (pergunto-me) se será verdade.
   to wonder at admirar-se de.
wonderful maravilhoso.
   wonderful city cidade maravilhosa.
wood madeira; floresta, lenha *(firewood)*; pl. selva, mato.
woodwork madeiramento *(around windows, etc.)*; carpintaria *(woodworking)*.
wool lã.
woolen de lã.
word palavra.
   word for word palavra por palavra.
   in other words em outras palavras.
   by word of mouth oralmente, verbalmente.
   upon my word palavra de honra.
   to leave word deixar (x = sh) recado.
work trabalho; obra *(of art)*.
   to be at work estar ocupado, estar trabalhando (a trabalhar).
   out of work desempregado.
workday dia útil, dia de trabalho.
work (to) trabalhar; funcionar, andar *(a machine)*; cultivar.
   to work out resolver *(a problem)*.
   the radio is not working o rádio não está funcionando (a funcionar).
worker trabalhador, operário, empregado.
workshop oficina.
world mundo.
   all over the world por todo o mundo.
   worldwide mundial.
   World War Guerra Mundial.
worm verme; minhoca, lombriga *(earthworm)*.

worn-out gasto *(object)*; estragado, batido *(tired)*.

worry preocupação, ansiedade.
    Don't worry. Não se preocupe.
    to be worried estar preocupado.

worse pior.
    to get worse piorar.
    so much the worse tanto pior.
    from bad to worse de mal a pior.
    to take a turn for the worse piorar.

worship adoração.

worship (to) adorar, venerar *(God)*; idolatrar *(money, etc.)*.

worst o pior.
    the worst o pior.
    at worst no pior dos casos.
    if worst comes to worst se acontecer o pior.

worth valor, mérito.
    What's it worth? Quanto vale?
    It's not worth that much. Não vale tanto.
    to be worthwhile valer a pena.

worthless inútil, sem valor.

worthwhile que vale a pena.

worthy digno, merecedor.

would The conditional tense is generally expressed by adding -ia, (-ias), -ia, -íamos, (íeis), -iam to the infinitive of the verb. The imperfect indicative is also used in this sense, especially in conversation. The verbs of the second and third conjugations (infinitives ending in -er, -ir) add the above endings to the stem of the infinitive to make the imperfect indicative tense. Verbs of the first conjugation (infinitives ending in -ar) add -ava, (-avas), -ava, -ávamos, (-áveis), -avam to the stem of the infinitive.
    I would go eu iria, eu ia.
    I would like to go. Gostaria de ir. Gostava de ir.
    I would go if I could. Eu iria (ia) se pudesse.
    She wouldn't come. Ela não quis vir.
    I wish she would come. Oxalá (x = sh) que venha.
    I would like to ask you a favor. Gostaria de lhe pedir (pedir-lhe) um favor.

wound ferida, ferimento.

wound (to) ferir.

wounded ferido.

Wow! Ena! Opa!

wrap (to) envolver, embrulhar *(package)*; enrolar *(to roll up)*.

wrapper envoltório, invólucro.

wrapping paper papel de embrulho.

wreath grinalda, coroa.

wreck destruição, ruína; naufrágio *(shipwreck)*.

wreck (to) arruinar, destruir; naufragar *(ship)*.

wrench chave inglesa *(tool)*.

wrench (to) torcer *(ankle, etc.)*; arrancar.

wrestle (to) lutar.

wring (to) torcer, espremer.

wrinkle ruga *(skin)*; prega.

wrinkle (to) enrugar(-se), franzir.
    she wrinkled her brow ela franzui a testa.

wrist pulso, munheca.
    wristwatch relógio-pulseira.

write (to) escrever.

writer escritor.

writing escrita, escrito, escritura; letra *(handwriting)*.
    in writing por escrito.
    writing desk escrivaninha, secretária.
    writing paper papel de escrever.

written escrito.

wrong *n.* mal; dano *(harm)*; injúria, injustiça; erro; trangressão, infração (infracção); *adj.* mau, incorreto (incorrecto), falso, errado, injusto; *adv.* mal.
    to do wrong fazer mal.
    You are wrong. Você não tem razão. Você está errado.
    to get up on the wrong side of the bed levantar-se com o pé esquerdo.
    That's wrong. Está mal escrito *(written)*. Está mal feito *(done)*.
    Something is wrong with the engine. O motor não funciona bem.
    wrong side out do lado do avesso.
    What's wrong with him? O que há com ele?

X ray raio X *(ray)*; radiografia *(x-ray picture)*.

yank (to) arrancar.

yard jarda *(measurement)*; pátio, quintal *(of a house)*.

yawn bocejo.

yawn (to) bocejar.

year ano.
    last year o ano passado.
    next year o ano que vem.
    many years ago há muitos anos.
    every year todos os anos.
    all year long o ano todo.
    I am 35 years old. Tenho trinta e cinco anos.

yearbook anuário.

yearly *adj.* anual; *adv.* anualmente.

yeast levedura, fermento.
yell grito, berro.
yell (to) gritar, berrar.
yellow amarelo.
yes sim.
yesterday ontem.
    the day before yesterday anteontem.
yet *adv.* ainda; *conj.* porém, todavia, não
    obstante.
    not yet ainda não.
    as yet até agora.
    I don't know yet. Ainda não sei.
yield rendimento, renda, produção, produto.
yield (to) render, produzir; ceder *(to give in).*
yoke jugo.
yolk gema.
you tu *(fam.);* você *(friendly);* o senhor, os
    senhores, a senhora, as senhoras *(polite).*
young jovem.
    young man jovem, moço.
    young lady jovem, moça.
    young people jovens.
    younger sister irmã mais nova.
your, yours teu, tua, teus, tuas *(fam.);* seu, sua,
    seus, suas, de você, de vocês, do senhor,
    dos senhores, da senhora, das senhoras.

    This book is yours. Este livro é seu.
    Sincerely yours. atenciosamente.
yourself você mesmo, o senhor mesmo, a
    senhora mesma, se.
    Wash yourself. Lave-se.
yourselves vocês mesmos, os senhores
    mesmos, as senhoras mesmas.
youth juventude, mocidade; jovem *(person).*
youthful jovem, juvenil.

Z

zeal zelo, fervor, ardor.
zealous zeloso, ardoroso.
zero zero.
zest entusiasmo, gosto.
zigzag ziguezague.
zinc zinco.
zit borbulha.
zone zona.
    time zone fuso horário.
zoo jardim zoológico.
zoological zoológico.
zoology zoologia.

GLOSSARY OF
PROPER NAMES

Adolph Adolfo
Alexander Alexandre
Alfred Alfredo
Alice Alice
Alphonse Afonso
Andrew André
Ann, Anna, Anne Ana
Anthony Antônio
   (António)
Arthur Artur
Augustus Augusto

Barbara Bárbara
Beatrice Beatriz
Bernard Bernardo

Caroline Carolina
Cecilia Cecília
Charles Carlos
Charlotte Carlota

Dorothy Dorotéia
   (Dorotcia)

Edward Eduardo
Eleanor Leonor
Elizabeth Isabel
Emily Emília
Ernest Ernesto
Esther Ester
Eugene Eugênio
   (Eugénio)

Francis Francisco
Frederick Frederico

George Jorge
Gertrude Gertrudes
Gloria Glória

Helen Helena
Henry Henrique

Inez Inês

John João
Joseph José
Josephine Josefa, Josefina
Julius Júlio

Leonard Leonardo
Louis Luís
Louise Luísa
Lucy Lúcia

Manuel Manuel
Margaret Margarida
Martha Marta
Mary Maria
Michael Miguel

Paul Paulo
Peter Pedro
Philip Filipe

Raymond Raimundo
Richard Ricardo
Robert Roberto
Rose Rosa

Theresa Teresa
Thomas Tomás

Vincent Vicente

William Guilherme

GLOSSARY OF GEOGRAPHICAL NAMES

Africa África
Alps Alpes
America América
Andes Andes
Angola Angola
Argentina Argentina
Asia Ásia
Athens Atenas
Atlantic Ocean Oceano Atlântico
Australia Austrália
Azores Açores

Barcelona Barcelona
Belgium Bélgica
Bolivia Bolívia
Brasilia Brasília
Brazil Brasil
Brussels Bruxelas (x = sh)
Buenos Aires Buenos Aires

Canada Canadá
Chile Chile
China China
Coimbra Coimbra
Colombia Colômbia
Costa Rica Costa Rica
Cuba Cuba
Czech Republic Republica Checa

Denmark Dinamarca
Dominican Republic República
    Dominicana

Ecuador Equador
Egypt Egito (Egipto)
El Salvador El Salvador
England Inglaterra
Estonia Estônia
Europe Europa

Finland Finlândia
France França

Galicia Galícia
Geneva Genebra
Germany Alemanha
Great Britain Grã Bretanha
Greece Grécia
Guatemala Guatemala

Haiti Haiti
Havana Havana
Hawaii Havaí
Hispanic America Hispano-América
Holland Holanda

Honduras Honduras
Hungary Hungria

Ireland Irlanda
Israel Israel
Italy Itália

Japan Japão

Latvia Letônia
Lisbon Lisboa
London Londres
Low Countries Países Baixos (x = sh)

Macao Macau
Madeira Madeira
Madrid Madri (Madrid)
Mediterranean Sea Mar
    Mediterrâneo
Mexico México (x = sh)
Moscow Moscou
Mozambique Moçambique

Netherlands Países Baixos (x = sh),
    Holanda
New York Nova Iorque
New Zealand Nova Zelândia
Nicaragua Nicarágua
North America América do Norte
Norway Noruega

Oceania Oceania

Pacific Ocean Oceano Pacífico
Panama Panamá
Paraguay Paraguai
Paris Paris
Peru Peru
Philippines Filipinas
Poland Polônia (Polónia)
Portugal Portugal
Puerto Rico Porto Rico
Pyrenees Pireneus

Rio de Janeiro Rio de Janeiro
Romania Romênia (Roménia)
Rome Roma
Russia Rússia

São Paulo São Paulo
Scandinavia Escandinávia
Scotland Escócia
Sicily Sicília
Slovakia Eslováquia
South America América do Sul
Spain Espanha
Spanish America América Espanhola.
    Hispano-América
Sweden Suécia

Switzerland Suíça

Turkey Turquia

Ukraine Ucrânia
United States of America Estados Unidos
da América

United Nations Organização
das Nações Unidas, ONU
Uruguay Uruguai

The Vatican O Vaticano
Venezuela Venezuela
Vienna Viena

"Entertaining. . . . Readers will enjoy spending time with the friendly folks of Tallulah Falls as well as Marcy's adorable Irish wolfhound." —Publishers Weekly

"This great cozy has a lively cast. . . . The pace is fast and the puns are amusing." —*RT Book Reviews* (4½ stars, top pick)

"[A] crafty mystery series that continues to successfully balance a light tone and humor with a dramatic plot." —Kings River Life Magazine

"Amanda Lee weaves an excellent cozy mystery that will keep the reader hooked from beginning to end." —Affaire de Coeur

"[T]here's never a dull moment . . . with . . . touches of humor and a hint of sensual romance." —Once Upon a Romance

"Well paced and a real page-turner . . . a great cozy mystery." —MyShelf.com

"A fun fast-paced mystery that will be hard to put down." —The Mystery Reader

"Fun, full of suspense, and . . . a satisfying conclusion— readers can hardly ask for more!" —Fresh Fiction

The
Calamity
Café

A Down South Café Mystery

GAYLE LEESON

AN OBSIDIAN MYSTERY

OBSIDIAN

Published by New American Library,
an imprint of Penguin Random House LLC
375 Hudson Street, New York, New York 10014

This book is an original publication of New American Library.

First Printing, June 2016

For more information about Penguin Random House, visit penguin.com.

ISBN 978-1-101-99078-0

Printed in the United States of America
10 9 8 7 6 5 4 3 2 1

Designed by Kelly Lipovich.

Penguin
Random
House

To Tim, Lianna, and Nicholas

Chapter 1

I took a deep breath, tightened my ponytail, and got out of my yellow Volkswagen Beetle. I knew from experience that the morning rush at Lou's Joint had passed and that the lunch crowd wouldn't be there yet. I put my letter of resignation in my purse and headed inside. Homer Pickens was seated at the counter with a cup of coffee. He was a regular . . . and when I say *regular*, I mean it. The man came to the café every morning at ten o'clock, lingered over a sausage biscuit and a cup of coffee, and left at ten forty. It was ten fifteen a.m.

"Good morning, Homer," I said. "Who's your hero today?"

"Shel Silverstein," he said.

"Good choice." I smiled and patted his shoulder. Homer was a retiree in his late sixties, and he chose a new hero every day.

You see, when Homer was a little boy, he noticed his

daddy wasn't around like other kids' daddies. So he asked his mom about him. She told him that his dad had died but that he'd been a great baseball player, which is why she'd named him Homer. When Homer was a teenager, she'd finally leveled with him and said his father hadn't been a baseball player . . . that he'd basically been a bum . . . but that Homer didn't need a father to inspire him. Heroes were everywhere. Since then, Homer had chosen a new hero every day. It was like his inspiration. I looked forward to hearing Homer's answer to my question every day I worked. When I was off from work, he told me who his hero was the day I asked plus the day I'd missed.

I could sympathize with Homer's desire for a heroic father figure. My dad left Mom and me when I was four. I don't really remember him at all.

"That apple tree? The one he wrote about? I have one like it in my backyard," Homer said. "I cherish it. I'd never cut it down."

"I'm sure the rain we've had the past couple of days has helped it grow. You bring me some apples off that tree this fall, and I'll make you a pie," I told him.

My cousin Jackie came from the back with a washcloth and a spray bottle of cleaner. She and I had waitressed together at the café for over a year. Jackie had been there for two years, and in fact, it was she who'd helped me get the job.

My mind drifted to when I'd come back home to work for Lou Lou. I'd just finished up culinary school in Kentucky. Nana's health had been declining for the past two or three years, but it had picked up speed. As

soon as I'd graduated, I'd come home and started working at Lou's Joint so I could be at Nana's house within ten minutes if I was needed. I was only biding my time at first, waiting for a chef's position to come open somewhere. But then Nana had died. And, although I knew I could've asked her for a loan to open a café at any time, I wouldn't have. I guess I got my streak of pride from my mother. But the money Nana had left me had made my dream a reality—I could open my café and stay right here at home.

"Morning, Amy!" said Jackie. "Guess what—Granny says she has a new Pinterest board. It's called *Things I'd Love to Eat but Won't Fix Because What's the Point Anyway Since I Don't Like to Cook Anymore.*"

I laughed. "I don't think they'd let her have a name that long."

"That's what I figured. It's probably called *Things I'd Love to Eat*, but she threw that last bit in there hoping we'll make some of this stuff for her."

"And we probably will."

Jackie's granny was my great-aunt Elizabeth, but Mom and I had always just called her "Aunt Bess." Aunt Bess was eighty-two and had recently discovered the wonders of the Internet. She had a number of Pinterest boards, had a Facebook page with a 1940s pinup for a profile pic, and trolled the dating sites whenever they offered a free weekend.

Lou Lou heard us talking and waddled to the window separating the kitchen from the dining room. She had a cigarette hanging from her bottom lip. She tucked it into the corner of her mouth while she spoke. "Thought I

heard your voice, Amy. You ain't here for your paycheck, are you? Because that won't be ready until tomorrow, and you ain't picking it up until after your shift."

"That's not why I'm here," I said. "Could we talk privately, please?"

"Fine, but if you're just wanting to complain about me taking half the waitresses' tips again, you might as well not waste your breath. If it wasn't for me, y'all wouldn't have jobs here, so I deserve half of what you get."

Jackie rolled her eyes at me and then got to cleaning tables before Lou Lou bawled her out.

We deserved *all* of our tips and then some, especially since Lou Lou didn't pay minimum wage and gave us more grief than some of the waitresses could bear. That's why I was here. Lou Lou Holman was a bully, and I aimed to put her out of business.

Speaking of daddies, Lou Lou had been named after hers—hence the Lou Lou, rather than Lulu—and according to my late grandmother, she looked just like him. He'd kept his hair dyed jet-black until he was put into the Winter Garden Nursing Home, and afterward, he put shoe polish on his head. According to Nana, he ruined many a pillowcase before the staff found his stash of shoe polish and did away with it.

Lou Lou wore her black hair in a tall beehive with pin curls on either side of her large round face. Her eyes were blue, a fact that was overpowered by the cobalt eye shadow she wore. She shaved her eyebrows, drew thin black upside-down Vs where they should have been, and added false eyelashes to complete the look.

Today Lou Lou wore a floor-length blue-and-white

floral-print muumuu, and she had a white plastic hibiscus in her hair just above the pin curl on the left. She shuffled into the office, let me go in ahead of her, and then closed the door. I could smell her perfume—a cloying jasmine—mixed with this morning's bacon and the cigarette, and I was more anxious than ever to get our business over with. She sat down behind her desk and looked at me.

I perched on the chair in front of the desk, reached into my purse, and took out the letter. As I handed it to her, I said, "I'm turning in my two-week notice."

"Well, I ain't surprised," she said, stubbing the cigarette into the ashtray. "I heard your granny left you some money when she passed last year. I reckon you've decided to take it easy."

"No. Actually, I'd like to buy your café."

Her eyes got so wide that her false eyelashes brushed against the tops of her inverted *V* eyebrows. "Is that a fact, Amy?"

"Yes, ma'am, it is." I lifted my chin. "I'm a good cook—better than good, as a matter of fact—and I want to put my skills . . . my passion . . . to work for me."

"If you think you can just waltz in here all high and mighty and take my daddy's business away from me, you've got another think coming," said Lou Lou.

"If you don't sell to me, I'm going to open up my own café. I just thought I should give you fair warning before I do."

Lou Lou scoffed. "You've got some nerve thinking you can run me out of business. You bring on the competition, girlie! We'll see who comes out ahead."

"All right." I stood. "Thank you for your time. I'll be here tomorrow for my shift."

"Don't bother. I'll mail you your final check."

"I'll be here," I said. "I don't want any of the other waitresses to have to work a double on my account."

"Suit yourself. But don't be surprised if I take the cost of putting an ad in the paper for a new waitress out of your salary."

I simply turned and walked out of the office. I knew that legally Lou Lou couldn't take her ad cost out of my pay. But Lou Lou did a lot of things that weren't right. I figured whatever she did to me in retaliation for my leaving wasn't worth putting up a fight over . . . not now. I'd pick my battles.

I'd also pick my wallpaper, my curtains, my flooring, my chairs, stools, and tables, my logo . . . My lips curled into a smile before I'd even realized it.

"Bye, Homer! Bye, Jackie!" I called over my shoulder on the way out.

"Bye, Amy!" They called in unison.

I went to the parking lot and got into my car. I glanced up at the sign—LOU'S JOINT—as I backed out into the road. The sign was as sad and faded as everything else about this place. If I could convince Lou Lou to change her mind, I'd start with a brand-new sign . . . a big yellow sign with DOWN SOUTH CAFÉ in blue cursive letters. I wanted everybody to know what to expect when they walked into my café—Southern food and hospitality.

I could do so much with this little place. Sure, I could also build a new café, but if I did, I'd also have to buy all-new equipment, get the building wired and up to code,

and basically spend a lot of extra money I'd rather save if at all possible. Besides, Lou's Joint was one of only two restaurants in town, and it was really close to my house—a definite plus once winter rolled in.

When I got home, I went straight to the kitchen. Rory, my little brown wirehaired terrier, met me at the door and followed me. Princess Eloise, the white Persian cat, barely looked up from her post in the living room picture-window sill. I bent and gave Rory kisses and then I got his box of dog treats. We play hide-and-seek with the treats before he eats them. Of course, they're in plain sight, but we act like they're hidden.

I scattered the treats in the foyer, hallway, and living room, repeating the word "Hide" each time I dropped one. When I placed the last treat on the marble hearth in the living room, I called, "Seek!" Rory sprang into action, backtracking to find all the treats.

This bought me a good five minutes to wash my hands and get started on an oatmeal pie. Oatmeal pies took a while to make—even when I had a frozen pie crust like the one I was using today—but they were worth it. Nana used to make them. Especially if I was feeling down, I could walk into her house, smell that oatmeal pie baking, and know that everything was gonna be all right.

I took my pie crust out of the freezer and preheated the oven. I got a small mixing bowl, put four eggs in it, and set it on the counter while I gathered the rest of my ingredients.

Lou Lou was right about my nana leaving me some money. The estate had been settled for quite a while, but I didn't want to rush to spend my inheritance. I'd wanted

to wait until I was absolutely sure I knew what I wanted to do.

Nana had a fairly sizable estate, or at least, sizable by Winter Garden, Virginia, standards. I'd always known my grandparents had money, but I hadn't realized how much Nana *did* have until she was gone. Of course, she'd bought me my car when I'd graduated high school, and it was brand-new then. I'd been impressed, but I'd thought maybe she'd been saving up for that for a long time. I'd been driving that little car for ten years now, and it was still going strong.

I smiled to myself, remembering the day she'd taken me to buy that car. We'd had to go all the way to Johnson City, Tennessee, but the dealership had given us Virginia sales tax on the vehicle. And the salesman had nearly fainted when Nana had paid cash!

I cracked the four eggs into the bowl and beat them until they were frothy. In a larger bowl, I mixed together sugar, cinnamon, flour, and salt. I then added the eggs. As I was pouring in the corn syrup, my phone rang. I'd placed the phone on the counter and could see that it was Sarah calling. She was one of my best friends. I hesitated, but when the oven clicked, indicating that it had reached 350 degrees, I let the call go to voice mail. I'd get back to Sarah as soon as I got the pie into the oven.

Sarah and I had become close when we were in elementary school, and we'd stayed that way. Her family was like one of those perfect television families. I used to wish I had a big family like hers, and whenever I said something along those lines, she'd assure me that I did—I had her family.

And I had Mom and Nana. They were wonderful.

Mom and I had lived in a smaller house on Nana and Pop's property. Despite her parents' abundance, Mom had taken as little from anybody as possible. She'd wanted to earn her own way, and she certainly had done that. And of course, Jackie and I had always been more like sisters than cousins, especially since Jackie had never known her dad and her mother had left her with Aunt Bess when Jackie was sixteen.

I poured the oatmeal mixture into the pie shell and slid it into the oven. Then I called Sarah.

"Hey, girl," she answered. "Did you throw down on the Big Bad Boss yet?"

"Yeah." I groaned. "Lou Lou was *not* happy when I offered to buy her café."

"I'd have loved to have seen the expression on her face!" Sarah laughed. "So . . . plan B?"

"I guess so. I'm nervous about it. It'll take longer than having a place that I only have to redecorate," I said.

"But starting from the ground up, you can get exactly what you want."

"That's true . . . but it's kinda scary."

"I'm sure it is, Amy, but you'll know what you're getting every step of the way," she said. "And you can afford to go with all-new stuff . . . good stuff!"

I laughed. "That's true. But I have to be smart. I won't have my salary to live on while the new place is being built. I gave Lou Lou my two weeks' notice. She didn't want me to come back at all, but I said I wouldn't do that to the other waitresses."

"Well, honey, it's not like you were making a fortune in that place."

"I know . . . but what will I *do* to keep from being

bored out of my mind while I'm waiting for my café to be built?"

"You'll help build it," Sarah said. "I've known you all your life. I can see you jumping right in there with your hammer and nails."

"You've got a point there. Plus, I'll be getting my permits and all that. Do you think we can get the construction done before winter?" I asked. "How long does something like that take?"

"I'd say it'll take four to six months . . . and it's June . . . so, yeah, you can be ready by winter."

I sighed. "Will people wait that long? I so wanted to go in, take over Lou Lou's place, shut down for a week or two for redecorating, and then have a grand opening on Independence Day."

"People won't wait," she said, "but they'll gladly leave Lou's Joint for something better as soon as that option becomes available to them."

"You're right," I said. "Come over after work and have some oatmeal pie with me."

"Is that what I smell?" she teased.

"Mmm-hmm."

She giggled. "I'll be there!"

"Want some fried chicken, biscuits, and mashed potatoes with gravy to go with it?" I asked.

"I'd be satisfied with just the pie . . . but I wouldn't hurt your feelings by not eating chicken and biscuits."

"Good. I'll see you after work, then."

Sarah was Billy Hancock's administrative assistant. In Winter Garden, that meant she was the secretary, bookkeeper, and paralegal to the town's only attorney-at-law. Billy was about fifty-five years old and had taken over the

business from his father, William. Being the only lawyer in town, Billy had plenty to keep him busy, but not so busy that he couldn't play golf in Abingdon with his friends two afternoons a week. He handled just about everybody's wills, estates, divorces, and misdemeanor charges. Not that everybody got divorced or had misdemeanors in Winter Garden, for goodness' sake . . . but there were enough to earn Billy a darned good living, and by extension Sarah too.

I closed my eyes and inhaled deeply. The aromas of the vanilla, cinnamon, and oatmeal were divine. I remembered standing on a chair at Nana's side watching her make her oatmeal pie at our house one Thanksgiving morning. Nana was strong and sturdily built, and I must've been only around five years old, because I felt tiny at her side. She was patiently explaining the pie making step by step. At the time, all I cared about was "Can I lick the spoon?" Now I'd love to have the opportunity to live that day over . . . to take in every detail, every loving nuance of her oatmeal pie preparation. But as the author of *Our Town* warned, reliving a day gone by might prove to be too painful.

I opened my eyes and wondered briefly if Thornton Wilder had ever been Homer's hero. I'd have to try to remember to ask Homer.

The pie still had a good thirty minutes to bake, so I went into my fancy room. My fancy room had once been my mother's bedroom. After Pop died, Aunt Bess moved in with Nana. After Nana died, Mom moved in with Aunt Bess. And then when Aunt Bess started getting forgetful— as in, accidentally leaving the stove on—Mom left her job as a sales associate for a retailer in Bristol to look after Aunt Bess full-time.

Nana's house was the biggest house in town, which wasn't saying a lot for the rural community. There were houses in Abingdon and Bristol that would make Nana's house look small in comparison. Most people in Winter Garden lived in farmhouses or small ranch houses. The people of Winter Garden were generally hardworking and proud. The majority thought it was beneath them to take handouts of any kind, and some lived a meager existence because of that.

Nana's house was situated on a hill so that a person could sit on the wraparound front porch and see the entire town of Winter Garden. The house hadn't been built until the early 1980s, when my grandpa had quit working in the coal mines and he and Nana moved here from Pocahontas.

After Mom had moved in with Aunt Bess, I'd remodeled her bedroom. Two of the walls were lined with oak bookshelves—not plasterboard, but real oak. My friend Roger was a construction worker, and he'd built them. There had always been the understanding that Roger would build my café if and when I decided to build. Before I'd given my notice to Lou Lou, I'd spoken with Roger to make sure he could work me in.

Roger had been friends with Sarah, Jackie, and me since we were children. In fact, I'd always thought he and Jackie would make a good couple.

In the center of the fancy room floor was a white velvet fainting couch, and I grinned every time I looked at it. The piece was just so girly and luxurious, and I loved it. I kept the door closed and didn't let Princess Eloise into this room at all for fear that she'd sharpen her claws on the legs of the couch. It was hard to slip off

from Rory, though, so I'd wound up putting a doggie bed beneath one of the windows so he could visit if he missed me when I was in the room. He generally liked to be by my side always. Princess Eloise could take me or leave me. She was Mom's cat, but Mom couldn't take her to live with Aunt Bess because Aunt Bess was allergic. So Princess Eloise tolerated me. When Mom came over, she was like a different Persian.

Off to the side of the fainting couch, I had an over-stuffed peacock blue chair with a matching ottoman. There was a floor lamp beside the chair, and when I'd curl up on the chair to read, it was like its big old arms just wrapped around me. I kept a pink-and-blue paisley throw on the ottoman. I had one of those old-fashioned rolltop desks at the window looking out onto the side yard. It too was oak, and I kept stationery supplies in it. I particularly liked personalized stationery, and Nana had made it a point to get me some every Christmas. Ever since seeing the old black-and-white movie *Rebecca*, I'd thought personalized stationery was the pinnacle of class. So what if the title character had turned out to be less than classy? She still had nice stationery.

Rory had long since found all his treats and was in a blissful sleep in front of the living room sofa, so I closed the door behind me when I went into the fancy room. I slipped my sandals off and stretched out on the fainting couch with my laptop. I checked Aunt Bess's Pinterest boards. One of my favorites was *Lord Have Mercy*. On that board, Aunt Bess pinned things that were, in her opinion, in need of grace: weird photos of celebrities, crime stories, strange phenomena, and multiple body piercings.

I'd been surfing the Web for several minutes when the phone rang. I didn't recognize the number that came up on my screen.

"Hello?"

"Yeah, Amy, hi. It's Pete Holman. How you doing?"

Pete was Lou Lou's son. He was several years older than I was, so I hadn't known him until I started working at Lou's Joint. Pete was nice enough, but he tended to be on the lazy side—did just enough to get by and didn't take much pride in his work. He'd always kinda struck me as an overgrown kid. Pete was a skinny balding man of forty who still lived with his momma and tried to pretend to her that he didn't have a girlfriend . . . because Lou Lou would definitely not have approved of the thirty-year-old woman Pete had been seeing. In fact, I doubted she would have approved of anyone Pete dated. Lou Lou liked keeping Pete under her thumb.

"I'm fine, Pete. How are you?"

"I'm all right. Momma told me that you offered to buy the Joint."

"I did. I imagine she also told you that she flat-out refused to sell it to me," I said.

"She did say that, but I believe I've got her talked into changing her mind."

"Really." It wasn't a question. It more like a nicer way of saying, *Fat chance*.

"Yeah. You see, she ain't as young as she used to be . . . and, well, I ain't either, for that matter. I never did want to spend my life slinging hash. Uh, not that you wouldn't enjoy it and all—that ain't what I'm saying," he said. "It's just, I'm saying I'd prefer a life on the open road. I want to drive a truck."

"Well, good for you, Pete. I hope that works out for you." I had a hard time buying what he was saying, much as I would have liked to.

"Thank you. I appreciate that, Amy. I really do. But, of course, for everybody to get what they want, Momma has to sell the Joint, right?"

"Um . . . okay."

"So I reminded her of how she's always wanted to go to Hawaii," Pete said. "She could take some of that money you're paying her and take right off, couldn't she?"

"I think that would be wonderful," I said. *For her and for everybody in Winter Garden . . . especially if Lou Lou decided to* stay *in the islands.* I had a vision of Lou Lou eating pupu, and I had to stifle a giggle.

"So you come on to the Joint right after closing tonight. I'll have Momma there, and the three of us will work out all the details. I'll even try to have Billy Hancock there to draw up the contract."

"Tonight at closing?" I asked, feeling my hopes rise, even though I knew better. "Can't we discuss the sale tomorrow morning?"

"No, Amy. We don't want Momma to have the chance to change her mind."

"I understand that, but—" The oven timer went off. "I have to go get my pie before it burns."

"See you tonight, then?" he asked.

"See you then."

It was a balmy night and, since it had stopped raining, I had my windows down as I drove to Lou's Joint. I'd had my fill of good food and fun conversation, and I

was feeling content. Sarah had stayed until just about an hour ago. We'd played a game of Yahtzee and had gone back to the drawing board on the existing café renovations, and we'd also dreamed about where I could buy land to build a new café and how it would look if tonight's deal fell through.

Sarah and I both felt as if this deal was more about Pete's hope that he could talk his momma into selling than any actual budging on Lou Lou's part. I'd worked for Lou Lou Holman for just over a year. She didn't budge. On anything. So I wasn't particularly optimistic about Lou Lou selling to me, but I had a plan B.

I pulled into the parking lot. The only other vehicle there was Lou Lou's old silver van. I wondered why she didn't get a nicer, more reliable car. The van seemed to be in the repair shop more than it was out. Despite having money, Lou Lou was stingy. Nana had once said that if you were really quiet, you could hear all the little Lincolns screaming in Lou Lou's pocket because the woman pinched her pennies so tightly.

I got out, locked the car, and walked up to the door. It was a cloudless night, and the moon was a waxing crescent. Nana used to tell me that when the moon looked like that, it was pouring out water . . . meaning it was going to rain again soon. A warm breeze blew, rustling the leaves of the sugar maples grouped on both sides of the café. I heard wings flap overhead. I shivered, wondering if it was a bat or a great horned owl. Either would scare the dickens out of me.

I quickly tried the door. The CLOSED sign had been turned toward the glass, but the door was unlocked.

Grateful, I slipped inside. All the lights were off except the one in the back.

"Lou Lou! Pete! It's me, Amy!"

I waited for one of them to come out and wave me on back into the office. I actually hoped that they'd come out, flip on a light, and we could meet in here either at the lunch counter or at a table. I didn't relish the thought of being confined in the stuffy, smoky office with Pete and Lou Lou.

No one answered, and no one emerged from the office. "Hello!" I headed toward the back. I'd simply suggest that we move into the dining area to give us all a bit more space. Come to think of it, I hadn't seen Pete's truck parked outside. Maybe Lou Lou had called off the deal, and he hadn't even bothered to come.

When I reached the office, I saw that Lou Lou was slumped over the desk. "Lou Lou, are you all right?"

She didn't look up.

I stepped closer and patted her arm. "Lou Lou?"

That's when I noticed the blood dripping from the desk pad onto the floor.

Chapter 2

I hurried over to my boss. "Lou Lou, you're bleed- ing!" I eased over to the desk and put an arm around her. "Here, sit up."

She was nonresponsive, and I wasn't strong enough to move her by myself. I gave her a little shake. "Lou Lou, come on."

I placed my index and middle fingers on her left wrist, but I was unable to find a pulse. I thought it was probably weak because she was unconscious.

I took out my phone and dialed the sheriff's office. It occurred to me that if someone had come into the café with the intention of robbing the place and had knocked Lou Lou out, he might still be here.

"Sheriff Billings's office," answered a woman's voice.

"Hi. I'm Amy Flowers. I'm at Lou's Joint, and some- thing has happened to Lou Lou, the owner. I need for you to send somebody over here right away."

"Okay. You stay put until they get there."

"I will. Please hurry!" As I ended the call, I wondered where Pete and Billy Hancock were. One or both of them should've been here by now. I heard a hoot coming from the large maple tree at the corner of the parking lot, and it sent a shiver down my spine.

It didn't take Sheriff Billings long to get to Lou's Joint. He'd been sheriff here in Winter Garden for the past ten years. When he and his deputy got out of their car, I hurried to the front door to meet them.

"I don't know if somebody broke in and hurt Lou Lou or what," I said. "She's in her office."

He nodded toward the kitchen. "Down that back hallway there?"

"Yes, sir."

"I'm going to go on to the office and have and look around. You stay here with Deputy Hall."

I turned from the tall, lanky sheriff to his deputy—a younger man with an athletic build. He had dark brown hair and brown eyes, and his muscles strained the fabric of his tan shirt. I hadn't seen him before.

"Could we please step outside?" I was shaking and on the verge of hyperventilating.

"Sure." Deputy Hall—R. Hall, according to his nameplate—took out a notebook and pen as we stepped just outside the door. "Could you please give me your name and your account of what happened here from the time you arrived until the time you called the sheriff's office?"

I was surprised his voice rivaled the timbre and depth of that of Sam Elliott.

"I'm Amy Flowers. Lou Lou's son Pete called me this afternoon and asked if I could be here tonight to meet with

him, his mother, and their attorney—Billy Hancock—
about buying the café."

He looked around the parking lot, obviously noting
that the only cars around were mine, Lou Lou's van, and
the police cruiser. "Was Ms. Holman the only person here
when you arrived?"

"As far as I know."

"Was she the only person inside?"

"She's the only one I saw."

"All right," he said. "Walk me through your arrival."

I told him how I'd gotten here and been surprised that
no one except Lou Lou seemed to be at the café. "And
then I walked through the café to the office and found
Lou Lou slumped over her desk."

"Did you call out to her?"

"Of course. When she didn't answer, I asked if she was
okay, and then I noticed the blood. I went over and tried
to get her to sit up, but she didn't answer me, so I called
you guys."

"All right. That's all the questions I have for the moment,
but I'd like for you to wait here with me until the sheriff
comes out."

The owl hooted again, and Deputy Hall glanced up
at the tree.

"That owl make you nervous too?" I asked with a
shaky grin.

"No, Ms. Flowers. I'd like to wait until we get an assess-
ment of Ms. Holman's condition before you leave."

"I was just kidding."

The ambulance—siren blaring and lights flashing—
pulled up beside the police car. The driver hopped out and
addressed Deputy Hall.

"Where's the patient?"

Deputy Hall held open the door. "Straight back and down the hall to the . . ." He looked at me.

"Left," I supplied.

"The sheriff is with her. I'll let him know you're here." He called Sheriff Billings on the radio clipped to his belt and told him the EMTs were there.

I heard the sheriff's reply. "No need to send them in. I'll be out in a minute. I've called Ivy Donaldson. She's on her way."

Deputy Hall relayed the information to the ambulance driver. "I think Sheriff Billings would appreciate it if y'all would hang around until he talks with you."

A black Buick sedan sped into the lot and stopped nearby without bothering with a parking space. Billy Hancock stepped out. Billy had looked the same for as long as I could remember—steel gray hair, light blue eyes, and black-framed glasses that were always sliding down on his long nose.

"I'm Billy Hancock. What's happening here?" he asked Deputy Hall.

"May I ask why you're here, sir?"

Deputy Hall already knew why Billy was here. He was confirming either Billy's story or mine—I wasn't sure which.

"Pete Holman called me and asked me to meet him, his mother, and Ms. Flowers—hello, Amy—at Lou's Joint for a meeting. I had a flat tire and was delayed. First of all, it took the tow truck a good twenty minutes to get to me, and then Wilma had to come and get me, and I had to take her home and then bring her car here."

"Where's Mr. Holman now?" Deputy Hall asked.

"I don't know. Isn't he here? What's going on?"

"No, Mr. Holman's not here, and something has happened inside the café."

"Oh, well . . . I'll call him." As Billy fished his phone out of his pocket, he said, "Congratulations on your decision to open your own café, Amy. I hope you know that I'll help you with the legalities. I won't even ask you to pay a retainer first . . . but, of course, you can if you'd like."

"The phone call?" Deputy Hall reminded.

"Yes, sure." Billy pulled up his contacts and called Pete Holman. "Pete, it's Billy. Where in blazes are you?"

Deputy Hall whispered, "Don't tell him anything's wrong. We don't want him alarmed while he's driving."

"All right," said Billy to Pete. "See you when you get here." He frowned at Deputy Hall. "He misplaced his car keys. Now would you please tell me what's going on?"

"When Ms. Flowers arrived, she found Ms. Holman slumped over her desk. Ms. Holman was bleeding."

Billy gasped. "That's awful. Is she going to be all right?"

"I don't think so."

The sheriff joined us then and confirmed Deputy Hall's suspicion. Lou Lou Holman was dead.

"What?" I asked. "Are you sure?" My head was spinning, and I staggered.

Deputy Hall put a hand on my back. "Are you all right?"

"Are you sure?" I repeated to the sheriff.

"Positive," he said.

The sheriff had turned to go talk with the EMTs when Pete arrived in his souped-up 1992 brown Ford Ranger. Why would anyone soup up a 1992 Ford Ranger, you ask? Who knows? Who knows why Pete Holman did anything he did?

Like Billy, Pete didn't park. He simply stopped the truck and got out.

Sheriff Billings had turned back around when Pete pulled into the parking lot. Now he met Pete halfway. "Pete, I need you to stay calm."

Pete looked at me, his eyes already wild. "Amy?"

I shook my head. I didn't want to be the one to tell him something had happened to his mother. I closed my eyes momentarily, fighting a wave of nausea.

Sheriff Billings took Pete gently but firmly by the shoulders. "I'm sorry to tell you this, but your mother is dead."

Pete looked stunned. "What? She's dead? What happened? Did she have a heart attack or something? I've told her she needs to take better care of herself."

"We don't know what happened yet," said Sheriff Billings. "But we aim to find out exactly what happened to her."

"What do you mean, you aim to find out what happened?"

"Because your mother didn't die of natural causes."

"Then what kind of causes *did* she die of?" He looked from the sheriff to the deputy to me and then to Billy. Poor Pete. He was grappling for answers, and no one really had any.

"I'm sorry, Pete, but it appears that somebody killed

your mother. That makes Lou's Joint a crime scene, Pete, and we're going to have to shut the café and its perimeter down for a day or so to be able to go over it thoroughly. Were you a joint owner of the café?"

"I guess," said Pete. "I don't know if my name was on anything or not, but I helped run the place." He looked dazed.

"Well, then, when you're permitted to return to the café, I want you to see if anything's missing. If there is, then please call us first so we can see whether or not we have the item in evidence. If not, then your mother's attacker likely took it."

Pete's brows drew together. "What do you mean, when I'm *permitted* to go back in? I want to go in now. I wanna see Momma."

"I'm afraid you can't go see her yet, son. The only person we can allow into the café at this time is Ivy Donaldson, our CST. I could have Ivy take a photo of your mother and bring it back outside so you can confirm that it *is* your mother in there. Would that be all right?"

"Y-yes, sir." He wobbled, and if Sheriff Billings hadn't been holding to Pete's shoulders, I think he would've fallen.

"Let's have a seat in my car and have a talk," said Sheriff Billings. "It doesn't look like your mother had either the front or the back door locked. Did she usually leave them unlocked?"

I didn't hear Pete's reply, since they'd opened the door and sat down in the police cruiser by then.

A blue convertible pulled into the lot and parked neatly beside my yellow Bug. Someone had a clear head

even in the midst of a crisis—it was bound to be Ivy. I knew Ivy from her visits to the café. She didn't come in often, but when she did, she typically ordered a burger—no mayo, extra pickles—and fries.

In her mid-thirties with shoulder-length auburn hair and gray eyes, Ivy was a no-nonsense kind of person. She got out of her car, nodded toward Ryan, Billy, and me, and then went to the driver's-side window of the sheriff's car. She leaned down and talked with Sheriff Billings for a moment, returned to her car, and opened her trunk. She pulled on white coveralls with a hood and took what looked to me like a toolbox out of the car. I supposed it was some sort of medical kit.

Ivy came over to the door of the café. "Hey, guys. How're you doing? You found the victim, right?"

I nodded.

She placed the back of her hand against my cheek. "Your skin isn't clammy. Do you feel dizzy or anything?"

"Not anymore. If anyone is in shock, it's Pete," I said.

She nodded. "Hopefully, Sheriff Billings can prevent that." She took a pair of surgical booties out of her pocket and put them over her shoes before going inside.

I looked at Deputy Hall. "May I please go home now?"

"The sheriff or I might have a couple more things to discuss with you," he said.

"What about me?" Billy asked. "Unless you think you might need an attorney, Amy."

"No, Billy, I'm fine."

"You may go, Mr. Hancock," said Deputy Hall. "But please make yourself available if the sheriff and I have any questions for you in the next couple of days."

"Will do." Without a backward glance, Billy hurried to his car—or, rather, his wife's car—and left.

"So what else do you want to know?" I asked Deputy Hall.

"You said Pete called you this afternoon to set up this meeting. Why didn't Ms. Holman call you herself if she was interested in selling?"

"I don't know. I thought the idea of selling was more Pete's idea and that he was trying to talk her into it. As a matter of fact, I figured my coming here tonight was a waste of my time. I'd talked with Lou Lou about selling me the Joint earlier today, and she'd made it clear she had no intention of doing so. I told her that I'd open my own café somewhere else."

Deputy Hall scribbled in his notebook. "And you don't think her son could've made her reconsider?"

"It's possible—he said he'd played the Hawaii angle . . . Lou Lou always wanted to go there—but even if he'd convinced her to sell, I can't imagine her selling to me."

"Why's that?"

"Because she knew I wanted the café. She'd rather have had someone buy it and bulldoze it than sell to me. That's why I thought I was wasting my time with the meeting. But I was trying to be optimistic."

"Didn't Ms. Holman like you?" he asked.

"She thought I was an upstart . . . that I was trying to get above my raising."

"Care to explain that?"

I winced and tried to choose my words carefully. I didn't want Deputy Hall to agree with Lou Lou. "I went away to school because I wanted to become a professional

chef. When my nana got sick, I came back home and took a job here to be closer to her. My house is only about ten minutes away from this place. Anyway, I took a job as a waitress. I made what I thought were helpful comments about the food and things I thought would help the café be more successful, but . . ."

"But Ms. Holman thought that you were trying to get above your raising," Deputy Hall finished after I'd trailed off. "Got it."

"Right. Plus, she thought the only people who needed to be cooking were her and Pete. And I knew I could do a better job. I didn't come right out and tell Lou Lou that, but I offered time and again to take a shift in the kitchen."

"When you threatened to open a café somewhere else—"

"It wasn't a threat, Deputy Hall. I *am* going to open my own café."

"Okay. But Ms. Holman saw that as competition."

"I guess. So what? Is there anything wrong with good, friendly competition?"

"Not so long as it's friendly," he said.

"If you're asking me if I came in here and knocked Lou Lou in the head—or whatever it was that happened to her—I can assure you I did not. I found her slumped over her desk and called the sheriff's office immediately."

"Duly noted." Deputy Hall held up his notebook to indicate that he had my statement written down.

"Is there anything else?" I asked.

"Not for now." He took a card from his back pocket. "Please call me if you think of anything else you think we should know."

I took the card. "Thank you. I will."

"And be careful going home. That owl could still be lingering around, you know."

I ignored his feeble attempt at humor and left.

When I got home, I was exhausted. It wasn't all that late, but the only thing I wanted to do was get into bed and read until I fell asleep. The trouble was that as I tried to read, I kept playing the evening over and over in my head.

I remembered walking into the office and seeing Lou Lou . . . her colossal beehive almost all the way to the other side of her cluttered desk.

Had she *really* changed her mind about selling to me? I found that hard to believe . . . unless the café was in financial trouble and Pete had been able to convince Lou Lou that he didn't want to work in the café for the rest of his life.

The café *could* be in financial trouble. Neither Lou Lou nor Pete had given much thought or care to their preparation of the food. And Lou Lou almost always had that cigarette hanging on her lip, even while she cooked. I never ate at the Joint, and neither did my friends. It was never terribly crowded. Let's face it—the place was a dive. Had I been able to buy the place, I'd have had to do a lot of PR work to raise the café's reputation to the point where most people—other than the regulars who had eaten there out of habit for so long—would even give me a chance. Maybe it was best that I start from scratch. Like Sarah had pointed out, I could choose everything from the ground up and know exactly what I was getting that way.

*   *   *

I awoke the next morning to Rory licking my face. I groaned. Couldn't he go out the doggie door? It opened onto a fenced yard where he could play and do his business without making me get up.

I reluctantly opened my eyes. "Rory, please. Not this morning. I got almost no sleep last night. Please just let me stay here for a few more minutes."

He whimpered.

I rose up onto my elbows, finally realizing what was wrong with the dog. Someone was at my door. I got up and went to the window. I didn't recognize the car that was in the driveway. Of course, that could possibly be attributed to brain fog.

"Coming!" I called, as I slipped on a robe and hurried to the door.

When I opened it, I saw Homer Pickens standing on my front porch.

"Morning, Homer." I'd known Homer pretty much all my life. He'd always worked odd jobs, and he did some interior painting for Nana the summers after Pop had died. But I'd never known him to just make a social call.

"Morning, Amy. I went by the Joint, but there was crime scene tape all over the place. I couldn't even get into the parking lot."

Last night came rushing back. "Yeah . . . something happened there last night, and they're having to close for a day or two."

"It's ten after ten," said Homer.

"Okay."

"Would you please make me my sausage biscuit?"

"Sure." I moved back so Homer could come on inside. Dealing with Homer's breakfast was a lot easier than coping with what had happened at the café last night. I felt a wave of sympathy for Pete and wondered if Ivy had found anything to tell the police who Lou Lou's killer might be. "Lucky for you, I went to the grocery store day before yesterday and stocked up. So, who's your hero today?"

"Winston Churchill. One of his quotes reminded me just this morning that 'A pessimist sees the difficulty in every opportunity; an optimist sees the opportunity in every difficulty.' It was a good thing I saw that."

"Yeah, I guess it was. I'm going to preheat the oven for the biscuits, and then I'm going to get dressed. You can make yourself at home here in the living room until I get back."

"Thank you, ma'am."

Chapter 3

I quickly dressed and hurried back out to the kitchen. I started a pot of coffee and got to work making the biscuits. By the time the oven light went off to let me know it had finished preheating, I had the biscuits ready to go in. I also had some sausage patties on hand.

"Homer, come on in here to the kitchen, and I'll pour you a cup of coffee." I was still surprised he'd come to my house, but I was also a little glad. Cooking always helped take my mind off my worries, and I sure had a bushel of them this morning.

"Thank you." He ambled into the kitchen. "May I wash my hands, please?"

"Sure." I nodded toward the sink before getting two cups out of the cabinet. "The soap's right there beside the sink, and you can dry your hands on a paper towel." I poured coffee into the two cups. I put Homer's cup on the table along with sugar and creamer. I added fat-free

vanilla creamer to mine and a packet of natural sweet-
ener. That's one thing I wanted to do with my café—offer
most of the items as usual but have some healthier choices
on hand too.

Homer washed his hands and sat down at the table while
I fried the sausage patties. "I see you have some coffee too.
Are you going to have breakfast with me?"

"I thought I would, if that's okay with you."

"That's plenty okay," he said. "I like having breakfast
at your house. The dog is sweet, your kitchen is clean, and
you're even going to eat with me."

I didn't want Homer to think this was our new everyday routine. "The café should be open and things should
be back to normal tomorrow."

"Oh." He looked crestfallen as he added two heaping
spoonfuls of sugar to his coffee.

I went to the stove and flipped the sausage patties
before turning back to Homer. "May I share a secret with
you?"

"Of course. And it will go no further. My mother
always taught me to be trustworthy."

"I'm going to open my own café. I wanted to buy Lou's
Joint." I sighed. "It looks like that's not going to happen
now. But I'm going to build a new café somewhere nearby."

"That's wonderful news! One of Churchill's famous
sayings dealt with the fact that not enough people see
private enterprise as a healthy horse pulling a sturdy
wagon."

"Okay." I wasn't quite sure what Homer meant by that,
but I supposed it was a good thing. I returned to the stove
and saw that the sausage patties were ready. I put them on

a plate and set them aside. Then I got the biscuits out of the oven. I put one of the patties on a biscuit, put the biscuit on a small plate, and set the plate in front of Homer. "Is there anything else I can get you?"

"No, thanks." He bit into the biscuit and then closed his eyes.

I placed the rest of the biscuits on a platter and brought it and the plate of sausage patties to the table.

"These are the most wonderful biscuits I've ever had in my life," said Homer. "They're so much better than Lou Lou's."

"Thanks. There's plenty. Eat all you want."

"I just need my one morning biscuit, but could I maybe take one with me for lunch? I'll pay you the extra."

"Now, Homer, you aren't paying for anything this morning. You aren't at the café. We're just two friends having breakfast together."

"You mean it?"

"I mean it." I smiled. "Just remember me when I open up my own café."

"I certainly will. And I'll tell everyone in town to do the same."

Homer left, and after I cleaned up the kitchen, I wasn't quite sure what to do with myself. I didn't want to spend the day being lazy, though, and I knew it was always best to be prepared. So I went online and searched for some small-business sites that would help me with getting my business off the ground. I knew how to cook—that wouldn't be a problem. It was the advertising, marketing,

accounting, payroll, and tax side of the business that had me concerned.

I hadn't been working long when the doorbell rang. I closed my laptop and went to see who was there. It was Dilly Boyd, another regular from Lou's Joint. Dilly was a wizened little creature who looked half sweet old lady and half impish gnome.

"Hey, Dilly."

"Hi, darlin'. I ran into Homer Pickens, and he said that you made him breakfast this morning. I don't reckon you're making lunch, are you?"

"Well, I wasn't planning on it."

"Shoot. Do you at least have any biscuits left over from this morning? You know, I have that little old raccoon that comes to my back porch every evening about dark, and he won't go away unless I give him a biscuit. Then he scampers on back up into the woods."

"I do have some leftover biscuits," I said. "Come on in."

Dilly followed me into the house and complimented me on my pretty place. "No wonder Homer liked it so good. And he said you sat right down with him and had breakfast with him. That must've been really nice. Shame the café's not open today."

"Give me just a second." I went into the kitchen and put the biscuits into a plastic bag. I was probably getting ready to make a big mistake, but Dilly had thrown such a guilt trip on me with that wistful "must've been really nice" comment. I checked my pantry, freezer, and refrigerator, and then I took her the biscuits.

"Thanks, hon. I appreciate this."

I hated to just send her off with a bag of leftover bis-

cuits, even if the biscuits were for a raccoon. Besides, it would be good practice for me to cook for someone other than my family.

"Dilly, do you think Homer and maybe one or two other people might like some lunch today?"

Her blue eyes sparkled to life, and her face became wreathed in smile wrinkles. "I believe I could round up a friend or two. What do you have in mind?"

"I'll make one meal out of what I have. People will have to eat what I make—they can't come in and ask for whatever they want. All right?"

She nodded. "What is it that we're having?"

"Meat loaf, macaroni salad, scalloped potatoes, creamed corn, collard greens, rolls, and preacher cookies." The no-bake cookies had gotten their name from being something simple to throw together if the preacher came to visit. I didn't mention the oatmeal pie I had left over from last night because I was afraid I wouldn't have enough.

"Oh boy!" She clutched her bag full of biscuits to her chest. "Won't this be fun?"

"Well, I hope it will. Be back in about an hour, all right?"

"See you then!"

When Dilly left, I called Jackie.

"Hi. So what's going on at the Joint?" she asked.

"I'll tell you all about it when you get to my house . . . that is, if you'll come to my house." I told her about Homer and then Dilly coming for food.

"Amy, these people can't expect you to feed you just because the café is closed today. And you can't let them guilt you into it."

"I didn't mean to. At first, it was just Homer wondering where he was going to get his morning sausage biscuit, and then Dilly came by and asked about lunch. I told her I didn't intend to make lunch. . . ."

"But she guilted you into it, didn't she?"

"A little."

"And are these people paying you?"

"Of course, not! That wouldn't be right."

Jackie made a little growly noise, and I could imagine her rubbing her forehead. Even though she was only a year older than me, she saw herself as the more logical and rational of the two of us and sometimes acted as if she were a decade older than I.

"You can't give people free food when you open your own place," she said.

"I won't." Probably. "But I can do this one meal. Maybe it could count as a promotional business expense. And, if you'll come and help me, I'll pay you."

"How could I possibly accept your money, knowing you aren't getting paid for this meal?"

"I'll make you accept it. Now would you please come give me a hand?"

I used Nana's recipe to make the meat loaf, and I was just getting it out of the oven when Dilly arrived.

"I wish I'd thought to make some deviled eggs," I said to Jackie.

"We've got plenty of food."

There wasn't enough room at my kitchen table—and I didn't have a dining room—so since it had turned out

to be a beautiful sunny day, I escorted our guests out to the picnic table in the backyard. There was an umbrella in the middle of the table, and it provided them some shade.

"Well, ain't this nice?" Dilly looked around like she was six years old and I'd thrown her a surprise birthday party.

She'd brought two other ladies who were regulars at the café.

"Just sit wherever you'd like, and Jackie and I will bring your plates out to you," I said. "Would everybody prefer sweet tea?"

One of the ladies requested ice water, but Dilly and the other one said tea would be fine.

When I went back into the kitchen, Jackie was busy buttering the rolls. I took our guests their drinks, and then I came back and started slicing the meat loaf.

"This would slice better if it was cold," I said. "It'll make a good sandwich tonight for dinner if there's any left over."

"That does sound good," said Jackie. "I'd like a couple of slices to take home too . . . if there is enough."

Nana's recipe made a big meat loaf, but I wasn't holding my breath.

We had no more than gotten our guests' plates out to them when someone rang the front doorbell.

"There go our sandwiches," Jackie told me.

I gave her an apologetic shrug and went to answer the door. I was surprised to see the more-gorgeous-than-I'd-remembered Deputy Hall standing on my porch. Maybe I'd been too traumatized to notice last night.

"Deputy Hall, what can I help you with?"

Before he could answer me, Homer came up onto the porch. "Hello, Amy. I hate to be a bother, but Dilly said you were serving lunch."

I nodded. "Go on through to the kitchen, and Jackie will fix you a plate." I stood aside to let Homer pass and then stepped out onto the porch. "Are you hungry, Deputy?"

"You know you can't be doing this," he said. "You don't have the proper permits to operate a café out of your home."

"I'm not operating a café out of my home. I've giving a few people a free meal. You want one or not?"

"I . . . uh. . . ."

"I promise it's clean. You can do an on-the-spot inspection if it'll make you feel better."

He hesitated.

"You like meat loaf?" I asked.

"Yeah, but I've had lunch already. I need to talk with you about the incident that occurred at Lou's Joint last night."

"Come on in." I walked back through the house, assuming he'd follow.

"Thank you." He looked around the kitchen. "Why are you doing all this?"

"I hadn't planned on it. Homer came to my door this morning at a little past ten. Not being able to go to Lou's Joint for his morning sausage biscuit threw him for a loop. He has a strict routine. I felt sorry for him and made him his breakfast. Dilly heard about it and wanted lunch. So here we are."

He grinned. "That little brown scruffy dog running around out there . . . was he a stray?"

"As a matter of fact, he was. His name is Rory, and he was at Lou's Joint one morning when I went in to work. I sneaked him some bacon—Lou Lou would've had my head had she known—and I looked for him when my shift was over. I was disappointed that he wasn't around. I guessed somebody had run him off. But when I started home, I saw him walking in the road. I called him, he came and got into the car, and he's been here ever since."

"I figured. It seems you have a thing for strays."

"I guess so." I nodded toward the table. "Have a seat."

His eyes flicked toward Jackie. "Maybe we could talk out on the porch. It's such a nice day and all."

Little did he know, I'd already told Jackie everything about last night . . . everything I knew anyway. "Sure. That'll be fine. Would you like a glass of water or tea?"

"A glass of tea would be nice. Thank you."

He was walking through to the front door when Jackie came back into kitchen from attending to our guests. She looked at me and then at Deputy Hall's retreating backside.

"Mercy, mercy, mercy," she said under her breath.

"Don't you 'mercy' me."

"Oh, don't worry. I'm not going to step on your toes. It's obviously not me he's interested in anyway."

I scoffed. "The only reason he's here is because of what I told you happened last night. He probably thinks I knocked Lou Lou over the head because she wouldn't sell me the café."

"I don't think that's the *only* reason he's here."

"Well, it's the main reason." I poured two glasses of tea.

"Do you know for sure that's what happened? That somebody hit her over the head?"

"I'm not sure exactly what happened. When I realized she was unconscious, I immediately called the police. I was afraid that whoever had knocked her out was still in the café."

"Still, nobody in his right mind would think you could knock out Lou Lou," Jackie said. "She was a huge woman. Not that you're a weakling or anything, but I'd imagine it would take a lot to fell Lou Lou Holman."

"I'd say you're right." I picked up the glasses. "Wish me luck."

Jackie held up her crossed fingers.

I pushed the screen door open and stepped out onto the porch. Deputy Hall was sitting on one of the white rockers. I handed him his drink.

I sat down on the other rocker. It felt good to relax for a moment. But then it felt good to have been able to provide a meal for some of Lou's Joint's regular customers too. "Am I a suspect in the . . . assault . . . or . . . whatever . . . of Lou Lou?" I asked quietly.

Instead of answering, the deputy took a sip of tea.

"Please be up-front with me. I'm being straight with you."

"I know you are," he said. "I guess we'd call you a person of interest because you found Ms. Holman"—he looked around to make sure none of the guests were coming around from the backyard—"and because you'd had a conflict with her. Of course, Sheriff Billings and I have been asking around, and a lot of people had some sort of conflict with Ms. Holman. She didn't appear to have been a very nice person."

I blew out a breath as I tried to decide what to say and what to hold back. I didn't want to come across as being mean, but I didn't want to paint an inaccurate picture of Lou Lou either.

"She was as tight as the skin on a sausage," I said. "She made us waitresses give her half our tips even though she paid the bare minimum she could get away with, so I doubt any of us would write to Santa on her behalf. She was nice enough when it came to the customers the biggest part of the time, but they could hear her yelling at us over every little thing, and I imagine most of them knew she was just flattering them to keep them coming around."

"You said you didn't work yesterday."

"Right. I only went in to give my notice and to talk with Lou Lou about buying the café."

"Did you notice anyone out of the ordinary—anyone who looked suspicious—while you were there?" he asked.

"No."

"Was Ms. Holman having any work done to the café that you know of?"

I shook my head. "Like I told you, she was stingy. Something would have to literally be falling down before she'd spend money to have it fixed."

"Did you happen to meet any cars coming from the café as you were driving toward it last night?"

"There was very little traffic. Come to think of it, I only met one car that I can recall. It was an SUV of some kind . . . red, I believe. I just remember it because one of the headlights was out."

He nodded and took another drink. "I'll make a note of that."

"What exactly happened to Lou Lou?" I asked. "I mean, I didn't look. I tried to get her to sit up, but I didn't lift up her head or anything. I saw the blood, and when I couldn't get a response, I called the sheriff's department."

"It was probably a good thing you didn't look. She'd been hit in the forehead with a blunt object."

"You mean, like a baseball bat or a golf club?"

"Likely something smaller—maybe a hammer or a crowbar."

I shuddered. "That's awful!" A hammer or a crowbar? I involuntarily shuddered at the thought of either of those weapons cracking open Lou Lou's skull. And why would someone bring something like that into her office anyway unless they were intending to harm her? "Is there anything I could've done for her?"

"No. Ivy said Ms. Holman likely died almost immediately upon suffering the blow."

I closed my eyes. "Oh my goodness. She must've been hit so hard." Then I thought about Lou Lou's son and my eyes flew open. "What about Pete? Does he know? I mean, you didn't let him go into the café last night, but did he see her like that, Deputy Hall?"

"Please call me Ryan. And, yeah, I'm afraid he did. The sheriff showed him the photo, remember?"

"That's right. And Pete had nearly fainted even before that."

"Yeah, he was in pretty bad shape last night."

"I should check on him . . . take him some food."

"That'd be nice." Ryan stood. "I have to get going. Thank you for your time."

"You're welcome."

I returned the glasses to the kitchen and put them in the dishwater.

"So he was here about the case?" Jackie asked.

"Yeah." I glanced out the window and saw that our little group was starting to disperse. "I'll tell you everything once they're gone."

Chapter 4

After everybody had gone and Jackie and I had cleaned up the kitchen, we went into the living room for a well-deserved break.

"I'm tired," I said. "But it's a good tired. We did a nice thing today."

"Yeah, we did. I'm proud of us . . . of you, in particular, because I wouldn't have dreamed of inviting those people to lunch . . . except maybe the cutie-pie policeman."

"I just felt bad for them, Jack. Unless they wanted to travel at least ten miles—and none of them did—they didn't have another restaurant to go to. I mean, lunch at the Joint is their thing. None of them work—at least, not full-time—and seeing one another at Lou's Joint is pretty much the extent of their social calendar." I blew out a breath. "How sad is that? I mean, people like Homer and Dilly are why I want to open my own café—to give the customers, as well as the staff, a better alternative to Lou's Joint."

"And you will."

Princess Eloise sauntered across the back of the sofa. Jackie reached up to stroke her long white fur. The cat gave her a reproachful glare and jumped down onto the floor.

"I don't think she likes me very much," Jackie remarked.

"She doesn't like anyone except Mom. She puts up with me, and to a lesser degree, Rory."

At the mention of his name, Rory popped his head up and wagged his tail. When he saw that no one was eating or offering him a treat, he plopped his head back down onto his paws.

I rested my head against the back of the armchair. "Deputy Hall said that Ivy Donaldson reported Lou Lou was killed with a blunt object."

"That's terrible. And you went in and saw her like that? No wonder you couldn't sleep last night."

"I didn't really see much."

"Thank goodness for that . . . given the circumstances, I mean."

"Pete saw her that way, though. The sheriff asked Ivy Donaldson to take a photo of Lou Lou and show it to Pete so Pete could confirm it was her. It was some sort of technicality, I guess, because we all knew it was Lou Lou."

"How awful."

"I know, right? I wish there'd been some other way. I thought I'd take some food over to Pete's in a little while . . . see if there's anything I can do to help."

"I'll go with you. What're you planning to take?"

"I thought I'd go with a chicken casserole and a pound cake."

"We'd better get started, then, hadn't we?"

* * *

Jackie and I were on our way over to the Holman house when my phone rang. Since I was driving, Jackie fished the phone out of my purse and handed it to me. I answered and was surprised that it was Pete.

"Pete, hi. Jackie and I are on our way to your house with some food. Is there anything you need for us to stop and get you?"

"Uh, no. Thanks, though. I appreciate the offer . . . and the food, of course. But I was calling to ask a favor. Would you care to go over to the funeral home with me to help pick out Momma's casket and make the other arrangements?"

"Yeah . . . sure." Why in the world would Pete ask *me* to help with his mother's funeral arrangements? Surely, there were better choices . . . his girlfriend, for one. Still, the man was grieving. I couldn't refuse. "We can do that. See you in a few." I ended the call and told Jackie what Pete wanted.

She groaned. "Do I have to go?"

"*You* don't. We could make the excuse that someone should stay there at the house in case anyone stops by."

"Are you sure? I hate to leave you stuck like that."

"It's fine. I know how you despise funeral homes."

When we got to the Holmans' small brick home, there were three vehicles besides Pete's truck in the driveway. I parked on the side of the road so I wouldn't block or get blocked in. I carried the casserole, and Jackie carried the cake. The Holmans' neighbor, Shirley Green, saw us coming and opened the door for us.

Ms. Green was a plump rosy-cheeked little woman

whose short gray curls clung to her head like a knit cap. Today she wore a pink floral housedress and a white apron. She lived for occasions like this, where she could insert herself into the situation and mother everyone involved.

"Aren't you girls precious? Come on in, and I'll show you to the kitchen." She lowered her voice. "Poor little old Pete. I don't know what'll become of him now that his momma is gone."

The kitchen reeked of cigarette smoke and a garbage can that needed to be emptied. The round wooden table was full of covered dishes and plates wrapped in aluminum foil that people had brought.

"Has Pete got any other family?" Jackie asked, as she added the cake to the foods on the table.

"Not from around here. And if he has any, they're distant relations at best." Ms. Green clucked her tongue. "Of course, I'll help take care of him as best I can."

I had to bite my tongue to keep from pointing out that the man was forty years old, for pity's sake. Instead, I put the casserole into the refrigerator and saw that it was almost as full as the table. At least Pete wouldn't starve for a good long while.

"Your momma and Bess came by a little while ago, Amy. They brought a lemon pie. It's there in the fridge." She turned to Jackie. "That granny of yours has some wild ideas about her computer stuff. She was telling us about some kinda *boards* she has on her computer?"

Jackie nodded. "She loves pinning things on her social media boards."

Ms. Green continued to look confused. "I don't know anything about computers."

We were saved from commenting further when Pete came into the kitchen.

Jackie gave him a brief hug. "I'm really sorry about your momma."

"Thanks. Amy. As soon as I can get Chris Anne to move her car, we can go."

"Go?" Ms. Green asked. "Go where?"

"To pick out Momma's casket. Amy's gonna help me."

"We can take my car," I offered.

He looked relieved. "I appreciate that. Ms. Green, we shouldn't be too long."

"I'll hold down the fort." She smiled and patted his shoulder.

"And I'll help her," Jackie said.

As Pete and I walked out to my car, I wondered why he hadn't solicited Chris Anne for this job, since she was his girlfriend.

"I'm grateful to you for doing this," he said as I pulled away from the curb. "Momma always appreciated your opinions."

That was hogwash, and we both knew it. But I kept that to myself. No need to speak ill of the dead.

"Chris Anne said she felt like she didn't know Momma well enough to help with the arrangements," he continued. "But I wanted a woman's opinion. I've never been good at picking out things."

Is anyone *good at choosing a casket?* "I understand," I mumbled.

"I guess I could've asked Ms. Green, but Momma always thought she was kind of a busybody."

So Pete's choices had come down to a busybody and an

upstart, as far as his mother was concerned. I suppose upstarts inched out busybodies in Pete's social hierarchy.

"I still want to go after my dream of driving a truck," he continued. "Me and Chris Anne thought maybe we could get married and buy a truck and go into business for ourselves. A lot of couples do that."

"I seem to have heard that somewhere."

"Chris Anne can learn to drive a truck in no time flat and get her commercial driver's license. I already know how to drive a big rig. All I have to do is take the test and get certified."

"That's great," I said. "I hope it works out for you."

"Me too." He paused. "So, naturally, I'll be selling Lou's Joint . . . and . . . uh . . . I was wondering if you're still interested in buying."

Was Pete really this crass? *Hey, Amy, let's go pick out my mother's casket and talk business at the same time.* Or were his supposed shock and grief over his mother's death for the benefit of the police? Or maybe he was simply awkward . . . or, as we used to say, "backward" socially.

"I am, Pete. But we can talk more about that in a few days when everything is settled."

"You mean, like the will? I talked to Billy Hancock, and Momma didn't leave no will."

"Actually, I meant we should give it a few days so you can recover from the blow of losing your mother so suddenly and be absolutely sure about what you want to do."

"Oh, I am sure," Pete said. "But I reckon you've got a point. We ought to get the funeral out of the way and everything before we talk business."

"Right." He'd certainly seemed to have recovered from

his shock and grief much more quickly than I'd expected. Or maybe he was using the business of selling the café and buying a truck as a way to get his mind off his mother's death.

"By the way, Sheriff Billings called, and we're clear to open the Joint back starting tomorrow morning. Would you care to man the grill for the first shift?"

"Of course. In fact, I can work both shifts. No one expects you to come back to work before you're ready, Pete."

"I'll see how I'm feeling tomorrow. Between you and me, I wouldn't step foot in Momma's office again for love or money." He shuddered. "You shouldn't need anything from in there to run the café, though."

"What about money for the cash register?" I asked. "Didn't Lou Lou keep that money in the safe in her office?"

"Yeah. I'll swing by the bank and get you enough to make change."

We arrived at the funeral home, which was a gray stone Colonial home built more than a hundred years ago. As such, it was reputed to be haunted, which is one reason the place freaked out Jackie. Every building a century old (some even less) in Winter Garden was said to be haunted.

When we stepped inside, the thought crossed my mind that maybe Lou Lou's ghost had joined the ranks of the funeral home's restless spirits. I shuddered. *Somebody just walked over my grave.*

U pon returning to Pete's house, Jackie was as glad to see me as I was to see her.

"Get me out of here," she whispered.

"Why don't we go by your place and grab a few things and you can stay over?" I asked on the way to the car. "I'd rather not be by myself tonight."

"Works for me. I'd rather not be alone either with thoughts of Lou Lou's death and the funeral home and Ms. Green's talk about killers so fresh in my mind. I believe that woman quoted statistics on everyone from Jack the Ripper to Ted Bundy."

Jackie lived in an apartment a few miles outside of Winter Garden. She liked to keep things simple—the bare minimum of furniture, no knickknacks, and no pets. Her living room consisted of two mismatched chairs, a coffee table, and a television. In the bedroom, she had a bed and a dresser. The kitchen contained a bistro set, a refrigerator, a coffeemaker, a stove, one frying pan, one saucepan, two sets of dinnerware, and utensils. I figured the only reason Jackie had more than two sets of flatware was because one typically had to buy an eight-, sixteen-, or twenty-four-piece set.

It wasn't just that Jackie preferred to live a simple life. She led a guarded life. Her dad had died in a car accident when Jackie was eight. Then her mother had taken off when Jackie was sixteen years old, leaving Aunt Bess to raise Jackie. Even though her mom, Renee, came around every once in a while, there was no regularity to her visits—one day she was in Winter Garden again, the next day she wasn't. So Jackie was particular about who she chose to trust. Me, Mom, Aunt Bess, Sarah, and Roger were about it.

She went into the bedroom, threw some things into a duffel, and we were off again.

"Was it scary?" she asked as we drove back toward Winter Garden.

"Your apartment? Heck, yeah. Way too uncluttered."

"You know what I meant."

"I'd say the whole funeral home experience was creepy rather than scary."

"I have to wonder why Pete asked you to go help him with the arrangements instead of taking Chris Anne. It might sound callous to say so, but now that Lou Lou is gone, they don't have to be secretive about their relationship anymore, right?"

"I got the impression she didn't want to do it. Pete said I knew his mother better than Chris Anne did and that he needed a woman's opinion," I said. "Plus, he took advantage of the opportunity to ask if I was still interested in buying the café."

"Dang," she said. "Let your mom get cold first, Pete. What'd you say? I mean, is he even sure he *can* sell the Joint this soon?"

"I told him that we should give it a few days . . . get the funeral behind him, let him adjust to the shock of losing his mother and all. He did ask me to man the grill tomorrow morning. That reminds me, did you bring your uniform?"

"No. I'll go get it before work. I figured Lou's Joint would be closed for a few days, didn't you?"

"Frankly, yes. But I'd rather go to the café tomorrow than have it come back to me."

"You've got a point there."

Jackie and I hadn't been at my house long when my mom and Aunt Bess came by. Mom was of average height and thin. She wore her highlighted dark blond hair in a pixie cut that set off her lovely green eyes. Aunt Bess

was on the plump side—but I'd never tell her so for a million dollars. I figured she was eighty-two, and she'd earned it. Plus, she looked great. She had a headful of curly white hair, silver-framed oval glasses, and a surprisingly smooth face. She never went out when she wasn't dressed to the nines, including jewelry and makeup.

Jackie and I hugged them both hello.

"Aunt Bess, you're looking as pretty as a pat of butter melting on a short stack," I said.

"Thank you, darlin'. There's no point in people going around like they do. Me and your momma went to the grocery store this morning, and people were walking around in there with their hair uncombed and some of them looked like they were wearing pajamas." She flattened her lips in disapproval. "And, Lord have mercy, what some of them girls were wearing! Or, should I say, *not* wearing. They ought to be ashamed."

"Yes, ma'am, they—"

"Now, I grew up in a time when girls were modest," she continued. "We didn't go around with our hineys and bosoms hanging out of our clothes. The only ones that did that were streetwalkers." She frowned. "And I don't think even *they* did, did they, Jenna?"

"I don't know," Mom said. "I wasn't there."

"No, but your mother was. Didn't she tell you about it?"

"She must not have." Mom was ready for a change in subject. "Tell us about Lou Lou. We didn't find out until just a few minutes ago that you were the one who found her, Amy. Why didn't you call me last night?"

"By the time I got home last night, I was exhausted, and I just wanted to go to bed."

Princess Eloise must've heard Mom's voice, because

she came into the living room and jumped onto Mom's lap, rubbing her head against Mom's chin.

"Hello, sweetums." Mom kissed the top of the cat's head.

"Did you get a picture of Lou's Joint with the crime scene tape up?" Aunt Bess asked.

"No, Aunt Bess, of course not! Why in the world would I do that?"

"I don't know. I just thought if you did, maybe I could start me a Pinterest board on small-town crime."

I exchanged looks of horror with Jackie. Maybe Shirley Green had been right about Aunt Bess's social media addiction getting out of hand. But given what Jackie had said about Ms. Green, the two might have more in common than Ms. Green thought.

"I—I didn't dream you'd want me to take a picture, Aunt Bess."

"Well, you'll know next time," she said.

I prayed there wouldn't be a next time.

"Are you all right?" Mom asked me. "It's bound to be a horrible experience to walk in on . . . on . . . you know, something like that."

"It was. I—"

"Did you see the killer?" Aunt Bess asked. "Do they know who did it? I wouldn't be a bit surprised if it was her boy, Pete. Maybe he finally got tired of taking her guff and just popped her one right in the head."

"Granny!" Jackie cried. "You don't really think Pete would kill his own mom, do you?"

"Why, young 'un, if you're gonna get killed by somebody, nine times out of ten, it's gonna be somebody you love."

She had a point.

"Hey! Why was your yard full of people earlier today?" Aunt Bess barely stopped to take a breath. "Did you have a party and not invite us?"

"Of course not," I said. Aunt Bess was always afraid of being left out of something. I told her and Mom about Homer coming for breakfast and then Dilly showing up wanting lunch.

"You can't let people take advantage of you like that," Mom said.

"That's what I told her," Jackie piped up. "But everything should be back to normal tomorrow. Pete wants us to get back to work."

"Before his mother's even in the ground?" Aunt Bess flattened her palm against her chest. "Lord, have mercy! That makes me want to go back over there and get my lemon pie back. We took that boy a lemon pie this morning, and now I'm wondering if he even deserves it."

"I'll make you another lemon pie," Mom told her.

"Well, I don't want you to go to any trouble on my account, Jenna. If I'd been you, I'd have made two to begin with . . . but that's just me."

Sometimes Mom and Aunt Bess got along great, and sometimes they acted like they couldn't stand each other.

"Amy and I'll be over to cook for you on Sunday, Granny," said Jackie. "And if you want a lemon pie, we'll make you one."

"Well, call me before you go to the store. I might've changed my mind by then."

Mom cut her eyes to Aunt Bess and then back to me. I know she was hoping she'd caught Aunt Bess between breaths. "So what's the sheriff saying about Lou Lou?"

"Not much to me," I said. "He and his deputy questioned me because I was the first on the scene. Neither of them shared any theories with me or anything."

"Do you reckon it was someone just driving by who saw her van there and decided to try to rob the place?" Mom asked. "I mean, Lou Lou usually didn't work late at night, did she?"

"Not often. She generally took the morning shift and left the afternoon shift to Pete. Any work she had to do, she tried to catch up on before she left in the morning."

"Why was she there, then?" Aunt Bess asked.

"I went in yesterday morning and asked to buy the café. She turned me down flat. Later on, Pete called me and asked me to come to a meeting last night. He said he'd talked his momma into selling but wanted to act fast, before she could change her mind. He was having Bobby Hancock come out too."

Aunt Bess squinted. "So Pete Holman was gung ho to sell Lou's Joint?"

"Yes, ma'am. He wants to go into the trucking business."

"Told you," she said, looking at the other three of us in turn. No one asked the question she was waiting for, so she said, "I told you Pete Holman killed that woman."

"Just because he wanted to sell the business?" Mom asked.

"*He* wanted to sell the business. Lou Lou didn't."

"But, Granny, he told Amy he'd gotten her to change her mind," Jackie said.

"He changed her mind by putting a hole in it." She gave a resolute nod of her head. "I reckon he can sell it now, can't he?"

Chapter 5

I was in the kitchen making dinner when Sarah showed up. She'd apparently gone home after work and changed into white shorts and a pink T-shirt. Being fair-skinned, Jackie and I had both always been a teensy bit jealous of Sarah's beautiful caramel-colored skin tone. She looked fantastic in shorts year-round.

"Hey, hey!" she called as she came into the kitchen and gave me a hug.

"You're in time for dinner. Meat loaf sandwiches, kettle-cooked chips, and preacher cookies."

"Sounds great," she said. "And I bet Jackie's in the living room setting up the Scrabble board."

"Yes, she is. Are you up for a game or two?"

"I am," she said. "I'm sorry I didn't call or come by this morning. I didn't know anything about Lou Lou until I got into work and Billy told me about it, and then after

that we were swamped. Plus, I heard about your impromptu luncheon. How'd that go?"

"Fine. It wasn't that big a deal. Deputy Hall came by and said I couldn't operate a café without a license. So I told him I was giving a very few people free food and invited him for lunch. But he said he'd already eaten."

She laughed. "You'd better be glad word didn't get out all over town, or else you'd *still* be serving food."

"True. I guess it's a good thing that Pete's opening the café back up tomorrow."

All traces of her laughter dissipated. "Have you seen him today?"

"Yeah. Why?"

"How'd he strike you?" she asked. While I contemplated my answer, she went on. "Did he seem like a guy who'd just lost his mother?"

"Not really," I said.

Jackie came into the kitchen. "Not really what?"

"Pete didn't really seem like a guy who'd just lost his mom today," I said. "But last night, he did. He nearly fainted when the sheriff told him the news."

"Then he recovered quickly," Sarah said. "He was in our office this morning to have Billy get the ball rolling on Lou Lou's estate."

We took our plates and glasses of tea and sat down at the table.

"He seems to be awfully anxious to marry Chris Anne so they can start their own trucking business," I said.

Sarah's eyes widened, and Jackie got strangled on a drink of her tea.

"Are you serious?" Jackie croaked.

"That's what he told me." I spread my hands. "I mean, he could be totally sad about his mom and yet . . . maybe . . . kinda excited about the new opportunities he can pursue now. Right? They say everyone deals with grief differently."

"How was he at the funeral home?" Jackie asked. "I mean, other than asking if you still want to buy the café?"

"Other than that, he was considerate. He wanted to make sure he got the things he thought—and that I thought—Lou Lou would've wanted for the service."

"So we can expect a Hawaiian blue floral-print coffin at the funeral?" Sarah asked.

"No. The Winter Garden Funeral Home would've had to special order that," I said. "We got a tasteful white coffin with a blue satin liner."

Sarah looked down at her plate. "I'm sorry. That was mean of me to say."

"You weren't being mean. You were being honest. How do you think I know for certain that the funeral home would've had to special order the blue floral coffin?"

She grinned at me.

"When will the funeral be?" Jackie asked.

"Day after tomorrow," I said.

Sarah ate a chip. "What did you tell Pete about the Joint?"

"I told him we'd talk about it in a few days. . . . You know, he should get the funeral behind him and make sure selling the café is what he's sure he wants to do." I sipped my tea. "Can Pete legally sell Lou's Joint now?

I'd have imagined there would be some sort of waiting period or something."

Sarah shook her head. "No. Although Lou Lou didn't have a will, Pete is her only heir. He inherits everything, so it's his to sell."

"Do you still want to buy the place?" asked Jackie as she wiped her mouth on her napkin. "I mean, Lou Lou *died* in there. Aren't you going to think about that every time you walk through the door?"

"I don't know," I said. "I guess I'll find out tomorrow."

J ackie left as soon as we'd had some toast and coffee the next morning. She had to go back home and get changed into her uniform before coming back to the café. We were the only two people we knew for certain were going to be working. Hopefully, Pete had called others—particularly Aaron, who bussed tables and washed dishes—but he hadn't mentioned anything about it when he'd lent me a key to the café yesterday.

I saw a police cruiser sitting in the parking lot and my heart began thumping against my rib cage. What were the police doing here? Weren't they done with me? Obviously Ryan had told me I was a person of interest, but I had hoped they would cross me off the list. Why were they here now? What if someone was here to arrest me? What would I do? I knew I was innocent, but I had no way to prove it. What if every cent Nana had left me went for a legal defense instead of for my café?

By the time I'd parked the car and stepped out, tears

had filled my eyes. Deputy Hall got out of the cruiser and came toward me.

He gently took my shoulders. "Hey, hey . . . don't cry. Everything's going to be all right."

"You're not here to arrest me?"

"Of course, not. I'm sorry if you thought that."

"But I *am* a suspect in Lou Lou's murder, aren't I? I found her."

"You are a suspect. But there's no hard evidence indicating you murdered Lou Lou Holman," he said. "Not really. As a matter of fact, off the record, I know you didn't do it."

"Wait. You said *not really.* Do you mean there was evidence found?"

He inclined his head. "Ivy found a necklace beneath Lou Lou's desk."

"What did it look like?"

"A pearl inside a heart. One of the waitresses we spoke with identified it as yours."

"That *is* mine. I lost it more than a month ago." Did he believe that? Or did he think I'd lost it the other night in a struggle with Lou Lou? "My nana gave me that necklace for my birthday one year. I thought I'd lost it for good."

"Well, I'll make sure you get it back . . . you know . . . when all this is over."

Tears filled my eyes again. "The sheriff thinks it's me, doesn't he? But I swear, I didn't hurt Lou Lou."

He spread his arms, and for a second, I thought he was going to hug me. Instead, he simply rested his hands on my forearms. "The sheriff has a lot of people on this case, and we're going to find Lou Lou's killer."

I nodded. "Thank you."

"I hope you'll confide to me any information you remember or come across—like who might've had the motive and the means to harm Ms. Holman," he said. "I also want to warn you. Since you were the first person to arrive at the café after Ms. Holman was murdered, the killer might think you know more than you do." He placed his hands on his hips. "And it's possible you *do* know more than you realize. I want you to take some time to yourself as soon as you can, and write down everything you remember."

"All right. I will."

"And be careful. If you even *think* somebody might be following you or creeping around your house, call the sheriff's department . . . or call me. It'd be better to run the risk of being wrong than to ignore it and be right."

"You're kinda scaring me."

"I don't want you to be scared, only aware."

"I will." I nodded toward the café. "I'd better get to work."

"Me too."

"Thanks for stopping by."

"Please call me if you think of anything I might need to know or if you feel threatened in any way," he said.

"Okay."

I went on into the café and hung my purse on a hook in the kitchen by the back door. Was this door how the killer had entered Lou's Joint that night, or had he—or she—come through the front? Going through the front door seemed awfully brazen to me, especially with the lights in the parking lot. It made more sense that the person would've come through the back. The back of the

café led out to just overgrown land. On the other hand, maybe the person had come in the front door, not realizing he'd get angry enough at Lou Lou to kill her.

I shook my head to try to dispel thoughts of that night. I had too much to do to dwell on it right now. Still, it was hard *not* to think about it. Lou Lou had been murdered not twenty feet from where I was standing. Besides, this was a remote area. Sure, it was beautiful, with oaks and maples that had stood for hundreds of years, fields of goldenrod, and cattle grazing in the pasture nearby. But the closest house was half a mile away.

Main Street was three times that distance. And while there were a small grocery store, the newspaper office, a general store, and a hair salon nestled together, none of those businesses were open at six o'clock in the morning.

My mouth suddenly went dry, and I got a drink of water. Jackie had been right. I hadn't realized how I'd be affected by returning to Lou's Joint this morning. I mean, I'd known it wouldn't be business as usual, but I hadn't thought I'd feel so afraid. Of course, Deputy Hall hadn't helped by saying that the killer might come after me. That was something I hadn't even considered.

I downed the rest of the water and made sure the back door was locked. The front door was open, but Jackie should be here any minute.

I had to pull myself together. Pete was counting on me. Lou's Joint patrons were counting on me.

I went out of the kitchen to the counter where the coffeepots were kept. I made two pots of regular coffee and one pot of decaffeinated. I felt better when the scent of brewing coffee filled the air.

I glanced toward the office door and thought about how Lou Lou had looked collapsed across her desk . . . the blood on the desk pad dripping onto the floor.

The front door opened, and I squealed and reeled backward.

"Amy!" Jackie hurried forward. "What is it? Are you okay?"

"You just startled me. That's all." I tried to laugh at myself, but my laugh came out sounding nearly hysterical.

She hugged me. "It's all right. Are you sure you can do this? If not, call Pete and tell him you're leaving. You don't even officially work here anymore, remember?"

"I'd still be working out my notice. Besides, that situation kinda changed night before last. Pete needs all the help he can get right now."

"But that's his problem, not yours."

"Jackie, his mom just died. And I'm the one who found her."

"In this café. Which is the best reason I can think of for you *not* to be here now. Why don't you go on back home? I can take care of things until Pete or somebody else can get here. Pete should have his butt kicked for not shutting down this place for a few days out of respect for his momma in the first place."

"Agreed, but still—"

Brooke, a nurse at Winter Garden Nursing Home, and one of my favorite regulars, came in then. "Am I missing out on a good argument?"

"No," I said. "We aren't arguing."

"Could've fooled me," said Brooke, tilting her head

and pushing her brown corkscrew curls off her right shoulder.

"I'm trying to get her to leave," Jackie told Brooke. "She's as jumpy as a frog dropped on a woodstove."

"Well, I don't doubt it." She turned to me. "I heard about you finding Lou Lou. I'm so sorry. I know that had to have been a shock."

"How do you do it?" I asked. "You go into work every day in a place where people have died."

"That's true, but in my case, they weren't murdered. I think that puts a whole different spin on things."

"Still, it doesn't creep you out to go into a room where some person just died?" Jackie asked. "I'd hate it."

"Well, it's not my favorite part of the job," said Brooke. "But I'm there to help the living. I concentrate on that."

"What about you, Jackie?" I asked. "Is it going to bother you to keep working here?"

"Not as long as I stay out of that office."

"Even if Pete sells, and I completely renovate the office?" Actually, the thought of renovating and using the office gave me pause as well.

"Hey, I heard you were going to open your own café," said Brooke. "I think that would be so cool."

"Thanks, Brooke," I said. "Pete wants me to buy this one, but I have to make sure everyone would be comfortable working here after . . . well, you know." I kept looking at Jackie because I wanted her to answer my question. If she couldn't work here, I wouldn't even consider buying this place anymore. I'd build my own café from scratch.

"I can work here," Jackie said. "We'll wipe away every trace of . . . anything bad that ever happened here, and we'll start all over."

I gave her a hug. "Then we'd better get started. I think we have our first customer of the day."

Jackie grabbed her notepad and pen. "What'll you have, Brooke?"

I went back into the kitchen. I wanted to prepare something different for Lou's Joint patrons today. I looked into the pantry and the refrigerator to see what I could make with the ingredients on hand. I decided to go with a Scottish shortbread.

Jackie brought me Brooke's order and, after making the pancakes, I began mixing up the shortbread. If I could start introducing patrons to new dishes, they'd come to not only accept but expect them . . . and, hopefully, look forward to them.

I thought back to the first time I'd made Scottish shortbread. The dean over the culinary institute was an intimidating man who reminded me of the film actor Robert Preston. Nana had loved older movies, and *The Music Man* had been one of her favorites.

But, anyway, the dean had been observing in our classroom that day. I'd been so nervous that when he'd asked me why the shortbread was baked at 350 degrees for ten minutes and then at 300 degrees for forty minutes, I couldn't sufficiently convey the proper answer—lowering the temperature makes for a flatter, crispier cookie. As I stood there struggling to answer the man, another student in the class stepped up and answered him. He praised her, and she turned to me with a smug smile. I'd decided then and there to stop being intimidated, to never let my

fear of failing or looking foolish stand in the way of my stepping up, answering the question, taking a chance.

That's what I was doing with the Down South Café— taking a chance. If I failed, I'd at least know that I'd tried.

Chapter 6

Homer was right on schedule at ten o'clock that morning, and by then, things were almost normal.

"Good morning, Homer. Who's your hero today?"

"Mr. John Lennon."

"Whoa. Are you going to sing 'Imagine' for me?"

"Unfortunately, I have no musical talent. But I do have a cute story to share. When he was in school, the teacher asked him what he wanted to be when he grew up. Mr. Lennon said he wanted to be happy. The teacher said he didn't understand the question. And guess what he said?"

I was familiar with the quote but didn't want to burst Homer's bubble. "What?"

"He said the teacher didn't understand life."

I smiled as I poured Homer a cup of coffee. "I'll have your sausage biscuit right out."

"Take your time."

When I returned with the biscuit, Homer placed a hand on my arm. "Are you nervous being here . . . you know, after what happened?"

"I am, a little." I glanced around to make sure no one was listening to us. "I wish I'd wake up and all of this would just be a bad dream, Homer. I wish I'd never come here that night."

"I know you do." He patted my arm. "John Lennon always said, 'Everything will be okay in the end. If it's not okay, it's not the end.'"

"Thanks. I hope he's right."

I was pressing out hamburger patties when Pete and Chris Anne arrived that afternoon. Chris Anne strode into the kitchen, put her not terribly clean-looking left hand in front of my face, and wagged her fingers.

"Lookie what I got!" she said in a singsong voice. "We're engaged. Pete took me over to the pawnshop and we got the ring last night."

"Congratulations," I said, shooting a look of desperation at Aaron, who had come in not long after Jackie arrived and who could usually interpret my expressions and the telepathy I was trying to convey with them.

"Let me see," Aaron said.

Chris Anne hurried over to show Aaron the ring, thankfully getting her away from the hamburger patties. I mouthed a thank-you to him behind her back.

"Pete says he'll get me an even bigger one once we get our trucking business off the ground."

"Heck, baby, you'll have rings on every finger then,"

Pete said from the doorway. "I appreciate you patting out them hamburgers, Amy. That'll make it easier on me today."

"I'm gonna help waitress," said Chris Anne, tucking a strand of her greasy hair behind her ear. "It'll help me find out what it's gonna be like working side by side with my man every day."

I glanced over her tight black jeans and black T-shirt. "Do you need a uniform?" I didn't think the goth look would go over all that well with our clientele.

"Nope. I'm good. Thanks, though."

"Did everything go all right this morning?" Pete asked.

"Yeah," I said. "I think we were all a little bit nervous at first, but we got through it."

"Good." He looked down the hallway toward the office. "I can't stand the thought of going in there."

"If you need anything, sugar, I'll get it for you." Chris Anne sashayed over to Pete and smiled up at him.

Stan Wheeler came into the café and called out to Pete. Stan rented a mobile home from Lou Lou, and he came into Lou's Joint to eat on occasion. I'd gleaned from overheard conversations between the two that Lou Lou wasn't the best landlord on the planet. But, then, Stan hadn't seemed to be a star renter either. He could be cantankerous, and I preferred to keep my distance from him.

"In the back," Pete answered.

Stan sauntered up and leaned against the other side of the doorjamb. "Need for you to get somebody over to the trailer and fix my leaky roof."

Chris Anne held out her hand. "Lookie what Pete got me."

"Yeah. Nice. About that roof, Pete."

"Stan, my momma just passed day before yesterday. I'm dealing with about everything I can handle."

"Then give me the money to get it fixed, and I'll hire somebody my own self."

I put the lid on the plastic container full of hamburger patties, slipped off my gloves, and put the container in the refrigerator. I was anxious to get out of there.

"How'd we do this morning?" Pete asked me.

"Not good enough to pay for a new roof," I said as I dropped my gloves into the trash.

"What about the safe?" Stan asked. "I know Lou Lou kept money in there."

"She did," said Pete. "But I ain't going in the office after it."

"I'll go," said Chris Anne.

"No, baby, you don't want to be going in there." Pete put his arm around her.

I could tell by the gleam in Chris Anne's eyes that Pete was wrong about that. Was it mere morbid curiosity that had her wanting to look around Lou Lou's office, or was it something more?

"Give me the combination, and I'll go." Stan held out his hand like it was a done deal.

Pete got out his wallet, took out a square of paper, and handed it to Stan. Frankly, I was surprised that he would trust Stan enough to have him go through his mother's safe. Maybe the two of them were closer than I'd thought.

"I never got to use the safe enough to memorize the combination," he said. "Just go ahead and clear it out while you're in there and bring everything out here to me."

"Fine."

"Is there anything else you need from the office?" Chris Anne asked.

"Well, I would like to have the accounts payable, accounts receivable, and payroll ledgers . . . if they're in there," said Pete. "The sheriff said they might have to take some of that kinda stuff for now . . . you know . . . until the person is caught or whatever. But I'm going to need all that stuff to settle the estate."

"I'll help Stan, then. He can't carry all that stuff by himself." She practically ran from the kitchen.

"Get anything else that looks important," Pete called down the hall.

I noticed he'd shut his eyes before turning toward the office.

I walked him into the dining room. "Come on out here and let me get you a cup of coffee. Or would you rather have some water, tea, or lemonade?"

"I don't need anything." He sat down at a table, and I saw that his hands were shaking. The man was an enigma—that was for sure. One minute, he's coming in here bragging with his fiancée that she'll soon have rings on every finger, and the next he's closing his eyes and trembling as he realizes his mother died just a few feet away.

"I can stay and handle the afternoon shift if you need me to," I said. "You don't have to be here today. In fact, I figure most of our patrons probably think we're closed."

"I'll stay," he said. "Thank you, though."

"You're welcome. In addition to patting out some hamburgers, I sliced some tomatoes and onions, shredded some lettuce, and made a chocolate crème pie."

He smiled slightly. "I appreciate that. I know you said you wanted to give me some time to think it over, but I'd like to know if you still want to buy Lou's Joint. If you're not, I'm going to go ahead and put it on the market."

And another emotional shift from Pete. Was he being manipulated by a puppet master who was throwing darts at a list of moods? "I am interested. Have you already scheduled the appraisal?"

"Billy said he'd handle all of that. I need some cash if I'm gonna buy me and Chris Anne that truck."

I nodded. "I wish you all the luck in the world with that."

"I do you too, Amy. I reckon you, me, and Chris Anne are all about to make our dreams come true. I wish Momma hadn't been too stubborn to make hers come true." His eyes filled with tears.

"I'm sure she had everything she wanted," I said. Who was I kidding? I wasn't sure of anything. I had no idea what sort of dreams Lou Lou might have had. Had someone asked me last week, I'd have guessed that maybe belittling her staff was her dream come true. And then I had a stab of guilt for thinking ill of the dead.

Stan and Chris Anne brought out armloads of stuff from Lou Lou's office: a metal bank box, three or four notebooks, a bunch of documents. . . . Chris Anne even had a coffee mug.

"Look," she said. "Still has your momma's lipstick print on the rim."

I managed to suppress a shudder. Jackie didn't.

"Jackie, are you ready to take off?" I asked.

She nodded. "I'll talk to you later."

* * *

I went home, showered, and changed into a navy blue business suit. I didn't have an appointment, but I hoped Billy Hancock would see me anyway. I headed for his office with high hopes.

The office building was small but elegantly decorated. Sarah was sitting at her desk looking beautiful in a pink dress. She loved pink, and the color looked terrific on her.

She smiled up at me. "Hi."

"Hi. Is Billy in?"

"Not back from lunch yet. Want to wait?"

"I do." I sat down on the chair nearest Sarah's desk. "Are you expecting anyone in this afternoon?"

"Not until two, so you have a little while. What do you want to see Billy about?"

"I just need some advice. Before I left Lou's Joint, Pete said he'd talked with Billy about getting the place appraised and that if I didn't want it, he was going to put it on the market."

"He was in here this morning—he and that insufferable Chris Anne. What does he see in her? Not that he's any big catch, but still . . ."

"I think you hit the nail on the head with that 'no big catch' comment. I mean, Pete's nice enough, but he's always struck me as being a sandwich or two short of a picnic. Plus, think about who his bride would have as a mother-in-law."

"That *is* scary," Sarah agreed. "Or was. Maybe Chris Anne is the one who knocked Lou Lou in the head."

We held each other's gazes.

"I was kidding," she said after a moment, "but that's not entirely out of the question."

"She was awfully ghoulish about wanting to go into Lou Lou's office a little while ago."

"Maybe she wanted to make sure she hadn't left any incriminating evidence behind."

I shook my head. "If she did, Ivy Donaldson has already scooped it up."

"Chris Anne might not know that."

It had me thinking. "Hey, can you come over to my house tonight? I'll see if Jackie and Roger can come too."

"Are we having a party?" Sarah asked with a grin.

"No. But what you said about Chris Anne makes sense. I want everybody to toss some theories around, write them down, and see what we can come up with."

"Honey, I'm sure the police are doing all of that."

"I'm sure they are too, but I'm on their list."

"What?"

"I'm a suspect," I said.

"That's total crap!"

"Not if you look at it from their point of view."

"Then let's Nancy Drew the fire out of this thing and get you off the hook."

Before she could say more, we heard Billy's car pull up.

"See you at six?" I asked.

"I'll be there."

"Hello, Amy," Billy said when he came in. "Did you and Sarah have lunch?"

"No, sir. I'm here to see you, if you have a minute."

"I believe I do . . . don't I, Sarah?"

"You're free until two," she told him.

"Good. Come on into my office, then."

I followed Billy into his office. Like the lobby, his office was decorated in forest green and burgundy. He had a high-backed leather desk chair, and there were two small matching chairs in front of the desk. With the exception of an in-box that was full stacked upon an out-box that was empty, the desk was uncluttered. It appeared all of Billy's current case files and other works in progress were on the credenza behind him.

"So how can I help you, Amy?"

"You tell me. I'm afraid I'm a suspect in a homicide, and I want to either buy Lou's Joint or build my own café. But you're probably already aware of all of that."

"I am." He folded his hands. "Whoever found Lou Lou was going to be a suspect in her murder. I don't feel there's anything to worry about unless you're formally accused."

"By 'accused,' do you mean 'arrested'?" My tone was matter-of-fact, but my heart was fluttering up into my throat.

"I do. Is there any reason for you to be arrested, Amy?"

"I didn't kill her, if that's what you mean."

"That's not what I meant. Good to know but not what I'm driving at. Do you have a motive?"

"I resigned from my job at Lou's Joint that morning, and I offered to buy the café. Lou Lou rejected my offer . . . rather soundly, I might add. I was surprised when Pete called to set up our meeting."

"I admit I thought the deed to Lou's Joint would have to be pried out of . . . well, you get my meaning."

"Then you were surprised too," I said.

"Sure, I was. And I let Pete know that I was billing him for the meeting even if his mother backed out."

"He told me this morning that he'd already asked you to get the café appraised."

Billy nodded. "I've called the commercial real estate appraiser, and she's going to get to it as soon as she can."

"Do you think I should buy the existing building or that I should buy a piece of land and build my own café?"

He sat back in his chair and clasped his hands behind his head. "I believe you'd be better off from a financial standpoint to buy Lou's Joint. All the power, water, and sewer lines are already in place. The location is established. And all you'd have to do is renovate." He lowered his arms and rubbed his chin. "Plus, if you don't buy the place, some fast-food franchise might come in and get a foothold while you're still trying to build."

"I hadn't considered that," I said.

"The other thing you have to think about, though, is this: are you going to have the heebie-jeebies working in Lou's Joint?"

"I had my reservations when I went in to work this morning," I began, but he cut in.

"What? Why were you working there? I thought you just said you'd quit."

"I had given my two weeks' notice. But I wouldn't leave Pete in the lurch. He doesn't have anybody else who can cook for him. If I hadn't taken the morning shift, he'd have had to cook all day."

"Or close the place like he had some sense," Billy muttered. "But maybe that's how he's dealing with his grief . . . staying busy."

"Maybe so. Either way, I feel I can't fully commit to buying or building a business until this black cloud I'm under goes away."

"Are you calling your being a murder suspect a black cloud?" Billy waved away that thought with the flick of his wrist. "That's ludicrous. I doubt you'll be arrested."

Doubt? I gulped. "Gee, thanks. I hope and pray you're right. But I'd like to go ahead and give you a retainer so that you can start either planning my defense or working on securing the paperwork I need for the café."

"I do feel the need to tell you that since one of the local churches boycotted Lou's Joint, the place hasn't been in the best financial shape."

"I figured I'd have to do a lot of promotion to let people know the café is something new and different from what they were used to with Lou's Joint. I mean, of course, many of the menu items will remain, but I take pride in my food and I'm looking forward to introducing lots of new dishes too."

"Sounds great. So let's go ahead and incorporate your business," he said. "That way, you'll have something to help distract you from Lou Lou's murder investigation until either the police find out who did it or the case grows cold. We can get the necessary permits and licenses in the business's name, and you can start making a list of your expenses even before you decide whether you'll build or buy. Sound good?"

"I guess so."

"So do you want your business name to be the same as the name of your café?"

"I want to call my café the Down South Café," I said. I'd been thinking on that for quite a while. I wanted people to think of Southern hospitality, a sweet home-town, and a small but bustling café when they thought of my restaurant.

"All righty. Want to call your business Down South Café, Incorporated?"

"Sure. That works."

"Good. I'll get Sarah to start on the paperwork. By this time tomorrow, you'll officially be an entrepreneur."

Chapter 7

I changed into a T-shirt and shorts as soon as I got home. Then I went into the fancy room and cuddled up in the blue chair with my old culinary school textbook. So I was almost an entrepreneur. As I'd mentioned to Billy Hancock, one of the main things I needed to do was establish that Down South Café wasn't simply Lou's Joint under new management . . . even if I wound up building a new restaurant rather than renovating Lou's Joint.

I wanted to continue to serve the foods that the café patrons expected and were accustomed to, but I wanted to give them some more exciting choices as well. My palate had become more sophisticated when I attended culinary school, but I realized that old habits died hard with many Southwest Virginians. Winter Garden residents liked the tried-and-true, and were reluctant to pay for something they might not like. So I'd have to allow

patrons to sample new dishes before I added them to the menu.

Also, I had to ensure that I could not only acquire all the ingredients I needed for a recipe, but that their cost wouldn't make the dish a loss for the café. For example, I loved cipollini onions, but I couldn't find a grocery store in our region that stocked them, and ordering them would be cost-prohibitive.

So as far as breakfast was concerned, I'd serve the typical fare, offer healthier options, such as turkey bacon and gluten-free pancakes, and introduce new dishes that would, hopefully, delight my customers. I made a souffléed cheddar omelet that would nearly melt in your mouth.

At lunch, I'd also have the menu staples patrons would expect, but I'd throw in a few surprises there as well. I felt that most of the patrons would love corn fritters made with cheddar cheese, but they might be reluctant to try fried plantain chips. Of course, they could surprise me. I wanted to give them the opportunity to try a variety of new foods. I truly felt that offering free samples was the key to seeing which items would do well on the menu.

I thumbed through the book until I came to the section on food and kitchen safety. That was something I would certainly need to go over with my staff, especially those—if any—who came with me from Lou's Joint. An image of Lou Lou with that ever-present cigarette dangling from her lip emerged, making me wonder for the umpteenth time what on earth happened just before I got to the café that night. And why had Pete been so willing to let Stan Wheeler pilfer through his mother's office? I understood why he hadn't wanted to go in there

himself, and I was certainly relieved that he hadn't asked me to go—because I'd have definitely turned him down—but why Stan?

R oger was the first to get to my house. I was surprised. Having his own construction business meant that Roger often worked late hours, especially in the summer. I was also glad he was the first to arrive because I had a lot of questions for him.

He was about five feet nine inches tall and solidly built. He had dark blond hair and brown eyes. I thought he'd been half in love with Jackie since middle school, but he wouldn't ask her out. Maybe one of these days.

I took Roger outside and put him in charge of watching the grill while I set the picnic table.

"I have some questions for you," I said.

"About what, Flowerpot?" The nickname harkened back to our childhood.

"Running your own business. It's difficult, isn't it?"

"Well, yeah. You learn pretty quickly that when you need a helping hand, it's at the end of your arm."

I struck a match to the citronella tiki torch I had standing in the yard. "You mean you don't have anyone you can count on to help you?"

"I have plenty of help . . . a lot of great workers. But at the end of the day, the business is my responsibility. There's nobody but me to worry about overhead and expenses and revenue."

"Is it scary?"

"Heck, yeah, it's scary." He winked and grinned at me. "But ain't anything worth having a little scary?"

I smiled. "You've got a point. Which actually brings me to another question: when are you going to ask Jackie out?"

"Now, don't start *that* again. Jackie's one of my best friends." He took the tongs and turned the steaks. "What if we'd go out and end up not getting along—or even worse, have a bad breakup—and never be able to go back to the way we were before? It would ruin things for our whole group."

"But, Roger, what if you're missing out on the love of your life? And what if Jackie is too?"

"If things are meant to work out between us, they will somehow. Now let's get back to talking about business. Did you ever decide whether you're going to build from the ground up or buy an existing building?"

"Pete's doing his best to get me to buy Lou's Joint, and Billy Hancock says that would be the way to go."

"Billy's right. And I can make that place look like new."

"I know you can." I surveyed the table. All the food was covered and waiting for us to dig in. In addition to the steaks and grilled vegetable kabobs, we were having potato salad, chips and salsa, corn on the cob, key lime pie, and watermelon slices.

"But?" Roger prompted.

"I'm a suspect in Lou Lou's murder. That's one reason I invited all of you over tonight. I have to get this figured out and clear my name."

He shook his head. "Honey, there's no way anyone could think you capable of murdering Lou Lou."

"You're wrong about that. I'm guessing I'm pretty high on the suspect list, since I found her body."

"That's stupid. Why would you kill her and then call

to say you'd found her? If you'd killed her, you'd have done exactly what her murderer did—take off."

"Amen," said Jackie, coming around the side of the house in time to hear what Roger had to say. She gave him a one-armed hug. "Long time, no see. Where've you been?"

"I've been working my butt off," he said.

She took a pointed look at his backside. "Nope, Roger, it's still there." She gave me the "okay" sign but made sure Roger couldn't see.

Sarah was the last to arrive. She'd brought a banana pudding because she said she didn't feel right not bringing anything. We gladly accepted.

"Where's John?" I asked.

John was Sarah's boyfriend. He was in law school at the Appalachian School of Law.

"Had a late class," she said. "Besides, I thought that since we were doing the Nancy Drew and Hardy Boys thing, it should just be us for dinner."

Roger turned the steaks again. "What? Do you think John did it?"

"Did what?" she asked.

"Killed Lou Lou."

She rolled her eyes. "Yes, Roger, I do."

"Good. Get him to confess, and we'll just enjoy our dinner."

"I was being sarcastic," said Sarah.

"I know, but it sounds like a plan. It'll test his legal skills."

"He hasn't graduated yet."

Jackie put an end to Roger's and Sarah's mock argument. "Smarty-pants, you got our steaks ready?"

Roger shook his behind in Jackie's direction. "Don't

rush perfection." Then he called me over to see if the steaks were done.

Once we were seated, I started my spiel. "I went to talk with Billy Hancock today, and he's incorporating my business."

Cheers and congratulations went up from around the table.

"But before I move forward, I need you guys to help me figure out who might've killed Lou Lou. I have to clear myself of any suspicion in her death," I continued. "Who's going to want to eat at the Down South Café if the proprietor is suspected of murdering the previous establishment's owner?"

"Hey, maybe Lou Lou ate some of her own food and died from that," Roger piped up. "I mean, I know they think she was hit on the head, but maybe she hit it on something as she was falling."

"I seriously doubt that," I said.

"No?" he asked. "No chance? I mean, Lou Lou's cooking was pretty nasty."

"That's why the whole town—and all the towns around here—are going to be thrilled with Amy's place," said Jackie. "What did you say you're calling it again?"

"The Down South Café," I said. "But let's be serious about Lou Lou for a minute. Do you guys know of anybody who disliked her enough to murder her?"

"I threw my card on the table when you were at the office today," said Sarah. "My money's on Chris Anne."

"Granny is bound and determined that it was Pete," Jackie said. "And that kinda makes sense too. I mean, Lou Lou was holding him back . . . didn't want him to

get married or leave the restaurant business. She wanted to keep him under her thumb."

"What about you, Roger? Any theories other than that she ate her own food and killed herself?" I asked.

He chewed his steak as he mulled over his answer. "Maybe it was a *Murder on the Orient Express*–type deal, and several people took a swing at her. I can imagine some of the waitresses being up for it, and Aaron asked me last week if I was hiring."

I nearly choked on my tea. "What did you tell him?"

"The truth—that I have everybody I need right now but would let him know if anything comes open," said Roger. "Fact is, I could use him while I build or renovate your café."

"You have a point. But I don't want to lose him. He's a great dishwasher and busboy."

Even before I'd approached Lou Lou about buying the Joint, I'd asked Roger to renovate the café for me or to build a new one if she wouldn't sell. The summer months were some of the busiest for him, but Roger had carved out that time for me.

Roger smiled. "Already got him hired, huh?"

"Well, no . . . but . . . I thought at least some of the staff would stay in place," I said.

"I'm only giving you a hard time."

"What do you think drove Aaron over the edge?" Sarah asked. "From what I've heard, Lou Lou was hateful to all of you."

"She was," I said. "I don't know what would've been the last straw for Aaron."

"I do," said Jackie. "Lou Lou accused him of stealing last week."

"When was this?" I asked. "I didn't hear anything about it."

"It was on Monday or Tuesday," she said. "I thought it was typical Lou Lou being Lou Lou, but it really upset Aaron. If he could've afforded to, I believe he'd have quit right there on the spot."

"So put him down on that little list you're making," Roger said.

"Aaron? No," I said. "He's a good kid. He's been helping his parents with their bills since his dad got sick. He wouldn't have killed Lou Lou."

"You said we were here to explore all possibilities. He's a possibility."

"Roger's right," said Sarah. "We need to list everybody with a motive."

"I might as well go ahead and put down half of the population of Winter Garden, then," I said. "How many people rented from Lou Lou?"

"She has the one trailer out on Huff's Pike that she rented to Stan Wheeler," said Roger. "And I believe she has a duplex out on Route Fifty-eight."

"She sold the duplex last year," said Sarah. "I remember drawing up the paperwork for the closing."

"So I guess Stan is her only renter," I said.

"Put him on the list," said Roger. "He's bad news."

"Why? What has he done?"

"According to one of my suppliers, he's a drug dealer. Stan apparently dealt to my friend's sister, and he went looking for Stan. I'd say Stan is lucky my friend didn't find him that night."

"How did I not hear about any of this before now?"

"You were gone, off at school, for quite a while,"

Jackie said. "And then after you came back, you were too busy with work and your nana to get too looped into the gossip."

"So read us that list," said Sarah.

"Me, Chris Anne, Pete, Aaron, and Stan."

Roger leaned across the table toward me. "I think it's that first one."

"*I'm* the first one," I protested.

"I know. Did you kill Lou Lou? I mean, what a shocker it would be if you had. We'd all be like . . ." He clutched at his chest.

"Roger, will you stop?" Jackie slapped his arm. "She's worried enough as it is."

He blew out a breath. "Good gravy! It was a joke! Would one of you *please* bring a boyfriend next time?" he teased. "Or, Amy, invite one of the neighbor men. I don't care if he's a hundred years old. Just get a little more testosterone at the table."

Jackie rolled her eyes. "I am man. See me beat my chest."

"Do not make me club you over the head and drag you back to my cave," he said with a grin.

She leaned back. "Oh, I would *love* to see you try."

"So what do we do now?" Sarah asked. "How do we find out where these people were, if they have alibis for the time of the murder or whatever? My only dealings with criminals are the ones that have already been caught."

"Good point," I said. "What *do* we do now?"

"I'll take Aaron," said Jackie. "I was there when Lou Lou accused him of stealing, and I can ask him in a round-about way what he was doing that night. Plus, he's not afraid to talk to me. You intimidate him, Amy. You're too pretty."

My jaw dropped. "I most certainly am not!"

"You are to him."

Roger tilted his head. "I can see it. If I hadn't known you since you had crooked teeth and skinned knees, I'd think you were pretty too."

I gave him a slow, exaggerated blink. "Thank you so much."

"You're welcome."

By the time everyone left, we still weren't quite sure what to do other than Jackie's plan to talk with Aaron to see what he'd been doing when Lou Lou was murdered. I needed to figure out what to do on my own. Like Roger had said about his business, at the end of the day, this was my own responsibility.

I went and got my phone and Ryan Hall's business card from my purse. As I punched in the number, I knew I was probably making a huge mistake. But I didn't know what else to do.

"Ryan Hall."

"Hi, Deputy Hall. It's Amy Flowers. How are you?"

"I'm fine, Amy. What can I do for you?"

"I've . . . um . . . I've kinda made a suspect list, and I'd like to go over it with you if you have a minute."

"A suspect list?"

I could hear the amusement in his tone, but I didn't let it deter me.

"Yes, a suspect list. Do you have time to talk with me about it, or not?"

"Sure. Let's have it."

I gave him every name on the list, starting with me. "As you know, I don't have an alibi for the time of the murder, other than the fact that I was with my friend Sarah only

minutes before I left for Lou's Joint. I haven't had anybody tell me an approximate time of death, but Sarah can verify the time I was with her."

"All right," he said. "Next."

I told him Sarah's theory about Chris Anne, but I didn't tell him it was Sarah's theory. I didn't want him to know I'd been talking about the case with my friends. I didn't think it was breaking any rules to talk with them about Lou Lou's murder, but just in case, I'd rather be safe than sorry.

"Pete also had motive to dispose of his mother," I continued.

"'Dispose of'? Interesting word choice."

"Well, I hate to say Pete had reason to *kill* his mother, but she was terribly hard on him. She wouldn't allow him to have a serious girlfriend, and he desperately wanted her to agree to sell the café so he could pursue other interests."

"She wouldn't 'allow' a forty-year-old man to have a serious girlfriend?" he asked.

"Apparently not. And he's already proposed to Chris Anne and asked me to buy the café so he can put the money toward starting a trucking business." I paused. "You think I'm a fruitcake, don't you?"

"I think you're scared, Amy. And I assure you, we're looking into all the people you've mentioned and then some. We'll find out who's responsible for Lou Lou Holman's death. Just let us do our jobs, all right?"

I didn't say anything. I wanted to trust Deputy Hall. Truly, I did. But this was my life we were talking about. How could I simply take a backseat?

"Please?" he asked. "Trust me."

"I'm trying to."

Chapter 8

Pete called me at just after ten o'clock that night. "Hey, Amy . . . whatcha doin', gal?" His words were slightly slurred.

"Pete, are you drunk?" He *had* to be drunk. And he was drunk-dialing *me*? What on earth for?

"I . . . I might be . . . the slightest bit . . . uh . . . wasted. Why? Is it . . . is it late?"

"What do you need?" I was not going to deal with him, not in his condition, and not at this time of night. I was trying to cut him some slack because of everything he'd been through, but enough was enough.

"Will you come in . . . in the morning . . . for the grill?"

"You didn't think to call me about this sooner?" I asked.

"I forgot. Sssorry."

"I'll man the grill tomorrow morning, but I don't have a key. Would you be able to meet me there and let

me in?" This was ridiculous. I thought—again, and like the rest of the town—that Pete should've had the courtesy to close the café for a few days to mourn. He apparently took his "leave no cent unearned" credo from his mother.

"Use the kitchen door," he said.

"What? Don't you keep it locked?"

"N-no. I mean, yeah. Key's unner the rock by the door."

"Okay. I'll look for it." And then I did something I'm not proud of. I tried to take advantage of his drunken state. "So Pete, do you know of anybody who'd want to hurt your mom?"

"Momma . . . poor Momma." He started blubbering. "Why would *anybody* hurt Momma? She was a saint! A saint, I tell you." He wheezed and coughed before blubbering again. "Except when she was mean. Sometimes she could be a little mean."

"I know, Pete. It's all right."

"It was for my own good. I never learned good judgment. Always hanging around . . . wrong people . . . bad decisions." He sniffled. "She just tried to take care of me. Momma was a saint. Poor, poor Momma!"

"I know," I said again. I didn't know what else to say. I wished I'd never mentioned it, but I thought he might tell me something I didn't know . . . something that he didn't *want* me—or anyone else to know. Now I felt pretty bad. At least he probably wouldn't remember this conversation tomorrow.

"Wh-when you . . . you buy the Joint, Amy . . . will you put a big p-painting of M-Momma on the wall? Y-you know . . . a memorial?"

Uh, no! I most certainly will not!

"Let's talk about it tomorrow, Pete," I said. "You get some rest."

"Nice b-big oil painting. We'll get somebody to do it up real nice. . . ."

"Good night."

"G'night, Amy."

As I got ready for bed, I thought about that key outside the kitchen door. I wondered how many other people knew about that key. It could've certainly allowed the killer to enter and leave the café without being spotted from the road.

The next morning, I found the key just where Pete had said it would be. The rock wasn't even one of those fake rocks used to hide a spare key. It was merely placed under a rock with a flat bottom. The key had apparently been there for a long time, because there was a perfect indentation of it in the earth beneath it. It crossed my mind that I might ought to call Ryan Hall and have him send Ivy Donaldson out to test the key for fingerprints, but I figured that would be useless. The key would have so many fingerprints—even if they were just those of Lou Lou and Pete—that I thought it would be hard to get a distinct print. Add to that the fact that after picking up the key, my own prints were on it. I put the thought aside, unlocked the door, and returned the key to the indentation beneath the rock.

I went into the dining room and retrieved the coffeepots. I thought about going ahead and unlocking the front door, but I decided against it. The café didn't open

for another thirty minutes, and I wanted to make sure that no one came in while I was doing the necessary prep work.

As I worked in the kitchen, I thought about uniforms. Should I have uniforms for the staff? Or should I allow the staff to wear their regular clothes covered by a DOWN SOUTH CAFÉ apron? I'd ask Jackie her opinion.

When I did go back through the dining room to unlock the front door, Dilly was standing there waiting for me.

"Good morning, Dilly. I'm sorry you had to wait."

"That's all right. Got any biscuits yet?"

"They're in the oven. Oh, and try this Scottish short-bread I made yesterday morning." I took the cover off the glass cake plate on which I had the cookies.

Dilly took a cookie and then sat at the counter. "I saw Pete Holman and Stan Wheeler going into the pizza parlor last night when I was on my way home from bingo. Why in the world would anybody be having supper that late? It was pert near ten o'clock."

"I don't know," I said. "My stomach would think my throat had been cut if I waited that long to eat my dinner."

"Me too." She shook her head. "And I imagine my raccoon would think I'd left home. He comes to that door every evening as soon as it starts getting dark. You can count on it."

"What happens if you don't have a biscuit for him?" I asked.

"He'll settle for a cookie if he has to. He doesn't like it as well, but he'll take it." She bit into the shortbread. "Oh my goodness! This is good. I bet he'd like this, but he's not getting mine."

I smiled. "Besides two biscuits, then, what would you like for breakfast this morning?"

"Just a scrambled egg, please."

"Hash browns?"

"Oh, yes. That'd be nice."

"Coming right up," I said as I poured Dilly a cup of coffee.

I thought it was interesting that Pete had been out last night with Stan instead of Chris Anne. Maybe the two men were celebrating Pete's engagement. Or maybe Pete had given in and handed over the deed to Stan's mobile home.

While I was preparing Dilly's breakfast, Preacher Robinson came in. He was the pastor of the Winter Garden First Methodist Church. Mom and I had always attended the Winter Garden First Baptist Church, but I was acquainted with Preacher Robinson because the two churches—especially since they were the only two in town—often came together during revivals and community events like buying for needy families during the holidays.

I was surprised to see Preacher Robinson this morning, though. During my time working at Lou's Joint, I'd never seen him in here before. It crossed my mind that he might be preaching Lou Lou's funeral.

"Good morning, Preacher Robinson," I said. "How are you this morning?"

"I'm fair to middling." He nodded to Dilly. "Morning, Missus Boyd."

"Howdy, Preacher."

It struck me that Preacher Robinson probably wasn't

as old as his manner would make him appear to be. He was a pencil-thin man of average height, with sparse brown hair and black-rimmed glasses. Even in this heat, he wore a brown three-piece suit with a tan shirt and a yellow-and-brown-striped tie.

He was standing awkwardly in the middle of the dining room, so I invited him to sit anywhere he'd like.

"I'll get you a menu in just a second," I said.

"That won't be necessary. I hadn't planned on staying to eat. I had some grits before I left the house this morning."

"Okay." I didn't have time to wait for him to tell me why he was here if it wasn't to eat, so I went ahead and plated Dilly's food. I brought it out for her and topped off her coffee.

Preacher Robinson peered down over his glasses at the meal. "That does look awfully good, though. I suppose it wouldn't hurt to have some scrambled eggs with a side of bacon." He grinned and patted his flat stomach. "Just this once."

"Coming right up," I said. "Coffee?"

"Please."

As I poured the coffee into a white stoneware mug, I asked, "If you didn't come in for breakfast, Preacher Robinson, then are you here about Lou Lou's funeral? Because Pete isn't here."

"Aw, shucks. I mean, I'm not here about the funeral—there's no way in heck she'd want *me* to preach it if I was the last pastor on earth anyhow—but I did want to have a word with Pete."

I glanced at Dilly, wondering if she knew what Lou Lou had against Preacher Robinson. She was so intent

on eating those hash browns that I doubt she'd even heard what he'd said.

"I can have him give you a call," I said, putting the mug in front of him. The curiosity was killing me. "May I tell him what it's about?"

He sheepishly avoided my eyes and put sugar and creamer into his coffee. As he stirred, he watched the black liquid turn to light brown. "I guess I should've given it a few more days, but our Bible study is coming up, and I'd love to be able to have the meeting here in town for the first time in two years."

"Where have you been meeting?" I asked.

"A diner over in Meadowview." He continued to stir. "Ms. Holman and I had a . . . well, a disagreement, you might say . . . back then, and she threw us out. Wouldn't let us come back either."

What in the world did a preacher and his Bible study group do to offend Lou Lou to the point that she wouldn't accept their business?

He finally looked up at me. "Yes, ma'am, eggs and a side of bacon would really hit the spot."

The conversation was over. I wasn't going to find out what happened from him. I told him I'd get his breakfast out to him right away.

We had a little lull at about a quarter to nine, and I pulled Jackie aside to ask how she felt about uniforms.

"It depends on what they look like. These things Lou Lou made us wear are ugly with a capital *U*." She spread her hands, indicating the pale orange–and-white-checked

uniforms. "I'd say she got them on sale somewhere because no one else wanted them. What have you got in mind?"

"I was thinking that the staff could either wear casual clothing covered by DOWN SOUTH CAFÉ aprons, or we could wear matching T-shirts with our logo."

Jackie nodded. "I like that idea. Plus, you could sell the T-shirts and aprons to customers for an additional source of income."

"You really think people would buy them?"

"Sure, they would. Tourists love things like that."

"I guess we could order some extra," I said.

"What about pants?"

"I was thinking jeans."

"Jeans are good," said Jackie.

"By the way, do you know anything about a disagreement between Preacher Robinson and Lou Lou? It would have happened about two years ago." I told Jackie about the pastor coming in this morning wanting to reinstate his Bible study sessions at the café.

Brow furrowed, she stared at the wall just above my head. Suddenly, her eyes widened. "Oh my gosh, I *do* remember that! In fact, it was just after I started working here, and I remember it like it was yesterday! During the Bible study, Preacher Robinson said that in four separate places in the Bible—Genesis, Matthew, Mark, and Ephesians—a man is instructed to leave his father and his mother and cleave unto his wife."

"And Lou Lou thought he was talking about her and Pete?"

Jackie nodded. "Apparently so, because she stormed out of that kitchen and told him that she and Pete were

none of his congregation's business and that he needed to do his Bible studying elsewhere."

"Wow. Is it just me, or does it seem kind of extreme that she would make that leap from one passage of the Bible to Pastor Robinson attacking her and her son because Pete still lived at home?"

"Oh, it was extreme, all right. But the thing was, Pete had been dating a woman in the congregation, and I believe her family was putting pressure on her to marry."

"And she was putting pressure on Pete," I guessed.

Jackie chuckled. "Poor woman. I don't know if she encouraged the preacher to have that particular study—and to have it here—or not, but that was the end of her dating Pete too."

"Who was she?" I asked.

"I don't know. She was quite a bit older than us, so neither of us had gone to high school with her. After that, the whole congregation boycotted Lou's Joint, and I think she finally started going to church in Abingdon. Hopefully, she met somebody there."

"Hopefully, someone not quite as henpecked." I shook my head. So maybe that explained why Pete had tried to keep his relationship with Chris Anne from his mom.

"Before I forget," Jackie said, lowering her voice, "I ran into Aaron yesterday evening at the grocery store and *casually* struck up a conversation about Lou Lou's murder. I told him I was at home watching television and had no clue anything had even happened until the next day. He said, 'Same here.'"

"Which, I guess, technically means he has no verifiable alibi."

She turned down the corners of her mouth. "Neither do I. Shouldn't you add me to the list?"

I half smiled. "Nah. If either of us had planned to do someone in, she'd have called on the other to help her."

Jackie laughed. "That's true."

Homer Pickens came into the café and sat on a stool at the counter. I went over to pour him some coffee.

"Good morning, Homer. Who's your hero today?"

"Liam Neeson."

I was eager to hear Homer's reasoning behind his choice. "I like his movies," I said. "If I'm ever kidnapped, I hope he'll come rescue me."

Homer nodded and smiled wistfully. "He's strong. And I love his voice. It can be gentle or menacing." Homer tried to affect Mr. Neeson's voice. He failed miserably. "And don't worry, Amy. If you *are* ever kidnapped, I'll find you. Maybe. I'll at least try."

"Thanks. Sausage biscuit coming right up."

Brooke came rushing into the Joint. "Amy, I need to talk with you for a minute. It's urgent."

I called to Jackie and asked her to make Homer his sausage biscuit, and then I joined Brooke at a table in the far corner.

"What's wrong?"

"Well, I know you were talking about buying this place from Pete Holman, so I thought this news might be of interest to you," she said. "Eddie March, a writer for the *Winter Garden News*, came into the nursing home to see his grandmother this morning. He said that the area immediately surrounding Lou's Joint is about to be designated a historical site because of some Civil War battle that was fought here."

"So what does that mean? Will the government buy Pete out and tear down the café to put up some kind of memorial or something?"

"I don't think so. From the way Eddie talked, it means the café will go up in value. He said that George Lincoln with the Chamber of Commerce had spoken to Lou Lou about buying the Joint, tearing it down, and building a bed-and-breakfast on this site."

"Wow. Thanks for letting me know. When was this?" I asked.

"Only about a week and a half to two weeks ago. It couldn't have been long before you made your offer."

"I wonder if Lou Lou had been considering accepting Mr. Lincoln's offer. She acted to me like she'd never sell her daddy's place, but I have to wonder if she was just holding out for more money."

"Either way, if you want to buy this place, you need to do it," said Brooke. "Mr. Lincoln will be talking with Pete soon if he hasn't done so already."

"Thanks, Brooke."

"You're welcome, Amy. I need to get back."

I passed by Homer and patted his shoulder. "Good?"

"The best. Thank you." He was still trying to talk like Liam Neeson, and it just sounded weird.

I went into the kitchen.

"What's up?" asked Jackie.

I told her about Brooke's news.

"I agree with Brooke." Jackie took off the gloves she'd been wearing while cooking. "If you want to buy this place, you'd better move on it today."

"I will."

"Really?" She smiled. "I'm so excited for you!"

I nodded.

Her smile faded slightly. "Wait. Aren't you excited?"

"Yeah, but I'm scared too. This is a big step."

"One big step for you," she said. "One giant leap for Winter Garden."

I smiled. Although I kept my thoughts to myself, I knew that if Pete could get more money, then he should. He was trying to start a new business too. I'd try to match George Lincoln's offer, but if I couldn't, I'd have to build elsewhere. I wanted to be fair to Pete.

Chapter 9

$\mathscr{P}$ete staggered in at about one thirty that afternoon looking like he'd been bear hunting with a switch. "I'm awfully sorry I didn't get here sooner." He rubbed his forehead. "I wasn't feeling very well this morning."

"You don't look like you're feeling very well now," I said. "Why don't I finish out the day here, and you go on back home?"

"I really would appreciate that. I'll make sure you're paid double time for it."

"Thank you. Also, if you're up to it later, I'd like to discuss buying the café from you."

His eyes sprang from their half-closed state to wide-open. "Are you serious?"

"Yes. If you're sure you want to sell, I'm sure I want to buy."

"Then close up the café an hour early this afternoon

and meet me up at Billy Hancock's office," said Pete. "I'll call him and get him to start drawing up the paperwork."

"Are you certain?" I asked. "You don't have any other offers to consider or anything?"

He frowned. "What do you mean?"

"I heard this morning that George Lincoln wanted to buy the café from your mom. I thought he might've made you an offer too. If he did, I'll try to match it, but—"

"George Lincoln wants to buy the Joint and tear it down. He told Momma that right to her face. He kept coming back and trying to change her mind, but she wouldn't have it, and I won't either. My granddaddy built this restaurant, and I won't have it torn down."

"You do realize that I'm planning on changing the name and the decor, don't you?"

"Sure, I do. But that's all right. I'll still be able to drive by here and see the building and know that it was started by my granddaddy and that there's a Holman legacy right on this very spot."

"All right."

"So I can go ahead and call Billy?" he asked.

"Yep. Just let me know if he can see us today. If he can, I'll close up early."

"Thanks, Amy. I'll call you as soon as I know something." And, with that, he was out the door.

As I stood there watching him back his pickup truck out into the road, Jackie put her hand on my shoulder.

"I heard most of that," she said. "And I'm proud of you. I'm really glad you've finally decided to make your café a reality."

"You don't think I'm hanging my basket higher than I can reach?"

"No way. And if you can't reach it, we'll get you a stepladder."

I hugged her. "I appreciate your confidence in me."

"Look around. See how much happier everybody has been when you've been running things? The waitresses get to keep all their tips. People are laughing and talking while they enjoy their food. Now imagine how much better it will be when we have a pretty new café with cool outfits."

I smiled. "It will be nice, won't it?"

"It'll be the best. You know it will."

That afternoon, I closed Lou's Joint early, and I hurried over to Billy Hancock's office. Like Jackie had been earlier, Sarah was brimming with excitement when she saw me.

"Can you believe it? It's really happening!" she said.

"I know. I'm nervous. I've never done anything like this before. Dang, I've never even bought a new car." I raised a trembling hand to my chest. "This is my first major purchase."

"But it's all right. You have the money to do it with. It's not like you're going into debt forever."

"I know, but what if I fail?" Why was my resolve so quick to run out on me?

"What if you do? You're young enough to start over with something else." She laughed. "Girl, grab that brass ring and hang on tight! You're doing this!"

I knew she was right. But I was just so scared. And Sarah could see that.

"Remember that time when we were about ten years old,

and we went with Roger to his uncle's farm?" she asked. "We all went to the hay barn, and we climbed up to the loft. Roger told us how fun it was to jump off into the hay. Remember?"

"I remember."

"He and I jumped again and again, but you were too afraid to jump. Finally, Roger pushed you. You screamed all the way down, and when you hit the bottom, you laughed. Then you immediately ran back up that ladder so you could jump again. This situation is just like that . . . except safer than jumping into a pile of hay." She smiled. "Making the initial leap is scary, but when you see how great it's going to be, you'll love it."

I laughed. "If I remember correctly, Roger's uncle told our parents and we got grounded for a month for that little stunt."

"Yeah. But it was worth it, wasn't it?"

"It was. Could you call Roger and see if he'd come over and push me into Billy's office?"

"If you need a push this time, I'll do it myself." She jerked her head toward the door. "Now go. They're waiting for you."

On Friday morning, I woke up with the thought, *I'm a business owner!* The truth was I wasn't *officially* yet—Pete and I still had to meet at Billy Hancock's office again that afternoon to sign the papers—but I was pretty much the proud owner of the soon-to-be Down South Café.

"Thanks, Nana," I said aloud. "If she couldn't hear that, would you tell her for me, God? I'd appreciate it." Like

God didn't have better things to do than to pass along messages to my grandmother.

What a week it had been. On Monday—had it truly been only Monday?—I had resigned from my job waitressing at Lou's Joint and offered to buy the place. Of course, later that same night, I'd found Lou Lou dead. And now I owned the café.

Geez, no wonder the police thought I might've killed Lou Lou. And they probably didn't even know about my actually buying the café yet. In my defense, it was Pete who'd insisted on selling so quickly.

He'd also insisted on manning the grill all day today since I'd handled it yesterday. I'd tried to get him to at least let me take the morning shift, but he wouldn't hear of it. He said that staying busy helped keep his mind off his momma's death. He also told me that after the funeral tomorrow, he wanted to focus on happy memories and moving forward with his life. So this was his last day at Lou's Joint. He said he'd probably feel sentimental, but he was glad the Joint was passing into good hands.

I got out of bed and went to the kitchen. I put food into the pets' bowls and made a to-do list while I ate my cereal. On the list, I put *join the Chamber of Commerce, choose my color scheme, set up a meeting with Roger, publish a website, get business cards made up, get laminated menus printed, prepare a budget.*

I decided to work my way down the list, starting with joining the Chamber of Commerce. I took a shower, French braided my hair, put on a sundress and sandals, and headed downtown.

The Chamber of Commerce was housed in a long,

two-story brick building along with the mayor's office, sheriff's office, and post office. Winter Garden was nothing if not efficient with the limited amount of space it had. The Chamber of Commerce was on the second floor. I took the stairs and met Deputy Hall leaving the post office. It struck me again how handsome he was. If only he didn't think I might be a murderer.

"Morning. Nice dress," he said, then looked a little bashful, like maybe he shouldn't have complimented me.

"Thank you."

"What brings you by?"

"I'm joining the Chamber of Commerce," I said. "Pete practically forced me into making a decision about the café, and I bought it. We sign the papers this afternoon."

"Congratulations." He smiled. "I'll have to stop in sometime."

"Please do." I looked around to make sure no one was paying any attention to us. "Any new leads?"

"I'm afraid not. But we're stringently pursuing the ones we do have. Have you . . . heard anything or come up with any new theories?"

"No, but I'll keep you posted."

"No threats or anything?"

"Not yet."

"That's good." He smiled again. "Although, if you need me, you know how to get in touch."

"Just whistle? Put my lips together and blow?" I laughed. "Sorry. I've seen that movie too many times."

"*To Have and Have Not*. It's one of my favorites too."

"You like old movies?" I asked.

"Yeah . . . I do." His eyes held mine for a long moment. I felt a blush creeping into my cheeks. "See you soon,"

I said as breezily as I possibly could. I felt his eyes still on me as I walked down the hall to the Chamber of Commerce. I wanted to turn and look back at him, but I didn't dare.

I pushed open the door and was immediately hit by a cool waft of air. The entire municipal office building was air-conditioned, of course, but this office must have turned its thermostat down to fifty. The slim short-haired receptionist wore a sweater over her summer dress, and she still had her shoulders hunched up to her ears like she was freezing.

"Hi," she said. "How can I help you today?"

"Well, I'm here to join the Chamber, but if you'd like, I can watch the phones for you for a few minutes if you want to go outside and warm up."

"Thanks for the offer, but the boss would have my hide." She handed me a form. "Just fill this out, and we'll make you official. What kind of business do you have?"

"A café. I'm calling it the Down South Café." I smiled. "I hope you'll drop in once I get it up and running."

"I sure will." She smiled. "It'll be nice to have a new café in town. Where are you located?"

"I bought Lou's Joint from Pete Holman. All I have to do is get it renovated."

A bulky man with a bad comb-over came rushing out of the office behind the reception area. "Did I hear you correctly, young lady? Did you say you'd purchased Lou's Joint?"

"Yes, sir."

"When was this?"

"Yesterday."

He gave his head two fast shakes as if he could

dislodge what he'd just heard. "You moved quickly, didn't you?"

"Actually, it was Pete Holman who wanted to sell the business," I said. "He wants to do something else, and he didn't want to delay."

"Could you come into my office, please?"

He was obviously furious, and I wasn't going anywhere with him. "Given your tone, I'd prefer to talk with you right here." I thought he could fling any accusations at me from behind the receptionist's desk as easily as he could from behind his own.

"I apologize. It appears we got off on the wrong foot. I'm George Lincoln, president of the Winter Garden Chamber of Commerce." He didn't sound all that contrite, and I didn't think his anger could've dissipated that quickly.

"I'm Amy Flowers." I didn't say it was nice to meet him, because it wasn't.

He extended his sweaty hand, and I shook it as briefly as possible.

"Ms. Flowers, I doubt you were aware, but I'd made an offer on Lou's Joint to Ms. Holman some few days ago."

He waited for a response from me, but I didn't know what to say.

"I was planning on speaking with Mr. Holman about the property on Monday, since his mother's funeral is tomorrow," Mr. Lincoln continued. "I felt it would be tacky to discuss business before then."

"As did I, Mr. Lincoln. But as I told you, Mr. Holman approached *me* . . . rather insistently, I might add."

"Very well. Would you consider selling the property and building your café elsewhere?"

"No, sir, I would not. I'm eager to get my business off

the ground and don't want to delay any longer than necessary."

"You might change your mind when you see how much work will go into your venture and how little profit will come out of it." He lifted his chin haughtily.

"If I do, I hope you'll still be willing to buy the café. If not, perhaps someone else will." I gave the receptionist my sweetest smile. "Thanks so much for your kindness. I hope you have a pleasant day. I'll fill out this application and get it back to you as soon as possible." I doubted it would do me any good, though, given the fact that the president of the Chamber of Commerce already had it in for me.

As I left, I decided I wasn't going to let George Lincoln get to me. Sure, the business would be slow starting out and would demand more work than profit, but wasn't that the case for all new entrepreneurial ventures?

Starting down the steps, I noticed Preacher Robinson coming out of the post office. I called to him and waited for him to join me at the stairs.

"Good morning, Amy. How'd you manage to get some time off?"

"Well, Pete wanted to man the grill all day today. It'll be his last time working at Lou's Joint."

He frowned. "Why's that?"

"He wants to go into the trucking business, and he sold the café to me. I'm going to renovate it and call it the Down South Café."

"That sounds charming," he said with a smile.

"And I want you to know that your Bible study group is welcome to meet at the café—once it's reopened—whenever you'd like."

"Well, that's kind of you. I appreciate that."

We began walking slowly down the steps. I wanted to ask about his disagreement with Lou Lou, but I didn't quite know how. I broached the subject tentatively.

"I'm sorry that you had to leave the café," I said. "I can't imagine your parishioners were happy about having to drive that extra twenty minutes or so, especially in winter."

"No. No, they were not."

"I . . . I hope you . . . and they . . . will have a better experience at the Down South Café."

"Yes, well, as a rule, we try not to single anyone out in our sermons or prayers," he said. "But even if we did, I seriously doubt you'd be offended if we called into question the suitability of a grown man not only living with his mother but not being allowed to date." He quickly glanced over his shoulder. "I'm sorry. My wicked tongue got away from me. You know, the Good Book calls the tongue a fire that corrupts the whole body. I'll have to repent of this gossip."

"Oh, now, Preacher Robinson, you didn't say anything that everybody in town didn't already know."

"I imagine not, but as the shepherd of a flock, I'm held to a higher standard, you know." He gently took my arm. "Please don't mention that I spoke out of turn."

"I won't."

"It's a bad habit I'm trying to break."

He looked so concerned that I had to wonder what other gossip had set his corrupt tongue to wagging.

My next stop was the hardware store. I went directly to the paint section and took swatches of yellow and blue. Who knew there were so many variations?

Did I want the interior of Down South Café to be *Sunny Day*, *Hay Bale*, *Daffodil*, *Custard*, *Lemonade*, or *Golden Delight*? And did I want the trim to be *Waterfall*, *Frost*, *Seascape*, or *Riviera*? Hopefully, Roger could help me decide. Yes, he was a construction worker, but I'd have sworn he was also part architect and part interior designer.

I was looking down at the paint swatches and wasn't watching where I was going when I ran headlong into Stan Wheeler. He took me by my upper arms to steady me.

"Hey, there. Somebody's got her head in the clouds."

"I'm so sorry, Stan! I was looking at these paint swatches."

"Oh yeah. Pete mentioned that you were buying the Joint." He snatched the swatches out of my hand. "I like that *Daffodil* and *Waterfall* myself. Of course, I ain't no artist or anything."

"Neither am I . . . but those two do look good together." He seemed in an unusually talkative mood, so I decided to see if I could get some information out of him. "Speaking of buying property, did Pete sell you the mobile home?"

"Uh, we're working on that." He handed back the swatches. "It's gonna take a lot of work to get it fixed back up."

"I heard you talking about the roof at the café the other day," I said.

"Yeah, it needs to be entirely reshingled. Darn thing leaks like a sieve. And not only that, the toilet in the half bath needs to be replaced."

"Owning property can be a money pit, can't it?"

He smiled. "Don't tell me you're having second thoughts already?"

"No. I guess it's too late for that now. At least, while you're renting, the repairs are the Holmans' problem, right?"

"You'd think," he said. "But you probably know how tight Ms. Holman was. She kept promising to send somebody out to patch the roof and to see what was wrong with the toilet, but she never did. I'd been fussing about both for going on three months."

"I do know how she could be," I said. "I'd have hoped she'd have taken better care of her tenants than she did her staff, but apparently she didn't."

"And Pete wouldn't admit it, but she wasn't even that good to him," said Stan. "I'm sorry the woman's dead, but I'm glad Pete has the chance to make a fresh start. I believe he'll do well in the trucking business."

"I hope so. Just don't you two go out partying too much."

He gave a little laugh. "You know about that?"

"Let's just say Pete kinda drunk-dialed me to ask me to work the next morning."

"Oh yeah. Well, Pete just needed to cut loose a little bit . . . let go of some of his grief."

"I understand," I said. "It's good he's got you and Chris Anne to help him through this."

"He's got you people at the Joint too. I mean, I know you wouldn't exactly say you were friends with Lou Lou, but most of you seem to like Pete."

"We do. Pete's a decent guy." I lowered my voice. "You don't know of anyone who might've wanted Lou Lou dead, do you?"

"Only everybody that ever met her. Am I right?" He

laughed again. "You know I'm joshing you. Why would you ask a thing like that?"

"Well, since I found Lou Lou, the police think I look pretty guilty."

"Aw, shucks. That's crazy. Her being hit in the head like that? Killed with one blow? A little thing like you couldn't have done that, and the police know it. I wouldn't worry about that, if I were you. You just concentrate on making the place nice and pretty for your customers."

"Thanks, Stan." I apologized again for nearly mowing him down and said I'd better get on with my rounds.

"That's all right. Just be careful."

The pneumatic doors opened when I approached, and I went from the lovely coolness of the hardware store into the oppressive heat. I was surprised that Stan had been so nice today. Of course, maybe he'd always been in a bad mood when he came into the Joint because of his disagreements with Lou Lou. Or maybe he was high or something today. Roger had said he thought Stan was a drug dealer. But I'd never seen him doing anything that struck me as shady. Was I naïve, or did I just want to think the best of people?

I got into my car and started the engine. Before backing out of the parking lot, I called Roger.

"Hi, Amy," he answered.

"Hi. Could I see you sometime today? I'm meeting with Pete at Billy's office later to sign the paperwork, and then I'll own the café."

"Congratulations, Flowerpot!"

"Thanks!"

"What time do you want to meet?"

"How about this—we'll meet at the café at around five thirty so you can get an idea of what kinds of renovations need to be done. And then I'll buy you dinner somewhere, and we can discuss everything."

"That works. I'll see you at *your* café at half past five."

Chapter 10

&Roger was already at the café when I got there. I parked my car, got out, and hurried over to him. He was standing under the front door awning in the shade. Grinning, I held up the café keys and shook them.

"I wish you'd show just a little enthusiasm about this place," he said.

I threw my arms around his neck and hugged him. "Eeeee! The café is officially mine!"

He chuckled. "Congratulations. Now, let's get in there and see what we can do to make it *look* like it's yours."

"All right."

My hand trembled so badly as I tried to put the key in the lock that Roger had to unlock the door himself.

"Calm down, Flowerpot." Roger held the door so I could be the first to step inside.

"We have a lot to do," I said as I looked around.

"I know."

"First things first." I took the paint swatches from my purse.

"Well, that's important, but the *first* thing is to clean out Lou Lou's office. I suggest you get a professional cleaning team to do that. Then once the office has been scrubbed and everything in it removed, we can redo it and you'll never . . ." His voice trailed off.

I smiled slightly. "Oh, I'll still know."

"And you're sure you'll be able to handle that?"

"Maybe you could somehow tear out the office and make it more of a storage room or something." I sighed. "I certainly can't see myself sitting in there working on the books. I'd rather do that from home anyway."

"We'll think of something. Did you talk with Pete about the things in his mother's office?"

"Not really . . . but I will. I know he took some ledgers and things that were in there, money from the safe, some documents. But he might want to keep her desk and the rest of the furniture."

"I have a cleaning team I use out of Bristol. They're really good, and they're reasonably priced. Would you mind if I went ahead and called them in?"

"Not at all. Would you like some coffee or water or something while we talk?" I asked.

"A bottle of water would be great."

I got each of us a bottle of water and sat down at the counter beside Roger. He had taken out a yellow legal pad and was making notes. I looked around the dining room. The walls needed repainting. These ugly chipped tables and chairs would have to go. The counter and stools needed to be replaced. We needed new light fixtures. I

wanted a display case for baked goods and specialty items. And, of course, the floor would have to be redone. If I just reopened this place rather than making the café my own, I'd have to call it "Calamity Café."

"Let's see those paint swatches," he said.

I put the swatches on the counter. Roger held different combinations side by side until he finally chose *Lemonade* and *Riviera*. "It's a paler yellow and a bolder blue. What do you think?"

"I defer to your expertise, and I think it'll look great."

"And a soft gray or muted orange for the counters and tables."

I didn't have any swatches for either color. "Which do you think would be best?"

"Personally, I'd go with the gray."

"Gray, it is."

He took out a measuring tape. "I'll need your help with this."

Together we measured the entire café with the exception of Lou Lou's office. Neither of us wanted to go in there until it had been cleaned, and Roger told me he'd be thinking of ways to renovate the café so that it wasn't necessary for anyone to use the office.

"So how do we do this?" I asked. "Do I put you on retainer?"

He smiled. "I'll open an account for you at the home store for all your supplies and everything, and they'll bill you for the materials. I have a contractor discount, so you'll get that too."

"I don't want you to be cheated out of part of your profit," I said.

"I won't be. I never make anyone pay extra for materials. As for the labor, how about I bill you weekly?"

"Sounds good."

"Have you made out a budget yet?" he asked.

"For the renovations? No. I thought you'd help me with that."

"I will. I'm talking about a budget for the café—payroll, supplies, electricity."

"I've got that all worked out."

"Great. I'll get you the renovation budget," said Roger. "I know your nana left you a nice chunk of change, but you won't have it for long unless you take care of it."

"I know, Roger." Once a guy adopts you as his baby sister, you're always his baby sister.

"I know you know, but I figured it would bear repeating. The first thing I'm going to do is change these locks. I took the liberty of stopping by earlier and seeing what kind of locks are used on the front and back doors, and I picked new ones up at the hardware store."

"Wow, thanks." He was a pretty good big brother.

"You don't want Pete or any of his buddies coming back in here when you're not around, now that you own the place," he said. "And I was *real* uncomfortable with that key under the rock at the back door. Who knows how many people knew about that."

"I wonder if that's how the killer got in on Monday night."

"I wouldn't be surprised . . . unless both doors were usually unlocked while Lou Lou was here. Regardless, it's likely that a lot of people know about that key." He

shook his head. "That was stupid on the Holmans' part. Why would they put a key right by the door like that?"

"I guess they trusted that the people who knew about the key wouldn't barge in without good reason."

"Well, some folks think hitting a woman over the head and robbing her café would be a sufficient reason."

"Yeah, but Lou Lou and Pete *obviously* trusted the people who knew about the key. I never knew about it until the night Pete drunk-dialed me and asked me to come in to work the next morning."

"I don't know about Lou Lou, but Pete doesn't always exercise the best judgment when it comes to people," Roger said. "Take his girlfriend, for example. She did a stint in jail for drugs."

"Chris Anne did? Are you kidding me?"

He gave an exaggerated blink. "Have you *met* Chris Anne?"

"Well, yeah. . . ." I thought about it for a moment. "I guess you're right. Pete doesn't hang out with the most reputable people."

"Face it. Pete isn't all that reputable either," he said. "You just told me he drunk-dialed you, and I've seen him a few times when I was sure his condition wasn't entirely due to alcohol consumption. And if you're hanging around with drug addicts . . ."

"I know . . . but he never missed work or anything, not that I knew of anyway."

He shrugged. "It just pays to be careful, Flowerpot. You can't be a hundred percent sure of who you're dealing with around here. Don't forget what happened to Lou Lou."

"How could I forget?"

*   *   *

The next morning, I opened the café early. The night before I'd printed up flyers saying that the café was under new management and would be closed while renovations were under way. I said we would close right after breakfast today so patrons could attend the funeral of Ms. Holman. I had the flyers on the counter, and I taped one to the front door.

Homer came in at his usual time, and I had his sausage biscuit just about ready when he came through the door.

"Am I that predictable?" he asked, as I sat the sausage biscuit in front of him.

"You're that steady." I smiled as I poured his coffee. "So, who's your hero?"

"Yesterday it was Dwight Eisenhower. Today it's Thomas Jefferson."

"You must be feeling presidential."

"Maybe. I've been thinking quite a bit about you and your predicaments."

"Predicaments?"

"Sure. Everybody knows you walked in and found Lou Lou dead, and I can see by this here paper that you've bought the café. Well, good for you. Jefferson once said, 'Do you want to know who you are? Don't ask. Act! Action will delineate and define you.' Do you see where I'm going with that advice?"

"Not exactly."

"You run your business the way it ought to be run and make it a source of pride and happiness to you," he said. "Before long, people will forget about Lou Lou

and everything bad that's happened . . . and so will you."

"It going to be pretty hard to forget, Homer. For me and for everybody else too."

He wagged a finger at me. "You can't stop a woman with the right mental attitude from achieving her goal. And you can't help one with the wrong attitude."

"Jefferson?"

"Paraphrased. I know it'll be hard to forget about Lou Lou and what happened here that night, but you have to do your best to put it behind you and move ahead. If you need to, talk with a therapist or something. There's no shame in that."

"I appreciate the advice," I said. "But I think I'll be okay."

"All right. I'm here if you need a friend."

"Thank you, Homer."

I fielded lots of questions throughout the morning about what I was naming the café, whether or not the staff would be kept on, and when the café would reopen. The last one was the only one I couldn't answer for sure. My answer was that I would try to have the café open—all shiny and new— in a month. I knew it was a stretch, but Roger seemed to think we could pull it off if we all worked together.

As soon as the stragglers from the breakfast crowd left, I locked up the café and went home to get ready for Lou Lou's funeral. I took a quick bath and then stood in front of my closet looking for something to wear that would be decent but that I wouldn't burn up in. I wound up choosing a black pencil skirt and a sleeveless black top. I went with black espadrilles because I knew they'd be easier to walk in than heels.

Stepping into the funeral home, I was more nervous than a long-tailed cat in a roomful of rocking chairs. Of course, I'd realized even before Homer mentioned it this morning that everyone knew I was the one who'd found Lou Lou. But there was nothing like somebody saying it out loud to truly drive the point home. Did anyone think I'd actually *killed* her?

Was it my imagination, or did people actually stop talking when they saw me approaching? Were their eyes shooting accusations my way?

I ducked out of the crowded lobby and into the bathroom. I wet a paper towel and cooled the back of my neck with it. I had to get a grip.

I tossed the paper towel into the wastebasket and freshened up my lipstick.

The door burst open and Chris Anne rushed in, threw open a stall, and then threw up her lunch.

"Oh my goodness," I said. "Are you all right? Is there anything I can do?"

Of course, she couldn't speak right then. She was still crouched over the toilet. I felt like an idiot. When she finally emerged from the stall, she was so weak and pale that I rushed to put my arm around her and lead her to a chair that was just inside the door. I got her a damp paper towel and handed it to her.

"Thank you," she whispered. "Do you have a mint or something?"

I did have a peppermint, and Chris Anne took it gratefully.

"Is it your nerves?" I asked.

She shook her head. "It's my baby."

I felt my eyes nearly pop out of my head.

"Don't say anything to anybody, please," she said. "I haven't even told Pete yet. I thought it'd be something good to tell him later today."

"I won't say a word. Congratulations."

"Thank you." She smiled. "I've suspected for a couple of weeks—even took a pregnancy test I got at the dollar store. But I wanted to be sure before saying anything. I knew Pete's momma would hit the ceiling."

"I don't know. She might've been glad."

"Are you serious? Pete was afraid to tell her anything about us. He'd have had to break the news about being in a relationship with me combined with the fact that I'm pregnant. That's why I didn't tell him until it was official. I went to the doctor yesterday."

"Well, I'm happy for you . . . and for Pete."

An odd expression must've crossed my face because Chris Anne said, "Don't worry. I'm not naming my baby 'Lou Lou.'"

I laughed. "Tell Pete that was a one-of-a-kind name for a one-of-a-kind lady. I think he'll understand."

"I sure hope so. Either way . . ."

"Are you feeling better?" I asked. "We should probably go into the chapel."

She nodded. "I think I can do it now. Would you please walk with me? Help hold me up?"

"Of course I will." I was as glad of the support as she was. It was easier for me not having to walk into the chapel alone too.

Either the stares were less accusing than they had been, or I wasn't as paranoid as I had been before. Chris Anne and I walked down the aisle. My plan was to hand her over to Pete and then find my mom, Aunt Bess, and Jackie,

and sit with them. But Chris Anne wouldn't let me go. She had an ally, and she was sticking with me for as long as possible.

The funeral service was long and obviously conducted by a preacher who didn't know Lou Lou Holman in the least. I don't know who he was, but he wasn't one of Winter Garden's pastors. I'm not saying it wasn't a nice service—the choir sang, and the preacher extolled Lou Lou's virtues—but it was generic. It was as if the preacher had been given a fill-in-the-blank form prior to preparing for the funeral.

Name of deceased: Lou Lou Holman
Occupation: Business owner
Mother of one

And then he simply recited from the list.

"Lou Lou Holman was a beloved business owner, a pillar of the community, and a respected member of the Winter Garden Chamber of Commerce. She was devoted to her only son . . ."

Naturally, my mind wandered as the man droned on. If Lou Lou was so devoted to Pete, why had he been afraid to tell her what was going on with his life? That he had a girlfriend, that he wanted to get married, that he wanted to buy a truck and go into business for himself? Granted, Lou Lou might not have agreed with all—or any—of Pete's decisions, but they were his choices to make. A forty-year-old man who was still frightened of his mother? What was up with that? Had he been afraid he'd hurt her feelings? Had he been scared she'd write him out of her will? Had he used Lou Lou as an excuse

to avoid growing up and having any responsibilities until life—or Chris Anne—had backed him against a wall?

I glanced over at Pete. He was staring at the floor between his shoes. Beside me, Chris Anne fanned herself with a tissue and patted Pete on the back. I merely hoped the service was almost over.

Chapter 11

After the service, I met up with Mom, Aunt Bess, and Jackie in the lobby. I explained that I was going to come and sit with them but that Chris Anne had held on to me for dear life.

"That's all right," said Mom. "We'll see you tomorrow for lunch."

"What're you making?" Aunt Bess asked.

"We haven't decided yet, Granny," said Jackie. "We'll get right on that."

"See that you do."

From the corner of my eye, I saw Sheriff Billings. He was looking straight at me. I nodded in lieu of a better greeting, and he nodded back.

Deputy Hall was behind the sheriff. "Ms. Flowers."

"Deputy."

It felt strange and uncomfortable addressing Ryan that way. Then again, it felt strange and uncomfortable to refer

to the deputy as "Ryan," even in my own head. But there was some sort of spark between us. He knew it, and I knew it. And yet, I hadn't been ruled out as a suspect in Lou Lou's murder, so we'd better just dump a bucket of water on that spark and forget about it for the time being.

"Amy?"

Jackie's voice drew me out of my reverie.

"Want to meet at your place and decide what to make for lunch tomorrow?" she asked.

"Sounds good," I said.

"I'll run home and change, and I'll see you in about forty-five minutes."

I nodded, my eyes trailing Deputy Hall as he stepped out into the blinding sunlight.

"He *is* a handsome one," Mom murmured in my ear.

"Who?"

She gave me the "oh, please" look, took Aunt Bess's arm, and left.

By the time Jackie had arrived, I had out the laptop and was looking at Aunt Bess's Pinterest board *Things I'd Love to Eat but Won't Fix*. I looked up at my cousin and shook my head.

"Aunt Bess *does* realize that there are food categories besides desserts, doesn't she?"

"I'm not so sure that she does. Have you made any decisions about what we're going to make?"

"I've narrowed it down. You can make the final choices." I turned the laptop so Jackie could see the screen. "Oven-fried catfish, stuffed shells, or country ham with redeye gravy."

"Let's go with the ham," she said. "I figure the funeral has her in a nostalgic mood thinking of everybody from Winter Garden that she used to know. Maybe the ham and gravy will give her the warm fuzzies."

"All right. We can make biscuits, grits, and maybe a bacon-cheddar quiche to go with it. What do you think?"

"Sounds good. And we can't forget that lemon pie."

"That'll do it." I smiled. "Unless she's changed her mind about the pie."

Jackie took her phone from her purse, called Aunt Bess, and confirmed that she did want a lemon pie.

"Now that we have our menu, should we head to the grocery store?" I asked.

"In a minute. First I want you to tell me what the deal was with Chris Anne. She was practically glued to you at the funeral. It's not like you two are friends or anything."

"We met up in the bathroom. I was having a fit of nerves, and she came in. She wasn't feeling well."

"Why wasn't she feeling well?"

I looked away. Jackie wasn't only my cousin. Being a year older than me, she'd been my best friend all my life. "I promised I wouldn't say anything to anyone."

"You know I won't tell anybody else." She paused. "Wait . . . in the bathroom not feeling well. Oh my gosh! She's pregnant?"

"I didn't say that."

"You didn't have to. Does Pete know?"

"If Chris Anne has any special news to share with Pete, I imagine she'll talk with him about it sometime today. Maybe she hopes to cheer him up . . . if whatever she has to tell him is happy news."

Jackie rolled her eyes. "Okay. Come off it. You didn't

tell me anything, so let's talk straight. Does she think Pete will be happy about her being pregnant?"

"She seemed to think so. And I hope he will be."

"I hope so too. But with all his talk about getting his trucking business started and Chris Anne being his partner . . . he might've preferred to wait a little while before having a family."

"That's true. I hadn't thought of that."

"Well, let's make a list of the ingredients we'll need and get to the store. We don't have time to worry about Pete and Chris Anne right now," she said.

To save us some time on Sunday, I'd gone ahead and made the lemon pie when I'd returned home from the store on Saturday. Now it was in a baker's box in the passenger seat of my car as I drove up to "the big house." The house was close enough that I usually walked when I visited, but I couldn't have carried the pie and the groceries without inevitably dropping something, so today I drove.

Mom heard me coming and opened the door. "Need any help with the groceries?"

"No, but if you'll get this pie, I can bring in all the groceries in one trip."

She took the pie, and I managed to stack the plastic bags onto my arms and muscle them into the kitchen.

I heard Aunt Bess hurrying into the kitchen like a little girl on Christmas morning. "What're we having?"

"Ham and redeye gravy, a bacon-and-cheddar quiche, biscuits, grits, and—by special request—a lemon pie."

She licked her lips. "Um-mmmm!"

"Where's Jackie?" Mom asked.

"I haven't talked with her this morning, but she should be here soon. I'll get started on the biscuits."

As I mixed up the ingredients for the biscuits, Mom and Aunt Bess sat down at the kitchen table to drink coffee and watch me work. I'd come by my culinary skills from Nana. Mom didn't like to cook. She did it when she had to, but she certainly didn't enjoy it. Same with Aunt Bess.

"That was a nice service yesterday," Aunt Bess said.

"I thought it was kinda sad." I mixed the dough with my hands. "The preacher didn't even know Lou Lou."

"Course he didn't! How else were they gonna get him to say nice things about her?"

"Aunt Bess!" Mom scolded.

"Now, Jenna, the truth'll stand when the world's on fire."

I hid my smile as I turned my dough out onto the floured board. "Were all of Lou Lou's people ornery, Aunt Bess?"

"Her daddy wasn't too awful bad. And he was nice-looking too. It was a shame Lou Lou and Pete turned out so homely."

"So Lou Holman was a nice man?" I prompted.

"I don't know that I'd call him nice, but he wasn't as bad as his daddy and his uncle," she said. "One time when I was young, I heard that Lou's daddy, Bo, and his uncle Grady had gone over to North Carolina and robbed a bank. That was along about the time that Lou was building the Joint."

I froze, doughy hands in the air. "Did you just say that Lou Lou's granddaddy robbed a bank?"

"That's what I heard. It was over in Boone or some-

where. But it might've just been a tale, honey. They weren't ever arrested, and I never heard tell of anybody finding the money they were supposed to have stolen. Maybe somebody just made it all up."

I washed the dough off my hands and got the rolling pin. "Why would somebody make up a story like that?"

"Aw, you know how things get started. They didn't have television or Internet. Plus, Grady and Bo—Lou's daddy—were as crooked as a dog's hind leg and twice as dirty. It wasn't hard to imagine them going across the border, robbing a bank, and hightailing it back home."

"Didn't the North Carolina police investigate the matter?" Mom asked.

"Of course, they did—at least, that's what I heard—but since they couldn't find the money and the men had worn masks while robbing the bank, the police couldn't prove the Holmans did any wrong."

Jackie was breathless when she rushed into the kitchen. "Sorry I'm late. I overslept."

"You've done missed out on a wild tale," I said.

"And I ain't repeating it." Aunt Bess gave a resolute nod.

Jackie merely rolled her eyes. "Granny tells lots of wild tales. What do you need me to do?"

"You can start frying the ham while I finish getting the biscuits ready to go into the oven."

"I grew up hearing wild tales," said Aunt Bess. "I'm just passing on the oral history of my people."

Mom laughed. "Whether they're true or not isn't the point."

Aunt Bess huffed. "Do you always believe what those people on television tell you? Or are they just telling you what they're paid to say?"

"Well, I think that depends," said Mom. "If they're tell-ing me to buy XYZ shampoo because it's the best thing on the market, I'm going to be suspicious. But if they're telling me someone's hair fell out after using XYZ sham-poo, then I'm going to think twice before I use the stuff."

"Either way, you're being swayed by the television. I was swayed by my parents, my grandparents, my aunts, and my uncles."

Jackie and I shared a glance. Aunt Bess had a point. But I knew that those old tales handed down from generation to generation could also become like that old game of telephone, where one person whispers something into someone's ear who then whispers it to someone else and by the time the story gets back to the originator, there's seldom much resemblance to that initial report.

By the time we were finishing lunch, all thoughts of wild tales had been replaced by the yumminess of lemon pie.

"Your meringue is always so good, Amy," said Mom.

"Yeah. Around here, nobody makes good meringue." Aunt Bess cut her eyes toward Mom. "What's your secret?"

"Well, for a cream pie like this, I make a Swiss meringue rather than a common meringue," I said.

"That's it, Jenna," said Aunt Bess. "Amy's meringue is uncommon. She does it like they do in Switzerland." Aunt Bess then nodded at me as if she, the Swiss, and I had it all figured out.

Later that afternoon, I was in the fancy room reading a small-business magazine when Roger dropped in. I took him to the kitchen. The fancy room wasn't Roger's

style, and I figured he'd want a glass of tea or a cup of coffee while we talked.

I was right. He wanted a cup of coffee and the last of the preacher cookies.

"I've got an idea." He brought out his yellow legal pad. "What would you think of this? We do away with the office completely. In its place, we build a screened-in porch with picnic tables. Patrons could enjoy the space most of three seasons out of the year." As he talked, he was drawing the café and how it would look with the screened-in side porch.

"I think that's a terrific idea! I love it."

"Really?"

"Really." I smiled. "You're a genius."

"Oh, I *know* that. I just thought this way, you wouldn't have to go into Lou Lou's office again. We can completely demolish it and turn it into something new. And the something new adds value and an additional aesthetic to the café."

"Brilliant. Thank you."

"That's what you're paying me the big bucks for." He popped the last bite of a preacher cookie into his mouth.

"Have you . . . have you looked at the office?"

He nodded, swallowed, and wiped his mouth on his napkin. "The cleaning crew spent hours in there yesterday. I went by before heading over here to make sure we won't have any trouble tearing out the office."

"Wh-what does it look like?"

"You'd never know what happened in there. The place is spotless." He took a sip of his coffee. "Here's the thing, though. You have to decide what you're going

to do with all the stuff still in that office. Do you want any of the furniture?"

"No. I don't want anything from that office. I don't need any reminders."

"That's what I figured. But we need to do something with it. Does Pete want it?"

"I don't know," I said. "I'll call him and ask him."

"He really needs to sort through the documents to see if there's anything important there. But, if he doesn't, we can simply take them to the recycling center. I can call and see if Goodwill or the Salvation Army would take the furniture if Pete doesn't want it. Find out today, and let me know in the morning."

"All right, I will. What time should we be there tomorrow?"

"Daylight," said Roger. "If you want to reopen the café in a month, we're going to have to put in a lot of hours."

"Fine by me. I'll bring sausage biscuits for everybody."

"They'd appreciate that." He finished off his coffee, stood, and patted my shoulder. "The Down South Café is going to be beautiful, Flowerpot."

"Thanks."

I put off calling Pete for as long as I could. He'd only buried his mother yesterday, and now here I was calling to ask if he'd like to go through the things in her office. I knew he'd said earlier that he'd gotten what he'd needed from Lou Lou's office; but I thought that maybe after the finality of her death had set in, he'd reconsider.

I finally dialed the Holman home at around nine

o'clock that night. The phone rang three times, and I was getting ready to hang up when Pete answered.

"Hello." His voice sounded flat and empty.

"Pete, hi. It's Amy. How are you?"

"I'm getting by. How are you?"

"I'm all right. I'm sorry to disturb you, but I need to ask you something. As you know, I'm renovating the café. The builders are going to take out your momma's office."

"Well, that's fine, Amy. Do whatever you want to do. It's yours now."

"Um . . . thanks . . . but I thought you might want to go through the contents of the office," I said. "You know . . . the furniture, the filing cabinet, the knickknacks . . . just to see if there's anything there you might want to save."

"I don't care about any of that. Just throw it all out."

"No, wait!"

Is that Chris Anne's voice?

It was. She'd grabbed the phone away from Pete.

"He doesn't know what he's saying, Amy. Save all Lou Lou's stuff for us somewhere on the property. We'll be there first thing in the morning to go through it all."

"Chris Anne, I don't want to," I heard Pete tell her.

"You might not right now, but if you let them throw away that stuff without even seeing what it was, you'll regret it."

I was inclined to agree with Chris Anne, but I kept my opinion to myself.

"If it's so important to you, *you* go!" he shouted.

"Fine! I will!"

She directed her next comment to me rather than Pete. "See you tomorrow, then. Thanks for holding that stuff for us."

"No problem," I said.

After I ended the call, I wondered about the couple. Had Chris Anne told Pete about the pregnancy? Had Jackie been right that Pete would be upset by the news? After all, his dream did involve him and Chris Anne hitting the open road in a tractor-trailer. That would be hard to do with Chris Anne pregnant, and it would be practically impossible once she'd had the baby.

Maybe she hadn't told him about the pregnancy yet and he was merely morose about his mother's death. I could understand his not wanting to go through her things, but I thought he should. They could bring him some comfort. I'd been consoled when I'd looked through some of the things Nana had left behind. They'd reminded me of her sense of humor, how much she'd loved us, how thoughtful she'd been. Those things had been in Nana's home, but if she'd had an office, I'd have wanted to see those things too. I'd have wanted to look at everything she'd left behind.

Of course, this was Lou Lou Holman we were talking about now. As far as I'd ever seen, she'd had no sense of humor and she'd certainly not been thoughtful. But, hopefully, she had been considerate toward her son, and he'd find something from her office that would make him smile.

Chapter 12

Since I had to be at the Down South Café so early—that sounded so cool in my head that I had to say it out loud just to bask in the words—I got up an hour before daylight so I could make the sausage biscuits I'd promised Roger. Of course, I'd chosen sausage biscuits because I thought it was likely that Homer would be coming by. And Dilly might also stop by so she could have her biscuit and take one to the raccoon.

I arrived at the café with a plastic container filled with sausage biscuits—I'd say I had about thirty-five. Roger and his crew were already there. He'd kept a key when he'd changed the locks so he could work whenever he wanted.

I put the biscuits on the counter and told the workers to help themselves while I made coffee. In addition to Roger's workers, Jackie, Aaron, and a couple of the other café staff came to help us. I was paying the café staff to

help. The ones who didn't come in either wanted time off or they intended to find jobs elsewhere. Either way was fine with me. I didn't want to have to replace any members of the existing staff, but I had a month to do so if need be.

After we'd had breakfast, I put the leftovers in the refrigerator.

"What do you want us to do?" I asked Roger.

"You guys need to move these tables and chairs out into the parking lot and stack them up. Since you're getting new ones, we'll have these hauled off."

"All right. If anyone comes by and wants a set, they can have them."

He nodded. "Okay. We're going to get started tearing down the office as soon as we move everything out of it. Did you talk with Pete?"

"I did. He told me to get rid of everything, but Chris Anne said they'd come by this morning and look through it first. I thought we could move it all outside and see whether or not they show up today." I put my hands on my hips. "After we get everything hauled out, then what?"

He pointed to a stack of paint cans, brushes, rollers, pans, and masking tape in the corner. "Get to taping off the dining room."

"Got it, chief."

Aaron and Jackie were already carrying chairs outside, so I began helping Roger bring everything out of the office. I still had the heebie-jeebies about returning to that room, but I was curious about what Lou Lou had been working on the night she was killed.

Either Roger or the cleaning crew had put everything into banker's boxes with openings on the sides so they

could be carried easily. I was lugging a box outside when
I noticed a sheet of notebook paper sticking out. It caught
my attention because it had STAN WHEELER written on it.
I set the box down and removed the sheet of paper. Beside
Stan's name, Lou Lou had drawn a fish.

I dug a little deeper into the box and found a list of
suppliers. I thought that would come in handy, although
I was still going to research suppliers of my own. When
possible, I wanted to buy from the local farmers. I also
found an old ledger with accounts payable and accounts
receivable. I knew Pete had the newest ones—which was
good, since he'd be dealing with those on behalf of Lou
Lou's estate—but I thought I might want to look through
it later just to see what Lou Lou's bookkeeping had been
like.

The café staff had just finished moving all the tables,
chairs, and other fixtures outside and stacking them
when Pete and Chris Anne arrived. Fortunately, Roger's
crew and I had moved everything from the office out
here too.

I went out to greet Pete and Chris Anne. "Hi. I'm glad
you decided to come by."

"She twisted my arm," Pete said.

"I figured as much."

Chris Anne simply smiled and then got started going
through Lou Lou's filing cabinet. I didn't really think
that was her place, but then it wasn't *my* place to say so.
I told them to let me know if they needed anything.

I went back inside, cringing at the sound of a sledgehammer pounding away at the office walls.

"So Aaron and I are going to start taping around the windows and doors," said Jackie.

"Okay. I'll help you."

Before I could begin helping Jackie and Aaron, Homer came in.

"Good morning, Homer," I said. "You're early today. Who's your hero?"

"Henry Ford. He once said that coming together is the beginning, keeping together is progress, and working together is success. I'm here to help."

"Oh, Homer, you don't have to do that. I do have a sausage biscuit for you, though."

"It isn't time for my biscuit yet, but I'd like to help you with your café. What can I do?"

"Will you give me a hand in taping around the trim?"

"I sure will." He beamed. "Like Mr. Ford always said, 'Nothing is particularly hard if you divide it into small jobs.'"

"He was a smart man."

"One of the smartest."

Homer and I had barely taped off one wall when Stan Wheeler poked his head into the café.

"Hey, Amy, can I see you for a second?" he asked.

"Sure." I wiped my hands on my shorts and stepped out into the parking lot. "What can I do for you?"

"Are you selling these tables and chairs?"

"Nope, but you can have a set if you'd like."

"I'll be glad to pay for them."

"Not for sale," I said. "But please take a set."

"I appreciate that."

"We're taking a set of them too, if that's all right," Chris Anne said. She was still busily loading things into

the back of Pete's pickup truck while he sat on a chair, looking miserable.

"That's fine." I went over to Pete. "May I get you anything? Coffee? Water?"

He shook his head. "Naw, I'm fine."

I knew he wasn't, but I also knew there was nothing I could do to help. "Let me know if you change your mind."

I went back inside to help Homer with the trim. I was relieved a few minutes later when I heard Pete's truck drive off . . . although I half expected to learn that Chris Anne had left in it, leaving poor Pete behind to wait for her to return for another load. I glanced out the window, and it appeared that she, Pete, and Stan were all gone.

Listening to Roger—or one of his crew members— pounding on that wall made me wish I'd thought to bring a radio or MP3 player this morning to give us something more pleasant to hear while we worked. But the slamming sledgehammer would still be audible above the music. I reminded myself of how great the screened-in porch would look when the work was finished.

"Amy! I need you in here!" Roger called.

I told Homer I'd be right back and hurried into the hallway. My steps faltered as I approached the open door to the office. "Wh-what do you need?"

He was holding a green metal lockbox. "This was in the wall."

"What is it?"

"I don't know. Let's go find out." He jerked his head toward the opening in the wall, and I followed him out to the backyard. He called out to his crew to keep busy and that he'd be right back.

Roger used a screwdriver and a hammer to break the lock. He glanced at me before opening the box.

My jaw dropped when I saw the contents of the box. "Is that *real*?"

The box contained stacks of hundred-dollar bills.

"Appears to be."

"Oh my gosh! What're we gonna do?"

"You're going to calm down," he said.

"Right. Right." I calmed down for nearly two seconds. "What're we gonna *do*?"

"Look, the money was hidden in the wall for a reason. I'd say there's something not right about it, wouldn't you?"

I bobbed my head. "Oh my *gosh*! The bank robbery! This is the money from the bank robbery!"

"What bank robbery? And keep your voice down."

"Aunt Bess told us Sunday that Lou's dad and uncle robbed a bank in North Carolina, but it was never proven and the money was never found." I shook both arms at the box. *"That's the money!"*

"We don't know that," he said.

"What're we gonna do?"

"Will you please stop asking me that? You sound like Prissy from *Gone with the Wind*."

"I'm sorry, but I don't know what to do." Tears welled in my eyes.

"Call that deputy you know."

"I don't *know* him, know him. I just *kinda* know him . . . because I'm a murder suspect." The tears spilled onto my cheeks.

Roger sighed and pulled me into a one-armed hug. "Stop crying. If most people found a box containing stacks of money in their wall, they'd be thrilled."

"I'm not most people. Most people didn't walk into an office to find their boss dead. Most people's necklaces aren't found beneath the dead woman's desk. Most people's great-aunts didn't tell them about a bank robbery that happened years ago when this café was being built." I just wanted to start my business. I didn't need any more drama. It was bad enough the building was part of a murder investigation. Was I now going to be slowed down for weeks while the police dug into a cold case—another investigation that involved *me*? It was too much.

"Calm down and call the deputy. You obviously had nothing to do with a bank robbery that occurred before you were even born."

"But what if the money *isn't* from the bank robbery? What if it's from something else?"

"Fine. I'll call the deputy," he said.

"No! I'll call him. I don't want him to think I'm trying to hide something."

Roger stared at me blankly. "I've slung a sledgehammer all morning, and now *you're* giving me a headache."

"Sorry. I'll make the call."

He handed me the box. "Keep this with you. Or, at least, put it in the kitchen. And don't mention it to anyone else until after the deputy tells you what to do with it."

"All right."

We went back around to the side of the building and stepped through the wall. I took the box into the kitchen, where Jackie was warming up Homer's sausage biscuit.

"What's that?" she asked.

"Just something Roger found."

She left with the plate, and I called Deputy Hall.

"Ryan Hall."

"Hi. This is Amy Flowers."

"Good morning, Ms. Flowers. What can I help you with?"

"Um . . . Could you come to the café? Alone, maybe? I mean, we—the workers . . . you know, the construction crew—they found something in the wall when they tore it out . . . and I don't know. . . . Could you come over?"

He chuckled. "What'd you find? A body?"

"No! I mean, not yet. There *is* one wall still standing. You don't think there's a body in there, do you?"

"It was a joke, Amy. I'm on my way."

"Th-thank you." With shaking hands, I ended the call.

I'd placed the box on the counter in front of me, and now I decided to look in it again. Maybe the money was fake. Maybe we'd been so surprised to find it that we had taken it at face value, when a closer examination would prove that we were all up in the air over nothing. Okay, so Roger wasn't up in the air, but I was in orbit.

I opened the box and peered inside. That money certainly looked legitimate. I mean, Ben Franklin's head wasn't enormous the way it was on newer bills, but it was Franklin. It wasn't some superhero or cartoon character. I wondered how much was there, but I didn't dare touch it. I quickly closed the box.

"Are you okay?" Jackie asked, returning Homer's plate. "You look pale."

"Yeah, fine. Hard work, I guess. Taking its toll on me."

She frowned. "You don't seem all right. You're talking like you've been sucking helium."

"Nope. No helium for me. I'm going to have some water. You want some water?"

"I'm good. I'm going to get back to taping. You should rest for a few minutes."

"Okay. Thanks."

She gave me another odd look before going back into the dining room. I needed to get back to work too. But I was going to have that water first. And try to get my trembling hands under control so my tape wouldn't be as crooked as a rainbow.

Luckily, Deputy Hall arrived before I'd even finished my water. I heard his car pull up, and I hurried to the doorway between the kitchen and the dining area and motioned him back. I didn't look directly at Jackie, but I could see from the corner of my eye that she was giving me the "I knew it!" look.

"Thank goodness you're here," I told Deputy Hall as I took his arm and pulled him the rest of the way into the kitchen.

He put his hands on my shoulders and examined my face. "Are you all right?"

"I'm better now."

He smiled.

"Here." I hurried over to the counter, got the box, and shoved it toward him.

"What is this?"

"Money."

He lifted the lid. "Wow." He put the box on the counter and slipped on some latex gloves. "Let's see how much is here." He took the stacks out of the box and began thumbing through one of them. "There appear to be fifty bills in a stack, so each of these stacks contains five thousand dollars."

I gasped. "And how many stacks are there?"

"There are four stacks here. That's twenty thousand dollars."

"Why would somebody have twenty thousand dollars stashed in a wall?"

"I don't know," said Deputy Hall. "But I'll take this with me and let you know what I can turn up."

"Thank you."

I watched him put the money back into the box.

"I want you to know I had nothing to do with any of this," I said.

He grinned at me. "I know."

"I wasn't even the one who found it in the wall. That was Roger."

"I believe you."

"You might want to check into a bank robbery that happened about the time those bills were minted." I told him Aunt Bess's story about the rumored North Carolina bank robbery.

"Thanks. I'll take all of this under advisement and be in touch when I know something. In the meantime, don't say a word about this to anyone. And caution your friend who found the box to keep it under wraps too. We don't want people to know we have this much money in the evidence locker at the jail."

"Right. Roger won't say anything. And, of course, I won't either. Neither of us will say anything about finding money stashed in the wall of Lou Lou's—*dead* Lou Lou's—office. I mean, first I stumble onto Lou Lou lying dead across her desk and now we find money hidden in the wall? What next?"

"There's really no need to be upset about this." He placed his hand gently on my arm.

"I—I know. It's just . . ." I took two deep breaths. "I've been through so much over the past week."

"Maybe whatever happens next will be something great," he said.

"I hope it will be." I gave him a bag to put the box in so no one would notice it when he left.

"So do I. I'll call you as soon as I know something."

Deputy Hall had barely backed out of the parking lot before Jackie hurried back into the kitchen.

"What's going on?"

"Nothing," I said.

She put her hands on her hips.

"Roger found something in the wall. We aren't supposed to talk about it. In fact, I need to go tell Roger not to say anything about it."

"What was it?" she asked.

"What did I just tell you?"

She pressed her lips together. "Fine. I won't say anything."

"I know. And I'll tell you all about it as soon as I can." I went out the kitchen door to find Roger.

Chapter 13

We stopped working at lunchtime and had ham sandwiches, and then we all—including Homer—resumed work on the café until five o'clock that afternoon. After that, I invited everybody to the pizza parlor for dinner. There were a couple of Roger's workers who had families to get home to or had already made other plans, but everyone else went to the pizza parlor.

It was a ragtag crew that ambled into Winter Garden Pizza, and we took the entire back corner of booths and tables. A waitress came over and took our drink orders, and I went ahead and ordered one of nearly every pizza on the menu.

As soon as the waitress left, I looked at Roger, who was seated to my left. "What's the plan for tomorrow?"

"You and I need to go to the restaurant furniture

wholesaler and pick out your tables, chairs, countertops, and stools . . . plus any other fixtures you might want."

"Okay. What about everyone else?"

"My workers know what they need to be doing," he said. "Do yours?"

Jackie was sitting directly across from me.

"Jackie, do you know what needs to be done in the dining room tomorrow?" I asked her.

"Sure do. Why? You bailing on us already?"

"I have to go with Roger to pick out furniture."

"We need flooring too," Roger said. "I'm thinking laminate wood flooring for the dining room and treated hardwood for the screened-in porch."

"And a sign," Jackie said. "See about getting your sign done."

"You want us to do all of that tomorrow?" I asked.

"You're the one who wants to be open in a month," Roger reminded me. "You need to get things ordered so they'll be finished and installed by then."

"All right. Do you have a list of what needs to be ordered?"

He tapped his temple. "It's all up here."

"Heaven help us," Jackie said. "You'd better make him write it down, Amy."

Roger blew her a kiss, and she countered with an un-ladylike gesture. Then they both laughed. Was I the only one who could see how crazy they were about each other? What a good couple they'd make?

The waitress brought our drinks then, and the group split into conversations about sports, television shows, and a new shopping center that was being built nearby.

We were all tired and weary of work. None of us really wanted to think about the café any more until tomorrow.

As soon as I got home from the pizza parlor, I took a long, relaxing shower. When I got out of the tub, I wrapped myself in a knee-length plush pink robe and went into the living room to curl up on the couch. I was reaching for the remote when my doorbell rang.

Rory went ballistic, barking and jumping near the door. Princess Eloise ran down the hall to parts unknown.

I wasn't expecting anyone. Remembering Deputy Hall's warning about the killer still being on the loose, I looked out the window and saw a red convertible in my driveway. Surely, Lou Lou's killer wouldn't drive a red convertible. Okay, so that was illogical. But, in my defense, I was tired and not thinking very clearly. I did, however, leave the chain on the door until I opened it and saw Deputy Hall standing there in faded jeans and a white T-shirt.

"Did I catch you at a bad time?" he asked.

"No. Please come in." I closed the door enough to undo the chain and then opened it to let Deputy Hall inside. "Have a seat, and I'll slip on some clothes and be right back."

I hurried to the bedroom and threw on some shorts and a sweatshirt. When I returned to the living room, he was sitting on the sofa with Princess Eloise perched on his lap and Rory lying by his feet. Rory I understood— he loved everybody—but Princess Eloise threw me for a loop.

"How'd you manage that?" I asked.

"Manage what?"

"To win the affection of Princess Eloise. She's not crazy about most people."

He shrugged. "Just lucky, I guess."

"May I get you something to drink? Are you hungry?"

"I'd love some water, please."

"Anything else?" I called over my shoulder as I went to the kitchen for two bottles of water.

"No, thanks."

I returned, handed him his water, and sat on the chair across from him. "What brings you by, Deputy Hall?"

"The money box. And please call me Ryan."

"Ryan," I repeated.

"As you can see, I'm here unofficially—plain clothes, my personal vehicle—and I'm not here to discuss the ongoing investigation of Lou Lou Holman's murder."

"All right." I drew the word out, indicating he should go ahead and make his point. Not that I minded sitting here looking at Mr. Handsome out of uniform, but I'd had an early morning today and there was another one ahead of me tomorrow.

"I just wanted to tell you that I was intrigued by that box you found and the story you told me. Since it was a slow day at work, I did some digging."

I leaned forward, elbows on my knees.

"There was a robbery in Surry County, North Carolina, in the spring of 1936."

"Do you think the robbery was committed by Lou Holman's dad and uncle like Aunt Bess said?" I asked.

"No one was ever convicted of the crime. I looked through some newspaper archives. You may be aware

that the *Winter Garden News* was pretty gossipy in the 1930s."

"Was?" I barked out a laugh. "It hasn't evolved much, then."

Ryan laughed too. "This is what I was able to piece together. Lou's dad's name was Bo, and Bo's brother was Grady. The bank was about to foreclose on Grady's farm."

I took a sip of my water. "The Surry County bank?"

"No, the local bank here in Winter Garden—or, rather, the bank that was in business at the time—is the one that was about to foreclose. But the men knew they'd likely be recognized if they robbed their own bank, even if they wore masks, so they went across the border."

"How did the newspaper say this stuff if the Holman brothers were never even arrested for the crime?"

"The newspaper was privately owned, and they put the information in their *gossip* column," Ryan said. "They basically said, 'this is all conjecture,' but I think they had the story right."

"So Bo and Grady robbed the bank in Surry County. How much did they get away with?"

"Twenty thousand dollars."

I frowned. "The exact amount in the lockbox? They didn't spend any of it. Were they lying low or what?"

"The gossip columnist said that Grady Holman had a change of heart. He felt like he'd besmirched the whole family's honor, and in fact, told a friend what had happened."

"Which is how the gossip columnist got his or her information. But wait. According to Aunt Bess, both Holman brothers were pretty mean. Why would Grady have a sudden change of heart?"

"Grady told this friend that he didn't want his brother to go to jail for Grady's mistakes and that he was going to turn himself in and give back the money," said Ryan. "He hoped the authorities would go easy on him. The friend didn't see Grady anymore after that."

"Why? Was Grady murdered? Did he run off somewhere?" I couldn't figure out why Grady's disappearance was a big deal.

Ryan inclined his head. "I'll get to that. As you already determined, Lou was building his café at the time and provided his dad with the perfect hiding place for the stolen money."

"How did Lou have the funds to build a café when his uncle's farm was being foreclosed on?" I asked. "That seems wrong somehow."

"It might seem unfair, but I have to think that Lou had also worked hard, saved his money for a down payment, and taken out a building loan. He had the right to pursue his dream as much as Grady had to pursue his, didn't he?"

"Of course. I'm sorry. I wasn't thinking."

"You're family-minded." He smiled and took a drink from his water bottle. "Had you been in Lou's position, you'd have used your money to try to help bail out your uncle."

"Yeah, but that doesn't mean Lou should have. Who knows? Maybe Grady had squandered all his money somehow, and Lou knew he would do the same with any more he received. So what happened to Grady?"

"The gossip columnist said Grady 'wasn't seen around these parts again.' He didn't know whether Grady had simply run off, committed suicide, or—and I quote—'met

a darker fate.' The columnist supposed that Bo and Grady might've argued—they were both known to drink a lot—and the argument might've escalated into a physical altercation."

"So I'm assuming that Grady never showed back up in Winter Garden," I said. "Aunt Bess didn't mention that. But, then, she's been known to leave bits out of her stories so she can come back with a jaw-dropper later on. I'll have to see what else she knows."

"I could find no record of Grady Holman after 1936."

"Okay, so let's say that Grady was dead. Why didn't Bo spend the money? Guilt?"

"Maybe. He could've also been waiting for news of the North Carolina robbery to die down. People would've likely forgotten it in a year or two, and he could've started to spend it a little at a time," Ryan said. "But Bo was killed when the tractor he was driving overturned on him in 1937."

"Wow. A lot of people around here would consider that money cursed, then."

"Maybe it is."

"You don't think it played into Lou Lou's murder?" I asked.

"I can't see a connection right now, but then, it *was* in the wall of the office where she was killed."

The thought gave me chills. "Do you think she knew about the money?"

"I don't know. I don't even know for sure that Lou knew. His dad might've put the money in the wall without Lou's knowledge."

"So what happens to the money now?"

"I turned it over to Sheriff Billings. We have no hard

evidence that this money even came from a robbery. That's conjecture. But since we're not sure what to do with the money, right now the box is sitting in an evidence locker."

"Thanks for sharing that story with me," I said.

"You're welcome. I thought you should know."

"My cousin Jackie is dying of curiosity about what was going on this morning. Do you mind if I tell her? And Roger—he found the box. I promise not to tell anyone else."

"You can tell Jackie and Roger, but I would appreciate it if you didn't spread the word that there's twenty thousand dollars sitting in evidence in our jail." He chuckled. "Sure as the world, some knucklehead would try to break in and steal it."

"Isn't that the truth?" I laughed.

"And I wouldn't put it past someone to try to break into the café to see if there was more money hidden there somewhere."

"The less said, the better."

"Right." He took Princess Eloise off his lap and stood. "I'd better be going."

"Thanks again for stopping by." I stood and walked him to the door. "And thank you for trusting me enough to talk with me about this stuff."

"I've already told you, I don't believe you murdered Lou Lou Holman." He lowered his eyes. "I'm anxious to get this case solved so . . ."

"So what?"

He brought his eyes back to mine. "So we can all move on."

He walked down the porch steps to the driveway. I

closed the door. I didn't want him to think I was weird for standing there watching him. Princess Eloise brushed against my ankle, gave me a haughty look, and left the room.

R oger and I had a good hour's drive the next morning to get to the restaurant furniture wholesaler. Along the way, I told him about Ryan's visit and the tale the gossip columnist had woven about the bank robbery.

"Ah, so the deputy finds an excuse to let you see his ripped muscles in a T-shirt and to show off his flashy car."

"That's not the subject we're addressing. We're talking about the money you found in the wall yesterday."

He laughed. "All right. All right. Ignore what's right in front of you in favor of a mystery that's what—eighty years old?"

"*I* ignore what's in front of *me*?"

"Yes, you do," he said.

"Well, Mr. Pot-Calling-the-Kettle-Black, I need a favor. Jackie was dying to know what was going on yesterday, and I didn't tell her because Ryan asked me not to."

Roger affected a falsetto voice. "Dreamy Ryan asked me to keep mum about the box in the wall." He then mimicked buttoning his lip.

I lightly slapped his arm. "Take Jackie to dinner tonight and tell her about the box. Just make sure that neither of you tells anyone else. The last thing I need is someone breaking into the café and tearing all the walls out to see if there's more money inside them."

"All right. Why do I have to take her to dinner, though? Can't I just pull her aside?"

"Roger, take Jackie to dinner already. How long are you two going to deny your feelings for each other?"

"We don't have those kinds of feelings for each other. We've been friends forever."

"So have we," I said. "But you and I don't look at each other the way you and Jackie do."

"Do you want me to?" He glanced away from the road to look cross-eyed at me.

"I'm serious."

"I am too. I don't want to ruin a perfectly good friendship."

"Then take Jackie to dinner as a friend."

"You're a pain in the butt, you know."

"I do know. And if you don't want me to sound like a broken record for the rest of the way to the wholesaler's shop and back, you'll agree to take Jackie to dinner this evening."

He sighed. "I'll see if she has plans. Satisfied?"

"Yes." I looked out the window at the wildflowers growing in the median. "How long do you think it'll take for our tables and chairs to be delivered?"

"Two months."

I jerked my head at him. "What?"

"Kidding. I owed you one."

Chapter 14

Roger and I got to the café around lunchtime. We brought burgers and potato chips for the entire crew.

I sat at the counter beside Homer to eat. "Did Jackie take care of your sausage biscuit this morning?"

"Yes, she did. Thank you for asking. And, in case you're wondering—Napoleon Hill is my hero for the day."

"How about that? I'm reading one of his books right now."

"Which one?"

"The Law of Success."

"That's a good one," he said. "I have *Think and Grow Rich*, if you'd like to borrow it after you finish the one you're reading."

"Thank you. I appreciate that. And I also appreciate all your hard work here." I'd had to insist on paying him

to the point of refusing to allow him to help if he didn't
accept a paycheck.

"Aw . . . it's like Mr. Hill once said: 'If you cannot
do great things, do small things in a great way.' By doing
small things, I'm helping y'all do something great."

"You sure are, Homer. And, trust me—where these
renovations are concerned, there are no small things."

Jackie came up and sat on the other side of me. "Roger
just cornered me and asked me to go to dinner tonight."

"Did you say yes?"

"Yeah, but that's weird, don't you think?"

"No, I don't." I debated on whether or not to tell her I'd
had to talk him into it, but I decided not to go there. He'd
asked and she'd accepted. That was all that mattered.

"Did you guys find everything you were looking for
at the wholesalers?"

"Yup. We ordered bamboo flooring. It's tongue-and-
groove hardwood but is the most durable and scratch-
resistant. Also, Roger was thrilled that it's environmentally
conscious. I mean, I am too, but I'd have thought all wood
was . . . well . . . green, you know?"

"I'd have thought so too." She looked down at the
scuffed brown linoleum. "It'll sure beat this all to pieces."

"Won't it, though? It'll be here tomorrow."

"Then we need to finish painting today," Jackie said.
"I'm so excited!"

She gave me a quick hug. "Me too. Hey, what about
the uniforms? What did you come up with there?"

"I thought I'd order blue T-shirts with DOWN SOUTH
CAFÉ written on them in yellow. We'll also have yellow
aprons. Other than that, you can wear jeans or a skirt—
whatever suits you."

"Jeans suit me. Don't forget to order extra T-shirts for the tourists."

"I'll do it," I said. "Even if the tourists don't buy them, we'll have them on hand when we need them."

"The tourists will buy the shirts. Trust me. We'll be famous."

"I'll buy one," Homer piped up.

"No way. You'll get yours for free. You're part of the staff now."

He puffed out his chest. "I'm proud to help."

"Lunch break is up, people!" Roger called from the other side of the room. "This café won't renovate itself!"

I was tidying up the kitchen area after everyone else had left that evening. The chime Roger had installed over the door alerted me to someone coming in the front. I wiped my hands on a dish towel and went to see who was there.

Stan Wheeler was standing in the middle of the dining room, gazing around and nodding. "This place is looking good."

"Thank you."

"Thank *you*. The table and chairs in my trailer were getting pretty ratty, so I was tickled to get one of those sets you were giving away."

"I'm glad it worked for you."

He nodded toward the window nearest where the screened-in porch would be. "I see that you've torn out the office."

"Yeah. We're going to make it additional dining space."

"Huh. Did Pete get everything he wanted or needed out of there?" He held up his hands. "I mean, I know you'd give him anything he'd want, but he acted the other night like he didn't want any of the stuff his momma had here."

"I know. I hope he and Chris Anne got what they wanted yesterday. A couple of Roger's guys hauled the rest of it off this morning."

"I imagine Chris Anne took everything she could carry," he said. "When I was here yesterday, it looked like she was packing that truck full."

"She was. Pete mainly just stood around looking sad. I think it bothered him to be here." I shrugged. "I guess Chris Anne was trying to look out for him."

Stan scoffed. "Make no mistake. If Chris Anne was looking out for anybody, it was for herself. I warned Pete when he started up with her that she was trouble."

"What makes you say so?"

"She served jail time for drug possession, for one thing. She's younger than Pete, but she's a lot harder than he is. He's been pretty much sheltered. And, you know, I served a nickel for drugs myself, but I'm clean now."

"You don't think Chris Anne is?"

"No, I don't. It'd take a miracle for that girl to get sober."

I thought about the miracle she had growing inside her and hoped it would be enough to convince her to change her ways, if she hadn't done so prior to finding out that she was going to be a mother.

I also wondered again if she'd told Pete about her pregnancy. Could that be why he seemed so distraught yesterday? Had he realized his mother wouldn't get to see her grandchild or be around to see the child grow up? Or

was he upset that Chris Anne's pregnancy interfered with his plans for the two of them to go on the road?

"I won't keep you any longer," said Stan. "You care if I walk around there and take a look at what the workers are doing with the office?"

"I don't mind. Just be careful. There might be nails lying around or something."

"I'll watch my step."

I locked the front door before going back to the kitchen. Even though Stan had been acting much nicer of late, and he'd just told me he wasn't doing drugs anymore, I didn't really trust him. And I didn't want to be caught off guard again.

After leaving the café, I went to Pete's house. He'd called earlier asking me to stop by, but he didn't say why.

I realized what a mess I was as I was knocking on the door. I hadn't brushed my hair—which now had paint in it—since this morning. My clothes were dusty and paint-flecked. I imagined I looked like a ragamuffin standing on the Holmans' doorstep.

Chris Anne came to the door. "Hey, Amy. How're you?"

"I'm fine. Is Pete here?"

"Not right now, but he'll be back in a minute. He went up to the pizza place to get us some dinner. We're tired of casseroles." Her eyes widened as if it had just dawned on her that I might've brought over one of those casseroles—which, of course, Jackie and I had. "I mean, we're keeping them in the freezer, and we'll certainly eat them. . . . We just wanted a change, is all."

"I understand. It's like a day or two after Thanksgiving when you don't want to even think about turkey again for a month."

"Exactly like that! Come on in. We'll talk while we wait for Pete."

I stepped into the living room. Even more than with the café, Lou Lou's influence was everywhere. A print of a Hawaiian landscape hung over the couch, and an Elvis clock sat atop the television. Chris Anne sat on the couch, and I sat on the chair across from her.

"Have you told Pete about the baby?"

"I have."

Was there a delicate way to ask her if she was sober? "Are you taking good care of yourself . . . and the baby?"

"I am." She grinned. "The doctor put me on them prenatal vitamins. They're big as half outdoors, and they taste nasty, but I'm taking them."

"That's good. I guess Pete's over the moon."

She studied her fingernails. "He wasn't as happy as I'd hoped he would be, but he'll come around."

"I'm sorry. It was probably bittersweet news for him, since he realizes his mother won't be around to see the baby."

Chris Anne looked surprised. "I hadn't thought of that. I figured he was just mad because it's going to be hard for me to drive a truck with a belly out to here." She held her hand out in front of her to show me how big she thought her stomach would get.

I laughed. "And I don't think tractor-trailers are particularly built for car seats either, are they?"

"No, I don't believe they are. I told Pete to get Stan

to go in with him. They've become like best friends or something here lately."

"Well, there you go. That sounds like the perfect solution."

She put her index finger to her lips. "Pete just pulled up. I don't want him to know what we've been talking about."

"Sure."

Pete came in carrying a pizza box. "Chris Anne, get this thing. It's hot."

Chris Anne hopped up off the couch and got the box. "I'll put it in the kitchen. Amy's here."

"Yeah, I saw her car. Hey, Amy." He took Chris Anne's vacated seat. "You doing all right?"

"I'm fine. How are you doing?"

"I'm okay. Getting there, anyway. It ain't easy."

"No, it's not. My nana dying was the hardest thing I've ever had to deal with. I can only imagine how hard this is for you."

He bobbed his head. "You want some pizza? We've got plenty."

"No. I need to leave here in a second. I only stopped by because I got your message."

"Oh yeah. I found another set of keys to the Joint. I'll get 'em for you." He went into the kitchen and got the keys.

"Thanks, Pete." I didn't tell him that Roger had already changed the locks. "You guys have a good evening."

"We will. Thanks for coming by."

The first thing I did when I got home was feed Rory and Princess Eloise. As soon as I'd done that, I took a shower. It felt good to wash away the grime and fatigue

of the day, but it also felt wonderful to have made so much progress on the café in such a short amount of time.

When I got out of the shower, I made myself a peanut butter sandwich. Luckily, Rory had gone out into the backyard after he'd eaten, so he didn't realize I had more food at his disposal.

While eating, I looked through my cookbooks to find something interesting I could make and take the crew for breakfast tomorrow morning. I decided on baked cinnamon-sugar doughnuts.

I preheated the oven, got out my doughnut pan, and sprayed the pan with nonstick spray. As I mixed up the batter for the doughnuts, I thought about Pete. He'd been so delighted with Chris Anne only a few days ago that he'd gotten engaged to her the day after his mother's murder. Now he seemed sullen and resentful toward her. What had happened between them since then? Was it her pregnancy? Or was there more to it?

I put the batter into a pastry bag and piped six doughnuts, filling the pan. I put that pan in the oven and melted a small bowl of butter in the microwave. I got another bowl and stirred together the cinnamon and sugar.

I planned on making two dozen doughnuts for the crew. I decided to make an additional half dozen and take them to Mom and Aunt Bess. I wanted to tell them about the money we found in the wall and its probable connection to the bank robbery Aunt Bess told us about on Sunday. I knew I was supposed to be keeping it a secret. But Ryan had said I could tell Roger and Jackie. Letting just two more people know—especially a pair as trustworthy as Aunt Bess and Mom—wouldn't make a difference.

* * *

A unt Bess was delighted with her box of doughnuts. "And it's not even Sunday!" she exclaimed. "Get us some plates, Jenna. And some milk too. I like milk with my doughnuts." She bit into one of the doughnuts. "Mmmm. Merciful goodness! These are still warm."

"I'm glad you like them."

Mom brought plates and glasses of milk for everybody. "We *could* go into the kitchen and eat, and I wouldn't have to vacuum crumbs up when we're done."

"Where'd be the fun in that?" Aunt Bess asked. "Besides, I can tell by the look on her face that Amy has some juicy gossip to fill us in on. I want to be on this comfy sofa when she does."

Mom arched a brow at me. "Do you have juicy gossip?"

"As a matter of fact, I do. Would you like for me to start with what Roger found hidden in the office wall of the Joint? Or would you like me to tell you about Pete and Chris Anne?"

"Tell us what was in the wall," Aunt Bess said, licking the sugar and cinnamon off her fingertips. "Was it Grady Holman's body? Did you get us some napkins, Jenna?"

She *had* known about Grady's disappearance and had left that out of her story.

Mom sighed. "Be right back. Don't start without me."

When Mom returned with napkins, I extracted promises from her and Aunt Bess not to say a word about what I was telling them to anyone. After they'd both sworn solemn oaths, I told them about the money in the lockbox hidden in the wall. I went on to tell them the story Ryan had told to me from the gossip columnist's point of view.

Aunt Bess looked up at the ceiling. "You know, for a fact, nobody saw Grady Holman around here right after the news about that bank robbery got stirred up. I didn't really know the Holmans and didn't give it much thought, but folks said they wouldn't be a bit surprised to find out that Bo killed Grady so he could keep all that money. So it very well could've been Grady you found holed up in the wall."

"I guess anything's possible, but it wasn't Grady," I said. "And Ryan said that Bo died in a tractor accident the next year."

Aunt Bess nodded. "I remember that well. The thing overturned and the back tires ran over his chest. Crushed him all to pieces."

"Why do you think Lou didn't spend the money?" I asked. "Why would he leave it hidden for all this time?"

"My guess is he didn't know about it," Mom said. "If I was going to hide ill-gotten gains in your café, I certainly wouldn't tell you about it."

"Gee, thanks."

"Where would you get these ill-gotten gains?" Aunt Bess asked. "Have you been up to something?"

"Of course not. But if I *had*, I wouldn't want to drag my daughter into it. Even if I had nowhere else to stash the money except her café, I wouldn't tell her. Then she'd have deniability if I was caught and the money was found."

"So you think it's been there all this time because Lou—and then Lou Lou and Pete—knew nothing about it," I said.

"I know Lou Lou Holman didn't know anything about money being hidden in that office, or else she'd have clawed through that wall years ago," said Aunt Bess. "She

sure wouldn't have left it alone. You know as well as I do that she was so tight her toes curled every time she blinked."

"That's true," I said. "But being as tight as she was, maybe she was keeping it there in case of an emergency."

"What news were you going to tell us about Pete and Chris Anne?" Mom asked.

"Chris Anne is pregnant."

Aunt Bess shook her head. "Saints preserve us. Those two need a baby like an alcoholic needs to tend bar. It's all they can do to take care of themselves."

"A lot of people never quite grow up until they have to," said Mom. "I actually thought I had until I had a child and realized how immature I was."

"Ain't that the truth? But you turned out just fine," said Aunt Bess. "And Amy did too."

Chapter 15

I got to the café the next morning even before Roger and his crew arrived. I preheated the oven to two hundred degrees so I could warm the doughnuts before everyone else got there.

I heard a truck pull into the parking lot and went out front, expecting to see Roger. To my surprise, it was Pete.

"Pete, is everything all right?" I asked when he stepped down out of the truck. "What on earth are you doing here at six o'clock?"

"Everything's fine. I was up anyway and got to wondering how the renovations are coming along."

"Come on inside and see for yourself."

He looked around the dining room. "I like these colors. They really brighten up the place."

"Thank you."

"Momma talked a lot about fixing up the Joint, but she never did," Pete said. "She just never had the time."

I nodded. "Time certainly can slip away from you in a hurry."

"Ain't that the truth? Seems like only yesterday, I was a little ol' thing running around here with dirty hands and skinned knees. Momma was waitressing, and Grandpa was at the grill." He grinned. "You don't know how good you've got it when you're a kid, you know? It's only looking back that you realize how nice it was."

I smiled. "I guess so."

His grin faded as he shook his head. "I can't quite come to grips with Momma being gone. She was always here. I know she could have an ornery turn to her sometimes, but she was always trying to do right by me."

"I know she was." I didn't really know whether she always tried to do right by Pete or not, but I felt that it was proper to say she did.

"I'm glad Chris Anne saved a bunch of the stuff from the office."

"I thought you would be," I said. "It helps you grieve when you have something to hold on to. It's not that you need something to remind you of her, but it's nice to have something of hers to sort of ground you to the past. I have one of my Nana's rings. I wear it sometimes when I want to feel especially close to her."

"Last night, Chris Anne got out Momma's photo albums. She wanted to see what I looked like as a baby and then as a boy." He blew out a breath. "I finally had to leave the room—brought up too many memories."

"It'll get easier. Congratulations on the baby."

"Thanks." He ran a hand through his thinning hair. "I wish me and Chris Anne could've done things differently, planned things out a little better, but I guess this is how

it's supposed to be. I mean, I'd have liked to have waited . . . just had it be me and her before having kids. But it is what it is."

"Chris Anne said you're thinking of asking Stan to be your business partner. I hope that works out for you."

"So do I. Maybe it's better not to be in business with my fiancée anyway, right?"

"Maybe." I told him that Aunt Bess had told me the legend of the Holman brothers who'd robbed a bank in North Carolina.

Pete did a snort-laugh combo. "Lordy mercy, I heard that story so many times growing up. At nearly every family reunion and every holiday, Grandpa would gather around anybody who'd listen and give them an earful." He gazed at the back wall as if seeing it all play out on a movie screen. "After he'd tell the bank-robbing story, he'd tell us that Uncle Grady disappeared after that and that maybe he took the money with him. Then he'd lean in like he was telling us a secret and say that maybe Uncle Grady had left that money hidden around here somewhere. Then all us kids would go on a treasure hunt."

"Did you ever find anything?"

"Poison ivy a time or two. Like as not, every cent of that money—if there ever was any—went for liquor or was gambled away two weeks after they got it."

I bobbed my head in a way that couldn't actually be called a nod. I didn't want to be mistaken for being in agreement with Pete when I knew full well that the money was in evidence at the Winter Garden Police Department.

"So what kind of tall tales did your grandpa tell you?" Pete asked.

"He mostly told us about working in the coal mines. And, with every story he told, I became more convinced that I never wanted to work in a dark, scary mine."

"I heard that."

Roger and his crew pulled into the parking lot.

"There's the boss," I told Pete. "Time to get to work."

"Thanks again for letting me look at the place. It's nice. Momma would be proud."

I knew that was a lie he could've kept from telling, but it was nice of him to say so all the same. "Thanks, Pete. Stop by anytime."

I brought out the warm doughnuts and hot coffee, and they were enjoyed by all. Homer still liked his ten-o'clock sausage biscuit, but he wouldn't turn down a warm doughnut at six thirty.

Homer's, Jackie's, and my job today was to tear out the old floor. We had heavy gloves and chisels.

"Who's your hero, Homer?" I asked.

"James Arthur Baldwin. Have you heard of him?"

"He wrote essays, right?"

"Novels too. And poems . . . plays."

"Sounds like an accomplished guy," said Jackie.

"Indeed he was."

"Pete stopped by today," I said. "He told me he was glad Chris Anne didn't let him throw out all of Lou Lou's things from the office."

"Yeah, I guess he was when he had time to stop and consider it," she said.

"Any word yet on who killed Ms. Holman?" Homer asked.

"Not yet." I pushed my chisel under a particularly well-glued stretch of linoleum. "I wish they'd find whoever did it, though. I'd love to know what the crime scene technician found."

"Let's think about who Lou Lou's enemies were," Jackie said.

"Mr. Baldwin said that people who treat others as less than human must not be surprised when the bread they've cast upon the waters comes floating back to them poisoned," said Homer.

"That guy had a good point." Jackie stopped in mid-scrape. "Lou Lou alienated almost everyone who'd ever met her."

"Even Pete said this morning that his mother could be ornery sometimes," I said. "But he said he knew she always had his best interests at heart."

"I'm not sure I believe that," said Jackie. "Do you?"

"I don't know. Maybe she *thought* she was doing the right thing for him, but she was actually smothering him." I frowned. "Is that the right word?"

"I believe the word you're looking for is 'overbearing,'" said Jackie. "But 'smothering' fits too. All the psychology and parenting articles warn that being too controlling really screws up your kids."

I dropped my chisel. "You've been reading parenting articles?"

She put the chisel back into my hand. "No. I mean, I thumbed through some when I was still in school and babysitting to pick up some extra money. And I did take a psychology course at the community college when I was taking secretarial classes."

I remembered that now. Jackie had dropped out of

college after one of her mother's visits to Winter Garden. It was the first time Renee had been back since she'd left Jackie with Aunt Bess, and Jackie had been devastated when her mom had left again.

"It shouldn't take a trained therapist to see that Pete's relationship with his mother was messed up," said Homer. "The man's forty and seemed to be afraid to tell his mother he had a serious girlfriend."

"No words of wisdom from Mr. Baldwin?" I asked.

"Only this—and I'm paraphrasing, of course. People pay for what they do and for what they've allowed themselves to become, and they pay for it by the lives they lead."

"Oh man, you're right. I never stopped to consider it, but Lou Lou must've been miserable," I said. "Maybe that's why she treated us all so badly."

Jackie stabbed her chisel into the linoleum with a vengeance. "I refuse to make excuses for that woman. She was wicked. I only went to the funeral because I felt sorry for Pete. After all, wasn't it ultimately her choice to be miserable?"

"Jackie, that's an awful thing to say!"

"I understand exactly what you mean, Jackie," said Homer. "Despite Ms. Holman's hardships, it was she who chose to wallow in self-loathing or self-pity or whatever other destructive emotions she was filled with rather than rising above them and making a better life for herself and her child."

Jackie smiled. "Homer, you are one deep dude."

"Thank you. I have my mom to thank for that . . . and my heroes." He smiled and went back to tearing up the floor.

"You grew up around here, right, Homer?" I asked.

"Nearby."

"Did you ever hear any stories about the Holmans? Aunt Bess told me that it was rumored that Lou Lou's grandfather and uncle robbed a bank in North Carolina once. Have you heard that story before?"

He shook his head. "Nope. Must've been before my time. The only stories I ever heard about the Holmans was that Lou—the original owner of this café—was a very hard man. He was said to have been rough on his wife and daughter. I always heard that he doted on his grandson, though. It seemed he'd wanted a boy when Lou Lou was born."

"So Lou Lou has no siblings," Jackie said.

"No." He looked at his watch. "It's ten o'clock."

I gratefully put down my chisel. "Let me get that sausage biscuit for you."

It did strike me odd, though, that Aunt Bess had believed Lou Holman to be such a peach of a guy when Homer had heard the exact opposite.

I didn't get a minute alone with Jackie until she and I were in the kitchen making sandwiches for everyone's lunch.

Speaking in hushed tones, I asked, "So?"

"So what?" She opened a loaf of bread and made a row of slices across the countertop.

I rolled my eyes. "How was your date with Roger?"

Jackie lowered her voice too. "I don't know that I'd classify it as a *date*. I mean, it was dinner with Roger. We've had dinner lots of times."

"Not by yourselves. Come on. His telling you about . . .

the thing we found . . . was just an excuse for the two of you to go out."

She tried to hide her smile. "Okay, okay. It was . . . nice."

"Nice?"

"It was *Roger*." She huffed. "We've known each other practically all our lives."

"But not like *this*. Not as dates. You've known each other as friends."

"I'd like to think we're still friends." She put mayo on half the slices she'd laid out and mustard on the other half.

"Jackie!" I wailed.

"Shhh!" She smiled. "It *was* nice. Maybe a little better than nice."

I squealed. "I knew it! You guys have liked each other for so long."

"Keep your cool. He might've had a lousy time."

"I'll do some recon later," I said.

Her eyes widened. "Don't you dare."

"Why not?"

"Because he'll know we've been talking about him . . . about our date," she said.

"As you pointed out, he's known us most of our lives. He already knows we've been talking about him and your date. He also knows I'm going to ask *him* about your date and that I'm then going to report back to you."

"Fair enough. But you know Roger well enough to know that he'll say it's none of your business."

I raised an index finger. "Unless he wants me to tell you something in particular."

She shook her head and took some turkey out of the refrigerator. "Do you think everybody's good with turkey?"

"I don't know. We'll make several turkey-and-cheese sandwiches and some peanut butter–and-jelly sandwiches too. That should cover everyone."

"So . . . what do you think he'll say?"

I made my own row of bread slices and got out the peanut butter. "Only one way to find out." My best guess was that Roger was dying to know what Jackie was saying about last night and that he'd seek *me* out after lunch. "Did you kiss good night?"

"None of your business."

"I'll take that as a yes." I spread peanut butter on the slice of bread nearest me.

"Fine. He kissed me once . . . when he dropped me off at home."

"And?" I looked up in time to see Jackie blush and drop her head.

"Tell me about your date with the deputy."

"What date?" I asked.

"The one where he came to your house to tell you all the important stuff about the thing that happened forever ago that couldn't wait until the next day."

"It was interesting . . . and it *was* important." I tried to concentrate hard on spreading my peanut butter to perfection. "I think it was great of Ryan to come to my house during his off-duty time to fill me in on what may be a . . . another . . . clue . . . or something in Lou Lou's case."

"Ah. Does *Ryan* think the box in the wall is a clue?"

"It certainly *could* be." I moved on to the next slice without looking up from my work.

"Sure. Because anything that happened—what—seventy-five . . . eighty . . . years ago would naturally have some bearing on a murder that took place just over a week

ago." She snorted. "That kind, thoughtful deputy . . . rushing over on his own time to make sure you were safe from the centenarian bandit killer!"

"Will you just hush and make your turkey sandwiches? We have hungry people to feed."

Chapter 16

After lunch, I went to take a look at the side porch to see how much progress had been made. I truly wasn't going to talk with Roger about his date. I knew he was busy and that I'd have plenty of time to speak with him after work.

"Amy . . . good . . . glad you're here," said Roger as I stepped around the side of the café. He pointed. "We need to turn that window into a door. The original door that opened into the office will be fine for staff taking dishes out or bringing them back inside, but you don't want your patrons having to use the same door."

"You're right. I hadn't considered that, but no, we don't want customers coming through the back, where we're working."

"I want to get that door cut out today. The flooring should be here later this afternoon, but we can't start putting it down until the door is finished."

"What about the painting we've already done?"

"It won't be a problem," said Roger. "If we mar any-thing, we'll touch it back up. But the molding around the door should hide where the window has been enlarged."

"Okay. So what do you need me to do?"

"Get out of here."

"Excuse me?"

He grinned. "You and the café staff should take the rest of the day off. I talked with Aaron about it over lunch, since he's been really interested in construction, and he'd like to stay."

I huffed. "Roger! I knew Aaron was interested in con-struction, but he's the best busboy and dishwasher we have!"

"He's really getting the hang of construction, and he's enjoying it. Would you prefer he stay a busboy forever?"

"No." I felt a stab of guilt for my poutiness. "Of course, I want Aaron to do whatever will make him happy. I'll talk with him."

"He's a good kid and a fast learner. I think he could do well in construction."

"I know, but I thought you didn't have an opening."

"I didn't, but I believe one of my guys will be leaving in late summer or early fall. That gives me time to get Aaron well trained."

"Then I guess I'm looking for a new busboy."

"I'm pretty sure you are, but talk with him first and make sure that's what he wants."

"I will." I turned to go back around the building to the café and saw Stan Wheeler pulling into the parking lot. "Wonder what he wants."

Roger stepped up next to me. "I don't know. Wait and we'll see."

Stan got out of his car and walked toward Roger and me. "Hey, folks, how're y'all doing?"

"Good, thanks," I said. "How are you, Stan?"

"To be honest, I'm as broke as a convict. I was wondering if Roger here could use an extra man."

"I don't know," Roger said. "Do you have any construction experience?"

"I do."

"Were you only wanting to work today? Or do you want to make it a regular thing?" asked Roger.

"Well, I'm mainly interested in helping with the café," Stan said. "Maybe we could see how it goes."

"All right. I could use some extra help for the next day or two." Roger nodded toward a tall, heavyset man holding a clipboard. "Go talk with Johnny and see where he'd like you to work today."

After Stan headed in Johnny's direction, Roger muttered to me under his breath, "Wish me luck."

"Good luck." Given Roger's warning about Stan, I had to wonder why he'd agree to take him on, even if it was only for a day or two. Could it be a case of keeping your friends close and your enemies closer? I left to find Aaron.

Aaron was in the café tearing up a section of flooring with Homer.

"I have good news," I said. "Roger wants us to clear out of here to let his guys turn a window into a door. So we can relax for the rest of the afternoon."

A little cheer went up.

"But," I continued, "I'm going to pay y'all for a full day. You guys have been working so hard, and I truly appreciate you."

"We're almost finished with what we're doing," Homer said. "Do you think Roger would mind if we clear this section here before we go?"

"Probably not. Aaron, could I talk with you for a second?"

"Yes, ma'am."

He was only a couple of years younger than me, but sometimes Aaron made me feel like I was ancient.

We walked over to the counter, and I handed him a bottle of water. He thanked me but looked at me expectantly rather than opening the bottle.

"Roger said he'd told you about converting the window to a door and that you'd like to stay and work with his crew this afternoon."

He nodded. "Yeah. That might be handy to know sometime . . . like if I buy a house and want to do my own renovations or something."

"True. Roger says you're a fast learner, and he's impressed with the work you've been doing."

He opened the bottle then and took a drink. "Thanks."

"What I'm asking is if you'd prefer to go to work with Roger."

His eyes widened. "You mean it? You wouldn't be mad?"

"Of course not. I'd miss you. You're our best busboy, but you need to follow your heart and do what you enjoy."

"Are you sure?"

"Positive," I said with a smile. "I would like to ask you something while I'm thinking of it, though. Were

you working that Monday afternoon? You know, *the* Monday?"

"Yes, ma'am."

"Did anyone come in acting angry toward Lou Lou or anything?"

"No. Pete almost always worked the afternoon shift, and Monday was no exception. If anybody would've been mad, they'd have been mad at Pete . . . right?"

"Good point. Did anyone come in acting like they had a beef with Pete?"

"Nah, Pete didn't make people mad. He just went along with whatever they said. It was his momma who ticked everybody off."

"That's true." I patted his shoulder. "Thanks again for all your hard work."

"The only person who came in who was disagreeable at all was that Mr. Lincoln from the Chamber of Commerce. He wanted to buy the Joint, but Pete told him his momma had already given him her answer." He looked toward the door. "Is it all right if I go ahead and tell Roger I'd like to work with him?"

"Sure." I had a couple of errands to run. I supposed I needed to add a stop at the *Winter Garden News* to the list.

The first errand on my agenda was to go to the print shop and order business cards and menus. Now that we had the colors for the café, I could take the swatches to the printer to get an exact match . . . or, at least, fairly close.

I thought this would be a simple, quick trip. I was

wrong. Once I'd explained to the printer what I wanted, she got out books to show me examples of business cards and menus. I looked through pages and pages of samples until I found the styles that I felt best exemplified Down South Café.

My choices made, I was ready to leave. And then the printer asked about letterhead and checks and envelopes— with windows for paychecks and without windows for correspondence. I told her I'd think about those and talk with her again when I returned to pick up the business cards and menus.

I had to take care of my budget. I knew it would be easy to spend a small fortune on things that would be nice to have but that I didn't necessarily need. A paycheck written on a plain check and put into a regular envelope would spend just as well as one written on a fancy check and put into a window envelope with a preprinted return address.

I still had checks and envelopes on my mind when I left the print shop and nearly collided with Chris Anne.

"Oh, goodness! I'm sorry, Chris Anne. I wasn't paying attention to where I was going."

"It's probably my fault. I'm so mad I could spit."

"What's wrong?"

"I went in there to the bank to get a loan. I want to build onto the house, get me some maternity clothes, buy a few things for the baby . . . stuff like that."

I was thinking, *Didn't Pete just come into an inheritance? And money from selling the café? Wouldn't that money buy you clothes and things you two need for the baby?* I didn't say anything, though. It wasn't any of my business.

Chris Anne anchored one bony fist to her hip. "Do you know they had the nerve to tell me that I couldn't use our house as collateral on a loan?"

"Your house?" I asked. "I thought you lived in an apartment building in Abingdon."

"I'm talking about my house with Pete. *Our* house."

"You and Pete bought a new house?"

She rolled her eyes. "Pete's house is now *our* house." She held up her left hand and waggled her fingers. "We're engaged?"

"True, but that doesn't make it your house too until Pete either adds you to the deed or the two of you get married."

She let out a growl of frustration. "Now you sound just like those bank people! They said I have no right to use Pete's home as collateral, and they wouldn't even tell me how much he has in his bank account."

"Huh." That's the only sound I could manage that wouldn't let her know that I was absolutely astounded by her incomprehension.

"I told them Pete was fine with it and told them to call him. They said he'd have to come to the bank in person." She huffed. "I told them he couldn't come today because he was out looking at trucks and getting ready to start his business. Don't they *know* they're dealing with a businessman now that could have a big impact on their bank?"

"I guess not." I wondered if Pete really *was* fine with Chris Anne trying to get a loan against his house. Did he even know?

"Oh well. I'll see you later, Amy."

"See you."

As I walked on up the street toward the *Winter Garden News* office, I marveled at Chris Anne's actions. Had she honestly thought that since she was Pete's fiancée, the bank employees would give her information on Pete's financial accounts? *And* a loan secured by his house?

And what about Pete and Stan? Both Pete and Chris Anne had indicated that Pete was considering asking Stan to go into the trucking business with Pete. Yet Stan had stopped by the café looking for work. If Stan was as broke as he said he was, how was he supposed to become a partner in a business? He couldn't afford to help pay for a truck. Maybe Pete intended to hire Stan as an employee rather than take him on as a partner. Or, it could be that they both thought they'd make so much money once the business got rolling that the truck would practically pay for itself.

I walked into the office of the *Winter Garden News* and was happy to see that it hadn't changed since the last time I'd visited, about nine years ago. I'd gone to have a classified ad put in proclaiming Mom's age on her birthday: *Lordy, lordy, Jenna's forty!* Mom had not been amused.

Anyway, the walls were still the same flat beige. The globe still stood in the corner, surrounded by floor-to-ceiling bookshelves to the left and right. And the scarred wooden desk stood in front of the office's only window—a picture window that looked out onto the street.

Ms. Peggy, who'd run the *Winter Garden News* for as long as anyone could remember, sat in her huge leather office chair with the wood scroll arms and the nail-head accents.

"Hello, dear," said Ms. Peggy in her reedy voice. "What can I do for you today?"

"I'd like to put in a classified ad to hire a busboy for the Down South Café."

I'd also put an ad on Craigslist. But even though not everyone in Winter Garden was computer savvy, everyone read the *News*. Hopefully, I could get my ad to run for a couple of weeks and have a few applicants by the time I needed to staff the café. Most of the high schoolers on summer break already had jobs, and there weren't many others beating a path to Winter Garden for its employment opportunities.

"All right." Ms. Peggy pushed away from the desk, got up, and handed me a pad of paper and a pen. "Twenty-five words or less, twenty dollars per week. Anything over twenty-five words will be an additional forty cents a word."

"Thank you." As I sat and tried to concentrate on what I wanted to say, I thought about how long Ms. Peggy had been here in Winter Garden. I got up and went to stand by the desk so she could hear me. "Ms. Peggy, have you lived here all your life?"

"Yep."

"My aunt Bess was telling me about a bank robbery that Lou Holman's dad, Bo, and his brother Grady were supposed to have committed back in the thirties."

"Over in North Carolina. I remember. What about it?"

"Do you believe the Holman brothers did it?"

"Course I do. Didn't she?" Ms. Peggy asked.

"I think she thought they were guilty."

"I'd bet you five dollars to ten they did it. Though why they didn't use that money to get Grady out of hock is beyond me."

"Aunt Bess said that Grady disappeared right after the robbery."

"Disappeared, my eye," she said. "Lou killed him."

"Lou?"

"Yeah, Lou. He was furious that Grady had dragged his daddy into something that could cause him to have to rot in prison for the rest of his life, and he killed Grady."

"Are you sure?" I asked.

"I wouldn't swear to it on a stack of Bibles or anything, but I'm fairly certain. And so was my father. He's the one who told me." She leaned back in her chair. "Lou Holman was a mean man. Why'd you think Lou Lou grew up with such a wicked look and a mouth that didn't spout nothing but vitriol?"

"Well, I figured it had something to do with her upbringing."

"Then you figured right. That little ol' girl never could do anything good enough to suit her daddy. And still, she worshipped the ground he walked on. It was a crying shame."

"I'm sorry," I said.

"Yeah, well, honey, what's done is done. Can't fix it now." She nodded toward the paper, which I hadn't even begun writing on. "You got that ad ready?"

After I got back home, I went into the fancy room, lay down on the sofa, and called Ryan.

"Hi," I said when he'd answered. "I was wondering if you've had any new leads on the Lou Lou Holman case."

"I haven't, but we're fully investigating the leads we

have. Is there anything new that has come to light on your end?"

"Not about this case, but maybe about one that happened around the time the lockbox was hidden in the office wall." I told Ryan about my visit with Ms. Peggy and what she'd told me about Lou Holman killing Grady.

"That's certainly possible. Of course, she has no proof, and it wouldn't matter if she did, since Lou Holman has been dead for more than sixty years."

"I know," I said. "I just wondered if Lou *had* known about the money hidden in the wall of his office. If so, isn't it possible that he told someone about the money? Or that he maybe left a note?"

"What're you getting at?"

"Let's say Lou did leave a note in case something happened to him. He'd want his family to have the money, right?"

"Maybe."

I huffed.

"Okay, probably," Ryan conceded.

"So the note gets lost for all this time, and then someone finds it and wants Lou Lou to cough up the money," I said.

"Doesn't it stand to reason that if her father had left a note, Lou Lou would be the most likely person to have found it?"

"Yeah, but what if she wasn't? What if someone else found the note and wanted that money? That could be the motive behind Lou Lou's death. Isn't that possible?"

"It is possible."

"So if Lou Lou didn't find it . . ." I gulped. And then

I swallowed again because my throat had become thick and dry. "Pete?"

"I'll look into it," Ryan said.

"Do you really think Pete could've had something to do with his mother's death?" I asked.

"He has always been a suspect. We typically look the hardest at the person with the most to gain from the victim's death. In this case, it was the victim's son."

"Wow."

"You had to have known we were looking at Pete."

"I did, but in my mind, the possibility was too unlikely to honestly consider. Now I'm not so sure."

"Why don't we discuss happy things? How are the renovations going?"

I began telling Ryan about what we'd got done so far. But in my mind, I was still ruminating over the idea that Pete could've killed his own mother.

Chapter 17

I decided it might be good for me to get out of Winter Garden for a little while. I could do some shopping, pick up some dinner . . . If it wasn't too late when I started back home, I could see if Mom and Aunt Bess wanted me to pick up something for them too.

Tucking a couple of foldable totes into my purse, I got into the Bug and backed out of the driveway. It was sunny, and since I had my hair in a ponytail, I put down my windows. The breeze not only felt good, it smelled like freshly mown grass. I turned on the radio and was delighted to hear Don Henley singing to me about the boys of summer.

On the way out of town, I drove by the mobile home Stan rented from Lou Lou . . . or Pete, I guessed, now. The roof had been patched in places using mismatched shingles. Hadn't Stan asked Pete for money to completely replace the roof? Maybe whoever he'd hired

hadn't got around to doing it yet, and Stan had just put the other shingles over the holes until the new roof was put on. It looked pretty bad. I hoped the roofer would get around to Stan's home soon.

I spent the rest of the afternoon looking at clothes, shoes, makeup, purses, linens, baking pans, and picnic tables with umbrellas—I made a mental note to ask Roger about what type of tables we planned to get for the patio. Fortunately for my wallet, I bought nothing.

Before heading back to Winter Garden, I called the big house. Aunt Bess answered.

"Hi, Aunt Bess. It's Amy. I was wondering if you and Mom would like me to swing by a drive-through and get us some burgers and fries for dinner."

"You're going to *buy* us some cheeseburgers and French fries when you could make better-tasting ones right here yourself?"

"Yes, I am. I'm not cooking this evening. So when I get my food, do you want me to pick y'all up something too?"

"Well, yeah. I'd appreciate that, and I imagine your mother and Jackie would too."

"I didn't realize Jackie was there," I said. "I'll get dinner for everybody and be there in about twenty minutes."

Mom had set the table by the time I got there with our bags of burgers and fries.

"The drinks are still in the car," I said, putting the bags on the dining room table.

"I'll grab them," said Jackie.

Aunt Bess instructed Mom to "light up the candles, since we're eating all fancy."

Whether it was out of spite or not, Mom lit the white taper candles. When Jackie returned with the drink tray, she passed out the drinks. We put our burgers and fries on the good china plates and used the linen napkins rather than the paper ones that came with the food.

Mom gave me a little smirk behind Aunt Bess's back, making me think that the fancy table *had* been an act of spite since Aunt Bess had disparaged my bringing us fast food for dinner. Mom was probably of the same mind as I was—it sure beat having to cook this evening.

"What have you done today?" Mom asked me.

I told her about tearing up linoleum all morning and then shopping this afternoon. "I didn't buy anything, but I feel that it did me good to have a change of scenery for a while."

"I bet it did," Jackie said. "I've been taking 'before' pictures of the café as well as photos of the progress we're making. I'm looking forward to seeing the café once all the work is done."

"How long do you think it'll take?" Mom asked.

"Roger told me it would take a month at the outset, but it seems to be going quicker than I thought it would. How about you, Jackie?"

"Yeah, I think that with us working too, Roger has had help he wasn't originally counting on."

Aunt Bess scoffed. "So you and Amy are doing the work of a whole crew of men?"

"No, Granny. But Amy is paying any of the café staff who wanted to help with the renovations to work."

"Yeah. Homer's even working for us," I said. "The only bad thing is that we've now lost Aaron as our busboy."

"What?" Jackie asked.

"He's found that he really enjoys construction work. He's going to work with Roger."

"That's good for Aaron and Roger, but what're *we* gonna do?" Jackie popped a fry into her mouth.

"I put an ad in the *Winter Garden News* before I came home after lunch. I put it on Craigslist too. Come to think of it, I'm not sure how many of our waitresses will be back either. There are only two who agreed to help renovate."

Jackie waved her hand dismissively. "We'll be fine."

Aunt Bess finished off her cheeseburger. "That was awfully tasty. We ought to do this more often."

When I went home, I got out my laptop. Ever since Roger had found the lockbox with the money hidden in the wall, I'd been curious about the bank robbery and the Holman brothers. So I did an Internet search for *Bo Holman, Winter Garden, Virginia*. As expected, there were genealogy sites with references to Bo's death, his marriage to Lou's mother, things like that. I hadn't expected the fount of information Ryan had been able to uncover, but I'd hoped for a little more than this.

Not getting my hopes up, I opened a new tab and typed *Grady Holman, Winter Garden, Virginia* into the search engine. Nothing. I went back to the results page for *Bo Holman* and found that he had a brother named *Grady Walter Holman*.

Thinking maybe Grady had started going by his middle name in an effort to remain hidden, I did a

search for *Walter Holman*. The first thing that popped
up was an obituary from 1984.

Walter Holman, 88, originally of Winter Garden, Virginia,
died today at his home near Boone, North Carolina.
Mr. Holman was preceded in death by his beloved wife,
Millicent, and is survived by his daughters, Anna and
Sadie; son, Philip; and numerous grandchildren. A
beloved member of the community, Mr. Holman . . .

I merely scanned the rest of the listing. Could this
really have been Lou Lou's great-uncle Grady? Had he
just walked away from Winter Garden and made a new
life for himself?

I did a search for *Philip Holman*. As the only boy, I
figured he'd be the easiest to find, because it was less
likely he might have changed his last name. There was
a phone number for a Philip Holman living in Knoxville,
Tennessee.

I grabbed my phone and punched in Mr. Holman's
number. As soon as this man answered, I could tell he
was too young to be Grady's son. Still, I soldiered on.

"Hello, Mr. Holman. My name is Amy Flowers, and
I live in Winter Garden, Virginia. I'm calling to ask if
your father was Grady or Walter Holman, who was also
originally from this area."

"No. My dad was from here in Tennessee."

I thanked him for his time and called two other rela-
tively local Philip Holmans. Both times, I struck out.

I put Anna Holman's name into the search engine. I
found an Anna Holman Carter who lived in Boone and
was sixty-nine years old.

Fingers crossed, I punched in Anna Carter's phone number. When she answered, I introduced myself and asked if her father was Grady or Walter Holman, originally of Winter Garden, Virginia.

"Yes, he was. He hated the name 'Grady' and went by 'Walter.' Why? What's this about?"

"Well, I've got a crazy story to tell you."

Ms. Carter laughed. "Daddy was full of crazy stories. Let's hear yours."

I told Ms. Carter about my buying the café from Lou Lou Holman, leaving out the part where I'd found the woman murdered in her office. "When we renovated the café, we found a lockbox hidden in the wall. Inside we found a little money." I didn't want to tell this woman we'd found twenty thousand dollars in the box. After all, Ryan had asked for my discretion.

"Oh, heavens!"

"We turned the lockbox over to the police because we didn't know what else to do with it. My aunt remembered hearing rumors of Bo and Grady Holman robbing a bank in North Carolina. It was never proven, of course," I added quickly, "and no money was ever recovered, but no one here in Winter Garden could seem to figure out what had happened to Grady. Frankly, I think many people were afraid that either his brother or his nephew had done him in."

Ms. Carter chuckled. "Our family heard all about that bank robbery growing up. You see, the bank there in Winter Garden was about to foreclose on Daddy's farm. His brother Bo offered to take him to a bank here in North Carolina to see if they'd give Daddy a loan.

Daddy didn't realize Bo intended to rob the bank until Bo handed him a ski mask and a pistol."

"Poor Grady . . . or *Walter*!"

"Well, I don't know if it was 'poor Walter' or not. He went along with the plan. Course, if you'd ever met Daddy, you'd have seen he was one of the most easygoing men in the world."

Given Aunt Bess's description of Grady, he must've really changed his ways after moving to North Carolina.

"He'd have gone along with Bo just because Bo was his older brother and wanted him to do it," Ms. Carter continued. "I mean, what kind of man allows his brother to rob a bank by himself?"

She laughed, and I did too.

"After they'd got back to Winter Garden, though, Daddy's conscience started to eat at him, and he wanted to give back the money. Bo told him no, they'd go to jail. To hear Daddy tell it, Daddy wanted to put the money in a sack and leave it by the bank's front door."

"Somebody else would've surely come along and got it if they'd done that," I said.

"That's exactly what Bo told him. Bo said he'd hide the money and that when things died down, they'd figure out how to get the money back to the bank. But Daddy figured Bo was lying, and he just left. He knew the bank would foreclose on the farm, and he didn't care. He just wanted to start over somewhere new."

"Well, I'm so glad nothing bad happened to him."

"Me too, or else I wouldn't be here." She chuckled again. "We didn't hear that story until all of us young 'uns were grown and had children of our own. My sister, Sadie,

was incensed that Daddy had taken part in a bank robbery, but my brother, Phil, and I thought it was kinda neat. We never would've dreamed Daddy had an adventurous streak."

"Did Sadie eventually forgive him?"

"Not until he was on his deathbed," she said, an edge to her voice. "By the way, what ever happened to Bo?"

"He died in a tractor accident the year after he and his brother robbed the bank."

"Huh. And Lou. Did you ever meet him?"

"No. I did know his daughter, though."

"What was she like?" Ms. Carter asked.

I paused, trying to think of a nice way to describe Lou Lou.

Ms. Carter giggled. "That bad, huh?"

"A little bit. She was . . . a rough person to have to work for."

"Which is why you bought the café?"

"That, and I wanted to either buy Lou Lou's café or build my own," I said. "Buying an existing café was easier in the long run."

"I imagine it was."

"I appreciate your talking with me. I was just so curious about what happened to Grady. The rumors were that he'd died. And when I did the search and found his obituary, I wondered if Walter was *the* Grady Holman."

"Well, he sure was. Do you have any photos of the Winter Garden Holmans?" she asked. "And I'd love to meet some of my relatives if they're amenable to it."

"I'm sure I can round up some pictures from the newspaper office."

"Thank you. I'd enjoy looking at them."

"Tell you what," I said. "I'll see what I can dig up, and I'll talk with Pete Holman—he'd be your great-nephew—and give him your number. And maybe once the café is renovated, I can come over and have coffee with you sometime. I'd like to look at your photos too."

"I'm going to be in Mountain City late tomorrow afternoon. I know you're in the middle of a big project, but you've got my curiosity up. Is there any way you could meet me for coffee there somewhere? Mountain City is about halfway for both of us, isn't it?"

She was right about my stirring her curiosity. Surely, Roger could spare me—and Jackie—for a couple of hours. I told Ms. Carter yes, I'd love to meet.

As soon as I was finished talking with Anna Carter, I called Jackie.

"What's up?"

"I'm calling to see if you're up for a road trip tomorrow afternoon," I said.

"Where are we going?"

"Mountain City."

"What's in Mountain City?"

"Grady Holman's daughter."

She was so quiet that for a second I thought we'd been disconnected. "Grady Holman's daughter?"

"Yes."

"Why would we want to go to Mountain City to see Grady Holman's daughter?"

"Why wouldn't we?" I explained about my search for Grady and then filled her in on my chat with his daughter Anna Holman Carter. "Who knows? Maybe whatever happened to Grady—or Walter, as he called himself after leaving Winter Garden—has some bearing on what

happened to Lou Lou. What if getting to the bottom of the old mystery could help us solve the new one? So what do you say? Will you go with me?"

"I guess. I don't know what good you think it'll do, though. An eighty-year-old crime has nothing to do with Lou Lou's death. Have you talked with your hunky deputy about this?"

"No, I haven't mentioned it to him yet. I want to see if anything comes of it first. I figure it can't do any harm to talk with this woman."

She blew out a breath. "Okay. I'll go."

Chapter 18

George Lincoln came by the café on his way to work the next morning. I was making coffee and didn't realize he was there until the café became dark, and I looked around to see where the sun had gone. It was being blocked by Mr. Lincoln standing in the doorway.

"May I help you with something this morning?" I asked.

"I was on my way to work and merely stopped by to see how the renovations are coming." His upper lip curled as he looked around at the café. "You do realize this paint will have to go, don't you?"

"Excuse me?"

He spread his hands as if he were dropping a basketball. "This color scheme doesn't fit in with the historical society's guidelines. I'm afraid you've wasted your time and money on your yellow and blue paint. If you'll come

by the Chamber of Commerce, I'll get you a list of acceptable colors."

"But my entire color scheme has already been established! Everything we've ordered complements these colors!" It would cost so much time and money to completely repaint the café. Who did George Lincoln think he was coming in here telling me what colors were suitable for the historical society?

I heard Roger's voice from behind George Lincoln. "Coming through with some flooring!"

Mr. Lincoln moved aside and allowed Roger to pass. I noticed a red SUV parked outside and realized it must be Mr. Lincoln's vehicle.

Roger set the box he carried onto the floor. "Did I hear you say something about Amy's color scheme not working?"

"Indeed you did. It won't do at all."

"Everyone is entitled to his opinion," Roger said. "I think it'll do nicely."

"Not according to the historical society guidelines." Mr. Lincoln raised his chin.

"And when was this café declared a historical site?" Roger asked.

"Well, it hasn't been yet. But only because the meeting isn't being held until next month. It's only a matter of time." Mr. Lincoln looked from Roger to me. "You could've saved yourself a great deal of trouble had you checked with me prior to choosing your colors. In fact, you could've saved yourself even more trouble had you sold this place to me as I asked you to."

"I'm not selling the café, Mr. Lincoln," I said.

"Suit yourself." He looked around the café again.

"Although if you change your mind, I might still consider taking the place off your hands." He nodded to both Roger and me, and then he left.

I waited until he'd started the engine on his car before asking Roger if what Mr. Lincoln had said about the color scheme was true.

"I doubt it. But you might want to call Sarah and find out what Billy thinks about it."

"I will. Thanks." I put my hand on Roger's arm because he was about to go back and get another box of flooring. "Wait. While it's just the two of us, I wanted to talk with you for a second."

He squinted at me.

"It's nothing bad, I promise," I said.

"I know what it is, and I don't want to discuss it with you."

I changed tactics. "Fine, then. I *won't* tell you that Jackie and I are going to Mountain City after work today to meet with Grady Holman's daughter."

"What?"

I nodded. "Yeah. I found the woman yesterday when I was poking around on the Internet trying to find out what happened to Grady. Turns out, he died in 1984, but he left behind three children. One of them is Anna Holman Carter, and Jackie and I are meeting her for coffee."

"Why?"

"Ms. Carter wants to look at photos of the Holmans she's never seen. I'm going to the newspaper office at lunch to see what I can find."

"Are you sure about this?" he asked. "What do you hope to gain from meeting this woman?"

"I'm hoping she can give me a little more insight into the

Holmans, the bank robbery, and the money we found." I huffed. "You sound like Jackie. And speaking of Jackie, how did your date go?"

"I *knew* that's what you wanted to talk with me about."

"Of course it is." I grinned. "So?"

"So you were kidding about meeting this woman?"

"No," I said. "We're meeting her."

"Do you want me to come with you?"

"No . . . unless you'd like to go."

"I'd *like* to work over this evening and get this as much of this floor done as possible," he said. "But you know absolutely nothing about this woman."

"I know that she's, like, seventy years old. I think the meeting will be fine."

"And the date was nice, but don't you *dare* repeat that, Flowerpot," he said over his shoulder as he strode outside to get another box.

Smiling, I went to the kitchen to check on the biscuits. They weren't quite done, and it was too early to call Sarah. I fried some sausage.

As I was assembling the sausage biscuits, everyone else started coming in to work. Jackie wandered into the kitchen to see how I was doing.

"Need any help?" she asked.

"Nope, I've about got it."

"Were you and Roger here alone this morning?"

"We usually are. I told him that you and I are going to meet Grady Holman's daughter. Like you, he didn't think that was such a swell idea. But I'm dropping by the newspaper office at lunchtime to see what old photos I can dig up to take to Ms. Carter."

"That's nice. What else did you guys talk about?"

"George Lincoln's assertion that my color scheme will violate some sort of historical society code. Which reminds me, I need to call Sarah." I handed her the tray of biscuits. "Would you mind taking these out to the workers?"

Jackie took the tray outside, and I called Sarah.

"Good morning. Hancock Law Offices. How may I help you?"

"Hi, Sarah." I told her about George Lincoln's visit to the café earlier this morning.

"I think that man is just trying another tactic to get you to sell him the café. Billy is walking in the door now. Let me put you on hold while I get his take on this situation."

I listened to some instrumental pop music while waiting for Sarah to talk the matter over with Billy.

"Hey," Sarah said when she came back on the line. "Billy says Lincoln is blowing smoke. The café hasn't been deemed a historic site, and you can do anything you want with it. Even if the *land* is deemed a historic site, that has nothing to do with the café. You aren't in a historic *district*. So you're good. If Lincoln keeps hounding you, we'll file a harassment suit."

"Works for me. You know, I'm beginning to think George Lincoln might be as big a bully as Lou Lou was. It makes me wonder what else he might've done to get his hands on the café." I blew out a breath. "Thanks for your help, Sarah."

"Anytime. How are the renovations coming, besides the inappropriate color scheme, I mean?"

"Things are going great. I can hardly wait for you to see the place."

"I'll come by soon," she said. "Got another call. See ya!"

I left the kitchen and joined everyone else in the dining room. They were either sitting on the floor or standing as they ate their biscuits and drank their coffee. I grabbed a cup of coffee and wandered over to Homer.

"I'm having my biscuit early today," he said.

"Good for you. Change can be a positive thing. Who's your hero today?"

"The great jazz saxophonist John Coltrane. He died young at only forty, you know. But he teaches us that men are here to grow into the best good that they can be," he said. "That's what I'm trying to do."

"I think you're doing a wonderful job, Homer."

Roger gathered us around in a circle and gave us our assignments. The café crew was going to be helping him and one other man put down flooring here in the dining room.

"Johnny and I will help with the harder areas—corners and edges. The rest of it should be simple and straightforward. We'll go over it with you a couple of times before we actually get started. Don't hesitate to let us know if you have questions. Better to ask than for us to have to tear something out and redo it."

The construction crew would be working on the patio.

I stood, dusted off my shorts, and slipped on my heavy canvas gloves.

Knowing I wouldn't have time to make lunch for the workers, given my planned trip to the newspaper office, I called the pizza parlor and had them deliver pizza and breadsticks for lunch. It was a good thing I

did. We weren't even halfway finished with the floor by then. The work was harder than it had looked.

I grabbed a breadstick and a bottle of water before heading out to search through the *Winter Garden News* archives.

Ms. Peggy looked up from her perusal of a crossword puzzle when I walked through the door. "Back to run another ad?"

"No, actually I'm here to see if the newspaper would have any old photographs of the Holmans."

She frowned. "Why in the world would you want those? Honey, let the past be. That café is your place now."

I smiled. "I know. But Grady Holman's daughter wants to see some of her Winter Garden relatives."

"Grady Holman's daughter!" Ms. Peggy brought her palm up to rest just below her throat. "I didn't know Grady had any children!"

"He had three—two daughters and a son . . . after he moved to North Carolina."

"Land's sakes! Grady didn't die way back in the thirties, then?"

"He didn't die until 1984."

"Well, I'll be," she mused. "I always thought Bo killed Grady. I'd have gone to my grave thinking it if you hadn't just told me different."

I quickly explained about doing an online search and finding Grady's obituary as Walter Holman and then locating Anna Carter from that.

Ms. Peggy took a business card out of her desk drawer. "Ask Ms. Carter to call me. I want to do a story on Grady and let people know what became of him."

"I'll tell her." I took the card and slipped it into my purse. "About those photos?"

"Your best bet would be to do a search for the grand opening of Lou's Joint. Also look for Lou Lou's engagement and marriage announcement."

"Lou Lou was married?" I asked.

"Well, sure she was. You know good and well that Pete's her son."

"I know. But since everybody in the family is named *Holman*, I assumed that Lou Lou had . . . you know . . . given birth out of wedlock."

"Nope. She was married to Sherman Harding," she said. "They didn't stay married long, though. And when they got divorced, Lou Lou took back her maiden name and gave the baby her name too, since she was no longer a Harding when Pete was born."

I went into the archive room and sat down at the computer. Ms. Peggy was right. There were photographs from the grand opening and ribbon-cutting ceremony of Lou's Joint. Lou Lou had looked a lot like her father. There was an older man standing next to Lou. The caption indicated it was Bo Holman, Lou's father. He had bushy white hair and the appearance of a mountain man, but he didn't strike me as a bank robber. I supposed looks could be deceiving.

Bo's obituary was in the *Winter Garden News*, of course, but there wasn't a photograph to accompany it.

The Holman–Harding engagement was announced. I pulled up that article and saw a photo of a younger, thinner, smiling—that was the strangest part, since the woman seldom smiled—Lou Lou and a man who didn't look half bad. In fact, there was something about him

that seemed familiar. The pair actually made a hand-some couple.

I looked at the wedding announcement. Lou Lou, again smiling, was in a tea-length white gown with a hat and gloves. Sherman Harding stood beside her in a black suit. They were looking at each other rather than at the photographer. I wondered what could've possibly gone so wrong between them that Lou Lou would even strip their son of Sherman's last name. And Pete had obviously not grown up with Sherman Harding being a part of his life . . . at least, as far as I knew.

I retrieved the photos I'd printed and went back out to the front office.

"Ms. Peggy, what happened between Lou Lou and Sherman Harding? They seemed so happy in their engagement and wedding photos."

She smiled. "Everybody looks happy in their engagement and wedding photos, don't you reckon?"

"Yeah, I guess they do."

"It's too bad they can't stay that way. With Lou Lou and Sherman, rumor had it that he never stopped loving his first girlfriend, Becky. Sherman had taken up with Lou Lou while he and Becky were broken up. Becky even left here for a while and went to stay with some relatives up north somewhere."

"And let me guess," I said. "Becky came back, and she and Sherman rekindled those old feelings?"

"She came back with a son. He was born just a few months before Pete was."

"Dang. Sherman must've been a fast worker."

"I reckon Becky's parents thought people would think the boy was adopted or something if she went away for

a few months, but everybody knew. Everybody always knows," she said. "But, anyhow, that was the end of his romance with Lou Lou. When he saw his first love with his firstborn child, he left Lou Lou for Becky." She nodded toward the papers in my hand. "Did you get everything you need?"

"Yes." I paid her for the copies. "Thanks for everything."

"Don't forget to ask Grady's daughter—Ms. Carter, did you say?—to call me. I'd bet she has an interesting story to tell."

Chapter 19

When I got back to the café, I went around the side of the building to look at the patio. The builders had made a lot of progress today. They'd put up support beams and should be able to construct the roof next.

"Looking nice, don't you think?" Stan said, coming to stand next to me.

"It sure is." I studied his profile. There was something so familiar about him . . . something I couldn't quite figure out. "Y'all are doing a fantastic job. Thank you."

"I just do what I'm told. I'm tickled Roger saw fit to give me this job, even if it *is* only for a few days. I'd like to earn enough money to go home for Independence Day."

"So you haven't always lived here in Winter Garden, Stan?"

There were very few people who lived here who weren't born here. Some were born here and stayed, some

left and later returned, but there weren't many transplants. Mainly because it was such small town. Folks had either never heard of Winter Garden, or they wanted to live closer to the shopping malls and restaurants.

"No, ma'am. I'm originally from Pulaski."

"And your parents are still there?" I asked.

"My mom's passed on, but my dad is. I can't imagine him ever leaving . . . though if I do ever make enough money, I'd like to have him come here and live with me."

"That'd be nice. I think he'd like it here."

He smiled. "Me too."

I went back into the café and got to work on the floor.

After we'd finished up for the day, Jackie and I went into the kitchen to pack ourselves some dinner to take with us. I was making ham sandwiches, and she was putting chips into plastic baggies.

Roger walked into the kitchen. "Getting ready for the road trip, I see."

"Yep," Jackie said.

He ran his hand lightly down her arm. "Be careful. I think it's weird that this woman wants to meet with strangers to compare notes about her family."

"*She* probably thinks it's weird that I called her out of the blue about her dead father," I said.

"You've got a point there," Roger said. "You're both weirdos."

"And what am I?" asked Jackie.

"I guess you're the person going with her to make sure she doesn't get killed."

"As long as I'm not a weirdo."

"I didn't say that," he corrected.

I put our sandwiches into baggies and then put the sandwiches, chips, and packages of apple slices into an insulated tote.

"Did you find lots of interesting photos to share with Anna Carter?" Jackie asked.

"Yeah. You'll find them interesting too."

She and Roger exchanged glances.

"One of you let me know when you get back," Roger said.

"I will." Jackie smiled.

Once we were in the car, I said, "I take it you and Roger had a talk."

"We did. And we're on the same page with wanting to take things slowly but to see if there's more between us than friendship. We're going out again on Saturday night."

"Oh, good. Glad you're taking it *slowly*."

"What did you mean about my finding the photos interesting?" She got our sandwiches out of the tote. She took mine from the baggie and handed it to me.

I accepted the sandwich. "After we eat, you can look through them, and you'll know exactly what I mean. They're on the backseat."

"I can wait." She dropped her sandwich back into the tote, undid her seat belt, and reached into the backseat for the manila envelope. She refastened the seat belt and slid the photos from the envelope.

I ate while Jackie flipped through the photographs.

"Oh my gosh!"

"I think you just found the most interesting one," I said.

"Can you believe Lou Lou was ever this thin?"

"I can't believe she ever looked that happy. I imagine she was devastated when Sherman left. You see how happy she looks in those photos."

"Yeah, but come on, Amy. Who looks sad in engagement and wedding photos?"

"That's what Ms. Peggy said."

"And she said Lou Lou's husband left her—while she was pregnant—for another woman?" Jackie asked.

"Apparently. And the other woman also had a child by him."

"Did this Harding guy know Lou Lou was pregnant when he abandoned her?"

"I don't know. Maybe he didn't realize it."

"I'd hope not. I'd hate to think the man would abandon his child as well as his wife, but this could explain why Lou Lou never wanted to cut those apron strings."

"Yeah. It looks as if Pete really was all she had."

Lou Lou had been a miserable person. And she'd held to her son so tightly that, in ways, she'd lost him too. He hadn't even been able to share some of the most important parts of his life with her. I felt that she'd have been happy—or, at least, I wanted to hope she would have been—to have known her grandchild. Maybe she'd have adored the baby and given Pete her blessing to start his trucking career.

The coffee shop was in the middle of a strip of store buildings. There was an antiques store on one side and an art gallery on the other. The Hill o' Beans was a tan building with kelly green trim. Inside, floral curtains

were pulled back to let the waning sunshine in, and there were sofas and armchairs in addition to bistro tables and chairs.

A waitress spotted Jackie and me standing just inside the front door, looking clueless. Smiling brightly, she hurried over.

"Hi, there! Is either one of you Amy Flowers?" she asked.

"I am," I said.

"Ms. Carter is waiting for you right over here." She led us to a table where Anna Carter sat nursing a cup of coffee.

Ms. Carter stood when Jackie and I reached the table. "Hello. Thank you so much for coming."

I introduced her to Jackie, and we all sat down around the table. Jackie and I ordered coffee from the waitress, and she scampered off to get it.

"I'm looking forward to seeing what some of Daddy's relatives looked like," said Ms. Carter. "Did you have a chance to talk with my great-nephew yet? Pete, did you say his name was?"

"I haven't had a chance to speak with Pete yet, but I will." I took Ms. Peggy's business card from my purse and slid it across the table. "When I went to the newspaper office to get the photos, Ms. Peggy was interested in doing a story on your dad. She thought people—especially the older folks—would enjoy knowing how he spent his life after leaving Winter Garden."

"Okay. I'll consider giving her a call." She took a photo album from a tote she had sitting on the floor beside her chair. She opened it. "This is Daddy."

The sepia photograph had been taken when Grady

Holman was in his early twenties. His hair was dark, and he was smiling impishly at the photographer. He had on overalls and what appeared to be a white shirt. I glanced up at Ms. Carter, but I didn't see much of a resemblance. I passed the photo album on down closer to Jackie.

"He was a cutie pie, wasn't he?" she said to Ms. Carter.

"He certainly was." She sat a little taller in her seat.

I opened the manila envelope and took out the photo taken at the grand opening of Lou's Joint. "I can see the resemblance between your dad and Bo." Grady hadn't been as tall or as broad as Bo, nor did he have a beard, but their faces looked similar.

"And Lou took after them too," said Ms. Carter, her lips slowly curving into a smile. "Daddy was the better-looking of the two brothers, though, don't you think?"

Jackie and I agreed that he was.

Ms. Carter flipped through the photos. "And this was Lou's daughter? Poor thing . . . to be named Lou Lou."

"I always heard Lou wanted a son," said Jackie.

"Apparently, he wanted two of them." Ms. Carter chuckled.

Jackie and I thumbed through the photo album.

"You must take after your mom's side of the family," I said, noting that the diminutive Ms. Carter looked nothing like the Holmans I knew.

"I do. My brother is tall and muscular." She grinned. "Mother always said thank goodness we girls took after her people."

"Did your dad ever talk about his family back in Winter Garden?" Jackie asked.

"He spoke of Bo pretty often. I believe he missed his brother." She ran a fingertip over the photocopy of Bo's

obituary. "I wonder if he knew Bo had died, or if he just thought his brother had forgotten about him."

"If Grady was in touch with anybody back home, then he knew what happened," I said. "You mentioned over the phone that Grady had told you about the bank robbery."

"He had." She shook her head. "I always figured it was one of his tall tales. I mean, some of the stories he told about growing up in that little town in Virginia with Bo . . . they couldn't possibly have been true." She looked again at the photo of Bo and Lou at the café's ribbon-cutting ceremony. "I thought there was maybe a grain of truth to them but that Daddy had exaggerated."

"So you didn't believe that he and Bo had robbed a bank?" Jackie asked.

"I thought maybe they'd tried . . . or even that they had made a teller slip them a few dollars. But Daddy told me his conscience bothered him too bad to keep it, and he gave the money back."

"I don't imagine Bo was very happy about that," I said.

"No, he wasn't. That drove the wedge between them that made Daddy leave Winter Garden and head for North Carolina to look for work," said Ms. Carter.

When Jackie and I were in the car on our way back home, I mentioned that Ms. Carter had changed her story about the bank robbery.

"Over the phone last night, she told me that Bo had driven Grady over to the bank in North Carolina and that Grady hadn't known they were going to rob the bank until Bo handed him a ski mask and a pistol."

"And then Grady just went along with it?"

"According to Ms. Carter, he did. She spoke as if Grady would've done anything his big brother wanted him to do."

"But she also told us that Grady had given the money back," Jackie said. "If that's the truth, where did the money in the lockbox come from?"

"I mentioned the lockbox to her over the phone too. I said there was money inside, but I didn't tell her how much. Now I wish I hadn't said anything about it."

"Amy! She might come looking for that money!"

"You saw her. Do you really believe she'd burst through the doors of the café, guns blazing, to demand her daddy's stolen money? Besides, I told her the money was in police custody."

"I don't think she'd do it herself, but her children might be like Bo, Grady, and Lou. Or, worse yet, Lou Lou!" Jackie said. "If they think there's anything to be gained here, they might come after you."

"I rather doubt it. I imagine the woman simply wanted to paint her father in the best possible light. Or what if Grady told his daughter the truth, and he really *did* return the money to the bank?" I asked. "Do you think the twenty thousand dollars was Bo's part of the money? Or do you think the money found in the lockbox had nothing to do with the bank after all? Maybe the money belonged to Lou."

"That's possible." She frowned. "Now I'm wondering what other skeletons linger in Lou Holman's closet."

"We know Sherman Harding was one. Wonder whatever became of him."

"I don't know, but I'm guessing you'll be burning up that laptop of yours tonight to try to find out."

"You've got that right," I said.

* * *

Jackie had been right. I wanted to find out more about this man who'd been married to Lou Lou Holman and had then thrown her over for another woman. So I got out my laptop as soon as I got home to see what I could learn.

I had no luck finding Sherman Harding until I downloaded a free trial for a genealogy site and searched for him there. That's where I found Sherman Harding, who had been married to Rebecca Minton Harding. And they had one son—Stanley Wheeler Harding.

Wait . . . what?!

I sat staring at my laptop as my cursor kept blinking on the name "Stanley Wheeler Harding." Stanley Harding. Stan Harding. Stan *Wheeler* Harding.

Oh my goodness. Was that true? It had to be. It's why Stan's profile had looked so familiar after I'd seen the photo of Sherman Harding. Stan Wheeler was Sherman Harding's son. He was Pete's half brother.

Had Lou Lou known? I thought back to the paper I'd seen in the box from her office. Was that why she'd written Stan's name and drawn the fish beside it? Did she think Stan was fishing for something? Or did she think there was something fishy about Stan?

At least, I now knew why, after seeing the photograph of Sherman Harding, something about Stan struck me as being familiar. And if I saw a resemblance, even though I couldn't quite recall why, surely Lou Lou—having been married to Sherman—could see his likeness in his son. Funny, though, Pete looked nothing like Sherman. He took after the Holman side of the family.

I thought about my conversation with Anna Carter and promising I'd talk with Pete to see if he'd be willing to talk with her. There might be another family member he'd be even more interested in speaking with.

So what was Stan doing in Winter Garden? Why was he here as Stan Wheeler rather than Stan Harding? And how long had he been here? It had obviously been long enough to establish a seedy reputation. Maybe I should talk with Ryan about this. He'd told me to let me know of any leads I came across. This could be considered a lead. I'd give him a call tomorrow.

Something very, very strange was going on with Stan Wheeler.

Chapter 20

The shrill noise woke me, but it was Rory's barking along with it that fully brought me from sleep to wakefulness. I rose up onto my elbow, gently pushed Rory's face out of mine, and answered the phone.

"Hello?"

"Morning, Flowerpot! Rise and shine!"

It was Roger. I looked at the clock. It was six a.m. "I refuse to rise or shine this early. What's wrong?" I had a sudden fear that the café was on fire.

"Nothing really. I just wondered if you'd give your staff the day off. It's pouring rain, and my guys can't work on the patio today, so I thought we'd work inside."

"And you don't want us in your way," I said.

"Precisely. You catch on quickly for a foggy-brained sleepyhead."

"What would you like me to bring for breakfast?"

"Nothing, thanks. I'll stop and get a box of dough-nuts. We wouldn't turn down lunch, though."

"You got it. Are sandwiches all right?"

"That'll be great," said Roger. "Thanks."

"Thank you. Not having to come in so early will be wonderful."

"Rub it in, why don't you?"

I laughed. "Do I need to tell Jackie, or does she know already?"

"I told her when we spoke last night that if it rained like the forecast was calling for, I was going to ask you to give the café staff the day off. You might want to remind her, though."

"I will. See you at lunchtime."

I hung up the phone. Rory had already snuggled back up against me. He was so warm and cozy. And I could hear the rain pounding against the roof. I dropped my head back onto my pillow. My alarm was set for six thirty. I'd snooze until then.

It was seven o'clock before I finally dragged my butt out of bed and called the café workers. Like me, they were thrilled not to have to work on such a rainy day. Jackie offered to come by and help with lunch, but I assured her that I had it under control. I'd planned to make sandwiches, potato wedges, and cookies. Easy to make, and easy to transport.

While I was at it, I thought I'd make a small tray of sandwiches to take to Pete and Chris Anne. I wanted to talk with Pete about his father and find out what he knew about Stan.

When I spoke with Homer, I promised to add a sausage biscuit to the lunch and have it for him at the café. He understood that he didn't have to work today, but he said he would drop by anyway to see if Roger needed his help. Homer was such a good guy.

I washed the potatoes, dried them, and cut them into wedges. I preheated the oven while gathering my spices. I put salt, pepper, and garlic powder into a large plastic baggie. I then added the potato wedges. I gave the mixture a good shake, added olive oil, and shook them again.

While the potatoes were baking, I made turkey, ham, tuna, and pimiento cheese sandwiches. I cut them into fourths, so they'd stand up nicely on the trays and the workers could see what kinds of sandwiches there were to choose from. When I took the potatoes from the oven, I sprinkled them with Parmesan cheese. I put the potato wedges in a pan lined with parchment paper to transport them to the café.

Fortunately, I had some frozen biscuits in my freezer, so it was no problem to add Homer's sausage biscuit to the food I was delivering. I also had frozen cookie dough, so while the oven was hot, I was able to make three dozen chocolate chip cookies.

I dropped off the food at the café. Homer was there, helping Roger's crew with something in the kitchen. I gave him his sausage biscuit, and he thanked me.

"Who's your hero today?"

"Jacques Cousteau, Mademoiselle."

I smiled. *"Fantastique!"*

I found Roger, told him I was delivering a sandwich tray to Pete and Chris Anne, and said I'd be back to help afterward.

"You don't have to do that. We've got everything under control. Enjoy today."

"But Homer is here. I can't *not* be here when Homer is here working. This is my café. I should be here."

"And, like Homer, you'll be underfoot and kinda in the way," Roger whispered. "And we'll have to give you something to do so you don't realize that you're under-foot and in the way."

"Fine, but I'll still come back by here after I go to Pete's house to make sure you don't need my help with anything."

"All right. Take your time," he said.

"Gee, you know how to make a girl feel appreciated."

"You want to feel appreciated? Be here when we dive into those boxes of food."

I laughed. "See you later."

I flipped the hood up on my jacket as I sprinted back out to the car. The rain was still coming down hard. I slid behind the wheel, put on my headlights, and drove to Pete's house.

I pulled into the driveway and was glad to see only Pete's brown pickup truck there. It might be easier to talk with him without Chris Anne around. I went to the door and rang the bell.

Pete answered the door and invited me inside.

"Where's Chris Anne?" I asked, carrying the sandwiches through to the kitchen. "I brought you two some lunch."

"That's thoughtful of you, and I'll try to save her some, but she's out garage-saling. I told her I doubted there'd be many people having sales today since it's raining so hard, but she hopes to find some bargains for the baby."

"Maybe she'll have good luck," I said. "I've heard you can find some great baby items at garage and thrift sales."

"That's what she's counting on."

"So, Pete, what are you hoping for? A boy or a girl?"

He shrugged his bony shoulders. "I don't reckon it matters. We're just praying the baby'll be healthy."

"How about your trucking business? Any luck finding a tractor and trailer yet?"

"I believe I've found the semi I want. Right now I'm dickering with the salesman to get him to come down a little on the price."

"Well, I'm glad you can haggle. I sure don't like to."

He chuckled. "Live with Momma for forty years. I don't know how *not* to haggle!"

I laughed but saw the opening I'd been waiting for. "What about your dad, Pete? Is he still in your life?"

His smile completely disappeared, and his lips curled in revulsion. "My daddy was never part of my life. He took off on Momma when she was pregnant."

"I'm so sorry to hear that."

"Yeah, well, that's just one of them things." He jerked his head toward the tray I'd sat on the table. "I appreciate the lunch. I'll save it until Chris Anne gets home. Does it need to go in the fridge?"

"It does," I said. "Just one other thing, Pete. I know you're considering Stan Wheeler for your partner. How well do you know him?"

"Pretty good, I guess. We've been friends since he moved here"—he squinted up at the ceiling—"a little over a year ago now."

"I don't know that I'd trust him enough to go into business with him," I said. "You've got this fresh new start. I don't want anything to jeopardize that for you."

He laughed. "Listen at you sounding like a baby

sister! I kinda like it. I always wanted a brother or a sister."

If he only knew. I wanted to tell him about Stan, but I was afraid to. For one thing, I wasn't sure what game Stan had been playing, coming here to Winter Garden under an assumed name . . . or, at least, not his full name. And for another, Pete had been through so much with his mother's death already. I didn't want to be the one to add to his stress.

"I'd better be getting back to the café. If y'all need anything, let me know."

"Thank you, Amy. We appreciate the kindness."

I got back into the car, shivering slightly from the onslaught of the cold rain, and backed out of Pete's driveway.

I couldn't imagine Pete would entertain friendly thoughts toward Stan Wheeler if he knew Stan was his half brother. He certainly had no warm, fuzzy feelings toward his father. Did he even know his father's name? I wondered what story Pete had been told . . . and who might know.

I went back to the café. The workers were taking their lunch break. Homer was sitting at the counter, sort of off to himself. I sat down beside him.

"Homer, may I ask you something?"

"You can ask me anything. I might not know the answer, but maybe I'll be able to help you find it."

I told him about my visit to Pete and my mentioning his father. "It's apparent that Pete can't stand his dad. I didn't know the Holmans personally until I came to work here last year. When Nana was living—before she got sick, I mean, and while I was growing up here in Winter

Garden—we didn't eat out much. Nana was an absolutely wonderful cook." I realized I was getting off track. "Anyway, I'd never heard anything about Pete's father or Lou Lou's situation. It had never really crossed my mind until now."

"Word around town at the time of Mr. Harding's departure was that he'd either been in an auto accident and had been placed in a rehab facility close to where his parents lived or that he'd returned to his first love," said Homer. "But, of course, Lou Lou went back to using her maiden name and gave the name to her child as well. That made us all believe that he'd just thrown Lou Lou over, and we correctly assumed that the Holman family didn't want mention made of Mr. Harding anymore."

"Pete told me his father ran out on his mother when she was pregnant. Why didn't anyone tell him the story about the auto accident?"

"Listen, *chérie*, Lou Holman was as hard as nails, and he laid down the law where his family was concerned. I have no doubt that he got rid of Sherman Harding—paid him to stay away or threatened him or something—and then told Lou Lou what she was to tell her son."

I glanced around to make sure Stan Wheeler wasn't within earshot, and lowered my voice. "Did you know that Stan is Pete's half brother?"

"I did not. I'm guessing no one else here does either. These people aren't Lou Lou's contemporaries; they're Pete's. Pete's father left Winter Garden before he was born. None of these younger people remember him."

"No, of course, they wouldn't." I told Homer about my findings the night before. "But Lou Lou *had* to have guessed who Stan Wheeler was . . . or, at least suspected.

He looks a lot like his father, judging from the photograph that was in the newspaper."

"I imagine she would have."

"Then why didn't she turn Stan away?" I asked. "Ask him to leave Winter Garden?"

"Perhaps Stan held the truth over her . . . threatened to tell Pete what he knew if she didn't do as he asked. Or maybe Lou Lou never recovered from her lost love, and she wanted news of Sherman. She might've even entertained thoughts of the two of them reuniting." He spread his hands. "The only person who could tell us her reasons has been silenced . . . that is, unless Stan knows."

"Yeah." I wondered if Sherman Harding might be able to give me some insight into Lou Lou's behavior. "I have to run. I'll check with Roger before I go to see if he needs anything."

"*À bientôt!*"

The French thing was odd. It was okay for a day, but I think it would wear thin after a while. Luckily, Homer would have a new hero tomorrow.

At home, I discussed the feasibility of calling Sherman Harding with Rory. I tried to include Princess Eloise in the discussion; but she merely gave me a disdainful look, turned her back, and glared out the window at the rain. I didn't know whether to interpret her silence as disapproval or not, so I continued to hash out my reasoning with Rory.

"What harm could it do?" I asked the furry little terrier. "I could tell Mr. Harding that I was going through some archives for a relative of Grady Holman—which

was true—and that I came across a wedding announcement for Lou Lou Holman and Sherman Harding. Then
I could ask if *he* is that Sherman Harding and then tell
him I thought he might be interested to know that Ms.
Holman passed away. And maybe he'll open up and give
me a clue as to what his son is doing here in Winter
Garden. What do you think?"

Rory barked.

"Okay." I got the phone. "Let's do this."

He wagged his tail and looked up at me expectantly.

"Let's see how this goes, and then I'll get you a treat.
I might need one myself."

I used the phone to look up listings for Sherman
Harding in Pulaski, Virginia. There was only one number. I called it.

After what seemed like forty rings but was probably
more like five, a gruff, wheezy male voice answered. "Hello."

"Hi. Is this Sherman Harding?"

"Yes. Who's this?"

"My name is Amy Flowers. I live in Winter Garden."

My announcement was met with silence, so I plunged on.

"I was going through some of the *Winter Garden News*
archives for a relative of Grady Holman, and I came
across a wedding announcement for Sherman Harding
and Lou Lou Holman," I said. "Were you ever married
to Lou Lou Holman?"

"For a very short while. Why do you ask?"

"Well, I thought you might want be interested to know
that she passed away about a week ago."

"Sorry to hear that."

He didn't seem surprised. He didn't sound particularly sorry either.

"Also, there's a man named Stan here in town, and I wondered if you were any relation."

"Yes, but I don't see how my relatives are any of your business," said Mr. Harding. "Anything else you need to know?"

"Well, actually, I wondered if Ms. Holman had been in touch with you before she died."

"Nope. Hadn't talked with any of the Holmans in years."

"Were you aware that Ms. Holman had a son named Pete?" I asked.

"Yep. Seems like that was her business."

"You're not Pete's father?"

"Didn't say that," he said. "I want to know how you figure any of this is *your* business, miss?"

"It isn't—"

"Right," Mr. Harding interrupted. "So stay out of it."

"But wait! Please!" I listened to make sure he hadn't ended the call.

"What?"

"Ms. Holman was murdered. I found her, and I'm trying to find out if anyone had a motive to kill her."

"And what? You think I did it?" He began to laugh, but it turned into a coughing fit.

"No, sir," I said once he'd recovered. "I don't suspect you at all. It's just that you have a history with the Holmans, so I thought you might be able to provide me with some insights."

"That girl should've never allowed her daddy to keep her under his thumb the way she did. But she made her choice. That's why I'm here and she and her boy are not. I imagine Lou Holman made a lot of enemies in his day,

and given Lou Lou's penchant for being the spitting image of him, she probably did too. I'd appreciate it if you don't call here again."

"All right. Thank you for your time."

He wheezed. "I'm sorry for your troubles, miss. But I can't help you."

"I know. Again, I appreciate your talking with me."

"You're welcome."

After talking with Sherman Harding, I felt deflated. I went into the kitchen and got Rory a treat, and I got myself a cookie. Then I went back to the living room and flopped onto the sofa.

I felt that what Mr. Harding *hadn't* said was as important as what he had said. He'd given me the impression that had Mr. Holman allowed it, he'd have stayed married to Lou Lou. But he'd been shut out—and possibly paid off—by Lou Holman. And Lou Lou had apparently let it happen.

So why had Lou Lou rented a home to Stan when he'd arrived in Winter Garden? Had she made the connection between Stan and her former husband? Or had she known that Stan was Sherman's son and had she rented the mobile home to him so she could find out why he'd come to town? Did Stan know about his father's brief marriage to Lou Lou and the fact that Pete was his half brother?

And had someone killed to make sure one or all of these secrets stayed buried?

Chapter 21

I called Ryan to get his thoughts on the situation. When I explained that I'd both met with Grady Holman's daughter and talked with Sherman Harding, he told me he was in the area and would stop by my house.

I put some chocolate chip cookies on a plate and made a fresh pitcher of iced tea. I also brushed my hair and freshened my makeup. I realized it was a police investigation and not a date, but that didn't mean I had to look my worst.

When Ryan arrived, we decided to speak on the front porch. I put the cookies, pitcher of tea, and plastic tumblers on a tray and placed it on the table between the two white rocking chairs.

"Thank you," he said with a grin. "Southern hospitality at its finest."

"I try. I hope that's what people will say about the

Down South Café once it's up and running. Well, that and that the food is delicious."

"If these cookies are any indication, your food is outstanding."

I smiled. "Thank you."

"So, you've been investigating, huh?"

"In a way . . . I guess I have."

"You do know that's the sheriff's department's job and that it's also our job to protect the citizens of Winter Garden—including you—right?"

I nodded.

"And unless I've missed some background on you somewhere, you aren't trained to investigate crimes."

"No, sir."

"All right," he said. "Tell me what you've got."

I told him about calling Grady Holman's daughter and later meeting her for coffee. "She told two different stories about the bank robbery, but in both versions, she said Grady gave the money back."

"It could be nothing," Ryan said. "Maybe Grady really did give the money back and the money found when the office wall was torn down belonged to either Bo or Lou. We're trying to track the money and see where it came from. But it's taking some time since it's so old and the original bank that was robbed back in the thirties is no longer there."

"When I was searching for photographs of the Holmans for Grady's daughter, I ran across Lou Lou's engagement and wedding announcements. That's when I realized she'd been married to Stan Wheeler's father." I took a drink of my tea. "I didn't know at first that he was Stan's father, but

now I do, and I can't help but think that somehow Lou Lou's secrets about her past played some part in her murder."

"We need to figure out where Lou Lou stood with regard to Sherman and Stan. Did she want to reconnect with her ex-husband?" He bit into a cookie while he studied the situation. "Who would Lou Lou have confided in? Who were those closest to her?"

"In the year that I worked with her, I don't know of anyone who struck me as being Lou Lou's friend. She had employees, suppliers, customers, and Pete. That was about the extent of her social circle."

"I'll see what Ivy confiscated from Lou Lou's office. Maybe there's a date book or something that might provide some answers for us."

I gazed at his profile. "Could I maybe help?"

"If there is a date book or planner among the items Ivy took from Lou Lou's office, it would be potential evidence, Amy. You aren't supposed to be around while I'm examining evidence."

"Please, Ryan. This is my life on the line here. I want to help."

He glanced over at me.

"Please."

His expression softened. "Of course, if you were to be at the library in half an hour and I happened to be there looking at the documents, I couldn't very well ask you to leave." He held up a hand. "I'm not going to let you look at anything, but you might be able to give me some insight into the names I'm not familiar with."

I smiled. "I'll see you then."

*   *   *

The Winter Garden Library was housed in a small brick building with floor-to-ceiling windows trimmed in white. The door was also white and heavy, and there were window panels on each side.

I walked inside, my sandaled feet clicking on the tile foyer until I reached the gray industrial carpet covering the floor inside the main part of the library. The building smelled fresh and clean. It had been remodeled since I'd been here as a little girl. Back then, the entire floor was tile and the library had smelled of leather book spines and old musty pages. I was sure there must still be some ancient leather-bound books around here somewhere, but most of the books sitting on the carts to be reshelved were brand-new, current bestsellers.

I looked around the room. Ryan hadn't said where he'd be. I supposed I could ask for him at the circulation desk, but he might not appreciate that. He might prefer I pretend our meeting was accidental. Either way, the clerk sitting behind the long wooden desk was chatting on the phone and didn't appear to be inclined to do anything else.

I spotted Ryan at a rectangular wooden table at the back of the room. He sat on the chair facing the door, and there was an empty chair in front of him.

"Is this seat taken?" I asked, pulling out the chair.

"Why, no. What brings you here, Ms. Flowers?"

"I thought I might take a look at some of the cookbooks of old to see if there's anything I might want to revive for the Down South Café."

"Then please grab a book and join me."

"Oh . . . yeah." I stood and took a book off the nearest shelf. It was a psychology textbook that had nothing to do with cooking. Still, it was a book. "Have you found anything?"

"There doesn't seem to be anything out of the ordinary in these ledgers."

"Wait. I thought Pete got the ledgers from the safe."

"The ledgers from the safe were probably old ones. These are current."

I tried not to look, but I couldn't help but see that the dates on the page Ryan was looking at were from two months ago. "Did Lou Lou have a date book?"

"She kept a calendar," he said. "It looks like she was seeing someone named Sissy every Wednesday. Do you know anyone named Sissy who might've visited Lou Lou at the café?"

I shook my head slowly. *Sissy . . . Sissy . . . Why did that name ring a bell?* "Sissy's Scissors!"

"Excuse me?"

I lowered my voice. "Sorry. Lou Lou left every Wednesday to have her hair done. She must've gone to Sissy's Scissors in Meadowview. Nana used to go there."

"Lots of women gossip with their hairstylists . . . or so I've heard. I'll see if anyone has talked with this woman yet, and if not, I'll get right on that. Thanks for your help."

I wasn't content to let the matter lie. I went out to my car, called Sissy, and learned that she had had a cancellation and would be able to see me in the next thirty minutes if I could get there by then. I said I'd be right over.

*   *   *

Apparently, Sissy had just finished giving an elderly woman a perm when I walked into her salon. The smell nearly brought tears to my eyes.

"Hi, hon!" Sissy, a woman with the top half of her hair platinum and the bottom half jet-black, called to me. "I'll be finished up here in a minute!" She was teasing the white tightly curled hair of the woman in the chair in front of her to the point where the hair was probably thinking it had had enough of this nonsense. She was about go from teasing it to making it downright mad.

I sat on a nearby black vinyl and stainless steel chair to watch Sissy—a wisp of a woman dressed in black capris, a black T-shirt, and silver ballet flats—poof up the rest of her client's hair. When she was finished, she instructed, "Close your eyes, sweetie!" before blasting the hair with so much hairspray that I could've sworn a mushroom cloud lingered over the poor lady's head.

"All done!" Sissy announced brightly. "You're beautiful!"

"Thank you." The woman reached into a large brown purse that she held on her lap and took out a wallet.

"No, sweetie, your daughter has done paid for you this week. Remember?"

"Oh. Well, here's a little something extra." She handed Sissy a dollar.

"You're so sweet. Thank you." She shoved the dollar into her pants pocket before helping the woman to the door and holding it open for her. "See you next time." When the woman left, Sissy turned to me. "What're we doing for you today, hon?"

"I thought I'd like an updo . . . something kind of intricate." I wanted to make sure I had adequate time to talk with Sissy.

She smiled. "Got a big date, huh? Good for you! Come on over and have a seat."

I sat down on the chair vacated by Ms. Perm, and Sissy draped me with a black cape. She took a book and showed me the hairstyle she had in mind. It appeared that it would certainly take a while, so I went with it.

"I don't think you've ever been here before," she said. "I never forget a face. Unless, of course, you were here when Tina or one of the other girls was working."

"No . . . this is my first time."

"How'd you hear about us?"

"Well, I worked for Lou Lou Holman," I said. "I know she came by here every week."

"Oh yeah . . . God rest her poor soul. What's gonna happen to the Joint now that Lou Lou's gone?"

"I bought it. Pete wants to go into the trucking business, so he sold Lou's Joint to me. I'm in the process of doing a little remodeling, and I hope to reopen as the Down South Café in a few weeks."

"Kudos to you, darling! It does my heart good to know somebody is going to run the place. The good Lord knows Winter Garden needs something better than that pizza place to keep us going . . . am I right? I mean, I like pizza all right, but theirs isn't the best in the world, and besides that, we need some variety. Am I right?"

"You're absolutely right," I said, wanting to steer the conversation back to my reason for being here. "Poor Lou Lou. I never knew her to miss a hair appointment."

"Yep. She had a standing Wednesday appointment.

Had it for as long as I've been in business, as a matter of fact." She took a small comb from a container of disinfecting solution, shook it out, and then began using it to separate my hair into sections. She took clips and secured the sections of my hair out of the way of the one she planned on working with first. "Gosh, I guess it's been twenty years since I started doing her hair."

"Wow. So you've known Lou Lou a long time."

"I reckon I have."

"I'm beginning to feel like I didn't know her at all," I said. "I mean, I'd been working for her for a year, but I didn't know anything about her marriage until just the other day."

"Oh yeah, that was a sore spot for her." Sissy began curling tiny sections of my hair and pinning them on top of my head.

"About that. I made the mistake of asking Pete about his father. You know, I wondered if maybe they were close. Pete took his mother's death so hard and everything."

"Hon, I know your heart was in the right place, but Pete knows absolutely nothing about his daddy. He thinks his daddy was some kind of jerk who just ran off and left his mother while she was pregnant," Sissy said. "Lou Lou said she told him his daddy's name was Joe Smith or something because she never wanted Pete to try to find the man."

"I can understand Lou Lou's pain, but didn't she think Pete deserved to know the truth about his father?"

"Well, you see, Lou Lou thought for years that Sherman had left her because he was in love with that other girl," said Sissy. "But he wasn't."

I winced as a bobby pin poked a little too enthusiastically into my scalp. "Then why did he marry the other girl?"

"I guess he figured he might as well. And he got to raise one of his children that way. Anyhow, Lou Lou's momma finally told her on her deathbed that her daddy was the reason Sherman left."

"Lou paid him off," I mused.

"I believe it started out that way, but Sherman wouldn't leave for money. Mrs. Holman told Lou Lou that Lou and Sherman had fought and that her daddy had stabbed Sherman. Sherman nearly died." Sissy nodded at my shocked expression in the mirror. "Lou and one of his friends took Sherman to the emergency room and dumped him out of the car. Then they took off. But they made it clear to Sherman that if he stayed in Winter Garden, they'd kill him. They told him to leave and never come back."

"And Lou was never arrested for the assault?"

Sissy shook her head. "Sherman just got out of town before Lou made good on his promise. Lou Lou said she wondered if Sherman had thought she'd reach out to him, but she didn't. She believed the tale her daddy had told her. And then she'd gone for so many years hating him for breaking her heart. . . ."

"It seems like she made sure that Pete hated him too," I said.

"Yep."

"Why didn't she tell Pete the truth when she found out what Lou had done?"

"She was afraid that Pete would go to Sherman . . . you know, meet him to see what he was like." She finished

pinning the tiny curls up onto my head and took down another section to work with. "See, by the time she learned what had really happened, Pete was all Lou Lou had. What if Pete blamed her for letting her daddy run Sherman off? What if he'd gotten to know Sherman and decided he could have a better life in Pulaski with Sherman and his family than with Lou Lou in Winter Garden?"

"I doubt that thought would've ever crossed his mind," I told her. "Pete adored his mother."

"But would he have if he'd found out the truth?" Sissy asked.

"Of course he would! He'd know that Lou Lou wasn't responsible for the actions of her father."

"Maybe and maybe not. Hon, losing Pete was Lou Lou Holman's biggest fear."

I could see that now. It was evident in everything she'd done.

I felt a pang of pity for Lou Lou. I could see now how she'd become the bitter woman I'd known.

Sissy handed me a mirror. "See what you think, gorgeous!"

"Wow." I hadn't seen hair this big since senior prom . . . photos of *Mom's* senior prom, to be exact.

Sissy was looking at me expectantly.

"Looks incredible!" I smiled, paid her for my enormous hair, gave her a tip, and left the salon.

It was a good thing Sissy had put enough pins in my hair to supply beauty pageants along the entire East Coast and had used half a can of spray to hold the updo in place, because it smushed against the top of the Beetle when I slid behind the wheel.

I called Ryan to ask him to give me some time before

heading to my house. I wanted to take my hair down and wash it before he saw me. But my call went to voice mail.

Oh well, when I got home, I could at least take a selfie—front and back—so that Jackie and I could laugh over the hair later. It wasn't that it was ugly. It was just big. Texas big. Sissy had done an excellent job of piling all of my hair up onto my head in a . . . well, an elaborate way.

W hen I pulled into my driveway, Ryan's red convertible was already there. And Ryan was sitting on my front porch. I groaned as I parked the car.

Dang.

He smirked as I maneuvered my head out of the car. "I knew you'd do it. I *knew* you'd do it!"

I raised my chin. "What did you expect? Like I told you, this is my life on the line."

He blew out a breath and shook his head. "You're impossible—you know that?"

I walked up the stairs and sat on the porch beside Ryan. "Have you been here long?"

"Only a few minutes. So did you learn anything valuable on your fishing expedition?"

"You mean, besides the answer to the question of how many bobby pins my head can hold without spraining my neck?" I smiled. "I found out that Lou Lou's mother confessed to her on her deathbed that her dad had been responsible for making Sherman Harding leave Winter Garden."

"After finding out, what did Lou Lou do with the information?"

"Apparently nothing. Sissy said that Lou Lou was afraid

to tell Pete the truth because she was scared that he'd want to meet his father and that, after meeting his father, Pete would want to go live with him."

"And then when Stan showed up, did she figure out the truth about his identity?" Ryan prompted.

"I don't know. Apparently, that was the one thing she didn't confide to her hairdresser. Incidentally, Lou Holman stabbed Sherman—he didn't pay him off. I think I should find out from Stan exactly what he knew before he came to Winter Garden and what he learned after he got here."

"I'll be the one talking with Stan."

I shook my head, which wasn't an easy feat, given its size and weight at this point. "He'd be more likely to talk with me. He said he'd been in jail before, so I imagine he'd be defensive around police officers."

"No dice. I'll tell him that we've learned that his father was once married to Lou Lou Holman and ask what his intentions were when he came to Winter Garden."

"Okay. I hope you find out something useful."

Chapter 22

After Ryan left, I went inside and fed the pets. I was getting ready to take the selfies for Jackie, and then wash my hair, when Stan Wheeler pulled into my driveway. I felt a chill run down my spine. I had no idea what this man was hiding, and I didn't want to be inside my house alone with him. I'd keep him out here on the porch, where all the neighbors could see us. I desperately hoped I could get my questions answered after all. I still thought the man would be more forthcoming with me than he would be with Ryan.

I stepped out onto the porch and pasted on a bright smile. "Hi, Stan!"

"Hey. I knocked off early because I wanted to talk with you. I heard about you calling my dad."

"I did. I . . . um . . . found out that Mr. Harding had been married to Lou Lou Holman, and I phoned to let him know she died last week."

"Why in the world would you do that?" he asked.

"Well . . ." I swallowed. "I thought maybe he'd like to know what happened to her."

"That was a long time ago," he said. "More than forty years, as a matter of fact. Why would he care? Why would *you*? Dad hadn't been in Lou Lou's life for nearly four decades."

"Um . . . yeah . . . looking back, it might not have been such a good idea. I learned he was your dad, though, because you two look so much alike. Or, at least, you know . . . you look like he looked when he was younger. I've obviously only seen the two photos . . . and those were grainy newspaper pictures . . . so what do I know?"

He shook his head. "What are you babbling on about?"

Stan was right. I *was* babbling. I needed to suck it up and to find out what I wanted to know. "Did Lou Lou know you were Sherman Harding's son?"

"Maybe. So what?"

"Did you know her history with your dad? And that Pete is your half brother?" I asked.

"Sure. Dad told me all of that before I left Pulaski."

"So, why did you come to Winter Garden? Did you want to meet your half brother . . . maybe make a connection with him?"

"I didn't give it a lot of thought." He put his hands on his hips. "I wanted to see them mainly . . . to just find out a little bit about who they were. I mean, they were important to Dad once . . . you know?"

"Of course. I can understand that. But you've been here for over a year. Why did you stay?"

"I don't see how any of this is your business," Stan said. "In fact, I'll call Roger tonight and tell him I'm

quitting because I don't want to work anywhere near you anymore." He turned to go.

"Wait, Stan. I'm sorry. I just . . . Why haven't you told Pete you're his half brother?"

He shrugged.

"But now that his mother is dead, don't you think Pete would like to know he still has family? Maybe he'd like to go to Pulaski and meet your dad."

"He might." He studied the tops of his work boots.

"I heard just today that Lou stabbed your dad and threatened to kill him if he didn't leave Winter Garden and never come back."

Stan raised his eyes to mine. "You calling my daddy a coward?"

"No. I'd never say that. But he was young and knew he could have a life with you and your mom. . . . I think he made the right choice."

A muscle worked in his jaw. "Like I've done told you, none of this is any of your business. So stay out of it."

After Stan left, I went into the bedroom and sat down at the vanity. I took photos of myself from the front and from the back and texted them to Jackie. Then I began the difficult task of undoing what Sissy had done to my hair. I took out a few pins, and yet the hair stayed where it was. I took out more pins, and the hair on one side drooped a little. Finally, all of the bobby pins were in a pile on my vanity. I swept them into a drawer, secure in the knowledge that I'd never again have to buy bobby pins.

I looked in the mirror and laughed at the disarray. Nana would've said I looked like I'd stuck my finger in

a light socket. I only hoped a shower, some shampoo, and conditioner would return my hair to normal. Before I went to the bathroom, however, I took another selfie and texted it to Jackie so she could see my mad-scientist hair.

I was chuckling as I went into the bathroom and turned on the shower. I retrieved a towel and washcloth from the closet.

I heard Rory's toenails click on the floor as he wandered into the hall to see what I was doing.

"What are you in the mood for this evening, Rory Borealis?" I asked him. "Wanna watch a movie when I get out?"

He turned and trotted toward the kitchen.

"Guess not. Maybe you'll change your mind."

I went into the bathroom and got into the shower. The weight of the water finally lost the battle with gravity and my hair once more fell to below my shoulders. I shampooed it twice and then one more time for good measure. Then I made sure to leave my conditioner on for a full minute while I sang a John Legend song to myself and thought about my nonexistent dating life.

I'd dated over the years, of course. I'd even had a steady relationship in college that had lasted for a few months. But then Nana had gotten sick, and I'd moved back to Winter Garden. The guy and I had planned to stay in touch, but the long-distance thing didn't really work out all that well for us. He finally called me and told me he was seeing someone else. It stung my pride, sure, but when I realized I didn't care as much as I should have, it underscored how little the relationship had meant to either of us.

And now here was Deputy Ryan Hall. I wondered what his story was . . . whether or not we could date once Lou Lou Holman's killer had been caught. Or should I

say *if* Lou Lou's killer was caught? What if he . . . or she . . . wasn't caught? The murder would remain an open case, and there would be a cloud of suspicion over my head from now on.

I got out of the shower, slipped on a terry robe, and wrapped my hair in a towel.

I couldn't let myself think that Lou Lou's killer wouldn't be caught. If her murderer went free, my reputation here in Winter Garden—as well as the reputation of the Down South Café—would be ruined. I sighed. I had to believe that everything would work out fine.

Stan had gotten so defensive. I remembered his asking me, "Are you calling my daddy a coward?" He'd looked furious . . . like he could kill me. If Lou Lou had belittled Sherman to Stan, it might've been just enough reason to push him over the edge. He could very well have struck her out of anger without intending to kill her.

I took down the towel, spritzed a styling spray onto my hair, ran a wide-tooth comb through it, and began blowing it dry. Thank goodness, it was beginning to look normal.

On the other hand, that might've been the reason Stan came to Winter Garden in the first place, to get revenge on Lou Lou for allowing her father to run Sherman out of town. I decided to call Ryan and talk my theory over with him.

I thought I heard something in the hall and switched off the dryer. I listened for a second, didn't hear anything else, and finished drying my hair. I ran my hands through it. It felt smooth and soft and free of gunk.

I heard a crash. This time I was positive it wasn't my imagination. And judging from the chill that ran down my spine, I didn't think it was one of the animals either.

Chapter 23

I tightened the belt to my robe and stepped out of the bathroom. My bedroom looked as I'd left it. The bed was made, the decorative pillows were as I usually placed them, and there was only a slight indentation on the bedspread where I'd sat to take off my shoes.

I eased into the hallway and looked into the kitchen. I gasped. Stan Wheeler was sitting at my table drinking a bottle of water.

He looked up and smiled humorlessly. "Sorry if I scared you."

"W-well, you s-sure did. What . . . what're you doing here, Stan?" My eyes darted around the kitchen. I saw that Stan had placed a chair in front of the doggie door so Rory couldn't come inside.

He followed my gaze. "The dog was outside when I came in. I thought it best that he stay out there."

"I see." My mind scrambled for some means of escape. "You know, Ryan—the deputy—is on his way over. I have a date with him this evening."

"We'd better get this over with, then."

"G-get what over with?"

"You've already made your mind up that I'm the one who killed Lou Lou. I mean, you've been digging around in my past, asking me all these questions . . . even calling my dad up in Pulaski and getting him all bent out of shape."

"N-no, I don't have any idea who killed Lou Lou . . . b-but I'm leaning toward Pete."

He nodded toward the chair opposite him. "Sit down."

"I . . . need to get ready . . . for my date."

"We both know that's a load of bull. Sit down."

I slumped onto the chair across from Stan. At least, maybe I could figure out a way to get out of the house . . . run screaming to a neighbor's. The man had broken into my house and had all but practically confessed to killing Lou Lou. There was no way he was planning to let me leave.

"Why do you say I've made up my mind that you killed Lou Lou?" I said. "Did you?"

He nodded. "Didn't mean to. I was out in the rain trying to patch that stupid roof, and I flew mad and left to go see her. When I drove by the Joint, I saw her van still there. I went in to have it out with her. And I took my hammer with me because I felt like she had something that belonged to me."

A hammer. "And I guess you did have it out with her."

"I sure did." He lifted his bottle and took a drink, keeping his eyes on me while he did so. "I told that

woman what I thought . . . about everything. She and her family had treated my daddy like dirt. Dad told me there was a secret compartment in the wall behind the desk. He'd heard that bank robbery story, and he'd seen Lou putting something in there once." He brought the hand that had been on his lap onto the table. In it, he clutched a claw hammer. "I took this hammer so I could get it."

I gulped. "Why didn't you get into the secret compartment, then?"

"We were arguing, and I told Lou Lou she wasn't going to treat me the way she'd done my daddy and that I intended to have what was coming to me. I raised up the hammer and started toward the wall behind the desk. Lou Lou said that was Pete's money. She was saving it for him. Well, I thought it should go to Daddy's other son."

"Why would she save the money for Pete?"

"Because the guy's lousy with money, and she knew it. When I shoved her out of the way so I could bust through the wall, she went to screaming and grabbed the phone. I knew she was going to call the police. So I hit her."

"Was the one blow all it took?" I asked.

"Yeah. I'm stronger than I look."

I clasped my hands together, desperately needing something to hold on to. "You could say it was self-defense, Stan. I'll back you up."

"How're you going to back me up?" he asked. "You weren't there."

"I know, but anyone could see how you . . . well, y-you had to defend yourself. Everybody in Winter Garden knows Lou Lou was a bully. They wouldn't be surprised if you told them she pulled a gun or a knife on you or something."

"I appreciate the thought, but I believe I'd be better off going with my own idea."

I gulped and dreaded for him to continue.

"After I left here a while ago, I knew it was only a matter of time before the police would come knocking," Stan said. "You'd found out too much about my past and my family's history with the Holmans. I thought a better story would be if you confessed to killing Lou Lou and then killed yourself."

"I had no reason to murder Lou Lou," I pointed out.

"Sure you did. You wanted the Joint, and she wouldn't sell it to you. You picked up the nearest thing you could find—this hammer—and struck out in a fit of rage. But, lately, your conscience has gotten the best of you, and you can't live with the guilt."

I shook my head. "Nobody'll buy that, Stan, and you . . . you'll go to prison for two murders. At least, you can try to pass off Lou Lou's death as something that happened in self-defense . . . or in the heat of the moment."

"You only want to *think* no one will buy that story, sweetie pie. Everyone knows you wanted Lou Lou to sell you the Joint and that she didn't want to. Pete was trying to talk her into it, but it's not likely he'd have been able to. Plus, you're the one who found her."

"Stan, I . . . I've told people about your connection to the Holmans and that you're Pete's half brother."

"It doesn't matter. You're getting ready to write a confession."

"No, I'm not."

"Yes, you are." He placed the hammer on the table, stood, and took a pistol from the waistband of his jeans.

"I'm not. I . . . I guess you'll have to shoot me without

the confession." The sound of my heartbeat was filling my ears.

Stan leveled the gun at me.

I made a whimpering sound, but I refused to break down or scream or beg. I was still thinking there might be a way I could get out of this.

Hedging my bets, I stood, pushing the table up and against Stan as hard as I could. He cursed as I spun around and ran back to my bedroom. I slammed the door, locked it, and climbed out the window. I heard him smashing through the door. I ran toward the street. I wondered how close Stan was to me, but I didn't dare look. I'd seen enough horror movies to know that when the girl looks back to see where her attacker is, she trips and falls and then gets cut to bits. Or, in my case, shot.

I'd just got to the road when headlights blinded me. I waved my arms to flag down the truck.

It was Roger and Jackie!

"Get me out of here!" I cried. "Stan's trying to kill me!"

As I leapt into the truck beside Jackie, Stan ran up beside the porch and began shooting at us.

Roger said a few choice words as we sped toward the police station.

The police apprehended Stan between my house and the trailer Stan had been renting from Lou Lou. I guessed he was going to grab whatever he could from his home and leave town.

Luckily for me, I'd sent that embarrassing selfie to Jackie. She saw a shadow at my bedroom window in the photo. She tried to call me right after that, but I was

in the shower. She convinced Roger that they should leave their dinner in Bristol and come to check on me. Good thing she did.

Pete was devastated to learn the story behind Stan and his father. He refused to go talk with Stan, but he did drive up to Pulaski to meet Sherman Harding. Pete also bought his truck, and Chris Anne's brother became his partner.

Sheriff Billings traced the money that had been hidden in the wall and discovered that it was the money that had been stolen from the bank in North Carolina all those years ago. Grady might've wanted to paint himself as a hero to his family—or maybe that had all been Ms. Carter's doing—but he hadn't given the money back. Still, he and Bo had fallen out over the money and had never reconciled. That was a shame.

Epilogue

It was a beautiful day—the last day of June, in fact—when we had the ribbon-cutting ceremony for the Down South Café. Aunt Bess was there in a yellow dress and a big blue hat. I wasn't sure if she thought she was going to the café's grand opening or to the Kentucky Derby, but she'd said she wanted to match the decor.

Mom was there. She wore the same outfit that Jackie, Roger, Homer, the café staff, and I wore—blue jeans with a Down South Café T-shirt. The construction crew had taken their lunch break during the ceremony. Sarah's boyfriend had even skipped class so he could be at the grand opening with her. Billy brought his wife. Pete and Chris Anne stopped by. Dilly and several of the regulars from Lou's Joint had come by to help us celebrate.

We'd invited everyone we could think of, including the media. Ms. Peggy was there to personally do a front-page write-up on the café. Her photographer was snapping

pictures left and right, and I was afraid we might all go blind from the flash. And there was a news crew from the local television station.

I was glad to see Sheriff Billings put in an appearance. And, of course, I was glad that Ryan was with him.

I gave a brief speech before cutting the yellow ribbon in front of the door of the café. I told guests about Nana and how much I appreciated her love, kindness, and generosity, and I got choked up. I thanked Mom, Aunt Bess, Roger, Jackie, and Sarah for their support, and I shed a tear or two. And I told Homer, the café staff, and the construction crew how grateful I was for their hard work. And then I welcomed everyone to the Down South Café before I really began crying in earnest.

Jackie, Mom, and I had set out a buffet along the counter so the guests could help themselves to lunch. I made sure the dishes were both familiar and diverse. We served potato salad, baked tomatoes with hazelnut bread crumbs, macaroni salad, roasted portobellos, beef and vegetable kebabs, fried chicken, biscuits, garlic herb bread twists, three-bean salad, mocha cake, and caramel apple pie. Our beverages were sweet tea, coffee, water, and pomegranate punch.

I proudly watched everyone go through the line. I felt someone beside me, and I turned to see Ryan there.

I smiled. "Hi."

"Hi," he said, returning my smile. "The place looks fantastic."

"Thank you. We—especially Roger and his crew—put a lot of work into it."

"Don't downplay your role. I was here on more than one occasion when you were covered in dust or paint or—"

"Panic." I laughed. "And you even saw me with giant hair. You're right. I did my part in making all this come together."

"And in crime solving."

I was glad he didn't say the actual words "solving Lou Lou's murder" out loud. I doubted anyone was paying attention to us, but I certainly didn't want to run the risk of reminding people of what was bound to be right beneath the surface anyway.

"Sheriff Billings would probably hire you on if you're interested," Ryan continued with a grin.

"I think I've got plenty to keep me busy right here."

He took a small clear bag out of his shirt pocket. Inside was the necklace Nana had given me and that I'd lost in Lou Lou's office so long ago. "As promised."

My eyes welled with tears for the umpteenth time. "Thank you."

Ryan took the necklace from the bag and held it up. "May I?"

I turned and held up my hair so he could fasten the necklace around my neck. I could practically feel Nana smiling down at me, proud of what I'd been able to accomplish.

Author's Note

When Amy shudders suddenly at the funeral home, she thinks, *Somebody just walked over my grave.* This saying originated in the eighteenth century from an English folk legend that stated an unexpected cold sensation was brought about when someone walked over the place where one was eventually to be buried.

Recipes from the Down South Café

Grandmother's Meat Loaf

Yield: 8 servings

1½ pounds ground beef
2 eggs
2 cups bread crumbs
¾ cup diced onions
1 tablespoon salt
⅛ teaspoon pepper
½ cup cracker crumbs
1 cup tomato juice

Preheat oven to 325 degrees F. Mix all ingredients except tomato juice well. Add tomato juice gradually, making mixture solid enough to handle. Form into a loaf. Bake in a loaf pan for 45 minutes.

Granny's Oatmeal Pie

(Contributed by Suzie Welker)

Yield: 10–12 servings

1 pie crust (Directions for pie crust below.)
4 large brown eggs
1 cup sugar
2 tablespoons flour
1 teaspoon ground cinnamon (You can take
   cinnamon sticks and grind them yourself for
   a better-tasting pie.)
¼ teaspoon salt
1 cup light corn syrup (Do not use dark.)
¼ cup softened butter (I use only butter, never
   margarine. Soften by leaving out of fridge about
   an hour; do not put into mixture hot/boiling,
   as this will cook the eggs, creating a
   bad-tasting pie.)
1 teaspoon vanilla
1 cup quick-cooking oatmeal, uncooked

Preheat oven to 350 for metal pan or 325 for glass.

Beat eggs until frothy. Sift sugar, flour, cinnamon, and salt in a small bowl. The sifting mixes the dry ingredients together for a better blend. Add eggs to the dry mixture. Stir well. Mix corn syrup, butter, and vanilla in a separate bowl. Add to the first mixture. Slowly mix in oatmeal. Stir 2–3 minutes to ensure even distribution of oatmeal.

Pour into pie crust and bake for 45 minutes.

(Optional diced apples, raisins, or cranberries can be added for additional flavor. If adding apples, use 1 cup, diced very small; 1½ cups if using cranberries or raisins. I prefer the golden raisins but any can be used.)

PIE CRUST

1¼ cups all-purpose flour (Do not use self-rising.)
¼ teaspoon salt
½ cup butter cut into small squares (cold, not warm/softened)
¼ cup cold water

Mix flour and salt then sift. Using a pastry cutter (a pastry cutter is best, but you can use your hands), cut in the butter until the dough resembles coarse crumbles. Slowly add ¼ cup water, 1 tablespoon at a time.

Roll into a ball and chill in freezer for 1 hour. After 1 hour, take out and roll out using a heavy rolling pin. Place in metal or glass pie dish, then crimp edges with fingers or mash down with a small fork.

Baked Cinnamon and Sugar Doughnuts

(Contributed by Jessica Potts of http://ahappyfooddance.com/)

*Yield: 12–15 regular-sized doughnuts
or about 30 minidoughnuts*

DOUGHNUTS

1 tablespoon baking powder
½ teaspoon salt
1½ cups all-purpose flour
1 egg
½ cup milk
1 teaspoon vanilla
5 tablespoons butter, softened
½ cup sugar

TOPPING

½ cup butter, melted
1 cup sugar
1 teaspoon cinnamon

Preheat oven to 350 degrees.

Lightly oil a doughnut pan.

In a medium bowl, combine baking powder, salt, and flour. Set aside.

In another bowl, add egg, milk, and vanilla and beat mixture lightly. Set aside.

In the bowl of a stand mixer, cream together the butter and sugar.

Add the wet ingredients in two parts, alternating with the dry ingredients, and finish by beating until everything is just combined.

Transfer the dough to a piping bag or a large plastic baggie with the tip cut off. Pipe into the doughnut pan, filling only halfway full.

Bake for 10–12 minutes, or until a toothpick inserted comes out clean.

Remove from the oven and transfer to a wire rack, allowing to cool just enough to handle.

While the doughnuts are baking, melt the ½ cup butter. In another bowl mix the cinnamon and sugar together for the topping,

To cover the doughnuts, dip each doughnut in the butter and then roll in the cinnamon-and-sugar mixture.

Country Ham with Redeye Gravy

(Contributed by Robin Coxon)

Yield: 2 servings

2 slices country ham (¼ inch thick)
2 tablespoons butter
½ cup strong brewed black coffee
⅓ cup water

In a large cast-iron skillet, fry the ham in butter over medium heat until lightly browned. Remove ham to a platter. Add the coffee and water to the skillet. Boil until reduced by about half, scraping up browned bits in the bottom of the pan. Pour gravy over the ham and serve with grits, biscuits, and eggs.

Preacher Cookies

Yield: 18–36 cookies, depending on size

2 cups sugar
1 stick butter
½ cup cream
2½ cups quick oatmeal
¾ cup peanut butter
1 teaspoon vanilla

For chocolate cookies, add one tablespoon of cocoa.

Mix and boil for 1½ minutes. Spread into greased pan.
Refrigerate.

Jeanne Robertson's
7-Up Pound Cake

(Contributed by humorist Jeanne Robertson—
http://www.jeannerobertson.com)

Can be frozen until someone you know is sick . . . or
has "passed." Jeanne's secret notes in italics.

2 sticks margarine
¼ cup shortening
3 cups sugar
1½ teaspoons lemon extract *(Give or take a little.)*
1½ teaspoons vanilla extract *(Sometimes Jeanne*
    pours in more.)
5 eggs
3 cups all-purpose flour—measure before sifting
7 ounces 7-Up *(Jeanne uses Diet 7-Up to cut*
    calories.)

Preheat oven to 300 degrees.

Cream margarine, shortening, and sugar. *(Put under*
kitchen light until soft. Beat with a mixer.)

Add lemon and vanilla extracts. *(Add now so you won't*
forget. Cake tastes funny without 'em. Beat some more.)

Add eggs one at a time. *(I throw all of them in at the*
same time. First, take off shells.)

Alternate adding flour and 7-Up, beating after each
addition. Finish with 7-Up. *(I don't alternate. Dump it all*
in. Go for it! Turn mixer to highest level. Stand back. Add

more 7-Up if it looks dry. Sprinkle in more flour if it looks too moist. This is not rocket science.)

Spray 10-inch tube pan with Baker's Joy. *(No need to flour. Important! Be generous. Trust me. Or split the batter and use two 8-inch tube pans. This will give you two cakes. Math.)*

Cook at 300 degrees for one hour or until it "tests done." *(To test, poke a knife or broom straw in and out of cake until nothing sticks. Note: It takes longer to cook one big cake than two smaller ones. Higher math. Think about it. Adapt.)*

Take whatever you cook out of the oven—let it sit for 30 minutes before flipping over on a plate. *(Flip the cake. Not you. Waiting a lot longer will require a chiseling step. It gets ugly.)*

Do you have a recipe you'd like to submit for an upcoming book? Email the author (gayle@gayletrent.com) for more information.

ʒ Just after crossing over . . . under . . . through . . .
 the covered bridge, I could see it. Barely. I could
make out the top of it, and that was enough at the moment
to make me set aside the troubling grammatical conun-
drum of whether one passes over, under, or through a
covered bridge.

"There it is," I told Angus, an Irish wolfhound who
was riding shotgun. "There's our sign!"

He woofed, which could mean anything from "I gotta
pee" to "Yay!" I went with "Yay!"

"Me, too! I'm so excited."

I was closer to the store now and could really see the
sign. I pointed. "See, Angus?" My voice was barely above
a whisper. "Our sign."

THE SEVEN-YEAR STITCH.

I had named the shop the Seven-Year Stitch for three
reasons. One, it's an embroidery specialty shop. Two, I'm

a huge fan of classic movies. And three, it actually took me seven years to turn my dream of owning an embroidery shop into a reality.

Once upon a time, in a funky-cool land called San Francisco, I was an accountant. Not a funky-cool job, believe me, especially for a funky-cool girl like me, Marcy Singer. I had a corner cubicle near a window. You'd think the window would be a good thing, but it looked out upon a vacant building that grew more dilapidated by the day. Maybe by the hour. It was majorly depressing. One year, a coworker gave me a cactus for my birthday. I set it in that window, and it died. I told you it was depressing.

Still, my job wasn't that bad. I can't say I truly enjoyed it, but I am good with numbers and the work was tolerable. Then I got the call from Sadie. Not *a* call, mind you; *the* call.

"Hey, Marce. Are you sitting down?" Sadie had said.

"Sadie, I'm always sitting down. I keep a stationary bike frame and pedal it under my desk so my leg muscles won't atrophy."

"Good. The hardware store next to me just went out of business."

"And this is good because you hate the hardware guy?"

She'd given me an exasperated huff. "No, silly. It's good because the space is for lease. I've already called the landlord, and he's giving you the opportunity to snatch it up before anyone else does."

Sadie is an entrepreneur. She and her husband, Blake, own MacKenzies' Mochas, a charming coffee shop on the Oregon coast. She thinks everyone—or, at least,

Marcy Singer—should also own a charming shop on the Oregon coast.

"Wait, wait, wait," I'd said. "You expect me to come up there to Quaint City, Oregon—"

"Tallulah Falls, thank you very much."

"—and set up shop? Just like that?"

"Yes! It's not like you're happy there or like you're on some big five-year career plan."

"Thanks for reminding me."

"And you've not had a boyfriend or even a date for more than a year now. I could still strangle David when I think of how he broke your heart."

"Once again, thank you for the painful reminder."

"So what's keeping you there? This is your chance to open up the embroidery shop you used to talk about all the time in college."

"But what do I know about actually running a business?"

Sadie had huffed. "You can't tell me you've been keeping companies' books all these years without having picked up some pointers about how to—and how not to—run a business."

"You've got a point there. But what about Angus?"

"Marce, he will *love* it here! He can come to work with you every day, run up and down the beach. . . . Isn't that better than the situation he has now?"

I swallowed a lump of guilt the size of my fist.

"You're right, Sadie," I'd admitted. "A change will do us both good."

That had been three months ago. Now I was a resident of Tallulah Falls, Oregon, and today was the grand opening of the Seven-Year Stitch.

A cool, salty breeze off the ocean ruffled my hair as I hopped out of the bright red Jeep I'd bought to traipse up and down the coast.

Angus followed me out of the Jeep and trotted beside me up the river-rock steps to the walk that connected all the shops on this side of the street. The shops on the other side of the street were set up in a similar manner, with river-rock steps leading up to walks containing bits of shells and colorful rocks for aesthetic appeal. A narrow, two-lane road divided the shops, and black wrought-iron lampposts and benches added to the inviting community feel. A large clock tower sat in the middle of the town square, pulling everything together and somehow reminding us all of the preciousness of time. Tallulah Falls billed itself as the friendliest town on the Oregon coast, and so far, I had no reason to doubt that claim.

I unlocked the door and flipped the CLOSED sign to OPEN before turning to survey the shop. It was as if I were seeing it for the first time. And, in a way, I was. I'd been here until nearly midnight last night, putting the finishing touches on everything. This was my first look at the finished project. Like all my finished projects, I tried to view it objectively. But, like all my finished projects, I looked upon this one as a cherished child.

The floor was black-and-white tile, laid out like a gleaming chessboard. All my wood accents were maple. On the floor to my left, I had maple bins holding cross-stitch threads and yarns. When a customer first came in the door, she would see the cross-stitch threads. They started in white and went through shades of ecru, pink, red, orange, yellow, green, blue, purple, gray, and black. The yarns were organized the same way on the opposite

side. Perle flosses, embroidery hoops, needles, and cross-stitch kits hung on maple-trimmed corkboard over the bins. On the other side of the corkboard—the side with the yarn—there were knitting needles, crochet hooks, tapestry needles, and needlepoint kits.

The walls were covered by shelves where I displayed pattern books, dolls with dresses I'd designed and embroidered, and framed samplers. I had some dolls for those who liked to sew and embroider outfits (like me), as well as for those who enjoy knitting and crocheting doll clothes.

Standing near the cash register was my life-size mannequin, who bore a striking resemblance to Marilyn Monroe, especially since I put a short curly blond wig on her and did her makeup. I even gave her a mole . . . er, beauty mark. I called her Jill. I was going to name her after Marilyn's character in *The Seven Year Itch*, but she didn't have a name. Can you believe that—a main character with no name? She was simply billed as "The Girl."

To the right of the door was the sitting area. As much as I loved to play with the amazing materials displayed all over the store, the sitting area was my favorite place in the shop. Two navy overstuffed sofas faced each other across an oval maple coffee table. The table sat on a navy, red, and white braided rug. There were red club chairs with matching ottomans near either end of the coffee table, and candlewick pillows with lace borders scattered over both the sofas. I made those, too—the pillows, not the sofas.

The bell over the door jingled, and I turned to see Sadie walking in with a travel coffee mug.

I smiled. "Is that what I think it is?"

"It is, if you think it's a nonfat vanilla latte with a hint of cinnamon." She handed me the mug. "Welcome to the neighborhood."

"Thanks. You're the best." The steaming mug felt good in my hands. I looked back over the store. "It looks good, doesn't it?"

"It looks fantastic. You've outdone yourself." She cocked her head. "Is that what you're wearing tonight?"

Happily married for the past five years, Sadie was always eager to play matchmaker for me. I hid a smile and held the hem of my vintage tee as if it were a dress. "You don't think Snoopy's Joe Cool is appropriate for the grand opening party?"

Sadie closed her eyes.

"I have a supercute dress for tonight," I said with a laugh, "and Mr. O'Ruff will be sporting a black tie for the momentous event."

Angus wagged his tail at the sound of his surname.

"Marce, you and that *pony*." Sadie scratched Angus behind the ears.

"He's a proud boy. Aren't you, Angus?"

Angus barked his agreement, and Sadie chuckled.

"I'm proud, too . . . of both of you." She grinned. "I'd better get back over to Blake. I'll be back to check on you again in a while."

Though we're the same age and had been roommates in college, Sadie clucked over me like a mother hen. It was sweet, but I could do without the fix-ups. Some of these guys she'd tried to foist on me . . . I have no idea where she got them—mainly because I was afraid to ask.

I went over to the counter and placed my big yellow

purse and floral tote bag on the bottom shelf before finally taking a sip of my latte.

"That's yummy, Angus. It's nice to have a friend who owns a coffee shop, isn't it?"

Angus lay down on the large bed I'd put behind the counter for him.

"That's a good idea," I told him. "Rest up. We've got a big day and an even bigger night ahead of us."

About the Author

Gayle Leeson lives in Virginia with her family, which includes a dog who adores her and a cat who can take her or leave her. She includes the meat loaf recipe in this book that her grandmother Marilyn Hicks taught her to make. For Gayle, a sandwich made with this meat loaf, fresh bread, and yellow mustard is a sentimental culinary delight.

Leeson, who is a native Virginian, also writes as Amanda Lee (the Embroidery Mystery series), Gayle Trent, and G. V. Trent. Please visit Leeson online at gayleleeson.com, gayletrent.com, on Facebook (facebook.com/gayletrentandamandalee), on Twitter (twitter.com/gayletrent), and on Pinterest (pinterest.com/gayletrent).